Sensation and Perception

NINTH EDITION

Sensation and Perception

E. Bruce Goldstein

University of Pittsburgh
University of Arizona

WADSWORTH
CENGAGE Learning·

Australia • Brazil • Japan • Korea • Mexico • Singapore • Spain • United Kingdom • United States

Sensation and Perception, Ninth Edition, International Edition
E. Bruce Goldstein

Executive Editor: Jaime Perkins

Developmental Editors: Kristin Makarewycz, Shannon LeMay-Finn

Assistant Editor: Paige Leeds

Editorial Assistant: Amelia Blevins

Media Editor: Mary Noel

Senior Brand Manager: Elisabeth Rhoden

Market Development Manager: Christine Sosa

Content Project Manager: Charlene M. Carpentier

Art Director: Vernon Boes

Manufacturing Planner: Karen Hunt

Rights Acquisitions Specialist: Dean Dauphinais

Production Service: Scratchgravel Publishing Services

Photo/Text Researcher: PreMedia Global

Copy Editor: Margaret C. Tropp

Art Editor: Lisa Torri, Precision Graphics

Illustrator: Precision Graphics/Integra

Text Designer: Lisa Buckley

Cover Image: Digital Vision, Fred Froese/Getty Images

Compositor: Integra

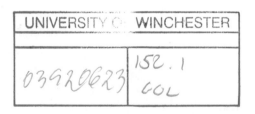
International Edition:

ISBN-13: 978-1-285-08514-2

ISBN-10: 1-285-08514-0

Cengage Learning International Offices

Asia
www.cengageasia.com
tel: (65) 6410 1200

Australia/New Zealand
www.cengage.com.au
tel: (61) 3 9685 4111

Brazil
www.cengage.com.br
tel: (55) 11 3665 9900

India
www.cengage.co.in
tel: (91) 11 4364 1111

Latin America
www.cengage.com.mx
tel: (52) 55 1500 6000

UK/Europe/Middle East/Africa
www.cengage.co.uk
tel: (44) 0 1264 332 424

Represented in Canada by Nelson Education, Ltd.
www.nelson.com
tel: (416) 752 9100/(800) 668 0671

Cengage Learning is a leading provider of customized learning solutions with office locations around the globe, including Singapore, the United Kingdom, Australia, Mexico, Brazil, and Japan. Locate your local office at: **www.cengage.com/global**

For product information and free companion resources:
www.cengage.com/international

Visit your local office: **www.cengage.com/global**

Visit our corporate website: **www.cengage.com**

Printed in Canada
1 2 3 4 5 6 7 16 15 14 13

To my wife, Barbara, more than ever
   and
To all of the students and teachers whose
suggestions helped shape this edition

About the Author

Christopher Baker

E. BRUCE GOLDSTEIN is Associate Professor Emeritus of Psychology at the University of Pittsburgh and Adjunct Professor of Psychology at the University of Arizona. He has received the Chancellor's Distinguished Teaching Award from the University of Pittsburgh for his classroom teaching and textbook writing. He received his bachelor's degree in chemical engineering from Tufts University and his PhD in experimental psychology from Brown University; he was a postdoctoral fellow in the Biology Department at Harvard University before joining the faculty at the University of Pittsburgh. Bruce has published papers on a wide variety of topics, including retinal and cortical physiology, visual attention, and the perception of pictures. He is the author of *Cognitive Psychology: Connecting Mind, Research, and Everyday Experience*, 3rd Edition (Wadsworth, 2011), and the editor of the *Blackwell Handbook of Perception* (Blackwell, 2001) and the two-volume *Sage Encyclopedia of Perception* (Sage, 2010).

Brief Contents

Contents

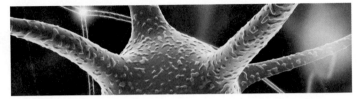

Neural Processing and Perception 53

Cortical Organization 77

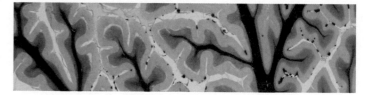

CHAPTER 13

Speech Perception **317**

CHAPTER 12

Auditory Localization and Organization **289**

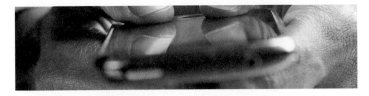

Virtual Lab Contents

Demonstrations

Preface

When I first began working on this book, Hubel and Wiesel were mapping orientation columns in the striate cortex and were five years away from receiving their Nobel Prize; Amoore's stereochemical theory, based largely on psychophysical evidence, was a prominent explanation for odor recognition; and one of the hottest new discoveries in perception was that the response properties of neurons could be influenced by experience. Today, specialized areas in the human brain have been mapped using brain imaging, olfactory receptors have been revealed using genetic methods, and the idea that the perceptual system is tuned to regularities in the environment is now supported by a wealth of both behavioral and physiological research.

But some things haven't changed. Teachers still stand in front of classrooms to teach students about perception, and students still read textbooks that reinforce what they are learning in the classroom. Another thing that hasn't changed is that teachers prefer texts that are easy for students to read, that present both classic studies and up-to-date research, and that present both the facts of perception and overarching themes and principles.

When I began teaching perception, I looked at the textbooks that were available and was disappointed, because none of them seemed to be written for students. They presented "the facts," but not in a way that seemed very interesting or inviting. I therefore wrote the first edition of *Sensation and Perception* with the idea of involving students in their study of perception by presenting the material as a story. The story is a fascinating one, because it is a narrative of one discovery following from another, a scientific "whodunit" in which the goal is to uncover the hidden mechanisms responsible for our ability to perceive.

Though my goal in writing this book has been to tell a story, this is, after all, a textbook designed for teaching. So in addition to presenting the story of perceptual research, this book also contains a number of features, all of which appeared in the eighth edition, that are designed to highlight specific material and to help students learn.

Features

- **Demonstrations.** *Demonstrations* have been a popular feature of this book for many editions. They are integrated into the flow of the text and are easy enough to be carried out with little trouble, thereby maximizing the probability that students will do them. Some examples: Becoming Aware of the Blind Spot (Chapter 2); Shape From Shading (Chapter 5); Perceiving Degraded Sentences (Chapter 13); "Tasting" With and Without the Nose (Chapter 15).

- **Methods.** It is important not only to present the facts of perception, but also to make students aware of how these facts were obtained. Highlighted *Methods* sections, which are integrated into the ongoing discussion, emphasize the importance of methods, and the highlighting makes it easier to refer back to them when referenced later in the book. Examples: Measuring Dark Adaptation (Chapter 2); Double Dissociations in Neuropsychology (Chapter 4); Measuring Tactile Acuity (Chapter 14); 2-Deoxyglucose Technique (Chapter 15).

- **Something to Consider.** This end-of-chapter feature offers the opportunity to consider especially interesting phenomena and new findings. Examples: The Mind–Body Problem (Chapter 3); Attention in Autism (Chapter 6); Connections Between Hearing and Vision (Chapter 12); The Proust Effect (Chapter 15).

- **Test Yourself.** *Test Yourself* questions appear in the middle and at the end of each chapter. These questions are broad enough that students have to unpack the questions themselves, thereby making students more active participants in their studying.

- **Think About It.** The *Think About It* section at the end of each chapter poses questions that require students to apply what they have learned and that take them beyond the material in the chapter.

- **Virtual Lab.** The *Virtual Lab* feature of this book enables students to view experimental stimuli, perceptual demonstrations, and short film clips about the research being discussed. The Virtual Lab has been updated in this edition. More than 50 new items have been added to the labs carried over from the eighth edition. Most of these new items have been generously provided by researchers in vision, hearing, and perceptual development. Each item is indicated in the chapters by this icon: **VL**. Students can access the Virtual Lab through Psychology CourseMate at www.cengagebrain.com.

- **Full-Color Illustrations.** Perception, of all subjects, should be illustrated in color, so I was especially pleased when the seventh edition became "full-color." What pleases me about the illustrations is not only how beautiful the color looks, but how well it serves pedagogy. There are 560 figures, 160 of them new to this edition.

Changes in This Edition

Here are some of the changes in this edition, which have been made both to make the book easier to read and to keep current with the latest research.

Taking Student Feedback Into Account

In past revisions, I have made changes based on feedback that professors have provided based on their knowledge of the field and their experience in teaching from the book. Beginning with the seventh edition, I began making use of feedback provided by students based on their experience in using the book. I continued this practice for the eighth edition and now this one, by asking each of the 150 students in my class to write a paragraph for each chapter in the eighth edition in which they described one thing they felt could be made clearer. My students identified where and why they were having problems, and often suggested changes in wording or organization. When just one or two students commented on a particular section, I often used their comments to make improvements, but I paid the most attention when many students commented on the same material. I could write a "Top Ten" list of sections students thought should be revised, but instead I'll just say that student feedback resulted in numerous changes to every chapter in the book. Because of these changes, this is the most "student friendly" edition yet.

Improving Organization

The organization of every chapter was evaluated to achieve a clearer and more logical flow from one topic to the next. Here are a few of the more extensive organizational changes:

Chapters 2–3 (The Beginnings of Perception; Neural Processing and Perception)
These chapters introduce students to a way of thinking about studying perception that sees perceptual experience as central, while also looking for underlying physiological

mechanisms. In the eighth edition, many of the physiological principles, including neural processing, receptive fields, coding, and the mind–body problem, were introduced in Chapter 2 (The Physiological Basis of Perception). Many students and reviewers felt this was "too much too soon," without proper concern for the connections to perception.

In this edition, the physiological material is introduced more gradually and within the context of the overall perceptual process. Chapter 2 opens by describing light, focusing, and how receptors affect perception. Electrical signals in neurons are then introduced, emphasizing the basic properties of action potentials. Chapter 3 then introduces neural processing, receptive fields, and the sensory code, while continually referring back to perception. This treatment reflects the general philosophy of the book, which is that neural processes are important, but only to the degree that they illuminate our understanding of perception.

Chapter 6 (Visual Attention)
This chapter has been completely reorganized. It opens with a discussion of what directs our attention and what happens when we attend; what happens when we don't attend (i.e., inattentional blindness) is now discussed later in the chapter. Also, physiological material has been integrated into the chapter rather than being placed in a separate section.

Chapter 8 (Perceiving Motion)
The corollary discharge/coincidence detector approach has been moved nearer to the beginning of the chapter, followed by a discussion of the aperture problem and higher-order motion perception.

Chapter 15 (The Chemical Senses)
The position of olfaction and taste have been reversed, with taste now opening the chapter and olfaction at the end. This results in a smoother transition to flavor perception, which is closely related to olfaction.

Developmental Dimensions
A new feature, *Developmental Dimension*, appears at the end of ten of the chapters. This feature includes material that appeared in Chapter 16, "Perceptual Development," in the eighth edition, plus new material. Some examples:

- Chapter 2 (The Beginnings of Perception): Infant visual acuity
- Chapter 5 (Perceiving Objects and Scenes): Infant face perception
- Chapter 6 (Visual Attention): Attention and perceptual completion
- Chapter 9 (Perceiving Color): Infant color vision
- Chapter 11 (Hearing): Infant hearing: audibility curve and voice recognition
- Chapter 13 (Speech Perception): Infant speech perception
- Chapter 15 (The Chemical Senses): Infant chemical sensitivity

Adding New Content

Every chapter has been updated. This updating is reflected in the inclusion of more than 100 new references, most of them to recent research. In addition, some earlier research has been added and some descriptions from the eighth edition have been updated. Here is a partial list of new "cutting-edge" research that has been added:

Chapter 4 (Cortical Organization)

- Response of human hippocampus neurons to remembering previously seen film clips (Gelbard-Sagiv et al., 2008)

Chapter 5 (Perceiving Objects and Scenes)

- "Brain reading" using fMRI voxel activation pattern to predict what a person is looking at (Naselaris et al., 2009)

Chapter 6 (Visual Attention)

- Attention in a dynamic environment (Jovancevic-Misic & Hayhoe, 2009)
- Attention maps in the brain (Datta & DeYoe, 2009)
- Load theory and inattentional blindness (Lavie, 2010)

Chapter 7 (Taking Action)

- Brain damage and wayfinding (Maguire et al., 2006; Schinazi & Epstein, 2010)
- Landmarks and wayfinding (Hamid et al., 2010)
- Parietal lobe neurons in monkey that respond to type of grip (Fattori et al., 2010)

Chapter 8 (Perceiving Motion)

- Event boundaries (Zacks et al., 2009)

Chapter 9 (Perceiving Color)

- Effect of seasonal wavelength distributions on color perception of scenes (Webster, 2011)
- Types of opponent neurons in the cortex (Johnson, Hawken, & Shapley, 2008; Tanigawa et al., 2010)

Chapter 10 (Perceiving Depth and Size)

- Creating depth perception in 3-D movies and TV
- Gaining stereovision as an adult: the case of "Stereo Sue" (Barry, 2011; Sacks, 2010)
- Infant perception of depth from cast shadows (Yonas & Granrud, 2006).

Chapter 11 (Hearing)

- Revised in collaboration with Christopher Plack, University of Manchester, author of *The Sense of Hearing* (Psychology Press, 2005). The revised chapter reflects current auditory research that emphasizes the temporal coding of pitch.

Chapter 12 (Auditory Localization and Organization)

- Broad interaural time difference tuning curves in mammals (Pecka et al., 2008; Recanzone et al., 2011)
- How lesioning or cooling the auditory cortex affects localization (Malhotra et al., 2008; Nodal et al., 2010)
- Rhythmic grouping and movement (Nozaradan et al., 2011; Trainor et al., 2009); grouping and language (Iversen & Patel, 2008)
- Brain activity in blind people during echolocation (Thaler et al., 2011)

Chapter 13 (Speech Perception)

- Effect of transcranial magnetic stimulation (TMS) of motor areas of the cortex on perceiving specific phonemes (D'Ausilio et al., 2009)
- "Brain reading" using the response of human temporal lobe neurons to predict the speech stimulus a person is hearing (Pasley et al., 2012)

Chapter 14 (The Cutaneous Senses)

- Updated treatment of somatosensory "mirror" phenomena (Keysers et al., 2010; Meyer et al., 2011; Osborn & Derbyshire, 2010)

Chapter 15 (The Chemical Senses)

- Chemotopic coding in the olfactory bulb (Johnson et al., 2010; Murthy, 2011)
- "Random" nature of odorant activation in the piriform cortex and the role of learning in the recognition of odor objects (Shepard, 2012; Wilson & Sullivan, 2011)
- Central neural interactions of taste and olfaction in determining flavor perception (Rolls et al., 2010; Small, 2012)
- Effect of pre- and postnatal learning on infant flavor preferences (Beauchamp & Mennella, 2009)

Epilogue

The Epilogue, at the end of the book, is new to this edition. It reinforces key concepts discussed in the book by highlighting a number of principles of perception that hold across senses.

Supplement Package

Instructor's Manual With Test Bank

For each chapter, this manual contains a detailed chapter outline, learning objectives, a chapter summary, key terms with page references, summary of virtual labs, and suggested websites, videos, demonstrations, activities, and lecture topics. The test bank includes 40 multiple-choice questions (with correct answer, page reference, and question type) and 5 to 10 essay questions per chapter.

Psychology CourseMate

Cengage Learning's Psychology CourseMate brings course concepts to life with interactive learning, study, and exam preparation tools that support the printed textbook. CourseMate includes an integrated ebook, glossaries, flashcards, quizzes, videos, virtual labs, and more—as well as EngagementTracker, a first-of-its-kind tool that monitors student engagement in the course. The accompanying instructor website, available through login.cengage.com, offers access to password-protected resources such as an electronic version of the instructor's manual, test bank files, and PowerPoint® slides. CourseMate can be bundled with the student text. Contact your Cengage sales representative for information on getting access to CourseMate.

Virtual Lab

The *Virtual Lab* enables students to view experimental stimuli, perceptual demonstrations, and short film clips about the research being discussed. Items are indicated in the chapters by this icon: **VL**. Students can access the Virtual Lab through Psychology CourseMate at www.cengagebrain.com.

PowerLecture With ExamView®

This one-stop digital library and presentation tool includes preassembled Microsoft® PowerPoint® lecture slides. In addition to a full Instructor's Manual and Test Bank, PowerLecture also includes ExamView® testing software with all the test items from the printed Test Bank in electronic format, enabling you to create customized tests in print or online, and all of your media resources in one place, including an image library of graphics from the book and videos.

WebTutor™

Jumpstart your course with customizable, rich, text-specific content within your Course Management System. Whether you want to Web-enable your class or put an entire course online, WebTutor™ delivers. WebTutor™ offers a wide array of resources, including access to the ebook, glossaries, flashcards, quizzes, videos, virtual labs, and more.

Acknowledgments

It is a pleasure to acknowledge the following people who worked tirelessly to turn my manuscript into an actual book. Without these people, this book would not exist, and I am grateful to all of them.

- Jaime Perkins, my editor, who has supported this book by providing resources and advice through a number of editions.

- Kristin Makarewycz, senior development editor. Thank you, Kristin, for listening to my concerns, for your support, for helping move things along, and for all of the things you did to make the book happen.
- Shannon LeMay-Finn, developmental editor extraordinaire, who has spoiled me with her attention to details, and with queries and suggestions that often amazed me. Many of the details of this edition of the book owe their existence to Shannon's perceptive feedback. Also thank you, Shannon, for your humor, for your appreciation of my humor, and for becoming interested in perception.
- Anne Draus of Scratchgravel Production Services, for taking care of the amazing number of details involved in turning my manuscript into a book in her usual efficient and professional way. But beyond professionalism, I want to thank you, Anne, for the way you dealt with my concerns and for your commitment to producing the best book possible.
- Lisa Torri, my art editor, for continuing the tradition of working on my book which started many editions ago and for all the care and creativity that went into making all of the illustrations happen.
- Vernon Boes, art guru, who directed the design for the book. Thanks, Vernon, for our continuing relationship, and the great design and cover.
- Lisa Buckley for the elegant design and Cheryl Carrington for the striking cover.
- Peggy Tropp, for her expert and creative copyediting.
- Mary Noel, senior media editor, for making all of the new additions to the Virtual Lab happen.
- Dean Dauphinais, Christie Barros, and Meg Shanahan for their relentless quests for permissions.
- Charlene Carpentier, senior content project manager, who coordinated all of the elements of the book during production and made sure everything happened when it was supposed to so the book would get to the printer on time.
- Precision Graphics and Integra Graphics for the beautiful art renderings.
- Mary Still, Missouri Western State University, for the Instructor's Manual and Test Bank.
- Paige Leeds, assistant editor, who coordinated the supplements for the ninth edition.

In addition to the help I received from all of these people on the editorial and production side, I also received a great deal of help from researchers and teachers. One of the things I have learned in my years of writing is that other people's advice is crucial. The field of perception is a broad one, and I rely heavily on the advice of experts in specific areas to alert me to emerging new research and to check my writing for accuracy. The following is a list of the "expert reviewers" who checked chapters for accuracy and completeness:

Martha Arterberry
Colby College

Sliman Bensmaia
University of Chicago

Marvin Chun
Yale University

Gregory DeAngelis
University of Rochester

Kalanit Grill-Spector
Stanford University

Emily Grossman
University of California, Irvine

Mark Hollins
University of North Carolina

Ruth Litovsky
University of Wisconsin, Madison

Andrew Lotto
University of Arizona

Mary Peterson
University of Arizona

Michael Webster
University of Nevada, Reno

Donald Wilson
New York University School of Medicine and Nathan
Kline Institute for Psychiatric Research

I also thank the following people who offered suggestions and answered my questions regarding specific sections of chapters.

Frank Durgin
Swarthmore College

Russell Epstein
University of Pennsylvania

Jay Neitz
University of Wisconsin

John Philbeck
George Washington University

Jessica Phillips-Silver
McGill University

Edmund Rolls
Oxford University

Maggie Shiffrar
Rutgers University

Dana Small
Yale University and Pierce Foundation

Laurel Trainor
McMaster University

Jessica Witt
Colorado State University

Jeffrey Zacks
Washington University in St. Louis

I also received especially important feedback from many teachers of perception, who rely on textbooks in their courses. They have read groups of chapters (and in a few cases the whole book), with an eye both to accuracy of the material and pedagogy. I owe a great debt of thanks to this group of reviewers for their advice about how to present the material to students.

Aneeq Ahmad
Henderson State University

Eric Amazeen
Arizona State University

Elan Barenholtz
Florida Atlantic University

Steve Buck
University of Washington

Meagan Curtis
Purchase College, State University of New York

Robert Dippner
University of Nevada, Las Vegas

Susan Dutch
Westfield State University

Sharon Guttman
Middle Tennessee State University

Katherine Hooper
University of North Florida

Jane Karwoski
University of Nevada, Las Vegas

Patrick Monnier
Colorado State University

Brian Pasley
University of California, Berkeley

John Philbeck
George Washington University

Elisabeth Ploran
George Mason University

Christy Porter
College of William and Mary

Lisa Renzi
University of Georgia

Thomas Sanocki
University of South Florida

Kenith V. Sobel
University of Central Arkansas

Mickie Vanhoy
University of Central Oklahoma

Scott Watamaniuk
Wright State University

Takashi Yamauchi
Texas A & M University

I also thank the following people who donated photographs and research records for illustrations that are new to this edition.

Frank Bremmer
Ruhr University–Bochum

Alessandro D'Ausilio
University of Ferrara

Luca Del Pero
University of Arizona

Stuart Derbyshire
University of Birmingham

Patrizia Fattori
University of Bologna

Jack Gallant
University of California, Berkeley

Tzvi Ganel
Ben-Gurion University of the Negev

Kalanit Grill-Spector
Stanford University

Marco Iacobonni
University of California, Los Angeles

Christian Keysers
University of Groningen

Michael Leon
University of California, Irvine

Kaspar Meyer
University of Southern California

Micah Murray
University of Lausanne

Thomas Naselaris
University of California, Berkeley

Alice O'Toole
University of Texas

Brian Pasley
University of California, Berkeley

Mary Peterson
University of Arizona

John Philbeck
George Washington University

Rodrigo Quiroga
California Institute of Technology

Pawan Sinha
Massachusetts Institute of Technology

Lore Thaler
University of Western Ontario

Michael Webster
University of Nevada

Albert Yonas
University of Minnesota

Finally, I thank all of the people who generously provided demonstrations and videos for the Virtual Lab.

Edward Adelson
Massachusetts Institute of Technology

Michael Bach
University of Freiburg

Mary Hayhoe
University of Texas

Laurie Heller
Brown University

George Hollich
Purdue University

Scott Johnson
University of California, Los Angeles

James Kalat
North Carolina State University

Fei Fei Li
Princeton University

Stephen Neely
Boys Town Hospital, Omaha

Thomas Papathomas
Rutgers University

Andrea Pierno
University of Padua

Lila Reddy
Massachusetts Institute of Technology

Ronald Rensink
University of British Columbia

Robert Sekuler
Brandeis University

Sensimetrics Corporation
Malden, Massachusetts

Ladan Shams
University of California, Los Angeles

Nikolaus Troje
Queen's University

Chris Urmson and Red Whittaker
Tartan Racing, Carnegie-Mellon University

Peter Wenderoth
Macquarie University

New to the ninth edition:

Karen Adolph
New York University

Marlene Behrmann
Carnegie-Mellon University

Ed Boyndon
McGovern Institute for Brain Research at MIT

Heinrich Bülthoff
Max-Planck-Institut für biologische Kybernetik
Max Planck Institute for Biological Cybernetics

Moran Cerf
California Institute of Technology

Nate Dappen
Days Edge Productions

Joshua Davis
Barnard College of Columbia University

James DiCarlo
McGovern Institute for Brain Research at MIT

Frank Durgin
Swarthmore College

Patrizia Fattori
University of Bologna

John Franchak
New York University

Jack Gallant
University of California, Berkeley

Tvzi Ganel
Ben-Gurion University of the Negev

Tim Harris
Writer/Director, The Professor Show

Douglas Whalen
Haskins Laboratory, Yale University

Karin Heineman
American Institute of Physics

Alex Huk
University of Texas

Nancy Kanwisher
McGovern Institute for Brain Research at MIT

Daniel Kersten
University of Minnesota

Kari Kretch
New York University

Thomas Naselaris
University of California, Berkeley

Shinji Nishimoto
University of California, Berkeley

Anthony Norcia
Stanford University

Brad Pasley
University of California, Berkeley

Olivier Pascalis
Université Pierre Mendes France

John Philbeck
George Washington University

Teresa Pinto
Take the Wind Productions & Portuguese Society for Neuroscience

Julie Prior
McGovern Institute for Brain Research at MIT

Arthur Shapiro
American University

Maggie Shiffrar
Rutgers University

Kokichi Sugihara
Meiji Institute for Advanced Study of Mathematical Sciences

Lore Thaler
University of Durham

Shawn Vecera
University of Iowa

Richard Warren
University of Wisconsin, Milwaukee

William Warren
Brown University

Jessica Witt
Colorado State University

Jeffrey Zacks
Washington University in St. Louis

Sensation and Perception

Introduction to Perception

VL The Virtual Lab icons direct you to specific animations and videos designed to help you visualize what you are reading about. Virtual Labs are listed at the end of the chapter, keyed to the page on which they appear, and can be accessed through Psychology CourseMate. Virtual Labs begin in Chapter 2.

◄ The Metropolitan Cathedral of Santiago, Chile, is represented here by its reflection on the glass façade of a modern building. The process of perception involves representations, such as when an object is represented by its image on the retina. Sometimes these representations are fragmented or distorted, as is this representation of the Cathedral, but somehow the perceptual system transforms these representations into the conscious experiences we call perceptions. This chapter begins describing how this process occurs.

Some Questions We Will Consider:

- Why should you read this book? (p. 4)
- How are your perceptions determined by processes that you are unaware of? (p. 5)
- What is the difference between perceiving something and recognizing it? (p. 8)
- How can we measure perception? (p. 12)

Imagine that you have been given the following hypothetical science project.

Project: Design a device that can *locate, describe,* and *identify* all objects in the environment, including their distance from the device and their relationships to each other. In addition, make the device capable of traveling from one point to another, avoiding obstacles along the way.

Extra credit: Make the device capable of having *conscious experience,* such as what people experience when they look out at a scene.

Warning: This project, should you decide to accept it, is extremely difficult. It has not yet been solved by the best computer scientists, even though they have access to the world's most powerful computers.

Hint: Humans and animals have solved these problems in a particularly elegant way. They use (1) two spherical sensors called "eyes," which contain a light-sensitive chemical, to sense light; (2) two detectors on the sides of the head, called "ears," which are fitted with tiny vibrating hairs to sense pressure changes in the air; (3) small pressure detectors of various shapes imbedded under the skin to sense stimuli on the skin; and (4) two types of chemical detectors to detect gases that are inhaled and solids and liquids that are ingested.

Additional note: Designing the detectors is just the first step in designing the system. An information processing system is also needed. In the case of the human, this information processing system is a "computer" called the brain, with 100 billion active units and interconnections so complex that they have still not been completely deciphered. Although the detectors are an important part of the project, the design of the computer is crucial, because the information that is picked up by the detectors needs to be analyzed. Note that the operation of the human system is still not completely understood and that the best scientific minds in the world have made little progress with the extra credit part of the problem. Focus on the main problem first, and leave conscious experience until later.

The "science project" just described is what this book is about. Our goal is to understand the human model, starting with the detectors—the eyes, ears, skin receptors, and receptors in the nose and mouth—and then moving on to the computer—the brain. We want to understand how we sense things in the environment and interact with them. The paradox we face is that although we still don't understand perception, perceiving is something that occurs almost effortlessly. In most situations, we simply open our eyes and see what is around us, listen and hear sounds, eat and taste, without expending any particular effort.

Because of the ease with which we perceive, many people see perception as something that "just happens" and don't see the feats achieved by our senses as complex or amazing. "After all," the skeptic might say, "for vision, a picture of the environment is focused on the back of my eye, and that picture provides all the information my brain needs to duplicate the environment in my consciousness." But the idea that perception is not very complex is exactly what misled computer scientists in the 1950s and 1960s to propose that it would take only about a decade or so to create "perceiving machines" that could negotiate the environment with humanlike ease. That prediction, made half a century ago, has yet to come true, even though a computer defeated the world chess champion in 1997 and defeated two *Jeopardy!* champions in 2010. From a computer's point of view, perceiving a scene is more difficult than playing world championship chess or accessing vast amounts of knowledge to answer quiz questions. In this chapter, we will consider a few practical reasons for studying perception, how perception occurs in a sequence of steps, and how to measure perception.

Why Read This Book?

The most obvious answer to the question "Why read this book?" is that it is required reading for a course you are taking. Thus, it is probably an important thing to do if you want to get a good grade. But beyond that, there are a number of other reasons for reading this book. For one thing, it will provide you with information that may be helpful in other courses and perhaps even your future career. If you plan to go to graduate school to become a researcher or teacher in perception or a related area, this book will provide you with a solid background to build on. In fact, many of the research studies you will read about were carried out by researchers who read earlier editions of this book when they were undergraduates.

The material in this book is also relevant to future studies in medicine or related fields, because much of our discussion is about how the body operates. Medical applications that depend on an understanding of perception include devices to restore perception to people who have lost vision or hearing and treatments for pain. Other applications include robotic vehicles that can find their way through unfamiliar environments, face recognition systems that can identify people as they pass through airport security, speech recognition systems that can understand what someone is saying, and highway signs that are visible to drivers under a variety of conditions.

But reasons to study perception extend beyond the possibility of useful applications. Studying perception can help you become more aware of the nature of your own perceptual experiences. Many of the everyday experiences that you take for granted—such as tasting food, looking at a painting in a museum, or listening to someone talking—can be appreciated at a deeper level by considering questions such as "Why do I lose my sense of taste when I have a cold?" "How do artists create an impression of depth in a picture?" and "Why does an unfamiliar language sound as if it is one continuous stream of sound, without breaks between words?" This book will not only answer these questions but will answer other questions that you may not have thought of, such as "Why don't I see colors at dusk?" and "How come the scene around me doesn't appear to move as I walk through it?" Thus, even if you aren't planning to become a physician or a robotic vehicle designer, you will come away from reading this book with a heightened appreciation of both the complexity and the beauty of the mechanisms responsible for your perceptual experiences, and perhaps even with an enhanced awareness of the world around you.

Because perception is something you experience constantly, knowing about how it works is interesting in its own right. To appreciate why, consider what you are experiencing right now. If you touch the page of this book, or look out at what's around you, you might get the feeling that you are perceiving exactly what is "out there" in the environment. After all, touching this page puts you in direct contact with it, and it seems likely that what you are seeing is what is actually there. But one of the things you will learn as you study perception is that everything you see, hear, taste, feel, or smell is created by the mechanisms of your senses.

Think about what this means. There are things out there that you want to see, hear, taste, smell, and feel. But the only way to achieve this is for these things to stimulate receptors designed to pick up light, sound energy, taste and smell stimuli, or touch stimuli. When you run your fingers over the pages of this book, you're feeling the page and its texture because the pressure and movement across the skin are activating small receptors just beneath the skin. Thus, whatever you are feeling depends on the activation of these receptors. If the receptors weren't there, you would feel nothing, or if they had different properties, you might feel something different than what you feel now. This idea that *perception depends on the properties of the sensory receptors* is one of the themes of this book.

A few years ago, I received an email from a student (not one of my own, but from another university) who was using an earlier edition of this book. In her email, "Jenny" made a number of comments about the book, but the one that struck me as being particularly relevant to the question "Why read this book?" is the following: "By reading your book, I got to know the fascinating processes that take place every second in my brain, that are doing things I don't even think about." Your reasons for reading this book may turn out to be totally different than Jenny's, but hopefully you will find out some things that will be useful, or fascinating, or both.

The Perceptual Process

Perception happens at the end of what can be described, with apologies to the Beatles, as a long and winding road (McCartney, 1970). This road begins outside of you, with stimuli in the environment—trees, buildings, birds chirping, smells in the air—and ends with the behavioral responses of perceiving, recognizing, and taking action. We picture this journey from stimuli to responses by the seven steps in **Figure 1.1**, called the **perceptual process**. The process begins with a stimulus

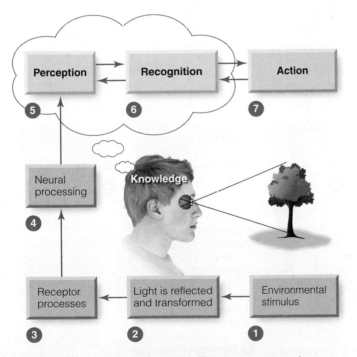

Figure 1.1 The perceptual process. These seven steps, plus "knowledge" inside the person's head, summarize the major events that occur between the time a person looks at an environmental stimulus (the tree in this example) and perceives the tree, recognizes it, and takes action toward it. Figures 1.2–1.5 describe the steps in the perceptual process in more detail. © Cengage Learning 2014

in the environment (a tree in this example) and ends with the conscious experiences of perceiving the tree, recognizing the tree, and taking action with respect to the tree.

Because we will be referring to this process in this chapter and the ones that follow, it is important to note that it is a simplified version of what happens. First, many things happen within each "box." For example, we could go far beyond "tree" to describe our example of an environmental stimulus. The tree has a particular configuration; its different parts reflect light in different ways (and so appear to have different colors, textures, and shapes); and it can be viewed from different angles. This complexity is even more obvious for boxes further down the line, such as "neural processing," which involves understanding not only how cells called neurons work, but how they interact with each other and how they operate within different areas of the brain.

Another reason we say the series of boxes in Figure 1.1 is simplified is that steps in the perceptual process do not always unfold in a one-follows-the-other order. For example, research has shown that perception ("I see something") and recognition (That's a tree) may not always happen one after another, but could happen at the same time, or even in reverse order (Gibson & Peterson, 1994). And when perception or recognition leads to action ("Let's have a closer look at the tree"), that action could change perception and recognition ("Looking closer shows that what I thought was an oak tree turns out to be a maple tree"). This is why there are reverse arrows between perception, recognition, and action.

Even though the process is simplified, Figure 1.1 provides a good way to think about how perception occurs and introduces some important principles that will guide our discussion of perception throughout this book. In the first part of this chapter, we will briefly describe each stage of the process; in the second part, we will consider ways of measuring the relationship between stimuli and perception. We begin the long and winding road that is the perceptual process by accompanying someone who is observing a tree in a field.

Stimuli (Steps 1 and 2)

There are stimuli within the body that produce internal pain and enable us to sense the positions of our body and limbs. But for the purposes of this discussion, we will focus on stimuli that exist "out there" in the environment, and we will consider what happens to stimuli in the first two steps of the perceptual process (**Figure 1.2**). We begin with the **environmental stimulus**, the tree that the person is observing (Step 1). The person's perception of the tree is based not on the tree getting into his eye (ouch!), but on light reflected from the tree (Step 2). The reflection of light from the tree introduces one of the central principles of perception, the **principle of transformation**, which states that *stimuli and responses created by stimuli are transformed, or changed, between the environmental stimulus and perception.*

The first transformation occurs when light hits the tree and is then reflected from the tree to the person's eyes. The

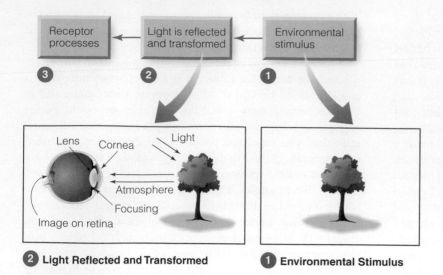

2 Light Reflected and Transformed　　**1** Environmental Stimulus

Figure 1.2 Steps 1 and 2 of the perceptual process. Step 1: *Environmental stimulus*. The tree is the stimulus. Step 2: *Light is reflected and transformed*. Information about the tree (the environmental stimulus) is carried by light, which is transformed when it is reflected from the tree, when it travels through the atmosphere, and when it is focused by the eye's optical system. The result is an image of the tree on the retina, which serves as a representation of the tree.
© Cengage Learning 2014

nature of the reflected light depends on properties of the light energy hitting the tree (is it the midday sun, light on an overcast day, or a spotlight illuminating the tree from below?), properties of the tree (its textures, shape, the fraction of light hitting it that it reflects), and properties of the atmosphere through which the light is transmitted (is the air clear, dusty, or foggy?).

When this reflected light reaches the eye, it is transformed as it is focused by the eye's optical system, which is the *cornea* at the front of the eye and the *lens* directly behind it. If these optics are working properly, they form a sharp image of the tree on the *receptors* of the person's *retina*, a 0.4-mm thick network of nerve cells that covers the back of the eye and that contains the receptors for vision. If the eye's optics are not working properly, the image that reaches the retina may be blurred.

The fact that an image of the tree is focused on the retina introduces another principle of perception, the **principle of representation**, which states that *everything a person perceives is based not on direct contact with stimuli but on representations of stimuli that are formed on the receptors and on activity in the person's nervous system.*

The distinction between the environmental stimulus (Step 1) and the stimulus on the receptors (Step 2) illustrates both transformation and representation. The environmental stimulus (the tree) is *transformed* into the image on the retina, and this image *represents* the tree in the person's eyes. But this transformation from "tree" to "image of the tree on the retina" is just the first in a series of transformations. The next transformation occurs within the receptors at the back of the eye.

Receptor Processes/Transduction (Step 3)

Sensory receptors are cells specialized to respond to environmental energy, with each sensory system's receptors specialized to respond to a specific type of energy. Visual receptors

respond to light, auditory receptors to pressure changes in the air, touch receptors to pressure transmitted through the skin, and smell and taste receptors to chemicals entering the nose and mouth. When the visual receptors that line the back of the eye receive the light reflected from the tree, they do two things: (1) They transform environmental energy into electrical energy; and (2) they shape perception by the way they respond to stimuli (**Figure 1.3**).

Visual receptors transform light energy into electrical energy because they contain a light-sensitive chemical called **visual pigment**, which reacts to light. The transformation of one form of energy (light energy in this example) to another form (electrical energy) is called **transduction**. Another example of transduction occurs when you touch the "withdrawal"

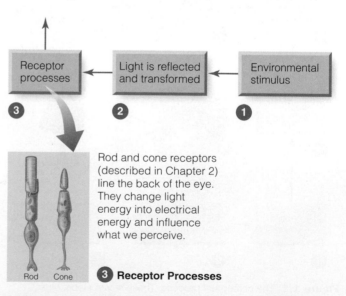

Rod and cone receptors (described in Chapter 2) line the back of the eye. They change light energy into electrical energy and influence what we perceive.

Rod　Cone　　**3** Receptor Processes

Figure 1.3 Step 3: *Receptor processes*. These processes include transduction (the transformation of light energy into electrical energy) and the shaping of perception by the properties of visual pigments in the receptor's outer segments. The end result is an electrical representation of the tree. © Cengage Learning 2014

button or icon on an ATM. The pressure exerted by your finger is transduced into electrical energy, which causes a device that uses mechanical energy to push your money out of the machine.

Transduction by the visual pigments is crucial for perception, because without it information about the representation of the tree formed on the retina would not reach the brain and perception would not occur. In addition, the visual pigments shape perception, both because the ability to see dim light depends on having a high concentration of pigment in the receptors and because there are different types of pigments. Some pigments respond better to light in the blue-green part of the spectrum; others respond better to the yellow-red part of the spectrum. We will describe both transduction and how the properties of pigments influence perception in Chapter 2.

Neural Processing (Step 4)

Once transduction occurs, the tree is represented by electrical signals in thousands of visual receptors, and these signals enter a vast interconnected network of neurons, first in the retina, then out the back of the eye, and then in the brain. This complex network of neurons (1) *transmits signals* from the receptors, through the retina, to the brain, and then within the brain; and (2) *changes* (or *processes*) these signals as they are transmitted. These changes occur because the pathway from receptors to the brain is typically far from a straight line. Instead, there are multiple routes, with some signals traveling in opposite directions, some signals becoming reduced or prevented from getting through, and others being amplified so they arrive at the brain with added strength.

The changes in these signals that occur as they are transmitted through this maze of neurons is called **neural** processing (**Figure 1.4**). Processing will be described in more detail in Chapters 2 and 3. For now, the main point is that processing continues the process of transformation that began when the tree was transformed into a small image inside the eye, which was then transformed into electrical signals in the visual receptors. A similar process of transduction followed by transmission occurs for other senses as well. For example, sound energy (pressure change in the air) is transformed into electrical signals inside the ear and is transmitted out of the ear along the auditory nerve and then through a series of structures on the way to the brain.

Electrical signals from each sense arrive at the **primary receiving area** for that sense in the cerebral cortex of the brain (as shown in Figure 1.4). The cerebral cortex is a 2-mm thick layer that contains the machinery for creating perceptions, as well as other functions, such as language, memory, and thinking. The primary receiving area for vision occupies most of the **occipital lobe**; the area for hearing is located in part of the **temporal lobe**; and the area for the skin senses—touch, temperature, and pain—is located in an area in the **parietal lobe**. The **frontal lobe** receives signals from all of the senses, and it plays an important role in perceptions that involve the coordination of information received through two or more senses. As we study each sense in detail, we will see that other areas in addition to the primary receiving areas are also associated with the neural processing of signals for each sense.

The sequence of transformations that occurs between the receptors and the brain, and then within the brain, means that the pattern of electrical signals in the brain is changed compared to the electrical signals that left the receptors. It is important to note, however, that although these signals have changed, they still represent the tree. In fact, the changes that occur as the signals are transmitted and processed are crucial for achieving the next step in the perceptual process, the *behavioral responses*.

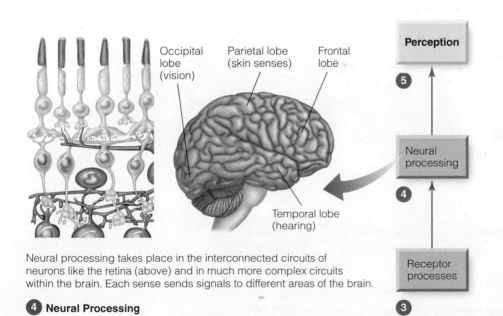

Neural processing takes place in the interconnected circuits of neurons like the retina (above) and in much more complex circuits within the brain. Each sense sends signals to different areas of the brain.

4 Neural Processing

Figure 1.4 Step 4: *Neural processing*. This involves interactions between the signals traveling in networks of neurons early in the system, in the retina; later, on the pathway to the brain; and finally, within the brain.
© Cengage Learning 2014

Behavioral Responses (Steps 5–7)

Finally, after all that reflection, focusing, transduction, transmission, and processing, we reach the behavioral responses (**Figure 1.5**). This transformation is perhaps the most miraculous of all of the transformations in the perceptual process, because the electrical signals from Step 4 are transformed into conscious experience: The person perceives the tree (Step 5) and recognizes it (Step 6). We can distinguish between **perception**, which is conscious awareness of the tree, and **recognition**, which is placing an object in a category, such as "tree," that gives it meaning, by considering the case of Dr. P., a patient described by neurologist Oliver Sacks (1985) in the title story of his book *The Man Who Mistook His Wife for a Hat.*

Dr. P., a well-known musician and music teacher, first noticed a problem when he began having trouble recognizing his students visually, although he could immediately identify them by the sound of their voices. But when Dr. P. began misperceiving common objects, for example addressing a parking meter as if it were a person or expecting a carved knob on a piece of furniture to engage him in conversation, it became clear that his problem was more serious than just a little forgetfulness. Was he blind, or perhaps crazy? It was clear from an eye examination that he could see well, and by many other criteria it was obvious that he was not crazy.

Dr. P.'s problem was eventually diagnosed as **visual form agnosia**—an inability to recognize objects—that was caused by a brain tumor. He perceived the parts of objects but couldn't identify the whole object, so when Sacks showed him a glove, Dr. P. described it as "a continuous surface unfolded on itself. It appears to have five outpouchings, if this is the word." When Sacks asked him what it was, Dr. P. hypothesized that it was "a container of some sort. It could be a change purse, for example, for coins of five sizes." The normally easy process of object recognition had, for Dr. P., been derailed by his brain tumor. He could perceive the object and recognize parts of it, but he couldn't perceptually assemble the parts in a way that would enable him to recognize the object as a whole. Cases such as this show that it is important to distinguish between perception and recognition.

The final behavioral response is **action** (Step 7), which involves motor activities. For example, the person might decide to walk toward the tree, have a picnic under it, or climb it. Even if he doesn't decide to interact directly with the tree, he is taking action when he looks at different parts of the tree, even if he is standing in one place.

Some researchers see action as an important outcome of the perceptual process because of its importance for survival. David Milner and Melvyn Goodale (1995) propose that early in the evolution of animals, the major goal of visual processing was not to create a conscious perception or "picture" of the environment but to help the animal control navigation, catch prey, avoid obstacles, and detect predators—all crucial functions for the animal's survival.

The fact that perception often leads to action—whether it be an animal's increasing its vigilance when it hears a twig snap in the forest or a person's deciding to interact with an object or just look more closely at something that looks interesting—means that perception is a continuously changing process. For example, the image of the tree on the back of the eye changes every time the person moves his body or his eyes relative to the tree, and this change creates new representations and a new series of transformations. Thus, although we can describe the perceptual process as a series of steps that "begins" with the environmental stimulus and "ends" with perception, recognition, and action, the overall process is dynamic and continually changing.

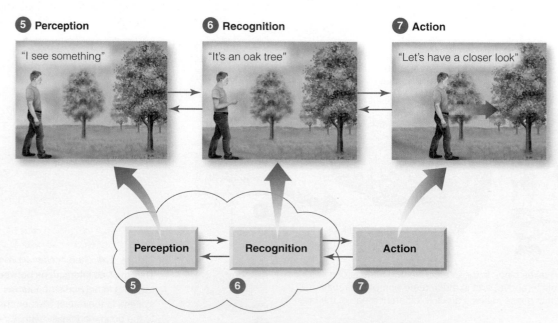

Figure 1.5 Steps 5–7: *Behavioral responses are perception, recognition, and action.* © Cengage Learning 2014

Figure 1.6 See Demonstration: Perceiving a Picture for instructions.

Adapted from "The Role of Frequency in Developing Perceptual Sets," by B. R. Bugelski and D. A. Alampay, 1961, *Canadian Journal of Psychology, 15,* 205–211. Copyright © 1961 by the Canadian Psychological Association. Reprinted with permission.

Knowledge

Our diagram of the perceptual process includes one more factor: *knowledge*. **Knowledge** is any information that the perceiver brings to a situation. Knowledge is placed inside the person's head in the diagram because it can affect a number of the steps in the perceptual process. Knowledge that a person brings to a situation can be information acquired years ago or, as in the following demonstration, information just recently acquired.

DEMONSTRATION
Perceiving a Picture

After looking at the drawing in **Figure 1.6**, close your eyes, turn to page 11, and open and shut your eyes rapidly to briefly expose the picture in **Figure 1.10**. Decide what the picture is; then open your eyes and read the explanation below it. Do this now, before reading further.

Did you identify Figure 1.10 as a rat (or a mouse)? If you did, you were influenced by the clearly rat- or mouselike figure you observed initially. But people who first observe **Figure 1.14** (page 13) instead of Figure 1.6 usually identify Figure 1.10 as a man. (Try this on someone else.) This demonstration, which is called the **rat–man demonstration**, shows how recently acquired knowledge ("that pattern is a rat") can influence perception.

An example of how knowledge acquired years ago can influence the perceptual process is the ability to categorize objects. This is something you do every time you name an object. "Tree," "bird," "branch," "car," and everything else you can name are examples of objects being placed into categories that you learned as a young child and that have become part of your knowledge base.

Another way to describe the effect of information that the perceiver brings to the situation is by distinguishing between bottom-up processing and top-down processing. **Bottom-up processing** (also called **data-based processing**) is processing that is based on the stimuli reaching the receptors. These stimuli provide the starting point for perception because, with the exception of unusual situations such as drug-induced perceptions or "seeing stars" from a bump to the head, without receptor activation there is no perception. The woman sees the moth on the tree in **Figure 1.7** because of processes triggered by the moth's image on her retina. The image is the "incoming data" that is the basis of bottom-up processing.

Top-down processing (also called **knowledge-based processing**) refers to processing that is based on knowledge. When the woman labels what she is seeing as a "moth" or perhaps a particular kind of moth, she is accessing what she has learned about moths. Knowledge such as this isn't always involved in perception, but as we will see, it often is—sometimes without our even being aware of it.

An example of the interaction between bottom-up and top-down processing occurs when a pharmacist reads what to you might look like an unreadable scribble on your doctor's prescription. She starts with the patterns that the doctor's handwriting creates on her retina. Once these bottom-up data have triggered the sequence of steps of the perceptual process, top-down processing can come into play as well. For example, the pharmacist might use her knowledge of the names of drugs, and perhaps past experience with this particular doctor's writing, to help her understand the unreadable (to you) squiggles on the prescription.

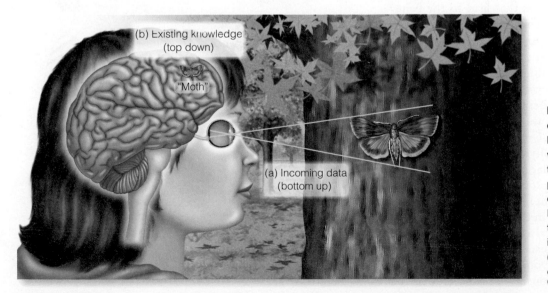

Figure 1.7 Perception is determined by an interaction between bottom-up processing, which starts with the image on the receptors, and top-down processing, which brings the observer's knowledge into play. In this example, (a) the image of the moth on the woman's retina initiates bottom-up processing; and (b) her prior knowledge of moths contributes to top-down processing.
© Cengage Learning

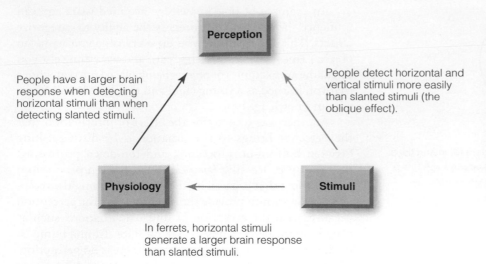

People have a larger brain response when detecting horizontal stimuli than when detecting slanted stimuli.

People detect horizontal and vertical stimuli more easily than slanted stimuli (the oblique effect).

In ferrets, horizontal stimuli generate a larger brain response than slanted stimuli.

Figure 1.8 Simplified perceptual process. The three boxes represent the three major components of the seven-step perceptual process: Stimuli (Steps 1 and 2); Physiology (Steps 3 and 4); and Perception, which stands for the three behavioral responses (Steps 5–7). The three relationships that are usually measured to study the perceptual process are the *psychophysical relationship* between stimuli and perception and the *physiological relationships* between stimuli and physiology and between physiology and perception. Results for research on the oblique effect described in the text are used as an example. © Cengage Learning 2014

My students often ask whether top-down processing is always involved in perception. The answer to this question is that it is "very often" involved. There are some situations, typically involving very simple stimuli, in which top-down processing is probably not involved. For example, perceiving a single flash of easily visible light is probably not affected by a person's prior experience. However, as stimuli become more complex, the role of top-down processing increases. In fact, a person's past experience is usually involved in perception of real-world scenes, even though in most cases the person is unaware of this influence. One of the themes of this book is that our knowledge of how things usually appear in the environment can play an important role in determining what we perceive.

How to Approach the Study of Perception

The goal of perceptual research is to understand each of the steps in the perceptual process that lead to the behavioral responses of perception, recognition, and action. (For simplicity, we will use the term *perception* to stand for all of these outcomes in the discussion that follows.) Toward this end, perception has been studied using two approaches: the *psychophysical approach* and the *physiological approach*.

To explain the difference between the psychophysical and physiological approaches, we simplify the seven-step perceptual process of Figure 1.1 into the simpler diagram shown in **Figure 1.8**. The **psychophysical approach**, also called **psychophysics**, measures the relationship between the stimuli (Steps 1–2 in our perceptual process of Figure 1.1) and the behavioral response (Steps 5–7 in Figure 1.1). This approach is indicated by the green arrow in Figure 1.8. An example of research using the psychophysical approach is an experiment in which subjects were tested to see how well they could see the fine lines in stimuli like the ones in **Figure 1.9** that were presented at different orientations. The result showed that

horizontal and vertical lines (stimuli) resulted in better detail vision (the behavioral response) than slanted lines. This better detail vision for verticals or horizontals compared to slanted lines is called the **oblique effect** (Appelle, 1972).

The **physiological approach** involves measuring two relationships, the relationship between stimuli (Steps 1–2) and physiological responses (Steps 3–4) (the orange arrow in Figure 1.8) and the relationship between physiological responses (Steps 3–4) and behavioral responses (Steps 5–7) (the red arrow in Figure 1.8). Researchers have used the physiological approach to understand the physiology behind the oblique effect. An example of measuring the

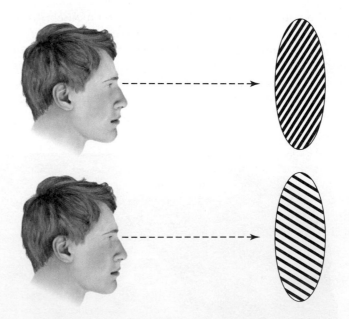

Psychophysical relationships are determined by measuring the relationship between stimuli and perception. In this example, *stimuli* are oriented bars, and *perception* is indicated by judgements of the bars' orientation.

Figure 1.9 Measuring the stimulus–perception (psychophysical) relationship between bar orientation and the ability to judge orientation. © Cengage Learning 2014

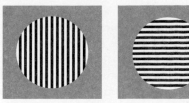

Stimuli: vertical, horizontal, slanted

Measure the relationship between stimuli (bars with different orientations) and physiological response (brain activity in ferret).

Figure 1.10 Did you see a "rat" or a "man"? Looking at the more ratlike picture in Figure 1.6 increased the chances that you would see this one as a rat. But if you had first seen the man version (Figure 1.14), you would have been more likely to perceive this figure as a man. Adapted from "The Role of Frequency in Developing Perceptual Sets," by B. R. Bugelski and D. A. Alampay, 1961, *Canadian Journal of Psychology, 15,* 205–211. Copyright © 1961 by the Canadian Psychological Association. Reprinted with permission.

Brain response: Bigger to vertical and horizontal orientations

Figure 1.11 Coppola and coworkers (1998) measured the relationship between bar orientation (stimuli) and brain activity (physiology) in ferrets.

stimulus–physiology relationship for the oblique effect is an experiment by David Coppola and coworkers (1998) in which they presented lines with different orientations to ferrets (**Figure 1.11**). Using a technique called *optical brain imaging* that measured activity over a large area of the ferret's visual cortex, researchers found that horizontal or vertical orientations (stimuli) caused larger brain responses (physiological responses) than slanted orientations, just as might be expected from the oblique effect that had been measured psychophysically in humans.[1]

An example of measuring the physiology–perception relationship for the oblique effect is an experiment by Christopher Furmanski and coworkers (2004) in which human subjects' brain activity was measured in a brain scanner while they carried out a task that involved detecting lines with different orientations. (We will describe the details of brain-scan technology in Chapter 4; see Figure 4.3, page 79, for a picture of the apparatus.) This experiment showed that the brain response (physiological) was larger when the subjects were detecting horizontals than when they were detecting slanted lines (perception) (**Figure 1.12**). Measuring physiological responding and perception in the same subjects determines the physiology–perception relationship.

As we study perception measuring the three relationships in Figure 1.8, we will also be concerned with how the knowledge, memories, and expectations that people bring to a situation influence their perceptions. These factors, which we have described as the starting place for top-down processing, are called **cognitive influences on perception**. These cognitive influences were represented by the word "knowledge" inside the person's head in the perceptual cycle

in Figure 1.1. Researchers study cognitive influences by measuring how knowledge and other factors, such as memories and expectations, affect all of the relationships in Figure 1.8.

For example, consider the rat–man demonstration. If we were to measure the stimulus–perception relationship by showing just Figure 1.10 to a number of people, we would probably find that some people see a rat and some people see a man. But when we add some "knowledge" by first presenting the more ratlike picture in Figure 1.6, most people see Figure 1.10 as a "rat" or "mouse." Thus, in this example, knowledge has affected the stimulus–perception relationship.

Perception: Better detection of horizontal   **Brain response:** Bigger to horizontal

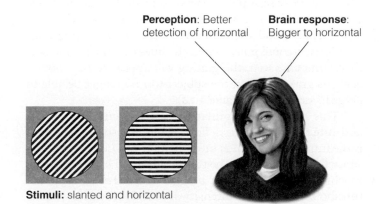

Stimuli: slanted and horizontal

Measure the relationship between physiological response (brain activity) and perception (detecting oriented lines)

Figure 1.12 Furmanski and coworkers (2004) measured the relationship between human subjects' brain responses (physiology) and their ability to judge the orientation of bars (perception).
© Cengage Learning 2014

---

[1]Because a great deal of physiological research has been done on animals, students often express concerns about how these animals are treated. All animal research in the United States follows strict guidelines for the care of animals established by organizations such as the American Psychological Association and the Society for Neuroscience. The central tenet of these guidelines is that every effort should be made to ensure that animals are not subjected to pain or distress. Research on animals has provided essential information for developing aids for people with sensory disabilities such as blindness and deafness and for helping develop techniques to ease severe pain.

One of the things that becomes apparent when we step back and look at the psychophysical and physiological approaches is that each one provides information about different aspects of the perceptual process. Thus, to truly understand perception, we have to study it using both approaches by measuring all three relationships in Figure 1.8. In the remainder of this chapter, we describe some ways to measure the stimulus–perception relationship using the psychophysical approach. In Chapters 2 and 3 we will introduce basic principles of the physiological approach.

TEST YOURSELF 1.1

1. What are some reasons for studying perception?

2. Describe the process of perception as a series of seven steps, beginning with the environmental stimulus and culminating in the behavioral responses of perceiving, recognizing, and acting.

3. What is the role of higher-level or "cognitive" processes in perception? Be sure you understand the difference between bottom-up and top-down processing.

4. What does it mean to say that perception can be studied using different approaches? Give an example of how each approach was applied to determine each of the relationships in Figure 1.8 for the oblique effect.

Measuring Perception

When we described the psychophysical experiment that demonstrated the oblique effect, we said that "subjects were tested to see how well they could see the fine lines in stimuli like the ones in Figure 1.12." But exactly how was this "seeing" measured? This is an important question, and it has led to the development of many different techniques to measure perception. For example, one way to measure the ability to see different orientations would be to present gratings with finer and finer lines and ask subjects to indicate the grating's orientation. At some point, when the lines become so fine that they cannot be seen, the grating will appear to be a homogeneous gray field, and the subject will no longer be able to judge its orientation (**Figure 1.13**).

This type of determination is a measurement of the **absolute threshold**. One definition of the absolute threshold is the minimum stimulus intensity that can just be detected. Thus, for seeing a light, the threshold would be the intensity at which the light can just barely be seen. For hearing, the threshold would be the intensity of sound that can just barely be heard. In the case of the grating task, the absolute threshold is defined as the smallest line width that can just barely be detected. In the discussion that follows, we will use the term *threshold* to refer to *absolute threshold*.

Returning to the oblique effect, measuring the threshold for detecting gratings of different orientations indicates

Figure 1.13 Measuring the finest line width at which a person can perceive the bars in a black-and-white grating stimulus. Stimuli with different line widths are presented one at a time, and the subject indicates the grating's orientation until the lines are so close together that the subject can no longer indicate the orientation. © Cengage Learning 2014

that the threshold is lower (finer lines can be detected) when the gratings are horizontal or vertical rather than slanted or oblique. This finding led to more experiments, both psychophysical and physiological, that were designed to determine why people perceive verticals and horizontals better. The answer, which we will return to in Chapter 5, is related to the fact that the development of the nervous system is influenced by the kinds of stimuli we experience in the environment. (Hint: There are more horizontals and verticals than oblique orientations in the environment.)

Measuring Thresholds

The importance of being able to accurately measure thresholds was recognized very early in the history of the scientific study of the senses. In 1860, Gustav Fechner (1801–1887), a German physicist interested in studying perceptual phenomena, published *Elements of Psychophysics*. This book was important at the time because many scientists and philosophers had stated that it was impossible to measure the mind. Fechner's book, which proposed a number of methods for measuring thresholds, proved this idea to be wrong and was thus an important step in the establishment of the field of scientific psychology.

Fechner proposed three main methods for measuring thresholds. They all have in common the idea that human perception can be variable, so measurements at one point in time might differ slightly from measurements at another point. Fechner's methods take this variability into account by having subjects make multiple judgments. These methods, which we describe below, are called the **classical psychophysical methods** because they were the original methods used to measure the relationship between stimuli and perception.

Figure 1.14 Man version of the rat–man stimulus. Adapted from "The Role of Frequency in Developing Perceptual Sets," by B. R. Bugelski and D. A. Alampay, 1961, *Canadian Journal of Psychology, 15,* 205–211. Copyright © 1961 by the Canadian Psychological Association. Reprinted with permission.

Note that every so often we will introduce a new method by describing it in a "Method" section like the following. Students are sometimes tempted to skip these sections because they think the content is unimportant. However, you should resist this temptation because these methods are essential tools for the study of perception. These "Method" sections will help you understand the experiment usually described immediately afterward and also provide the background for understanding other experiments later in the book.

METHOD
Determining the Threshold

Fechner's classical psychophysical methods for determining the threshold are the methods of *limits*, *adjustment*, and *constant stimuli*. In the **method of limits**, the experimenter presents stimuli in either ascending order (intensity is increased) or descending

Intensity	1 ↓	2 ↑	3 ↓	4 ↑	5 ↓	6 ↑	7 ↓	8 ↑
103	Y		Y		Y		Y	
102	Y		Y		Y		Y	
101	Y		Y		Y		Y	Y
100	Y	Y	Y	Y	Y		Y	Y
99	Y	N	Y	N	Y	Y	Y	Y
98	N	N	Y	N	N	N	N	Y
97		N	N	N		N		N
96		N		N		N		N
95		N		N		N		N

Crossover values → 98.5 99.5 97.5 99.5 98.5 98.5 98.5 97.5

Threshold = Mean of crossovers = 98.5

Figure 1.15 The results of an experiment to determine the threshold using the method of limits. The dashed lines indicate the crossover point for each sequence of stimuli. The threshold—the average of the crossover values—is 98.5 in this experiment. © Cengage Learning 2014

order (intensity is decreased), as shown in **Figure 1.15**, which indicates the results of an experiment that measures a person's threshold for hearing a tone.

On the first series of trials, the experimenter begins by presenting a tone with an intensity of 103, and the observer indicates by a "yes" response that he hears the tone. This response is indicated by a Y at an intensity of 103 in the far left column of the table. The experimenter then presents another tone, at a lower intensity, and the observer responds to this tone. This procedure continues, with the observer making a judgment at each intensity until he responds "no," he did not hear the tone. This change from "yes" to "no," indicated by the dashed line, is the *crossover point*, and the threshold for this series is taken as the mean between 99 and 98, or 98.5. The next series of trials begins below the observer's threshold, so that he says "no" on the first trial (intensity 95), and continues until he says "yes" (when the intensity reaches 100). Notice that the crossover point when starting below the threshold is slightly different. Because the crossover points may vary slightly, this procedure is repeated a number of times, starting above the threshold half the time and starting below the threshold half the time. The threshold is then determined by calculating the average of all of the crossover points.

The **method of adjustment** is similar to the method of limits in that the stimulus intensity is either increased or decreased until the stimulus can just be detected. However, in the method of adjustment, the observer (not the experimenter) adjusts the stimulus intensity continuously until he or she can just barely detect the stimulus. For example, the observer might be told to turn a knob to decrease the intensity of a sound until the sound can no longer be heard, and then to turn the knob back again so the sound is just barely audible. This just barely audible intensity is taken as the threshold. This procedure can be repeated several times and the threshold determined by taking the average setting.

In the **method of constant stimuli**, the experimenter presents five to nine stimuli with different intensities in random order. For example, in a hypothetical experiment designed to determine the threshold for seeing a light, intensities of 150, 160, 170, 180, 190, and 200 are presented one at a time. On each trial, the observer says "yes" or "no" to indicate whether he or she sees the light. The experimenter chooses light intensities so that the lowest intensity is never detected and the highest one is always detected. The intensities in between are detected on some trials and not on others. The result from presenting each intensity many times and determining the percentage of trials on which the light was detected is shown in **Figure 1.16**. The threshold is usually defined as the intensity that results in detection on 50 percent of the trials. Applying this definition to the results in Figure 1.16 indicates that the threshold is an intensity of 180.

The choice among the methods of limits, adjustment, and constant stimuli is usually determined by the degree of accuracy needed and the amount of time available. The method of constant stimuli is the most accurate method because it involves many observations and stimuli are presented in random order, which minimizes how presentation on one trial can affect the observer's judgment of the stimulus presented on the next trial. The disadvantage of this method is that it is time-consuming. The method of adjustment is faster because observers can determine their threshold in just a few trials by adjusting the intensity themselves.

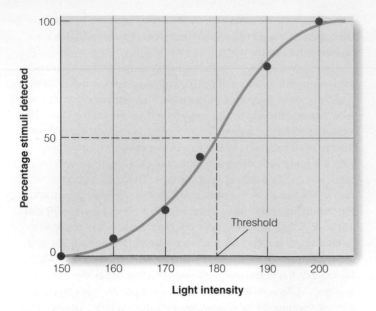

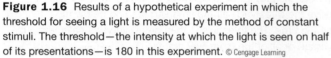

Figure 1.16 Results of a hypothetical experiment in which the threshold for seeing a light is measured by the method of constant stimuli. The threshold—the intensity at which the light is seen on half of its presentations—is 180 in this experiment. © Cengage Learning

When Fechner published *Elements of Psychophysics*, he not only described his methods for measuring the absolute threshold but also described the work of Ernst Weber (1795–1878), a physiologist who, a few years before the publication of Fechner's book, measured another type of threshold, the **difference threshold**. The absolute threshold measures the stimulus level above zero that is necessary for detecting a stimulus. There is also a minimum *difference* that must exist *between* two stimuli before we can tell the difference between them. This just detectible difference is the difference threshold (called DL from the German *Differenze Limen*, which is translated as "difference threshold.")

Measuring instruments, such as an old-fashioned balance scale, can detect very small differences. For example, imagine that a scale is balanced when four 50-penny rolls are placed on each pan. When just one additional penny is placed on one side, the scale succeeds in detecting this very small difference between the two weights. The human sensory system is not as sensitive to weight differences as this type of scale, so a human comparing the weight of 201 pennies to 200 pennies would not be able to tell the difference. The difference threshold for weight is about 2 percent, which means that under ideal conditions, we would have to add 4 pennies to one side before the difference could be detected.

The idea that the difference threshold is a *percentage* of the weights being compared was discovered by Weber, who proposed that the ratio of the DL to the standard is constant. This means that if we doubled the number of pennies to 400, the DL would also double, becoming 8. The ratio DL/Standard for lifting weights is 0.02, which

is called the Weber fraction, and the fact that the Weber fraction remains the same as the standard is changed is called Weber's law. Modern investigators have found that Weber's law is true for most senses, as long as the stimulus intensity is not too close to the absolute threshold (Engen, 1972; Gescheider, 1976).

The Weber fraction remains relatively constant for a particular sense, but each type of sensory judgment has its own Weber fraction. For example, from **Table 1.1** we can see that people can detect a 1 percent change in the intensity of an electric shock but that light intensity must be increased by 8 percent before they can detect a difference.

We have noted that Fechner's proposal of three psychophysical methods for measuring the threshold and his statement of Weber's law for the difference threshold were extremely important because they demonstrated that mental activity could be measured quantitatively. Perhaps the most significant thing about these methods, however, is that even though they were proposed in the 1800s, they are still used today. In addition to being used to determine thresholds in research laboratories, simplified versions of the classical psychophysical methods are used to measure people's detail vision when determining prescriptions for glasses and measuring people's hearing when testing for possible hearing loss.

The classical psychophysical methods were developed to measure absolute and difference thresholds. But most of our everyday experience consists of perceptions that are far above threshold, when we can easily see and hear what is happening around us. How do we measure these above-threshold perceptions? One method is a technique called *magnitude estimation*.

Estimating Magnitude

If we double the intensity of a tone, does it sound twice as loud? If we double the intensity of a light, does it look twice as bright? Although a number of researchers, including Fechner, proposed equations that related perceived magnitudes, such as the brightness of a light or the loudness of a tone, to stimulus intensity, it was not until 1957 that S. S. Stevens developed a technique called scaling, or magnitude estimation, that accurately measured this relationship (Stevens, 1957, 1961, 1962).

TABLE 1.1 Weber Fractions for a Number of Different Sensory Dimensions

Electric shock	0.01
Lifted weight	0.02
Sound intensity	0.04
Light intensity	0.08
Taste (salty)	0.08

Source: Teghtsoonian (1971).

METHOD
Magnitude Estimation

The procedure for a magnitude estimation experiment is relatively simple: The experimenter first presents a "standard" stimulus to the subject (let's say a light of moderate intensity) and assigns it a value of, say, 10. He or she then presents lights of different intensities, and the subject is asked to assign a number to each of these lights that is proportional to the brightness of the original light. This number for "brightness" is the perceived magnitude of the stimulus. If the light appears twice as bright as the standard, it gets a rating of 20; half as bright, a 5; and so on. Thus, each light intensity has a brightness assigned to it by the subject.

It is important to note that *intensity* is a physical measure—related to *how much* light energy is present. (For example, a 200-watt lightbulb has twice the energy of a 100-watt bulb.) *Brightness* or *perceived magnitude*, on the other hand, is a perceptual measure that indicates what the observer *experiences*.

The results of a magnitude estimation experiment on brightness are plotted as the red curve in **Figure 1.17**. This graph plots the average magnitude estimates made by a number of observers of the brightness of a light. This curve indicates that doubling the intensity does not necessarily double the perceived brightness. For example, when the intensity is 20, perceived brightness is 28. If we double the intensity to 40, perceived brightness does not double to 56, but instead increases only to 36. This result, in which the increase in perceived magnitude is smaller than the increase in stimulus intensity, is called **response compression**.

Figure 1.17 also shows the results of magnitude estimation experiments for the experience caused by an elec-

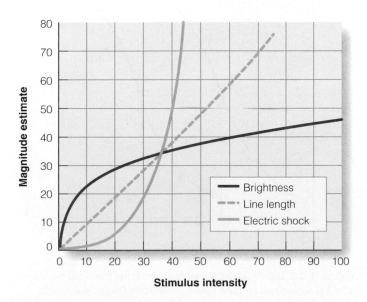

Figure 1.17 The relationship between perceived magnitude and stimulus intensity for electric shock, line length, and brightness. Adapted from "The Surprising Simplicity of Sensory Metrics" by S. S. Stevens, 1962, *American Psychologist, 17,* 29–39. Copyright © 1962 by American Psychological Association.

tric shock presented to the finger and for the perception of length of a line. The electric shock curve bends up, indicating that doubling the strength of a shock more than doubles the perceived magnitude of the shock. Increasing the intensity from 20 to 40 increases perception of shock magnitude from 6 to 49. This is called **response expansion**. As intensity is increased, perceptual magnitude increases more than intensity. The curve for estimating line length is straight, with a slope of close to 1.0, meaning that the magnitude of the response almost exactly matches increases in the stimulus, so if the line length is doubled, an observer says it appears to be twice as long.

The beauty of the relationships derived from magnitude estimation is that the relationship between the intensity of a stimulus and our perception of its magnitude follows the same general equation for each sense. These functions, which are called **power functions**, are described by the equation $P = KS^n$. Perceived magnitude, P, equals a constant, K, times the stimulus intensity, S, raised to a power, n. This relationship is called **Stevens's power law**.

For example, if the exponent, n, is 2.0 and the constant, K, is 1.0, the perceived magnitude, P, for intensities 10 and 20 would be calculated as follows:

Intensity 10: $P = (1.0) \times (10)^2 = 100$

Intensity 20: $P = (1.0) \times (20)^2 = 400$

In this example, doubling the intensity results in a fourfold increase in perceived magnitude, an example of response expansion.

The exponent of the power function, n, tells us something important about the way perceived magnitude changes as intensity is increased. Exponents less than 1.0 are associated with response compression (as occurs for the brightness of a light), and exponents greater than 1.0 are associated with response expansion (as occurs for sensing shocks).

Response compression and expansion illustrate how the operation of each sense is adapted to how organisms function in their environment. Consider, for example, your experience of brightness. Imagine you are inside reading a book, when you turn to look out the window at a sidewalk bathed in intense sunlight. Your eyes may be receiving thousands of times more light from the sidewalk than from the page of your book, but because of response compression, the sidewalk does not appear thousands of times brighter than the page. It does appear brighter, but not so much that you are blinded by the sunlit sidewalk.[2]

The opposite situation occurs for electric shock, which has an exponent of 3.5, so small increases in shock intensity cause large increases in pain. This rapid increase in pain associated with response expansion serves to warn us of impending danger, and we therefore tend to withdraw even from weak shocks.

---

[2]Another mechanism that keeps you from being blinded by high-intensity lights is the process of *adaptation*, which adjusts the eye's sensitivity in response to different light levels.

Beyond Thresholds and Magnitudes

There are many other ways of measuring the behavioral response to a stimulus besides measuring thresholds and magnitudes. One common technique is the **phenomenological method**, in which a person is asked to describe what he or she is perceiving or to indicate when a particular perception occurs. Describing what is being perceived can be at a very basic level, such as when we notice that we can perceive some objects as being farther away than others, or that there is a perceptual quality we call "color," or that there are different qualities of taste, such as bitter, sweet, and sour. These are such common observations that we take them for granted because they occur routinely every day, but this is where the study of perception begins, because these observations describe the basic properties that we are seeking to explain. Many of the experiments described in this book involve the phenomenological method. For example, a person might be asked to name the color of a light or to indicate whether a particular taste is bitter or sweet.

The phenomenological method is often used when testing the perception of people with brain damage. Thus, Dr. P., the musician with visual form agnosia described earlier, was able to *describe* a glove as a "continuous surface unfolded on itself. It appears to have five outpouchings." Although this is an awkward way to describe the object, it does show that Dr. P. was able to perceive some of its characteristics. However, when asked to *recognize* the object, Dr. P. was stymied. Even though he could see it and describe it, he could not recognize it as a glove. Description involves noting what is seen (or heard, felt, smelled, or tasted); testing for *recognition* goes a step further, requiring that the person name the object.

Another method used to study perceptual mechanisms is **visual search**, in which the observer's task is to find one stimulus among many, as quickly as possible. An everyday example of visual search would be searching for a friend's face in a crowd. If you've ever done this, you know that sometimes it is easy (if you know your friend is wearing a bright red hat and no one else is), and sometimes it is difficult (if there are lots of people and your friend doesn't stand out). When we consider visual attention in Chapter 6, we will describe visual search experiments in which the observer's task is to find a target stimulus that is hidden among a number of other stimuli. We will see that measuring **reaction time**—the time between presentation of the stimulus and the observer's response to the stimulus—has provided important information about mechanisms responsible for perception.

Numerous other methods have been used to measure the stimulus–perception relationship. For example, in some experiments, observers are asked to decide whether two stimuli look the same or different, or to adjust the brightness or the colors of two lights so they appear the same, or to close their eyes and walk, as accurately as possible, to a distant target stimulus in a field. We will encounter methods such as these, and others as well, as we describe perceptual research in the chapters that follow.

SOMETHING TO CONSIDER:
Threshold Measurement Can Be Influenced by How a Person Chooses to Respond

We've seen that by randomly presenting lights of different intensities, we can use the method of constant stimuli to determine a person's threshold—the intensity to which the person reports "I see the light" 50 percent of the time. What determines this threshold intensity? Certainly, the physiological workings of the person's eye and visual system are important. But some researchers have pointed out that perhaps other characteristics of the person may also influence the determination of threshold intensity.

To illustrate this idea, let's consider a hypothetical experiment in which we use the method of constant stimuli to measure Julie's and Regina's thresholds for seeing a light. We pick five different light intensities, present them in random order, and ask Julie and Regina to say "yes" if they see the light and "no" if they don't see it. Julie thinks about these instructions and decides that she wants to be sure she doesn't miss any presentations of the light. She therefore decides to say "yes" if there is even the slightest possibility that she sees the light. However, Regina responds more conservatively because she wants to be totally sure that she sees the light before saying "yes." She is not willing to report that she sees the light unless it is clearly visible.

The results of this hypothetical experiment are shown in **Figure 1.18**. Julie gives many more "yes" responses than Regina

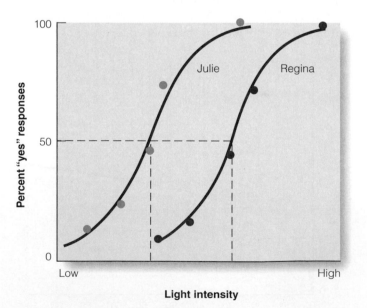

Figure 1.18 Data from experiments in which the threshold for seeing a light is determined for Julie (green points) and Regina (red points) by means of the method of constant stimuli. These data indicate that Julie's threshold is lower than Regina's. But is Julie really more sensitive to the light than Regina, or does she just appear to be more sensitive because she is a more liberal responder? © Cengage Learning

and therefore ends up with a lower threshold. But given what we know about Julie and Regina, should we conclude that Julie's visual system is more sensitive to the lights than Regina's? It could be that their actual sensitivity to the lights is exactly same, but Julie's apparently lower threshold occurs because she is more willing than Regina to report that she sees a light. A way to describe this difference between these two people is that each has a different **response criterion**. Julie's response criterion is low (she says "yes" if there is the slightest chance a light is present), whereas Regina's response criterion is high (she says "yes" only when she is sure that she sees the light).

What are the implications of the fact that people may have different response criteria? If we are interested in how one person responds to different stimuli (for example, measuring how a person's threshold varies for different colors of light), then we don't need to take response criterion into account because we are comparing responses within the same person. Response criterion is also not very important if we are testing many people and averaging their responses. However, if we wish to compare two people's responses, their differing response criteria could influence the results. Luckily, there is a way to take differing response criteria into account. This procedure is described in the Appendix, which discusses **signal detection theory**.

The Road From Here

In Chapter 2, "Beginnings of Perception," we follow the stimulus from when it is in the environment (a tree in a field) to what it becomes in the nervous system (electrical signals in the eye). Most of the chapter focuses on Steps 1–3, and then neural processing (Step 4) is introduced at the end of the chapter. Note that although we will be describing the process using the example of vision, every step in this process also holds for each of the other senses—hearing, touch, taste, and smell—that we will be describing in this book.

Chapter 3 elaborates on the introduction to neural processing (Step 4) from the end of Chapter 2, beginning with what happens in the eye and moving on to what happens in the brain. Chapter 4 again focuses on Step 4 by looking at how processing is affected by the way the brain is organized.

If, at this point, you are thinking that we are going to be spending a lot of pages considering the physiology of perception, you are right. The purpose of Chapters 2, 3, and 4 is, in fact, to orient you to the perceptual process and to introduce the basic physiological principles you will need to understand the rest of the book. But although we will be focusing on neurons, we never lose sight of perception, because the goal of this book is to explain what is responsible for our perceptions. Thus, as we describe the physiological mechanisms of perception, we will continually be asking "How does the physiology relate to perception?"

TEST YOURSELF 1.2

1. Describe the three methods for measuring the absolute threshold.

2. What is the difference threshold? What is the Weber fraction? Weber's law?

3. What is the purpose of magnitude estimation? Describe the procedure for a magnitude estimation experiment.

4. What is a power function? What does the exponent of a power function indicate about how perceived magnitude increases with stimulus intensity? How is this related to how the senses are adapted to the environment?

5. Describe other ways of measuring perception besides methods for determining thresholds and magnitudes.

6. What does it mean to say that a person's threshold may be determined by more than the physiological workings of his or her sensory system?

THINK ABOUT IT

1. This chapter argues that although perception seems simple, it is actually extremely complex when we consider "behind the scenes" activities that are not obvious as a person is experiencing perception. Cite an example of a similar situation from your own experience, in which an "outcome" that might seem as though it was achieved easily actually involved a complicated process that most people are unaware of.

2. Describe a situation in which you initially thought you saw or heard something but then realized that your initial perception was in error. What was the role of bottom-up and top-down processing in this example of first having an incorrect perception and then realizing what was actually there?

KEY TERMS

Absolute threshold (p. 12)
Action (p. 8)
Bottom-up processing (data-based processing) (p. 9)
Classical psychophysical methods (p. 12)
Cognitive influences on perception (p. 11)
Difference threshold (p. 14)
Environmental stimulus (p. 5)
Frontal lobe (p. 7)
Knowledge (p. 9)
Magnitude estimation (p. 14)
Method of adjustment (p. 13)
Method of constant stimuli (p. 13)
Method of limits (p. 13)
Neural processing (p. 7)
Oblique effect (p. 10)

Occipital lobe (p. 7)
Parietal lobe (p. 7)
Perceived magnitude (p. 15)
Perception (p. 8)
Perceptual process (p. 5)
Phenomenological method (p. 16)
Physiological approach to perception (p. 10)
Power function (p. 15)
Primary receiving area (p. 7)
Principle of representation (p. 6)
Principle of transformation (p. 5)
Psychophysical approach to perception (p. 10)
Psychophysics (p. 10)
Rat–man demonstration (p. 9)
Reaction time (p. 16)
Recognition (p. 8)

Response compression (p. 15)
Response criterion (p. 17)
Response expansion (p. 15)
Sensory receptors (p. 6)
Signal detection theory (p. 17)
Stevens's power law (p. 15)
Temporal lobe (p. 7)
Top-down processing (knowledge-based processing) (p. 9)
Transduction (p. 6)
Visual form agnosia (p. 8)
Visual pigment (p. 6)
Visual search (p. 16)
Weber fraction (p. 14)
Weber's law (p. 14)

MEDIA RESOURCES

CourseMate 🖥

Go to CengageBrain.com to access Psychology CourseMate, where you will find the Virtual Labs plus an interactive eBook, flashcards, quizzes, videos, and more.

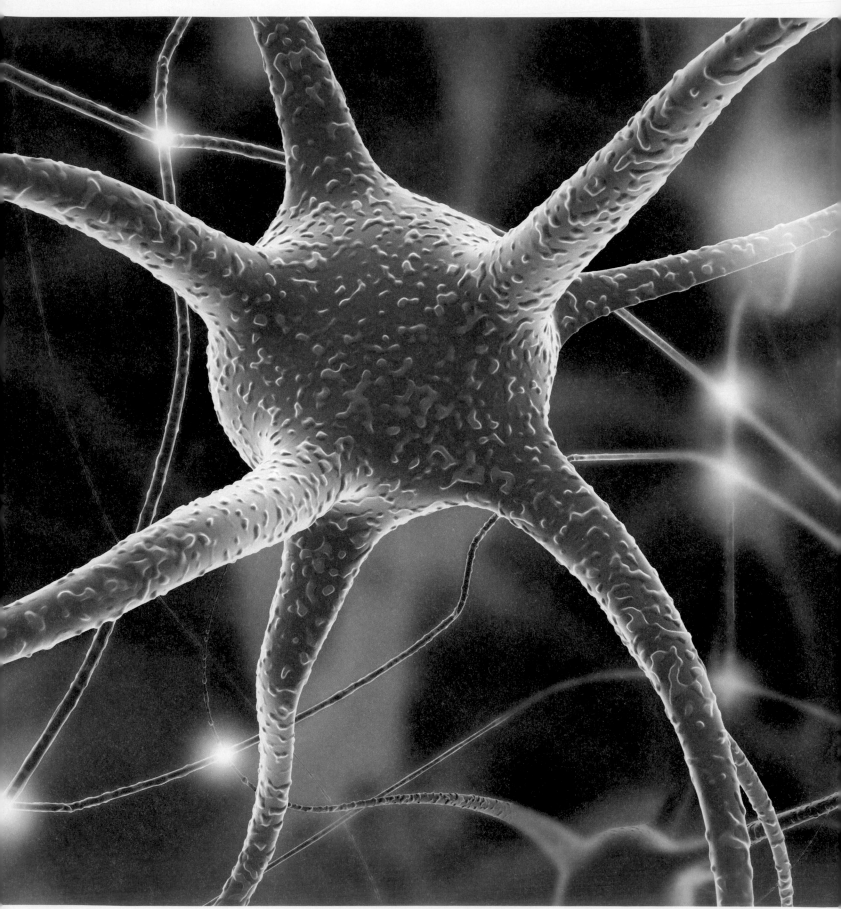

The Beginnings of Perception

VL The Virtual Lab icons direct you to specific animations and videos designed to help you visualize what you are reading about. Virtual Labs are listed at the end of the chapter, keyed to the page on which they appear, and can be accessed through Psychology CourseMate

◀ This spiderlike object is an artist's conception of a neuron, a type of cell that is responsible for communication within the nervous system. In this chapter, we consider the beginning of the perceptual process, and then introduce neurons and begin to see how essential they are for the creation of perceptions.

Some Questions We Will Consider:

- How does the focusing system at the front of our eye affect our perception? (p. 22)
- How do chemicals in the eye called visual pigments affect our perception? (p. 23)
- How can the way neurons are "wired up" affect perception? (p. 40)

When the person we met in Chapter 1 opens his eyes to see the tree, he sets in motion the sequence of events of the perceptual process that we introduced in Figure 1.1. This chapter starts at the beginning of the process.

Starting at the Beginning

The idea that perception starts at the beginning of the perceptual process may sound obvious. But as we will see, there is enough going on right at the beginning of the perceptual process to fill a whole chapter and more, and most of what goes on can affect perception. So, the first step in understanding perception is to take a close look at the processes that begin, in the case of vision, with light reflected from an object into the eye.

The purpose of this chapter is to look at these initial processes. We will use visual examples, but many of the principles we will be describing hold for the other senses as well. Just as the person from Chapter 1 sees the tree because light is reflected from it into his eyes, he hears the rustle of its branches because sound energy in the form of pressure changes in the air enters his ears. In both cases, stimuli trigger a process that ends up with perception occurring due to activity in the brain, and similar events occur for feeling the texture of the tree's bark, smelling its blossoms, and tasting its fruit. By the time you finish this book, you will see that

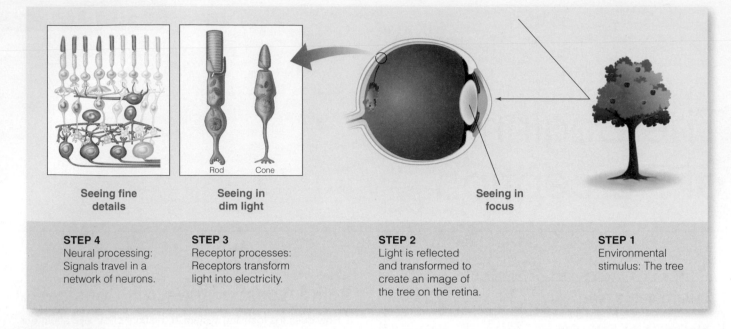

Figure 2.1 Chapter preview. This chapter will describe the first three steps of the perceptual process for vision and will introduce Step 4. Physical processes are indicated in black; the perceptual outcomes of these processes are indicated in blue. © Cengage Learning 2014

STEP 4
Neural processing: Signals travel in a network of neurons.

STEP 3
Receptor processes: Receptors transform light into electricity.

STEP 2
Light is reflected and transformed to create an image of the tree on the retina.

STEP 1
Environmental stimulus: The tree

Seeing fine details

Seeing in dim light

Rod   Cone

Seeing in focus

although there are numerous differences between the senses, they all operate according to similar principles.

Figure 2.1 shows the beginning of the visual process, when light enters the eye and becomes transformed in a number of ways. We start with Step 1, the environmental stimulus (the tree); then move to Step 2, how light reflected from the tree is transformed on the way to the visual receptors; then to Step 3, how the properties of the receptors transform light into electrical signals and determine our sensitivity to light and which portion of the reflected light we see. Finally, we introduce Step 4, in which electrical signals are "processed" as they travel in neurons.

Note that we have been describing the *physical events* indicated in black on the figure. But the only reason we are interested in these physical events is because of their role in creating perceptions, indicated in blue. For example, the physical events of Steps 1 and 2 affect the visibility of the tree (without light we don't see the tree) and the sharpness of our perception (the nature of the air and the operation of the eye's focusing system determine whether the tree appears sharp or fuzzy). Every time we refer to physical events, we will be interested in exploring how these events affect perception. We begin describing this connection between physical and perceptual by considering the nature of light and how it is focused by the eye.

Light and Focusing

The ability to see a tree, or any other object, depends on information contained in light reflected from that object into the eye.

Light: The Stimulus for Vision

Vision is based on visible light, which is a band of energy within the electromagnetic spectrum. The **electromagnetic spectrum** is a continuum of electromagnetic energy that is produced by electric charges and is radiated as waves (**Figure 2.2**). The energy in this spectrum can be described by its **wavelength**—the distance between the peaks of the electromagnetic waves. The wavelengths in the electromagnetic spectrum range from extremely-short-wavelength gamma rays (wavelength = about 10^{-12} meters, or one ten-billionth of a meter) to long-wavelength radio waves (wavelength = about 10^4 meters, or 10,000 meters).

Visible light, the energy within the electromagnetic spectrum that humans can perceive, has wavelengths ranging from about 400 to 700 nanometers (nm), where 1 nanometer = 10^{-9} meters, which means that the longest visible wavelengths are slightly less than one-thousandth of a millimeter long. For humans and some other animals, the wavelength of visible light is associated with the different colors of the spectrum, with short wavelengths appearing blue, middle wavelengths green, and long wavelengths yellow, orange, and red. Although we will usually specify light in terms of its wavelength, light can also be described as consisting of small packets of energy called *photons*, with one photon being the smallest possible packet of light energy.

The Eye

The **eyes** contain the receptors for vision. The first eyes, back in the Cambrian period (570–500 million years ago), were

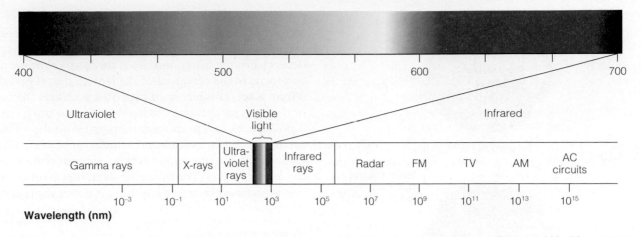

Figure 2.2 The electromagnetic spectrum, showing the wide range of energy in the environment and the small range within this spectrum, called visible light, that we can see. The wavelength is in nanometers (nm), where 1 nm = 10^{-9} meters. © Cengage Learning

eyespots on primitive animals such as flatworms that could distinguish light from dark but couldn't detect features of the environment. Detecting an object's details didn't become possible until more sophisticated eyes evolved to include optical systems that could produce images and therefore provide information about shapes and details of objects and the arrangement of objects within scenes (Fernald, 2006).

Light reflected from objects in the environment enters the eye through the **pupil** and is focused by the **cornea** and **lens** to form sharp images of the objects on the **retina**, the network of neurons that covers the back of the eye and that contains the receptors for vision (**Figure 2.3a**).

These visual receptors, the **rods** and **cones**, contain light-sensitive chemicals called **visual pigments** that react to light and trigger electrical signals. Signals from the receptors flow through the network of neurons that make up the retina (**Figure 2.3b**) and emerge from the back of the eye in the **optic nerve**, which conducts signals toward the brain. The cornea

and lens at the front of the eye and the receptors and neurons in the retina lining the back of the eye shape what we see by creating two transformations: (1) the transformation from light reflected from an object into an image of the object; and (2) the transformation from the image of the object into electrical signals. **VL**

Light Is Focused by the Eye

Light reflected from an object into the eye is focused onto the retina by a two-element optical system: the cornea and the lens. The cornea, the transparent covering of the front of the eye, accounts for about 80 percent of the eye's focusing power, but like the lenses in eyeglasses, it is fixed in place so can't adjust its focus. The lens, which supplies the remaining 20 percent of the eye's focusing power, can change its shape to adjust the eye's focus for objects located at different distances. This change in shape is achieved by the action of *ciliary muscles*,

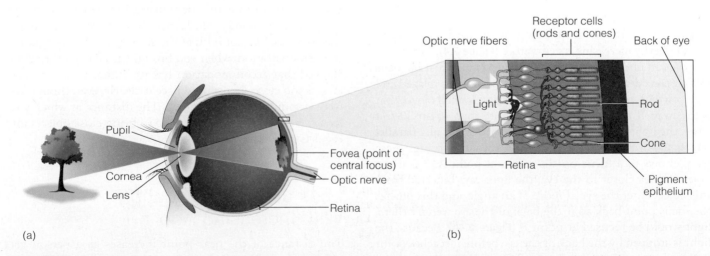

(a)   (b)

Figure 2.3 An image of the tree is focused on the retina, which lines the back of the eye. The close-up of the retina on the right shows the receptors and other neurons that make up the retina. © Cengage Learning

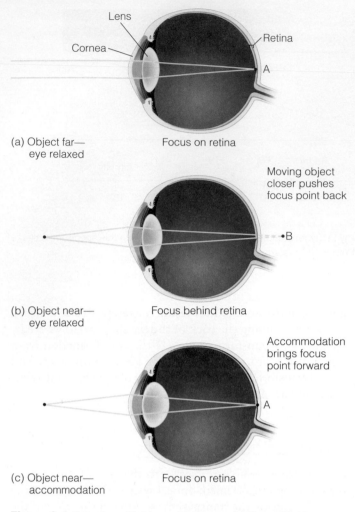

**(a) Object far—
eye relaxed**

Lens
Cornea
Retina
A

Focus on retina

**(b) Object near—
eye relaxed**

Moving object
closer pushes
focus point back

•B

Focus behind retina

**(c) Object near—
accommodation**

Accommodation
brings focus
point forward

A

Focus on retina

Figure 2.4 Focusing of light rays by the eye. (a) Rays of light coming from a small light source that is more than 20 feet away are approximately parallel. The focus point for parallel light is at A on the retina. (b) Moving an object closer to the relaxed eye pushes the focus point back. Here the focus point is at B, but light is stopped by the back of the eye. (c) Accommodation of the eye (indicated by the fatter lens) increases the focusing power of the lens and brings the focus point for a near object back to A on the retina. © Cengage Learning

which increase the focusing power of the lens (its ability to bend light) by increasing its curvature (**Figure 2.4**).

We can understand why the eye needs to adjust its focus by first considering what happens when the eye is relaxed and a person with normal (20/20) vision views a small object that is far away. If the object is located more than about 20 feet away, the light rays that reach the eye are essentially parallel (**Figure 2.4a**), and the cornea–lens combination brings these parallel rays to a focus on the retina at point A. But if the object moves closer to the eye, the light rays reflected from this object enter the eye at more of an angle, and this pushes the focus point back so if the back of the eye weren't there, light would be focused at point B (**Figure 2.4b**). Because the light is stopped by the back of the eye before it reaches point B, the image on the retina is out of focus. If things remained in this state, the person would see the object as blurred.

The adjustable lens, which controls a process called *accommodation*, comes to the rescue to help prevent blurring. **Accommodation** is the change in the lens's shape that occurs when the ciliary muscles at the front of the eye tighten and increase the curvature of the lens so that it gets thicker (**Figure 2.4c**). This increased curvature increases the bending of the light rays passing through the lens so the focus point is pulled back to A to create a sharp image on the retina. This means that as you look around at different objects, your eye is constantly adjusting its focus by accommodating, especially for nearby objects. The following demonstration shows that this is necessary because everything is not in focus at once.

DEMONSTRATION
Becoming Aware of What Is in Focus

Accommodation occurs unconsciously, so you are usually unaware that the lens is constantly changing its focusing power to let you see clearly at different distances. This unconscious focusing process works so efficiently that most people assume that everything, near and far, is always in focus. You can demonstrate that this is not so by holding a pen or a pencil, point up, at arm's length, closing one eye, and looking past the pencil at an object that is at least 20 feet away. As you stay focused on the faraway object, notice the pencil point without actually looking at it (be sure to stay focused on the far object). The point will probably appear slightly blurred.

Then slowly move the pencil toward you while still looking at the far object. Notice that as the pencil moves closer, the point becomes more blurred. When the pencil is about 12 inches away, shift your focus to the pencil point. Notice that when the pencil point comes into focus, it is difficult to see the details of the far object that was previously in focus.

Now bring the pencil even closer, looking directly at the point. Eventually, even though you are looking directly at the point, it may become difficult to see the point sharply no matter how hard you try. Notice the strain in your eyes as you try to bring the point into focus.

When you changed focus from far away to the nearby pencil point during this demonstration, you were changing your accommodation. Either the near or the far object was in focus, but not both at the same time. The last part of the demonstration, when you brought the pencil very close, showed that accommodation has its limits. When the pencil was too close, you couldn't see it clearly, even though you were straining to accommodate. The distance at which your lens can no longer accommodate to bring close objects into focus is called the **near point**.

Loss of Accommodation With Increasing Age

The distance of the near point increases as a person gets older, a condition called **presbyopia** (for "old eye"). The near point for most 20-year-olds is at about 10 cm, but it increases

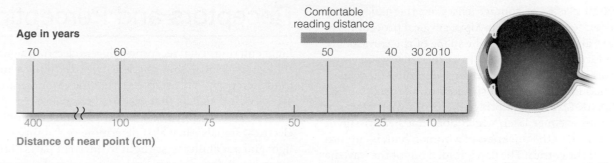

Comfortable
reading distance

Age in years

70   60   50   40   30 20 10

400   100   75   50   25   10

Distance of near point (cm)

Figure 2.5 Vertical lines show how the distance of the near point (green numbers) increases with increasing age. When the near point becomes farther than a comfortable reading distance, corrective lenses (reading glasses) become necessary. © Cengage Learning

to 14 cm by age 30, 22 cm at 40, and 100 cm at 60 (**Figure 2.5**). This loss of the ability to accommodate occurs because the lens hardens with age and the ciliary muscles become weaker. These changes make it more difficult for the lens to change its shape for vision at close range.

Though this gradual decrease in accommodative ability poses little problem for most people before the age of 45, at around that age the ability to accommodate begins to decrease rapidly, and the near point moves beyond a comfortable reading distance. There are two solutions to this problem. One is to hold reading material farther away. If you've ever seen someone holding a book or newspaper at arm's length, the person is employing this solution. The other solution is to wear reading glasses to replace the focusing power that can no longer be provided by the "old," poorly accommodating lens.

Myopia

Of course, many people who are far younger than 45 need to wear glasses to see clearly. Most of these people have **myopia**, or **nearsightedness**, an inability to see distant objects clearly. The reason for this difficulty, which affects more than 70 million Americans, is illustrated in **Figure 2.6a**. The myopic optical system brings parallel rays of light into focus at a point in front of the retina, so the image that reaches the retina is blurred. This problem can be caused by either of two factors: (1) **refractive myopia**, in which the cornea and/or the lens bends the light too much, or (2) **axial myopia**, in which the eyeball is too long. Either way, images of faraway objects are not focused sharply, so objects look blurred.

How can we deal with this problem? One way to create a focused image on the retina is to move the object closer. Remember that moving an object closer pushes the focus point further back (see Figure 2.4b), so if we move the object close enough, we can push the focus point onto the retina (**Figure 2.6b**). The distance at which light becomes focused on the retina is called the **far point**. When an object is at the far point, a person with myopia can see it clearly.

Although a person with myopia can see nearby objects clearly (which is why a myopic person is called *nearsighted*), objects beyond the far point are still out of focus. The solution to this problem is well known to anyone with myopia: corrective eyeglasses or contact lenses. These corrective lenses

bend incoming light so that it is focused as if it were at the far point, as illustrated in **Figure 2.6c**. Notice that the lens placed in front of the eye causes the light to enter the eye at exactly the same angle as light coming from the far point in Figure 2.6b.

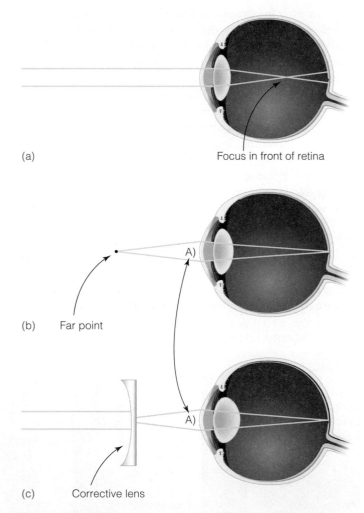

(a)   Focus in front of retina

(b)   Far point

(c)   Corrective lens

Figure 2.6 Focusing of light by the myopic (nearsighted) eye. (a) Parallel rays from a distant spot of light are brought to a focus in front of the retina, so distant objects appear blurred. (b) As the spot of light is moved closer to the eye, the focus point is pushed back until, at the far point, the rays are focused on the retina, and vision becomes clear. (c) A corrective lens, which bends light so that it enters the eye at the same angle as light coming from the far point, brings light to a focus on the retina. Angle A is the same in (b) and (c). © Cengage Learning

Although glasses or contact lenses are the major route to clear vision for people with myopia, surgical procedures in which lasers are used to change the shape of the cornea have been introduced that enable people to experience good vision without corrective lenses. More than 1 million Americans a year have had **laser-assisted in situ keratomileusis (LASIK)** surgery. LASIK involves sculpting the cornea with a type of laser called an excimer laser, which does not heat tissue. A small flap, less than the thickness of a human hair, is cut into the surface of the cornea. The flap is folded out of the way, the cornea's curvature is sculpted by the laser so that it focuses light onto the retina, and the flap is then folded back into place. The result, if the procedure is successful, is good vision without the need for glasses.

Hyperopia

A person with **hyperopia**, or **farsightedness**, can see distant objects clearly but has trouble seeing nearby objects. In the hyperopic eye, the focus point for parallel rays of light is located behind the retina, usually because the eyeball is too short. For young people this usually isn't a problem because they can accommodate to bring the focus point forward onto the retina. However, as noted earlier, as a person gets older, the constant need to accommodate when looking at nearby objects (as in reading or doing close-up work) becomes more difficult. The resulting symptoms of eyestrain and headaches, which occur because of the constant effort needed to accommodate, can be eliminated by corrective lenses that bring the focus point forward onto the retina.

Focusing an image clearly onto the retina is the initial step in the process of vision, but although a sharp image on the retina is essential for clear vision, we do not see the image on the retina. Vision occurs not in the retina but in the brain. Before the brain can create vision, the light on the retina must activate the visual receptors in the retina.

Receptors and Perception

Light entering visual receptors triggers electrical signals when the light is absorbed by light-sensitive *visual pigment* molecules in the receptors. This step is crucial for vision because it creates electrical signals that eventually signal the properties of the tree to the brain. These visual pigments not only trigger electrical signals, they also determine our ability to see dim light and our ability to see light in different parts of the visual spectrum. Before describing these perceptual effects of visual receptors, we consider the all-important process of transduction that transforms light energy into electrical energy.

Transforming Light Energy Into Electrical Energy

Transduction is the transformation of one form of energy into another form of energy (see Chapter 1, page 6). The process of transduction for vision—the transformation of light energy into electrical energy—occurs in the receptors for vision: the *rods* and *cones* (**Figure 2.7a**). The starting point for understanding how the rods and cones create electricity are the millions of molecules of a light-sensitive visual pigment that are contained in the **outer segments** of the receptors (**Figure 2.7b**). Visual pigments have two parts: a long protein called *opsin* and a much smaller light-sensitive component called *retinal*. **Figure 2.8a** shows a model of a retinal molecule attached to opsin (Wald, 1968). Note that only a small part of the opsin is shown here; it is actually hundreds of times longer than the retinal. **VL**

Despite its small size compared to the opsin, retinal is the crucial part of the visual pigment molecule, because when the retinal and opsin are combined, the resulting molecule absorbs visible light (see Figure 2.2). When a visual pigment molecule absorbs one photon of light, the retinal changes its

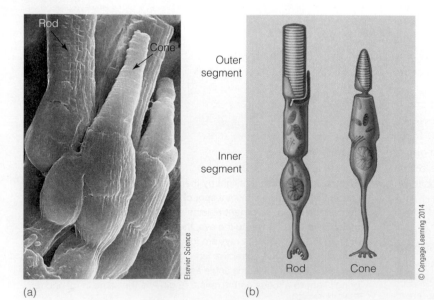

(a)

(b)

Figure 2.7 (a) Scanning electromicrograph of the rod and cone receptors in the retina, showing the rod-shaped and cone-shaped receptor outer segments; (b) Rod and cone receptors, showing the inner and outer segments. The outer segments contain the light-sensitive visual pigment.

From "Scanning Electron Microscopy of Vertebrate Visual Receptors," by E. R. Lewis, Y. Y. Zeevi, & F. S. Werblin, *Brain Research, 15,* 559–562. Copyright © 1969 Elsevier Science Publishers, B. V. Reprinted with permission.

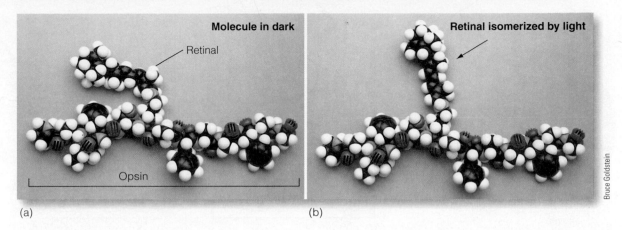

Molecule in dark

Retinal

Opsin

(a)

Retinal isomerized by light

Bruce Goldstein

(b)

Figure 2.8 Model of a visual pigment molecule. The horizontal part of the model shows a tiny portion of the huge opsin molecule near where the retinal is attached. The smaller molecule on top of the opsin is the light-sensitive retinal. (a) The retinal molecule's shape before it absorbs light. (b) The retinal molecule's shape after it absorbs light. This change in shape, which is called isomerization, triggers a sequence of reactions that culminates in generation of an electrical response in the receptor.

shape, from being bent, as shown in Figure 2.8a, to straight, as shown in **Figure 2.8b**. This change of shape, called **isomerization**, creates a chemical chain reaction, illustrated in **Figure 2.9**, that activates thousands of charged molecules to create electrical signals in receptors. (Remember that light can be described either in terms of its wavelength or as small packets of energy called photons. Generally, we will specify light by its wavelength, but occasionally, as when describing how light interacts with the visual pigment, photons are more appropriate.)

What is important about the chain reaction that follows isomerization is that it amplifies the effect of isomerization.

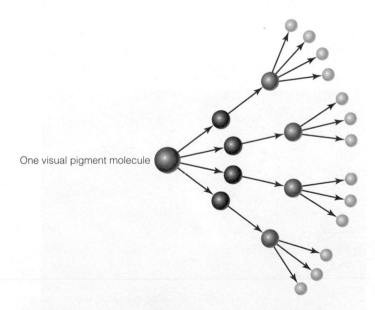

One visual pigment molecule

Figure 2.9 This sequence symbolizes the chain reaction that is triggered when a single visual pigment molecule is isomerized by absorption of a single photon of light. In the actual sequence of events, each visual pigment molecule activates hundreds more molecules, which, in turn, each activate about a thousand molecules. Isomerization of just one visual pigment molecule activates about a million other molecules, which activates the receptor. © Cengage Learning

Isomerizing one visual pigment molecule triggers a chain of chemical reactions that releases as many as a million charged molecules, which leads to activation of the receptor (Baylor, 1992; Hamer et al., 2005).

Visual pigments not only create electrical signals in the receptors, they also shape specific aspects of our perceptions. For example, properties of the pigments help determine how well we are able to adjust to darkness and how well we are able to see light in different parts of the visible spectrum. We will demonstrate how properties of the pigments influence perception by comparing perceptions caused by the two different types of receptors, rods and cones (Figure 2.7). As we will see, the different pigments in these two types of receptors result in different perceptual outcomes.

Adapting to the Dark

An important feature of the visual system is its ability to adapt to the dark by increasing its sensitivity to light. Consider, for example, a person in a darkened movie theater noticing that the aisle is lit by small lights on the sides of the chairs. Later, after the person's visual system has adapted to the dark, the small lights appear brighter, as if the theater manager had turned up the power. In reality, however, the lights are exactly the same as before. They look brighter not because they are more intense, but because the person's visual system has become more sensitive. This process of increasing sensitivity in the dark is called **dark adaptation**.

Experiments have shown that rod receptors and cone receptors adapt to the dark at different rates and that these differences occur because of differences in their visual pigments. The first challenge in comparing rod adaptation and cone adaptation is to find a way to measure rod and cone vision separately. Luckily, the visual system comes to our rescue by distributing the rods and cones differently across the retina.

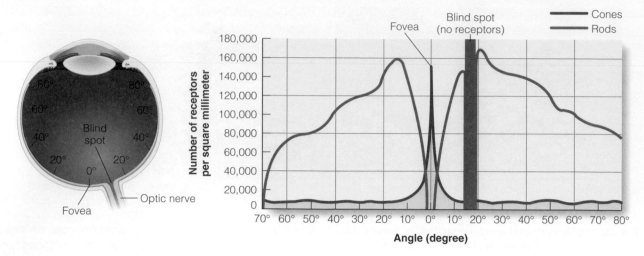

Figure 2.10 The distribution of rods and cones in the retina. The eye on the left indicates locations in degrees relative to the fovea. These locations are repeated along the bottom of the chart on the right. The vertical brown bar near 20 degrees indicates the place on the retina where there are no receptors because this is where the ganglion cells leave the eye to form the optic nerve. Adapted from *Human Information Processing*, by P. Lindsay and D. A. Norman, 1977, 2nd ed., p. 126. Copyright © 1977 Academic Press, Inc. Adapted with permission.

Distribution of the Rods and Cones From the picture of rods and cones in Figure 2.7a, you can see that the rods and cones are interspersed in the retina. In the parts of the retina shown in this picture, there are more rods than cones. The ratio of rods and cones depends, however, on the location in the retina. **Figure 2.10** shows how the rods and cones are distributed in the retina.

1. One small area, the **fovea**, contains only cones. When we look directly at an object, the object's image falls on the fovea.

2. The **peripheral retina**, which includes all of the retina outside of the fovea, contains both rods and cones. It is important to note that although the fovea has *only* cones, there are also many cones in the peripheral retina. The fovea is so small (about the size of this "o")

that it contains only about 1 percent, or 50,000, of the 6 million cones in the retina (Tyler, 1997a, 1997b).

3. The peripheral retina contains many more rods than cones because there are about 120 million rods and only 6 million cones in the retina.

One way to appreciate the fact that the rods and cones are distributed differently in the retina is by considering what happens when functioning receptors are missing from one area of the retina. A condition called **macular degeneration**, which is most common in older people, destroys the cone-rich fovea and a small area that surrounds it. (*Macula* is a term usually associated with medical practice that includes the fovea plus a small area surrounding the fovea.) This creates a blind region in central vision, so when a person looks directly at something, he or she loses sight of it (**Figure 2.11a**).

(a)

(b)

Bruce Goldstein

Figure 2.11 (a) In a condition called macular degeneration, the fovea and surrounding area degenerate, so the person cannot see whatever he or she is looking at. (b) In retinitis pigmentosa, the peripheral retina initially degenerates and causes loss of vision in the periphery. The resulting condition is sometimes called "tunnel vision."

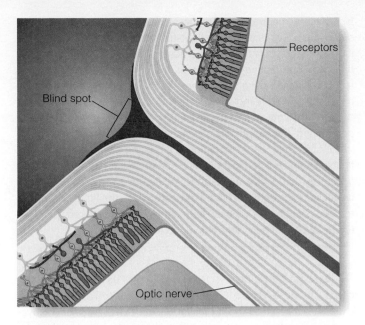

Figure 2.12 There are no receptors at the place where the optic nerve leaves the eye. This enables the receptor's ganglion cell fibers to flow into the optic nerve. The absence of receptors in this area creates the blind spot. © Cengage Learning

Another condition, called **retinitis pigmentosa**, is a degeneration of the retina that is passed from one generation to the next (although not always affecting everyone in a family). This condition first attacks the peripheral rod receptors and results in poor vision in the peripheral visual field (**Figure 2.11b**). Eventually, in severe cases, the foveal cone receptors are also attacked, resulting in complete blindness.

Before leaving the rod–cone distribution shown in Figure 2.10, note that there is one area in the retina, indicated by the vertical brown bar, where there are no receptors. **Figure 2.12** shows a close-up of the place where this occurs, which is where the optic nerve leaves the eye. Because of the absence of receptors, this place is called the **blind spot**. Although you are not normally aware of the blind spot, you can become aware of it by doing the following demonstration.

DEMONSTRATION
Becoming Aware of the Blind Spot

Place the book on your desk. Close your right eye, and position yourself above the book so that the cross in **Figure 2.13** is aligned with your left eye. Be sure the page is flat and, while looking at the cross, slowly move closer. As you move closer, be sure not to move your eye from the cross, but at the same time keep noticing the circle off to the side. At some point, around 3 to 9 inches from the book, the circle should disappear. When this happens, the image of the circle is falling on your blind spot.

Figure 2.13 © Cengage Learning

Why aren't we usually aware of the blind spot? One reason is that the blind spot is located off to the side of our visual field, where objects are not in sharp focus. Because of this and because we don't know exactly where to look for it (as opposed to the demonstration, in which we are focusing our attention on the circle), the blind spot is hard to detect.

But the most important reason that we don't see the blind spot is that some mechanism in the brain "fills in" the place where the image disappears (Churchland & Ramachandran, 1996). The next demonstration illustrates an important property of this filling-in process.

DEMONSTRATION
Filling in the Blind Spot

Close your right eye and, with the cross in **Figure 2.14** lined up with your left eye, move the "wheel" toward you. When the center of the wheel falls on your blind spot, notice how the spokes of the wheel fill in the hole (Ramachandran, 1992).

These demonstrations show that the brain does not fill in the area served by the blind spot with "nothing"; rather, it creates a perception that matches the surrounding pattern—the white page in the first demonstration, and the spokes of the wheel in the second one.

Measuring the Dark Adaptation Curve We are now ready to move our attention back to the receptors to show how the rods and cones control an important aspect of vision: the ability of the visual system to adjust to dim levels of illumination. The first step in the study of dark adaptation is to measure the **dark adaptation curve**, which is the function relating sensitivity to light to time in the dark, beginning when the lights are extinguished.

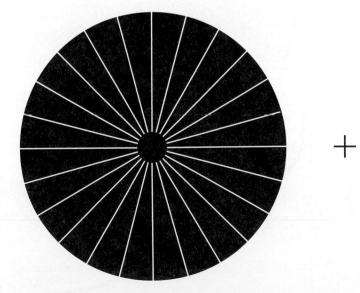

Figure 2.14 View the pattern as described in the text, and observe what happens when the center of the wheel falls on your blind spot.

Adapted from "Blind Spot" by Vilaynaur S. Ramachandran. Copyright © 1992 by Scientific American, Inc.

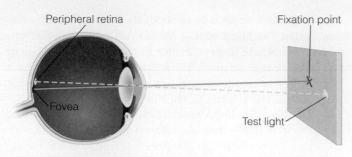

Peripheral retina

Fixation point

Fovea

Test light

Figure 2.15 Viewing conditions for a dark adaptation experiment. The image of the fixation point falls on the fovea, and the image of the test light falls on the peripheral retina. © Cengage Learning

METHOD
Measuring the Dark Adaptation Curve

The first step in measuring a dark adaption curve is to have the observer look at a small fixation point while paying attention to a flashing test light that is off to the side (**Figure 2.15**). Because the observer is looking directly at the fixation point, its image falls on the fovea, so the image of the test light falls on the peripheral retina, which contains both rods and cones. While still in the light, the observer measures his or her threshold for seeing the light by turning a knob that adjusts the intensity of the flashing light until it can just barely be seen. This threshold, the minimum amount of energy necessary to just barely see the light, is converted to *sensitivity*. Because sensitivity = 1/threshold, this means that a

high threshold corresponds to *low sensitivity*. The sensitivity measured in the light is called the **light-adapted sensitivity**, because it is measured while the eyes are adapted to the light. Because the room (or adapting) lights are on, the intensity of the flashing test light has to be high to be seen. At the beginning of the experiment, then, the threshold is high and the sensitivity is low.

Once the light-adapted sensitivity to the flashing test light is determined, the adapting light is extinguished so the observer is in the dark. The observer continues adjusting the intensity of the flashing light so it can just barely be seen, tracking the increase in sensitivity that occurs in the dark. As the observer becomes more sensitive to the light, he or she must decrease the light's intensity to keep it just barely visible. The result, shown as the red curve in **Figure 2.16**, is a dark adaptation curve.

The dark adaptation curve shows that as adaptation proceeds, the observer becomes more sensitive to the light. Note that higher sensitivity is at the bottom of this graph, so movement of the dark adaptation curve downward means that the observer's sensitivity is increasing. The red dark adaptation curve indicates that the observer's sensitivity increases in two phases. It increases rapidly for the first 3 to 4 minutes after the light is extinguished and then levels off. At about 7 to 10 minutes, it begins increasing again and continues to do so until observers have been in the dark for about 20 or 30 minutes (Figure 2.16). The sensitivity at the end of

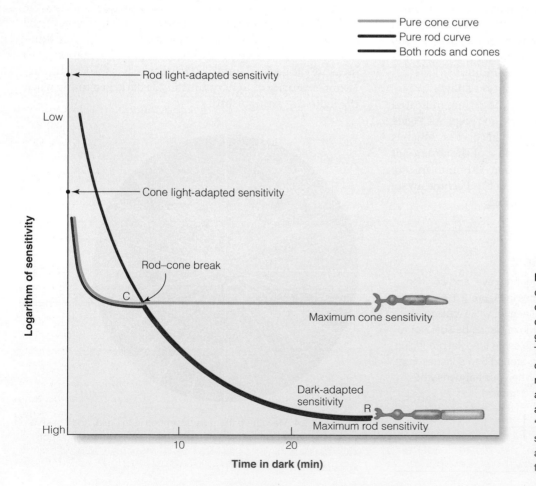

Pure cone curve
Pure rod curve
Both rods and cones

Rod light-adapted sensitivity

Low

Cone light-adapted sensitivity

Logarithm of sensitivity

Rod–cone break

C

Maximum cone sensitivity

Dark-adapted sensitivity

R

High

Maximum rod sensitivity

10   20

Time in dark (min)

Figure 2.16 Three dark adaptation curves. The red line is the two-stage dark adaptation curve, with an initial cone branch and a later rod branch. The green line is the cone adaptation curve. The purple curve is the rod adaptation curve. Note that the downward movement of these curves represents an *increase* in sensitivity. The curves actually begin at the points indicating "light-adapted sensitivity," but there is a slight delay between the time the lights are turned off and when measurement of the curves begin. © Cengage Learning

dark adaptation, labeled **dark-adapted sensitivity**, is about 100,000 times greater than the light-adapted sensitivity measured before dark adaptation began.

Dark adaptation was involved in an episode of the *Mythbusters* program on the Discovery Channel (2007), which was devoted to investigating myths about pirates. One of the myths was that pirates wore eye patches to preserve night vision in one eye so that when they went from the bright light outside to the darkness below decks, removing the patch would enable them to see.

To determine whether this would work, the Mythbusters carried out some tasks in a dark room just after both of their eyes had been in the light and did some different tasks with an eye that had previously been covered with a patch for 30 minutes. It isn't surprising that they completed the tasks much more rapidly when using the eye that had been patched. Anyone who has taken a course on sensation and perception could have told the Mythbusters that the eye patch would work because keeping an eye in the dark triggers the process of dark adaptation, which causes the eye to increase its sensitivity in the dark. (Whether pirates actually used patches to dark adapt their eyes to help them see below decks remains an unproven hypothesis. One argument against this idea is that the loss of depth perception caused by patching one eye might be a serious disadvantage when the pirate is working on deck.)

Although the Mythbusters showed that dark adapting one eye made it easier to see with that eye in the dark, we have a more specific goal. We are interested in showing that the first part of the dark adaptation curve is caused by the cones and the second part is caused by the rods. We will do this by running two dark adaptation experiments, one measuring adaptation of the cones and another measuring adaptation of the rods.

Measuring Cone Adaptation The reason the red dark adaptation curve in Figure 2.16 has two phases is that the test light fell on the peripheral retina, which contains both rods and cones. To measure dark adaptation of the cones alone, we have to ensure that the image of the test light falls only on cones. We achieve this by having the observer look directly at the test light so its image will fall on the all-cone fovea, and by making the test light small enough so that its entire image falls within the fovea. The dark adaptation curve determined by this procedure is indicated by the green line in Figure 2.16. This curve, which measures only the activity of the cones, matches the initial phase of our original dark adaptation curve but does not include the second phase. Does this mean that the second part of the curve is due to the rods? We can show that the answer to this question is "yes" by doing another experiment.

Measuring Rod Adaptation We know that the green curve in Figure 2.16 is due only to cone adaptation because our test light was focused on the all-cone fovea. Because the cones are more sensitive to light at the beginning of dark adaptation, they control our vision during the early stages of adaptation, so we can't see what the rods are doing. In order to reveal how the sensitivity of the rods is changing at the very beginning of dark adaptation, we need to measure dark adaptation in

a person who has no cones. Such people, who have no cones due to a rare genetic defect, are called **rod monochromats**. Their all-rod retinas provide a way for us to study rod dark adaptation without interference from the cones. (Students sometimes wonder why we can't simply present the test flash to the peripheral retina, which contains mostly rods. The answer is that there are a few cones in the periphery, which influence the beginning of the dark adaptation curve.)

Because the rod monochromat has no cones, the light-adapted sensitivity we measure just before we turn off the lights is determined by the rods. The sensitivity we determine, which is labeled "rod light-adapted sensitivity" in Figure 2.16, indicates that the rods are much less sensitive than the cone light-adapted sensitivity we measured in our original experiment. We can also see that once dark adaptation begins, the rods increase their sensitivity, as indicated by the purple curve, and reach their final dark-adapted level in about 25 minutes (Rushton, 1961). The end of this rod adaptation measured in our monochromat matches the second part of the two-stage dark adaptation curve.

Based on the results of our dark adaptation experiments, we can summarize the process of dark adaptation. As soon as the light is extinguished, the sensitivity of *both* the cones *and* the rods begins increasing. However, because the cones are much more sensitive than the rods at the beginning of dark adaptation, we see with our cones right after the lights are turned out. One way to think about this is that the cones have "center stage" at the beginning of dark adaptation, while the rods are working "behind the scenes." However, after about 3 to 5 minutes in the dark, the cones have reached their maximum sensitivity, as indicated by the leveling off of the dark adaptation curve. Meanwhile, the rods are still adapting, behind the scenes, and by about 7 minutes in the dark, the rods' sensitivity finally catches up to the cones'. The rods then become more sensitive than the cones, and rod adaptation, indicated by the second branch of the dark adaptation curve, becomes visible. The place where the rods begin to determine the dark adaptation curve is called the **rod–cone break**.

Why do the rods take about 20 to 30 minutes to reach their maximum sensitivity (point R on the curve), compared to only 3 to 4 minutes for the cones (point C)? The answer to this question involves a process called *visual pigment regeneration,* which occurs more rapidly in the cones than in the rods.

Visual Pigment Regeneration From our description of transduction earlier in the chapter, we know that light causes the retinal part of the visual pigment molecule to change its shape. Eventually, after this shape change, the retinal separates from the *opsin* part of the molecule. This change in shape and separation from the opsin causes the molecule to become lighter in color, a process called **visual pigment bleaching**. This bleaching is shown in **Figure 2.17**. Figure 2.17a is a picture of a frog retina that was taken moments after it was illuminated with light. The red color is the visual pigment. As the light remains on, more and more of the pigment's retinal is isomerized and breaks away from the opsin, so the retina's color changes as shown in Figures 2.17b and c.

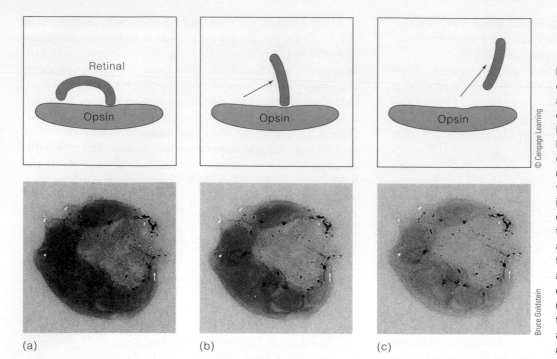

© Cengage Learning

(a) (b) (c)

Figure 2.17 A frog retina was dissected from the eye in the dark and then exposed to light. The top diagrams show the relationship between retinal and opsin. The bottom photographs show the color of the retina. (a) This picture of the retina was taken just after the light was turned on. The dark red color is caused by the high concentration of visual pigment in the receptors that are still in the unbleached state, as indicated by the closeness of the retinal and opsin in the diagram above the retina. Only a small part of the opsin molecule is shown. (b, c) As the pigment isomerizes, the retinal and opsin break apart, and the retina becomes *bleached*, as indicated by the lighter color.

When the pigments are in their lighter bleached state, they are no longer useful for vision. In order to do their job of changing light energy into electrical energy, the *retinal* needs to return to its bent shape and become reattached to the *opsin*. This process of reforming the visual pigment molecule is called **visual pigment regeneration**.

When you are in the light, as you are now as you read this book, some of your visual pigment molecules are isomerizing and bleaching, as shown in Figure 2.17, while at the same time, others are regenerating. This means that in most normal light levels, your eye always contains some bleached visual pigment and some intact visual pigment. When you turn out the lights, the bleached visual pigment continues to regenerate, but there is no more isomerization, so eventually your retina contains only intact (unbleached) visual pigment molecules.

This increase in visual pigment concentration that occurs as the pigment regenerates in the dark is responsible for the increase in sensitivity we measure during dark adaptation. This relationship between pigment concentration and sensitivity was demonstrated by William Rushton (1961), who devised a procedure to measure the regeneration of visual pigment in humans by measuring the darkening of the retina that occurs during dark adaptation. (Think of this as Figure 2.17 proceeding from right to left.)

Rushton's measurements showed that cone pigment takes 6 minutes to regenerate completely, whereas rod pigment takes more than 30 minutes. When he compared the course of pigment regeneration to the dark adaptation curve, he found that the rate of cone dark adaptation matched the rate of cone pigment regeneration and the rate of rod dark adaptation matched the rate of rod pigment regeneration. These results demonstrated two important connections between perception and physiology:

1. Our sensitivity to light depends on the concentration of a chemical—the visual pigment.
2. The speed at which our sensitivity increases in the dark depends on a chemical reaction—the regeneration of the visual pigment.

What happens to vision if something prevents visual pigments from regenerating? This is what occurs when a person's retina becomes detached from the *pigment epithelium* (see Figure 2.3), a layer that contains enzymes necessary for pigment regeneration. This condition, called **detached retina**, can occur as a result of traumatic injuries of the eye or head, as when a baseball player is hit in the eye by a line drive. When this occurs, the bleached pigment's separated *retinal* and *opsin* can no longer be recombined, and the person becomes blind in the area of the visual field served by the separated area of the retina. This condition is permanent unless the detached area of retina is reattached, which can be accomplished by laser surgery.

Our discussion of rods and cones has focused on how they control our vision as we adapt to darkness. Rods and cones also differ in the way they respond to light in different parts of the *visible spectrum* (Figure 2.2). The differences in the rod and cone responses to the spectrum have been studied by measuring the **spectral sensitivity** of rod vision and cone vision, where spectral sensitivity is the eye's sensitivity to light as a function of the light's wavelength.

Spectral Sensitivity

How well can we see different wavelengths in the visible spectrum? To answer this question we need to measure **spectral sensitivity curves**—the relationship between wavelength and sensitivity.

Spectral Sensitivity Curves The following is the psychophysical method used to measure a spectral sensitivity curve.

METHOD
Measuring a Spectral Sensitivity Curve

To measure sensitivity to light at each wavelength across the spectrum, we present one wavelength at a time and measure the observer's sensitivity to each wavelength. Light of a single wavelength, called **monochromatic light**, can be created by using special filters or a device called a *spectrometer*. To determine a person's spectral sensitivity, we determine the person's threshold for seeing monochromatic lights across the spectrum using one of the psychophysical methods for measuring threshold described in Chapter 1. The threshold is usually not measured at *every* wavelength, but at regular intervals. Thus, we might measure the threshold first at 400 nm, then at 410 nm, and so on. The result is the curve in **Figure 2.18a**, which shows that the threshold is higher at short and long wavelengths and lower in the middle of the spectrum; that is, less light is needed to see wavelengths in the middle of the spectrum than to see wavelengths at either the short- or long-wavelength end of the spectrum.

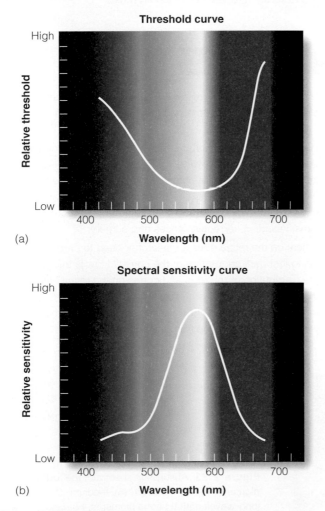

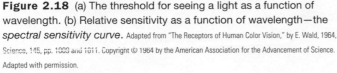

(a)

(b)

Figure 2.18 (a) The threshold for seeing a light as a function of wavelength. (b) Relative sensitivity as a function of wavelength—the *spectral sensitivity curve.* Adapted from "The Receptors of Human Color Vision," by E. Wald, 1964, *Science, 145,* pp. 1009 and 1011. Copyright © 1964 by the American Association for the Advancement of Science. Adapted with permission.

The ability to see wavelengths across the spectrum is often plotted not in terms of *threshold* versus wavelength, as in Figure 2.18a, but in terms of *sensitivity* versus wavelength. Using the equation, sensitivity = 1/threshold, we can convert the threshold curve in Figure 2.18a into the curve in **Figure 2.18b**, which is called the spectral sensitivity curve.

We measure the **cone spectral sensitivity curve** by having an observer look directly at a test light so that it stimulates only the cones in the fovea. We measure the **rod spectral sensitivity curve** by measuring sensitivity after the eye is dark adapted (so the rods control vision because they are the most sensitive receptors) and presenting test flashes in the peripheral retina, off to the side of the fixation point.

The cone and rod spectral sensitivity curves in **Figure 2.19** show that the rods are more sensitive to short-wavelength light than are the cones, with the rods being most sensitive to light of 500 nm and the cones being most sensitive to light of 560 nm. This difference in the sensitivity of cones and rods to different wavelengths means that as vision shifts from the cones to the rods during dark adaptation, we become relatively more sensitive to short-wavelength light—that is, light nearer the blue and green end of the spectrum.

You may have noticed an effect of this shift to short-wavelength sensitivity if you have observed how green foliage seems to stand out more near dusk. A shift from cone vision to rod vision occurs at dusk because your eye begins dark adapting in low light levels, so the rods begin to influence vision. This enhanced perception of short wavelengths during dark adaptation is called the **Purkinje** (Pur-kin'-jee) **shift** after Johann Purkinje, who described this effect in 1825. You can experience this shift in color sensitivity during dark adaptation by closing one eye for 5 to 10 minutes so it dark adapts, then switching back and forth between your eyes and

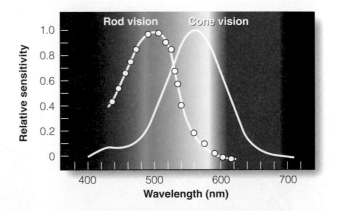

Figure 2.19 Spectral sensitivity curves for rod vision (left) and cone vision (right). The maximum sensitivities of these two curves have been set equal to 1.0. However, the relative sensitivities of the rods and the cones depend on the conditions of adaptation: The cones are more sensitive in the light, and the rods are more sensitive in the dark. The circles plotted on top of the rod curve are the absorption spectrum of the rod visual pigment. From "Human Rhodopsin," by G. Wald and P. K. Brown, 1958, *Science, 127,* pp. 222–226, Figure 6, and "The Receptors of Human Color Vision," by E. Wald, 1964, *Science, 145,* pp. 1007–1017. Copyright © 1964 by the American Association for the Advancement of Science. Adapted with permission.

Figure 2.20 Flowers for demonstrating the Purkinje shift. See text for explanation. © Cengage Learning

noticing how the blue flower in **Figure 2.20** is brighter compared to the red flower in your dark-adapted eye.

Rod and Cone Absorption Spectra Just as we can trace the difference in the rate of rod and cone dark adaptation to a property of the visual pigments (the cone pigment regenerates faster than the rod pigment), we can trace the difference in the rod and cone spectral sensitivity curves to another property of the visual pigments: the rod and cone *absorption spectra*. A pigment's **absorption spectrum** is a plot of the amount of light absorbed versus the wavelength of the light. The absorption spectra of the rod and cone pigments are shown in **Figure 2.21**. The rod pigment absorbs best at 500 nm, the blue-green area of the spectrum.

There are three absorption spectra for the cones because there are three different cone pigments, each contained in its own receptor. The short-wavelength pigment (S) absorbs light best at about 419 nm; the medium-wavelength pigment (M) absorbs light best at about 531 nm; and the long-wavelength pigment (L) absorbs light best at about 558 nm.

The absorption of the rod visual pigment closely matches the rod spectral sensitivity curve (Figure 2.19), and the short-, medium-, and long-wavelength cone pigments that absorb best at 419, 531, and 558 nm, respectively, add together to result in a psychophysical spectral sensitivity curve that peaks at 560 nm. Because there are fewer short-wavelength receptors and therefore much less of the short-wavelength

pigment, the spectral sensitivity curve is determined mainly by the medium- and long-wavelength pigments (Bowmaker & Dartnall, 1980; Stiles, 1953). (We will have more to say about the three cone pigments in Chapter 9, because they are the basis of our ability to see colors.)

It is clear from the evidence we have presented that sensitivity in the dark (dark adaptation) and sensitivity to different wavelengths (spectral sensitivity) are determined by the properties of the rod and cone visual pigments. Thus, even though perception does not *occur* in the eye, what we see is definitely affected by what happens there.

We have now traveled through the first three steps in the perceptual process. The tree (Step 1) reflects light, which is focused onto the retina by the eye's optical system (Step 2). The visual receptors shape perception because of the concentration and absorption properties of their visual pigments as they transform light energy into electrical energy (Step 3). We are now ready to move to Step 4, the transmission and processing of electrical signals. But before we can begin describing electrical signals and what happens to them on their journey from receptors to the brain, we need to spend a few pages describing these electrical signals.

TEST YOURSELF 2.1

1. Describe the structure of the eye and how moving an object closer to the eye affects how light reflected from the object is focused on the retina.

2. How does the eye adjust the focusing of light by accommodation? Describe the following conditions that can cause problems in focusing: presbyopia, myopia, hyperopia. Be sure you understand the difference between the near point and the far point and can describe the various solutions to focusing problems, including corrective lenses and surgery.

3. Where on the retina does a researcher need to present a stimulus to test dark adaptation of the cones? How is this related to the distribution of the rods and cones on the retina? How can the adaptation of cones be measured without any interference from the rods? How can adaptation of the rods be measured without any interference from the cones?

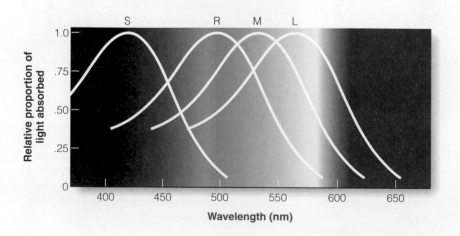

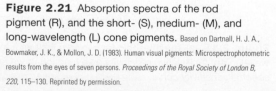

Figure 2.21 Absorption spectra of the rod pigment (R), and the short- (S), medium- (M), and long-wavelength (L) cone pigments. Based on Dartnall, H. J. A., Bowmaker, J. K., & Mollon, J. D. (1983). Human visual pigments: Microspectrophotometric results from the eyes of seven persons. *Proceedings of the Royal Society of London B, 220*, 115–130. Reprinted by permission.

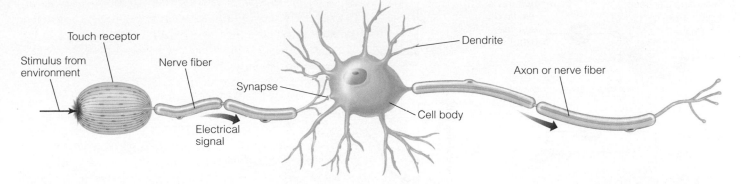

Figure 2.22 The neuron on the right consists of a cell body, dendrites, and an axon, or nerve fiber. The neuron on the left that receives stimuli from the environment has a receptor in place of the cell body. © Cengage Learning

4. Describe how rod and cone sensitivity changes starting when the lights are turned off and how this change in sensitivity continues for 20 to 30 minutes in the dark. When do the rods begin adapting? When do the rods become more sensitive than the cones?

5. What happens to visual pigment molecules when they (a) absorb light and (b) regenerate? What is the connection between visual pigment regeneration and dark adaptation?

6. What is spectral sensitivity? How is a cone spectral sensitivity curve determined? A rod spectral sensitivity curve?

7. What is an absorption spectrum? How do rod and cone pigment absorption spectra compare, and what is their relationship to rod and cone spectral sensitivity?

Electrical Signals in Neurons

Electrical signals occur in structures called **neurons**, like the ones shown in **Figure 2.22**. The key components of neurons, shown in the neuron on the right in Figure 2.22, are the **cell body**, which contains mechanisms to keep the cell alive; **dendrites**, which branch out from the cell body to receive electrical signals from other neurons; and the **axon**, or **nerve fiber**, which is filled with fluid that conducts electrical signals. There are variations on this basic neuron structure: Some neurons have long axons; others have short axons or none at all. Especially important for perception are **sensory receptors**, which are neurons specialized to respond to environmental stimuli. In Figure 2.22, the receptor on the left responds to touch stimuli.

Individual neurons do not, of course, exist in isolation. There are hundreds of millions of neurons in the nervous system and, as we will see, each neuron is connected to many other neurons. In the case of vision, each eye contains more than 100 million receptors, each of which transmits signals to neurons within the retina. These signals are transmitted out of the back of the eye in the optic nerve to a group of neurons called the *lateral geniculate nucleus* and then to the *visual receiving area* in the cortex (**Figure 2.23**). All along this pathway from eye to cortex, and then within the cortex, individual neurons are transmitting messages about the tree.

One of the most important ways of studying how the tree is represented by electrical signals is to record the signals from single neurons. We can appreciate the importance of being able to record from single neurons by considering the following analogy: You walk into a large room in which hundreds of people are talking about a political speech they have just heard. There is a great deal of noise and commotion in the room as people react to the speech. Based on hearing this "crowd noise," all you can say about what is going on is that the speech seems to have generated a great deal of excitement. To get more specific information about the speech, you need to listen to what individual people are saying.

Just as listening to individual people provides valuable information about what is happening in a large crowd,

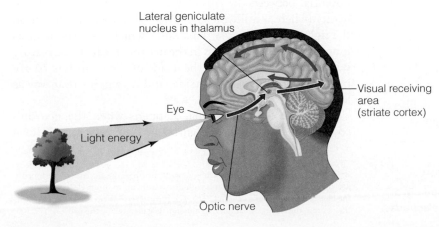

Figure 2.23 Side view of the visual system showing the three major sites along the primary visual pathway: the eye, the lateral geniculate nucleus, and the visual receiving area in the cortex. © Cengage Learning

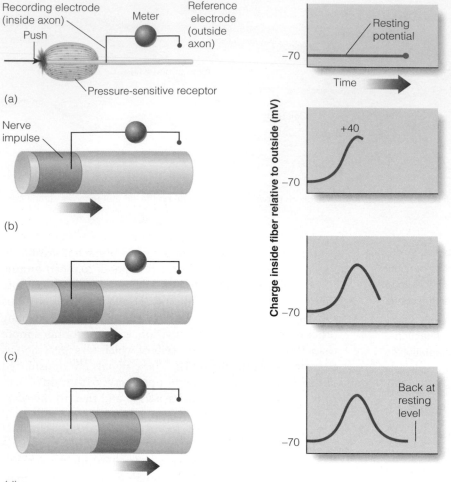

(a)

(b)

(c)

(d)

Figure 2.24 (a) When a nerve fiber is at rest, there is a difference in charge of –70 mV between the inside and the outside of the fiber. This difference is measured by the meter indicated by the blue circle; the difference in charge measured by the meter is displayed on the right. (b) As the nerve impulse, indicated by the red band, passes the electrode, the inside of the fiber near the electrode becomes more positive. This positivity is the rising phase of the action potential. (c) As the nerve impulse moves past the electrode, the charge inside the fiber becomes more negative. This is the falling phase of the action potential. (d) Eventually the neuron returns to its resting state. © Cengage Learning

recording from single neurons provides valuable information about what is happening in the nervous system. Recording from single neurons is like listening to individual voices. It is important to record from as many neurons as possible, of course, because just as individual people may have different opinions about the speech, different neurons may respond differently to a particular stimulus or situation.

The ability to record electrical signals from individual neurons ushered in the modern era of brain research, and in the 1950s and 1960s, development of sophisticated electronics and the availability of computers made possible more detailed analysis of how neurons function.

Recording Electrical Signals in Neurons

Electrical signals are recorded from the axons (or nerve fibers) of neurons using small electrodes to pick up the signals.

METHOD
The Setup for Recording From a Single Neuron

Figure 2.24a shows a typical setup used for recording from a single neuron. There are two electrodes: a *recording electrode*,

shown with its recording tip inside the neuron,[1] and a *reference electrode*, located some distance away so it is not affected by the electrical signals. These two electrodes are connected to a meter that records the difference in charge between the tips of the two electrodes. This difference is displayed on a computer screen, like the one shown in **Figure 2.25**, which shows electrical signals being recorded from a neuron in a laboratory setting.

When the axon, or nerve fiber, is at rest, the difference in potential between the tips of the two electrodes is –70 millivolts (where a millivolt is 1/1,000 of a volt), as shown on the right in Figure 2.24a. This value, which stays the same as long as there are no signals in the neuron, is called the **resting potential**. In other words, the inside of the neuron is 70 mV more negative than the outside, and it remains that way as long as the neuron is at rest. **VL**

Figure 2.24b shows what happens when the neuron's receptor is stimulated so that a signal is transmitted down

---

[1] In practice, most recordings are achieved with the tip of the electrode positioned just outside the neuron because it is technically difficult to insert electrodes into the neuron, especially if it is small. However, if the electrode tip is close enough to the neuron, the electrode can pick up the signals generated by the neuron.

Figure 2.25 Electrical signals being displayed on a computer screen, in an experiment in which responses are being recorded from a single neuron. The signal on the screen shows the difference in voltage between two electrodes as a function of time. In this example, many signals are superimposed on one another, creating a thick white tracing. (Photographed in Tai Sing Lee's laboratory at Carnegie Mellon University.)

the axon. As the signal passes the recording electrode, the charge inside the axon rises to +40 millivolts compared to the outside. As the signal continues past the electrode, the charge inside the fiber reverses course and starts becoming negative again (**Figure 2.24c**), until it returns to the resting level (**Figure 2.24d**). This signal, which is called the **action potential**, lasts about 1 millisecond (1/1,000 second).

Basic Properties of Action Potentials

An important property of the action potential is that it is a **propagated response**—once the response is triggered, it travels all the way down the axon without decreasing in size. This means that if we were to move our recording electrode in Figure 2.24 to a position nearer the end of the axon, the response recorded when the action potential passed the electrode would still be an increase from –70 mV to +40 mV and then a decrease back to –70 mV. This is an extremely important property of the action potential because it enables neurons to transmit signals over long distances.

Another property is that the action potential remains the same size no matter how intense the stimulus is. We can demonstrate this by determining how the neuron fires to different stimulus intensities. **Figure 2.26** shows what happens when we do this. Each action potential appears as a sharp spike in these records because we have compressed the time scale to display a number of action potentials.

The three records in Figure 2.26 represent the axon's response to three intensities of pushing on the skin. Figure 2.26a shows how the axon responds to gentle stimulation applied to the skin, and Figures 2.26b and 2.26c show how the response changes as the pressure is increased. Comparing these three records leads to an important conclusion: Changing the stimulus intensity does not affect the *size* of the action potentials but does affect the *rate* of firing.

Although increasing the stimulus intensity can increase the rate of firing, there is an upper limit to the number of nerve impulses per second that can be conducted down an axon. This limit occurs because of a property of the axon called the **refractory period**—the interval between the time one nerve impulse occurs and the next one can be generated in the axon. Because the refractory period for most neurons is about 1 ms, the upper limit of a neuron's firing rate is about 500 to 800 impulses per second.

Another important property of action potentials is illustrated by the beginning of each of the records in Figure 2.26. Notice that a few action potentials are occurring even before the pressure stimulus is applied. Action potentials that occur in the absence of stimuli from the environment are called

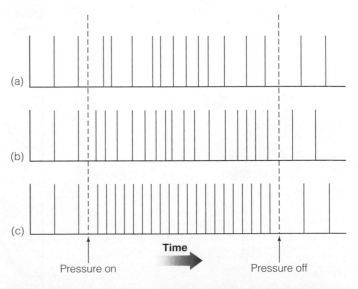

Figure 2.26 Response of a nerve fiber to (a) soft, (b) medium, and (c) strong stimulation. Increasing the stimulus strength increases both the rate and the regularity of nerve firing in this fiber. © Cengage Learning

spontaneous activity. This spontaneous activity establishes a baseline level of firing for the neuron. The presence of stimulation usually causes an increase in activity above this spontaneous level, but under some conditions, which we will describe shortly, it can cause firing to decrease below the spontaneous level.

Chemical Basis of Action Potentials

What causes these rapid changes in charge that travel down the axon? Because this is a traveling electrical charge, we might be tempted to equate it to the electrical signals that are conducted along electrical power lines or the wires used for household appliances. But action potentials create electricity not in the dry environment of metal wires, but in the wet environment of the body.

The key to understanding the "wet" electrical signals transmitted by neurons is understanding the components of the neuron's liquid environment. Neurons are bathed in a liquid solution rich in **ions**, molecules that carry an electrical charge (**Figure 2.27**). Ions are created when molecules gain or lose electrons, as happens when compounds are dissolved in water. For example, adding table salt (sodium chloride, NaCl)

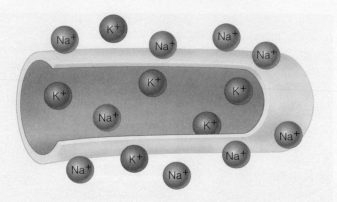

Figure 2.27 A nerve fiber, showing the high concentration of sodium outside the fiber and potassium inside the fiber. Other ions, such as negatively charged chlorine, are not shown. © Cengage Learning

to water creates positively charged sodium ions (Na^+) and negatively charged chlorine ions (Cl^-). The solution outside the axon of a neuron is rich in positively charged sodium (Na^+) ions, whereas the solution inside the axon is rich in positively charged potassium (K^+) ions.

You can understand how these ions result in the action potential by imagining yourself just outside an axon next to a recording electrode (**Figure 2.28a**). (You will have to shrink

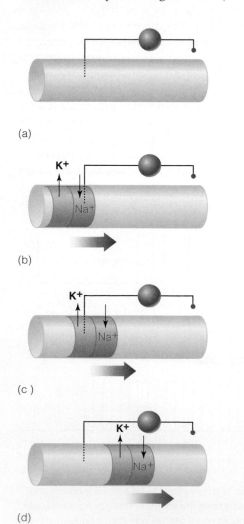

(a)

(b)

(c)

(d)

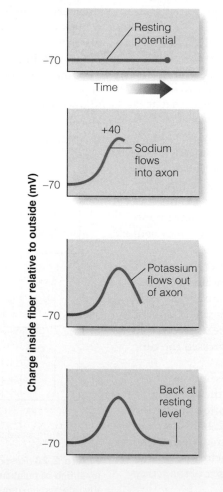

Charge inside fiber relative to outside (mV)

Resting potential

−70

Time

+40

Sodium flows into axon

−70

Potassium flows out of axon

−70

Back at resting level

−70

Figure 2.28 How the flow of sodium and potassium creates the action potential. (a) When the fiber is at rest, there is no flow of ions, and the record indicates the resting potential. The ion flow will occur when an action potential travels down the fiber. (b) As positively charged sodium (Na^+) flows into the axon, the inside of the neuron becomes more positive (rising phase of the action potential). (c) As positively charged potassium (K^+) flows out of the axon, the inside of the axon becomes more negative (falling phase of the action potential). (d) The fiber's charge returns to the resting level after the flow of Na^+ and K^+ has moved past the electrode. © Cengage Learning

yourself down to a very small size to do this!) Everything is quiet until an action potential begins traveling down the axon. As it approaches, you see Na+ ions rushing into the axon (**Figure 2.28b**). This occurs because channels in the membrane have opened to allow Na+ to flow across the membrane. This opening of sodium channels represents an increase in the membrane's **permeability** to sodium, where permeability refers to the ease with which a molecule can pass through the membrane. In this case, permeability is selective, which means that the fiber is highly permeable to one specific type of molecule (Na+ in this case), but not to others. The inflow of positively charged sodium causes an increase in the positive charge inside the axon from the resting potential of –70 mV until it reaches the peak of the action potential of +40 mV. This increase in potential from –70 mV to +40 mv is the **rising phase of the action potential** (Figure 2.28b).

Continuing your vigil, you notice that once the charge inside the neuron reaches +40 mV, the sodium channels close (the membrane becomes impermeable to sodium), and potassium channels open (the membrane becomes selectively permeable to potassium). Positively charged potassium rushes out of the axon, causing the charge inside the axon to become more negative. This increase in negativity from +40 mV back to –70 mV is the **falling phase of the action potential** (**Figure 2.28c**). Once the potential has returned to the –70 mV resting level, the K+ flow stops (**Figure 2.28d**).

After reading this description of ion flow, students often ask why the sodium-in, potassium-out flow that occurs during the action potential doesn't cause sodium to build up inside the axon, and potassium to build up outside. The answer is that a mechanism called the *sodium-potassium pump* keeps this buildup from happening by continuously pumping sodium out and potassium into the fiber.

Transmitting Information Across a Gap

We have seen that action potentials caused by sodium and potassium flow travel down the axon without decreasing in size. But what happens when the action potential reaches the end of the axon? How is the action potential's message transmitted to other neurons? The problem is that there is a very small space between neurons, known as a **synapse** (**Figure 2.29**). The discovery of the synapse raised the question of how the electrical signals generated by one neuron are transmitted across the space separating the neurons. As we will see, the answer lies in a remarkable chemical process that involves molecules called *neurotransmitters*.

Early in the 1900s, it was discovered that when action potentials reach the end of a neuron, they trigger the release of chemicals called **neurotransmitters** that are stored in structures called *synaptic vesicles* in the sending neuron (**Figure 2.29b**). The neurotransmitter molecules flow into the synapse to small areas on the receiving neuron called **receptor sites** that are sensitive to specific neurotransmitters

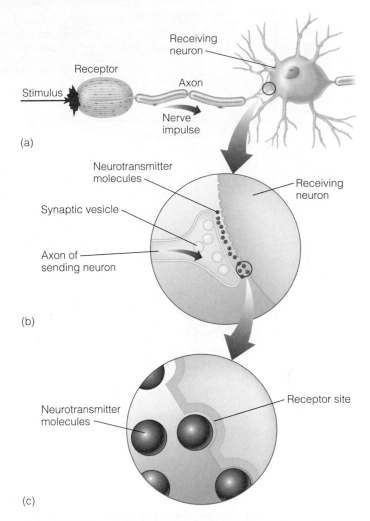

Figure 2.29 Synaptic transmission from one neuron to another. (a) A signal traveling down the axon of a neuron reaches the synapse at the end of the axon. (b) The nerve impulse causes the release of neurotransmitter molecules from the synaptic vesicles of the sending neuron. (c) The neurotransmitters fit into receptor sites and cause a voltage change in the receiving neuron. © Cengage Learning

(**Figure 2.29c**). These receptor sites exist in a variety of shapes that match the shapes of particular neurotransmitter molecules. When a neurotransmitter makes contact with a receptor site matching its shape, it activates the receptor site and triggers a voltage change in the receiving neuron. A neurotransmitter is like a key that fits a specific lock. It has an effect on the receiving neuron only when its shape matches that of the receptor site.

Thus, when an electrical signal reaches the synapse, it triggers a chemical process that causes a new electrical signal in the receiving neuron. The nature of this signal depends on both the type of transmitter that is released and the nature of the receptor sites in the receiving neuron. Two types of responses can occur at these receptor sites, *excitatory* and *inhibitory*. An **excitatory response** occurs when the inside of the neuron becomes more positive, a process called **depolarization**. **Figure 2.30a** shows this effect.

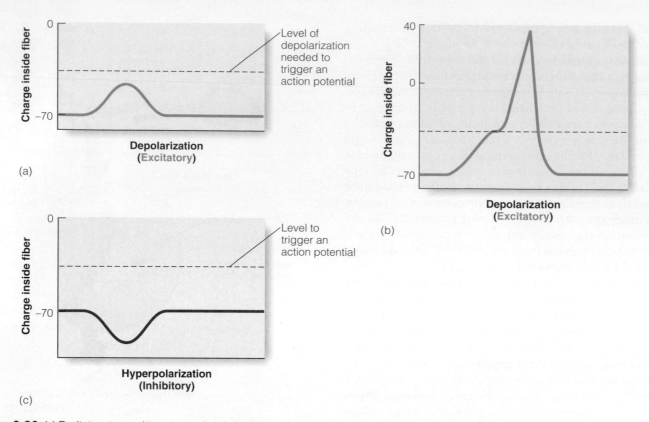

Figure 2.30 (a) Excitatory transmitters cause depolarization, an increased positive charge inside the neuron. (b) When the level of depolarization reaches threshold, indicated by the dashed line, an action potential is triggered. (c) Inhibitory transmitters cause hyperpolarization, an increased negative charge inside the axon. © Cengage Learning

Notice, however, that this response is much smaller than the positive action potential. To generate an action potential, enough excitation must occur to increase depolarization to the level indicated by the dashed line. Once depolarization reaches that level, an action potential is triggered (**Figure 2.30b**). Depolarization is an an excitatory response because it causes the charge to change in the direction that triggers an action potential.

An **inhibitory response** occurs when the inside of the neuron becomes more negative, a process called **hyperpolarization**. **Figure 2.30c** shows this effect. Hyperpolarization is an inhibitory response because it causes the charge inside the axon to move away from the level of depolarization, indicated by the dashed line, needed to generate an action potential.

We can summarize this description of the effects of excitation and inhibition as follows: Excitation increases the chances that a neuron will generate action potentials and is associated with increasing rates of nerve firing. Inhibition decreases the chances that a neuron will generate action potentials and is associated with lowering rates of nerve firing. Since a typical neuron receives both excitation and inhibition, the response of the neuron is determined by the interplay of excitation and inhibition, as illustrated in **Figure 2.31**. In **Figure 2.31a**, excitation (E) is much stronger than inhibition (I), so the neuron's firing rate is high.

However, as inhibition becomes stronger and excitation becomes weaker, the neuron's firing decreases, until in **Figure 2.31e**, inhibition has eliminated the neuron's spontaneous activity and has decreased firing to zero.

Why does inhibition exist? If one of the functions of a neuron is to transmit its information to other neurons, what would be the point of decreasing or eliminating firing in the next neuron? The answer to this question is that the function of neurons is not only to transmit information but also to *process* it, and, as we will see in Chapter 3, both excitation and inhibition are involved in this processing. **VL**

Neural Convergence and Perception

Now, with some background about neurons and the electrical signals in neurons, we are ready to look for more connections between physiology and perception. Step 4 in the perceptual process, the transmission and processing of electrical signals, is the topic of Chapters 3 and 4. But before we leave the receptors to consider events happening further along in the visual system, we will introduce the neural processing that occurs in Step 4 by considering how perception

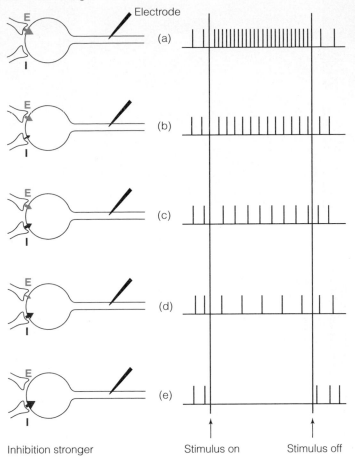

Excitation stronger

Electrode

(a)

(b)

(c)

(d)

(e)

Inhibition stronger

Stimulus on   Stimulus off

Figure 2.31 Effect of excitatory (E) and inhibitory (I) input on the firing rate of a neuron. The amount of excitatory and inhibitory input to the neuron is indicated by the size of the arrows at the synapse. The responses recorded by the electrode are indicated by the records on the right. The firing that occurs before the stimulus is presented is spontaneous activity. In (a), the neuron receives only excitatory transmitter, which causes the neuron to fire. In (b) to (e), the amount of excitatory transmitter decreases while the amount of inhibitory transmitter increases. As inhibition becomes stronger relative to excitation, firing rate decreases, until eventually the firing rate becomes zero. © Cengage Learning

is related to the way the rods and cones are "wired up" in the retina.

Figure 2.32a is a cross section of the retina that has been stained to reveal the retina's layered structure. **Figure 2.32b** shows the five types of neurons that make up these layers and that create **neural circuits**—interconnected groups of neurons—within the retina. Signals generated in the receptors (R) travel to the **bipolar cells** (B) and then to the **ganglion cells** (G). The receptors and bipolar cells do not have long axons, but the ganglion cells have axons like the neurons in Figure 2.22. These axons transmit signals out of the retina in the optic nerve (see Figure 2.12). **VL**

In addition to the receptors, bipolar cells, and ganglion cells, there are two other types of neurons that connect neurons across the retina: **horizontal cells** and **amacrine cells**.

Signals can travel between receptors through the horizontal cells, and between bipolar cells and between ganglion cells through the amacrine cells. We will return to the horizontal and amacrine cells in Chapter 3. For now we will focus on the direct pathway from the receptors to the ganglion cells. We focus specifically on the property of **neural convergence** (or just **convergence** for short).

Convergence occurs when a number of neurons synapse onto a single neuron. A great deal of convergence occurs in the retina because each eye has 126 million receptors but only 1 million ganglion cells. Thus, on the average, each ganglion cell receives signals from 126 receptors. We can show how convergence can affect perception by returning to our comparison of rods and cones. An important difference between rods and cones is that the signals from the rods converge more than do the signals from the cones. We can appreciate this difference by noting that there are 120 million rods in the retina, but only 6 million cones. Thus, on the average, about 120 rods send their signals to one ganglion cell, but only about 6 cones send signals to a single ganglion cell.

This difference between rod and cone convergence becomes even greater when we consider the cones in the fovea. (Remember that the fovea is the small area that contains only cones.) Many of these foveal cones have "private lines" to ganglion cells, so that each ganglion cell receives signals from only one cone, with no convergence. The greater convergence of the rods compared to the cones translates into two differences in perception: (1) the rods result in better sensitivity than the cones, and (2) the cones result in better detail vision than the rods.

Convergence Causes the Rods to Be More Sensitive Than the Cones

In the dark-adapted eye, rod vision is more sensitive than the cone vision (see "dark-adapted sensitivity" in the dark adaptation curve of Figure 2.16). This is why in dim light conditions we use our rods to detect faint stimuli. A demonstration of this effect, which has long been known to astronomers and amateur stargazers, is that some very dim stars are difficult to detect when looked at directly (because the star's image falls on the cones in the fovea), but these same stars can often be seen when they are located off to the side of where the person is looking (because then the star's image falls on the rod-rich peripheral retina). One reason for this greater sensitivity of rods, compared to cones, is that it takes less light to generate a response from an individual rod receptor than from an individual cone receptor (Barlow & Mollon, 1982; Baylor, 1992). But there is another reason as well: The rods have greater convergence than the cones.

Keeping this basic principle in mind, we can see how the difference in rod and cone convergence translates into differences in the maximum sensitivities of the rods and the cones.

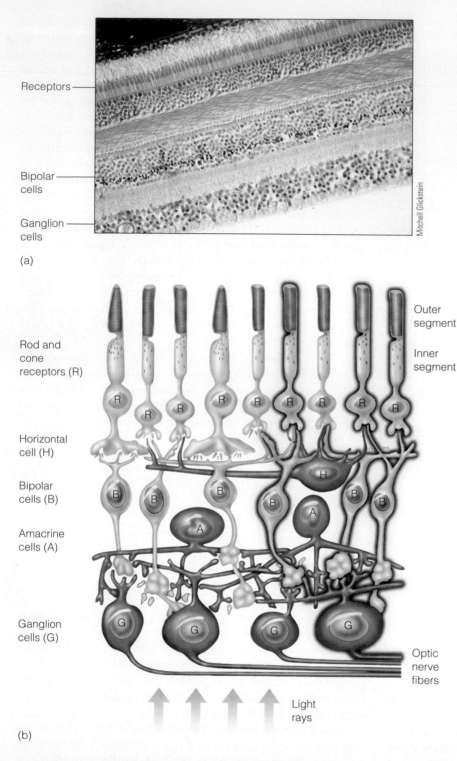

Receptors

Bipolar
cells

Ganglion
cells

Mitchell Glickstein

(a)

Rod and
cone
receptors (R)

Outer
segment

Inner
segment

Horizontal
cell (H)

Bipolar
cells (B)

Amacrine
cells (A)

Ganglion
cells (G)

Optic
nerve
fibers

Light
rays

(b)

Figure 2.32 (a) Cross section of a monkey retina, which has been stained to show the various layers. Light is coming from the bottom. The red circles are cell bodies of the receptors, bipolar cells, and ganglion cells. (b) Cross section of the primate retina showing the five major cell types and their interconnections: receptors (R), bipolar cells (B), ganglion cells (G), horizontal cells (H), and amacrine cells (A). Signals from the three highlighted rods on the right reach the highlighted ganglion cell. This is an example of convergence. Based on "Organization of the Private Retina," by J. E. Dowling and B. B. Boycott, *Proceedings of the Royal Society of London, B, 1966,* 166, pp. 80–111. Used by Permission of the Royal Society of London and John Dowling.

In the two circuits in **Figure 2.33**, five rod receptors converge onto one ganglion cell and five cone receptors each send signals onto their own ganglion cells. We have left out the bipolar, horizontal, and amacrine cells in these circuits for simplicity, but our conclusions will not be affected by these omissions.

For the purposes of our discussion, we will assume that we can present small spots of light to individual rods and cones. We will also make the following additional assumptions:

1. *One unit of light intensity* causes the release of *one unit of excitatory transmitter*, which causes *one unit of excitation* in the ganglion cell.

2. The ganglion cell fires when it receives 10 units of excitation.

3. When the ganglion cell fires, the light is perceived.

When we present spots of light with an intensity of 1 to each receptor, the rod ganglion cell receives 5 units of excitation, 1 from each of the 5 rod receptors. In contrast, each cone ganglion cell receives 1 unit of excitation, 1 from each cone receptor. Thus, when intensity = 1, the rod ganglion cell receives more excitation than the cone ganglion cells because of convergence, but not enough to cause it to fire. If, however, we increase the intensity to 2, as shown in the figure, the rod

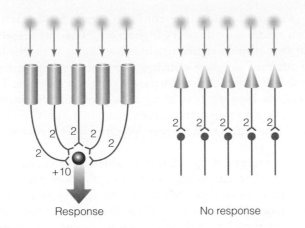

Figure 2.33 The wiring of the rods (left) and the cones (right). The dot and arrow above each receptor represents a "spot" of light that stimulates the receptor. The numbers represent the number of response units generated by the rods and the cones in response to a spot intensity of 2. © Cengage Learning

ganglion cell receives 2 units of excitation from each of its 5 receptors, for a total of 10 units of excitation. This causes the ganglion cell to fire, and the light is perceived. Meanwhile, at the same intensity, the cones' ganglion cells are each receiving only 2 units of excitation. For the cones' ganglion cells to fire, we must increase the intensity to 10. **VL**

The operation of these circuits demonstrates how the rods' high sensitivity compared to the cones' is caused by the rods' greater convergence. Many rods sum their responses by feeding into the same ganglion cell, but only one or a few cones send their responses to any one ganglion cell. The fact that rod and cone sensitivity is determined not by individual receptors but by groups of receptors converging onto other neurons means that when we describe "rod vision" and "cone vision" we are actually referring to the way *groups* of rods and cones participate in determining our perceptions.

Lack of Convergence Causes the Cones to Have Better Acuity Than the Rods

While rod vision is more sensitive than cone vision because the rods have *more* convergence, the cones have better **visual acuity** because they have *less* convergence. Acuity refers to the ability to see details; thus, being able to see very small letters on an eye chart in the optometrist or ophthalmologist's office translates into high acuity.

One way to appreciate the high acuity of the cones is to think about the last time you were looking for one thing that was hidden among many other things. This could be searching for your cell phone on the clutter of your desk or locating a friend's face in a crowd. To find what you are looking for, you usually need to move your eyes from one place to another. When you move your eyes to look at different things in this way, what you are doing is scanning with your cone-rich fovea (remember that when you look directly at something, its image falls on the fovea). This is necessary because

your visual acuity is highest in the fovea; objects that are imaged on the peripheral retina are not seen as clearly.

In the demonstration above, we showed that acuity is better in the fovea than in the periphery. Because you were light adapted, the comparison in this demonstration was between the foveal cones, which are tightly packed, and the peripheral cones, which are more widely spaced. Comparing the foveal cones to the rods results in even greater differences in acuity. We can make this comparison by noting how acuity changes during dark adaptation.

The picture of the bookcase in **Figure 2.34** simulates the change in acuity that occurs during dark adaptation. The

Figure 2.34 Simulation of the change from colorful sharp perception to colorless fuzzy perception that occurs during the shift from cone vision to rod vision during dark adaptation.

books on the top shelf represent the details we see when viewing the books in the light, when our cones are controlling vision. The books on the middle shelf represent how we might perceive the details midway through the process of dark adaptation, when the rods are beginning to determine our vision, and the books on the bottom shelf represent the poor detail vision of the rods. The poor detail vision of the rods is why it is difficult to read in dim illumination. (Also note that color has disappeared. We will describe why this occurs in Chapter 9.) **VL**

We can understand how differences in rod and cone wiring explain the cones' greater acuity by returning to our rod and cone neural circuits. First consider the rod circuit in **Figure 2.35a**. When we present two spots of light next to each other, as on the left, the rod's signals cause the ganglion cell to fire. When we separate the two spots, as on the right, the two separated rods feed into the same ganglion cell and cause it to fire. In both cases, the ganglion cell fires. Thus, firing of the ganglion cell provides no information about whether there are two spots close together or two separated spots.

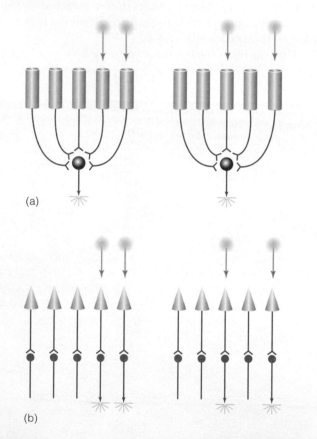

(a)

(b)

Figure 2.35 How the wiring of the rods and cones determines detail vision. (a) Rod neural circuits. On the left, stimulating two neighboring rods causes the ganglion cell to fire. On the right, stimulating two separated rods causes the same effect. (b) Cone neural circuits. On the left, stimulating two neighboring cones causes two neighboring ganglion cells to fire. On the right, stimulating two separated cones causes two separate ganglion cells to fire. This firing of two neurons, with a space between them, indicates that two spots of light have been presented to the cones. © Cengage Learning

We now consider the cones in **Figure 2.35b**, each of which synapses on its own ganglion cell. When we present a light that stimulates two neighboring cones, as on the left, two adjacent ganglion cells fire. But when we separate the spots, as on the right, two separate ganglion cells fire. This separation between two firing cells provides information that there are two separate spots of light. Thus, the cones' lack of convergence causes cone vision to have higher acuity than rod vision.

Convergence is therefore a double-edged sword. High convergence results in high sensitivity but poor acuity (the rods). Low convergence results in low sensitivity but high acuity (cones). The way the rods and cones are wired up in the retina, therefore, influences what we perceive. In Chapter 3 we will provide more examples of how neural wiring can influence perception, and we will show how the addition of inhibition adds another dimension to neural processing.

SOMETHING TO CONSIDER:
Early Events Are Powerful

In 1990, a rocket blasted off from Cape Canaveral to place the Hubble space telescope into earth orbit. The telescope's mission was to provide high-resolution images from its vantage point above the interference of the earth's atmosphere. But it took only a few days of data collection to realize that something was wrong. Images of stars and galaxies that should have been extremely sharp were blurred (**Figure 2.36a**). The cause of the problem, it turned out, was that the telescope's lens was ground to the wrong curvature. Although a few of the planned observations were possible, the telescope's mission was severely compromised. Three years later, the problem was solved when a corrective lens was fitted over the original one. The new Hubble, with its "eyeglasses," could now see stars as sharp points (**Figure 2.36b**).

This diversion to outer space emphasizes that what happens early in a system can have a large, often crucial, effect on the outcome. No matter how sophisticated Hubble's electronic computer and processing programs were, the distorted image caused by the faulty lens had fatal effects on the quality of the telescope's image. Similarly, if problems in the eye's focusing system deliver degraded images to the retina, no amount of processing by the brain can create sharp perception.

What we see is also determined by the energy that can enter the eye and can activate the receptors. Although there is a huge range of electromagnetic energy in the environment, the visual pigments in the receptors limit our sensitivity by absorbing only a narrow range of wavelengths. One way to think about the effect of pigments is that they act like filters, only making available for vision the wavelengths they absorb. Thus, at night, when we are perceiving with our rods, we see only wavelengths between about 420 and 580 nm, with the best sensitivity at 500 nm. However, in daylight, when we

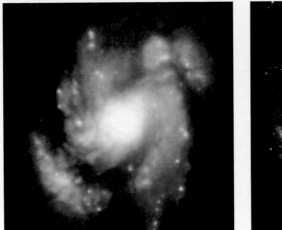

Wide field planetary camera 1
(a) **Before**

Wide field planetary camera 2
(b) **After correction**

NASA Images

Figure 2.36 (a) Image of a galaxy taken by the Hubble telescope before the lens was corrected. (b) The same galaxy after the lens was corrected.

(a)

(b)

Bjørn Rørslett

Figure 2.37 (a) A black-and-white photograph of a flower as seen by a human. (b) The same flower, showing markings that become visible to sensors that can detect ultraviolet light. Although we don't know exactly what honeybees see, their short-wavelength cone pigment makes it possible for them to sense these markings. © 2014 Cengage Learning

are perceiving with our cones, we become more sensitive to longer wavelengths, as the best sensitivity shifts to 560 nm.

This idea of visual pigments as limiting our range of seeing is dramatically illustrated by the honeybee, which, as we will see in the chapter on color vision, has a visual pigment that absorbs light all the way down to 300 nm (see Figure 9.43).

This very-short-wavelength pigment enables the honeybee to perceive ultraviolet wavelengths that are invisible to us, so the honeybee can see markings on flowers that reflect ultraviolet light (**Figure 2.37**). Thus, as we noted earlier in this chapter, although perception does not *occur* in the eye, what we see is affected by what happens there.

DEVELOPMENTAL DIMENSION: Infant Visual Acuity

Some chapters in this book will include "Developmental Dimensions," which describe the perceptual capacities of infants and young children that are related to material in the chapter. In this Developmental Dimension, we will see that infants have lower visual acuity than adults and that this lower acuity is related to the structure of the infant's cones.

One of the challenges of determining infant capacities is that infants can't respond by saying "yes, I perceive it" or

"no, I don't perceive it" in reaction to a stimulus. But this difficulty has not stopped developmental psychologists from devising clever ways to determine what infants or young children are perceiving. One method that has been used to measure infant visual acuity is the **preferential looking (PL) technique**.

METHOD
Preferential Looking VL

The key to measuring infant perception is to pose the correct question. To understand what we mean by this, let's consider how we might determine infants' *visual acuity*, their ability to see details. To test adults, we can ask them to read the letters or symbols on an eye chart. But to test infant acuity, we have to ask another question and use another procedure. A question that works for infants is "Can you tell the difference between the stimulus on the left and the one on the right?" The way infants answer this question is by looking more at one of the stimuli. In the preferential looking (PL) technique, two stimuli like the ones the infant is observing in **Figure 2.38** are presented, and the experimenter watches the infant's eyes to determine where the infant is looking. In order to guard against bias, the experimenter does not know which stimulus is being presented on the left or right. If the infant looks at one stimulus more than the other, the experimenter concludes that he or she can tell the difference between them.

The reason preferential looking works is that infants have *spontaneous looking preferences*; that is, they prefer to look at certain types of stimuli. For example, infants choose to look at objects with contours over ones that are homogeneous (Fantz et al., 1962). Thus, when we present a grating stimulus (alternating white and black bars like the one shown in Figure 2.38) with large bars on one side, and a gray field that reflects the same total amount of light that the grating would reflect on the other side (again, like the one shown in Figure 2.38), the infant can easily see the bars and therefore looks at the side with the bars more than the side with the gray field. If the infant looks preferentially at the side with the bars when the bars are switched randomly from side to side on different trials, he or she is telling the experimenter "I see the grating."

But decreasing the size of the bars makes it more difficult for the infant to tell the difference between the grating and gray stimulus. Eventually, the infant begins to look equally at each display,

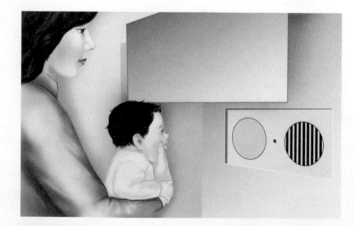

Figure 2.38 An infant being tested using the preferential looking technique. The mother holds the infant in front of the display, which consists of a grating on the right and a homogeneous gray field on the left. The grating and the gray field have the same average light intensity. An experimenter, who does not know which side the grating is on in any given trial, looks through the peephole between the grating and the gray field and judges whether the infant is looking to the left or to the right. © Cengage Learning

which tells the experimenter that very fine lines and the gray field are indiscriminable. Therefore, we can measure the infant's acuity by determining the narrowest stripe width that results in looking more at the grating stimulus.

How well can infants see details? The red curve in **Figure 2.39** shows acuity over the first year of life measured with the preferential looking technique, in which infants are tested with gratings, as in Figure 2.38. The blue curve indicates acuity determined by measuring an electrical signal called the **visual evoked potential (VEP)**, which is recorded by disc electrodes placed on the infant's head over the visual cortex. For this technique, researchers alternate a gray field with a grating or checkerboard pattern. If the stripes or checks are large enough to be detected by the visual system, the visual cortex generates an electrical response called the *visual evoked potential*. If, however, the stripes are too fine to be detected by the visual system, no response is generated. Thus, the VEP provides an objective measure of the visual system's ability to detect details.

The VEP usually indicates better acuity than does preferential looking, but both techniques indicate that visual

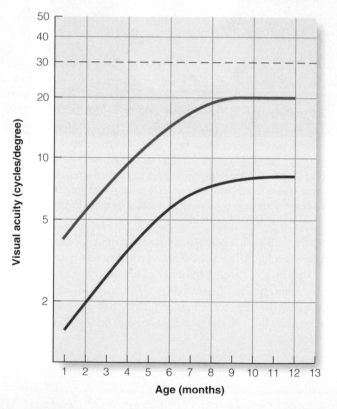

Figure 2.39 Acuity over the first year of life, measured by the visual evoked potential technique (top curve) and the preferential looking technique (bottom curve). The vertical axis indicates the fineness, in cycles per degree, of a grating stimulus that the infant can detect. One cycle per degree corresponds to one pair of black and white lines on a circle the size of a penny viewed from a distance of about a meter. Higher numbers indicate the ability to detect finer lines on the penny-sized circle. The dashed line is adult acuity (20/20 vision). (VEP curve adapted from Norcia & Tyler, 1985; PL curve adapted from Gwiazda et al., 1980, and Mayer et al., 1995.) © Cengage Learning

acuity is poorly developed at birth (about 20/400 to 20/600 at 1 month). (The expression 20/400 means that the infant must view a stimulus from 20 feet to see the same thing that an adult with normal vision can see from 400 feet.) Acuity increases rapidly over the first 6 to 9 months (Banks & Salapatek, 1978; Dobson & Teller, 1978; Harris et al., 1976; Salapatek et al., 1976). This rapid improvement of acuity is followed by a leveling-off period, and full adult acuity is not reached until sometime after 1 year of age.

From our discussion of how adult rod and cone visual acuity depends on the wiring of the rods and cones, it would make sense to consider the possibility that infants' low acuity might be traced to the development of their receptors. If we look at the newborn's retina, we find that this is the case. Although the rod-dominated peripheral retina appears adultlike in the newborn, the all-cone fovea contains widely spaced and very poorly developed cone receptors (Abramov et al., 1982).

Figure 2.40a compares the shapes of newborn and adult foveal cones. Remember from our discussion of transduction that the visual pigments are contained in the receptor's outer segments. These outer segments sit on top of the other part of the receptor, the inner segment. The newborn's cones have fat inner segments and very small outer segments, whereas the adult's inner and outer segments are larger and are about the same diameter (Banks & Bennett, 1988; Yuodelis & Hendrickson, 1986). These differences in shape and size have a number of consequences. The small size of the outer segment means that the newborn's cones contain less visual pigment and therefore do not absorb light as effectively as adult cones. In addition, the fat inner segment creates the coarse receptor lattice shown in **Figure 2.40b**, with large spaces between the outer segments. In contrast, when the adult cones have become thin, they can become packed closely together to create a fine lattice that is well suited to detecting small details. Martin Banks and Patrick Bennett (1988) calculated that the cone receptors' outer segments effectively cover 68 percent of the adult fovea but only 2 percent of the newborn fovea. This means that most of the light entering the newborn's fovea is lost in the spaces between the cones and is therefore not useful for vision.

Thus, adults have good acuity because the cones have low convergence compared to the rods and the receptors in the fovea are packed closely together. In contrast, the infant's poor acuity can be traced to the fact that the infant's cones are spaced far apart. Another reason for the infant's poor acuity is that the visual area of the brain is poorly developed at birth, with fewer neurons and synapses than in the adult cortex. The rapid increase in acuity that occurs over the first 6 to 9 months of life can thus be traced to the fact that during that time, more neurons and synapses are being added to the cortex, and the infant's cones are becoming more densely packed.

TEST YOURSELF 2.2

1. Describe the basic structure of a neuron.
2. Describe how to record electrical signals from a neuron.
3. What are some of the basic properties of action potentials?
4. Describe what happens when an action potential travels along an axon. In your description, indicate how the charge inside the fiber changes, and how that is related to the flow of chemicals across the cell membrane.

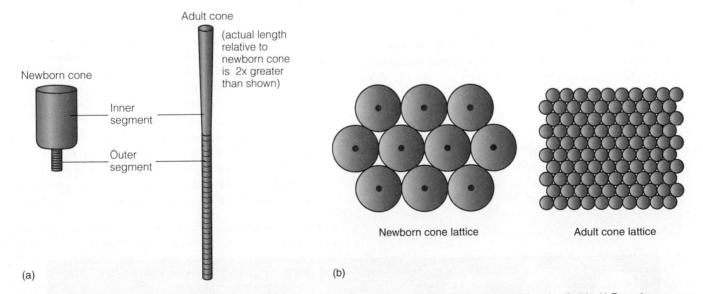

(a)

Adult cone
(actual length relative to newborn cone is 2x greater than shown)

Newborn cone

Inner segment

Outer segment

(b)

Newborn cone lattice

Adult cone lattice

Figure 2.40 (a) Idealized shapes of newborn and adult foveal cones. (Real cones are not so perfectly straight and cylindrical.) Foveal cones are much narrower and longer than the cones elsewhere in the retina, so these look different from the one shown in Figure 2.7. (b) Receptor lattices for newborn and adult foveal cones. The newborn cone outer segments, indicated by the red circles, are widely spaced because of the fat inner segments. In contrast, the adult cones, with their slender inner segments, are packed closely together. Adapted from Banks, M. S., & Bennett, P. J. (1988). Optical and photoreceptor immaturities limit the spatial and chromatic vision of human neonates. *Journal of the Optical Society of America, A5,* 2059–2079.

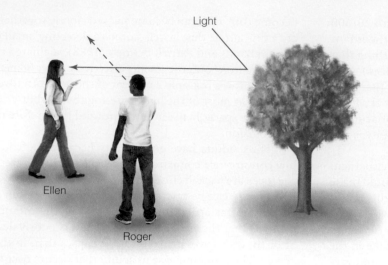

Figure 2.41 Ellen sees the tree because light is reflected from the tree into her eyes. Roger doesn't see the tree because he is not looking at it, but he is looking directly across the space where light from the tree is reflected into Ellen's eyes. Why isn't he aware of the information contained in this light? © Cengage Learning 2014

5. How are electrical signals transmitted from one neuron to another? Be sure you understand the difference between excitatory and inhibitory responses.

6. What is convergence, and how can the differences in the convergence of rods and cones explain (a) the rods' greater sensitivity in the dark and (b) the cones' better detail vision?

7. What does it mean to say that early events are powerful shapers of perception? Give examples.

8. What is the young infant's visual acuity, and how does it change over the first year of life? What is the reason for (a) low acuity at birth and (b) the increase in acuity over the first 6 to 9 months?

THINK ABOUT IT

1. Ellen is looking at a tree. She sees the tree because light is reflected from the tree into her eyes, as shown in **Figure 2.41**. One way to describe this is to say that information about the tree is contained in the light. Meanwhile, Roger is off to the side, looking straight ahead. He doesn't see the tree because he is looking away from it. He is however, looking right at the space through which the light that is carrying information from the tree to Ellen is passing. But Roger doesn't see any of this information. Why does this occur? (Hint #1: Consider the idea that "objects make light visible." Hint #2: Outer space contains a great deal of light, but it looks dark, except where there are objects.)

2. In the demonstration "Becoming Aware of What Is in Focus" on page 24, you saw that we see things clearly only when we are looking directly at them so that their image falls on the cone-rich fovea. But consider the common observation that the things we aren't looking at do not appear "fuzzy," that the entire scene appears "sharp" or "in focus." How can this be, in light of the results of the demonstration?

3. Here's an exercise you can do to get more in touch with the process of dark adaptation: Find a dark place where you will make some observations as you adapt to the dark. A closet is a good place to do this because it is possible to regulate the intensity of light inside the closet by opening or closing the door. The idea is to create an environment in which there is dim light (no light at all, as in a darkroom with the safelight out, is too dark). Take this book into the closet, opened to this page. Close the closet door all the way so it is very dark, and then open the door slowly until you can just barely make out the white circle on the far left in **Figure 2.42** but can't see the others or can see them only as being very dim. As you sit in the dark,

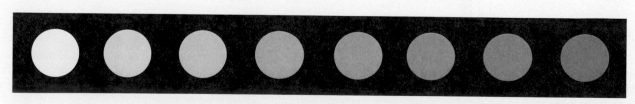

Figure 2.42 Dark adaptation test circles. © Cengage Learning

become aware that your sensitivity is increasing by noting how the circles to the right in the figure slowly become visible over a period of about 20 minutes. Also note that once a circle becomes visible, it gets easier to see as time passes. If you stare directly at the circles, they may fade, so move your eyes around every so often. Also, the circles will be easier to see if you look slightly above them.

4. Because the long axons of neurons look like electrical wires, and both neurons and electrical wires conduct electricity, it is tempting to equate the two. Compare the functioning of axons and electrical wires in terms of their structure and the nature of the electrical signals they conduct.

KEY TERMS

Absorption spectrum (p. 34)
Accommodation (p. 24)
Action potential (p. 37)
Amacrine cells (p. 41)
Axial myopia (p. 25)
Axon (p. 35)
Bipolar cells (p. 41)
Blind spot (p. 29)
Cell body (p. 35)
Cone (p. 23)
Cone spectral sensitivity curve (p. 33)
Convergence (p. 41)
Cornea (p. 23)
Dark adaptation (p. 27)
Dark adaptation curve (p. 29)
Dark-adapted sensitivity (p. 31)
Dendrites (p. 35)
Depolarization (p. 39)
Detached retina (p. 32)
Electromagnetic spectrum (p. 22)
Excitatory response (p. 39)
Eye (p. 22)
Falling phase of the action potential (p. 39)
Far point (p. 25)
Farsightedness (p. 26)
Fovea (p. 28)
Ganglion cells (p. 41)

Horizontal cells (p. 41)
Hyperopia (p. 26)
Hyperpolarization (p. 40)
Inhibitory response (p. 40)
Ions (p. 38)
Isomerization (p. 27)
Laser-assisted in situ keratomileusis (LASIK) (p. 26)
Lens (p. 23)
Light-adapted sensitivity (p. 30)
Macular degeneration (p. 28)
Monochromatic light (p. 33)
Myopia (p. 25)
Near point (p. 24)
Nearsightedness (p. 25)
Nerve fiber (p. 35)
Neural circuits (p. 41)
Neural convergence (p. 41)
Neuron (p. 35)
Neurotransmitter (p. 39)
Optic nerve (p. 23)
Outer segment (p. 26)
Peripheral retina (p. 28)
Permeability (p. 39)
Preferential looking technique (p. 45)
Presbyopia (p. 24)
Propagated response (p. 37)
Pupil (p. 23)

Purkinje shift (p. 33)
Receptor sites (p. 39)
Refractive myopia (p. 25)
Refractory period (p. 37)
Resting potential (p. 36)
Retina (p. 23)
Retinitis pigmentosa (p. 29)
Rising phase of the action potential (p. 39)
Rod (p. 23)
Rod monochromat (p. 31)
Rod spectral sensitivity curve (p. 33)
Rod–cone break (p. 31)
Sensory receptor (p. 35)
Spectral sensitivity (p. 32)
Spectral sensitivity curve (p. 32)
Spontaneous activity (p. 38)
Synapse (p. 39)
Transduction (p. 26)
Visible light (p. 22)
Visual acuity (p. 43)
Visual evoked potential (p. 46)
Visual pigment (p. 23)
Visual pigment bleaching (p. 31)
Visual pigment regeneration (p. 32)
Wavelength (p. 22)

MEDIA RESOURCES

CourseMate 🖥

Go to CengageBrain.com to access Psychology CourseMate, where you will find the Virtual Labs plus an interactive eBook, flashcards, quizzes, videos, and more.

Virtual Labs ⱽᴸ

The Virtual Labs are designed to help you get the most out of this course. The Virtual Lab icons direct you to specific media demonstrations and experiments designed to help you visualize what you are reading about. The numbers below indicate the number of the Virtual Lab you can access through Psychology CourseMate.

2.1 The Human Eye (p. 23)
A drag-and-drop exercise to test your knowledge of parts of the eye.

2.2 Vision: Light and Neural Activity (p. 26)
A video describing the structure of the retina and how the receptors transform light energy into electrical energy that is then transmitted from the eye to the brain. (Courtesy of Teresa Pinto)

2.3 Resting Potential (p. 36)
Illustrates how ions inside and outside the neuron are related to the resting potential.

2.4 Optogenetics (p. 40)
Describes a new method called optogenetics that uses genetic cloning techniques to implant light-sensitive molecules onto neurons. These implanted neurons can then be activated by light. (Courtesy of McGovern Institute, MIT)

2.5 Cross-Section of the Retina (p. 41)
A drag-and-drop exercise to test your knowledge of the neurons in the retina.

2.6 Visual Path Within the Eyeball (p. 41)
How electrical signals that start in the rods and cones are transmitted through the retina and out the back of the eye in the optic nerve.

2.7 Receptor Wiring and Sensitivity (p. 43)
A neural circuit that explains why rod ganglion cells fire to lower light intensities than cone ganglion cells.

2.8 Receptor Wiring and Acuity (p. 44)
A neural circuit that explains why cone receptors result in better detail vision than do rod receptors.

2.9 Curveball Illusion (p. 44)
A demonstration that shows how perception of the direction in which a ball is moving depends on whether it is seen in foveal or peripheral vision. (Courtesy of Arthur Shapiro)

2.10 Preferential Looking (p. 46)
A film showing how a child moves his eyes between two stimuli in a preferential looking experiment. (Courtesy of George Hollich)

2.11 Testing Perception in Infants (p. 46)
A film showing a child being tested in a preferential looking experiment in which the child can choose between two films: one of a talking face with no sound and the other of a talking face with sound. (Courtesy of George Hollich)

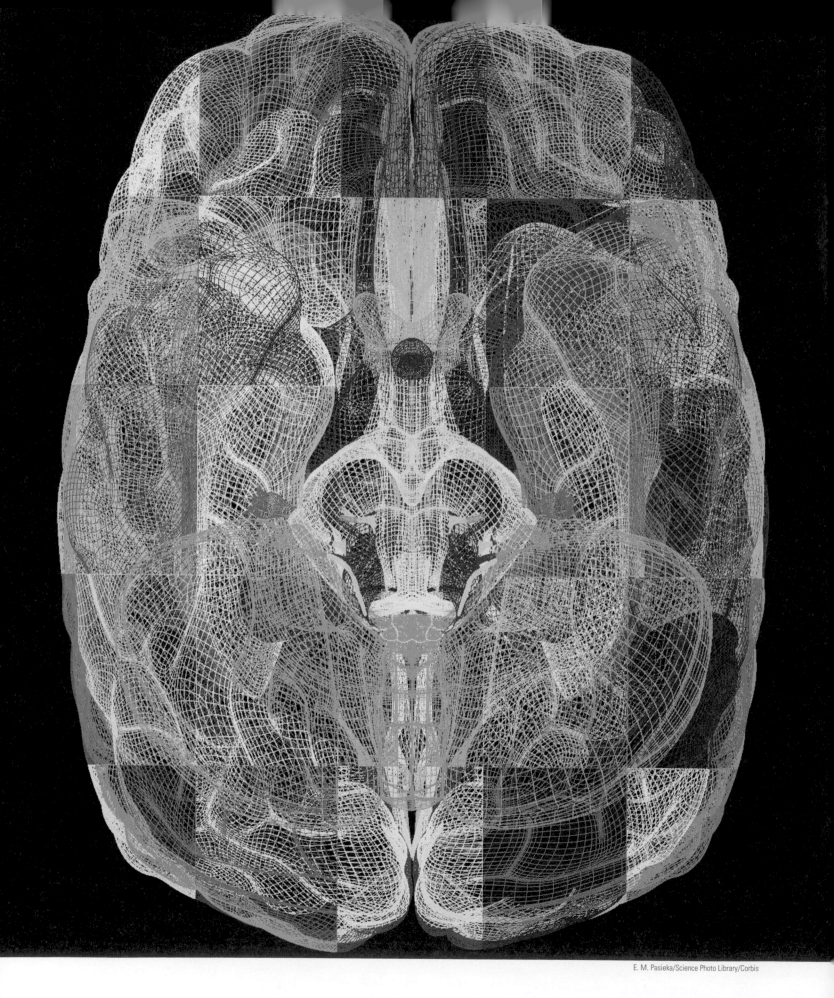

Neural Processing and Perception

VL The Virtual Lab icons direct you to specific animations and videos designed to help you visualize what you are reading about. Virtual Labs are listed at the end of the chapter, keyed to the page on which they appear, and can be accessed through Psychology CourseMate.

◀ This picture of the brain as seen from the bottom has been artistically embellished with colors and patterns that don't exist in real brains. The beauty of this fanciful image is in the way it symbolizes the mysteries of the brain's operation. As we will see in this chapter, researchers have begun to unlock these mysteries by recording from single neurons and by considering how groups of neurons work together to create our perceptions.

Some Questions We Will Consider:

- How do both excitation and inhibition determine how a neuron fires to different types of stimuli? (p. 62)
- How do the responses of neurons change as we move higher in the visual system? (p. 64)
- How are objects in the environment represented by the firing of neurons in the cortex? (p. 70)
- Is it possible to explain how sodium and potassium ions moving into and out of neurons can result in our perception of the color "red" or a friend's face? (p. 72)

Two cars start at the same place and drive to the same destination. Car A takes the turnpike, stopping only briefly for gas and to pay a toll. Car B takes the "scenic" route—back roads that go through the countryside and small towns, stopping a number of times along the way to see some sights and meet some people. Each of Car B's stops can influence its route, depending on the information its driver receives. Stopping at a small-town General Store, the driver of Car B hears about a detour up the road, so he changes his route accordingly. Meanwhile, Car A is speeding directly to its destination.

The way electrical signals travel through the nervous system is more like Car B's journey. The pathway from receptors to brain is not a nonstop turnpike. Every signal leaving a receptor travels through a complex network of interconnected neurons, often meeting, and being affected by, other signals along the way.

What is gained by taking a complex, indirect route? If the goal were just to send a signal to the brain that a particular receptor had been stimulated, then the straight-through method would work. But the purpose of electrical signals in the nervous system goes beyond signaling that a receptor was stimulated. The information that reaches the brain and that then continues its journey within the brain is much richer than this. There are neurons in the brain that respond to slanted lines, faces, bodies, and movement in a specific direction. These neurons didn't achieve these properties by

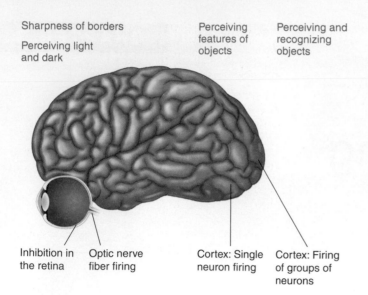

Sharpness of borders

Perceiving light and dark

Perceiving features of objects

Perceiving and recognizing objects

Inhibition in the retina | Optic nerve fiber firing | Cortex: Single neuron firing | Cortex: Firing of groups of neurons

Figure 3.1 Chapter preview. Physical processes are indicated in black. Perceptual outcomes are indicated in blue. © Cengage Learning 2014

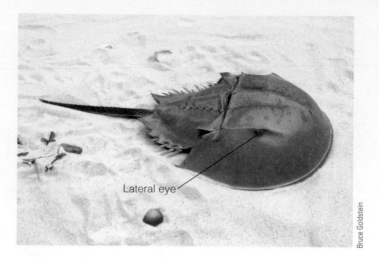

Bruce Goldstein

Lateral eye

Figure 3.2 A *Limulus*, or horseshoe crab. Its large eyes are made up of hundreds of ommatidia, each containing a single receptor.

receiving signals through a straight-line transmission system from receptors to brain. They achieve these properties by **neural processing**—the interaction of the signals in many neurons.

This chapter and the next describe the relationship between neural processing and perception. We begin by going back to the retina, where, at the end of Chapter 2, we introduced neural processing by showing how differences in neural convergence of the rods and cones affect sensitivity (rods: high convergence = high sensitivity) and detail vision (cones: low convergence = high visual acuity). We now move from the receptors into the wiring of the retina to show how inhibition in the retina can affect the perception of border sharpness and how light or dark an area appears (**Figure 3.1**, left). We then move to the optic nerve, to the lateral geniculate nucleus, and then to the cortex. At each of these places, we will show how the responses of single neurons provide information for the perception of object features and for recognizing objects. Finally, we will describe the connection between the responding of groups of neurons and recognizing objects (Figure 3.1, right).

Lateral Inhibition and Perception

What happens when both convergence and inhibition are present? We begin answering that question by considering **lateral inhibition**—inhibition that is transmitted *across* the retina—and will show how inhibition can cause perceptual effects. The pioneering work on lateral inhibition was carried out on a primitive animal called the *Limulus*, more familiarly known as the horseshoe crab (**Figure 3.2**).

Lateral Inhibition in the *Limulus*

In an experiment that is now considered a classic, Keffer Hartline, Henry Wagner, and Floyd Ratliff (1956) used the *Limulus* to demonstrate how lateral inhibition can affect the response of neurons in a circuit. They chose the *Limulus* because the structure of its eye makes it possible to stimulate individual receptors. The *Limulus* eye is made up of hundreds of tiny structures called **ommatidia**, and each ommatidium has a small lens on the eye's surface that is located directly over a single receptor. Each lens and receptor is roughly the diameter of a pencil point (very large compared to human receptors), so it is possible to illuminate and record from a single receptor without illuminating its neighboring receptors.

When Hartline and coworkers recorded from the nerve fiber of receptor A, as shown in **Figure 3.3**, they found that illumination of that receptor caused a large response (**Figure 3.3a**). But when they added illumination to the three nearby receptors at B, the response of receptor A decreased (**Figure 3.3b**). They also found that further increasing the illumination of B decreased A's response even more (**Figure 3.3c**). Thus, illumination of the neighboring receptors at B inhibited the firing caused by stimulation of receptor A. This decrease in the firing of receptor A is caused by lateral inhibition that is transmitted from B to A across the *Limulus*'s eye by the fibers of the *lateral plexus*, shown in Figure 3.3.

Just as the lateral plexus transmits signals laterally in the *Limulus*, the horizontal and amacrine cells transmit signals across the human retina. We will now see how lateral inhibition transmitted by the horizontal and amacrine cells (see Figure 2.32b) may influence how humans perceive light and dark.

Lateral Inhibition and Lightness Perception

We will now describe some perceptual phenomena that have been explained by lateral inhibition. Each of these phenomena

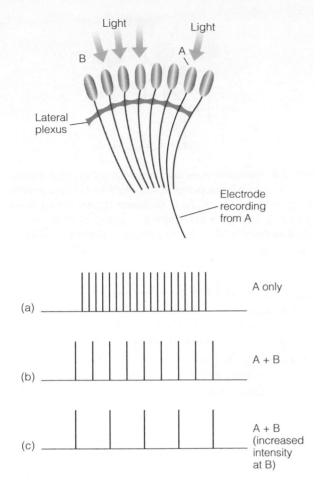

Figure 3.3 A demonstration of lateral inhibition in the *Limulus*. The records show the response recorded by the electrode in the nerve fiber of receptor A: (a) when only receptor A is stimulated; (b) when receptor A and the receptors at B are stimulated together; (c) when A and B are stimulated, with B at an increased intensity. Adapted from *Mach Bands: Quantitative Studies on Neural Networks in the Retina*, by F. Ratliff, 1965, figure 3.25, p. 107. Copyright © 1965 Holden-Day, Inc. Reprinted with permission.

involves the perception of **lightness**—the perception of shades ranging from white to gray to black.

The Hermann Grid: Seeing Spots at Intersections

Notice the ghostlike gray images at the intersections of the white "corridors" in the **Hermann grid** in **Figure 3.4**. You can prove that this grayness is not physically present by noticing that it is reduced or vanishes when you look directly at an intersection or, better yet, when you cover two rows of black squares with white paper.

Figures 3.5 through 3.8 show how the dark spots at the intersections can be explained by lateral inhibition. **Figure 3.5a** shows four squares of the grid, imaged on the surface of the retina. The green circles are receptors. **Figure 3.5b** is a perspective view of the grid, showing the receptors (in green) and the bipolar cells (in blue) that receive signals from the receptors. Because the receptors are all illuminated by the white of the "corridors," each receives the same illumination and generates the same response. For this example, we assume the response of each receptor is 100. **VL**

Figure 3.4 The Hermann grid. Notice the gray "ghost images" at the intersections of the white areas, which decrease or vanish when you look directly at an intersection. © Cengage Learning

Our goal is to determine the response associated with the receptor at the intersection of the crossroads, where the dark spot appears and where receptor A is located. Perception is determined, however, not by the response of the receptors, but by the response of neurons farther down the system, in the retina or the brain. For the purposes of this example, let's assume that perception of lightness is determined by the output of the bipolar cells, which receive signals from the receptors. We focus our attention on the bipolar cells in **Figure 3.6** and assume that the *initial response* of each bipolar is the same as the response of the receptor associated with it. Thus, bipolars A, B, C, D, and E would initially each have a response of 100.

The final response of bipolar A is determined by starting with its initial response and subtracting any decrease caused

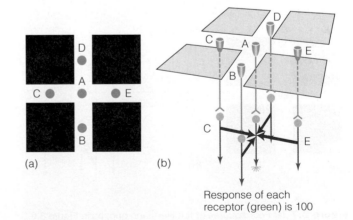

Figure 3.5 (a) Four squares of the Hermann grid, showing five of the receptors under the pattern. Receptor A is located at the intersection, and B, C, D, and E have a black square on either side. (b) Perspective view of the grid and five receptors, showing how the receptors (green) connect to bipolar cells (blue). The response of all five receptors is 100. The initial response of the bipolars matches the response of the receptors. Lateral inhibition travels to bipolar cell A along the red pathways. © Cengage Learning

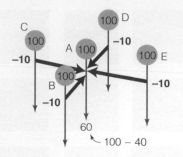

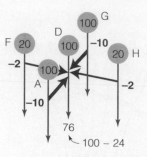

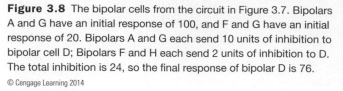

Figure 3.6 The bipolar cells from the circuit in Figure 3.5. Each bipolar cell has an initial response of 100. Bipolar cells B, C, D, and E each send 10 units of inhibition to bipolar cell A, as indicated by the red arrows. Because the total inhibition is 40, the final response of bipolar A is 60. © Cengage Learning 2014

Figure 3.8 The bipolar cells from the circuit in Figure 3.7. Bipolars A and G have an initial response of 100, and F and G have an initial response of 20. Bipolars A and G each send 10 units of inhibition to bipolar cell D; Bipolars F and H each send 2 units of inhibition to D. The total inhibition is 24, so the final response of bipolar D is 76.
© Cengage Learning 2014

by lateral inhibition, which is indicated by the red arrows. We will assume for this example that the amount of lateral inhibition sent by neurons B, C, D, and E to bipolar A is one-tenth the neuron's initial response. Thus, each bipolar cell sends 100 × 0.1 = 10 units of inhibition to bipolar A (red arrows), and the total lateral inhibition sent to A is 10 + 10 + 10 + 10 = 40. This means that the final response of bipolar A is Initial Response (100) – Inhibition (40) = 60.

We now look at **Figure 3.7** and focus our attention on receptor D, which is not located at the intersection of the corridors. In this example, receptors A, D, and G receive white light from the corridor, so they will have an initial response of 100. But receptors F and H are illuminated by the black part of the grid, so their response is lower, let's say 20.

Focusing on the bipolars in **Figure 3.8**, we make the same assumption as before that the initial response of the bipolars matches the response received from the receptors. The red arrows show how much inhibition each bipolar sends to D.

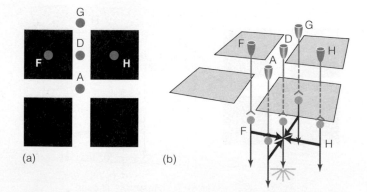

Figure 3.7 (a) Four squares of the Hermann grid, as in Figure 3.5, but now focusing on receptor D, which is flanked by two black squares. Receptor D is surrounded by receptors A, F, G, and H. Notice that receptors F and H are located under the two black squares, so they receive less light than the other receptors. (b) Perspective view of the grid and five receptors, showing how the receptors (green) connect to bipolar cells (blue). The response of receptors A and G is 100, and the response of F and H is 20. Lateral inhibition travels to bipolar D along the red pathways. © Cengage Learning

A and G each send 100 × 0.1 = 10 units of inhibition. F and H each send 20 × 0.1 = 2 units of inhibition. Thus, the total inhibition sent to D is 10 + 10 + 2 + 2 = 24, and bipolar D's final response is, therefore, (100) – (24) = 76.

Comparing the final responses of A and D enables us to make a prediction about perception: Because the response of 60 associated with receptor A (at the intersection) is smaller than the response of 76 associated with receptor D (in the corridor between the black squares), the intersection should appear darker than the corridor. This is exactly what happens—we perceive gray images at the intersections. Although the *initial* responses of bipolars A and D are the same, their *final* responses are different, *because D receives less lateral inhibition than A*. Lateral inhibition, therefore, explains the dark images at the intersection. (Although the fact that these images disappear when we look at the intersection directly must be explained by some other mechanism.)

Mach Bands: Seeing Borders More Sharply Another perceptual effect that can be explained by lateral inhibition is **Mach bands**, illusory light and dark bands near a light–dark border. Mach bands were named after the Austrian physicist and philosopher Ernst Mach, who also lent his name to the "Mach number" that indicates speed compared to the speed of sound (Mach 2 = twice the speed of sound). You can see the light Mach band in **Figure 3.9a** along the border just to the right of B and the dark band along the border just to the left of C. (There are also bands at the other two borders in this figure.)

DEMONSTRATION
Creating Mach Bands in Shadows

Mach bands can be demonstrated using gray stripes, as in Figure 3.9, or by casting a shadow, as shown in **Figure 3.10**. When you do this, you will see a dark Mach band near the border of the shadow and a light Mach band on the other side of the border. The light Mach band is often harder to see than the dark band.

Like the dark spots in the Hermann grid, Mach bands are not actually present in the pattern of light and so are an illusion.

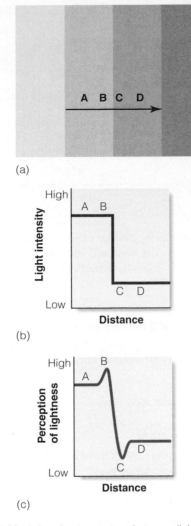

(a)

(b)

(c)

Figure 3.9 Mach bands at a contour between light and dark. (a) Just to the left of the contour, near B, a faint light band can be perceived, and just to the right at C, a faint dark band can be perceived. (b) The physical intensity distribution of the light, as measured with a light meter. (c) A plot showing the perceptual effect described in (a). The bump in the curve at B indicates the light Mach band, and the dip in the curve at C indicates the dark Mach band. The bumps that represent our perception of the bands are not present in the physical intensity distribution. © Cengage Learning

This is illustrated in **Figure 3.9b**, which shows the light intensity measured as we move along the line from A to D. Notice that the light intensity remains the same across the entire distance between A and B, then at the border drops to a lower level and remains the same between C and D. Thus, the intensity distribution gives no hint of Mach bands at the borders. If perception followed intensity, we would see a light rectangle on one side and a darker rectangle on the other side, with no Mach bands. But we do see these bands, so they must be an illusion created by our visual system.

Our perception of these illusory bands is represented graphically in **Figure 3.9c**, which indicates the lightness we perceive as we move along the line from A to D. The lightness is high as we begin moving to the right across the lighter stripe, but then, near the border at B, the lightness becomes

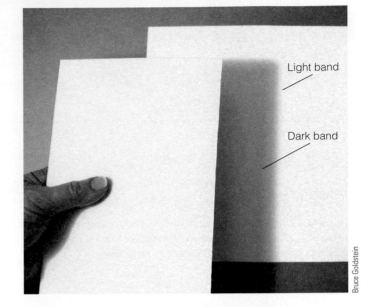

Figure 3.10 Shadow-casting technique for observing Mach bands. Illuminate a light-colored surface with your desk lamp and cast a shadow with a piece of paper.

even higher. The upward bump at B represents this slight *increase* in lightness we see just to the left of the border. Once across the border, we encounter the dark Mach band, indicated by the downward bump at C that represents the slight *decrease* in lightness we see just to the right of the border. **VL**

By using the circuit in **Figure 3.11** and doing a calculation like the one we did for the Hermann grid, we can show that Mach bands can be explained by lateral inhibition. Each of the six receptors in this circuit sends signals to bipolar cells, and each bipolar cell sends lateral inhibition to its neighbors on both sides. Receptors A and B correspond to A and B in Figure 3.9, which are on the light side of the border and so receive intense illumination; receptors C and D are on the darker side and receive dim illumination. Receptors X and Y

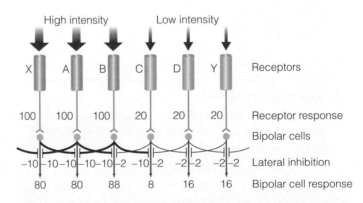

Figure 3.11 Circuit to explain the Mach band effect based on lateral inhibition. The circuit works like the one for the Hermann grid in Figure 3.5, with each bipolar cell sending inhibition to its neighbors. If we know the initial output of each receptor and the amount of lateral inhibition, we can calculate the final output of each bipolar cell.

© Cengage Learning

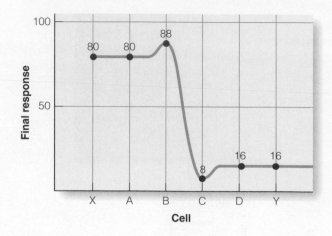

Bipolar	Initial Response	Inhibition From Left	Inhibition From Right	Total Inhibition	Final Output
X	100	10	10	20	80
A	100	10	10	20	80
B	100	10	2	12	88 (bright band)
C	20	10	2	12	8 (dark band)
D	20	2	2	4	16
Y	20	2	2	4	16

Figure 3.12 Table for determining the final output of the bipolar cells in Figure 3.11, by starting with the initial response and subtracting inhibition coming from the left and right. © Cengage Learning

Figure 3.13 A plot showing the final receptor output calculated for the circuit in Figure 3.11. The bump at B and the dip at C correspond to the light and dark Mach bands, respectively. © Cengage Learning

have been added to this circuit for the purposes of this calculation, so A and D will receive inhibition from both sides.

Let's assume that receptors X, A, and B generate responses of 100, whereas C, D, and Y generate responses of 20, as shown in Figure 3.11. X, A, and B result in an initial response of 100 in their bipolar cells, and C, D, and Y cause an initial response of 20 in their bipolar cells. If perception were determined only by these responses, we would see a bright bar on the left with equal intensity across its width (corresponding to response = 100) and a dimmer bar on the right with equal intensity across its width (corresponding to response = 20). But, as we saw in the Hermann grid example, we need to take lateral inhibition into account to determine what we perceive. We do this with the following calculation (**Figures 3.11** and **3.12**):

1. Start with the initial response of each bipolar cell: 100 for X, A, and B; 20 for C, D, and Y.

2. Determine the amount of inhibition that each bipolar cell sends to its neighbor on each side. As with the Hermann grid, we will assume that the amount of inhibition each cell sends to the cells on either side is equal to one-tenth of that cell's initial response. Thus, cells X, A, and B send 100 × 0.1 = 10 units of inhibition to their neighbors on each side, and cells C, D, and Y send 20 × 0.1 = 2 units of inhibition to their neighbors on each side.

3. Determine the output of each cell by starting with its initial response and subtracting the amount of inhibition received from the left and from the right.

Plotting the numbers in the final output results in the graph in **Figure 3.13**, similar to the one in Figure 3.9c, which represents the increase in lightness on the light side of the border at C and a decrease in lightness on the dark side at D. The lateral inhibition in our circuit has therefore created a neural pattern that looks like the Mach bands we perceive. A circuit similar to this one, but of much greater complexity, is probably responsible for the Mach bands that we see.

Lateral Inhibition and Simultaneous Contrast Simultaneous contrast occurs when our perception of the brightness or color of one area is affected by the presence of an adjacent or surrounding area.

DEMONSTRATION
Simultaneous Contrast

When you look at the two small squares in **Figure 3.14**, the one on the left appears much darker than the one on the right. Now, in a card or a piece of paper, punch two holes that are separated by the distance between the centers of the small squares. Position the two holes over the squares so you are viewing the centers of the two small squares with the background masked off. Now compare your perception of lightness as seen through the left and right holes. **VL**

You may have been surprised to see that the small squares look the same when viewed through the holes.

Figure 3.14 Simultaneous contrast. The two center squares reflect the same amount of light into your eyes but look different because of simultaneous contrast. © Cengage Learning

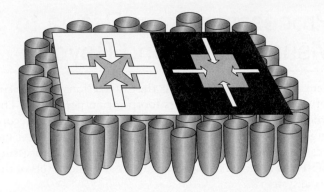

Figure 3.15 How lateral inhibition has been used to explain the simultaneous contrast effect. The size of the arrows indicates the amount of lateral inhibition. Because the square on the left receives more inhibition, it appears darker. © Cengage Learning

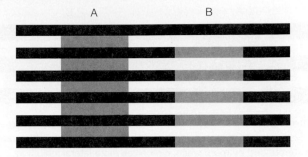

Figure 3.16 White's illusion. The rectangles at A and B appear different, even though they are printed from the same ink and reflect the same amount of light. From White, M. (1981). The effect of the nature of the surround on the perceived lightness of grey bars within square-wave test gratings. *Perception*, 10, 215–230.

This perception occurs because the two small squares are actually identical shades of gray. The illusion that they are different, which is created by the differences in the areas surrounding each square, is the simultaneous contrast effect.

An explanation for simultaneous contrast that is based on lateral inhibition is diagrammed in **Figure 3.15**, which shows an array of receptors that are stimulated by a pattern like the one in Figure 3.14. The receptors under the two small squares receive the same illumination. However, the light area surrounding the square on the left causes receptors under that area to respond rapidly and to send large amounts of inhibition to the neurons below the center square (large arrows). The dark area surrounding the square on the right causes the receptors under that area to fire less rapidly, so they send less inhibition to the neurons under the right square (small arrows). Because the cells under the left square receive more inhibition than the cells under the right square, their response is decreased more. This smaller response compared to the response of the neurons under the right square causes the left square to appear darker.

This explanation, based on lateral inhibition, makes sense and is still accepted by some researchers, but it is difficult for lateral inhibition to explain the following perception: If we start at the edge of one of the center squares and move toward the middle of the square, the lightness appears to be the same, all across the square. However, because lateral inhibition would affect the square more strongly near the edge, we would expect that the square would look lighter near the border and darker in the center. The fact that this does not occur suggests that lateral inhibition cannot be the whole story behind simultaneous contrast. In fact, psychologists have created other displays that result in perceptions that can't be explained by the spread of lateral inhibition.

A Display That Can't Be Explained by Lateral Inhibition

Look at the two rectangles in **Figure 3.16**, which is called **White's illusion** (White, 1981). Rectangle A, on the left,

which appears to be resting on the white area under the black bars, looks much darker than rectangle B, on the right, which appears to be located on the black bars. However, rectangles A and B reflect the same amount of light. This is hard to believe because the two rectangles look so different, but you can prove this to yourself by using white paper to mask off part of the display and comparing parts of rectangles A and B, as in **Figure 3.17**. **VL**

What causes the rectangles on the left and right to look so different, even though they are reflecting the same amount of light? We can determine if lateral inhibition might explain this effect by determining the amount of lateral inhibition received by rectangles A and B. **Figure 3.18** shows part of rectangle A, on the left, and part of rectangle B, on the right. The amount of lateral inhibition that affects each area is indicated by the arrows, with larger arrows indicating more inhibition, just as in Figure 3.15. It is clear that area B receives more lateral inhibition, because more of its border is surrounded by white. Because area B receives more lateral inhibition than area A, an explanation based on lateral inhibition would predict that area B should appear darker, like the left square in the simultaneous contrast display in Figure 3.15. But the opposite happens—rectangle B appears lighter! Clearly, White's illusion can't be explained by lateral inhibition.

What's happening here, according to Alan Gilchrist and coworkers (1999), is that our perception of lightness in

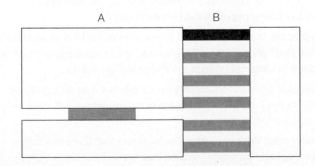

Figure 3.17 When you mask off part of the White's illusion display, as shown here, you can see that rectangles A and B are actually the same. (Try it!) © Cengage Learning

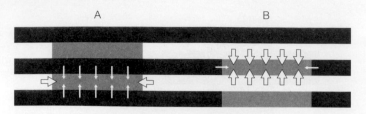

Figure 3.18 The arrows indicate the amount of lateral inhibition received by parts of rectangles A and B. Because the part of rectangle B is surrounded by more white, it receives more lateral inhibition. This would predict that B should appear darker than A (as in the simultaneous contrast display in Figure 3.14), but the opposite happens. This means that lateral inhibition cannot explain our perception of White's illusion. © Cengage Learning

influenced by a principle called **belongingness**, which states that an area's appearance is influenced by the part of the surroundings to which the area appears to belong. According to this idea, our perception of rectangle A would be affected by the white background, because it appears to be resting on the white background that is behind the black bars. Similarly, our perception of rectangle B would be affected by the dark bars, because it appears to be resting on them. Thus, the principle of belongingness proposes that the light area makes area A appear darker and the dark bars make area B appear lighter.

Regardless of whether the idea of belongingness turns out to be the correct explanation, there is no question that some mechanism other than lateral inhibition is involved in our perception of White's illusion and many other displays (see Adelson, 1993; Benary, 1924; Knill & Kersten, 1991; Williams et al., 1998). It isn't surprising that we can't explain some perceptions based only on what is happening in the retina, because there is still much more processing to be done before perception occurs. This processing happens later in the visual system, in the visual receiving area of the cortex and beyond.

TEST YOURSELF 3.1

1. Describe the experiment that demonstrated the effect of lateral inhibition in the *Limulus*.

2. How can lateral inhibition explain the "spots" that are perceived at the intersections of the Hermann grid?

3. What are Mach bands, and how can lateral inhibition explain our perception of them? Be sure to understand the calculations used in conjunction with the circuit in Figure 3.11.

4. What is simultaneous contrast? How has it been explained by lateral inhibition? What are some problems with this explanation?

5. How does White's illusion demonstrate that there are some perceptual "lightness" effects that lateral inhibition cannot explain? What principle has been used to explain White's illusion? What does this mean about the location of the mechanism that determines lightness perception?

Processing From Retina to Visual Cortex and Beyond

Neural processing caused by the interactions that occur between neurons can leave its footprint on perception. The processing we have already considered has involved convergence and lateral inhibition located at or near the visual receptors. We are now ready to consider how processing affects the responses of single neurons at higher levels of the visual system.

Responding of Single Fibers in the Optic Nerve

Figure 3.19 shows the optic nerve leaving the back of the eye, with the cross section showing that the nerve is made up of many individual nerve fibers traveling together. These fibers are the axons of the retinal ganglion cells (also see Figure 2.12). Our story begins with H. Keffer Hartline, whose work on lateral inhibition in the *Limulus* we described at the beginning of this chapter.

Before beginning on his *Limulus* research, Hartline (1938, 1940) used the preparation diagramed in **Figure 3.20**—the opened eye cup of a frog. He isolated a single fiber in the optic nerve by teasing apart the optic nerve near where it leaves the eye. While recording from this teased-out fiber, Hartline illuminated different areas of the retina and found that the fiber he was recording from responded only when a small area of the retina was illuminated. He called the area that caused the neuron to fire the nerve fiber's **receptive field** (**Figure 3.20a**), which he defined as follows:

> The region of the retina that must receive illumination in order to obtain a response in any given fiber. (Hartline, 1938, p. 410)

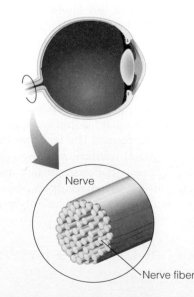

Nerve

Nerve fiber

Figure 3.19 The optic nerve, which leaves the back of the eye, contains about one million optic nerve fibers in the human. © Cengage Learning

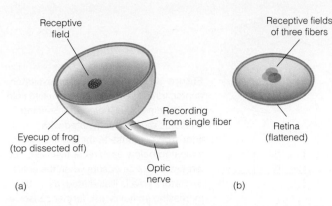

Figure 3.20 (a) Hartline's experiment in which he determined which area of a frog's retina caused firing in a single optic nerve fiber. This area is called the receptive field of that optic nerve fiber. (b) Receptive fields of three optic nerve fibers. These receptive fields overlap, so stimulating at a particular point on the retina will generally activate a number of fibers in the optic nerve. © Cengage Learning 2014

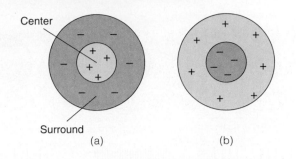

Figure 3.21 Center-surround receptive fields. (a) Excitatory center, inhibitory surround; (b) inhibitory center, excitatory surround. © Cengage Learning 2014

Hartline went on to emphasize that a fiber's receptive field covers a much greater area than a single rod or cone receptor. The fact that a fiber's receptive field covers hundreds or even thousands of receptors means that the fiber is receiving converging signals from all of these receptors. Finally, Hartline noted that the receptive fields of many different fibers overlap (**Figure 3.20b**). This means that shining light on a particular point on the retina activates many ganglion cell fibers.

One way to think about receptive fields is to imagine a football field and a grandstand full of spectators, each with a pair of binoculars trained on one small area of the field. Each spectator is monitoring what is happening in his or her own small area, and all of the spectators together are monitoring the entire field. Since there are so many spectators, some of the areas they are observing will wholly or partially overlap.

To relate this "football analogy" to Hartline's receptive fields, we can equate each spectator to an optic nerve fiber, the football field to the retina, and the small areas viewed by each spectator to receptive fields. Just as the spectators each monitor a small area but collectively take in information about what is happening on the entire football field, each optic nerve fiber monitors a small area of retina, and all of them together take in information about what is happening over the entire retina. Of course, perception doesn't occur based just on the responses of optic nerve fibers, but the optic nerve fibers do contain information about everything that is happening on the retina. Researchers after Hartline, who studied the responses of neurons in the cat and the monkey at different levels of the visual system, bring us closer to the neural responses that are associated with perception.

Researchers studying the responding of optic nerve fibers in the cat discovered a property of receptive fields that Hartline had not observed in the frog. The cat receptive fields, it turns out, are arranged in a **center-surround organization**, in which the area in the "center" of the receptive field responds differently to light than the area in the "surround"

of the receptive field (Barlow et al., 1957; Hubel & Wiesel, 1965; Kuffler, 1953).

For the receptive field in **Figure 3.21a**, presenting a spot of light to the center increases firing, so it is called the **excitatory area** of the receptive field. In contrast, stimulation of the surround causes a decrease in firing, so it is called the **inhibitory area** of the receptive field. This receptive field is called an **excitatory-center, inhibitory-surround receptive field**. The receptive field in **Figure 3.21b**, which responds with inhibition when the center is stimulated and excitation when the surround is stimulated, is an **inhibitory-center, excitatory-surround receptive field**.

The discovery that receptive fields can have oppositely responding areas made it necessary to modify Hartline's definition of receptive field to *the retinal region over which a cell in the visual system can be influenced (excited or inhibited) by light* (Hubel & Wiesel, 1961). The word "influences" and reference to excitation and inhibition make it clear that *any* change in firing—either an increase or a decrease—needs to be taken into account in determining a neuron's receptive field.

The discovery of **center-surround receptive fields** was also important because it showed that neural processing could result in neurons that respond best to specific patterns of illumination. This is illustrated by an effect called **center-surround antagonism**, illustrated in **Figure 3.22**. A small spot of light presented to the excitatory center of the receptive field causes a small increase in the rate of nerve firing (a), and increasing the light's size so that it covers the entire center of the receptive field increases the cell's response, as shown in (b).

Center-surround antagonism comes into play when the spot of light becomes large enough that it begins to cover the inhibitory area, as in (c) and (d). Stimulation of the inhibitory surround counteracts the center's excitatory response, causing a decrease in the neuron's firing rate. Thus, because of center-surround antagonism, this neuron responds best to a spot of light that is the size of the excitatory center of the receptive field.

We can explain center-surround receptive fields and center-surround antagonism in terms of neural processing by describing the operation of a *neural circuit*, which, as you will recall from Chapter 2, is a group of interconnected neurons. **Figure 3.23** shows a neural circuit consisting of seven receptors.

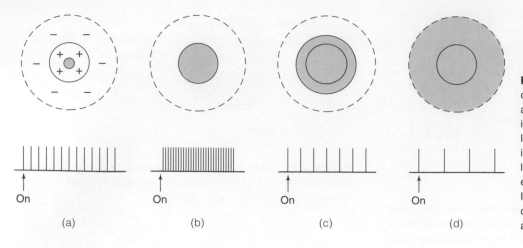

Figure 3.22 Response of an excitatory-center, inhibitory-surround receptive field as stimulus size is increased. Shading indicates the area stimulated with light. The response to the stimulus is indicated below each receptive field. The largest response occurs when the entire excitatory area is illuminated, as in (b). Increasing stimulus size further causes a decrease in firing due to center-surround antagonism. © Cengage Learning

These neurons, working together, help create the excitatory-center, inhibitory-surround receptive field of neuron B.

Receptors 1 and 2 synapse on neuron A; receptors 3, 4, and 5 synapse on neuron B; and receptors 6 and 7 synapse on neuron C. All of these synapses are excitatory, as indicated by the Y's and + signs. Additionally, neurons A and C synapse on neuron B, with both of these synapses being inhibitory, as indicated by the vertical lines and – signs. Let's now consider how stimulating these receptors will affect the firing of B. Stimulating receptors 3, 4, and 5 causes B's firing to increase because their synapses with B are excitatory. This is what we would expect, because receptors 3, 4, and 5 are located in the excitatory center of the receptive field.

Now consider what happens when we stimulate receptors 1 and 2. Both of these receptors connect to A with excitatory synapses, so illuminating these receptors causes A's firing to increase. A's signal then travels to neuron B, but because its synapse onto B is inhibitory, this signal causes B's firing to decrease. This is what we would expect, because receptors 1 and 2 are located in the inhibitory surround of the receptive field. The same thing happens when we illuminate receptors 6 and 7, which are also located in the inhibitory surround. Thus, stimulating anywhere in the center (green area) causes B's firing to increase. Stimulating anywhere in the surround (red area) causes B's firing to decrease.

It is easy to see that neuron B would respond poorly when all of the receptors are illuminated simultaneously,

because the excitation from 1, 2, and 3 and the inhibition from A and C would counteract each other, causing center-surround antagonism. Although an actual ganglion cell neuron receives signals from many more than seven receptors, and the wiring diagram is much more complex than shown in our example, the basic principle described here operates. Center-surround receptive fields are created by the interplay between excitation and inhibition.

Research on receptive fields ushered in a new era of research on neural processing because researchers realized that they could follow the effects of processing through different levels of the visual system by determining which patterns of light are most effective in generating a response in neurons at each level. This was the strategy adopted by David Hubel and Thorsten Wiesel, who extended the study of receptive fields into the cortex.

Hubel and Wiesel's Rationale for Studying Receptive Fields

Hubel and Wiesel (1965) state their tactic for understanding vision as follows:

> One approach … is to stimulate the retina with patterns of light while recording from single cells or fibers at various points along the visual pathway. For each cell, the optimum stimulus can be determined, and one can note the characteristics common to cells at each level in the visual pathway, and compare a given level with the next. (Hubel & Wiesel, 1965, p. 229)

Hubel and Wiesel's research, which earned them the Nobel Prize in Physiology and Medicine in 1981, showed how neurons at higher levels of the visual system become tuned to respond best to more and more specific kinds of stimuli. To do this, Hubel and Wiesel modified Hartline's procedure for presenting light to the retina. Instead of shining light directly into the animal's eye, Hubel and Wiesel had animals look at a screen on which they projected stimuli.

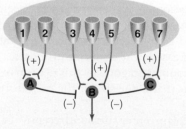

Figure 3.23 A seven-receptor neural circuit underlying a center-surround receptive field. Receptors 3, 4, and 5 are in the excitatory center, and receptors 1, 2, 6, and 7 are in the inhibitory surround.

© Cengage Learning 2014

METHOD
Presenting Stimuli to Determine Receptive Fields

A neuron's receptive field is determined by presenting a stimulus, such as a spot of light, to different places on the retina to determine which areas result in no response, an excitatory response, or an inhibitory response. Hubel and Wiesel projected stimuli onto a screen (**Figure 3.24**). The animal, usually a cat or monkey, was anesthetized and looked at the screen, its eyes focused with glasses so that whatever was presented on the screen would be in focus on the back of the eye.

Because the cat's eye remains stationary, each point on the screen corresponds to a point on the cat's retina. Thus, a stimulus at point A on the screen creates an image on point A on the retina, B creates an image on B, and C on C. There are many advantages to projecting an image on a screen. Stimuli are easier to control compared to projecting light directly into the eye (especially for moving stimuli); they are sharper; and it is easier to present complex stimuli such as faces or scenes.

An important thing to remember about receptive fields, which is always true no matter what method is used, is that *the receptive field is always on the retina*. It doesn't matter where the *neuron* is—the neuron can be in the retina, the visual cortex, or elsewhere in the brain, but the receptive field is always on the retina, because that is where the stimuli are *received*.

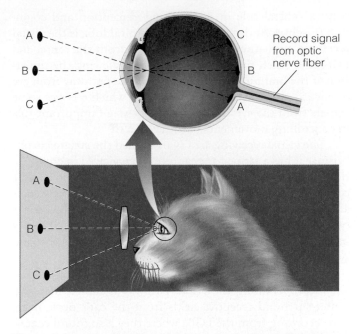

Figure 3.24 Recording electrical signals from a fiber in the optic nerve of an anesthetized cat. Each point on the screen corresponds to a point on the cat's retina. © Cengage Learning

Figure 3.25a repeats the overall view of the visual system from Chapter 2, which shows how signals leaving the eye in the optic nerve travel to the **lateral geniculate nucleus (LGN)**, and then from the LGN to the *occipital lobe* of the **cerebral cortex**, the 2–4 mm thick covering of the brain that

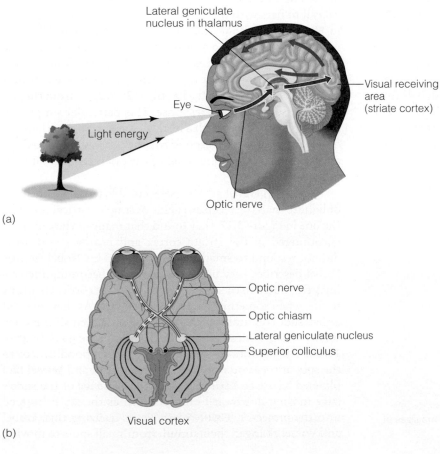

Figure 3.25 (a) Side view of the visual system, showing the major sites along the primary visual pathway where processing takes place: the eye, the optic nerve, the lateral geniculate nucleus, and the visual receiving area of the cortex. (b) Visual system seen from underneath the brain, showing the superior colliculus, which receives some of the signals from the eye. © Cengage Learning

plays a central role in determining perception and cognition (Fischl & Anders, 2000). The **occipital lobe** is the **visual receiving area**—the place where signals from the retina and LGN first reach the cortex (Figure 1.5). Viewing the underside of the brain in **Figure 3.25b** shows the pathway from eye to cortex, plus the **superior colliculus**, which receives some signals from the eye. This structure plays an important role in controlling movements of the eyes. **VL**

The visual receiving area is also called the **striate cortex**, because it has a striped appearance when viewed in cross section, or **area V1** to indicate that it is the first visual area in the cortex. As indicated by the blue arrows in Figure 3.25a, signals also travel to other places in the cortex, but for now we focus on the pathway from the eye to the LGN to the visual cortex because this pathway was the staging ground for Hubel and Wiesel's pioneering experiments.

Hubel and Wiesel's strategy of recording from different locations along the visual pathway included mapping center-surround receptive fields from the cat's optic nerve and recording from the LGN, where they also found center-surround receptive fields. The fact that little change occurred in receptive fields when moving from the optic nerve fibers to neurons in the LGN made researchers wonder about the function of the LGN. Something must be going on there, because the LGN receives 90 percent of the optic nerve fibers that leave the eye (the other 10 percent travel to the superior colliculus) and it is a complex structure containing millions of neurons.

One proposal of LGN function is based on the observation that the signal sent from the LGN to the cortex is smaller than the input the LGN receives from the retina (**Figure 3.26**). This decrease in the signal has led to the suggestion that one of the purposes of the LGN is to regulate neural information as it flows from the retina to the cortex (Casagrande & Norton, 1991; Humphrey & Saul, 1994). Another important characteristic of the LGN is that it receives more signals from the cortex than from the retina (Sherman & Koch, 1986; Wilson et al., 1984). This "backwards" flow of information, called *feedback*, could also be involved in regulation of information flow, the idea being that the information the LGN

receives back from the brain may play a role in determining which information is sent up to the brain. As we will see later in the book, there is good evidence for the role of feedback in perception. For now, we will continue our journey up the visual pathway, traveling from the LGN to the visual receiving area.

Receptive Fields of Neurons in the Visual Cortex

Hubel and Wiesel's initial research on cortical neurons focused on the striate cortex (area V1) because this is where signals first arrive in the cortex. By flashing spots of light on different places in the retina, Hubel and Wiesel found cells in the striate cortex with receptive fields that, like center-surround receptive fields of neurons in the retina and LGN, have excitatory and inhibitory areas. However, these areas are arranged side by side rather than in the center-surround configuration (**Figure 3.27a**). Cells with these side-by-side receptive fields are called **simple cortical cells**.

We can tell from the layout of the excitatory and inhibitory areas of the simple cell shown in Figure 3.27a that a cell with this receptive field would respond best to vertical bars. As shown in **Figure 3.27b**, a vertical bar that illuminates only the excitatory area causes high firing, but as the bar is tilted so the inhibitory area is illuminated, firing decreases (**Figure 3.27c**).

The relationship between orientation and firing is indicated by a neuron's **orientation tuning curve**, which is determined by measuring the responses of a simple cortical cell to bars with different orientations. The tuning curve in **Figure 3.27d** shows that the cell responds with 25 nerve impulses per second to a vertically oriented bar and that the cell's response decreases as the bar is tilted away from the vertical and begins stimulating inhibitory areas of the neuron's receptive field. Notice that a bar tilted 20 degrees from the vertical elicits only a small response. This particular simple cell responds best to a bar with a vertical orientation, but there are other simple cells that respond to other orientations, so there are neurons that respond to all of the orientations that exist in the environment.

Although Hubel and Wiesel were able to use small spots of light to map the receptive fields of simple cortical cells like the one in Figure 3.27, they found that many of the cells they encountered in the striate cortex and nearby visual areas did not respond to small spots of light. In his Nobel lecture, Hubel describes how he and Wiesel were becoming increasingly frustrated in their attempts to get these cortical neurons to fire, when something startling happened: As they inserted a glass slide containing a spot stimulus into their slide projector, a cortical neuron "went off like a machine gun" (Hubel, 1982). The neuron, as it turned out, was responding not to the spot at the center of the slide that Hubel and Wiesel had planned to use as a stimulus, but to the image of the slide's edge moving downward on the screen as the slide dropped into the projector (**Figure 3.28**). Upon realizing this, Hubel and Wiesel changed their stimuli from small spots to moving

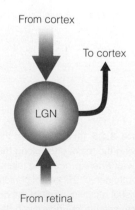

Figure 3.26 Information flow into and out of the LGN. The sizes of the arrows indicate the sizes of the signals. © Cengage Learning

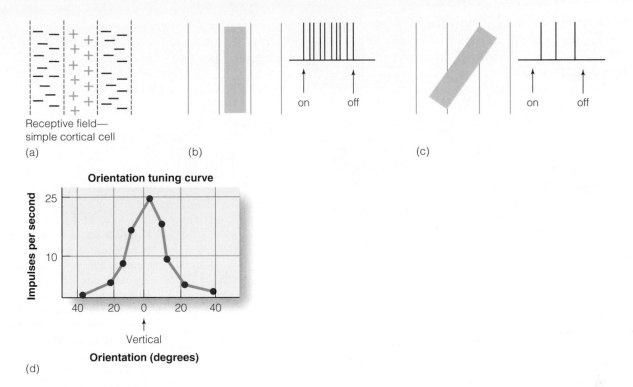

Receptive field—
simple cortical cell

(a)   (b)   (c)

Orientation tuning curve

(d)

Impulses per second

25

10

40   20   0   20   40

↑
Vertical

Orientation (degrees)

Figure 3.27 (a) The receptive field of a simple cortical cell. (b) This cell responds best to a vertical bar of light that covers the excitatory area of the receptive field. (c) The response decreases as the bar is tilted so that it also covers the inhibitory area. (d) Orientation tuning curve of a simple cortical cell for a neuron that responds best to a vertical bar (orientation = 0). © Cengage Learning 2014

lines and were then able to find cells that responded to oriented moving bars. As with simple cells, a particular neuron had a preferred orientation.

Hubel and Wiesel (1965) discovered that many cortical neurons respond best to moving barlike stimuli with specific orientations. **Complex cells**, like simple cells, respond best to bars of a particular orientation. However, unlike simple cells, which respond to small spots of light or to stationary stimuli, most complex cells respond only when a correctly oriented bar of light moves across the entire receptive field.

Edge of slide

Figure 3.28 When Hubel and Wiesel dropped a slide into their slide projector, the image of the edge of the slide moving down unexpectedly triggered activity in a cortical neuron. © Cengage Learning

Further, many complex cells respond best to a particular direction of movement (**Figure 3.29a**). Because these neurons don't respond to stationary flashes of light, their receptive fields are indicated not by pluses and minuses but by outlining the area that, when stimulated, elicits a response in the neuron.

Another type of cell, called **end-stopped cells**, fire to moving lines of a specific length or to moving corners or angles. **Figure 3.29b** shows a light corner stimulus that is being moved up and down across the retina. The records to the right indicate that the neuron responds best to a medium-sized corner that is moving upward.

Hubel and Wiesel's finding that some neurons in the cortex respond only to oriented lines and others respond best to corners was an extremely important discovery because it extended the idea first proposed in connection with center-surround receptive fields that neurons respond to some patterns of light and not to others. This makes sense because the purpose of the visual system is to enable us to perceive objects in the environment, and many objects can be at least crudely represented by simple shapes and lines of various orientations. Thus, Hubel and Wiesel's discovery that neurons respond selectively to oriented lines and stimuli with specific lengths was an important step toward determining how neurons respond to more complex objects.

Because simple, complex, and end-stopped cells fire in response to specific features of the stimulus, such as orientation or direction of movement, they are sometimes called

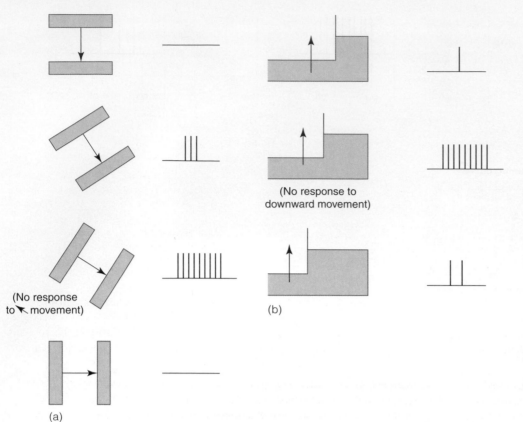

(No response to downward movement)

(No response to ↖ movement)

(a)

(b)

Figure 3.29 (a) Response of a complex cell recorded from the visual cortex of the cat. The stimulus bar is moved back and forth across the receptive field. The cell fires best when the bar is positioned with a specific orientation and is moved in a specific direction. (b) Response of an end-stopped cell recorded from the visual cortex of the cat. The stimulus is indicated by the light area on the left. This cell responds best to a medium-sized corner that is moving up. © Cengage Learning 2014

feature detectors. Table 3.1, which summarizes the properties of the neurons we have described so far, illustrates an important fact about neurons in the visual system: As we travel farther from the retina, neurons fire to more complex stimuli. Retinal ganglion cells respond best to spots of light, whereas cortical end-stopped cells respond best to bars of a certain length that are moving in a particular direction.

TABLE 3.1 Properties of Neurons in the Optic Nerve, LGN, and Cortex

TYPE OF CELL	CHARACTERISTICS OF RECEPTIVE FIELD
Optic nerve fiber (ganglion cell)	Center-surround receptive field. Responds best to small spots, but will also respond to other stimuli.
Lateral geniculate	Center-surround receptive fields very similar to the receptive field of a ganglion cell.
Simple cortical	Excitatory and inhibitory areas arranged side by side. Responds best to bars of a particular orientation.
Complex cortical	Responds best to movement of a correctly oriented bar across the receptive field. Many cells respond best to a particular direction of movement.
End-stopped cortical	Responds to corners, angles, or bars of a particular length moving in a particular direction.

© Cengage Learning

Do Feature Detectors Play a Role in Perception?

Neural processing endows neurons with properties that make them feature detectors that respond best to a specific type of stimulus. When researchers show that neurons respond to oriented lines, they are measuring the *stimulus–physiology relationship* (**Figure 3.30**). But just measuring this relationship does not prove that these neurons have anything to do with the perception of oriented lines. To demonstrate a link between physiology and perception, it is necessary to measure the *physiology–perception relationship*. One way this has been accomplished is by using a psychophysical procedure called *selective adaptation*.

Selective Adaptation

When we view a stimulus with a specific property, neurons tuned to that property fire. The idea behind **selective adaptation** is that this firing causes neurons to eventually become fatigued, or adapt. This adaptation causes two physiological effects: (1) the neuron's firing rate decreases, and (2) the neuron fires less when that stimulus is immediately presented again. According to this idea, presenting a vertical line causes neurons that respond to vertical lines to respond, but as these presentations continue, these neurons eventually begin to fire less to vertical lines. Adaptation is *selective* because only the

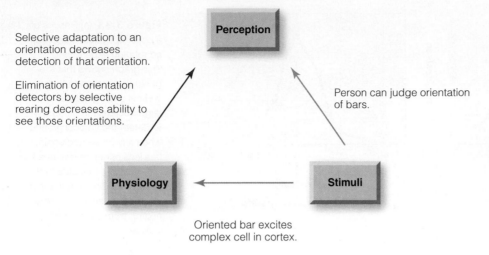

Selective adaptation to an orientation decreases detection of that orientation.

Elimination of orientation detectors by selective rearing decreases ability to see those orientations.

Person can judge orientation of bars.

Oriented bar excites complex cell in cortex.

Figure 3.30 Three-part version of the perceptual process, showing the three basic relationships: stimulus–perception (green arrow); stimulus–physiology (orange), and physiology–perception (red). The descriptions refer to experiments described in the chapter that are relevant to the role of neural feature detectors in perception. © Cengage Learning 2014

neurons that were responding to verticals or near-verticals adapt, and neurons that were not firing do not adapt.

METHOD

Psychophysical Measurement of the Effect of Selective Adaptation to Orientation

Measuring the effect of selective adaptation to orientation involves the following three steps:

1. Measure a person's *contrast threshold* to gratings with a number of different orientations (**Figure 3.31a**). A grating's **contrast threshold** is the minimum intensity difference between two adjacent bars that can just be detected. The contrast threshold for seeing a grating is measured by changing the intensity difference between the light and dark bars until the bars can just barely be seen. For example, it is easy to see the four gratings on the left of **Figure 3.32**, because the

difference in intensity between the bars is above threshold. However, there is only a small intensity difference between the bars of the grating on the far right, so it is close to the contrast threshold. The intensity difference at which the bars can just barely be seen is the contrast threshold.

2. Adapt the person to one orientation by having the person view a high-contrast *adapting stimulus* for a minute or two. In this example, the adapting stimulus is a vertical grating (**Figure 3.31b**).

3. Remeasure the contrast threshold of all the test stimuli presented in step 1 (**Figure 3.31c**).

The rationale behind the above procedure is that if the adaptation to the high-contrast grating in step 2 decreases the functioning of neurons that normally respond to verticals, this will cause an increase in contrast threshold so it is more difficult to see low-contrast vertical gratings. In other words, when vertical feature detectors are adapted, it is necessary to increase the difference between the black and white vertical bars in order to see them. **Figure 3.33a** shows that this is exactly what happens. The peak of the contrast threshold curve, which indicates that a large increase in the difference between the bars was needed to see the bars, occurs at the vertical adapting orientation. The important result of this experiment is that our psychophysical curve shows that adaptation selectively affects only some orientations, just as neurons selectively respond to only some orientations. In fact, comparing the psychophysically determined selective adaptation curve (Figure 3.33a) to the orientation tuning

(a) Measure contrast threshold at a number of orientations.

(b) Adapt to a high-contrast grating.

(c) Remeasure contrast thresholds for same orientations as above.

Figure 3.31 Procedure for carrying out a selective adaptation experiment. See text for details. © Cengage Learning

Figure 3.32 The contrast threshold for a grating is the minimum difference in intensity at which the observer can just make out the bars. The grating on the left is far above the contrast threshold. The ones in the middle have less contrast, but are still above threshold. The grating on the far right is near the contrast threshold. © Cengage Learning

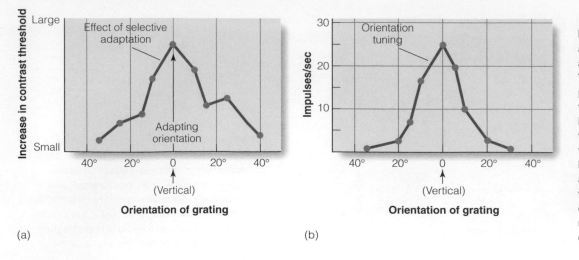

(a)

(b)

Figure 3.33 (a) Results of a psychophysical selective adaptation experiment. This graph shows that the person's adaptation to the vertical grating causes a large decrease in her ability to detect the vertical grating when it is presented again, but has less effect on gratings that are tilted to either side of the vertical. (b) Orientation tuning curve of the simple cortical neuron from Figure 3.27.

© Cengage Learning 2014

curve for a simple cortical neuron (**Figure 3.33b**) reveals that they are very similar. (The psychophysical curve is slightly wider because the adapting stimulus affects some neurons that respond to orientations near the adapting orientation.)

The near match between the orientation selectivity of neurons and the perceptual effect of selective adaptation supports the idea that orientation detectors play a role in perception. The selective adaptation experiment is measuring how a physiological effect (adapting the feature detectors that respond to a specific orientation) causes a perceptual result (decrease in sensitivity to that orientation). This evidence that feature detectors have something to do with perception means that when you look at a complex scene, such as a city street or a crowded shopping mall, feature detectors that are firing to the orientations in the scene are helping to construct your perception of the scene.

Selective Rearing

Further evidence that feature detectors are involved in perception is provided by selective rearing experiments. The idea behind **selective rearing** is that if an animal is reared in an environment that contains only certain types of stimuli, then neurons that respond to these stimuli will become more prevalent. This follows from a phenomenon called **neural plasticity** or **experience-dependent plasticity**—the idea that the response properties of neurons can be shaped by perceptual experience. According to this idea, rearing an animal in an environment that contains only vertical lines should result in the animal's visual system having neurons that respond predominantly to verticals.

This result may seem to contradict the results of the selective adaptation experiment just described, in which exposure to verticals *decreases* the response to verticals. However, adaptation is a short-term effect. Presenting the adapting orientation for a few minutes decreases responding to that orientation. In contrast, selective rearing is a longer-term effect. Presenting the rearing orientation over a period

of days or even weeks keeps the neurons that respond to that orientation active. Meanwhile, neurons that respond to orientations that aren't present are not active, so they lose their ability to respond to those orientations.

One way to describe the results of selective rearing experiments is "Use it or lose it." This effect was demonstrated in a classic experiment by Colin Blakemore and Grahame Cooper (1970) in which they placed kittens in striped tubes like the one in **Figure 3.34a**, so that each kitten was exposed to only one orientation, either vertical or horizontal. The kittens were kept in the dark from birth to 2 weeks of age, at which time they were placed in the tube for 5 hours a day; the rest of the time they remained in the dark. Because the kittens sat on a Plexiglas platform, and the tube extended both above and below them, there were no visible corners or edges in their environment other than the stripes on the sides of the tube. The kittens wore cones around their head to prevent them from seeing vertical stripes as oblique or horizontal stripes by tilting their heads; however, according to Blakemore and Cooper, "The kittens did not seem upset by the monotony of their surroundings and they sat for long periods inspecting the walls of the tube" (p. 477).

When the kittens' behavior was tested after 5 months of selective rearing, they seemed blind to the orientations that they hadn't seen in the tube. For example, a kitten that was reared in an environment of vertical stripes would pay attention to a vertical rod but ignore a horizontal rod. Following behavioral testing, Blakemore and Cooper recorded from cells in the visual cortex and determined the stimulus orientation that caused the largest response from each cell.

Figure 3.34b shows the results of this experiment. Each line indicates the orientation preferred by a single neuron in the cat's cortex. This cat, which was reared in a vertical environment, has many neurons that respond best to vertical or near-vertical stimuli, but none that respond to horizontal stimuli. The horizontally responding neurons were apparently lost because they hadn't been used. The opposite result occurred for the horizontally reared cats. The parallel between the orientation selectivity of neurons in the cat's

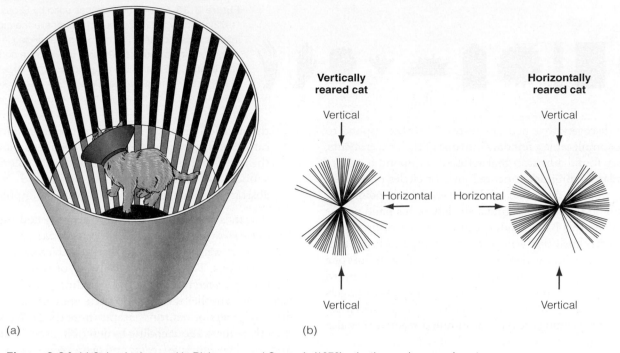

(a)

(b)

Figure 3.34 (a) Striped tube used in Blakemore and Cooper's (1970) selective rearing experiments. (b) Distribution of optimal orientations for 72 cells from a cat reared in an environment of vertical stripes, on the left, and for 52 cells from a cat reared in an environment of horizontal stripes, on the right.

Reprinted by permission from Macmillan Publishers Ltd: *Nature,* from Blakemore, C., & Cooper, G. G., Development of the brain depends on the visual environment, 228, 477–478. Copyright 1970.

cortex and the cat's behavioral response to the same orientation provides more evidence that feature detectors are involved in the perception of orientation. This connection between feature detectors and perception was one of the major discoveries of vision research in the 1960s and 1970s.

Higher-Level Neurons

The idea that perception can be explained in terms of feature detectors that respond to straight lines or corners was popular in the 1970s because, as anyone who has played with building blocks or Legos knows, many objects can be created from rectangular shapes. Objects could, according to this idea, be represented by the firing of feature detectors that responded to these rectangular shapes that make up the objects.

But the idea that perception was based solely on what might be called "stick-figure physiology" was not to last. Although researchers continued to study feature detectors in the striate cortex and nearby areas, vision researchers were beginning to pay attention to brain areas far outside of the striate cortex. One of these researchers was psychologist Charles Gross, who decided that the **inferotemporal (IT) cortex** in the temporal lobe was ripe for study (**Figure 3.35a**). He based this decision on research that showed that removing parts of the IT cortex in monkeys affected the monkeys' ability to recognize objects, as well as on research on a human condition called **prosopagnosia**, in which people with temporal lobe damage were unable to recognize faces.

Gross's experiments, in which he recorded from single neurons in the monkey's IT, required a great deal of endurance by the experimenters, because the experiments typically lasted 3 or 4 days. In these experiments, Gross's research team presented a variety of different stimuli to anesthetized monkeys. Using the projection screen procedure, they presented lines, squares, and circles. Some stimuli were light, and some dark. The dark stimuli were created by placing cardboard cutouts against the transparent projection screen.

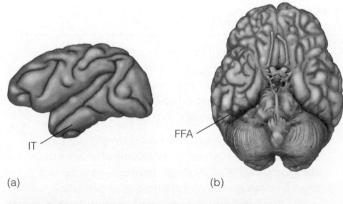

(a)

(b)

Figure 3.35 (a) Location of the inferotemporal (IT) cortex in the monkey. (b) Location of the fusiform face area (FFA) in the human, just under the temporal lobe. Both of these areas are rich in neurons that respond to faces. © Cengage Learning

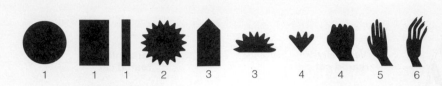

Figure 3.36 Some of the shapes used by Gross et al. (1972) to study the responses of neurons in the monkey's inferotemporal cortex. The shapes are arranged in order of their ability to cause the neuron to fire, from none (1) to little (2 and 3) to maximum (6). From Gross, C. G., Rocha-Miranda, C. E., & Bender, D. B. (1972). Visual properties of neurons in inferotemporal cortex of the macaque. *Journal of Neurophysiology*, 5, 96–111. © The American Physiological Society (APS). All rights reserved.

The discovery that neurons in the IT cortex respond to complex stimuli came a few days into one of their experiments, when they found a neuron that refused to respond to any of the standard stimuli like oriented lines or circles or squares. Nothing worked, until one of the experimenters pointed at something in the room, casting a shadow of his hand on the screen. When this hand shadow caused a burst of firing, the experimenters knew they were on to something and began testing the neuron with a variety of stimuli, including cutouts of a monkey's hand. After a great deal of testing, they determined that this neuron responded to a handlike shape with fingers pointing up (**Figure 3.36**) (Rocha-Miranda, 2011; also see Gross, 2002). After expanding the types of stimuli presented, they also found some neurons that responded best to faces.

Finding neurons that responded to real-life objects like hands and faces was a revolutionary result. Apparently, neural processing that occurred beyond the initial receiving areas studied by Hubel and Wiesel had created these neurons. But sometimes revolutionary results aren't accepted immediately, and Gross's results were largely ignored when they were published in 1969 and 1972 (Gross et al., 1969, 1972). Finally, in the 1980s, other experimenters began recording from neurons in the IT cortex of the monkey that responded to faces and other complex objects (Rolls, 1981; Perrett et al., 1982), and in the 1990s, researchers discovered an area on the underside of the temporal lobe of the human cortex that was named the **fusiform face area** because it responded strongly to faces (Kanwisher et al., 1997; McCarthy et al., 1997) (**Figure 3.35b**). We will see in the chapters that follow that neurons that respond to complex real-world stimuli are now considered the norm in vision research.

The Sensory Code

One of the goals of our discussion so far has been to explore the electrical signals that are the link between the environment and perception. The idea that nerve impulses can represent things in the environment is what is behind the following statement, written by Bernita Rabinowitz, a student in my class.

> A human perceives a stimulus (a sound, a taste, etc.). This is explained by the electrical impulses sent to the brain. This is so incomprehensible, so amazing. How can one electrical impulse be perceived as the taste of a sour lemon, another impulse as a jumble of brilliant blues and greens and reds, and still another as bitter, cold wind? Can our whole complex range of sensations be explained by just

the electrical impulses stimulating the brain? How can all of these varied and very concrete sensations— the ranges of perceptions of heat and cold, colors, sounds, fragrances and tastes—be merely and so abstractly explained by differing electrical impulses?

Bernita's question is refering to **sensory coding**: *how the firing of neurons represents various characteristics of the environment*. So far, we have described feature detectors and higher-order neurons. The idea that the firing of single neurons is the key to understanding sensory coding is called *specificity coding*. But another idea—that objects are represented by the firing of *groups* of neurons—seems more likely. We will consider these ideas about coding by describing specificity theory first and then *distributed coding* and *sparse coding*, both of which involve groups of neurons.

Specificity Coding: Representation by the Firing of a Specialized Neuron

Specificity coding proposes that a particular object is represented by the firing of a neuron that responds *only* to that object and to no other objects. This is illustrated in **Figure 3.37**, which shows that only neuron #4 responds to Bill's face, only

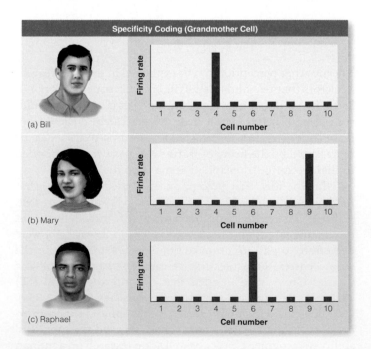

Figure 3.37 Specificity coding, in which each face causes a different neuron to fire. © Cengage Learning 2014

#9 responds to Mary's face, and only #6 responds to Raphael's face. Also note that the neuron specialized to respond only to Bill, which we can call a "Bill neuron," does not respond to Mary or Raphael. No other faces or types of objects would affect this neuron; it fires only to Bill's face.

One of the requirements of specificity coding is that there are neurons that are specifically tuned to each object in the environment. The idea that there are single neurons that each respond only to a specific stimulus was proposed in the 1960s by Jerzy Konorski (1967) and Jerry Lettvin (see Barlow, 1995; Gross, 2002; Rose, 1996). Lettvin coined the term *grandmother cell* to describe this highly specific type of cell. A **grandmother cell**, according to Lettvin, is a neuron that responds only to a specific stimulus. This stimulus could be a specific image, such as a picture of your grandmother, or a concept, such as the idea of grandmothers in general (Gross, 2002). The neurons in Figure 3.37 would qualify as grandmother cells.

Although the simplicity of the idea of grandmother cells has its appeal, it should be pointed out that when Jerry Lettvin proposed the term *grandmother cell*, he did it "tongue in cheek" (Gross, 2002), which presumably means that he was stating it as a possibility, but he didn't really believe such neurons existed. Certainly, when he proposed the idea, no such neurons were known. We have seen that neurons have been discovered that respond to faces, but even these neurons respond to many different faces. Most researchers feel that specificity coding is an unlikely possibility. There are just too many different objects (and colors and tastes and smells and sounds) in the world to have a separate neuron dedicated to each object. An alternative to the idea of specificity coding is that a number of neurons are involved in representing an object.

Distributed Coding: Representation by the Firing of Large Groups of Neurons

Distributed coding is the representation of a particular object by the pattern of firing of a large number of neurons. According to this idea, Bill's face might be represented by the pattern of firing shown in **Figure 3.38a**, Mary's face would be represented by a different pattern (**Figure 3.38b**), and Raphael's face by another pattern (**Figure 3.38c**). An advantage of distributed coding is that a large number of stimuli can be represented, because groups of neurons can create a huge number of different patterns. We will see that there is good evidence for distributed coding in all of the senses. But for some functions, a large number of neurons isn't necessary. *Sparse coding* occurs when small groups of neurons are involved.

Sparse Coding: Representation by the Firing of a Small Number of Neurons

Sparse coding occurs when a particular object is represented by a pattern of firing of only a small group of neurons, with the

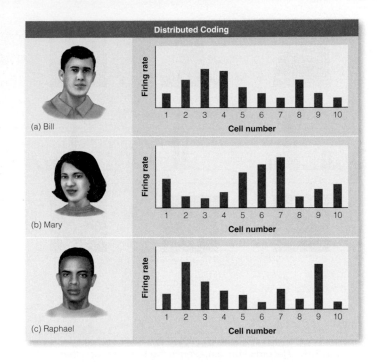

Figure 3.38 Distributed coding, in which the face's identity is indicated by the pattern of firing of a large number of neurons. © Cengage Learning 2014

majority of neurons remaining silent. As shown in **Figure 3.39**, sparse coding would represent Bill's face by the pattern of firing of a few neurons. Mary's face would be signaled by the pattern of firing of a few different neurons, but possibly with some overlap with the neuron's representing Bill, and Raphael's face would have yet another pattern. Notice that a

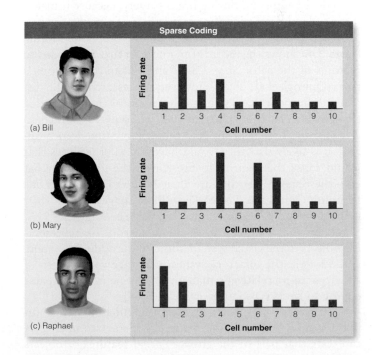

Figure 3.39 Sparse coding, in which the face's identity is indicated by the pattern of firing of a small group of neurons. © Cengage Learning 2014

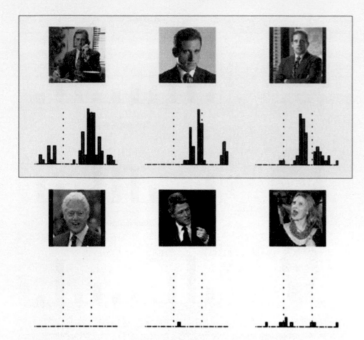

Figure 3.40 Records from a neuron in the temporal lobe that responded to different views of Steve Carell (top records) but did not respond to pictures of other well-known people (bottom records). From Quiroga, R. Q., Reddy, L., Kreiman, G., Koch, C., & Fried, I. (2008). Sparse but not "grandmother-cell" coding in the medial temporal lobe. *Trends in Cognitive Sciences, 12,* 87–91. Reproduced by permission.

particular neuron can respond to more than one stimulus. For example, neuron #4 responds to all three faces, although most strongly to Mary's.

Recently, neurons were discovered when recording from the temporal lobe of patients undergoing brain surgery for epilepsy. (Stimulating and recording from neurons is a common procedure before and during brain surgery, because it makes it possible to determine the exact layout of a particular person's brain.) These neurons responded to very specific stimuli. **Figure 3.40** shows the records for a neuron that responded to pictures of the actor Steve Carell and not to other people's faces (Quiroga et al., 2008). However, the researchers who discovered this neuron (as well as other neurons that responded to other people) point out that they had only 30 minutes to record from these neurons, and that if more time were available, it is likely that they would have found other faces that would cause this neuron to fire. Given the likelihood that even these special neurons are likely to fire to more than one stimulus, Quiroga and coworkers (2008) suggested that their neurons are probably an example of sparse coding. **VL**

There is also other evidence that the code for representing objects in the visual system, tones in the auditory system, and odors in the olfactory system may involve a pattern of activity across a relatively small number of neurons, as sparse coding suggests (Olshausen & Field, 2004).

Returning to Bernita's question about how neural firing can represent various features in the environment, we can state that part of the answer is that features or objects are represented by the pattern of firing of groups of neurons. Sometimes the groups are small (sparse coding), sometimes

large (distributed coding). But this is just the beginning of the answer to Bernita's question. As we will see in the next chapter, another part of the answer involves considering how neurons in sensory systems are organized.

SOMETHING TO CONSIDER:
The Mind–Body Problem

One of the most famous problems in science is called the **mind–body problem**: How do physical processes such as nerve impulses or sodium and potassium molecules flowing across membranes (the body part of the problem) become transformed into the richness of perceptual experience (the mind part of the problem)?

The mind–body problem is what my student Bernita was asking about when she posed her question about how heat and cold, colors, sounds, fragrances, and tastes can be explained by differing electrical impulses. One way to answer Bernita's question is to describe how stimuli are represented by a sensory code, as we did above. Research on sensory coding, which focuses on the relationship between stimuli in the environment and how neurons fire, is often referred to as research on the **neural correlate of consciousness (NCC)**, where consciousness can roughly be defined as our experiences.

Does determining the NCC qualify as a solution to the mind–body problem? Researchers often call finding the NCC the **easy problem of consciousness** because it has been possible to discover many connections between neural firing and experience (**Figure 3.41a**). For example, Quiroga's experiment showed a connection between the firing of some neurons in the hippocampus and Steve Carell's face. Later in the book, we will see that there is a connection between the firing of certain neurons and experiencing different colors.

But if NCC is the "easy" problem, what is the "hard" problem? We encounter the hard problem when we approach Bernita's question at a deeper level by asking not how physiological responses *correlate* with experience, but how physiological responses *cause* experience. To put it another way, how do physiological responses *become transformed* into experience? We can appreciate why this is called the **hard problem of consciousness** by stating it in terms of the flow of sodium and potassium ions we described in Chapter 2 (see page 38): How are sodium and potassium flows across a membrane or the nerve impulses that result from this flow turned into experiencing a person's face or the color red (**Figure 3.41b**)?

Although researchers have been working to determine the physiological basis of perception for more than a century, the hard version of the mind–body problem is still unsolved. The first difficulty lies in figuring out how to go about studying the problem. Just looking for relationships between nerve firing and experience may not be enough to determine how physiological processes *cause* experience. Because of the hard problem's difficulty, most researchers have focused on determining the NCC. That doesn't mean the hard version of the

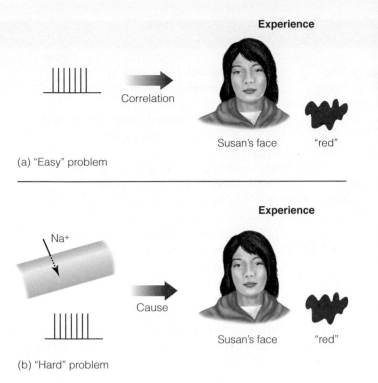

Experience

Correlation

Susan's face   "red"

(a) "Easy" problem

Experience

Na+

Cause

Susan's face   "red"

(b) "Hard" problem

Figure 3.41 (a) Solving the "easy" problem of consciousness involves looking for *connections* between physiological responding and experiences such as perceiving "Susan's face" or "red." This is also called the search for the *neural correlate of consciousness*. (b) Solving the "hard" problem of consciousness involves determining how physiological processes, such as ions flowing across the nerve membrane, *cause* us to have experiences. © Cengage Learning

mind–body problem will never be solved. Many researchers believe that doing research on the easy problem (which, after all, isn't really that easy) will eventually lead to a solution to the hard problem (see Baars, 2001; Block, 2009; Crick & Koch, 2003). For now, there is quite a bit of work to be done

on the easy problem. This approach to the physiology of perception is what the rest of this book is about.

THINK ABOUT IT

1. Ralph, who is skeptical about the function of lateral inhibition, says, "OK, so lateral inhibition causes us to see Mach bands and the spots at the intersections of the Hermann grid. Even though these perceptual effects are interesting, they don't seem very important to me. If they didn't exist, we would see the world in just about the same way as we do with them." (a) How would you respond to Ralph if you wanted to make an argument for the importance of lateral inhibition? (b) What is the possibility that Ralph could be right? (p. 56)

2. Look for shadows, both inside and outside, and see if you can see Mach bands at the borders of the shadows.

Remember that Mach bands are easier to see when the border of a shadow is slightly fuzzy. Mach bands are not actually present in the pattern of light and dark, so you need to be sure that the bands are not really in the light but are created by your nervous system. How can you accomplish this? (p. 57)

3. Cell A responds best to vertical lines moving to the right. Cell B responds best to 45-degree lines moving to the right. Both of these cells have an excitatory synapse with cell C. How will cell C fire to vertical lines? To 45-degree lines? What if the synapse between B and C is inhibitory? (p. 65)

KEY TERMS

Area V1 (p. 64)
Belongingness (p. 60)
Center-surround antagonism (p. 61)
Center-surround organization (p. 61)
Center-surround receptive field (p. 61)
Cerebral cortex (p. 63)
Complex cells (p. 65)
Contrast threshold (p. 67)
Distributed coding (p. 71)
Easy problem of consciousness (p. 72)
End-stopped cell (p. 65)
Excitatory area (p. 61)
Excitatory-center, inhibitory-
  surround receptive field (p. 61)
Experience-dependent plasticity
  (p. 68)
Feature detectors (p. 66)

Fusiform face area (p. 70)
Grandmother cell (p. 71)
Hard problem of consciousness
  (p. 72)
Hermann grid (p. 55)
Inferotemporal (IT) cortex
  (p. 69)
Inhibitory area (p. 61)
Inhibitory-center, excitatory-surround
  receptive field (p. 61)
Lightness (p. 55)
Lateral geniculate nucleus (LGN) (p. 63)
Lateral inhibition (p. 54)
Mind–body problem (p. 72)
Neural correlate of consciousness
  (NCC) (p. 72)
Neural plasticity (p. 68)

Neural processing (p. 54)
Occipital lobe (p. 64)
Ommatidia (p. 54)
Orientation tuning curve (p. 64)
Prosopagnosia (p. 69)
Receptive field (p. 60)
Selective adaptation (p. 66)
Selective rearing (p. 68)
Sensory coding (p. 70)
Simple cortical cell (p. 64)
Simultaneous contrast (p. 58)
Sparse coding (p. 71)
Specificity coding (p. 70)
Striate cortex (p. 64)
Superior colliculus (p. 64)
Visual receiving area (p. 64)
White's illusion (p. 59)

MEDIA RESOURCES

CourseMate

Go to CengageBrain.com to access Psychology CourseMate, where you will find the Virtual Labs plus an interactive eBook, flashcards, quizzes, videos, and more.

Virtual Labs **VL**

The Virtual Labs are designed to help you get the most out of this course. The Virtual Lab icons direct you to specific media demonstrations and experiments designed to help you visualize what you are reading about. The numbers below indicate the number of the Virtual Lab you can access through Psychology CourseMate.

3.1 Lateral Inhibition in the Hermann Grid (p. 55)
Demonstration of how lateral inhibition can create the "spots" in the Hermann grid by affecting the firing rate of neurons in a neural circuit.

3.2 Vasarely Illusion (p. 57)
A demonstration of how lateral inhibition can create illusory lines on squares that are stacked on top of one another. (Courtesy of Edward Adelson)

3.3 Pyramid Illusion (p. 57)
Another way of demonstrating the Vasarely illusion. (Courtesy of Michael Bach)

3.4 Simultaneous Contrast (p. 58)
How perception of a small field can be changed by different backgrounds. (Courtesy of Edward Adelson)

3.5 White's Illusion (p. 59)
A demonstration of White's illusion, which, as described in the text, illustrates a lightness effect that can't be explained by lateral inhibition. (Courtesy of Edward Adelson)

3.6 Craik-Obrien-Cornsweet Effect (p. 59)
A demonstration of how the lightness of two adjacent squares can be determined by the fact that the visual system responds best to sharp changes of intensity. This effect is, therefore, another demonstration of a lightness effect that isn't explained by lateral inhibition. (Courtesy of Edward Adelson)

3.7 Criss-Cross Illusion (p. 59)
Illustration of a another lightness illusion that can't be explained by lateral inhibition. (Courtesy of Edward Adelson)

3.8 The Corrugated Plaid (p. 59)
A demonstration showing how the orientation of a surface can affect lightness perception (Courtesy of Edward Adelson)

3.9 Snake Illusion (p. 59)
Yet another lightness demonstration that can't be explained by lateral inhibition. (Courtesy of Edward Adelson)

3.10 Koffka Ring (p. 59)
A demonstration showing how the spatial configuration of a pattern can affect lightness perception. (Courtesy of Edward Adelson)

3.11 The Visual Pathways (p. 64)
A drag-and-drop exercise that tests your knowledge of visual structures.

3.12 Neurons That Respond to Specific Faces (p. 72)
Shows the response of one neuron that responds to Marilyn Monroe and another neuron that responds to Josh Brolin. (Courtesy of Moran Cerf)

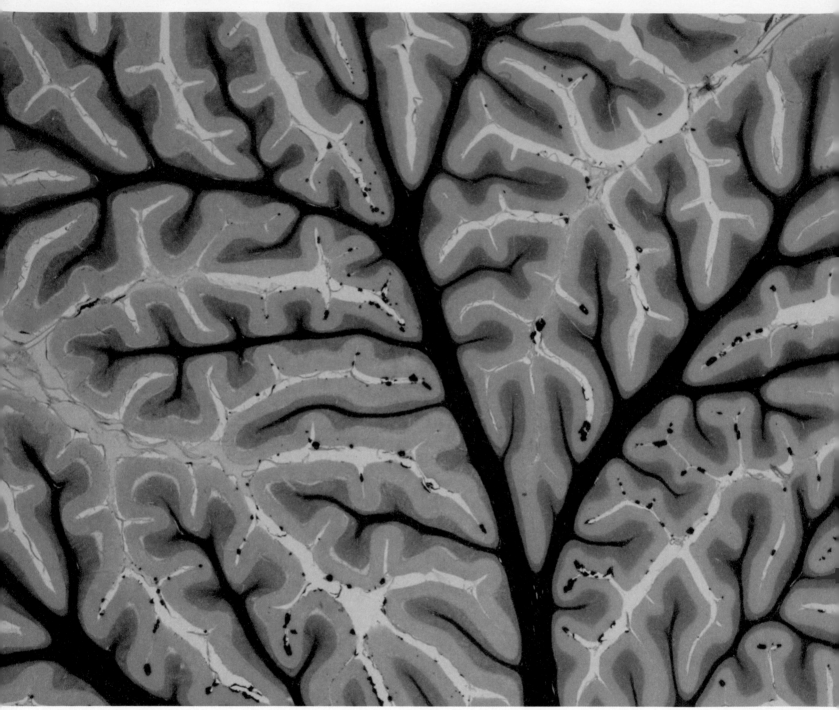

Cortical Organization

◄ This beautiful pattern is a cross-section of a small area of the brain. The black, tree-like areas are air spaces, and the white and orange areas are brain tissue. The white areas, called white matter, are mainly nerve fibers; the orange areas, called gray matter, are mainly the cell bodies of neurons. The white and gray matter, taken together, contain the mechanisms not only for perception, but for everything else the brain controls and creates. In this chapter we consider how different perceptual functions are organized within the brain.

Some Questions We Will Consider:

- Do electrical signals that represent objects at different places in a scene go to different places in the brain? (p. 78)
- How can brain damage affect a person's perception? (p. 85)
- Are there separate brain areas that determine our perception of different qualities? (pp. 84, 87)

Research on the physiology of vision has been dominated by two major themes: (1) describing the types of stimuli that cause neurons at different levels of the visual system to respond; and (2) describing how neurons in the visual system are organized. We considered the first theme in Chapter 3 when we showed how neurons at higher levels of the visual system respond to more and more complex stimuli. This chapter considers the problem of organization. As we will see, this problem has been approached in a number of ways, all of which are important for understanding how the visual system processes information.

The Organized Visual System

Organization is important. We need to "get organized." Companies have an organizational chart. The military has a chain of command. Organizing information in a file cabinet or in your computer makes it easier to access information when you need it.

The need for organization is especially important in the visual system because of the tasks the visual system faces. One task is to process information about various characteristics, or features, of objects, such as size, shape, orientation, color, movement, and location in space. We will see that each characteristic is served by separate mechanisms located at different places in the brain. Once this information is processed, how are all of an object's features combined? We don't see "red," "truck," "long," "moving to the left," separately. We see a red fire engine speeding up the street. Organization plays a central role in achieving the tasks of both processing specific information and combining information to create coherent perceptions. The visual system accomplishes this organization in a number of different ways. We begin by considering *spatial organization*—how different locations in the environment and on the retina are represented in the brain.

An Exploration of Spatial Organization

Spatial organization refers to the way stimuli at specific locations in the environment are represented by activity at specific locations in the nervous system. For example, when we look out at a scene, things are organized across our visual field. There are objects to the left and right, high and low. This organization in visual space then becomes transformed into organization in the eye, when an image of the scene is created on the retina. It is easy to appreciate spatial organization at the level of the retinal image because this image is essentially a picture of the scene. But when the picture is transformed into electrical signals, a new type of organization occurs in the form of "electronic maps" of the retina in structures higher up in the system.

The Electronic Map on V1

To begin, let's ask how points in the retinal image are represented *spatially* on the striate cortex. We will determine this by stimulating various places on the retina and determining where neurons fire in the cortex. **Figure 4.1** shows a man

looking at the top of a tree so that points A, B, C, and D on the tree stimulate points A, B, C, and D on his retina. Moving to the cortex, the image at point A on the retina causes neurons at point A to fire in the cortex. The image at point B causes neurons at point B to fire, and so on.

This example shows how points on the retinal image cause activity in the cortex. But we can also reverse the process by recording from a neuron in the cortex and determining the location of its receptive field on the retina (see Chapter 3, page 61). Thus, if we record from a neuron at point A in the cortex, its receptive field will be located at point A on the retina; if we record from point B, the receptive field is at point B; and so on. These examples show that locations on the cortex correspond to locations on the retina. This electronic map of the retina on the cortex is called a **retinotopic map**. This organized spatial map means that two points that are close together on an object and on the retina will activate neurons that are close together in the brain (Silver & Kastner, 2009).

But let's look at this retinotopic map a little more closely, because it has a very interesting property that is relevant to perception. Although points A, B, C, and D in the cortex correspond to points A, B, C, and D on the retina, you might notice something about the *spacing* of these locations. Considering the retina, we note that the man is looking at the top of the tree, so points A and B are both near the fovea and the images of points C and D at the bottom of the trunk are in the peripheral retina. But although the spacing between A and B and between C and D are the same on the retina, the spacing is not the same on the cortex. A and B take up more space on the cortex than C and D. What this means is that the map on the cortex is distorted, with more space being allotted to locations near the fovea than to locations in the peripheral retina. Even though the fovea accounts for only 0.01 percent of the retina's area, signals from the fovea account for 8 to 10 percent of the retinotopic map on the cortex (Van Essen & Anderson, 1995). This apportioning to the small fovea of a large area on the cortex is called **cortical magnification** (**Figure 4.2**).

The cortical magnification factor has been determined in the human cortex using a technique called *brain imaging*,

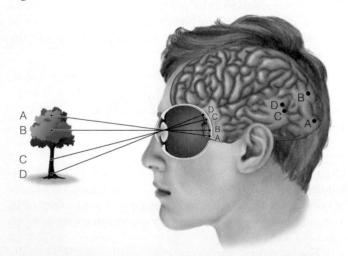

Figure 4.1 A person looking at a tree, showing how points A, B, C, and D are imaged on the retina and where these retinal activations cause activity in the brain. Although the distances between A and B and between C and D are about the same on the retina, the distance between A and B is much greater on the cortex. This is an example of cortical magnification, in which more space is devoted to areas of the retina near the fovea. © Cengage Learning

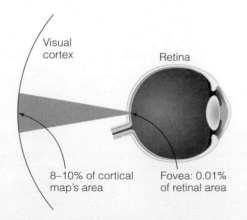

Figure 4.2 The magnification factor in the visual system. The small area of the fovea is represented by a large area on the visual cortex.
© Cengage Learning

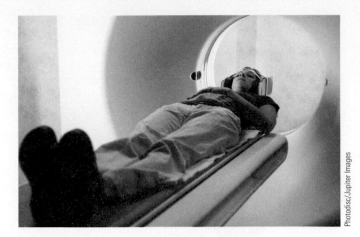

Figure 4.3 A person in a brain scanning apparatus.

which makes it possible to create pictures of the brain's activity (**Figure 4.3**). We will describe the procedure of brain imaging and how this procedure has been used to measure the cortical magnification factor in humans.

METHOD
Brain Imaging

Brain imaging refers to a number of techniques that result in images that show which areas of the brain are active. One of these techniques, **positron emission tomography (PET)**, was introduced in the mid-1970s (Hoffman et al., 1976; Ter-Pogossian et al., 1975). In the PET procedure, a person is injected with a low dose of a radioactive tracer that is not harmful. The tracer enters the bloodstream and indicates the volume of blood flow. The basic principle behind the PET scan is that the parts of the brain that are active will require more "fuel" from the blood than other, less active parts of the brain. Thus, changes in the activity of the brain are accompanied by changes in blood flow, so monitoring the radioactivity of the injected tracer provides a measure of brain activity.

Another neuroimaging technique is **functional magnetic resonance imaging (fMRI)**. Like PET, fMRI is based on the measurement of blood flow. Because hemoglobin, which carries oxygen in the blood, contains an iron molecule and therefore has magnetic properties, presenting a magnetic field to the brain causes the hemoglobin molecules to line up like tiny magnets.

fMRI indicates the presence of brain activity because the hemoglobin molecules in areas of high brain activity lose some of the oxygen they are transporting. This makes the hemoglobin more magnetic, so these molecules respond more strongly to the magnetic field. The fMRI apparatus determines the relative activity of various areas of the brain by detecting changes in the magnetic response of the hemoglobin that occurs when a person perceives a stimulus or engages in a specific behavior. Because fMRI doesn't require radioactive tracers and because it is more precise, this technique has become the main method for localizing brain activity in humans.

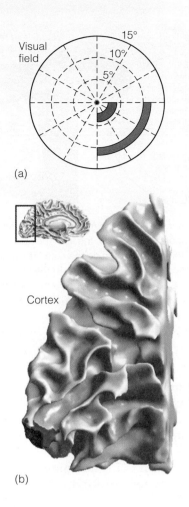

Figure 4.4 (a) Red and blue areas show the extent of stimuli that were presented while a person was in an fMRI scanner. (b) Red and blue indicate areas of the brain activated by the stimulation in (a).

From Dougherty, R. F., et al. (2003). Visual field representations and locations of visual areas V1/2/3 in human visual cortex. *Journal of Vision, 3,* 586–598. Copyright © 2003 by ARVO. All rights reserved. Reproduced by permission.

Robert Dougherty and coworkers (2003) used brain imaging to determine the magnification factor in the human visual cortex. **Figure 4.4a** shows the stimulus display viewed by the observer, who was in an fMRI scanner. The observer looked directly at the center of the screen, so the dot at the center fell on the fovea. During the experiment, stimulus light was presented in two places: (1) near the center (red area), which illuminated a small area near the fovea; and (2) farther from the center (blue area), which illuminated an area in the peripheral retina. The areas of the brain activated by these two stimuli are indicated in **Figure 4.4b**. This activation illustrates the magnification factor because stimulation of the small area near the fovea activated a greater area on the cortex (red) than stimulation of the larger area in the periphery (blue). (Also see Wandell, 2011.)

The large representation of the fovea in the cortex is also illustrated in **Figure 4.5**, which shows the space that would be allotted to words on a page (Wandell et al., 2009). Notice that the letter "a," which is near where the person is looking (red arrow), is represented by a much larger area in the cortex than letters that are far from where the person is looking.

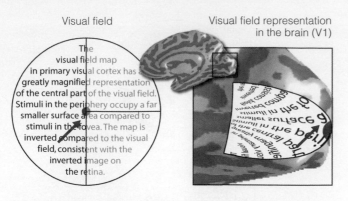

Visual field

Visual field representation in the brain (V1)

The visual field map in primary visual cortex has a greatly magnified representation of the central part of the visual field. Stimuli in the periphery occupy a far smaller surface area compared to stimuli in the fovea. The map is inverted compared to the visual field, consistent with the inverted image on the retina.

Figure 4.5 Demonstration of the magnification factor. A person looks at the red spot on the text on the left. The area of brain activated by each letter of the text is shown on the right. The arrows point to the letter *a* in the text on the left, and the area in the brain activated by the *a* on the right. Reprinted from Wandell, B. A., Dumoulin, S. O., & Brewer, A. A. (2009). Visual areas in humans. In L. Squire (Ed.), *Encyclopedia of neuroscience*, Fig. 6, with permission from Elsevier.

The extra cortical space allotted to letters and words at which the person is looking provides the extra neural processing needed to accomplish tasks such as reading that require high visual acuity (Azzopardi & Cowey, 1993).

What the magnification factor means when you look at a scene is that information about the part of the scene you are looking at takes up a larger space on your cortex than an area of equal size that is off to the side. Another way to appreciate the magnification factor is to do the following demonstration.

DEMONSTRATION
Cortical Magnification of Your Finger

Hold your left hand at arm's length, holding your index finger up. As you look at your finger, hold your right hand at arm's length, about a foot to the right of your finger and positioned so the back of your hand is facing you. When you have done this, your left index finger (which you are still looking at) activates an area of cortex as large as the area activated by your whole right hand.

One of the interesting things about the above demonstration is that when your finger is imaged on the fovea it takes up about the same space on the cortex as your hand imaged on the peripheral retina, but you do not perceive your finger as being as large as your hand. Instead, you see the details of your finger far better than you can see details on your hand. The fact that more space on the cortex translates into better detail vision rather than larger size is an example of the fact that what we perceive doesn't exactly match the "picture" in the brain. We will return to this idea shortly.

The Cortex Is Organized in Columns

Determining the retinotopic map and the magnification factor has kept us near the surface of the cortex. We are now going to consider what is happening below the surface by

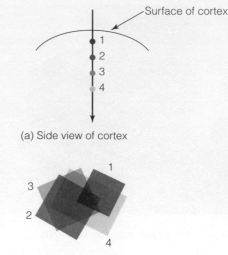

Surface of cortex

(a) Side view of cortex

(b) Receptive field locations on retina

Figure 4.6 Location column. When an electrode penetrates the cortex perpendicularly, the receptive fields of the neurons encountered along this track overlap. The receptive field recorded at each numbered position along the electrode track is indicated by a correspondingly numbered square. © Cengage Learning

looking at the results of experiments in which a recording electrode was lowered into the cortex.

Location and Orientation Columns Hubel and Wiesel (1965) carried out a series of experiments in which they recorded from neurons they encountered as they lowered electrodes into the cortex. When they positioned an electrode perpendicular to the surface of a cat's cortex, they found that every neuron they encountered had its receptive field at about the same location on the retina. Their results are shown in **Figure 4.6a**, which shows four neurons along the electrode track, and **Figure 4.6b**, which shows that these neurons' receptive fields are all located at about the same place on the retina. From this result, Hubel and Wiesel concluded that the striate cortex is organized into **location columns** that are perpendicular to the surface of the cortex, so that all of the neurons within a location column have their receptive fields at the same location on the retina.

As Hubel and Wiesel lowered their electrodes along perpendicular tracks, they noted not only that the neurons along this track had receptive fields with the same location on the retina, but that these neurons all preferred stimuli with the same orientation. Thus, all cells encountered along the electrode track at A in **Figure 4.7** fired the most to horizontal lines, whereas all those along electrode track B fired the most to lines oriented at about 45 degrees. Based on this result, Hubel and Wiesel concluded that the cortex is organized into **orientation columns**, with each column containing cells that respond best to a particular orientation.

Hubel and Wiesel also showed that adjacent orientation columns have cells with slightly different preferred orientations. When they moved an electrode through the cortex obliquely (not perpendicular to the surface), so that the

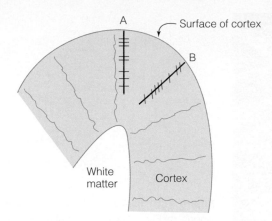

Figure 4.7 Orientation columns. All of the cortical neurons encountered along track A respond best to horizontal bars (indicated by the red lines cutting across the electrode track). All of the neurons along track B respond best to bars oriented at 45 degrees. © Cengage Learning

electrode cut across orientation columns, they found that the neurons' preferred orientations changed in an orderly fashion, so a column of cells that respond best to 90 degrees is right next to the column of cells that respond best to 85 degrees (**Figure 4.8**). Hubel and Wiesel also found that as they moved their electrode 1 millimeter across the cortex, their electrode passed through orientation columns that represented the entire range of orientations. Interestingly enough, this 1-mm dimension is the size of one location column.

One Location Column: Many Orientation Columns This 1-mm dimension for location columns means that one location column is large enough to contain orientation columns that cover all possible orientations. Thus, the location column shown in **Figure 4.9** serves one location on the retina (all the neurons in the column have their receptive fields at about the same place on the retina) *and* contains neurons that respond to all possible orientations.

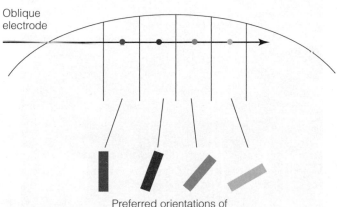

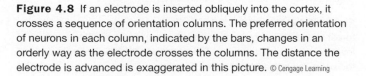

Figure 4.8 If an electrode is inserted obliquely into the cortex, it crosses a sequence of orientation columns. The preferred orientation of neurons in each column, indicated by the bars, changes in an orderly way as the electrode crosses the columns. The distance the electrode is advanced is exaggerated in this picture. © Cengage Learning

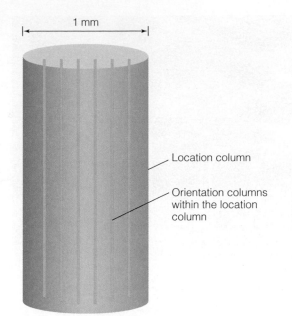

Figure 4.9 A location column that contains the full range of orientation columns. A column such as this, which contains a full array of orientation columns, was called a *hypercolumn* by Hubel and Wiesel. A column such as this receives information about all possible orientations that fall within a small area of the retina. © Cengage Learning 2014

Think about what this means. Neurons in that location column receive signals from a particular location on the retina, which corresponds to a small area in the visual field. Because this location column contains some neurons that respond to each orientation, any oriented object that falls within the location column's area on the retina will cause some of the neurons in this location column to fire.

A location column with all of its orientation columns, which has been called a **hypercolumn** by Hubel and Wiesel, receives information about all possible orientations that fall within a small area of the retina, and it is therefore well suited for processing information from a small area in the visual field.[1]

How Do Feature Detectors Respond to a Scene?

Determining how the millions of neurons in the cortex respond when we look at a scene such as the one in **Figure 4.10a** is an ambitious undertaking. We will simplify the task by focusing on one small part of the scene—the tree trunk in **Figure 4.10b**. We focus specifically on the part of the trunk shown passing through the three circles, A, B, and C.

---

[1]In addition to location and orientation columns, Hubel and Wiesel also described **ocular dominance columns**. Most neurons respond better to one eye than to the other. This preferential response to one eye is called **ocular dominance**, and neurons with the same ocular dominance are organized into ocular dominance columns in the cortex. This means that each neuron encountered along a perpendicular electrode track responds best to either the left eye or the right eye. There are two ocular dominance columns within each hypercolumn, one for the left eye and one for the right.

(a)

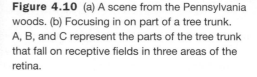

(b)

Figure 4.10 (a) A scene from the Pennsylvania woods. (b) Focusing in on part of a tree trunk. A, B, and C represent the parts of the tree trunk that fall on receptive fields in three areas of the retina.

Figure 4.11a shows how the image of this part of the tree trunk is imaged on the retina. Each of the circles represents the area served by a location column. **Figure 4.11b** shows the location columns in the cortex. Remember that each of these location columns contains a complete set of orientation columns (Figure 4.9). This means that the vertical tree trunk will activate the 90-degree orientation columns in each location column, as indicated by the orange areas in each column.

Thus, the continuous tree trunk is represented by the firing of neurons in a number of separated columns in the cortex. Although it may be a bit surprising that the tree is represented by separate columns in the cortex, it simply confirms a property of our perceptual system that we mentioned earlier: The cortical representation of a stimulus does not have to *resemble* the stimulus; it just has to contain information that *represents* the stimulus. The representation of the tree in the visual cortex is contained in the firings of neurons in separate cortical columns. At some point in the cortex, the information in these separated columns must be combined to create our perception of the tree.

Before leaving our description of how objects are represented by feature detectors, let's return to our scene (**Figure 4.12**). Each circle or ellipse in the scene represents an area that sends information to one location column. Working together, these columns cover the entire visual field, an effect called **tiling**. Just as a wall can be covered by adjacent tiles, the visual field is served by adjacent (and often overlapping) location columns (Nassi & Callaway, 2009). (Does this sound familiar? Remember the "football analogy" for optic nerve fiber receptive fields in Chapter 3, in which each spectator was observing a small area of the field. In that example, the spectators were tiling the football field.)

The idea that any scene is represented by activity in many location columns means that a scene is represented in the striate cortex by an amazingly complex pattern of firing. Just imagine the process we described for the three small areas

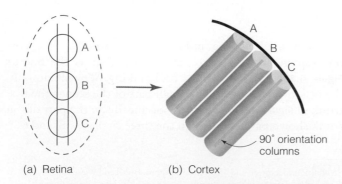

(a) Retina   (b) Cortex

Figure 4.11 (a) Receptive fields for the three sections of the tree trunk from Figure 4.10b. The neurons associated with each of these receptive fields are in different location columns. (b) Three location columns in the cortex. Neurons that fire to the tree trunk's orientation are within the orange areas of the location column. © Cengage Learning 2014

Figure 4.12 The yellow circles and ellipses superimposed on the forest scene each represent an area that sends information to one location column in the cortex. The way these location columns cover the entire receptive field is called *tiling*.

on the tree trunk multiplied by hundreds or thousands. Of course, this representation in the striate cortex is only the first step in representing the tree. As we will now see, signals from the striate cortex travel to a number of other places in the cortex for further processing.

TEST YOURSELF 4.1

1. How is the retina mapped onto the striate cortex? What is the cortical magnification factor, and what function does it serve?

2. Describe the technique of brain imaging. How has it been used to determine the retinotopic map in humans? How do the results of the brain imaging experiment provide evidence for cortical magnification in the human cortex?

3. Describe location columns and orientation columns. What do we mean when we say that location columns and orientation columns are "combined"? What is a hypercolumn?

4. How do feature detectors respond to a scene? Start by describing how a tree trunk is represented in the cortex and then expand your view to the whole forest scene.

5. What does it mean to say that the cortical representation of a scene does not have to resemble the scene, but just has to contain information that represents the scene?

Streams: Pathways for What, Where, and How

So far, as we have been looking at types of neurons in the cortex and how the cortex is spatially organized into maps and columns, we have been describing research primarily from the 1960s and 1970s. Most of the research during this time was concerned with the striate cortex or areas near the striate cortex. Although a few pioneers had looked at visual functioning outside the striate cortex (Gross et al., 1969, 1972; see Chapter 3, page 69), it wasn't until the 1980s that a large number of researchers began investigating how visual stimulation causes activity in areas far beyond the striate cortex.

One of the most influential ideas to come out of this research is that there are pathways, or "streams," that transmit information from the striate cortex to other areas in the brain. This idea was introduced in 1982, when Leslie Ungerleider and Mortimer Mishkin described experiments that distinguished two streams that served different functions.

Streams for Information About What and Where

Ungerleider and Mishkin (1982) used a technique called *ablation* (also called *lesioning*). **Ablation** refers to the destruction or removal of tissue in the nervous system.

METHOD
Brain Ablation

The goal of a brain ablation experiment is to determine the function of a particular area of the brain. First an animal's capacity is determined by testing it behaviorally. Most ablation experiments have used monkeys because of the similarity of their visual system to that of humans and because monkeys can be trained in ways that enable researchers to determine perceptual capacities such as acuity, color vision, depth perception, and object perception.

Once the animal's perception has been measured, a particular area of the brain is ablated (removed or destroyed), either by surgery or by injecting a chemical that destroys tissue near the place where it is injected. Ideally, one particular area is removed and the rest of the brain remains intact. After ablation, the monkey is retrained to determine which perceptual capacities remain and which have been affected by the ablation.

Ungerleider and Mishkin presented monkeys with two tasks: (1) an object discrimination problem and (2) a landmark discrimination problem. In the **object discrimination problem**, a monkey was shown one object, such as a rectangular solid, and was then presented with a two-choice task like the one shown in **Figure 4.13a**, which included the "target"

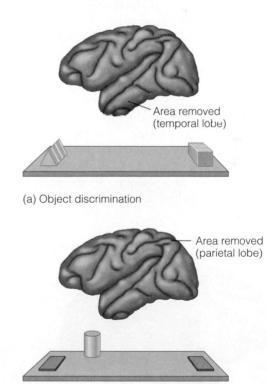

(a) Object discrimination

(b) Landmark discrimination

Figure 4.13 The two types of discrimination tasks used by Ungerleider and Mishkin. (a) Object discrimination: Pick the correct shape. Lesioning the temporal lobe (shaded area) makes this task difficult. (b) Landmark discrimination: Pick the food well closer to the cylinder. Lesioning the parietal lobe makes this task difficult.

From "Object Vision and Spatial Vision: Two Central Pathways," by M. Mishkin, L. G. Ungerleider, & K. A. Makco, 1983, *Trends in Neuroscience, 6,* 414–417, figure 2. Copyright © 1983, with permission from Elsevier.

object (the rectangular solid) and another stimulus, such as the triangular solid. If the monkey pushed aside the target object, it received the food reward that was hidden in a well under the object. The **landmark discrimination problem** is shown in **Figure 4.13b**. Here, the monkey's task was to remove the cover of the food well that was closest to the tall cylinder.

In the ablation part of the experiment, part of the temporal lobe was removed in some monkeys. After ablation, behavioral testing showed that the object discrimination problem was very difficult for monkeys with their temporal lobes removed. This result indicates that the pathway that reaches the temporal lobes is responsible for determining an object's identity. Ungerleider and Mishkin therefore called the pathway leading from the striate cortex to the temporal lobe the *what* pathway (**Figure 4.14**). ▄VL▄

Other monkeys had their parietal lobes removed, and they had difficulty solving the landmark discrimination problem. This result indicates that the pathway that leads to the parietal lobe is responsible for determining an object's location. Ungerleider and Mishkin therefore called the pathway leading from the striate cortex to the parietal lobe the *where* pathway (Figure 4.14).

The *what* and *where* pathways are also called the **ventral pathway** (what) and the **dorsal pathway** (where), because the lower part of the brain, where the temporal lobe is located, is the ventral part of the brain, and the upper part of the brain, where the parietal lobe is located, is the dorsal part of the brain. The term *dorsal* refers to the back or the upper surface of an organism; thus, the dorsal fin of a shark or dolphin is the fin on the back that sticks out of the water. **Figure 4.15** shows that for upright, walking animals such as humans, the dorsal part of the brain is the top of the brain. (Picture a person with a dorsal fin sticking out of the top of his or her head!) *Ventral* is the opposite of dorsal, hence it refers to the lower part of the brain.

The discovery of two pathways in the cortex—one for identifying objects (what) and one for locating objects

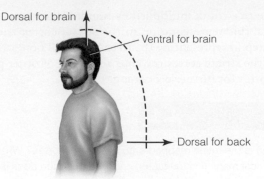

Figure 4.15 *Dorsal* refers to the back surface of an organism. In upright standing animals such as humans, dorsal refers to the back of the body *and* to the top of the head, as indicated by the arrows and the curved dashed line. Ventral is the opposite of dorsal. © Cengage Learning

(where)—led some researchers to look back at the retina and LGN. Using the techniques of both recording from neurons and ablation, they found that properties of the ventral and dorsal streams are established by two different types of ganglion cells in the retina, which transmit signals to different layers of the LGN. Thus, the cortical ventral and dorsal streams can actually be traced back to the retina and LGN.

Although there is good evidence that the ventral and dorsal pathways serve different functions, it is important to note that (1) the pathways are not totally separated, but have connections between them; and (2) signals flow not only "up" the pathway toward the parietal and temporal lobes, but "back" as well (Merigan & Maunsell, 1993; Ungerleider & Haxby, 1994). It makes sense that there would be communication between the pathways because in our everyday behavior we need to both identify and locate objects, and we routinely coordinate these two activities every time we identify something (for example, a pen) and take action with regard to it (picking up the pen and writing with it). Thus, there are two distinct pathways, but some information is shared between them. The "backward" flow of information, called *feedback* (see page 64), provides information from higher centers that can influence the signals flowing into the system. This feedback is one of the mechanisms behind top-down processing, introduced in Chapter 1 (page 10).

Streams for Information About What and How

Although the idea of ventral and dorsal streams has been generally accepted, David Milner and Melvyn Goodale (1995; see also Goodale & Humphrey, 1998, 2001) have suggested that the dorsal stream does more than just indicate where an object is. Milner and Goodale propose that the dorsal stream is for taking action, such as picking up an object. Taking this action would involve knowing the location of the object, consistent with the idea of *where*, but it goes beyond *where* to involve a physical interaction with the object. Thus, reaching to pick up a pen involves information about the pen's

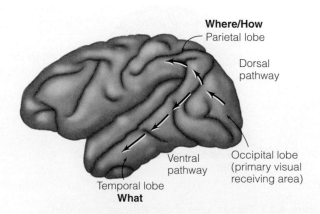

Figure 4.14 The monkey cortex, showing the *what*, or ventral, pathway from the occipital lobe to the temporal lobe, and the *where*, or dorsal, pathway from the occipital lobe to the parietal lobe. The *where* pathway is also called the *how* pathway. From "Object Vision and Spatial Vision: Two Central Pathways," by M. Mishkin, L. G. Ungerleider, & K. A. Makco, 1983, *Trends in Neuroscience, 6*, 414–417, figure 1. Copyright © 1983, with permission from Elsevier.

location *plus* movement of the hand toward the pen. According to this idea, the dorsal stream provides information about *how* to direct action with regard to a stimulus.

Evidence supporting the idea that the dorsal stream is involved in how to direct action is provided by the discovery of neurons in the parietal cortex that respond (1) when a monkey looks at an object and (2) when it reaches toward the object (Sakata et al., 1992; also see Taira et al., 1990). But the most dramatic evidence supporting the idea of a dorsal *how* or *action* stream comes from **neuropsychology**—the study of the behavioral effects of brain damage in humans.

METHOD
Double Dissociations in Neuropsychology

One of the basic principles of neuropsychology is that we can understand the effects of brain damage by determining **double dissociations**, which involve two people: In one person, damage to one area of the brain causes function A to be absent while function B is present; in the other person, damage to another area of the brain causes function B to be absent while function A is present.

Ungerleider and Mishkin's monkeys provide an example of a double dissociation. The monkey with damage to the temporal lobe was unable to discriminate objects (function A) but had the ability to solve the landmark problem (function B). The monkey with damage to the parietal lobe was unable to solve the landmark problem (function B) but was able to discriminate objects (function A). These two findings, taken together, are an example of a double dissociation. The fact that object discrimination and the landmark task can be disrupted separately and in opposite ways means that these two functions operate independently of one another.

An example of a double dissociation in humans is provided by two hypothetical patients. Alice, who has suffered damage to her temporal lobe, has difficulty naming objects but has no trouble indicating where they are located (Table 4.1a). Bert, who has parietal lobe damage, has the opposite problem—he can identify objects but can't tell exactly where they are located (Table 4.1b). The cases of Alice and Bert, taken together, represent a double dissociation and enable us to conclude that recognizing objects and locating objects operate independently of each other.

The Behavior of Patient D.F. The method of determining dissociations was used by Milner and Goodale (1995) to study D.F., a 34-year-old woman who suffered damage to her ventral pathway from carbon monoxide poisoning caused by a gas

TABLE 4.1 A Double Dissociation

	NAMING OBJECTS	DETERMINING OBJECT'S LOCATION
(a) ALICE: Temporal lobe damage (ventral stream)	NO	YES
(b) BERT: Parietal lobe damage (dorsal stream)	YES	NO

© Cengage Learning 2014

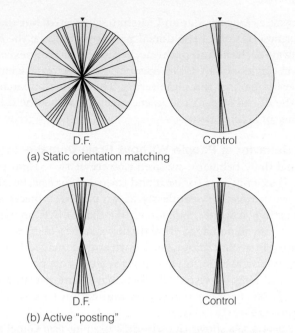

(a) Static orientation matching

(b) Active "posting"

Figure 4.16 Performance of D.F. and a person without brain damage on two tasks: (a) judging the orientation of a slot; and (b) placing a card through the slot. See text for details. From *The Visual Brain in Action* by A. D. Milner and M. A. Goodale. Copyright © 1995 by Oxford University Press. Reprinted by permission.

leak in her home. One result of the brain damage was that D.F. was not able to match the orientation of a card held in her hand to different orientations of a slot. This is shown in the left circle in **Figure 4.16a**. Each line in the circle indicates the orientation to which D.F. adjusted the card. Perfect matching performance would be indicated by a vertical line for each trial, but D.F.'s responses are widely scattered. The right circle shows the accurate performance of the normal controls.

Because D.F. had trouble orienting a card to match the orientation of the slot, it would seem reasonable that she would also have trouble *placing* the card through the slot, because to do this she would have to turn the card so that it was lined up with the slot. But when D.F. was asked to "mail" the card through the slot, she could do it! Even though D.F. could not turn the card to match the slot's orientation, once she started moving the card toward the slot, she was able to rotate it to match the orientation of the slot (**Figure 4.16b**). Thus, D.F. performed poorly in the *static orientation-matching task* but did well as soon as *action* was involved (Murphy et al., 1996). Milner and Goodale interpreted D.F.'s behavior as showing that there is one mechanism for judging orientation and another for coordinating vision and action.

These results for D.F. demonstrate a double dissociation when compared with other patients whose symptoms are the opposite of D.F.'s, and such people do, in fact, exist. These people can judge visual orientation, but they can't accomplish the task that combines vision and action. As we would expect, whereas D.F.'s ventral stream is damaged, these other people have damage to their dorsal streams.

Based on these results, Milner and Goodale suggested that the ventral pathway should still be called the *what* pathway, as Ungerleider and Mishkin suggested, but that a better description of the dorsal pathway would be the *how* **pathway**, or the **action pathway**, because it determines *how* a person carries out an *action*. As sometimes occurs in science, not everyone uses the same terms. Thus, some researchers call the dorsal stream the *where* pathway, and some call it the *how* or *action* pathway.

The Behavior of People Without Brain Damage In our normal daily behavior, we aren't aware of two visual processing streams, one for *what* and the other for *how*, because they work together seamlessly as we perceive objects and take actions toward them. Cases like that of D.F., in which one stream is damaged, reveal the existence of these two streams. But what about people without damaged brains? Psychophysical experiments that measure how people perceive and react to visual illusions have demonstrated the dissociation between perception and action that was evident for D.F.

Figure 4.17a shows the stimulus used by Tzvi Ganel and coworkers (2008) in an experiment designed to demonstrate a separation of perception and action in non-brain-damaged subjects. This stimulus creates a visual illusion: Line 1 is actually longer than line 2 (see **Figure 4.17b**), but line 2 *appears* longer. **VL**

Ganel and coworkers presented subjects with two tasks: (1) a *length estimation task* in which they were asked to indicate how they perceived the lines' length by spreading their thumb and index finger, as shown in **Figure 4.17c**; and (2) a *grasping task* in which they were asked to reach toward the lines and grasp each line by its ends. Sensors on the subjects' fingers measured the separation between the fingers as the subjects grasped the lines. These two tasks were chosen because they depend on different processing streams. The length estimation task involves the ventral or *what* stream. The grasping task involves the dorsal or *how* stream.

The results of this experiment, shown in **Figure 4.17d**, indicate that in the length estimation task, subjects judged line 1 (the longer line) as looking shorter than line 2, but in the grasping task, they separated their fingers farther apart for line 1. Thus, the illusion works for perception (the length estimation task), but not for action (the grasping task). These results support the idea that perception and action are served by different mechanisms. An idea that originated with observations of patients with brain damage is supported by the performance of observers without brain damage.

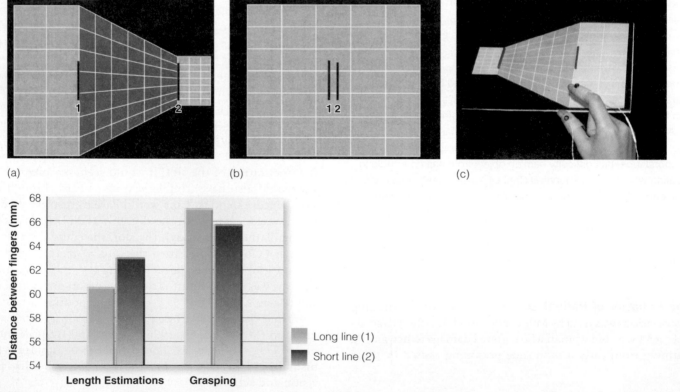

(a)   (b)   (c)

(d)

Figure 4.17 (a) The size illusion used by Ganel and coworkers (2008) in which line 2 looks longer than line 1. The numbers were not present in the display seen by the subjects. (b) The two vertical lines from (a), showing that line 2 is actually shorter than line 1. (c) Subjects in the experiment adjusted the space between their fingers either to estimate the length of the lines (length estimation task) or to reach toward the lines to grasp them (grasping task). The distance between the fingers is measured by sensors on the fingers. (d) Results of the length estimation and grasping tasks in the Ganel et al. experiment. The length estimation task indicates the illusion, because the shorter line (line 2) was judged to be longer. In the grasping task, subjects separated their fingers more for the longer line (line 1), which was consistent with the physical lengths of the lines. From Ganel, T., Tanzer, M., & Goodale, M. A. (2008). A double dissociation between action and perception in the context of visual illusions. *Psychological Science, 19,* 221–225. Copyright © 2008 by SAGE Publications. Reprinted by permission of SAGE Publications.

Modularity: Structures for Faces, Places, and Bodies

We have seen how the study of the visual system has progressed from Hubel and Wiesel's discovery of neurons in the striate cortex and nearby areas that respond to oriented bars to the pioneering early experiments of Charles Gross and coworkers (1969, 1972), described in Chapter 3 (see page 69), that showed that neurons in the monkey's inferotemporal (IT) cortex respond to complex stimuli like cutouts of hands and pictures of faces.

Although there was a delay between the publication of Gross's work and when other researchers began finding neurons that responded to complex stimuli, once they started, the floodgates opened, and one research study after another described neurons that responded to complex stimuli. For example, Keiji Tanaka and his coworkers (Ito et al., 1995; Kobatake & Tanaka, 1994; Tanaka, 1993; Tanaka et al., 1991) recorded from cells in the temporal cortex that responded best to complex stimuli, as shown in **Figure 4.18a**. This cell, which responds best to a circular disc with a thin bar, responds poorly to the bar alone (**Figure 4.18b**) or the disc alone (**Figure 4.18c**). The cell does respond to the square shape with the bar (**Figure 4.18d**), but not as well as to the circle and bar.

In addition to discovering neurons that respond to complex stimuli, researchers also found evidence that neurons that respond to similar stimuli are often grouped together in one area of the brain. A structure that is specialized to process information about a particular type of stimulus is called a **module**. There is a great deal of evidence that specific areas in the temporal lobe respond best to particular types of stimuli.

Face Neurons in the Monkey's IT Cortex

Edmund Rolls and Martin Tovee (1995) measured the response of neurons in the monkey's inferotemporal (IT) cortex (see Figure 3.35a). When they presented pictures of faces and pictures of nonface stimuli (mostly landscapes and food), they found many neurons that responded best to faces.

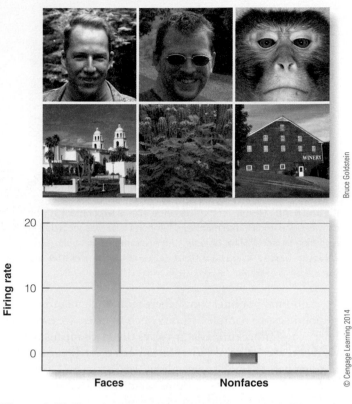

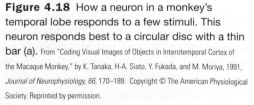

Figure 4.19 Size of response of a neuron in the monkey's IT cortex that responds to face stimuli but not to nonface stimuli. (Based on data from Rolls & Tovee, 1995.)

Figure 4.19 shows the results for a neuron that responded briskly to faces but hardly at all to other types of stimuli.

What is particularly significant about "face neurons" is that there are areas in the monkey temporal lobe that are particularly rich in these neurons. Doris Tsao and coworkers (2006) presented 96 images of faces, bodies, fruits, gadgets, hands, and scrambled patterns to two monkeys while recording from cortical neurons inside this face area. They classified neurons as "face selective" if they responded at least twice as strongly to faces as to nonfaces. Using this criterion, they found that 97 percent of the cells were face selective. The high level of face selectivity within this area is illustrated in **Figure 4.20**, which shows the average response for both monkeys to each of the 96 objects. The response to the 16 faces, on the left, is far greater than the response to any of the other objects.

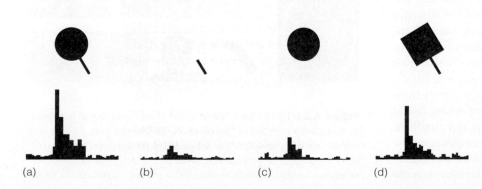

(a)　　　　(b)　　　　(c)　　　　(d)

Figure 4.18 How a neuron in a monkey's temporal lobe responds to a few stimuli. This neuron responds best to a circular disc with a thin bar (a). From "Coding Visual Images of Objects in Interotemporal Cortex of the Macaque Monkey," by K. Tanaka, H-A. Siato, Y. Fukada, and M. Moriya, 1991, *Journal of Neurophysiology, 66,* 170–189. Copyright © The American Physiological Society. Reprinted by permission.

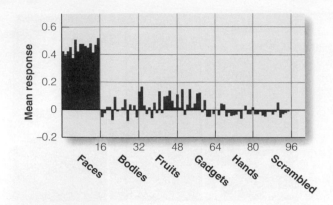

Figure 4.20 Results of the Tsao et al. (2006) experiment in which activity of neurons in the monkey's temporal lobe was recorded in response to faces, other objects, and a scrambled stimulus. From Tsao, D. Y., Freiwald, W. A., Tootell, R. B., & Livingstone, M. S. (2006). A cortical region consisting entirely of face-selective cells. *Science, 311*, 670–674., Fig. 2b, right. Reprinted with permission from AAAS.

You may wonder how there could be neurons that respond best to complex stimuli such as faces. We have seen how neural processing that involves the mechanisms of convergence, excitation, and inhibition can create neurons that respond best to small spots of light (see Figure 3.21, page 61). The same mechanisms are presumably involved in creating neurons that respond to more complex stimuli. Of course, the neural circuits involved in creating a "face-detecting" neuron must be extremely complex. However, the potential for this complexity is there, because there are a hundred billion (10^{11}) neurons and each neuron in the cortex receives inputs from an average of 1,000 other neurons. Based on these numbers, it has been estimated that there are several hundred trillion synaptic connections between neurons in the brain (Marois & Ivanoff, 2005). When we consider the vast complexity of the neural interconnections that must be involved in creating a neuron that responds best to faces, it is easy to agree with the description of the brain by William James, professor of psychology at Harvard and author of one of the first psychology textbooks (James, 1890/1981), as "the most mysterious thing in the universe."

Areas for Faces, Places, and Bodies in the Human Brain

Brain imaging (see Method, page 79) has been used to identify areas of the human brain that contain neurons that respond best to faces, and others that respond best to pictures of scenes and human bodies. In one of these experiments, Nancy Kanwisher and coworkers (1997) used fMRI to determine brain activity in response to pictures of faces and other objects, such as scrambled faces, household objects, houses, and hands. When they subtracted the response to the other objects from the response to the faces, Kanwisher and coworkers found that activity remained in an area they called the **fusiform face area (FFA)**, which is located in the fusiform gyrus on the underside of the brain directly below the IT cortex (see Figure 3.35b). This area is roughly equivalent to the face areas in the

temporal cortex of the monkey. Kanwisher's results, plus the results of many other experiments, have shown that the FFA is specialized to respond to faces (Kanwisher, 2010). **VL**

Additional evidence of an area specialized for the perception of faces is that damage to the temporal lobe causes *prosopagnosia*—difficulty recognizing the faces of familiar people. Even very familiar faces are affected, so people with prosopagnosia may not be able to recognize close friends or family members—or even their own reflection in the mirror—although they can easily identify such people as soon as they hear them speak (Burton et al., 1991; Hecaen & Angelerques, 1962; Parkin, 1996).

In addition to the FFA, which contains neurons that are activated by faces, two other specialized areas in the temporal cortex have been identified. The **parahippocampal place area (PPA)** is activated by pictures depicting indoor and outdoor scenes like those shown in **Figure 4.21a** (Aguirre et al., 1998; Epstein et al., 1999; Epstein & Kanwisher, 1998). Apparently what is important for this area is information about spatial layout, because increased activation occurs both to empty rooms and to rooms that are completely furnished (Kanwisher, 2003). The other specialized area, the **extrastriate body area (EBA)**, is activated by pictures of bodies and parts of bodies (but not by faces), as shown in **Figure 4.21b** (Downing et al., 2001).

The existence of neurons that are specialized to respond to faces, places, and bodies brings us closer to being able to explain how perception is based on the firing of neurons. It is likely that our perception of faces, landmarks, and people's bodies depends on specifically tuned neurons in areas such as the FFA, PPA, and EBA. But it is also important to recognize that even though stimuli like faces and buildings activate specific areas of the brain, these stimuli also activate other

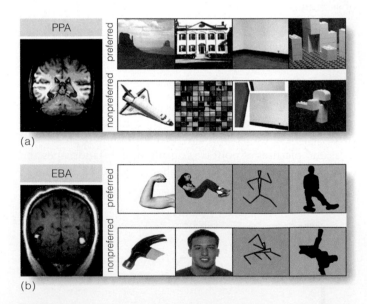

Figure 4.21 (a) The parahippocampal place area (PPA) is activated by places (top row) but not by other stimuli (bottom row). (b) The extrastriate body area (EBA) is activated by bodies (top), but not by other stimuli (bottom). Chalupa, Leo M., and John S. Werner, eds., *The Visual Neurosciences*, 2-vol. set, figure from pages 1179–1189, © 2003 Massachusetts Institute of Technology, by permission of The MIT Press.

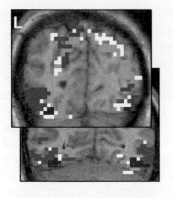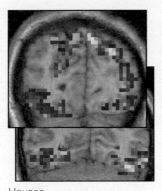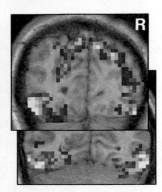

Houses   Faces   Chairs

(a) Segregation by category   (b) Response magnitude

Maximal Respose to:

■ Houses   ■ Faces

■ Chairs   □ No difference

Percent Activation

−1   0   +1   +2

Figure 4.22 fMRI responses of the human brain to various types of stimuli: (a) areas that were most strongly activated by houses, faces, and chairs; (b) all areas activated by each type of stimulus.

From Alumit Ishai, Leslie G. Ungerleider, Alex Martin, & James V. Haxby, "The representation of objects in the human occipital and temporal cortex," *Journal of Cognitive Neuroscience, 12*:2 (2000), 35–51. © 2000 by the Massachusetts Institute of Technology.

areas of the brain as well. This is illustrated in **Figure 4.22**, which shows the results of an fMRI experiment on humans.

Figure 4.22a shows that pictures of houses, faces, and chairs cause maximum activation in three separate areas in the IT cortex. However, each type of stimulus also causes substantial activity within the other areas, as shown in the three panels limited to just these areas (Ishai et al., 1999, 2000). Thus, objects such as faces may cause a large focus of activity in an area specialized for faces, such as the FFA, but they also cause additional activity that is distributed over a wide area of the cortex (Cohen & Tong, 2001; Riesenhuber & Poggio, 2000, 2002).

We can summarize what we know about organization in the visual system by noting that the visual system is organized both *spatially* and *functionally*. The spatial map is retinotopic, which means that points on the LGN or cortex correspond to specific points on the retina or in a scene. But spatial organization becomes weaker as we move to higher cortical areas, because in areas such as IT cortex, neurons have very large receptive fields that extend over large areas of the retina and visual field. Most of the face neurons respond when the face is imaged on the fovea, which makes sense, because when we want to identify a face we usually look directly at it.

The visual system is organized *functionally*, with different streams for *what* and *where/how* and with specific cortical areas that are rich in neurons that respond to specific types of stimuli such as faces, places, and bodies. It is no coincidence that the stimuli that have specific areas in the brain are ones we see all the time (faces and bodies) and that are important for helping us find our way through the environment (place neurons).

From our story so far, it might be tempting to say that the IT cortex, with its neurons for faces and other complex objects, is "the end of the line" for processing information about objects. As we will now see, this conclusion may be partially correct, but signals from the IT cortex also continue on to other structures that may be involved in remembering objects.

SOMETHING TO CONSIDER:
Where Vision Meets Memory

Some of the signals leaving the IT cortex reach structures in the medial temporal lobe (MTL), such as the parahippocampal cortex, the entorhinal cortex, and the hippocampus (**Figure 4.23a**). These MTL structures are extremely important for memory. The classic demonstration of the importance of one of the structures in the MTL, the hippocampus, is the case of H.M., who had his hippocampus on both sides of his brain removed in an attempt to eliminate epileptic seizures that had not responded to other treatments (Scoville & Milner, 1957).

The operation eliminated H.M.'s seizures, but it also eliminated his ability to store experiences in his memory. Thus, when H.M. experienced something, such as a visit from his doctor, he was unable to remember the experience, so the next time the doctor appeared, H.M. had no memory of having seen him. H.M.'s unfortunate situation occurred because in 1953, the surgeons did not realize that the hippocampus is crucial for the formation of long-term memories. Once they realized the devastating effects of removing the hippocampus on both sides of the brain, H.M.'s operation was never repeated.

The connection between the hippocampus and vision was demonstrated in experiments by R. Quian Quiroga and coworkers (2005, 2008) that we introduced in Chapter 3 (page 72). These experiments showed that there are neurons in the hippocampus that respond to faces of specific people, like Steve Carell (see Figure 3.40), and also to specific structures such as the Eiffel Tower or the Sydney Opera House. Let's now look at these experiments in more detail.

Quiroga recorded from eight patients with epilepsy who, in preparation for surgery, had electrodes implanted in their

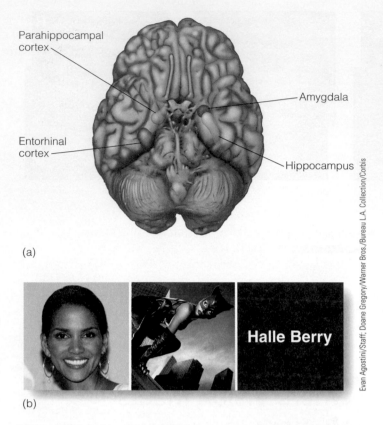

Parahippocampal cortex

Amygdala

Entorhinal cortex

Hippocampus

(a)

Halle Berry

(b)

Evan Agostini/Staff; Doane Gregory/Warner Bros./Bureau L.A. Collection/Corbis

Figure 4.23 (a) Location of the hippocampus and some of the other structures that were studied by Quiroga and coworkers (2005). (b) Some of the stimuli that caused a neuron in the hippocampus to fire.

hippocampus or other areas in the medial temporal lobe to help localize precisely where their seizures originated. Patients saw a number of different views of specific individuals and objects plus pictures of other things, such as faces, buildings, and animals. Not surprisingly, a number of neurons responded to some of these stimuli. What was surprising, however, was that some neurons responded to a number of different views of just one person or building or to a number of ways of representing that person or building. For example, one neuron responded to all pictures of the actress Jennifer Aniston, but did not respond to faces of other famous people, nonfamous people, landmarks, animals, or other objects. As we noted in Chapter 3, another

neuron responded to pictures of actor Steve Carell. Still another neuron responded to photographs of Halle Berry, to drawings of her, to pictures of her dressed as Catwoman from *Batman*, and also to the words "Halle Berry" (**Figure 4.23b**).

According to Quiroga, the MTL—and especially the hippocampus—is not responsible for recognizing objects. Patient H.M. for example, who had no hippocampus, could still recognize objects. He just couldn't remember them later. Thus, just because a hippocampus neuron responds to a visual stimulus doesn't mean it is responsible for seeing. What it is responsible for is remembering.

The possible role of these neurons in memory is supported by the way they respond to many different views of the stimulus, different modes of depiction, and even words signifying the stimulus. These neurons are not responding to visual features of the pictures, but to *concepts*—"Jennifer Aniston," "Halle Berry," "Sydney Opera House"—that the stimuli represent. Thus, the fact that the neuron that responded to Jennifer Aniston also responded to Lisa Kudrow was not a coincidence, because both appeared on the *Friends* TV series. The response of these MTL neurons to visual stimuli appears to depend, therefore, on a particular person's past experiences. Thus, a football fan could conceivably have a neuron that responds to seeing a picture of Tom Brady, and this same neuron might also respond to Aaron Rogers.

The link between these MTL neurons that respond to visual stimuli and memory has received additional support from the results of an experiment by Hagan Gelbard-Sagiv and coworkers (2008). These researchers had epilepsy patients view a series of 5- to 10-second video clips a number of times while recording from neurons in the MTL. The clips showed famous people, landmarks, and nonfamous people and animals engaged in various actions. As the person was viewing the clips, some neurons responded better to certain clips. For example, a neuron in one of the patients responded best to a clip from *The Simpsons* TV program.

The firing to specific video clips is similar to what Quiroga found for viewing still pictures. However, this experiment went a step further by asking the patients to think back to any of the film clips they had seen while the experimenter continued to record from the MTL neurons. One result is shown in **Figure 4.24**, which indicates the response

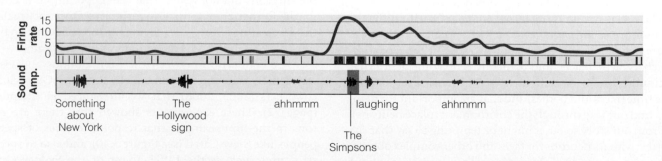

Firing rate

Sound Amp.

Something about New York

The Hollywood sign

ahhmmm

The Simpsons

laughing

ahhmmm

Figure 4.24 Activity of a neuron in the MTL of an epilepsy patient as he remembered the things indicated below the record. A response occurs when the person remembered *The Simpsons* TV program. Earlier, this neuron had been shown to respond to viewing a video clip of *The Simpsons*. From Gelbard-Sagiv, H., Mukamel, R., Harel, M., Malach, R., & Fried, I. (2008). Internally generated reactivation of single neurons in human hippocampus during free recall. *Science, 322*, 96–101. Reprinted with permission from AAAS.

of the neuron that fired to *The Simpsons*. The patent's description of what he was remembering is shown at the bottom of the figure. First the patient remembered "something about New York," then "the Hollywood sign." The neuron responds weakly or not at all to those two memories. However, remembering *The Simpsons* causes a large response, which continues as the person continues remembering the episode (indicated by the laughter). Results such as this support the idea that the neurons in the MTL that respond to *perceiving* specific objects or events may also be involved in *remembering* these objects and events. Moran Cerf and coworkers (2010) have provided another demonstration of how thoughts can influence the firing of neurons. Go to CourseMate to view videos describing this research.

DEVELOPMENTAL DIMENSION: Experience and Neural Responding

In this chapter we have seen that the brain is organized based on function, with neurons specialized to respond to faces, places, and bodies located in specific areas of the brain. Here we consider the role of experience in creating these specialized neurons. There is evidence, which we will be describing in later Developmental Dimensions, that some perceptual capacities, such as the ability to perceive movement, light–dark contrasts, faces, depth, tastes, and smells, are present at or near birth, although not at adult levels. Other capacities, such as color perception, depth that can be seen with one eye, and visual attention, emerge slightly later, also not at adult levels. Over time, these capacities improve—some rapidly, such as visual acuity, which reaches near adult levels by 9 months of age, and some over a longer time, such as recognizing faces, which continues developing into adolescence (Grill-Spector et al., 2008; Sherf et al., 2007).

What causes this improvement over time? Biological maturation is clearly involved, as we saw when we described the connection between improvement of visual acuity and the development of the rod and cone receptors. On a longer time scale, there is evidence that some aspects of face recognition depend on the emergence of the fusiform face area (FFA), which is not fully developed until adolescence.

In addition to biological maturation, experience in perceiving the environment also plays a role in perceptual development. One line of evidence supporting the role of experience is the research on *experience-dependent plasticity* that we described in Chapter 3. Blakemore and Cooper's experiments, in which they reared kittens in striped tubes, showed that these kittens' visual systems were shaped by the environment in which they were raised, so kittens reared seeing only vertical stripes had neurons that responded only to vertical or near vertical orientations.

Humans aren't usually reared in deprived environments, but we do grow up in an environment in which many features occur regularly, and these repeating features of the environment can influence how our visual system develops and, therefore, how we perceive. One example of this, which we described in Chapter 1, is the finding that people perceive horizontal and vertical orientations more easily than other orientations, called the *oblique effect*. There is evidence that the oblique effect occurs because there are more cortical neurons that respond to horizontal and vertical orientations, and it is no coincidence that horizontals and verticals occur more frequently in the environment than slanted orientations.

The fact that experience with the environment can shape the nervous system is the basis of the **expertise hypothesis**, which proposes that our proficiency in perceiving certain things can be explained by changes in the brain caused by long exposure, practice, or training (Bukach et al., 2006; Gauthier et al., 1999). Isabel Gauthier and coworkers (1999) demonstrated an expertise effect by using fMRI to determine the level of activity in the fusiform face area (FFA) in response to faces and to objects called *Greebles*—families of computer-generated "beings" that all have the same basic configuration but differ in the shapes of their parts (**Figure 4.25a**). Initially, the observers were shown both human faces and Greebles. The results for this part of the experiment, shown by the left pair of bars in **Figure 4.25b**, indicate that the FFA neurons responded poorly to the Greebles but well to the faces.

The participants were then trained in "Greeble recognition" for 7 hours over a 4-day period. After the training sessions, participants had become "Greeble experts," as indicated by their ability to rapidly identify many different Greebles by the names they had learned during the training. The right pair of bars in Figure 4.25b shows how becoming a Greeble expert affected the neural response in the participants' FFA. After the training, the FFA neurons responded about as well to Greebles as to faces.

This result shows that the FFA area of the cortex responds not just to faces but to other complex objects as well, and that the objects that the neurons respond to can be established

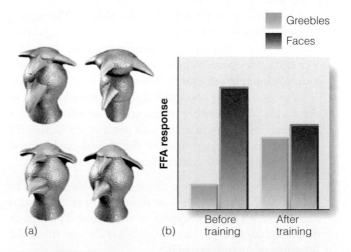

Figure 4.25 (a) Greeble stimuli used by Gauthier. Participants were trained to name each different Greeble. (b) Brain responses to Greebles and faces before and after Greeble training. Reprinted by permission from Macmillan Publishers Ltd, Copyright 1999: *Nature Neuroscience, 2,* 568–573. From Figure 1a, p. 569, from Gauthier, I., Tarr, M. J., Anderson, A. W., Skudlarski, P. L., & Gore, J. C., "Activation of the middle fusiform 'face area' increases with experience in recognizing novel objects," 1999.

by experience with those objects. In fact, Gauthier has also shown that neurons in the FFA of people who are experts in recognizing cars or birds respond well not only to human faces but to cars (for the car experts) and to birds (for the bird experts; Gauthier et al., 2000). Recently, another study showed that viewing the positions of chess pieces on a chess board causes a larger activation of the FFA in chess experts than in non-experts (Bilalic et al., 2011). Results such as these have led many researchers to suggest that that the reason the FFA responds well to faces is because we are all "face experts."

It is important to note that although there is good evidence that experience can influence the types of stimuli to which a neuron responds, the role of experience in establishing the FFA as a module for faces is controversial. Some researchers agree with Gauthier that experience is important for establishing the FFA as a module for faces (Bukach et al., 2006); others argue that the FFA's role as a face area does not depend on experience (Kanwisher, 2010).

Whatever the outcome of this ongoing debate about the FFA, there is no question that properties of neurons are influenced by our experience with stimuli in the environment. This experience, which "tunes" our perceptual system to respond best to what is usually present in the environment, is likely to play a role in determining the improvements in perception that occur from infancy into adulthood.

Now that you have finished this chapter, you have the background necessary to understand the physiological material in the chapters that follow. In the next six chapters we will continue discussing the visual system, with each chapter devoted to a specific visual quality or process. Chapter 5 continues our discussion of how we perceive objects. We will still be concerned with faces, but our main focus will be objects in general, as well as how we perceive many objects that are organized to create scenes. One thing you will notice as you read the next chapter is that you won't encounter the word *neuron* until two-thirds of the way through the chapter. One of the messages of Chapter 5 is that a large amount of research in perception occurs at the behavioral level, measuring the relationship between stimuli and perception. Of course, we never get away from neurons, because physiology is part of the story. But when neurons reappear, you will be ready for them!

TEST YOURSELF 4.2

1. How has ablation been used to demonstrate the existence of the ventral and dorsal processing streams? What is the function of these streams?

2. How has neuropsychology been used to show that one of the functions of the dorsal stream is to process information about coordinating vision and action? How do the results of a behavioral experiment support the idea of two primary streams in people without brain damage?

3. What is the evidence that there are modules for faces, places, and bodies? What is the evidence that stimuli like faces and places also activate a wide area of the cortex?

4. Describe the connection between vision and memory, as illustrated by experiments that recorded from neurons in the MTL and hippocampus. Describe both the experiments using still pictures and those using film clips.

5. Describe the possible role of experience-dependent plasticity in determining how neurons and brain areas respond to (a) horizontal, vertical, and slanted lines; and (b) Greebles.

THINK ABOUT IT

1. Ralph is hiking along a trail in the woods. The trail is bumpy in places, and Ralph has to avoid tripping on occasional rocks, tree roots, or ruts in the trail. Nonetheless, he is able to walk along the trail without constantly looking down to see exactly where he is placing his feet. That's a good thing because Ralph enjoys looking out at the woods to see whether he can spot interesting birds or animals. How can you relate this description of Ralph's behavior to the operation of the dorsal and ventral streams in the visual system? (p. 83)

2. Although most neurons in the striate cortex respond to stimulation of small areas of the retina, many neurons in the temporal lobe respond to areas that represent as much as half of the visual field. What do you think the function of such neurons is?

3. We have seen that the neural firing associated with an object in the environment does not necessarily look like, or resemble, the object. Can you think of situations that you encounter in everyday life in which objects or ideas are represented by things that do not exactly resemble those objects or ideas?

4. We have seen that there are neurons that respond to complex shapes and also to environmental stimuli such as faces, bodies, and places. Which types of neurons do you think would fire to the stimulus in **Figure 4.26**? How would your answer to this question be affected if this stimulus were interpreted as a human figure? ("Howdy, pardner!") What role would top-down processing play in determining the response to a cactus-as-person stimulus? (p. 88)

Figure 4.26 "Howdy, pardner."

KEY TERMS

Ablation (p. 83)
Action pathway (p. 86)
Brain imaging (p. 79)
Cortical magnification (p. 78)
Dorsal pathway (p. 84)
Double dissociation (p. 85)
Expertise hypothesis (p. 91)
Extrastriate body area (EBA) (p. 88)
Functional magnetic resonance imaging (fMRI) (p. 79)

Fusiform face area (FFA) (p. 88)
How pathway (p. 86)
Hypercolumn (p. 81)
Landmark discrimination problem (p. 84)
Location column (p. 80)
Module (p. 87)
Neuropsychology (p. 85)
Object discrimination problem (p. 83)
Ocular dominance (p. 81)
Ocular dominance column (p. 81)

Orientation column (p. 80)
Parahippocampal place area (PPA) (p. 88)
Positron emission tomography (PET) (p. 79)
Retinotopic map (p. 78)
Spatial organization (p. 78)
Tiling (p. 82)
Ventral pathway (p. 84)
What pathway (p. 84)
Where pathway (p. 84)

MEDIA RESOURCES

CourseMate 🖥

Go to CengageBrain.com to access Psychology CourseMate, where you will find the Virtual Labs plus an interactive eBook, flashcards, quizzes, videos, and more.

Virtual Labs 🆅🅛

The Virtual Labs are designed to help you get the most out of this course. The Virtual Lab icons direct you to specific media demonstrations and experiments designed to help you visualize what you are reading about. The numbers below indicate the number of the Virtual Lab you can access through Psychology CourseMate.

4.1 fMRI Procedure in Perception Experiment (p. 79)
Shows a subject in an experiment in which the subject's brain activation is measured while the subject views pictures in an fMRI scanner.

4.2 What and Where Streams (p. 84)
A drag-and-drop exercise to test your knowledge of the *what* and *where* visual pathways.

4.3 Ganel Experiment (p. 86)
The procedure for Ganel's experiment that is described on page 86. (Courtesy of Tzvi Ganel)

4.4 Meet Nancy Kanwisher (p. 88)
Describes Nancy Kanwisher's research on modularity and some practical applications of this research. (Courtesy of McGovern Institute for Brain Research, MIT)

4.5 On-line Voluntary Control of Human Temporal Lobe Neurons (p. 91)
Describes neurons recorded from epilepsy patients that respond to photos of Marilyn Monroe and Josh Brolin, and how the patients can use their minds to influence the firing of these neurons (Courtesy of Moran Cerf)

4.6 Thought Projection by Neurons in the Human Brain (p. 91)
A shorter description of the research involving thought control of Marilyn Monroe and Josh Brolin neurons. (Courtesy of Moran Cerf)

Bruce Goldstein

Perceiving Objects and Scenes

VL The Virtual Lab icons direct you to specific animations and videos designed to help you visualize what you are reading about. Virtual Labs are listed at the end of the chapter, keyed to the page on which they appear, and can be accessed through Psychology CourseMate.

◄ We see this landscape easily. But beneath the ease of our perception are complex processes that enable us to perceive the shapes of objects, to separate one object from another, and to know that the row of trees in the foreground extends behind the tower on the rooftop. Most amazingly, we can tell that the small white shapes hidden among the far row of trees are buildings. This chapter considers some of the mechanisms, both mental and neural, that enable us to perceive objects and scenes.

Some Questions We Will Consider:

- Why are even the most sophisticated computers unable to match a person's ability to perceive objects? (p. 97)

- Why do some perceptual psychologists say "The whole differs from the sum of its parts"? (p. 101)

- Can we tell what people are perceiving by monitoring their brain activity? (p. 116)

- What is special about faces? (p. 119)

- How do infants perceive faces? (p. 120)

Sitting in the upper deck in PNC Park, home of the Pittsburgh Pirates, Roger looks out over the city (**Figure 5.1**). He sees a group of about 10 buildings on the left and can easily tell one building from another. Looking straight ahead, he sees a small building in front of a larger one, and has no trouble telling that they are two separate buildings. Looking down toward the river, he notices a horizontal yellow band above the right field bleachers. It is obvious to him that this is not part of the ballpark but is located across the river.

All of Roger's perceptions come naturally to him and require little effort. But when we look closely at the scene, it becomes apparent that the scene poses many "puzzles." The following demonstration points out a few of them.

DEMONSTRATION
Perceptual Puzzles in a Scene

The questions below refer to the areas labeled in **Figure 5.2**. Your task is to answer each question and indicate the reasoning behind each answer:

- What is the dark area at A?

- Are the surfaces at B and C facing in the same or different directions?

- Are areas B and C on the same or on different buildings?

- Does the building at D extend behind the one at A?

Figure 5.1 It is easy to tell that there are a number of different buildings on the left and that straight ahead there is a low rectangular building in front of a taller building. It is also possible to tell that the horizontal yellow band above the bleachers is across the river. These perceptions are easy for humans but would be quite difficult for a computer vision system.

Figure 5.2 A city "puzzle." See Demonstration for instructions.

Although it may have been easy to answer the questions, it was probably somewhat more challenging to indicate what your "reasoning" was. For example, how did you know the dark area at A is a shadow? It could be a dark-colored building that is in front of a light-colored building. Or on what basis might you have decided that building D extends behind building A? It could, after all, simply end right were A begins. We could ask similar questions about everything in this scene because, as we will see, a particular pattern of shapes can be created by a large number of objects.

One of the messages of this chapter is that it is necessary to go beyond the pattern of light and dark that a scene creates on the retina to determine what is "out there." One way to appreciate the importance of this "going beyond" process is to consider how difficult it has been to program even the most powerful computers to accomplish perceptual tasks that humans achieve with ease.

Consider, for example, the robotic vehicles that were designed to compete in the "Urban Challenge" race that occurred on November 3, 2007, in Victorville, California. This race, which was sponsored by the Defense Advanced Research Project Agency (DARPA), required that vehicles drive for 55 miles through a course that resembled city streets, with other moving vehicles, traffic signals, and signs. The vehicles had to accomplish this feat on their own, with human involvement limited to entering global positioning coordinates of the course's layout into the vehicle's guidance

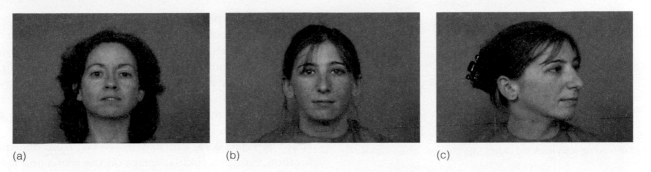

(a)   (b)   (c)

Figure 5.3 A computer or a person can determine whether the two straight-on views in (a) and (b) are the same person, but the person outperforms the computer when comparing a straight-on view to a face at an angle, as in (c). From O'Toole, A. J., Harms, J., Snow, S. L., Hurst, D. R., Pappas, M. R., & Abdi, H. (2005). A video database of moving faces and people. *IEEE Transactions on Pattern Analysis and Machine Intelligence, 27*(5), 812–816.

system. Vehicles had to stay on course and avoid unpredictable traffic without any human intervention, based only on the operation of onboard computer systems.

The winner of the race, a vehicle from Carnegie Mellon University, succeeded in staying on course and avoiding other cars while maintaining an average speed of 14 miles per hour. Vehicles from Stanford, Virginia Tech, MIT, Cornell, and the University of Pennsylvania also successfully completed the course, out of a total of 11 teams that qualified for the final race. **VL**

The feat of navigating through the environment, especially one that contains moving obstacles, is extremely impressive. However, even though these robotic vehicles were able to avoid obstacles along a defined pathway, they weren't able to identify most of the objects they were avoiding. For example, even though the Carnegie-Mellon car was able to avoid an obstacle in the middle of the road, it couldn't tell whether the obstacle was a pile of rocks, a bush, or a dog.

One object that has received a tremendous amount of attention from computer vision researchers is faces, in an effort to develop computer surveillance systems that can recognize faces. With large amounts of research invested in computer face recognition systems, new programs have been developed that can determine, as well as humans can, whether two faces that are seen straight on, as in **Figure 5.3a** and **b**, are the same or different people (O'Toole, 2007; O'Toole et al., 2007). However, when one of the faces is seen at an angle, as in **Figure 5.3c**, humans outperform computers.

Finally, computer vision systems specifically designed to determine the location of a room's walls and to locate furniture within the room are able to achieve these tasks crudely for some photographs, as in **Figure 5.4a**, but they often make large errors, as in **Figure 5.4b** (Pero et al., 2011). Although the location and extent of the bed in Figure 5.4b may be obvious to a person, it isn't so obvious to a computer, even though the computer program was specifically designed to detect objects like the bed that are defined by straight lines. Even if it could find the borders of the bed, determining the identity of other objects in the room is far beyond the capabilities of this state-of-the-art program.

Why Is It So Difficult to Design a Perceiving Machine?

We will now describe a few of the difficulties involved in designing a "perceiving machine." Remember that the point of these descriptions is that although they pose difficulties for computers, humans solve these problems easily.

The Stimulus on the Receptors Is Ambiguous

When you look at the page of this book, the image cast by the borders of the page on your retina is ambiguous. It may seem strange to say that, because once we know the shape of the

(a)   (b)

Figure 5.4 (a) The lines represent the attempt of a computer vision program to determine the corners of the room and the places where the wall, ceiling, and floor meet. In this example, the computer does a fairly good job. (b) Another example for the same computer vision program, in which the program's indications of the locations of straight-line contours in the room was inaccurate. From Pero, L. Del, Guan, J., Brau, E., Schlecht, J., & Barnard, K. (2011). Sampling bedrooms. *IEEE Computer Society Conference on Computer Vision and Pattern Recognition (CVPR)*, pp. 2009–2016. Reproduced by permission.

Image on retina

Figure 5.5 Determining the projection of an object on the retina is just a matter of extending rays from the object into the eye. © Cengage Learning

object and its distance from the eye, determining an object's image on the retina is a simple geometry problem, which can be solved by extending "rays" from the corners of the object into the eye, as shown in **Figure 5.5**.

But the perceptual system is not concerned with determining an object's image on the retina. It *starts* with the image on the retina, and its job is to determine the object "out there" that created the image. The task of determining the object responsible for a particular image on the retina is called the **inverse projection problem**, because it involves starting with the retinal image and extending rays *out* from the eye. When we do this, as shown in **Figure 5.6**, we see that

the rectangular page (in red) could have created the retinal image, but that a number of other objects, including a tilted trapezoid, a much larger rectangle, and an infinite number of other objects, could also have created that image. When we consider that a particular image on the retina can be created by many different objects in the environment, it is easy to see why we say that the image on the retina is ambiguous. **VL**

The ambiguity of the image on the retina is also illustrated by **Figure 5.7a**, which, when viewed from one specific location, creates a circular image on the retina and appears to be a circle of rocks. However, moving to another viewpoint reveals that the rocks aren't arranged in a circle after all (**Figure 5.7b**). Thus, just as a rectangular image on the retina can be created by trapezoids and other nonrectangular objects, a circular image on the retina can be created by objects that aren't circular.

The "environmental rock sculpture" in Figure 5.7 is designed to fool us by creating a special condition (viewing from a specific place) that results in an erroneous perception. But most of the time, erroneous perceptions such as this don't occur; the visual system solves the inverse projection problem and determines which object out of all the possible objects is responsible for a particular image on the retina.

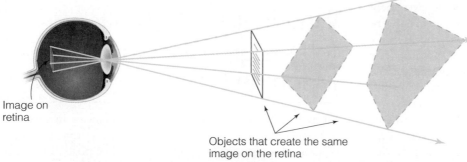

Image on retina

Objects that create the same image on the retina

Figure 5.6 The principle behind the inverse projection problem, in which the task is to determine which object created the image on the retina. This problem is difficult to solve because a particular image on the retina can be created by an infinite number of objects, among them the two rectangles and the tilted trapezoid shown here. This is why we say that the image on the retina is ambiguous.
© Cengage Learning

(a)　　　　　　　　　　　　　　(b)

Courtesy of Thomas Macaulay, Blackhawk Mountain School of Art, Blackhawk, CO

Figure 5.7 An environmental sculpture by Thomas Macaulay. (a) When viewed from exactly the right vantage point (the second-floor balcony of the Blackhawk Mountain School of Art, Black Hawk, Colorado), the stones appear to be arranged in a circle. (b) Viewing the stones from the ground floor reveals a truer indication of their configuration.

However, as easy as this is for the human perceptual system, solving the inverse projection problem poses serious challenges to computer vision systems.

Objects Can Be Hidden or Blurred

Sometimes objects are hidden or blurred. Can you find the pencil and eyeglasses in **Figure 5.8**? (Stop and try this before reading further.) Although it might take a little searching, people can find the pencil in the foreground and the glasses frame sticking out from behind the computer, even though only a small portion of these objects is visible. People also easily perceive the book, scissors, and paper as whole objects, even though they are partially hidden by other objects.

This problem of hidden objects occurs any time one object obscures part of another object. This occurs frequently in the environment, but people easily understand that the part of an object that is covered continues to exist, and they are able to use their knowledge of the environment to determine what is likely to be present.

People are also able to recognize objects that are not in sharp focus, such as the faces in **Figure 5.9**. See how many of these people you can identify, and then consult the answers on page 123. Despite the degraded nature of these images, people can often identify most of them, whereas computers perform poorly on this task (Sinha, 2002).

Objects Look Different From Different Viewpoints

Another problem facing any perceiving machine is that objects are often viewed from different angles. This means that the images of objects are continually changing, depending on the angle from which they are viewed.

Bruce Goldstein

Figure 5.8 A portion of the mess on the author's desk. Can you locate the hidden pencil (easy) and the author's glasses (hard)?

Figure 5.9 Who are these people? See page 123 for the answers.

From Sinha, P. (2002). Recognizing complex patterns. *Nature Neuroscience, 5,* 1093–1097. Reproduced by permission.

Although humans continue to perceive the object in **Figure 5.10** as the same chair viewed from different angles, this isn't so obvious to a computer. The ability to recognize an object seen from different viewpoints is called **viewpoint invariance**. We've already seen that viewpoint invariance enables people to tell whether faces seen from different angles

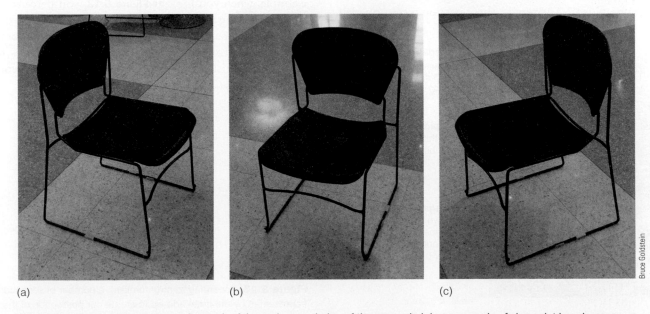

(a) (b) (c)

Bruce Goldstein

Figure 5.10 Your ability to recognize each of these views as being of the same chair is an example of viewpoint invariance.

are the same person, but this task is difficult for computers (refer back to Figure 5.3).

The difficulties facing any perceiving machine illustrate that the process of perception is more complex than it seems (something you already knew from the perceptual process in Figure 1.1 and the physiological material in Chapters 2–4). But how do humans overcome these complexities? We begin answering this question by considering *perceptual organization*.

Perceptual Organization

Perceptual organization is the process by which elements in the environment become perceptually grouped to create our perception of objects. During this process, incoming stimulation is organized into coherent units such as objects. The process of perceptual organization involves two components, *grouping* and *segregation* (**Figure 5.11**; Peterson & Kimchi, 2012). **Grouping** is the process by which visual events are "put together" into units or objects. Thus, when Roger sees each of the buildings in Pittsburgh as an individual unit, he has grouped the visual elements in the scene to create each building. If you can perceive the Dalmatian dog in **Figure 5.12**, you have perceptually grouped some of the dark areas to form a Dalmatian, with the other dark areas being seen as shadows on the ground. **VL**

The process of grouping works in conjunction with **segregation**, which is the process of separating one area or object from another. Thus, seeing two buildings in Figure 5.11 as separated from one another, with borders indicating where one building ends and the other begins, involves segregation.

The Gestalt Approach to Perceptual Grouping

What causes some elements to become grouped so they are part of one object? Answers to this question were provided

Figure 5.12 Some black and white shapes that become perceptually organized into a Dalmatian.

in the early 1900s by the **Gestalt psychologists**—where *Gestalt*, roughly translated, means *configuration*. "How," asked the Gestalt psychologists, "are configurations formed from smaller elements?"

Structuralism We can understand the Gestalt approach by first considering an approach that came before Gestalt psychology, called *structuralism*, which was proposed by Wilhelm Wundt, who established the first laboratory of scientific psychology at the University of Leipzig in 1879. **Structuralism** distinguished between **sensations**—elementary processes that occur due to stimulation of the senses—and *perceptions*, more complex conscious experiences such as our awareness of objects. Sensations might be linked to very simple experiences, such as seeing a single flash of light, but perception accounts for the vast majority of our sensory experiences. For example, when you look at **Figure 5.13**, you perceive a face, but the starting point, according to structuralism, would be many sensations, which are indicated by the small dots.

The structuralists saw sensations as analogous to the atoms of chemistry. Just as atoms combine to create complex

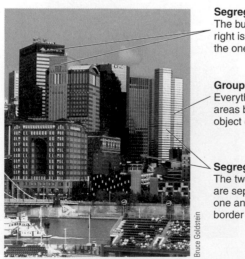

Segregation
The building on the right is in front of the one on the left.

Grouping
Everything in the white areas belongs to one object (the building).

Segregation
The two buildings are separated from one another, with a border between them.

Figure 5.11 Examples of grouping and segregation in a city scene.

Figure 5.13 According to structuralism, a number of sensations (represented by the dots) add up to create our perception of the face.
© Cengage Learning

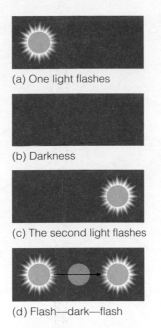

(a) One light flashes

(b) Darkness

(c) The second light flashes

(d) Flash—dark—flash

Figure 5.14 The conditions for creating apparent movement. (a) One light flashes, followed by (b) a short period of darkness, followed by (c) another light flashing in a different position. The resulting perception, symbolized in (d), is a light moving from left to right. Movement is seen between the two lights even though there is only darkness in the space between them. © Cengage Learning 2014

Corbis Bridge/Alamy

Figure 5.15 The stock ticker in Times Square, New York. The letters and numbers that appear to be moving smoothly across the screen are created by hundreds of small lights that are blinking on and off.

molecular structures, sensations combine to create complex perceptions. Another principle of structuralism is that the combination of sensations to form perceptions is aided by the observer's past experience.

The Gestalt psychologists rejected the idea that perceptions were formed by "adding up" sensations and also rejected past experience as playing a major role in perception. To see why the Gestalt psychologists felt that perceptions could not be explained by adding up small sensations, consider the experience of psychologist Max Wertheimer, who was on vacation taking a train ride through Germany in 1911 (Boring, 1942). When he got off the train to stretch his legs at Frankfurt, he bought a toy stroboscope from a vendor who was selling toys on the train platform. The stroboscope, a mechanical device that created an illusion of movement by rapidly alternating two slightly different pictures, caused Wertheimer to wonder how the structuralist idea that experience is created from sensations could explain the illusion of movement he observed.

Apparent Movement **Figure 5.14** diagrams the principle behind the illusion of movement created by the stroboscope, which is called **apparent movement** because although movement is perceived, nothing is actually moving. There are three components to stimuli that create apparent movement: (1) One image flashes on and off (**Figure 5.14a**); (2) there is a period of darkness, lasting a fraction of a second (**Figure 5.14b**); and (3) the second image flashes on and off (**Figure 5.14c**). Physically, therefore, there are two images flashing on and off

separated by a period of darkness. But we don't see the darkness because our perceptual system adds something during the period of darkness—the perception of an image moving through the space between the flashing images (**Figure 5.14d**). A modern example of apparent movement is provided by electronic signs like the one in **Figure 5.15**, which display moving advertisements or news headlines. The perception of movement in these displays is so compelling that it is difficult to imagine that they are made up of stationary lights flashing on and off.

Wertheimer drew two conclusions from the phenomenon of apparent movement. First, apparent movement can't be explained by sensations, because there is nothing in the dark space between the flashing images. Second, *the whole is different than the sum of its parts*, because the perceptual system creates the perception of movement where there actually is none. This idea that the whole is different than the sum of its parts became the battle cry of the Gestalt psychologists. "Wholes" were in. "Sensations" were out!

Illusory Contours Another demonstration that argues against sensations and for the idea that the whole is different than the sum of its parts is shown in **Figure 5.16**. This demonstration involves circles with a "mouth" cut out, which resemble "Pac Man" figures from the classic video game introduced in the 1980s. We begin with the Pac Men in **Figure 5.16a**. You may see an edge running between the "mouths" of the Pac Men, but if you cover up one of them, the edge vanishes. This single edge becomes part of a triangle when we add the third Pac Man, in **Figure 5.16b**. The three Pac Men have created the perception of a triangle, which becomes more obvious by adding lines, as shown in **Figure 5.16c**. The edges that create the triangle are called **illusory contours** because there are actually no physical edges present. Sensations can't explain illusory contours, because there aren't any sensations along the contours. This demonstration provides more evidence that the whole is different than the sum of its parts.

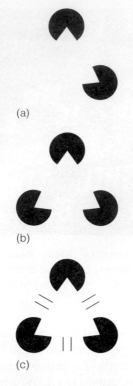

(a)

(b)

(c)

Figure 5.16 The illusory contours clearly visible in (b) and (c) cannot be caused by sensations, because there is only white there. © Cengage Learning 2014

Gestalt Organizing Principles

Having questioned the idea that perceptions are created by adding up sensations, the Gestalt psychologists proposed that perception depends on a number of **organizing principles**, which determine how elements in a scene become grouped together. The starting points for these principles are things that usually occur in the environment. Consider, for example, how you perceive the rope in **Figure 5.17a**. Although there are many places where one strand is overlapped by another strand, you probably perceive the rope not as a number of separate pieces but as a continuous strand, as illustrated by the highlighted segment of rope in **Figure 5.17b**. The Gestalt psychologists, being keen observers of perception, used this kind of observation to formulate the *principle of good continuation*.

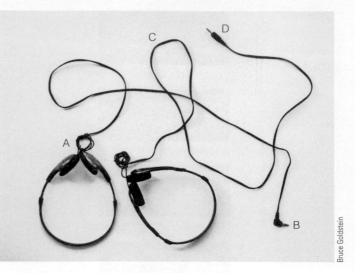

Figure 5.18 Good continuation helps us perceive two separate wires, even though they overlap.

Good Continuation According to the **principle of good continuation**, *points that when connected result in straight or smoothly curving lines are seen as belonging together, and the lines tend to be seen in such a way as to follow the smoothest path*. The principle operates on surfaces as well: *Objects that are partially covered by other objects are seen as continuing behind the covering object*. The rope in Figure 5.17 illustrates how covered objects are seen as continuing behind the object that covers them. The wire starting at A in **Figure 5.18** flowing smoothly to B is an example of lines following the smoothest path. The path from A does not go to C or D because those paths would violate good continuation by making sharp turns.

Pragnanz *Pragnanz*, roughly translated from the German, means "good figure." The **principle of pragnanz**, also called the **principle of good figure** or the **principle of simplicity**, is the central principle of Gestalt psychology: *Every stimulus pattern is seen in such a way that the resulting structure is as simple as possible*. The familiar Olympic symbol in **Figure 5.19a** is an example of the principle of simplicity at work. We see this display as five circles and not as a larger number of more complicated shapes such as the ones in **Figure 5.19b**.

(a)

(b)

Figure 5.17 (a) Rope on the beach. (b) Good continuation helps us perceive the rope as a single strand.

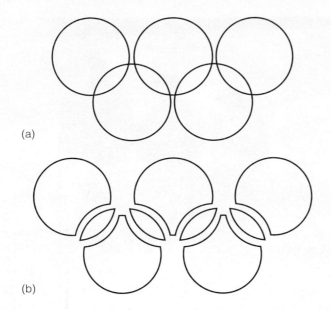

(a)

(b)

Figure 5.19 (a) This is usually perceived as five circles, not as the nine shapes in (b). © Cengage Learning

Figure 5.21 This photograph, *Waves*, by Wilma Hurskainen, was taken at the exact moment that the front of the white water aligned with the white area on the woman's clothing. Similarity of color causes grouping; differently colored areas of the dress are perceptually grouped with the same colors in the scene. Also notice how the front edge of the water creates grouping by good continuation across the woman's dress.

Good continuation is also at work here, creating the perception of smoothly curving lines that result in circles.

Similarity Most people perceive **Figure 5.20a** as either horizontal rows of circles, vertical columns of circles, or a square filled with evenly spaced dots. But when we change the color of some of the columns, as in **Figure 5.20b**, most people perceive vertical columns of circles. This perception illustrates the **principle of similarity**: *Similar things appear to be grouped together.* This law causes circles of the same color to be grouped together. A striking example of grouping by similarity of color is shown in **Figure 5.21**. Grouping can also occur because of similarity of shape, size, or orientation.

Grouping also occurs for auditory stimuli. For example, notes that have similar pitches and that follow each other closely in time can become perceptually grouped to form a melody. We will consider this and other auditory grouping effects when we describe organizational processes in hearing in Chapter 12.

Proximity (Nearness) Our perception of **Figure 5.22** as three groups of candles illustrates the **principle of proximity**,

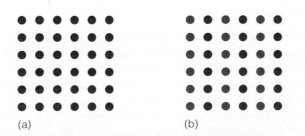

(a)   (b)

Figure 5.20 Perceived as horizontal rows or vertical columns or both. (b) Perceived as vertical columns. © Cengage Learning

Figure 5.22 The candles are grouped by proximity to create three separate groups. Can you identify additional Gestalt principles in the patterns on the menorah?

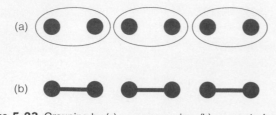

(a)

(b)

Figure 5.23 Grouping by (a) common region; (b) connectedness.
© Cengage Learning

Bruce Goldstein

Figure 5.24 A usual occurrence in the environment: Objects (the men's legs) are partially hidden by another object (the gray boards). In this example, the men's legs continue in a straight line and are the same color above and below the boards, so it is highly likely that they continue behind the boards.

or **nearness**: *Things that are near each other appear to be grouped together.*

Common Fate According to the **principle of common fate**, *things that are moving in the same direction appear to be grouped together.* Thus, when you see a flock of hundreds of birds all flying together, you tend to see the flock as a unit, and if some birds start flying in another direction, this creates a new unit. Note that common fate can work even if the objects in a group are dissimilar. The key to common fate is that a group of objects are moving in the same direction.

The principles we have just described were proposed by the Gestalt psychologists in the early 1900s. The following additional principles have been proposed by modern perceptual psychologists.

Common Region **Figure 5.23a** illustrates the **principle of common region**: *Elements that are within the same region of space appear to be grouped together.* Even though the circles inside the ovals are farther apart than the circles that are next to each other in neighboring ovals, we see the circles inside the ovals as belonging together. This occurs because each oval is seen as a separate region of space (Palmer, 1992; Palmer & Rock, 1994). Notice that in this example, common region overpowers proximity, because proximity would predict that the nearby circles would be perceived together. But even though the circles that are in different regions are close to each other in space, they do not group with each other, as they did in Figure 5.22.

Uniform Connectedness According to the **principle of uniform connectedness**, *a connected region of the same visual properties, such as lightness, color, texture, or motion, is perceived as a single unit* (Palmer & Rock, 1994). For example, in **Figure 5.23b**, the connected circles are perceived as grouped together, just as they were when they were in the same region in Figure 5.23a. Again, connectedness overpowers proximity.

The Gestalt principles we have described predict what we will perceive, based on what usually happens in the environment. Many of my students react to this idea by saying that the Gestalt principles aren't therefore anything special, because all they are doing is describing the obvious things we see every day. When they say this, I remind them that the reason we perceive scenes like the city buildings in Figure 5.2 or the scene in **Figure 5.24** so easily is because we use observations about commonly occurring properties of the environment

to organize the scene. Thus, we assume, without even thinking about it, that the men's legs in Figure 5.24 extend behind the gray board, because generally in the environment when two visible parts of an object (like the men's legs) have the same color and are "lined up," they belong to the same object and extend behind whatever is blocking it.

People don't usually think about how we perceive situations like this as being based on assumptions, but that is, in fact, what is happening. The reason the "assumption" seems so obvious is that we have had so much experience with things such as this in the environment. That the "assumption" is actually almost a "sure thing," may cause us to take the Gestalt principles for granted, and label them as "obvious." But the reality is that the Gestalt principles are nothing less than the basic operating characteristics of our visual system that determine how our perceptual system organizes elements of the environment into larger units.

Perceptual Segregation

The Gestalt psychologists were also interested in determining characteristics of the environment responsible for **perceptual segregation**—the perceptual separation of one object from another, as occurred when you saw the buildings in Figure 5.1 as separate from one another. The question of what causes perceptual segregation is often referred to as the problem of **figure–ground segregation**. When we see a separate object, it is usually seen as a **figure** that stands out from its background, which is called the **ground**. For example, you

Figure 5.25 A version of Rubin's reversible face-vase figure.
© Cengage Learning

would probably see a book or papers on your desk as figure and the surface of your desk as ground. The Gestalt psychologists were interested in determining the properties of the figure and the ground and what causes us to perceive one area as figure and the other as ground.

Properties of Figure and Ground One way the Gestalt psychologists studied the properties of figure and ground was by considering patterns like the one in **Figure 5.25**, which was introduced by Danish psychologist Edgar Rubin in 1915. This pattern is an example of **reversible figure–ground** because it can be perceived alternately either as two dark blue faces looking at each other, in front of a gray background, or as a gray vase on a dark blue background. Some of the properties of the figure and ground are:

■ The figure is more "thinglike" and more memorable than the ground. Thus, when you see the vase as figure, it appears as an object that can be remembered later. However, when you see the same light area as ground, it does not appear to be an object but is just "background" and is therefore not particularly memorable.

■ The figure is seen as being in front of the ground. Thus, when the vase is seen as figure, it appears to be in front of the dark background (**Figure 5.26a**), and when the

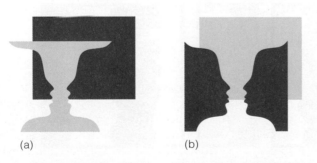

(a)   (b)

Figure 5.26 (a) When the vase is perceived as figure, it is seen in front of a homogeneous dark background. (b) When the faces are seen as figure, they are seen in front of a homogeneous light background.
© Cengage Learning

faces are seen as figure, they are on top of the light background (**Figure 5.26b**).

■ Near the borders it shares with the figure, the ground is seen as unformed material, without a specific shape, and seems to extend behind the figure. This is not to say that grounds lack shape entirely. They are often shaped by borders distant from those they share with the figure; for instance, the backgrounds in Figure 5.26 are square.

■ The border separating the figure from the ground appears to belong to the figure. Consider, for example, the Rubin face-vase in Figure 5.25. When the two faces are seen as figure, the border separating the blue faces from the grey background belongs to the faces. This property of the border belonging to one area is called **border ownership**. When perception shifts so the vase is perceived as figure, border ownership shifts as well, so now the border belongs to the face.

Image-Based Factors That Determine Which Area Is Figure The Gestalt psychologists specified a number of factors within the image that determine which areas are perceived as figure. This idea that information *in the image* determines perception is similar to the approach the Gestalt psychologists took to grouping, in which their principles all referred to how properties of the image determined which elements were seen as being grouped together.

One image-based factor proposed by the Gestalt psychologists was that areas lower in the field of view are more likely to be perceived as figure (Ehrenstein, 1930; Koffka, 1935). This idea was confirmed experimentally years later by Shaun Vecera and coworkers (2002), who flashed stimuli like the ones in **Figure 5.27a** for 150 milliseconds (ms) and

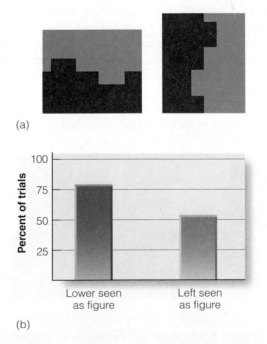

Figure 5.27 (a) Stimuli from Vecerra et al. (2002). (b) Percentage of trials on which lower or left areas were seen as figure. © Cengage Learning

Figure 5.28 The scene, in the bottom half of the visual field, is seen as figure. The sky, in the upper half of the visual field, is seen as ground.

determined which area was seen as figure, the red area or the green area. The results, shown in **Figure 5.27b**, indicate that for the upper–lower displays, observers were more likely to perceive the lower area as figure, but for the left–right displays, they showed only a small preference for the left region. From this result, Vecera concluded that there is no left–right preference for determining figure, but there is a definite preference for seeing objects lower in the display as figure. The conclusion from this experiment, that the lower region of a display tends to be seen as figure, makes sense when we consider a scene like the one in **Figure 5.28**, in which the lower part of the scene is figure and the sky is ground. What is significant about this scene is that it is typical of scenes we perceive every day. In our normal experience, the "figure" is much more likely to be below the horizon. **VL**

Another Gestalt proposal was that figures are more likely to be perceived on the convex side of borders (borders that bulge out) (Kanisza & Gerbino, 1976). Mary Peterson and Elizabeth Salvagio (2008) demonstrated this by presenting displays like the one in **Figure 5.29a** and asking observers to indicate whether the red square was "on" or "off" a perceived figure. Thus, if they perceived the dark area in this example as being a figure, they would say "on." If they perceived the dark area as ground, they would say "off." The result, in agreement with the Gestalt proposal, was that convex regions, like the

dark region in Figure 5.29a, were perceived as figure 89 percent of the time.

But Peterson and Salvagio went beyond simply confirming the Gestalt proposals by also presenting displays like the ones in **Figure 5.29b** and **c**, which had fewer components. Doing this greatly decreased the likelihood that convex displays would be seen as figure, with the convex region containing the red square in the two-component display being seen as figure only 58 percent of the time. What this result means, according to Peterson and Salvagio, is that to understand how segregation occurs we need to go beyond simply identifying factors like convexity. Apparently, segregation is determined not by just what is happening at a single border but by what is happening in the wider scene. This makes sense when we consider that perception generally occurs in scenes that extend over a wide area. We will return to this idea later in the chapter when we consider how we perceive scenes.

Subjective Factors That Determine Which Area Is Figure

Remember that the Gestalt psychologists disagreed with the structuralists' idea that perceptions were created by adding up sensations. They also disagreed with the idea that a person's past experience played an important role in determining perception, so visual elements that had been grouped previously would be more likely to be grouped when seen again.

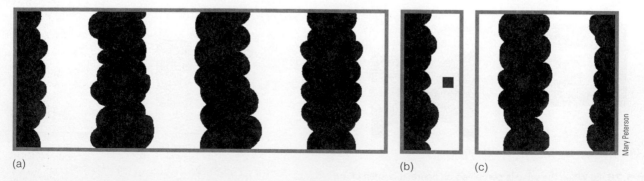

(a) (b) (c)

Figure 5.29 Stimuli from Peterson and Salvagio's (2008) experiment. (a) 8-component display; (b) 2-component display; (c) 4-component display. The red squares appeared on different areas on different trials. The subject's task was to judge whether the area the red square was on was "figure" or "ground."

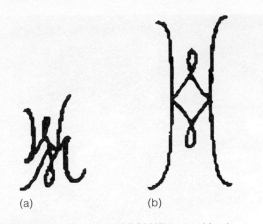

(a)   (b)

Figure 5.30 (a) "W" on top of "M." (b) When combined, a new pattern emerges, overriding the meaningful letters. From Wertheimer, M. (1912). Experimentelle Studien über das Sehen von Beuegung. *Zeitschrift für Psychologie, 61,* 161–265.

The following demonstration by the Gestalt psychologist Max Wertheimer (1912) illustrates how the Gestalt psychologists downplayed experience.

Wertheimer notes that we tend to perceive the display in **Figure 5.30a** as a "W" sitting on top of an "M," largely because of our past experiences with those two letters. However, when the *W* and *M* are arranged as in **Figure 5.30b**, we see two uprights with a pattern in between. Although we can tell where the *W* and *M* are if we look closely, the pattern with the two uprights is the dominant perception. Returning to the Gestalt organizing principles, Wertheimer said that the uprights are created by the principle of good continuation, and that this principle overrides any effects of past experience due to having seen *W*s or *M*s before.

The Gestalt idea that past experience and the meanings of stimuli (like the *W* and *M*) play a minor role in perceptual organization is also illustrated by the Gestalt proposal that one of the first things that occurs in the perceptual process is the segregation of figure from ground. They contended that the figure must stand out from the ground before it can be recognized. In other words, the figure has to be separated from the ground before we can assign a meaning to the figure.

But Bradley Gibson and Mary Peterson (1994) did an experiment that argued against this idea by showing that figure–ground formation can be affected by the meaningfulness of a stimulus. They demonstrated this by presenting a display like the one in **Figure 5.31a**, which can be perceived in two ways: (1) a standing woman (the black part of the display) or (2) a less meaningful shape (the white part of the display). When they presented stimuli such as this for a fraction of a second and asked observers which region seemed to be the figure, they found that observers were more likely to say that the meaningful part of the display (the woman, in this example) was the figure.

Why were the observers more likely to perceive the woman? One possibility is that they recognized that the black area was a familiar object. In fact, when Gibson and Peterson turned the display upside down, as in **Figure 5.31b**, so that it was more difficult to recognize the black area as a woman,

(a)   (b)

Figure 5.31 Gibson and Peterson's (1994) stimulus. (a) The black area is more likely to be seen as figure because it is meaningful; (b) this effect doesn't occur when meaningfulness is decreased by turning the picture upside down.

subjects were less likely to see that area as being the figure. The fact that meaningfulness can influence the assignment of an area as figure means that the process of recognition must be occurring either before or at the same time as the figure is being separated from the ground (Peterson, 1994, 2001).

Gibson and Peterson were studying rapid processes that operate on a time scale of fractions of a second to determine figure and ground. The next demonstration illustrates how meaning can influence perceptual organization on a longer time scale, when it is initially difficult to perceive figures hidden in the scene.

DEMONSTRATION

Finding Faces in a Landscape

Consider the picture in **Figure 5.32**. At first glance, this scene appears to contain mainly trees, rocks, and water. But on closer inspection, you can see some faces in the trees in the background, and if you look more closely, you can see that a number of faces are formed by various groups of rocks. See if you can find all 13 faces hidden in this picture.

Some people find it difficult to perceive the faces at first, but then suddenly they succeed. The change in perception from "rocks in a stream" or "trees in a forest" to "faces" is a change in the perceptual organization of the rocks and the trees. The two shapes that you at first perceive as two separate

Figure 5.32 *The Forest Has Eyes* by Bev Doolittle (1984). Can you find 13 faces in this picture? Email the author at bruceg@email.arizona.edu for the solution.

The Forest Has Eyes by Bev Doolittle (1984)

rocks in the stream become perceptually grouped together when they become the left and right eyes of a face. In fact, once you perceive a particular grouping of rocks as a face, it is often difficult *not* to perceive them in this way—they have become permanently organized into a face. This is similar to the process we observed for the Dalmatian. Once we see the Dalmatian, it is difficult not to perceive it.

The principles and research we have been describing have focused largely on how our perception of individual objects depends on organizing principles and on the principles that determine which parts of a display will be seen as figure and which will be seen as ground. If you look back at the illustrations in this section, you will notice that most of them are simple displays designed to illustrate a specific principle of perceptual organization. But to truly understand perception as it occurs in the environment, we need to expand our view to consider not just individual objects, but more complex scenes as well.

TEST YOURSELF 5.1

1. What are some of the problems that make object perception difficult for computers but not for humans?

2. What is structuralism, and why did the Gestalt psychologists propose an alternative to this way of explaining perception?

3. How did the Gestalt psychologists explain perceptual organization?

4. How did the Gestalt psychologists describe figure–ground segregation? What are some basic properties of figure and ground?

5. What image-based properties of a stimulus tend to favor perceiving an area as "figure"? Be sure you understand Vecera's experiment that showed that the lower region of a display tends to be perceived as figure, and why Peterson and Salvagio stated that to understand how segregation occurs we have to consider what is happening in the wider scene.

6. Describe the Gestalt ideas about the role of meaning and past experience in determining figure–ground segregation.

7. Describe Gibson and Peterson's experiment that showed that meaning can play a role in figure–ground segregation.

8. What does the Bev Doolittle scene in Figure 5.32 demonstrate?

Perceiving Scenes and Objects in Scenes

Our discussion of organization and figure–ground described how our perception is influenced by characteristics such as nearness, good continuation, and similarity; higher or lower in the visual field; convexity or concavity of borders. But at the end of this discussion, we also noted that the *meaning* of a stimulus can affect both figure–ground formation (Gibson and Peterson's experiment) and our perception of objects in a scene (the "Finding Faces" demonstration). Meaning now takes center stage in our discussion, as we describe modern research on how observers perceive objects and scenes.

A **scene** is a view of a real-world environment that contains (1) background elements and (2) multiple objects that are organized in a meaningful way relative to each other and the background (Epstein, 2005; Henderson & Hollingworth, 1999). One way of distinguishing between objects and scenes is that objects are compact and are *acted upon*, whereas scenes are extended in space and are *acted within*. For example, if we are walking down the street and mail a letter, we would be *acting upon* the mailbox (an object) and *acting within* the street (the scene).

Perceiving the Gist of a Scene

Perceiving scenes presents a paradox. On one hand, scenes are often large and complex. However, despite this size and complexity, you can identify most scenes after viewing them for only a fraction of a second. This general description of the type of scene is called the **gist of a scene**. An example of your ability to rapidly perceive the gist of a scene is the way you can rapidly flip from one TV channel to another, yet still grasp the meaning of each picture as it flashes by—a car chase, quiz contestants, or an outdoor scene with mountains—even though you may be seeing each picture for a second or less and so may not be able to identify specific objects. When you do this, you are perceiving the gist of each scene (Oliva & Torralba, 2006).

Research has shown that it is possible to perceive the gist of a scene within a fraction of a second. Mary Potter (1976) showed observers a target picture and then asked them to indicate whether they saw that picture as they viewed a sequence of 16 rapidly presented pictures. Her observers could do this with almost 100 percent accuracy even when the pictures were flashed for only 250 ms (milliseconds; 1/4 second). Even when the target picture was only specified by a written description, such as "girl clapping," observers achieved an accuracy of almost 90 percent (**Figure 5.33**).

Another approach to determining how rapidly people can perceive scenes was used by Li Fei-Fei and coworkers (2007), who presented pictures of scenes for exposures ranging from 27 ms to 500 ms and asked observers to write a description of what they saw. This method of determining the observer's response is a nice example of the phenomenological method, described on page 17. Fei-Fei used a procedure called *masking* to be sure the observers saw the pictures for exactly the desired duration.

METHOD
Using a Mask to Achieve Brief Stimulus Presentations

What if we want to present a stimulus that is visible for only 100 ms? Although you might think that the way to do this would be a flash a stimulus for 100 ms, this won't work because of a phenomenon called persistence of vision—the perception of a visual stimulus continues for about 250 ms (1/4 second) after the stimulus is extinguished. Thus, a picture that is presented for 100 ms will be *perceived* as lasting about 350 ms. But the persistence of vision can be eliminated by presenting a visual masking stimulus, usually a random pattern that covers the original stimulus, so if a picture is flashed for 100 ms followed immediately by a masking stimulus, the picture is visible for just 100 ms. A masking stimulus is therefore often presented immediately after a test stimulus to stop the persistence of vision from increasing the duration of the test stimulus.

Typical results of Fei-Fei's experiment are shown in **Figure 5.34**. At brief durations, observers saw only light and dark areas of the pictures. By 67 ms they could identify some large objects (a person, a table), and when the duration was increased to 500 ms (half a second) they were able to identify smaller objects and details (the boy, the laptop). For a picture of an ornate 1800s living room, observers were able to identify the picture as a room in a house at 67 ms and to identify details, such as chairs and portraits, at 500 ms. Thus, the overall gist of the scene is perceived first, followed by perception of details and smaller objects within the scene. **VL**

Girl clapping

Description   250 ms   250 ms   250 ms

Figure 5.33 Procedure for Potter's (1976) experiment. She first presented either a target photograph or, as shown here, a description, and then rapidly presented 16 pictures for 250 ms each. The observer's task was to indicate whether the target picture had been presented. In this example, only 3 of the 16 pictures are shown, with the target picture being the second one presented. On other trials, the target picture is not included in the series of 16 pictures.

27 ms	Looked like something black in the center with four straight lines coming out of it against a white background. (Subject: AM)
40 ms	The first thing I could recognize was a dark splotch in the middle. It may have been rectangular-shaped, with a curved top... but that's just a guess. (Subject: KM)
67 ms	A person, I think, sitting down or crouching. Facing the left side of the picture. We see their profile mostly. They were at a table or where some object was in front of them (to their left side in the picture). (Subject: EC)
500 ms	This looks like a father or somebody helping a little boy. The man had something in his hands, like a LCD screen or a laptop. They looked like they were standing in a cubicle. (Subject: WC)

Figure 5.34 Observer's description of a photograph presented in Fei Fei's (2007) experiment. Viewing durations are indicated on the left. From Fei-Fei, L., Iyer, A., Koch C., & Perona, P. (2007). What do we perceive in a glance of a real world scene? *Journal of Vision*, 7, 1–29, Figure 13. © ARVO.

What enables observers to perceive the gist of a scene so rapidly? Aude Oliva and Antonio Torralba (2001, 2006) propose that observers use information called **global image features**, which can be perceived rapidly and are associated with specific types of scenes. Some of the global image features proposed by Oliva and Torralba are:

- *Degree of naturalness.* Natural scenes, such as the ocean and forest in **Figure 5.35**, have textured zones and undulating contours. Man-made scenes, such as the street, are dominated by straight lines and horizontals and verticals.

- *Degree of openness.* Open scenes, such as the ocean, often have a visible horizon line and contain few objects. The street scene is also open, although not as much as the ocean scene. The forest is an example of a scene with a low degree of openness.

- *Degree of roughness.* Smooth scenes (low roughness) like the ocean contain fewer small elements. Scenes with high roughness like the forest contain many small elements and are more complex.

- *Degree of expansion.* The convergence of parallel lines, like what you see when you look down railroad tracks that appear to vanish in the distance, or in the street scene in Figure 5.35, indicates a high degree of expansion. This feature is especially dependent on the observer's viewpoint. For example, in the street scene, looking directly at the side of a building would result in low expansion.

- *Color.* Some scenes have characteristic colors, like the ocean scene (blue) and the forest (green and brown) (Goffaux et al., 2005).

Global image features are *holistic* and *rapidly perceived.* They are properties of the scene as a whole and do not depend on time-consuming processes such as perceiving small details, recognizing individual objects, or separating one object from another. Another property of global image features is that they contain information about a scene's structure and spatial layout. For example, the degree of openness and the degree of expansion refer directly to characteristics of a scene's layout, and naturalness also provides layout information that comes from knowing whether a scene is "from nature" or contains "human-made structures."

Global image properties not only help explain how we can perceive the gist of scenes based on features that can be seen in brief exposures, they also illustrate the following general property of perception: Our past experiences in perceiving properties of the environment play a role in determining our perceptions. We learn, for example, that blue is associated with open sky, that landscapes are often green and smooth, and that verticals and horizontals are associated with buildings. Characteristics of the environment such as this, which occur frequently, are called **regularities in the environment**. We will now describe these regularities in more detail.

Regularities in the Environment: Information for Perceiving

Although people make use of regularities in the environment to help them perceive, they are often unaware of the specific information they are using. This aspect of perception is similar to what occurs when we use language. Even though people

Figure 5.35 Three scenes that have different global image properties. See text for description.

Courtesy of Aude Oliva

Figure 5.36 Objects in the environment often have homogeneous colors. See text for details.

easily string words together to create sentences in conversations, they may not know the rules of grammar that specify how these words are being combined. Similarly, we easily use our knowledge of regularities in the environment to help us perceive, even though we may not be able to identify the specific information we are using. We can distinguish two types of regularities: *physical regularities* and *semantic regularities*. **VL**

Physical Regularities Physical regularities are regularly occurring physical properties of the environment. For example, there are more vertical and horizontal orientations in the environment than oblique (angled) orientations. This occurs in human-made environments (for example, buildings contain many horizontals and verticals) and also in natural environments (trees and plants are more likely to be vertical or horizontal than slanted) (Coppola et al., 1998). It is, therefore, no coincidence that people can perceive horizontals and

verticals more easily than other orientations—the oblique effect we introduced in Chapter 1 (see page 11) (Appelle, 1972; Campbell et al., 1966; Orban et al., 1984).

Another physical regularity is that objects in the environment often have homogeneous colors and nearby objects have different colors. Thus, if we pick a point on the scene in **Figure 5.36** (such as A) and move slightly away from that point (to B), it is likely that the two points are on the same object if the color is the same. If, however, we move to C, the color changes, which means it is likely we are looking at a different object. While you are looking at this scene, see if you can find examples of good continuation and good figure.

The following demonstration illustrates yet another physical regularity.

DEMONSTRATION
Shape From Shading

What do you perceive in **Figure 5.37a**? Do some of the discs look as though they are sticking out, like parts of three-dimensional spheres, and others appear to be indentations? If you do see the discs in this way, notice that the ones that appear to be sticking out are arranged in a square. After observing this, turn the page over so the small dot is on the bottom. Does this change your perception?

Figures 5.37b and c show that if we assume that light is coming from above (which is usually the case in the environment), then patterns like the circles that are light on the top would be created by an object that bulges out (**Figure 5.37b**), but a pattern like the circles that are light on the bottom would be created by an indentation in a surface (**Figure 5.37c**). The assumption that light is coming from above has been called the **light-from-above assumption** (Kleffner & Ramachandran, 1992). Apparently, people make the light-from-above assumption because most light in our environment comes from above. This includes the sun, as well as most artificial light sources.

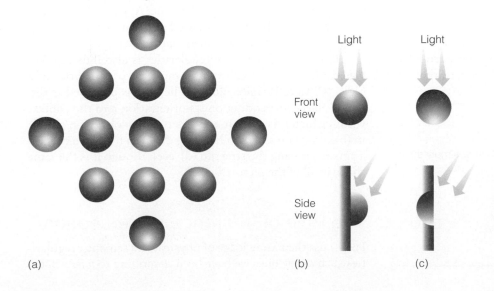

Figure 5.37 (a) Some of these discs are perceived as jutting out and some are perceived as indentations. (b) Explanation for your perception of (a). Light coming from above will illuminate the top of a shape that is jutting out and (c) the bottom of an indentation. © Cengage Learning

(a)

(b)

Figure 5.38 Why does (a) look like indentations in the sand and (b) look like mounds of sand? See the text for explanation.

Bruce Goldstein

Another example of the light-from-above assumption at work is provided by the two pictures in **Figure 5.38**. **Figure 5.38a** shows indentations created by people walking in the sand. But when we turn this picture upside down, as in **Figure 5.38b**, then the indentations in the sand become rounded mounds.

It is clear from these examples of physical regularities in the environment that one of the reasons humans are able to perceive and recognize objects and scenes so much better than computer-guided robots is that our system is customized to respond to the physical characteristics of our environment. But this customization goes beyond physical characteristics. It also occurs because we have learned about what types of objects typically occur in specific types of scenes.

Semantic Regularities In language, *semantics* refers to the meanings of words or sentences. Applied to perceiving scenes, semantics refers to the meaning of a scene. This meaning is often related to the function of a scene—what happens within it. For example, food preparation, cooking, and perhaps eating occur in a kitchen; waiting around, buying tickets, checking luggage, and going through security checkpoints happens in airports. **Semantic regularities** are the characteristics associated with the functions carried out in different types of scenes.

One way to demonstrate that people are aware of semantic regularities is simply to ask them to imagine a particular type of scene or object, as in the following demonstration.

DEMONSTRATION
Visualizing Scenes and Objects

Your task in this demonstration is simple—visualize or simply think about the following scenes and objects:

1. An office
2. The clothing section of a department store
3. A microscope
4. A lion

Most people who have grown up in modern society have little trouble visualizing an office or the clothing section of a department store. What is important about this ability, for our purposes, is that part of this visualization involves details within these scenes. Most people see an office as having a desk with a computer on it, bookshelves, and a chair. The department store scene may contain racks of clothes, a changing room, and perhaps a cash register.

What did you see when you visualized the microscope or the lion? Many people report seeing not just a single object, but an object within a setting. Perhaps you perceived the microscope sitting on a lab bench or in a laboratory, and the lion in a forest or on a savannah or in a zoo.

An example of the knowledge we have of things that typically belong in certain scenes is provided by a classic experiment by Stephen Palmer (1975), using stimuli like the picture in **Figure 5.39**. Palmer first presented a context scene such as the one on the left and then briefly flashed one of the target pictures on the right. When Palmer asked observers to identify the object in the target picture, they correctly identified an object like the loaf of bread (which is appropriate to the kitchen scene) 80 percent of the time, but correctly identified the mailbox or the drum (two objects that don't fit into the scene) only 40 percent of the time. Apparently, Palmer's observers were using their knowledge about kitchens to help them perceive the briefly flashed loaf of bread.

The effect of semantic regularities is also illustrated in **Figure 5.40**, which is called "the multiple personalities of a blob" (Oliva & Torralba, 2007). The blob is perceived as different objects depending on its orientation and the context within which it is seen. It appears to be an object on a table in (b), a shoe on a person bending down in (c), and a car and a person crossing the street in (d), even though it is the same shape in all of the pictures. **VL**

The Role of Inference in Perception

People use their knowledge of physical and semantic regularities such as the ones we have been describing to *infer* what is

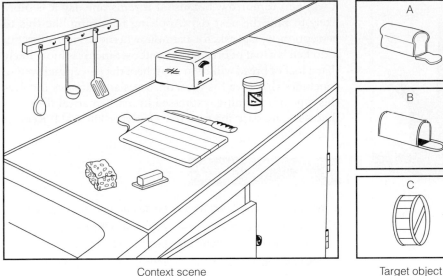

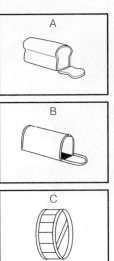

Figure 5.39 Stimuli used in Palmer's (1975) experiment. The scene at the left is presented first, and the observer is then asked to identify one of the objects on the right. © Cengage Learning

present in a scene. The idea that perception involves inference is nothing new; it was proposed in the 18th century by Hermann von Helmholtz (1866/1911), who was one of the preeminent physiologists and physicists of his day.

Helmholtz made many discoveries in physiology and physics, developed the ophthalmoscope (the device that an optometrist or ophthalmologist uses to look into your eyes), and proposed theories of object perception, color vision, and hearing. One of his proposals about perception is a principle called the **theory of unconscious inference**, which states that some of our perceptions are the result of unconscious assumptions we make about the environment.

The theory of unconscious inference was proposed to account for our ability to create perceptions from stimulus information that can be seen in more than one way. For example, what do you see in the display in **Figure 5.41a**? Most people perceive a blue rectangle in front of a red rectangle, as shown in **Figure 5.41b**. But as **Figure 5.41c** indicates, this display could have been caused by a six-sided red shape positioned either in front of or behind the blue rectangle. According to the theory of unconscious inference, we infer that Figure 5.41a is a rectangle covering another rectangle because of experiences we have had with similar situations in the past. A corollary of the theory of unconscious inference is the **likelihood principle**, which states that we perceive the object that is *most likely* to have caused the pattern of stimuli we have received. Thus, we perceive Figure 5.41a as a blue rectangle in front of a red rectangle because it is *most likely*, based on our past experience, to have caused that pattern.

One reason that Helmholtz proposed the likelihood principle is to deal with the ambiguity of the perceptual stimulus that we described at the beginning of the chapter. Helmholtz viewed the process of perception as being similar

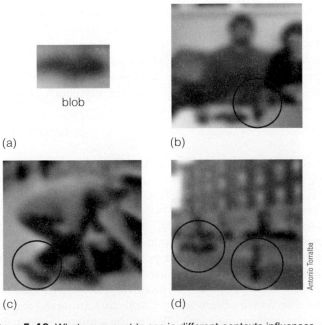

blob

(a)

(b)

(c)

(d)

Antonio Torralba

Figure 5.40 What we expect to see in different contexts influences our interpretation of the identity of the "blob" inside the circles.

Part (d) adapted from Oliva, A., & Torralba, A., The role of context in object recognition, *Trends in Cognitive Sciences*, Vol. 11, 12. Copyright 2007, with permission from Elsevier.

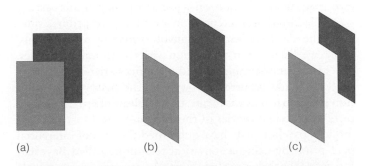

(a)

(b)

(c)

Figure 5.41 The display in (a) is usually interpreted as being (b) a blue rectangle in front of a red rectangle. It could, however, be (c) a blue rectangle and an appropriately positioned six-sided red figure.

© Cengage Learning

Figure 5.42 (a) What lurks behind the tree? (b) It is two strangely shaped tree trunks, not an animal! © Cengage Learning

to the process involved in solving a problem. For perception, the task is to determine which object caused a particular pattern of stimulation, and this problem is solved by a process in which the observer brings his or her knowledge of the environment to bear in order to infer what the object might be.

Consider, for example, the following situation: As you are hiking in the woods, you stop cold in your tracks because not too far ahead you see what appears to be an animal lurking behind a tree (**Figure 5.42a**). This conclusion is based on a number of factors. Seeing the shapes to the left and right of the tree as a single object is inferred from the Gestalt organizing principles of similarity (both shapes are the same color so it is likely that they are part of the same object) and good continuation (the line across the top of the object extends smoothly from one side of the tree to another). In addition, the image resembles animals you've seen before. Because you fear the animal might be dangerous, you take a different path. As your detour takes you around the tree, you notice that the dark shapes aren't an animal after all, but are two oddly shaped tree stumps (**Figure 5.42b**). So in this case, the outcome of your inferential process has led you astray. This should be no surprise, because not all inferences are true. But because perceptual inferences are based on our vast storehouse of information about what usually occurs in the environment, they are right more often than not. (And what if the object behind the tree was an unfriendly creature? Perhaps erring on the side of caution is the best policy in this case.)

This idea that inference is involved in perception is similar to the idea that perception involves making assumptions, which we discussed in connection with the Gestalt principles. The idea that assumptions and inferences are important for perception has recurred throughout the history of perception research in various forms, from Helmholtz to the Gestalt principles to regularities of the environment. Most recently, modern psychologists have quantified the idea of inferential perception by using a statistical technique called **Bayesian inference** that takes probabilities into account (Kersten et al., 2004; Yuille & Kersten, 2006). For example, let's say we want to determine how likely it is that it will rain tomorrow. If we know it rained today, then this increases the chances that

it will rain tomorrow, because if it rains one day it is more likely to rain the next day. Applying reasoning like this to perception, we can ask, for example, whether a given object in a kitchen is a loaf of bread or a mailbox. Since it is more likely that a loaf of bread will be in a kitchen, the perceptual system concludes that bread is present. Bayesian statistics involves this type of reasoning, expressed in mathematical formulas that we won't describe here (see Geisler, 2008, 2011; Kersten et al., 2004).

TEST YOURSELF 5.2

1. What is a "scene," and how is it different from an "object"?
2. What is the evidence that we can perceive the gist of a scene very rapidly? What information helps us identify the gist?
3. What are regularities in the environment? Give examples of physical regularities, and discuss how these regularities are related to the Gestalt laws of organization.
4. What are semantic regularities? How do semantic regularities affect our perception of objects within scenes? What is the relation between semantic regularities and the idea that perception involves inference?
5. What did Helmholtz have to say about inference and perception?
6. What is Bayesian inference, and how is it related to Helmholtz's ideas about inference?

Connecting Neural Activity and Object Perception

So far in our discussion of objects and scenes, we have focused on how perception is determined by aspects of *stimuli*. In fact, the words *neuron* and *brain* haven't appeared even once! Now it is time to consider the relationship between physiological processes and the perception of objects. This relationship has been studied in a number of different ways, both in animals (mostly monkeys) and in humans.

Brain Activity and Identifying a Picture

In the first experiment we will describe, Kalanit Grill-Spector and coworkers (2004) were interested in determining the relationship between the brain activation that occurs when looking at an object and a person's ability to identify the object. The "object" they used were pictures of Harrison Ford's face. They presented pictures, as shown in **Figure 5.43**, to observers in a brain scanner while measuring the response of the fusiform face area (FFA) in the temporal lobe to each picture. On each trial, observers saw either (a) a picture of Harrison Ford, (b) a picture of another person's face, or (c) a random texture. Each of these stimuli was presented briefly

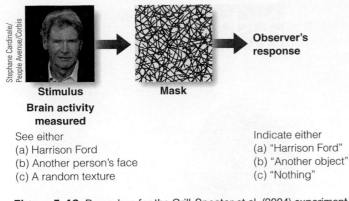

Brain activity measured

See either
(a) Harrison Ford
(b) Another person's face
(c) A random texture

Indicate either
(a) "Harrison Ford"
(b) "Another object"
(c) "Nothing"

Figure 5.43 Procedure for the Grill-Spector et al. (2004) experiment. See text for details. © Cengage Learning

(about 50 ms), followed immediately by a random-pattern mask, which limited the visibility of each stimulus to just 50 ms (see Method: Using a Mask to Achieve Brief Stimulus Presentations, page 109).

Limiting the visibility to 50 ms made the stimuli difficult to identify, so the observer's task, to indicate whether each picture was "Harrison Ford," "another object," or "nothing," was not easy. **Figure 5.44** shows the course of brain activation for the trials in which Harrison Ford's face was presented. The top curve (red) shows that activation was greatest when observers correctly identified the picture as Harrison Ford's face. The next curve shows that activation was less when they responded "other object" to Harrison Ford's face. In this case, they detected the picture as a face but were not able

to identify it as Harrison Ford's face. The lowest curve indicates that there was little activation when observers could not even tell that a face was presented.

Remember that all of the curves in Figure 5.44 represent the brain activity that occurred *during presentation of Harrison Ford's face*. These results therefore show that neural activity that occurs *as a person is looking at a stimulus* is related to that person's ability to identify the stimulus. A large neural response is associated with processing that results in the ability to *identify* the stimulus; a smaller response, with *detecting* the stimulus; and the absence of a response with missing the stimulus altogether. This is important because it shows that how the brain reacts to a stimulus *as it is being presented* determines our ability to identify the stimulus.

Brain Activity and Seeing

The Harrison Ford experiment presented stimuli that were quickly flashed and so were difficult to see. Another approach to studying the relationship between brain activity and vision is to look for connections between brain activity and stimuli that are easy to see. We will describe two experiments, one on a monkey and one on a human, both of which make use of a technique in which different images are presented to the left and right eyes.

In normal everyday perception, our two eyes receive slightly different images because the eyes are in two slightly different locations. These two images are, however, similar enough so they can be combined into a single perception by the brain. (We will describe this process of combining these images, which is called *binocular fusion*, in Chapter 10, when we discuss depth perception.)

But if each eye receives totally different images, the brain can't fuse the two images and a condition called **binocular rivalry** occurs, in which the observer perceives either the left-eye image or the right-eye image, but not both at the same time.

D. L. Sheinberg and Nikos Logothetis (1997) used this principle, presenting a sunburst pattern to a monkey's left eye and simultaneously presenting a picture of a butterfly to the monkey's right eye (**Figure 5.45**). Presenting different pictures to each eye caused the monkey to see the sunburst for part of the time and the butterfly for part of the time, but not both together.[1]

To determine what the monkey was perceiving, they trained the monkey to pull one lever when it perceived the sunburst pattern and another lever when it perceived the butterfly. As the monkey was reporting what it was perceiving, they simultaneously recorded the activity of a neuron in the inferotemporal (IT) cortex that had previously been shown to respond to the butterfly but not to the sunburst. The result

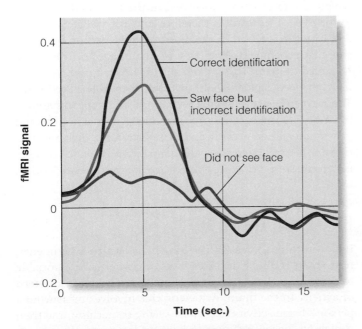

Figure 5.44 Results of Grill-Spector et al. (2004) experiment for trials in which Harrison Ford's face was presented. From Grill-Spector, K., Knouf, N., & Kanwisher, N., The fusiform face area subserves face perception, not generic within-category identification, *Nature Neuroscience, 7,* 555–562. Reprinted by permission from Macmillan Publisher Ltd. Copyright 2004.

---

[1]This "all or none" effect of rivalry, in which one image is seen at a time (either the sunburst or the butterfly), occurs most reliably when the images presented to each eye cover a small area of the visual field. When larger images are presented, observers sometimes see parts of the two images at the same time. In the experiments described here, observers generally saw either one image or the other, alternating back and forth.

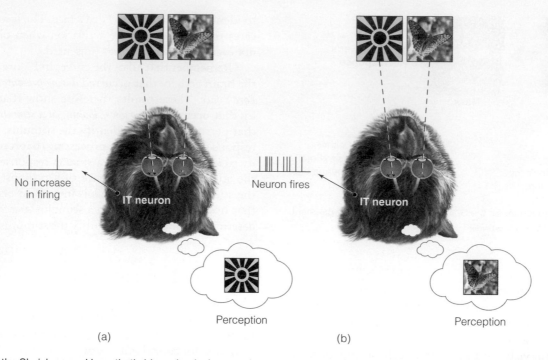

(a)   (b)

Figure 5.45 In the Sheinberg and Logothetis binocular rivalry experiment a "sunburst" stimulus was presented to the monkey's left eye, and a butterfly was presented to the right eye. Both eyes were stimulated at the same time, but because of binocular rivalry the monkey perceived either the sunburst or the butterfly at any given time. (a) When the monkey perceived the sunburst, the rate of firing of the neuron in the IT cortex remained the same. (b) When perception shifted to the butterfly, firing increased. In both situations, the images on the retina remained the same. What changed was the monkey's perception and neural firing. Based on Sheinberg, D. L., & Logothetis, N. K. (1997). The role of temporal cortical areas in perceptual organization. *Proceedings of the National Academy of Sciences, 94*, 3408–3413. Butterfly photo: Randy Baker.

of this experiment is indicated by the firing pattern in Figure 5.45: Whenever the monkey perceived the sunburst, the neuron's firing rate was low, but when the monkey's perception shifted to the butterfly, firing increased.

Consider what happened in this experiment. The images on the monkey's retinas remained the same throughout the experiment—the sunburst was always imaged on the left retina, and the butterfly was always imaged on the right retina. The change in perception from "sunburst" to "butterfly" must therefore have been happening in the monkey's brain, and these changes in the perception were linked to changes in the firing of a neuron in the brain.

This binocular rivalry procedure has also been used to connect perception and neural responding in humans by using fMRI. Frank Tong and coworkers (1998) presented a picture of a person's face to one eye and a picture of a house to the other eye, by having observers view the pictures through colored glasses, as shown in **Figure 5.46**. The colored glasses caused the face to be presented to the left eye and the house to the right eye. Because each eye received a different image, binocular rivalry occurred, so while the images remained the same on the retina, observers perceived just the face or just the house, and these perceptions alternated back and forth every few seconds.

The subjects pushed one button when they perceived the house and another button when they perceived the face, while Tong used fMRI to measure activity in the subject's

parahippocampal place area (PPA) and fusiform face area (FFA). When observers were perceiving the house, activity increased in the PPA (and decreased in the FFA); when they were perceiving the face, activity increased in the FFA (and decreased in the PPA). This result is therefore similar to what Sheinberg and Logothetis found in the monkey single neuron butterfly-sunburst experiment. Even though the images on the retina remained the same throughout the experiment, activity in the brain changed depending on what the person was experiencing. These experiments generated a great deal of excitement among brain researchers because they measured brain activation and perception simultaneously and demonstrated a dynamic relationship between perception and brain activity in which changes in perception and changes in brain activity mirrored each other.

Reading the Brain

Following the success of the binocular rivalry experiments, researchers took the next step by asking whether it is possible to determine what a person is seeing by analyzing the pattern of activity in the brain. Achieving this involves measuring a person's brain activity as they are seeing something, and then somehow "decoding" that activity to determine the perception associated with it.

An early "brain reading" experiment simplified the problem by limiting what the subject sees to oriented grating

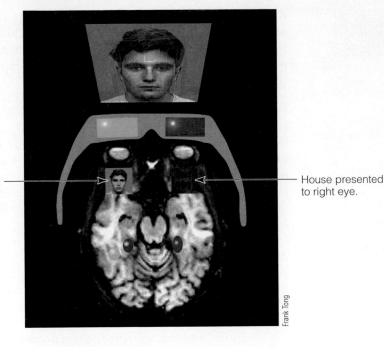

Face presented to left eye.

House presented to right eye.

Frank Tong

Figure 5.46 Observers in Tong et al.'s (1998) experiment viewed the overlapping red house and green face through red–green glasses, so the house image was presented to the right eye and the face image to the left eye. Because of binocular rivalry, the observers' perception alternated back and forth between the face and the house. When the observers perceived the house, activity occurred in the parahippocampal place area (PPA) in the left and right hemispheres (red ellipses). When observers perceived the face, activity occurred in the fusiform face area (FFA) in the left hemisphere (green ellipse). From Tong, F., Nakayama, K., Vaughn, J. T., & Kanwisher, N., 1998, Binocular rivalry and visual awareness in human extrastriate cortex. *Neuron, 21,* 753–759.

stimuli like the one in **Figure 5.47**. Kamitani and Tong (2005) recorded their subjects' fMRI responses to a number of gratings with different orientations (the one in **Figure 5.47a** is 45 degrees to the right) and determined the response to the gratings in a number of fMRI voxels. A *voxel* is a small cube-shaped area of the brain about 2 or 3 mm on each side. (The size of a voxel depends on the resolution of the fMRI scanner. Scanners are being developed that will be able to resolve areas smaller than 2 or 3 mm on a side.) **VL**

Kamitani and Tong determined the pattern of voxel activity generated by each orientation and used the relationship between voxel activity and orientation to create an "orientation decoder." This decoder was designed to determine, from a person's brain response, which orientation the person was seeing. To test the decoder, they presented oriented gratings to a subject, fed the resulting fMRI response into the decoder, and had the decoder predict the grating's orientation. The results, shown in **Figure 5.47b**, indicate that the decoder accurately predicted the orientations that were presented.

The development of a decoder that could determine what orientation a person was perceiving was an impressive achievement. But what about complex stimuli like scenes in the environment? Expanding our stimulus set from eight grating orientations to every possible scene in the environment is quite a jump! But recent work toward creating such a "scene decoder" has had some success.

Thomas Naselaris and coworkers (2009) created a brain-reading device by developing two methods for analyzing the patterns of voxel activation recorded from visual areas of an observer's brain. The first method, called **structural encoding**, is based on the relationship between voxel activation and structural characteristics of a scene, such as lines, contrasts, shapes,

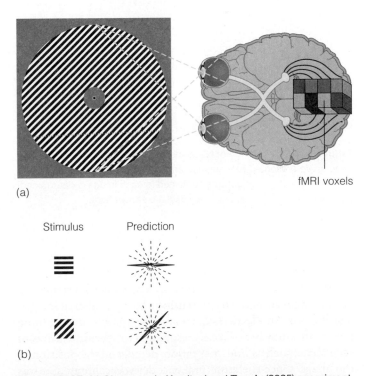

(a)

Stimulus   Prediction

(b)

fMRI voxels

Figure 5.47 (a) Observers in Kamitani and Tong's (2005) experiment viewed oriented gratings like the one on the left. The cubes in the brain represent the response of 6 voxels. The activity of 400 voxels was monitored in the experiment. (b) Results for two orientations. The gratings are the stimulus presented to the observer. The line is the orientation predicted by the orientation decoder. The decoder was able to accurately predict the presentation of all eight of the orientations tested. Reprinted by permission of Macmillan Publishers Ltd: *Nature Neuroscience,* Decoding the visual and subjective contents of the human brain, Kamitani, Y., & Tong, F., 8, 679–685, Copyright 2005.

Present 1,750 images

Measure response of a large number of voxels to all 1,750 images

One of the voxels

Response properties of this voxel calculated based on its response to the images

Bruce Goldstein

Figure 5.48 Calibration of Nasalaris's structural decoder. Natural images are presented to a subject, and the way a large number of voxels respond to the features contained in each image is determined. Just three of the images and one voxel are shown here.

and textures. Just as Kamitani and Tong's orientation decoder was calibrated by determining the voxel activation patterns generated by eight different orientations, Naselaris's structural decoder was calibrated by presenting a large number of images, like the ones in **Figure 5.48**, to an observer and determining how a large number of voxels responded to specific features of each scene, such as line orientation, detail, and the position of the image. Once the structural encoder was calibrated, it was "reversed" to make predictions in the opposite direction, using the patterns of voxel responses to predict the features of the image that the subject was viewing. **VL**

The second method, called **semantic encoding**, is based on the relationship between voxel activation and the *meaning* or *category* of a scene. The semantic encoder is calibrated by measuring the pattern of voxel activation to a large number of images that have previously been classified into categories such as "crowd," "portrait," "vehicle," and "outdoor." From

this calibration, the relationship between the pattern of voxel activation and image category is determined. This makes it possible to use the voxel responses that occur when a subject is viewing a scene to make predictions about the type of scene the subject is viewing.

The information provided by the structural decoder and by the semantic decoder provides a clue to what the subject is seeing. For example, the structural encoder might indicate that there are straight lines of various orientations on the left of the scene, that there are curved contours in some places and that there are few straight or curved contours in another area. The semantic decoder, which provides a different type of information, might indicate that the subject is looking at an outdoor scene.

But knowing the features of a scene and the type of scene doesn't tell us what the scene actually looks like. This step is achieved when the decoder consults a database of 6 million natural images and picks the images that most closely match the information determined from analyzing the person's brain activity. **Figure 5.49a** shows the results when just the structural encoder was used. The encoder has picked the three images on the right as the best match for the target image in the red box, which is the image the person was observing. The structure of all of the matching images is similar, with objects appearing on the left of the image and open spaces in the middle and right. However, whereas the target image contains buildings, buildings are either absent or difficult to see in the matching images.

Thus, the structural encoder alone does a good job of matching the *structure* of the target image, but a poor job of matching the *meaning* of the target image. Adding the semantic encoder improves performance, as shown in **Figure 5.49b**. It is easy to see the effect of the semantic encoder, because now

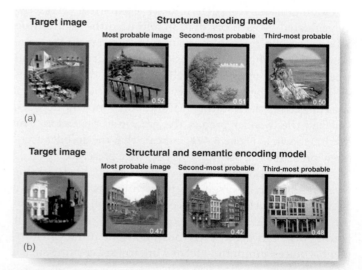

Figure 5.49 (a) The subject viewed the image in the red square. The structural decoder picked the other three images as the best match from the database of 6 million images. (b) Another image viewed by the subject and the three images picked by structural and semantic decoders as the best matches from the database. From Naselaris, T., Prenger, R. J., Kay, K. N., Oliver, M., & Gallant, J. L. (2009). Bayesian reconstruction of natural images from human brain activity. *Neuron, 63,* 902–915.

the meanings of the match images are much closer to the test image, with all of the matches showing the sides of buildings.

The ability to pick pictures that come this close to matching what a person is looking at, based only on analysis of the pattern of activation of the person's brain, is quite an accomplishment. One reason the images picked as matches are not exactly the same as the target is that the target images are not contained in the 6-million-picture database of images from which the encoder selected. Eventually, according to Naselaris, much larger image databases will result in matches that are much closer to the target. Accuracy will also increase as we learn more about how the neural activity of various areas of the brain represents the characteristics of environmental scenes.

Of course, the ultimate decoder won't need to compare its output to huge image databases. It will just analyze the voxel activation patterns and recreate the image of the scene. Presently, there is only one "decoder" that has achieved this, and that is your own brain! (Although it is worth noting that your brain does make use of a "database" of information about the environment, as we know from the role of regularities of the environment in perceiving scenes.) Achieving this ultimate decoder in the laboratory falls into the category of the "science project" described at the beginning of this book (see page 3) and is still far from being achieved. However, the decoders that presently exist are amazing achievements, which only recently might have been classified as "science fiction."

SOMETHING TO CONSIDER:
Are Faces Special?

Having described perceptual organization and how we perceive objects and scenes, we now focus on one specific type of object: faces. Why should faces get their own section?

The answer to this question is, as the title of this section implies, that there is something special about faces. There are a number of things that lead to this conclusion. First, faces are pervasive in the environment. Unless you avoid people, faces are everywhere. But what makes them special is that they are important sources of information. Faces establish a person's identity, which is important for social interactions (who is the person who just said hello to me?) and for security surveillance (checking people as they pass through airport security). Faces also provide information about a person's mood, where the person is looking, and can elicit evaluative judgments in an observer (the person seems unfriendly, the person is attractive, and so on).

Faces are also special because, as we've discussed in previous chapters, there are neurons that respond selectively to faces, and there are specialized places in the brain, such as the fusiform face area, that are rich in these neurons. Furthermore, when people are given a task that involves moving their eyes as rapidly as possible to look at a picture of either a face, an animal, or a vehicle, faces elicit the fastest eye movements, occurring within 138 ms, compared to 170 ms for animals and 188 ms for vehicles (Crouzet et al., 2010). Results such as these have led to the suggestion that faces have special status that allows them to be processed more efficiently and faster than other classes of objects (Crouzet et al., 2010; Farah et al., 1998).

One research finding that had been repeated many times is that inverting a picture of a face (turning it upside down) makes it more difficult to identify the face or to tell if two inverted faces are the same or different (Busigny & Rossion, 2010). Similar effects occur for other objects, such as cars, but the effect is much smaller (**Figure 5.50**).

Because inverting a face makes it more difficult to process configurational information—the relationship between features such as the eyes, nose, and mouth—the inversion

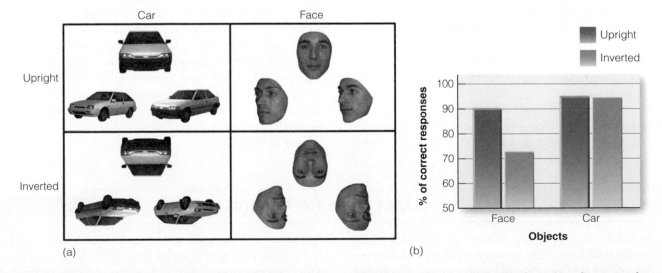

Figure 5.50 (a) Stimuli from Busigny and Rossion's (2010) experiment in which subjects were presented with a front view of a car or a face and were asked to pick the three-quarter view that was the same car or face. For example, the car on the right in the upper panel is the same car as the one shown in front-view above. (b) Performance for upright cars and faces (blue bars) and inverted cars and faces (orange bars). Notice that inverting the cars has little or no effect on performance but that inverting faces causes performance to decrease from 89 percent to 73 percent.

From Busigny, T., & Rossion, B. (2010). Acquired prosopagnosia abolishes the face inversion effect. *Cortex, 46*, 965–981. By permission of Elsevier.

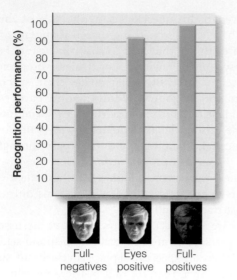

Figure 5.51 Ability to recognize faces of well-known people who were familiar to the subjects. Each type of image (negative and negative with eyes changed to positive) was shown to different groups of subjects, followed by the full-positive image. The subjects' task was to identify the face (Newt Gingrich in this example). Changing just the eyes in the negative image to positive causes a large increase in performance. From Gilad, S., Meng, M., & Sinha, P. (2009). Role of ordinal contrast relationships in face encoding. *Proceedings of the National Academy of Sciences, 106,* 5353–5358.

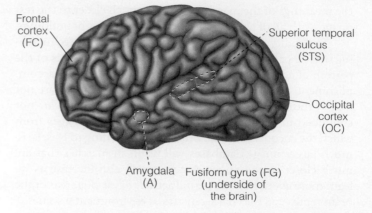

Figure 5.52 The human brain, showing some of the areas involved in perceiving faces. See text for the function of each area. Note that the labels indicate a general area of cortex but not the overall extent of an area. Also, the amygdala is located deep inside the cortex, approximately under the label shown here. © Cengage Learning

effect has been interpreted as providing evidence that faces are processed holistically (Freire et al., 2000). Thus, while all faces contain the same basic features—two eyes, a nose, and a mouth—our ability to distinguish thousands of different faces seems to be based on our ability to detect the configuration of these features—how they are arranged relative to each other on the face.

But features are not totally irrelevant. Changing a photograph of a face into a negative image, as in **Figure 5.51**, makes it much more difficult to recognize; changing only the eyes back to positive greatly increases the ability to recognize the face (Gilad et al., 2009). This suggests that eyes are an important cue for facial recognition and may explain why it is difficult to recognize someone who is wearing a mask that covers just the eyes.

Finally, although the existence of areas of the brain that respond specifically to faces provides evidence for specialized modules in the brain (see Chapter 4, page 87), faces

provide evidence for distributed processing as well. Initial processing of faces occurs in the occipital cortex, which sends signals to the fusiform gyrus, where visual information concerned with identification of the face is processed (Grill-Spector et al., 2004; **Figure 5.52**). Emotional aspects of the face, including facial expression and the observer's emotional reaction to the face, are reflected in activation of the amygdala, which is located deep within the brain (Gobbini & Haxby, 2007; Ishai et al., 2004). Evaluation of where a person is looking is linked to activity in the superior temporal sulcus; this area is also involved in perceiving movements of a person's mouth as the person speaks (Calder et al., 2007; Puce et al., 1998) and general movement of faces (Pitcher et al., 2011). Evaluation of a face's attractiveness is linked to activity in the frontal area of the brain (Winston et al., 2007), and the pattern of activation across many areas of the brain differs in familiar faces compared to unfamiliar faces, with familiar faces causing more activation in areas associated with emotions (Natu & O'Toole, 2011). Faces, it appears, are special both because of the role they play in our environment and because of the widespread activity they trigger in the brain.

DEVELOPMENTAL DIMENSION: Infant Face Perception

What do newborns and young infants see? Research using the preferential looking effect to measure infant visual acuity show that infants have poor detail vision compared to adults but that the ability to see details increases rapidly over the first year of life (see Developmental Dimension: Infant Visual Acuity, page 45). We should not conclude from young infants' poor vision, however, that they can see nothing at all.

At very close distances, a young infant can detect some gross features, as indicated in **Figure 5.53**, which simulates how infants perceive from a distance of about 2 feet. At birth, the contrast perceived between light and dark areas is so low that it is difficult to determine it is a face, but it is possible to see very high contrast areas. By 8 weeks, however, the infant's ability to perceive the contrast between light and dark

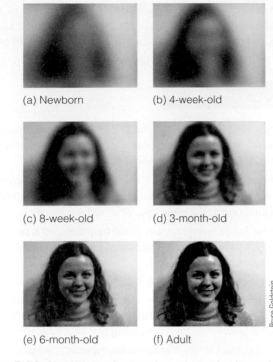

(a) Newborn

(b) 4-week-old

(c) 8-week-old

(d) 3-month-old

(e) 6-month-old

(f) Adult

Bruce Goldstein

Figure 5.53 Simulations of perceptions of a mother located 24 inches from an observer, as seen by newborns and various ages. Simulations courtesy of Alex Wade.

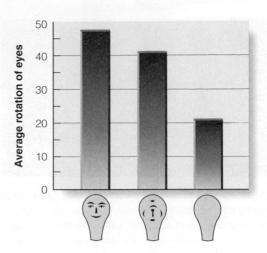

Figure 5.54 The magnitude of infants' eye movements in response to movement of each stimulus. The average rotation of the infants' eyes was greater for the facelike stimulus than for the scrambled-face stimulus or the blank stimulus. Adapted from Morton, J., & Johnson, M. H. (1991). CONSPEC and CONLEARN: A two-process theory of infant face recognition. *Psychological Review, 98,* 164–181.

perception has improved so that the image looks clearly facelike. By 3 to 4 months, infants can tell the difference between faces that look happy and those that show surprise, anger, or are neutral (LaBarbera et al., 1976; Young-Browne et al., 1977) and can also tell the difference between a cat and a dog (Eimas & Quinn, 1994). **VL**

Human faces are among the most important stimuli in an infant's environment. As a newborn or young infant stares up from the crib, numerous faces of interested adults appear in the infant's field of view. The face that the infant sees most frequently is usually the mother's, and there is evidence that young infants can recognize their mother's face shortly after they are born.

Using preferential looking in which 2-day-old infants were given a choice between their mother's face and a stranger's, Ian Bushnell and coworkers (1989) found that newborns looked at the mother about 63 percent of the time. This result is above the 50 percent chance level, so Bushnell concluded that the 2-day-olds could recognize their mother's face.

To determine what information the infants might be using to recognize the mother's face, Olivier Pascalis and coworkers (1995) showed that when the mother and the stranger wore pink scarves that covered their hairline, the preference for the mother disappeared. The high-contrast border between the mother's dark hairline and light forehead apparently provide important information about the mother's physical characteristics that infants use to recognize the mother (see Bartrip et al., 2001, for another experiment that shows this). **VL**

In an experiment that tested newborns within an hour after they were born, John Morton and Mark Johnson (1991) presented stimuli (see bottom of **Figure 5.54**) to the newborns and then moved the stimuli to the left and right. As they did this, they videotaped the infant's face. Later, scorers who were unaware of which stimulus had been presented viewed the tapes and noted whether the infant turned its head or eyes to follow the moving stimulus. The results in Figure 5.54 show that the newborns looked at the moving face more than at the other moving stimuli, which led Morton and Johnson to propose that infants are born with some information about the structure of faces.

But there is also evidence for a role of experience in infant face perception. Ian Bushnell (2001) observed newborns over the first 3 days of life to determine whether there was a relationship between their looking behavior and the amount of time they were with their mother. He found that at 3 days of age, when the infants were given a choice between looking at a stranger's face or their mother's face, the infants who had been exposed to their mother longer were more likely to prefer her over the stranger. The two infants with the lowest exposure to the mother (an average of 1.5 hours) divided their looking evenly between the mother and stranger, but the two infants with the longest exposure (an average of 7.5 hours) looked at the mother 68 percent of the time. Analyzing the results from all of the infants led Bushnell to conclude that face perception emerges very rapidly after birth, but that experience in looking at faces does have an effect.

Although the infant's ability to recognize faces develops rapidly over the first few months, these impressive gains are only a starting point, because even though 3- to 4-month-old infants can recognize some facial expressions, their ability to identify faces doesn't reach adult levels until adolescence or early adulthood (Mondlach et al., 2003, 2004; Grille-Spector, 2008).

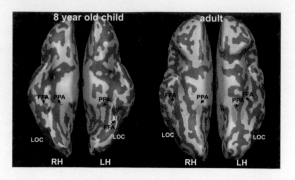

Figure 5.55 Face (red), place (green), and object (blue) selective activations for one representative 8-year-old and one representative adult. The place and object areas are well developed in the child, but the face area is small compared to the adult. From Grill-Spector, K., Golarai, G., & Gabrieli, J. (2008). Developmental neuroimaging of the human ventral visual cortex. *Trends in Cognitive Sciences, 12,* 152–162.

One reason for this prolonged course of the development of face perception can be traced to physiology. **Figure 5.55** shows that the fusiform face area (FFA), indicated by red, is small in an 8-year-old child compared to the FFA in an adult (Golarai et al., 2007; Grill-Spector et al., 2008). In contrast, the parahippocampal place area (PPA), indicated by green, is similar in the 8-year-old child and the adult.

It has been suggested that this slow development of the specialized face area may be related to the maturation of the ability to recognize faces and their emotions, and especially the ability to perceive the overall configuration of facial features (Scherf et al., 2007). Thus, the specialness of faces extends from birth, when newborns can react to some aspects of faces, to late adolescence, when the true complexity of our responses to faces finally emerges. **VL**

TEST YOURSELF 5.3

1. Describe Grill-Spector's "Harrison Ford" experiment. What do the results indicate about the connection between brain activity and the ability to recognize faces?

2. Describe Sheinberg and Logothetis's binocular rivalry experiment in which they presented a picture of a butterfly to one eye and a sunburst to the other eye. What did the results indicate?

3. Describe Tong's experiment in which he presented a picture of a house to one eye and a picture of a face to the other eye. What did the results indicate?

4. Describe how "decoders" have enabled researchers to use the brain's response, measured using fMRI, to predict what orientation or what picture a person is looking at. Be sure you understand the difference between semantic encoding and structural encoding.

5. Why is it correct to say that faces are "special"? What do the face inversion experiments show? Do faces activate the brain mainly in one place or in many different places?

6. What is the evidence that newborns and young infants can perceive faces? What is the evidence that perceiving the full complexity of faces does not occur until late adolescence or adulthood?

THINK ABOUT IT

1. Consider this situation: We saw in Chapter 1 that top-down processing occurs when perception is affected by the observer's knowledge and expectations. Of course, this knowledge is stored in neurons and groups of neurons in the brain. In this chapter, we saw that there are neurons that have become tuned to respond to specific characteristics of the environment. We could therefore say that some knowledge of the environment is built into these neurons. Thus, if a particular perception occurs because of the firing of these tuned neurons, does this qualify as top-down processing?

2. Reacting to the results of the recent DARPA race, Harry says, "Well, we've finally shown that computers can perceive as well as people." How would you respond to this statement? (p. 96)

3. Biological evolution caused our perceptual system to be tuned to the Stone Age world in which we evolved. Given this fact, how well do we handle activities like downhill skiing or driving, which are very recent additions to our behavioral repertoire?

4. Vecera showed that regions in the lower part of a stimulus are more likely to be perceived as figure. How does this result relate to the idea that our visual system is tuned to regularities in the environment? (p. 105)

5. The blue area in the painting in **Figure 5.56** is a silhouette of a mountain. The dark area in the foreground represents trees. What happens to your perception of these

Courtesy of Bernie Baker

Figure 5.56 Detail of *Winter Twilight* (2011) by Bernie Baker. Look at this painting right side up and upside down. What changes?

Figure 5.57 Is there something wrong with these people's legs? (Or is it just a problem in perception?)

two areas when you turn the picture upside down? (Hint: Can you see yellow mountains in the foreground of the upside-down picture?) Relate the changes in perception you experience to the determinants of figure and ground discussed in this chapter.

6. When you first look at **Figure 5.57**, do you notice anything funny about the walkers' legs? Do they initially appear tangled? What is it about this picture that makes the legs appear to be perceptually organized in that way? Can you relate your perception to any of the laws of perceptual organization? To cognitive processes based on assumptions or past experience? (pp. 102, 110)

Answers for Figure 5.9
Faces from left to right: Prince Charles, Woody Allen, Bill Clinton, Saddam Hussein, Richard Nixon, Princess Diana.

KEY TERMS

Apparent movement (p. 101)
Bayesian inference (p. 114)
Binocular rivalry (p. 115)
Border ownership (p. 105)
Figure (p. 104)
Figure–ground segregation (p. 104)
Gestalt psychologist (p. 100)
Gist of a scene (p. 109)
Global image features (pp. 110)
Ground (p. 104)
Grouping (p. 100)
Illusory contour (p. 101)
Inverse projection problem (p. 98)
Light-from-above assumption (p. 111)
Likelihood principle (p. 113)
Organizing principles (p. 102)

Perceptual organization (p. 100)
Perceptual segregation (p. 104)
Persistence of vision (p. 109)
Physical regularities (p. 111)
Principle of common fate (p. 104)
Principle of common region (p. 104)
Principle of good continuation (p. 102)
Principle of good figure (p. 102)
Principle of pragnanz (p. 102)
Principle of proximity (nearness) (p. 103)
Principle of similarity (p. 103)
Principle of simplicity (p. 102)
Principle of uniform connectedness (p. 104)

Regularities in the environment (p. 110)
Reversible figure–ground (p. 105)
Scene (p. 109)
Segregation (p. 100)
Semantic encoding (p. 118)
Semantic regularities (p. 112)
Sensations (p. 100)
Structural encoding (p. 117)
Structuralism (p. 100)
Theory of unconscious inference (p. 113)
Viewpoint invariance (p. 99)
Visual masking stimulus (p. 109)

MEDIA RESOURCES

CourseMate 🖥

Go to CengageBrain.com to access Psychology CourseMate, where you will find the Virtual Labs plus an interactive eBook, flashcards, quizzes, videos, and more.

Virtual Labs 🆅🅻

The Virtual Labs are designed to help you get the most out of this course. The Virtual Lab icons direct you to specific media demonstrations and experiments designed to help you visualize what you are reading about. The numbers below indicate the number of the Virtual Lab you can access through Psychology CourseMate.

5.1 Robotic Vehicle Navigation: DARPA Urban Challenge (p. 97)
Video showing Carnegie-Mellon's robotic car "Boss" as it navigates a course in the DARPA urban challenge in California. (Courtesy of Red Whittaker and the Tartan Racing Team)

5.2 Ambiguous Reversible Cube (p. 98)
Illustration of a stimulus that can be perceived in a number of different ways and that does strange things when it moves. (Courtesy of Michael Bach)

5.3 Reversible Pattern (p. 98)
Still picture of display that flips back and forth between two perceptions. (Courtesy of Anthony Norcia)

5.4 Windows and a Bar (p. 98)
Three-dimensional objects that are not what they appear to be. (Courtesy of Kokichi Sugihara)

5.5 Perches and a Ring (p. 98)
Another type of three-dimensional object that has a deceiving appearance. (Courtesy of Kokichi Sugihara)

5.6 Impossible Motion: Antigravity Ramps (p. 98)
How to make a ball appear to roll uphill. (Courtesy of Kokichi Sugihara)

5.7 Impossible Motion: Magnet-like Slopes (p. 98)
Illusion in which balls appear to roll uphill. (Courtesy of Kokichi Sugihara)

5.8 Perceptual Organization: Dalmatian (p. 100)
How a black and white pattern can be perceived as a Dalmatian. (Courtesy of Michael Bach)

5.9 Figure-Ground Trials (p. 106)
Example of the stimulus used in Vecera's figure-ground experiment. (Courtesy of Shaun Vecera)

5.10 Perceiving Rapidly Flashed Stimuli (p. 109)
Some rapidly flashed stimuli like those used in the Fei-Fei experiment described on page 109, which investigated what people perceive when viewing rapidly flashed pictures. (Courtesy of Li Fei Fei)

5.11 Visual Object Recognition—Jim DeCarlo (p. 111)
Talks about some basic principles of how the brain solves the problem of visual object recognition, emphasizing the importance of how experience helps us learn about how objects appear when viewed from different angles. (Courtesy of McGovern Institute for Brain Research, MIT)

5.12 Rotating Mask 1 (p. 112)
Illustrates how our assumption about the three-dimensional shape of a face can create an error of perception. (Courtesy of Michael Bach)

5.13 Rotating Mask 2 (p. 112)
Another rotating face. (Courtesy of Heinrich Bülthoff)

5.14 Rotating Mask 3 (p. 112)
An example of the rotating mask effect, which includes a nose ring on the face. (Courtesy of Thomas Papathomas)

5.15 Visual Mind Reading (p. 117)
Description of an experiment that shows how recording brain activity can indicate which one of two possible stimuli a person is perceiving.

5.16 Reconstructing Movies From Brain Activity (p. 118)
Neuroscientist Jack Gallant describes experiments in which data collected while people watch movies while in a brain scanner were used to reconstruct the images from new movies based on brain activity generated by these new movies. (Courtesy of Jack Gallant)

5.17 Reconstructed Movies (p. 118)
A short film showing the results of the experiments discussed by Gallant. (Courtesy of Jack Gallant)

5.18 Newborn Hearing and Vision (p. 121)
Shows newborns responding to sounds and visual stimuli.

5.19 Infant Face Preference Test (p. 121)
Stimuli used by Olivier Pascalis to measure infant preference for faces. (Courtesy of Olivier Pascalis)

5.20 Development of Whole-Part Perception (p. 122)
Describes research on how children perceive parts and wholes of objects, and how the development of the ability to perceive parts is related to brain development and brain plasticity.

Charles Feil

Visual Attention

VL The Virtual Lab icons direct you to specific animations and videos that will help you visualize what you are reading about. Virtual Labs are listed at the end of the chapter, keyed to the page on which they appear, and can be accessed through Psychology CourseMate.

◄ One of the things that influences how we direct our attention is salience: physical characteristics of a scene that make certain things stand out. In this scene our attention is drawn to the tree because of its isolation and color, and to the sunlit part of the background because of its contrast with the darker background and its jagged shape. In this chapter we will consider what attracts our attention, how attending enhances perception, and the consequences of not attending.

Some Questions We Will Consider:

■ Why do we pay attention to some parts of a scene, but not to others? (p. 129)

■ Does paying attention to an object make the object "stand out"? (p. 134)

■ Do we have to pay attention to something to perceive it? (p. 140)

We have come a long way from Chapter 1, when we described light entering the eye at the very beginning of the perceptual process. By Chapter 4, we had reached areas in the cortex that are specialized for perceiving faces, places, and bodies. Chapter 5 continued where Chapter 4 left off by considering objects and scenes and by introducing the idea that perception is an active process that involves making inferences based on knowledge gained from a lifetime of experiencing characteristics of the environment.

This chapter expands upon the idea that the observer is actively involved in creating perceptions. We don't just passively sit there as stimuli create images of objects or scenes in our eyes. Instead, we direct our attention toward specific objects or locations within a scene and ignore other objects or locations. This process of focusing on specific objects while ignoring others is the process of **attention**. We will see, however, that attention is far more than just "looking around" at things. The act of attending not only brings an object into view; it enhances the processing of that object and therefore our perception of the object.

The effects of attention were described in the 19th century by William James, the first professor of psychology at Harvard. James relied not on the results of experiments but rather on his own personal observations when making statements such as the following description of attention, from his 1890 textbook *Principles of Psychology*:

Millions of items . . . are present to my senses
which never properly enter my experience.
Why? Because they have no interest for me.

My experience is what I agree to attend to. . . .
Everyone knows what attention is. It is the taking
possession by the mind, in clear and vivid form,
of one out of what seem several simultaneously
possible objects or trains of thought. . . . It implies
withdrawal from some things in order to deal
effectively with others.

Thus, according to James, we focus on some things to the
exclusion of others. As you walk down the street, the things you
pay attention to—a classmate you recognize, the "Don't Walk"
sign at a busy intersection, and the fact that just about everyone except you seems to be carrying an umbrella—stand out
more than many other things in the environment. The reason
you are paying attention to those things is that saying hello to
your friend, not crossing the street against the light, and your
concern that it might rain later in the day are important to you.

But there is also another reason for paying attention to
some things and ignoring others. Your perceptual system has
a limited capacity for processing information (Chun et al.,
2011). Thus, to prevent overloading the system and therefore
not processing anything well, the visual system, in James's
words, "withdraws from some things in order to deal more
effectively with others." One of the mechanisms for selecting
certain things in the visual environment is **visual scanning**—
looking from one place to another. This scanning is necessary
because there is only one place on the retina—the cone-rich
fovea—that creates good detail vision.

Scanning a Scene

The following demonstration illustrates the importance of
scanning for finding one object in a cluttered scene.

DEMONSTRATION
Looking for a Face in the Crowd

Your task in this demonstration is to find Justin Bieber's face in
the group of people in **Figure 6.1**. Notice how long it takes to
accomplish this task.

Unless you were lucky and just happened to look at Justin Bieber immediately, you probably had to scan the scene,
checking each face in turn, before finding him. What you
were doing is aiming your fovea at one face after another.
Each time you briefly paused on one face you were making a
fixation. When you moved your eye to observe another face,
you were making a **saccadic eye movement**—a rapid jerky
movement from one fixation to the next.

It isn't surprising that you were moving your eyes from
one place to another, because you were consciously looking
for a particular target (Justin Bieber). But it may surprise
you to know that even when you are freely viewing an object
or scene without searching for a target, you move your eyes
about three times per second. This rapid scanning is shown
in **Figure 6.2**, which is a pattern of fixations (dots) separated

Figure 6.1 Where is Justin Bieber? (Extra credit: Where is Rihanna? Miley Cyrus?)

First fixation

Figure 6.2 Scan path of an observer freely viewing a picture. Fixations are indicated by the yellow dots and saccadic eye movements by the red lines. Notice that this person looked preferentially at areas of the picture such as the statues and lights but ignored areas such as the fence and the sky.

Reproduced with permission from John Henderson, South Carolina.

by saccadic eye movements (lines) that occurred as a subject viewed a picture of the fountain.

Scanning involves **overt attention**—attention that involves looking directly at the attended object. Although we often look directly at the objects of our attention, objects can also be attended even when they are off to the side. **Covert attention** is attention without looking. Covert attention is an important part of many sports. Consider, for example, the basketball player in **Figure 6.3**, who looks to the right but then suddenly throws a dead-on pass to a teammate he was covertly attending to off to the left.

We will describe a number of experiments that involve covert attention, in which observers are told to keep looking at a small dot or "X" without moving their eyes, and to pay attention to an area off to the side.

We are constantly monitoring our environment by shifting our attention both overtly, by making eye movements, and covertly, by noticing what is happening off to the side. But what determines where we attend? One answer to that question, as suggested by James, is that we attend to what interests us. But, as we will now see, there are also other factors that determine where we attend.

Kamil Krzaczynski/epa/Corbis

Figure 6.3 When a basketball player looks to the right while paying attention to a teammate off to the left, he is covertly attending to the teammate.

What Directs Our Attention?

Where we direct attention can be caused by an involuntary process, in which stimuli that stand out capture our attention, and by voluntary processes, in which attention is guided by our goals and intentions (Anderson et al., 2011). We first consider attention that is determined by stimuli that stand out because of their physical properties.

Stimulus Salience

Stimulus salience refers to physical properties such as color, contrast, movement, and orientation that make a particular object or location conspicuous. When attention due to stimulus salience causes an involuntary shift of attention, this shift is called **attentional capture** (Anderson et al., 2011). For example, attention can be drawn away from what we are doing by a bright flash or a loud noise off to the side. This capturing of attention could be important if it serves as a warning of something dangerous like an explosion, a dangerous animal, or an object moving rapidly toward us.

On a less dramatic level, some things draw our attention because they stand out in a scene. Thus, the man in the red shirt in the crowd in **Figure 6.4** attracts our attention because the shirt's color contrasts with the light colors in the rest of the scene. Procedures for determining how saliency influences how we scan a scene typically analyze characteristics such as color, orientation, and intensity at each location in a scene, and combine these values to create a **saliency map** of the scene (Itti & Koch, 2000; Parkhurst et al., 2002; Torralba et al., 2006). For example, the highly salient red-shirted man in **Figure 6.4** would be indicated by a light area on a saliency map.

Figure 6.5 shows a scene and its saliency map as determined by Derrick Parkhurst and coworkers (2002). When Parkhurst calculated saliency maps for a number of pictures and then measured observers' fixations as they observed the pictures, he found that the first few fixations were closely associated with the light areas on the saliency map, with fixations being more likely on high-saliency areas. But after the first few fixations, scanning begins to be influenced by top-down, or cognitive, processes that depend on things such as an observer's goals and expectations. As we will see in the next section, these goals and expectations are influenced by the observer's past experiences in observing the environment.

Selection Based on Cognitive Factors

One way to show that where we look isn't determined only by saliency is by checking the eye movements of the subject looking at the fountain in Figure 6.2. Notice that the person never looks at the fence in the foreground, even though it is very salient because of its high contrast and its position near the front of the scene. Instead, the person focuses on aspects of the fountain that might be more interesting, such as the

Figure 6.4 The red shirt is highly salient because of its color compared to the rest of the scene.

Ales Fevzer/CORBIS

(a) Visual scene

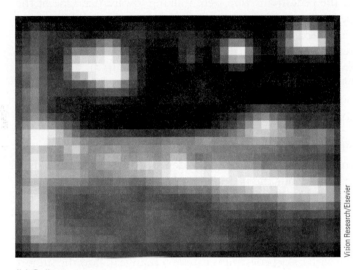

(b) Saliency map

Figure 6.5 (a) A visual scene. (b) Saliency map of the scene determined by analyzing the color, contrast, and orientations in the scene. Lighter areas indicate greater salience. Adapted from Parkhurst, D., Law, K., & Niebur, E. (2002). Modeling the role of salience in the allocation of overt visual attention. *Vision Research, 42,* 107–123.

horses. It is likely that the *meaning* of the horses has attracted this particular person's attention.

It is important to note, however, that just because this person looked at the horses doesn't mean everyone would. Just as there are large variations between people, there are variations in how people scan scenes (Castelhano & Henderson, 2008; Noton & Stark, 1971). Thus, another person, who might be interested in wrought iron fences, might look less at the horses and more at the fence.

Top-down processing is also associated with **scene schemas**—an observer's knowledge about what is contained in typical scenes (remember *regularities in the environment* from Chapter 5, page 110). Thus, when Melissa Vo and John Henderson (2009) showed observers pictures like the ones in **Figure 6.6**, observers looked longer at the printer in **Figure 6.6b** than the pot in **Figure 6.6a** because a printer is less likely to

Figure 6.6 Stimuli used by Vo and Henderson (2009). Observers spent more time looking at the printer (in B) than at the pot (in A), shown inside the yellow rectangles (which were not visible to the observers). From Vo, M. L. H., & Henderson, J. M. (2009). Does gravity matter? Effects of semantic and syntactic inconsistencies on the allocation of attention during scene perception. *Journal of Vision, 9*(3), 1–15. Reproduced with permission.

be found in a kitchen. The fact that people look longer at things that seem out of place in a scene means that attention is being affected by their knowledge of what is usually found in the scene.

You can probably think of other situations in which your knowledge about specific types of scenes might influence where you look. You probably know a lot, for example, about kitchens, college campuses, automobile instrument panels, and shopping malls, and your knowledge about where things are usually found in these scenes can help guide your attention through each scene (Bar, 2004).

Another example of how cognitive factors based on knowledge of the environment influences scanning is an experiment by Hiroyuki Shinoda and coworkers (2001) in which they measured observers' fixations and tested their ability to detect traffic signs as they drove through a computer-generated environment in a driving simulator. They found that the observers were more likely to detect stop signs positioned at intersections than those positioned in the middle of a block, and that 45 percent of the observers' fixations occurred close to intersections. In this example, the observers are using learning about regularities in the environment (stop signs are usually at corners) to determine when and where to look for stop signs.

Task Demands

The examples in the last section demonstrate how knowledge of various characteristics of the environment can influence how people direct their attention. However, the last example, in which subjects drove through a computer-generated environment, was different from the rest. The difference is that instead of looking at pictures of stationary scenes, subjects were interacting with the environment. This kind of situation, in which people are shifting their attention from one place to another as they are doing things, occurs when people are moving through the environment, as in the driving example, and when people are carrying out specific tasks.

Some researchers have focused, therefore, on determining where people look as they are carrying out tasks. Since most tasks require attention to different places as the task unfolds, it isn't surprising that the timing of when people look at specific places is determined by the sequence of actions involved in the task. Consider, for example, the pattern of eye movements in **Figure 6.7** that were measured as a person was making a peanut butter sandwich. The process of making the sandwich begins with the movement of a slice of bread from the bag (A) to the plate (B). Notice that this operation is accompanied by an eye movement from the bag to the plate. The observer then looks at the peanut butter jar just before the jar is lifted, looks at the top just before it is removed (C). Attention then shifts to the knife, which is picked up and used to scoop the peanut butter and spread it on the bread (Land & Hayhoe, 2001). **VL**

The key finding of these measurements, and also of another experiment in which eye movements were measured as a person prepared tea (Land et al., 1999), is that the person's eye movements were determined primarily by the task. The person fixated on few objects or areas that were irrelevant to the task, and eye movements and fixations were closely linked to the action the person was about to take. Furthermore, the eye movement usually preceded a motor action by a fraction of a second, as when the person first fixated on the peanut butter jar and then reached over to pick it up. This is an example of the "just in time" strategy—eye movements occur just before we need the information they will provide (Hayhoe & Ballard, 2005; Tatler et al., 2011).

When making a peanut butter sandwich, everything is stationary or under the direct control of the person making the sandwich. What about tasks in which other things are moving and the situation isn't entirely predictable? Such a situation occurs when walking down a busy sidewalk or when crossing the street in the middle of traffic. Jelena Jovancevic-Misic and Mary Hayhoe (2009) did a study to investigate how attention might be determined by people's sensitivity to properties of a dynamic environment.

A subject walked along an elliptical path that went around a partition that partially blocked her view. As the subject walked along this path, she encountered three "pedestrians" who were walking in the opposite direction. The key factor in this experiment was what the subject learned about the behavior of each of the pedestrians who were walking toward her. One of the pedestrians, called "Rogue," veered toward the subject every time he passed her, although no collisions happened, as Rogue returned to his original path before a collision occurred. Pedestrian "Risky" veered on every fourth circuit, and pedestrian "Safe" never veered toward the subject. The subject, who was not informed about the behavior of the pedestrians, was simply told to walk around the path and to avoid other pedestrians.

When Jovancevic-Misic and Hayhoe measured how long the subject looked directly at each pedestrian, they found that the subject's attention depended on what they had learned about the pedestrians. Rogue was most likely to be looked at, followed by Risky and Safe. Near the end of the experiment, when the subject had learned what to expect from each pedestrian, she was looking at Rogue four times more than Safe. Thus, the probability of potentially colliding with risky pedestrians caused a change in how the subject allocated her attention.

These results can be interpreted in terms of the observer's knowledge of **scene statistics** of dynamic events, where scene statistics are the probability of various things occurring in a dynamic environment. This is similar to the idea that scene schemas—our knowledge of characteristics of specific scenes—influence where we look when we view still pictures. This experiment extends this idea to dynamic environments where events can become unpredictable.

What Happens When We Attend?

The answer to this question may seem obvious. When we attend to something, we become aware of it. But the effects of attention extend beyond creating awareness.

Returning to William James (who is getting a lot of attention!), remember his statement that attending to an object enables us to "deal effectively" with it. In line with that statement, researchers have found that attention enhances our

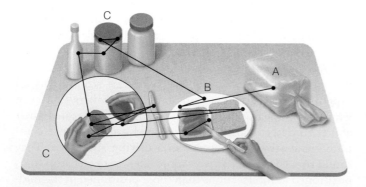

Figure 6.7 Sequence of fixations of a person making a peanut butter sandwich. The first fixation is on the loaf of bread. From Land, M. F., Mennie, N., & Rusted, J., 1999, "The roles of vision and eye movements in the control of activities of daily living," *Perception, 28*(11), 1311–1328. Copyright © 1999 by Pion Ltd, London. Reproduced by permission. www.pion.co.uk and www.envplan.com.

response to objects (we respond faster to things that are located where we are attending), perception of objects (attention can make it easier to see an object), and physiological responding (attention can enhance neural firing to objects).

Attention Speeds Responding

We often pay attention to specific locations, as when paying attention to what is happening in the road directly in front of your car when driving. Paying attention informs us about what is happening at a location, and also enables us to respond more rapidly to anything that happens in that location.

Speeding Responding to Locations Attention to a specific location is called **spatial attention**. In a classic series of studies on spatial attention, Michael Posner and coworkers (1978) asked whether paying attention to a location improves a person's ability to respond to stimuli presented there. To answer this question, Posner used the **precueing** procedure, as shown in **Figure 6.8**.

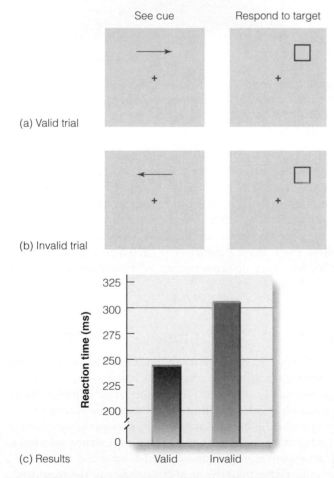

(a) Valid trial

(b) Invalid trial

(c) Results

Figure 6.8 Procedure for the (a) valid task and (b) invalid task in Posner and coworkers' (1978) precueing experiment. See text for details. (c) The results of the experiment. The average reaction time was 245 ms for valid trials but was 305 ms for invalid trials. From Posner, M. I., Nissen, M. J., & Ogden, W. C. (1978). Attended and unattended processing modes: The role of set for spatial location. In H. L. Pick & I. J. Saltzman (Eds.), *Modes of perceiving and processing information*. Hillsdale, NJ: Erlbaum. Reproduced by permission.

METHOD
Precueing

The general principle behind a precueing experiment is to determine whether presenting a cue indicating where a test stimulus will appear enhances the processing of the test stimulus. The participants in Posner and coworkers' (1978) experiment kept their eyes stationary throughout the experiment, always looking at the + in the display in **Figure 6.8**. They first saw an arrow cue (as shown in the left panel) indicating on which side of the target a stimulus was likely to appear. In Figure 6.8a, the arrow cue indicates that they should focus their attention to the right. (Remember, they do this without moving their eyes, so this is an example of covert attention.) The participant's task was to press a key as rapidly as possible when a target square was presented off to the side (as shown in the right panel). The trial shown in Figure 6.8a is a *valid trial* because the square appears on the side indicated by the cue arrow. The location indicated by the cue arrow was valid 80 percent of the time, so 20 percent of the trials were invalid. That is, the cue arrow indicated that the target was going to be presented on one side but it actually appeared on the other side, as shown in **Figure 6.8b**. For this *invalid trial*, the cue arrow indicates that the observer should attend to the left, but the target is presented on the right.

The results of this experiment, shown in **Figure 6.8c**, indicate that subjects reacted more rapidly on valid trials than on invalid trials. Posner interpreted this result as showing that information processing is more effective *at the place where attention is directed*. This result and others like it gave rise to the idea that attention is like a spotlight or zoom lens that improves processing when directed toward a particular location (**Figure 6.9**; Marino & Scholl, 2005).

Speeding Responding to Objects We also attend to specific objects in the environment. You see a person you know in a crowd and focus your attention on that person. You are looking at a table of items for sale at a flea market and focus your attention on one object after another.

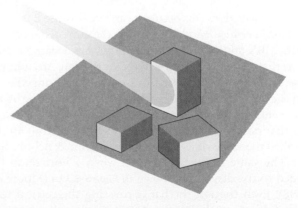

Figure 6.9 Spatial attention can be compared to a spotlight that scans a scene. From Goldstein, E. B., *Cognitive Psychology*, 3rd ed. © 2011 Wadsworth, a part of Cengage Learning, Inc. Reproduced by permission. www.cengage.com/permissions

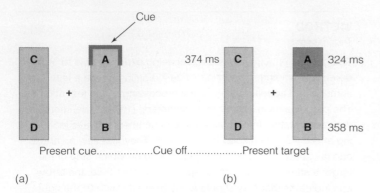

Figure 6.10 In Egly and coworkers' (1994) experiment, (a) a cue signal appears at one place on the display, then the cue is turned off and (b) a target is flashed at one of four possible locations, A, B, C, or D. Numbers are reaction times in ms for positions A, B, and C, when the cue appeared at position A. © Cengage Learning

We will now consider some experiments that show (1) that attention can enhance our response to objects and (2) that when attention is directed to one place on an object, the enhancing effect of that attention spreads to other places on the object.

Consider, for example, the experiment diagrammed in **Figure 6.10** (Egly et al., 1994). As participants kept their eyes on the +, one end of the rectangle was briefly highlighted (**Figure 6.10a**). This was the cue signal that indicated where a target, a dark square (**Figure 6.10b**), would probably appear. In this example, the cue indicates that the target is likely to appear in position A, at the upper part of the right rectangle, and the target is, in fact, presented at A. (The letters used to illustrate positions in our description did not appear in the actual experiment.)

The subjects' task was to press a button when the target was presented anywhere on the display. The numbers indicate the reaction times, in milliseconds, for three target locations when the cue signal had been presented at A. Not surprisingly, subjects responded most rapidly when the target was presented at A, where the cue had been presented. However, the most interesting result is that subjects responded more rapidly when the target was presented at B (reaction time = 358 ms) than when the target was presented at C (reaction time = 374 ms). Why does this occur? It can't be because B is closer to A than C, because B and C are exactly the same distance from A. Rather, B's advantage occurs because it is located *within the object* that was receiving the subject's attention. Attending at A, where the cue was presented, causes the maximum effect at A, but the effect of this attention spread throughout the object so some enhancement occurred at B as well. The faster responding that occurs when enhancement spreads within an object is called the **same-object advantage** (Marino & Scholl, 2005).

The same result occurs even when a horizontal bar is added to the display, as shown in **Figure 6.11a** (Moore et al., 1998). Even though the bar is covering the vertical rectangles, presenting the cue at A still results in enhancement at B. What this means is that enhancement still spreads throughout the object. This "spreading enhancement" may

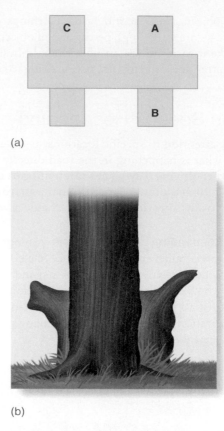

Figure 6.11 (a) Stimulus in Figure 6.10 but with a horizontal bar added (Moore et al., 1998). (b) Possible animal lurking behind a tree (see Chapter 5, page 114). © Cengage Learning

help us perceive partially obscured objects, such as our "animal" lurking behind the tree from Chapter 5 (**Figure 6.11b**). Because the effects of attention spread behind the tree, our awareness spreads throughout the object, thereby enhancing the chances we will interpret the interrupted shape as being a single object. (Also see Baylis & Driver, 1993; Driver & Baylis, 1989, 1998; Katzner et al., 2009; and Lavie & Driver, 1996, for more demonstrations of how attention spreads throughout objects.)

Attention Can Influence Appearance

Does the fact that attention can result in faster reaction times show that attention can change the *appearance* of an object? Not necessarily. It is possible that the target stimulus always appears identical, but attention enhances the observer's ability to press the button quickly. To answer the question of whether attention affects an object's appearance, we need to do an experiment that measures the *perceptual response* to a stimulus rather than the *speed of responding* to the stimulus.

A study by Marissa Carrasco and coworkers (2004) was designed to measure the perceptual response to grating stimuli with alternating light and dark bars, like the ones in **Figure 6.12c**. She was interested in determining whether attention affected the *perceived contrast* between the bars, where perceived contrast refers to how different the light and dark bars

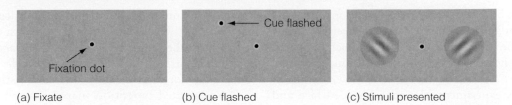

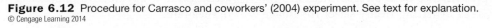

(a) Fixate   (b) Cue flashed   (c) Stimuli presented

Figure 6.12 Procedure for Carrasco and coworkers' (2004) experiment. See text for explanation.
© Cengage Learning 2014

appear. Carrasco's hypothesis was that attention would cause an *increase* in the perceived contrast of the gratings.

The procedure for Carassco's experiment, shown in **Figure 6.12**, was as follows: (a) Subjects were instructed to keep their eyes fixed on the small fixation dot at all times; (b) a cue stimulus was flashed for 67 ms either on the left or on the right. Subjects were told that this cue had no relation to the stimuli that followed it; (c) a pair of gratings was flashed for 40 ms. The gratings were tilted in different directions (one to the left and one to the right).

The contrast between the bars of the gratings was randomly varied from trial to trial, so sometimes the contrast of the right grating was higher, the contrast of the left grating was higher, or both gratings were identical. The subjects' task was to indicate on each trial whether the grating stimulus with the greatest contrast was tilted to the left or to the right. Thus, the subject first decided which grating had a higher contrast, and then indicated the orientation of that grating. Carrasco had subjects indicate orientation, rather than directly reporting how they perceived the gratings' contrast, to reduce the chances they might be influenced by any expectation they might have that attention might enhance the grating's perceived contrast.

Carrasco found that when two gratings were different, the attention-capturing dot had no effect. However, when two gratings were physically identical, subjects were more likely to report the orientation of the one that was on the same side as the flashed cue. Thus, when the two gratings

were the same, the one that received attention appeared to have more contrast. More than 100 years after William James suggested that attention makes an object "clear and vivid," Carrasco provided experimental evidence that attention does, in fact, enhance the appearance of an object. (Also see Carrasco, 2011; Carrasco et al., 2006.)

From the experiments we have described, it is clear that attention can affect both how a person *responds* to a stimulus and how a person *perceives* a stimulus. It should be no surprise that these effects of attention are accompanied by changes in physiological responding.

Attention Can Influence Physiological Responding

A large number of experiments have shown that attention affects physiological responding in a number of ways. We begin by considering evidence that attention increases the neural response to an attended item.

Attention to Objects Increases the Response of Specific Areas in the Brain In an experiment by Kathleen O'Craven and coworkers (1999), subjects saw a face and a house superimposed (**Figure 6.13a**). You may remember the experiment from Chapter 5 in which a picture of a house was presented to one eye and a picture of a face was presented to the other eye (Figure 5.47). In that experiment, presenting different images

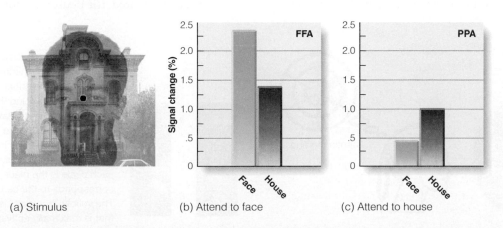

(a) Stimulus   (b) Attend to face   (c) Attend to house

Figure 6.13 (a) Superimposed face and house stimulus used in O'Craven and coworkers' (1999) experiment. (b) FFA activation when the subject attended to the face or the house. (c) PPA activation for attention to the face or the house. Based on data from O'Craven, K. M., Downing, P. E., & Kanwisher, N. (1999). fMRI evidence for objects as the units of attentional selection. *Nature, 401*, 584–587. Reproduced by permission.

to each eye created binocular rivalry, so perception alternated between the two images. When the face was perceived, activation occurred in the fusiform face area (FFA). When the house was perceived, activation occurred in the parahippocampal place area (PPA).

In O'Craven's experiment, the superimposed face and house stimuli were presented to both eyes, so there was no binocular rivalry. Instead of letting rivalry select the image that is visible, O'Craven asked subjects to direct their attention to one stimulus or the other. For each pair, one of the stimuli was stationary and the other was moving slightly back and forth. When looking at a pair, subjects were told to attend to either the moving or stationary house, the moving or stationary face, or to the direction of movement. As they were doing this, activity in their FFA, PPA, and MT/MST (the area specialized for movement) was measured.

The results for when subjects attended to the house or the face show that attending to the moving or stationary *face* caused enhanced activity in the FFA (**Figure 6.13b**) and attending to the moving or stationary *house* caused enhanced activity in the PPA (**Figure 6.13c**). In addition, attending to the movement caused activity in the movement areas, MT/MST, for both moving face and moving house stimuli. Thus, attention to different types of objects influences the activity in areas of the brain that process information about that type of object.

Attention to Locations Increases the Response at Specific Locations in the Brain

What happens in the brain when people shift their attention to different locations while keeping their eyes stationary? Ritobrato Datta and Edgar DeYoe (2009) answered this question by measuring how brain activity changed when covert attention was focused on different locations. They measured brain activity using fMRI as subjects kept their eyes fixed on the center of the display in **Figure 6.14a** and shifted their attention to different locations in the display. They found that the area of the brain that was activated depended on where the subject was directing his or her attention.

The colors in the circles in **Figure 6.14b** indicate the area of brain that was activated when the subject directed his or her attention to different locations indicated by the numbers

on the stimulus in Figure 6.14a. Notice that the yellow "hot spot," which is the place of greatest activation, moves out from the center and also becomes larger as attention is directed farther from the center. By collecting brain activation data for all of the locations on the stimulus, Datta and DeYoe created "attention maps" that show how directing attention to a specific area of space activates a specific area of the brain.

The attention maps are like the retinotopic map we described in Chapter 4 (see Figure 4.1), in which presenting objects at different locations on the retina activates different locations on the brain. However, in Datta and DeYoe's experiment, brain activation is changing not because images are appearing on different places on the retina, but because the subject is directing his or her mind to different places in the visual field.

What makes this experiment even more interesting is that after attention maps were determined for a particular subject, that subject was told to direct his or her attention to a "secret" place, unknown to the experimenters. Based on the location of the resulting yellow "hot spot," the experimenters were able to predict, with 100 percent accuracy, the "secret" place where the subject was attending. This is similar to the "mind reading" experiment we described on page 117 of Chapter 5, in which brain activity caused by an oriented line was analyzed to determine what orientation the person was seeing. In the attention experiments, brain activity caused by *where the person was attending* was analyzed to determine where the person was directing his or her mind!

Attention Can Shift the Location of a Neuron's Receptive Field

Another physiological effect of attention was demonstrated by Thilo Womelsdorf and coworkers (2006), who showed that attention can cause a monkey's receptive field to shift toward the place where attention is directed.

Remember from Chapter 3 that a neuron's receptive field is the area of retina that, when stimulated, influences the response of the neuron. The idea behind the receptive fields we described in Chapter 3 was simple: A particular neuron receives signals from a specific area on the retina, so when that area is stimulated, the neuron responds.

Figure 6.14 (a) Subjects in Datta and DeYoe's (2009) experiment directed their attention to different areas of this circular display while keeping their eyes fixed on the center of the display. (b) Activation of the brain that occurred when the subjects attended to the areas indicated by the numbers on the stimulus. The center of each circle is the place on the brain that corresponds to the center of the stimulus. The yellow "hot spot" is the area of the brain that is maximally activated. From Datta, R., & DeYoe, E. A. (2009). I know where you are secretly attending! The topography of human visual attention revealed with fMRI. *Vision Research, 49,* 1037–1044. Reproduced with permission.

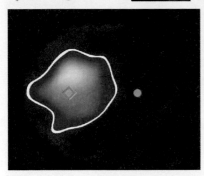
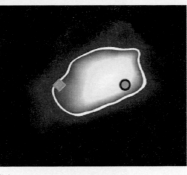

◆ S1 ● S2 0 ▬▬▬▬ 50 spikes per s

(a)   (b)

Figure 6.15 Receptive field maps on the retina determined when a monkey was attending to locations corresponding to (a) the small diamond and (b) the small circle. The yellow areas are areas of the receptive field that generate the largest response. Notice that the receptive field map shifts to the right when the monkey shifts its attention from the diamond to the circle. From Womelsdorf, T., Anton-Erxleben, K., Pieper, F., & Treue, S. (2006). Dynamic shifts of visual receptive fields in cortical area MT by spatial attention. *Nature Neuroscience, 9,* 1156–1160. Reproduced with permission.

In our discussion in Chapter 3, we never considered the possibility that a neuron's receptive field could change. But Womelsdorf showed that attention can cause slight shifts in a receptive field's location on the retina. He demonstrated this by recording from neurons in a monkey's middle temporal (MT) cortex, an area in the temporal lobe responsible for processing information about motion. Womelsdorf mapped the receptive fields of a neuron as the monkey shifted its attention to locations that correspond to different locations on the retina. **Figure 6.15** shows maps of the receptive fields on the monkey's retina, which were determined (a) when the monkey was attending to a location that corresponded to the small diamond and (b) when the monkey was attending to a location corresponding to the small circle. Yellow indicates the area of retina that, when stimulated, causes greatest response.

Notice that the receptive field is shifted to the left when the monkey is attending to the diamond on the left and is shifted to the right when the monkey shifts its attention to the circle on the right. This is an amazing result because it means that attention is changing the organization of part of the visual system. Receptive fields, it turns out, aren't fixed in place but can move in response to where the monkey is attending. This concentrates neural processing power right at the place that is important to the monkey at that moment.

TEST YOURSELF 6.1

1. What are the two main points that William James makes about attention? (Hint: what it is and what it does.) What are two reasons for paying attention to some things and ignoring others?

2. What does the demonstration that involved finding Justin Bieber's face tell us about attention and scanning?

3. What are fixations? Saccadic eye movements? Overt attention? How is overt attention measured? What is covert attention?

4. Describe the following factors that determine where we look: stimulus factors, cognitive factors, and task demands. Describe the examples or experiments that illustrate each

factor. (Be sure you understand the role of stimulus saliency, attentional capture, scene schemas, and scene statistics.)

5. What is spatial attention? Describe Posner's experiment on speeding response to locations. Be sure you understand the precueing procedure, covert attention, and what Posner's results demonstrated.

6. Describe Egly's and Moore's experiments on speeding response to objects (see Figures 6.10 and 6.11). What is the same-object advantage?

7. Describe Carrasco's experiment that showed an object's appearance can be changed by attention. Why did Carrasco have subjects report the *orientations* of the gratings rather than the *contrast* of the gratings?

8. Describe O'Craven's experiment that showed how attention to faces or houses affects responding of areas specialized to respond to faces or houses.

9. Describe Datta and DeYoe's experiment on how attending to different locations activates the brain. What is an attention map? What was the point of the "secret place" experiment? Compare this experiment to the "mind reading" experiments described at the end of Chapter 5.

10. Describe Womelsdorf's experiment that demonstrated how receptive fields are affected by attention.

What Happens When We Don't Attend?

We have seen that paying attention affects both responding to stimuli and perceiving them. But what happens when we don't pay attention? One idea is that you don't perceive things your aren't attending to. After all, if you're looking at something over to the left, you're not going to see something else that is far to the right. But research has shown not only that we miss things that are out of our field of view, but that not attending can cause us to miss things even if we are looking directly at them. One example of this is a phenomenon called **inattentional blindness**.

Inattentional Blindness

In 1998, Arien Mack and Irvin Rock published a book titled *Inattentional Blindness*, in which they described experiments that showed that subjects can be unaware of clearly visible stimuli if they aren't directing their attention to them. In an experiment based on one of Mack and Rock's experiments, Ula Cartwright-Finch and Nilli Lavie (2007) presented the cross stimulus shown in **Figure 6.16**. The cross was presented for five trials, and the observer's task was to indicate which arm of the briefly flashed cross was longer, the horizontal or the vertical. This is a difficult task because the cross was flashed rapidly, the arms were just slightly different in length, and the arm that was longer changed from trial to trial. On the sixth trial, a small outline of a square was added to the display (**Figure 6.16b**). Immediately after the sixth trial, subjects were asked whether they noticed if anything had appeared on the screen that they had not seen before. Out of 20 subjects, only 2 reported that they had seen the square. In other words, most of the subjects were "blind" to the small square, even though it was located right next to the cross. **VL**

This demonstration of inattentional blindness used a rapidly flashed geometric test stimulus. But similar effects occur for more naturalistic stimuli that are visible for longer periods of time. For example, imagine looking at a display in a department store window. When you focus your attention on the display, you probably fail to notice the reflections on the surface of the window. Shift your attention to the reflections, and you become less aware of the display inside the window.

The idea that attention can affect perception of overlapping scenes was tested in an experiment by Daniel Simons and Christopher Chabris (1999), who created a 75-second film that showed two "teams" of three players each. One team, dressed in white, was passing a basketball around, and the other was "guarding" that team by following them

Figure 6.17 Frame from Simons and Chabris's (1999) experiment.
Figure provided by Daniel Simons. Simons, D. J., & Chabris, C. F. (1999). Gorillas in our midst: Sustained inattentional blindness for dynamic events. *Perception, 28*, 1059–1074. Used by permission.

around and putting their arms up as in a basketball game (**Figure 6.17**). Observers were told to count the number of passes, a task that focused their attention on the team wearing white. After about 45 seconds, one of two events occurred. Either a woman carrying an umbrella or a person in a gorilla suit walked through the "game," an event that took 5 seconds.

After seeing the video, observers were asked whether they saw anything unusual happen or whether they saw anything other than the six players. Nearly half of the observers—46 percent—failed to report that they saw the woman or the gorilla. This experiment demonstrated that when observers are attending to one sequence of events, they can fail to notice another event, even when it is right in front of them (also see Goldstein & Fink, 1981; Neisser & Becklen, 1975).

Change Detection

Following in the footsteps of the superimposed image experiments, researchers developed another way to demonstrate how a lack of attention can affect perception. Instead of presenting several stimuli at the same time, they first presented one picture, then another slightly different picture. To appreciate how this works, try the following demonstration. **VL**

DEMONSTRATION
Change Detection

When you are finished reading these instructions, look at the picture in **Figure 6.18** for just a moment, and then turn the page and see whether you can determine what is different in **Figure 6.20**. Do this now.

Were you able to see what was different in the second picture? People often have trouble detecting the change even though it is obvious when you know where to look.

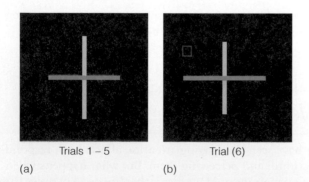

Trials 1 – 5   Trial (6)

(a)   (b)

Figure 6.16 Inattentional blindness experiment. (a) The cross display is presented for five trials. One arm of the cross is slightly longer on each trial. The subject's task is to indicate which arm (horizontal or vertical) is longer. (b) On the sixth trial, the subjects carry out the same task, but a small square is included in the display. After the sixth trial, subjects are asked if they saw anything different than before. Adapted from Lavie, N. (2010). Attention, distraction, and cognitive control under load. *Current Directions in Psychological Science, 19*, 143–148. Reproduced with permission.

Figure 6.18 Stimulus for change blindness demonstration. See text.

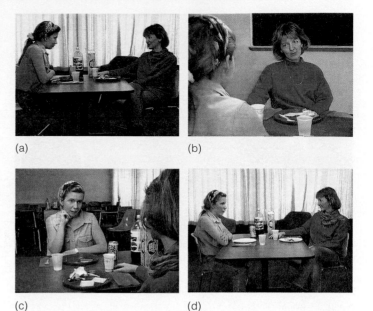

(a)   (b)

(c)   (d)

Figure 6.19 Frames from a video that demonstrates change blindness. The woman on the right is wearing a scarf around her neck in shots (a), (c), and (d), but not in shot (b). Also, the color of the plates changes from red in the first three frames to white in frame (d), and the hand position of the woman on the left changes between shots (c) and (d). From Levin, D., & Simons, D. (1997). Failure to detect changes to attended objects in motion pictures. *Psychonomic Bulletin and Review, 4,* 501–506.

(See the bottom of page 149 for a hint and then try again.) Ronald Rensink and coworkers (1997) did a similar experiment in which they presented one picture, followed by a blank field, followed by the same picture but with an item missing, followed by a blank field, and so on. The pictures were alternated in this way until observers were able to determine what was different about the two pictures. Rensink found that the pictures had to be alternated back and forth a number of times before the difference was detected.

This difficulty in detecting changes in scenes is called **change blindness** (Rensink, 2002). The importance of attention (or lack of it) in determining change blindness is demonstrated by the fact that when Rensink added a cue indicating which part of a scene had been changed, participants detected the changes much more quickly (also see Henderson & Hollingworth, 2003).

The change blindness effect also occurs when the scene changes in different shots of a film. **Figure 6.19** shows successive frames from a video of a brief conversation between two women. The noteworthy aspect of this video is that changes take place in each new shot. In (b), the woman's scarf has disappeared; in (c), the other woman's hand is on her chin, although seconds later, in (d), both arms are on the table. Also, the plates change color from red in the initial views to white in (d).

Although participants who viewed this video were told to pay close attention, only 1 of 10 participants claimed to notice any changes. Even when the participants were shown the video again and were warned that there would be changes in "objects, body position, or clothing," they noticed fewer than a quarter of the changes that occurred (Levin & Simons, 1997).

This blindness to change in films is not just a laboratory phenomenon. It occurs regularly in popular films, in which some aspect of the scene, which should remain the same, changes from one shot to the next, just as objects changed in the film shots in Figure 6.19. These changes in films, called *continuity errors*, are spotted by viewers who are looking for them, usually by viewing the film multiple times, but are usually missed by viewers in theaters who are not looking for these errors.

For example, in the film *Oceans 11* (2001), Rusty, the character played by Brad Pitt, is talking to Linus, the character played by Matt Damon. In one shot, Rusty is holding a cocktail glass full of shrimp in his hand, but in the next shot, which moves in closer and is from a slightly different angle, the glass has turned into a plate of fruit, and then in the next shot the plate changes back to the cocktail glass full of shrimp! If you are interested in exploring continuity errors further, you can find websites devoted to them by searching for "continuity errors in movies."

We have seen from the inattentional blink and change detection experiments that people can miss things that they aren't attending to. But does the fact that attention is important for perception mean that it is always necessary? Some researchers have concluded that it is possible to perceive the gist of a scene and to detect objects in a scene without attention. We will now consider two experiments: one that concludes attention is not necessary for perceiving objects in scenes and another that comes to the opposite conclusion.

Is Attention Necessary for Perceiving Scenes?

One reason it seems reasonable to suppose that attention may not be necessary for perceiving scenes is that people can identify the gist of a scene after seeing a picture for less than a quarter of a second (see page 109; also see Van Rullen & Thorpe, 2001). Fei Fei Li and coworkers (2002) took this as their starting point for an experiment using the **dual-task procedure**, in which subjects are required to carry out simultaneously a

Figure 6.20 Stimulus for change blindness demonstration. See text.

central task that demands attention and a *peripheral task* that involves making a decision about the contents of a scene.

Li's subjects looked at the + on a fixation screen (**Figure 6.21a**) and then saw the central stimulus, an array of five letters (**Figure 6.21b**). On some trials, all of the letters were the same; on other trials, one of the letters was different from the other four. The letters were followed immediately by the peripheral stimulus—either a disc that was half green and half red or a picture of a scene—flashed for 27 ms at a random position on the edge of the screen (**Figure 6.21c**).

The subjects' central task was to indicate if all of the letters in the central stimulus were the same, and their peripheral task was to indicate whether the scene contained an animal (for the picture) or whether the colored discs were red–green or green–red (for the discs). Even though subjects had to keep their attention focused on the letters in the middle in order

to carry out the central letter task, their performance was 90 percent on the peripheral picture task, but only 50 percent on the peripheral colored-disc task (**Figure 6.21d**). Thus, performance on the colored discs was reduced to chance levels by the central task but stayed high for the pictures. Li concluded from this result that properties of scenes can be perceived with little or no attention (see also Tsuchiya & Koch, 2009).

Recently, however, Michael Cohen and coworkers (2011) wondered if Li's central letter task did not distract attention enough. To test this idea, Cohen created a letter–number task in which a series of letters and numbers were rapidly flashed (for example, G, N, W, 4, A, Y, 5, T) and subjects indicated how many numbers they saw. While they were doing this central task, subjects indicated if a rapidly flashed picture contained an animal or a vehicle. When the peripheral animal–vehicle task was presented alone, without the central task, subjects were correct 89 percent of the time. However, their performance dropped to 63 percent when their attention was distracted by the central letter–number task. From this result, Cohen concluded that "the perception of natural scenes does require attention" (p. 1170). **VL**

But Cohen also noted that even though performance dropped when attention was distracted from the scene, it was still above chance. Perhaps, suggests Cohen, a more difficult central task would have caused a larger decrease in performance, or perhaps there are some aspects of scene perception that require attention and some that don't.

What can we conclude from this? Cohen states that perceiving scenes requires attention, but then leaves open the possibility that some aspects of scene perception may not require attention. Another recent experiment confirms Cohen's finding that a distracting task can decrease the ability to perceive scenes (Mack & Clarke, 2012). Clearly, further research is needed to determine whether attention is necessary for perceiving scenes.

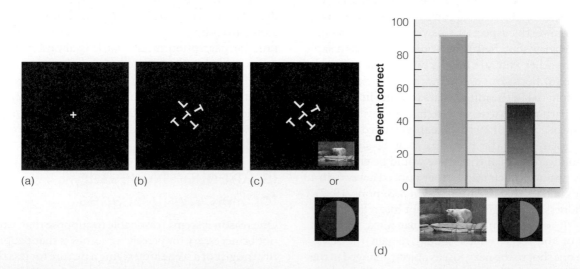

Figure 6.21 (a–c) Procedure for Li and coworkers' (2002) experiment. See text for details. (d) Results of the experiment. Performance is the percent correct when carrying out the central task compared to the percent correct when not carrying out the central task. Performance drops only slightly for the scene task but drops to near chance for the colored-disc task. Adapted from Li, F., VanRullen, R., Koch, C., & Perona, P. (2002). Rapid natural scene categorization in the near absence of attention. *Proceedings of the National Academy of Sciences, 99,* 9596–9601. Photo of polar bear: Barbara Goldstein.

The Distracting Effect of Task-Irrelevant Stimuli

We mentioned earlier in the chapter that stimuli that are highly salient, such as a bright flash, can capture our attention and possibly warn us of a dangerous situation that we want to avoid (see page 130). But sometimes when unattended stimuli attract our attention, they simply distract us from something we are doing. For example, a colorful pop-up ad for a dating service that suddenly appears on your computer screen might interfere with your search for a recently received email in your inbox; or an eye-catching billboard along the side of the highway might distract your attention from the traffic situation on the road in front of you (Forster & Lavie, 2008).

Stimuli that don't provide information relevant to the task with which we are involved are **task-irrelevant stimuli**. Examples such as the computer pop-up or the billboard are *distracting* task-irrelevant stimuli, which can potentially decrease our performance of a task. It isn't surprising that the amount of distraction depends on properties of the distracting stimulus, with highly salient stimuli being more likely to cause distraction. However, the effect of a potentially distracting stimulus also depends on the characteristics of the task.

Distraction and Task Characteristics

The idea that the effect of an unattended stimulus depends on the nature of the task was suggested by Nilli Lavie (1995, 2006, 2010), who showed, in a number of experiments, that

if the task is easy, then task-irrelevant stimuli have an effect on performance. However, if the task is hard, task-irrelevant stimuli have little or no effect on performance.

An experiment by Sophie Forster and Lavie (2008) illustrates this result. The subjects' task was to respond as quickly as possible when they identified a target, either X or N, in displays like the ones in **Figure 6.22a**. Subjects pressed one key if they saw the X and another key if they saw the N. This task is easy for displays like the one on the left in which the target is surrounded by just one type of letter, like the o's. However, the task becomes harder when the target is surrounded by different letters, as in the display on the right. This difference is reflected in the reaction times, with the hard task resulting in slower reaction times than the easy task. However, when a task-irrelevant stimulus is flashed off to the side, like the cartoon character in the displays in **Figure 6.22b**, responding slows for the easy task and is affected only slightly for the hard task. **VL**

Attention and Perceptual Load

Lavie explains results such as the ones in Figure 6.22b in terms of her **load theory of attention**, which involves two key concepts: *perceptual capacity* and *perceptual load*. **Perceptual capacity** refers to the idea that a person has a certain capacity that can be used for carrying out perceptual tasks. **Perceptual load** is the amount of a person's perceptual capacity needed to carry out a particular perceptual task. Some tasks, especially easy, well-practiced ones, have low perceptual loads; these **low-load tasks** use up only a small amount of the person's

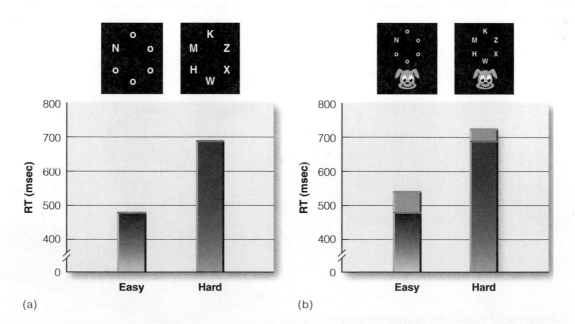

(a)   (b)

Figure 6.22 The task in Forster and Lavie's (2008) experiment was to indicate the identity of a target (X or N) as quickly as possible. (a) The reaction time for the easy condition like the display on the left, in which the target is accompanied by small o's, is faster than the reaction time for the hard condition, in which the target is accompanied by other letters. (b) Flashing a distracting cartoon character increases the reaction time for the easy task but has a smaller effect on the hard task. The increase for each task is indicated by the blue extensions of the bars. Adapted from Forster, S., & Lavie, N. (2008). Failures to ignore entirely irrelevant distractors: The role of load. *Journal of Experimental Psychology: Applied, 14*, 73–83.

perceptual capacity. Other tasks, those that are difficult and perhaps not as well practiced, are **high-load tasks** and use more of a person's perceptual capacity. Lavie proposes that the amount of perceptual capacity that remains as a person is carrying out a task determines how well the person can avoid being distracted by task-irrelevant stimuli.

This idea is illustrated in **Figure 6.23**. The circle in this figure represents a person's total perceptual capacity, and the shading represents the portion that is used up by a task. In **Figure 6.23a**, only part of the person's resources are being used by a low-load task, leaving resources available for processing other stimuli that may be present, as was the case for the "easy" or low-load task in Forster and Lavie's experiment (Figure 6.22).

Figure 6.23b shows a situation in which all or most of a person's perceptual capacity is being used by a high-load task, such as the hard task in the experiment. When this occurs, no resources remain to process other stimuli, so irrelevant stimuli can't be processed and they have little effect on performance of the task.

One way to understand the idea that load is important is to think about situations in which you have been totally focused on something, because it is either extremely interesting or difficult to carry out. Saying that such a situation is demanding all your attention is another way of saying that you are using all your cognitive resources and therefore are less likely to be distracted by task-irrelevant stimuli.

We can also apply Lavie's load theory to the phenomenon of inattentional blindness we described earlier. Remember that when subjects had to decide which line in a display like Figure 6.16 was longer, only 10 percent of the subjects were aware of the small square presented near the cross. In terms of load theory, the difficult length estimation task is a high-load task that uses up most of a person's perceptual

capacity, so there are few resources left to detect the small, unattended stimulus. However, when the task was turned into a low-load task by asking subjects to indicate which of the cross-hairs was green (horizontal or vertical), then 55 percent of the subjects reported seeing the unattended object (Cartwright-Finch & Lavie, 2007; Lavie, 2010).

Attention and Experiencing a Coherent World

We have seen that attention is an important determinant of what we perceive. Attention brings things to our awareness and can enhance our ability to perceive and to respond. We now consider yet another function of attention, one that is not obvious from our everyday experience. This function of attention is to help create **binding**, which is the process by which features—such as color, form, motion, and location—are combined to create our perception of a coherent object.

Why Is Binding Necessary?

We can appreciate why binding is necessary by remembering our discussion of modularity in Chapter 4, when we saw that separated areas of the brain are specialized for the perception of different qualities. In Chapter 4 we focused on the inferotemporal (IT) cortex, which is associated with perceiving forms. But there are also areas associated with motion, location, and possibly color (the exact locations of areas for color are still being researched) located at different places in the cortex.

Thus, when the person in **Figure 6.24** observes a red ball roll by, cells sensitive to the ball's shape fire in his IT cortex, cells sensitive to movement fire in his middle temporal

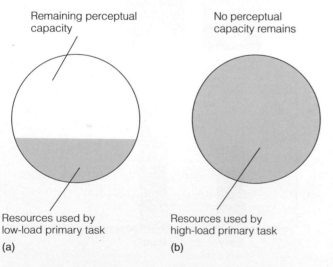

Figure 6.23 The rationale for the idea that (a) low-load tasks that use few cognitive resources may leave resources available for processing unattended task-irrelevant stimuli, whereas (b) high-load tasks that use all of a person's cognitive resources don't leave any resources to process unattended task-irrelevant stimuli. © Cengage Learning 2014

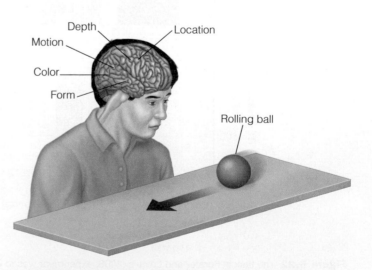

Figure 6.24 Any stimulus, even one as simple as a rolling ball, activates a number of different areas of the cortex. Binding is the process by which these separated signals are combined to create a unified perception. © Cengage Learning

cortex, and cells sensitive to color fire in other areas. But even though the ball's shape, movement, and color cause firing in different areas of the person's cortex, he doesn't perceive the ball as separated shape, movement, and color perceptions. He experiences an integrated perception of a ball, with all of the ball's features being bound together to create a coherent perception of a "rolling red ball." The question of how an object's individual features become bound together, which is called the **binding problem**, has been addressed by Anne Treisman's (1986, 1988, 1999) *feature integration theory*.

Feature Integration Theory

Treisman's **feature integration theory** tackles the question of how we perceive individual features as part of the same object. In her theory, the first step in processing an image of an object is the **preattentive stage** (the first box in the flow diagram in **Figure 6.25**). In the preattentive stage, objects are analyzed into separate features. For example, the rolling red ball would be analyzed into the features color (red), shape (round), and movement (rolling to the right). Because each of these features is processed in a separate area of the brain, they exist independently of one another at this stage of processing.[1]

The idea that an object is automatically broken into features may seem counterintuitive because when we look at an object, we see the whole object, not an object that has been divided into its individual features. The reason we aren't aware of this process of feature analysis is that it occurs early in the perceptual process, before we have become conscious of the object. Thus, when you see this book, you are conscious of its rectangular shape, but you are not aware that before you saw this rectangular shape, your perceptual system analyzed the book into individual features such as lines with different orientations.

Evidence That Objects Are Analyzed Into Features To provide some perceptual evidence that objects are, in fact, analyzed into features, Anne Treisman and H. Schmidt (1982) did an ingenious experiment to show that early in the perceptual process, features may exist independently of one another. Treisman and Schmidt's display consisted of four objects flanked by two black numbers (**Figure 6.26**). They flashed this display onto a screen for one-fifth of a second, followed by a random-dot masking field designed to eliminate any residual perception that might remain after the

Figure 6.26 Stimuli similar to those used in Treisman and Schmidt's (1982) experiment. When participants first attended to the black numbers and then to the other objects, some illusory conjunctions, such as "green triangle," occurred. © Cengage Learning

stimuli were turned off. Participants were told to report the black numbers first and then to report what they saw at each of the four locations where the shapes had been.

In 18 percent of the trials, participants reported seeing objects that were made up of a combination of features from two different stimuli. For example, after being presented with the display in Figure 6.26, in which the small triangle is red and the small circle is green, they might report seeing a small red circle and a small green triangle. These combinations of features from different stimuli are called **illusory conjunctions**. Illusory conjunctions can occur even if the stimuli differ greatly in shape and size. For example, a small blue circle and a large green square might be seen as a large blue square and a small green circle.

Although illusory conjunctions are usually demonstrated in laboratory experiments, they can occur in other situations as well. Recently I ran a class demonstration to illustrate that observers sometimes make errors in eyewitness testimony. In the demonstration, a male wearing a green shirt burst into the class, grabbed a yellow purse that was sitting on a desk (the owner of the purse was in on the demonstration), and left the room. This event happened very rapidly and was a surprise to students in the class. Their task was to describe what had happened as eyewitnesses to a "crime." Interestingly enough, one of the students reported that a male wearing a yellow shirt grabbed a green purse from the desk! Interchanging the colors of these objects is an example of illusory conjunctions (Treisman, 2005).

According to Treisman, illusory conjunctions occur because at the beginning of the perceptual process, each feature exists independently of the others. That is, features such as "redness," "curvature," or "tilted line" are, at this early stage of processing, not associated with a specific object. They are, in Treisman's (1986) words, "free floating," as shown in **Figure 6.27**, and can therefore be incorrectly combined if there is more than one object, especially in laboratory situations when briefly flashed stimuli are followed by a masking field.

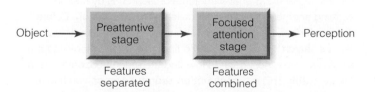

Figure 6.25 Flow diagram of Treisman's (1988) feature integration theory. © Cengage Learning

---

[1]This is a simplified version of feature integration theory. For a more detailed description of the model, which also includes "feature maps" that code the location of each of an object's features, see Treisman (1999).

"Free-Floating" Features

Small Triangle Red   Circle Large Yellow

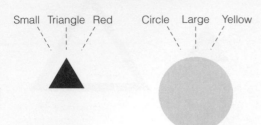

Figure 6.27 Illustration of the idea that in the preattentive stage, an object's features are "free floating." Because they are not attached to a particular object, they can potentially become associated with any object in a display. When this happens, an illusory conjunction is created. © Cengage Learning

You can think of these features as components of a visual "alphabet." At the very beginning of the process, perceptions of each of these components exist independently of one another, just as the letter tiles in a game of Scrabble exist as individual units when the tiles are scattered at the beginning of the game. However, just as the individual Scrabble tiles are combined to form words, the individual features combine to form perceptions of whole objects.

Focused Attention Stage According to Treisman's model, these features are combined in the second stage, called the **focused attention stage** (Figure 6.25). Once the features have been combined in this stage, we perceive the object.

During the focused attention stage, the observer's attention plays an important role in combining the features to create the perception of whole objects. To illustrate the importance of attention for combining the features, Treisman repeated the illusory conjunction experiment using the stimuli in Figure 6.26, but this time she instructed her participants to ignore the black numbers and to focus all of their attention on the four target items. This focusing of attention eliminated illusory conjunctions so that all of the shapes were paired with their correct colors.

When I describe this process in class, some students aren't convinced. One student said, "I think that when people look at an object, they don't break it into parts. They just see what they see." To convince this student (and the many others who, at the beginning of the course, are not comfortable with the idea that perception sometimes involves rapid processes we aren't aware of), I describe the case of R.M., a patient who had parietal lobe damage that resulted in a condition called **Balint's syndrome**. A crucial characteristic of Balint's syndrome is an inability to focus attention on individual objects.

According to feature integration theory, lack of focused attention would make it difficult for R.M. to combine features correctly, and this is exactly what happened. When R.M. was presented with two different letters of different colors, such as a red T and a blue O, he reported illusory conjunctions such as "blue T" on 23 percent of the trials, even when he was able to view the letters for as long as 10 seconds

Figure 6.28 Stimuli used to show that top-down processing can reduce illusory conjunctions. © Cengage Learning

(Friedman-Hill et al., 1995; Robertson et al., 1997). The case of R.M. illustrates how a breakdown in the brain can reveal processes that are not obvious when the brain is functioning normally.

The feature analysis approach involves mostly bottom-up processing because knowledge is usually not involved. In some situations, however, top-down processing can come into play. For example, when Treisman and Schmidt (1982) did an illusory conjunction experiment using stimuli such as the ones in **Figure 6.28** and asked participants to identify the objects, the usual illusory conjunctions occurred; the orange triangle, for example, would sometimes be perceived to be black. However, when she told participants that they were being shown a carrot, a lake, and a tire, illusory conjunctions were less likely to occur, and participants were more likely to perceive the triangular "carrot" as being orange. In this situation, the participants' knowledge of the usual colors of objects influenced their ability to correctly combine the features of each object. In our everyday experience, in which we often perceive familiar objects, top-down processing combines with feature analysis to help us perceive things accurately.

Visual Search Another approach to studying the role of attention in binding has used a task called visual search. **Visual search** is something we do anytime we look for an object among a number of other objects, such as looking for Justin Bieber in a group of musicians or trying to find Waldo in a "Where's Waldo?" picture (Handford, 1997). A type of visual search called a *conjunction search* has been particularly useful in studying binding.

DEMONSTRATION
Searching for Conjunctions

We can understand what a conjunction search is by first describing another type of search called a **feature search**. Before reading further, find the horizontal line in **Figure 6.29a**. This is a feature search because you could find the target by looking for a single feature—"horizontal." Now find the green horizontal line in **Figure 6.29b**. This is a conjunction search because you had to search for a combination (or conjunction) of two or more features in the same stimulus—"horizontal" and "green." In Figure 6.29b, you couldn't focus just on green because there are vertical green lines, and you couldn't focus just on horizontal because there are horizontal red lines. You had to look for the *conjunction* of horizontal and green.

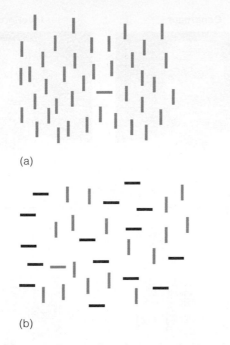

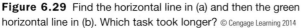

(a)

(b)

Figure 6.29 Find the horizontal line in (a) and then the green horizontal line in (b). Which task took longer? © Cengage Learning 2014

Conjunction searches are useful for studying binding because finding the target in a conjunction search involves scanning a display in order to focus attention at a specific location. To test the idea that attention to a location is required for a conjunction search, a number of researchers have tested the Balint's patient R.M. and have found that he cannot find the target when a conjunction search is required (Robertson et al., 1997). This is what we would expect because of R.M's difficulty in focusing attention. R.M. can, however, find targets when only a feature search is required, as in Figure 6.29a, because attention-at-a-location is not required for this kind of search. Feature integration theory therefore considers attention to be an essential component of the mechanism that creates our perception of objects from a number of different features.

SOMETHING TO CONSIDER:
Attention in Autism

Not only is attention important for detecting objects in the environment, as described above, it is also a crucial component of social situations. People pay attention not only to what others are saying, but also to their faces (Gullberg & Holmqvist, 2006) and to where they are looking (Kuhn & Land, 2006; Tatler & Kuhn, 2007), because these things provide information about the other person's thoughts, emotions, and feelings.

The link between attention and perceptions of social interactions becomes especially evident when we consider a situation in which that link is disturbed, as occurs in people with **autism.** Autism is a serious developmental

disorder in which one of the major symptoms is the withdrawal of contact from other people. People with autism typically do not make eye contact with others and have difficulty telling what emotions others are experiencing in social situations.

Research has revealed many differences in both behavior and brain processes between autistic and nonautistic people (Grelotti et al., 2002, 2005). Ami Klin and coworkers (2003) note the following paradox: Even though people with autism can often solve reasoning problems that involve social situations, they cannot function when placed in an actual social situation. One possible explanation is differences in the way autistic people observe what is happening. Klin and coworkers (2003) demonstrated this by comparing eye fixations of autistic and nonautistic people as they watched the film *Who's Afraid of Virginia Woolf?*

Figure 6.30 shows fixations on a shot of the actor's faces. The shot occurs just after another character has smashed a bottle. The nonautistic observers fixated on the male actor's eyes in order to access his emotional reaction, but the autistic observers looked near the female actor's mouth or off to the side.

Another difference between how autistic and nonautistic observers direct their attention is related to the tendency of nonautistic people to direct their eyes to the place where a person is pointing. **Figure 6.31** compares the fixations of a nonautistic person (shown in white) and an autistic person (shown in black). In this scene, the male character points to the painting and asks the actor on the right, "Who did the painting?" The nonautistic person follows the pointing movement from the finger to the painting and then looks at the actor's face to await a reply. In contrast, the autistic observer looks elsewhere first, then back and forth between the pictures.

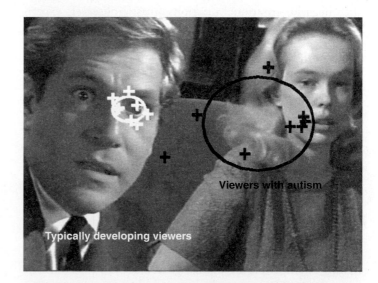

Figure 6.30 Where people look when viewing this image from the film *Who's Afraid of Virginia Woolf?* Nonautistic viewers: white crosses; autistic viewers: black crosses. From Klin, A., Jones, W., Schultz, R., & Volkmar, F. (2003). The enactive mind, or from actions to cognition: Lessons from autism. *Philosophical Transactions of the Royal Society of London B, 358,* 345–360.

Figure 6.31 Scan paths for nonautistic viewers (white path) and autistic viewers (black path) in response to the picture and dialogue while viewing this shot from *Who's Afraid of Virginia Woolf?* From Klin, A., Jones, W., Schultz, R., & Volkmar, F. (2003). The enactive mind, or from actions to cognition: Lessons from autism. *Philosophical Transactions of the Royal Society of London B, 358,* 345–360.

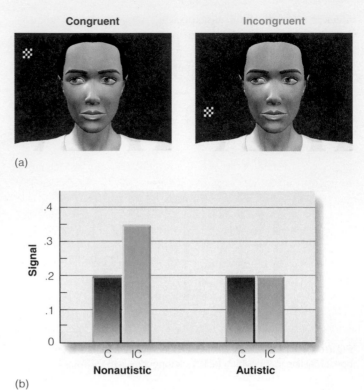

Figure 6.32 (a) Observers in Pelphrey and coworkers' (2005) experiment saw either the congruent condition, in which the animated character looked at the checkerboard 1 second after it appeared, or the incongruent condition, in which the character looked somewhere else 1 second after the checkerboard appeared. (b) Response of the STS in nonautistic and autistic observers to the two conditions. C = congruent; IC = incongruent. From Pelphrey, K. A., Morris, J. P., & McCarthy, G. (2005). Neural basis of eye gaze processing deficits in autism. *Brain, 128,* 1038–1048. By permission of Oxford University Press.

These results indicate that because of the way autistic people attend to events as they unfold in a social situation, they may perceive the environment differently than normal observers. Autistic people look more at things, whereas non-autistic observers look at other people's actions and especially at their faces and eyes. It is likely, therefore, that autistic observers create a mental representation of a situation that does not include much of the information that nonautistic observers usually use in interacting with others.

The exact cause of the differences in eye movement patterns of autistic and nonautistic observers is, however, not clear. One suggestion is that the differences may have to do with negative emotional reactions autistic observers experience when looking at or interacting with other people. These negative emotions influence where they look, which influences how well they can understand what is happening, which in turn makes it even more difficult to function in social situations. Another idea is that autistic observers process face stimuli differently, so when they do look at faces they focus on individual features or details within the face and don't see faces as whole (Behrmann et al., 2006). The most likely explanation is that attentional differences are caused by a combination of social and perceptual factors.

Other experiments provide clues to physiological differences in attention between autistic and nonautistic people. Kevin Pelphrey and coworkers (2005) measured brain activity in the superior temporal sulcus (STS; see Figure 5.52), an area in the temporal lobe that has been shown to be sensitive to how other people direct their gaze in social situations. For example, the STS is strongly activated when a passerby makes eye contact with a person, but is more weakly activated if the passerby doesn't make eye contact (Pelphrey et al., 2004).

Pelphrey measured STS activity as autistic and nonautistic people watched an animated character's eyes move 1 second after a flashing checkerboard appeared (**Figure 6.32a**). The character either looked at the checkerboard (congruent condition) or in a direction away from the checkerboard (incongruent condition). To determine whether the observers saw the eye movements, Pelphrey asked his observers to press a button when they saw the character's eyes move. Both autistic and nonautistic observers performed this task with 99 percent accuracy.

But even though both groups of observers saw the character's eyes move, there was a large difference between how the STS responded in the two groups. The STS of the nonautistic observers was activated more for the incongruent situation (left pair of bars in **Figure 6.32b**), but the STS of the autistic observers was activated equally in the congruent and incongruent situations (right pair of bars).

What does this result mean? Since both groups saw the character's eyes move, the difference may have to do with how observers *interpreted* what the eye movements meant. Pelphrey suggests that there is a difference in autistic and nonautistic people's ability to read other people's *intentions*. The nonautistic observers expected that the character would look at the checkerboard, and when that didn't happen, this caused a large STS response. Autistic observers, on the other hand, may not have expected the observer to look at the checkerboard, so the STS responded in the same way to both the congruent and incongruent stimuli.

The idea that neural responding may reflect cognitive factors, such as what people *expect* will happen in a particular situation, is something we will encounter again in the next chapter when we consider the connection between perception and how people interact with the environment.

DEVELOPMENTAL DIMENSION: Attention and Perceptual Completion

Although newborns have limited visual acuity (see Developmental Dimension: Infant Visual Acuity in Chapter 2, page 46), they show by their looking behavior that they prefer to look at some objects more than others. They look more at contours and high contrasts, and exhibit a preference for faces (see Developmental Dimension: Infant Face Perception in Chapter 5, page 120). However, many attentional processes don't begin emerging until after 3 months of age, and the full development of processes such as scanning the details of scenes continues well unto childhood and early adolescence (Amso, 2010).

Our concern here is not to survey the research on the development of attention, but to consider a possible link between the early emergence of attentional processes and **perceptual completion**—the perception of an object as extending behind occluding objects, such as the horizontal boards that partially block the view of the three men in Figure 5.24 (see page 104). (This is also referred to as achieving *object unity*.)

When adults look at a scene like the one in Figure 5.24, they perceive the men's bodies as continuing behind the boards on which they are leaning. But would a young infant perceive the upper, middle, and lower parts of the bodies as separate units or as parts of a single object that continues behind the boards? Research on this question has used the *habituation procedure*, which is based on the following fact about infant looking behavior: When given a choice between a familiar stimulus and a novel one, an infant is more likely to look at the novel one (Fagan, 1976; Slater et al., 1984).

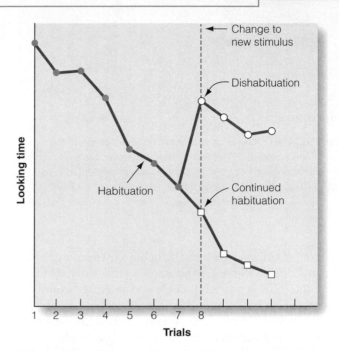

Figure 6.33 Possible results of a habituation experiment. See text for details. © Cengage Learning

If, however, the infant cannot tell the difference between the two stimuli, he or she will continue to habituate to the new stimulus (because it will not be perceived as novel), as indicated by the open blue squares. Remember that the occurrence of dishabituation means that the second stimulus appears different to the infant from the habituation stimulus.

METHOD
Habituation

Because infants are more likely to look at a novel stimulus, we can create a preference for one stimulus over another by familiarizing the infant with one stimulus but not with the other. For this technique, which is called **habituation**, one stimulus is presented to the infant repeatedly, and the infant's looking time is measured on each presentation (**Figure 6.33**). As the infant becomes more familiar with the stimulus, he or she habituates to it, looking less and less on each trial, as indicated by the green circles in Figure 6.33.

Once the infant has habituated to this stimulus, we determine whether the infant can tell the difference between it and another stimulus by presenting a new stimulus. In Figure 6.33, the new stimulus is presented on the eighth trial. If the infant can tell the difference between the habituation stimulus and the new stimulus, he or she will exhibit **dishabituation**, an increase in looking time when the stimulus is changed, as shown by the open red circles.

Habituation has been used to study the development of perceptual completion by presenting stimuli like the one in **Figure 6.34a**, which is a rod moving back and forth behind a rectangular occluder. Adults perceive the gray bars as part of a single rod that extends behind the rectangle. To determine how 4-month-old infants perceive this display, Philip Kellman and Elizabeth Spelke (1983) first habituated the infants to the rod moving back and forth behind a block, so the infants looked less and less at this stimulus. They then presented either two separated moving rods (top stimulus in **Figure 6.34b**) or a single longer moving rod (bottom stimulus in Figure 6.34b).

Remember that the principle of habituation is that after habituation to a stimulus, the infant looks longer at a new stimulus that is perceived as *different* from the habituation stimulus. Thus, looking longer at the *separated bars* on top would indicate that the infants perceived the display in

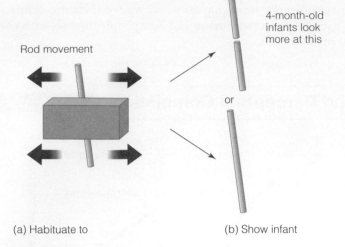

(a) Habituate to   (b) Show infant

4-month-old infants look more at this

or

Rod movement

Figure 6.34 (a) Stimulus used in the habituation phase of the Kellman and Spelke (1983) experiment. A rod moves back and forth behind a rectangular occluder. (b) Stimuli that are presented in the dishabituation phase of the experiment. Reprinted from Kellman, P. J., & Spelke, E. S. Perception of partly occluded objects in infancy. *Cognitive Psychology, 15*, 483–524, figure 3. Copyright © 1983, with permission from Elsevier.

Figure 6.34a as a *single bar* moving behind the rectangle. Kellman and Spelke obtained this result, and concluded that the infants had perceived a single rod moving behind the rectangle and therefore are capable of perceptual completion. This result did not occur, however, when the infant was habituated to a stationary rod and rectangle display. Thus, movement helped the 4-month-old infants infer that the bar extended behind the block. **VL**

If 4-month-olds perceive a moving object as continuing behind an occluding stimulus, can younger infants do this as well? When Alan Slater and coworkers (1990) repeated Kellman and Spelke's experiment with newborns, they found that when the newborns saw the moving rod during habituation, they looked more at the single rod when given the choice between the segmented or single rod. This suggests that they saw the moving rods as two separate units and not as a single rod extending behind the occluder. Apparently newborns do *not* make the inference that 4-month-olds make about the moving display.

Thus, the capacity demonstrated at 4 months does not exist (or can't be measured using this particular procedure) at birth. But when does it appear? Scott Johnson and Richard Aslin (1995) helped determine the answer when they tested 2-month-olds and obtained results for some of the infants that was similar to those for the 4-month-olds. Apparently, the ability to use movement as a way to organize the perceptual world develops rapidly over the first few months of life.

The fact that young infants demonstrate perceptual completion only when the rod stimulus is moving has led to the hypothesis that perceptual completion depends on the infants' development of the ability to perceive motion, and specifically the common motion of objects such as the rods (Johnson et al., 2008). But further research suggests that perhaps motion perception isn't the crucial variable. For example, Johnson and

coworkers (2008) traced the development of infants' ability to detect the direction of motion and to follow moving objects with their eyes and found that there was no connection between the development of these aspects of motion perception and performance on the perceptual completion task.

But Johnson and coworkers (2004) found evidence for a connection between perceptual completion and attention. They first determined that at the age of 3 months, some infants perceived the moving rod as continuing behind the occluder and some did not. They labeled the infants who demonstrated perceptual completion *perceivers* and those who did not, *nonperceivers*. They then determined the eye fixation patterns for the two groups. **Figure 6.35** shows eye

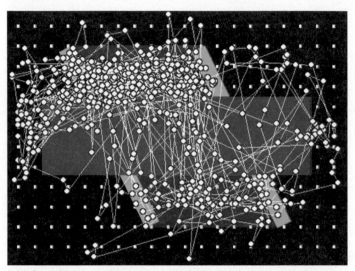

(a) Infants who perceived rod as continuing behind the occluder

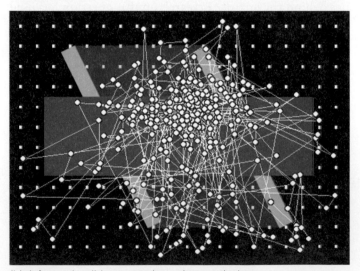

(b) Infants who did not perceive rod as continuing

Figure 6.35 How infants looked at a display during habituation, in which a rod moved back and forth behind a rectangular occluder. (a) Fixations for an infant who perceived the moving rod as a single object (a "perceiver"). (b) Fixations for an infant who did not perceive the moving rod as a single object (a "nonperceiver"). From Johnson, S. P., Slemmer, J. A., & Amso, D. (2004). Where infants look determines how they see: Eye movements and object perception performance in 3-month olds. *Infancy*, Vol. 6, Issue 2, pp. 185–201, Taylor & Francis. Records courtesy of Scott Johnson.

fixation records measured during habituation for a perceiver (**Figure 6.35a**) and a nonperceiver (**Figure 6.35b**). The two rods in each figure indicate the left- and right-most positions of the moving rod.

Notice that the perceiver fixated mainly on the rod, whereas the nonperceiver fixated on the rectangular occluder. Eye movement records also showed that, as a group, perceivers made more horizontal eye movements than nonperceivers. The perceivers, therefore, tended to look at the rod and follow its movement, whereas the nonperceivers looked more at the stationary occluder and other parts of the display that were not related to perceiving the rod as extending behind the occluder. Based on these results and others, Johnson and coworkers (2008) concluded that the infants' ability to achieve perceptual completion is most closely linked to the development of scanning patterns that enable them to actively explore the display and pick up the information necessary to infer that the two separated rods are actually one. Not surprisingly, there is a connection between how infants attend and what they perceive.

TEST YOURSELF 6.2

1. Describe the following two situations that illustrate how not attending can result in not perceiving: (1) inattentional blindness and (2) change detection.

2. Describe Li's experiment that shows that under certain conditions we can perceive qualities of things that we are not attending. How does the situation in Li's experiment differ from the situation in the change blindness experiments?

3. Describe the study by Forster and Lavie that shows that the distracting effect of a task-irrelevant stimulus depends on the nature of the task.

4. How is Forster and Lavie's result explained by Lavie's load theory of attention? Be sure you understand the concepts of perceptual resources and perceptual load.

5. How has load theory been applied to inattentional blindness experiments?

6. What are the two stages in feature integration theory? What does feature integration theory propose about the role of attention in perception and binding?

7. What evidence links attention and binding? Describe evidence that involves both illusory conjunctions and conjunction search in normal subjects and patients with Balint's syndrome.

8. Describe the results of experiments that measured (a) eye movements in autistic and nonautistic observers while they watched a film; (b) the response of the STS to "congruent" and "incongruent" conditions. What can we conclude from these results?

9. What is perceptual completion? Describe the experiment that demonstrates the existence of perceptual completion in infants. What is the role of movement in this experiment? What is the role of attention in determining perceptual completion?

THINK ABOUT IT

1. If salience is determined by characteristics of a scene such as contrast, color, and orientation, why might it be correct to say that paying attention to an object can increase its salience? (p. 130)

2. How is the idea of regularities of the environment that we introduced in Chapter 5 (see page 110) related to the cognitive factors that determine where people look? (p. 130)

3. Can you think of situations from your experience that are similar to the change detection experiments in that you missed seeing an object that became easy to see once you knew it was there? What do you think was behind your initial failure to see this object? (p. 138)

4. The "Something to Consider" section discussed differences between how autistic and nonautistic people direct their attention. Do you think differences in directing attention may also occur in nonautistic people? Can you think of situations in which you and another person perceived the same scene or event differently? (p. 145)

5. In describing the habituation procedure, it was stated that when given a choice between a familiar stimulus and a novel one, an infant is more likely to look at the novel one. But in the Developmental Dimension of Chapter 5, we saw that young infants tend to look more at a mother's face than at a stranger's face. Why do you think this would occur if infants usually tend to prefer looking at novel objects? (p. 147)

Hint for change detection demonstration on page 138: Pay attention to the sign near the lower left portion of the picture.

KEY TERMS

Attention (p. 127)
Attentional capture (p. 130)
Autism (p. 145)
Balint's syndrome (p. 144)
Binding (p. 142)
Binding problem (p. 143)
Change blindness (p. 139)
Conjunction search (p. 144)
Covert attention (p. 129)
Dishabituation (p. 147)
Dual-task procedure (p. 139)
Feature integration theory (p. 143)
Feature search (p. 144)

Fixation (p. 128)
Focused attention stage (p. 144)
Habituation (p. 147)
High-load task (p. 142)
Illusory conjunction (p. 143)
Inattentional blindness (p. 137)
Load theory of attention (p. 141)
Low-load task (p. 141)
Overt attention (p. 129)
Perceptual capacity (p. 141)
Perceptual completion (p. 147)
Perceptual load (p. 141)

Preattentive stage (p. 143)
Precueing (p. 133)
Saccadic eye movement (p. 128)
Saliency map (p. 130)
Same-object advantage (p. 134)
Scene schema (p. 131)
Scene statistics (p. 132)
Spatial attention (p. 133)
Stimulus salience (p. 130)
Task-irrelevant stimuli (p. 141)
Visual scanning (p. 128)
Visual search (p. 144)

MEDIA RESOURCES

CourseMate 🖥

Go to CengageBrain.com to access Psychology CourseMate, where you will find the Virtual Labs plus an interactive eBook, flashcards, quizzes, videos, and more.

Virtual Labs **VL**

The Virtual Labs are designed to help you get the most out of this course. The Virtual Lab icons direct you to specific media demonstrations and experiments designed to help you visualize what you are reading about. The numbers below indicate the number of the Virtual Lab you can access through Psychology CourseMate.

6.1 Task-driven Eye Movements (p. 132)
Eye movements made by a person making a peanut butter and jelly sandwich. (Courtesy of Mary Hayhoe)

6.2 Eye Movements: Adult Walking (p. 132)
Eye movements made as a person walks through a room. (Courtesy of John Franchak, Karen Adolph, and Kara Kretch)

6.3 Eye Movements: Infant Crawling (p. 132)
Eye movements made by an infant while retrieving objects to give to mother. (Courtesy of John Franchak, Karen Adolph, and Kara Kretch)

6.4 Inattentional Blindness Stimuli (p. 138)
Stimuli presented in Mack and Rock's (1998) inattentional blindness experiment. (Courtesy of Arien Mack)

6.5 Change Detection: Gradual Change (p. 138)
Demonstration of difficulty of detecting changes in a scene that is gradually changing.

6.6 Change Detection: Airplane (p. 138)
Change detection demonstration with picture of airplane. (Courtesy of Ronald Rensink)

6.7 Change Detection: Farm (p. 138)
Change detection demonstration with picture of farm. (Courtesy of Ronald Rensink)

6.8 Change Detection: Harborside (p. 138)
Change detection demonstration with picture of harborside. (Courtesy of Ronald Rensink)

6.9 Change Detection: Money (p. 138)
Change detection demonstration with picture of money. (Courtesy of Ronald Rensink)

6.10 Change Detection: Sailboats (p. 138)
Change detection demonstration with picture of sailboats. (Courtesy of Ronald Rensink)

6.11 Change Detection: Tourists (p. 138)
Change detection demonstration with picture of tourists. (Courtesy of Ronald Rensink)

6.12 Change Detection: Watch the Cards (p. 138)
Count the red cards.

6.13 Change Blindness (p. 138)
Demonstration of a change detection experiment carried out in the environment, focusing on experiments by Daniel Levin.

6.14 Perception Without Focused Attention: Reddy (2007) Experiment (p. 140)
Stimulus from an experiment that tested observers' ability to identify stimuli presented while carrying out a competing task. (Courtesy of Lila Reddy)

6.15 Perception Without Focused Attention: Cohen (2011) Experiment (p. 140)
Stimulus from another experiment that tested observers' ability to identify stimuli presented while carrying out a competing task. (Courtesy of Michael Cohen)

6.16 **Effect of Distracting Contrast** (p. 141)
A demonstration that shows how a distracting contrast-stimulus can affect perception of two flashing dots. (Courtesy of Arthur Shapiro)

6.17 **Rod Moving Behind Occluder** (p. 148)
Stimulus used to habituate infants to a rod moving back and forth behind a block. (Courtesy of Scott Johnson)

6.18 **Eye Movements Following a Ball** (p. 148)
How 4- and 6-month-old infants follow a moving ball that disappears behind an occluder and then reappears. (Courtesy of Scott Johnson)

Taking Action

VL The Virtual Lab icons direct you to specific animations and videos designed to help you visualize what you are reading about. Virtual Labs are listed at the end of the chapter, keyed to the page on which they appear, and can be accessed through Psychology CourseMate.

◄ How did McKayla Maroney of the U.S. gymnastics team, vaulting at the 2012 London Olympics, get into this position, and how did she execute a successful landing just moments later? As we will see in this chapter, the answer involves a close connection between perception and action, and this connection holds not just for spectacular athletic feats, but also for everyday actions such as walking across campus or reaching across a table to pick up a cup of coffee.

Some Questions We Will Consider:

■ What is the connection between perceiving and moving through the environment? (p. 154)

■ What is the connection between somersaulting and vision? (p. 155)

■ How do neurons called mirror neurons respond when a person perceives an action and when the person watches someone else perceive the same action? (p. 166)

Serena straps on her helmet for what she anticipates will be a fast, thrilling, and perhaps dangerous ride. As an employee of the Speedy Delivery Package Service, her mission is to deliver the two packages strapped to the back of her bicycle to an address 30 blocks uptown. Once on her bike, she weaves through traffic, staying alert to close calls with cars, trucks, pedestrians, and potholes. Seeing a break in traffic, she reaches down to grab her water bottle to take a quick drink before having to deal with the next obstacle. "Yes," Serena thinks, "I can multitask!" As she replaces the water bottle, she downshifts and keeps a wary eye out for the pedestrian ahead who looks as though he might decide to step off the curb at any moment.

Serena faces a number of challenges that involve both perception—using her sight and hearing to monitor what is happening in her environment—and action—staying balanced on her bike, staying on course, reaching for her water bottle, and being ready to avoid the pedestrian who does, as Serena predicted, step off the curb just as she is approaching.

We have discussed some of these things in the last two chapters: perceiving a scene and individual objects within it, scanning the scene to shift attention from one place to another, focusing on what is important and ignoring what is not, and relying on prior knowledge about characteristics of the environment. This chapter takes all of these things a step further by considering the processes involved in being *physically active* and interacting with objects within a scene. In other words, we are taking perception out into the world, where perception often occurs "on the run," as in Serena's bike trip, or in a more relaxed setting, as when Serena, resting in a coffee shop after her ride, reaches across the table to pick up her coffee cup. As we explain how Serena is able to stay on course, grab her water bottle, predict what is going to happen ahead, and reach for her cup of coffee, we will be describing how perceiving and taking action interact with one another. We will see, in this chapter, that we need to consider action to truly understand perception. To begin our discussion of perception and action, we consider an early and influential approach proposed by J. J. Gibson, who founded the ecological approach to perception.

The Ecological Approach to Perception

During World War II, J. J. Gibson studied the kind of perceptual information that airplane pilots use when coming in for a landing. In his first book, *The Perception of the Visual World* (1950), Gibson proposed that pilots use information that is created by their own movement. What this means is that they look out the window and, because of their movement, the terrain is rushing by beneath them. The perceived movement of the terrain provides information that helps the pilot guide the plane in for a landing. We will consider how pilots might use this information in a moment, but first it is important to note the difference between Gibson's approach and the way perception was being studied in the mid-20th century (Goldstein, 1981).

From the 1950s until the 1980s, the dominant way perception research was carried out was by having stationary observers look at stimuli in a laboratory situation. Gibson's idea was that this traditional way of studying perception couldn't explain perception as experienced by moving observers, such as pilots landing an airplane or people riding a bike or walking down the street. The correct approach, suggested Gibson, was to study how people perceive as they move through the environment. This focus on observers moving through the environment was the starting point for the **ecological approach to perception**. The ecological approach focuses on studying moving observers and on determining how their movement creates perceptual information that both guides further movement and helps observers perceive the environment.

The Moving Observer Creates Information in the Environment

To understand what it means to say that movement creates perceptual information, imagine that you are driving down the street. No other cars or people are visible, so everything around you—buildings, trees, traffic signals—is stationary. But even though the objects are stationary, your movement *relative to the objects* causes you to see the houses and trees moving past when you look out the side window. And when you look at the road ahead, you see the road moving toward the front of your car. As your car hurtles forward when crossing a bridge, everything around you—the sides and top of the bridge and

the road below—moves past you in a direction opposite to the direction you are moving (**Figure 7.1**). All of the movement you are seeing is called **optic flow**. According to Gibson, optic flow provides information about how rapidly we are moving and where we are headed. Optic flow has two characteristics:

1. Optic flow is more rapid near the moving observer, as indicated by the length of the arrows in Figure 7.1, with longer arrows indicating more rapid flow. The different speed of flow—fast near the observer and slower farther away—is called the **gradient of flow**. According to Gibson, the gradient of flow provides information about how fast the observer is moving.

2. There is no flow at the destination toward which the observer is moving. The absence of flow at the destination point is called the **focus of expansion (FOE)**. In Figure 7.1 the FOE, marked by the dot, is at the end of the bridge, and in **Figure 7.2**, which shows optic flow lines for an airplane coming in for a landing, the FOE is indicated by a small red dot. The FOE indicates the place where the plane will touch down on the runway if it maintains its present course. **VL**

Figure 7.1 The side and top of the bridge and the road below appear to move toward a car that is moving forward. This movement is called optic flow.

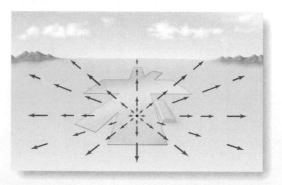

Figure 7.2 Optic flow created by an airplane coming in for a landing. The focus of expansion (FOE), indicated by the red dot, is the place where the plane will touch down on the runway. From Gibson, J. J. *The perception of the visual world.* Boston: Houghton Mifflin. 1950. Figure 58, page 128.

Another important concept of the ecological approach is the idea of **invariant information**—information that remains constant even when the observer is moving. Optic flow provides invariant information because flow information is present as long as the observer is moving through the environment. Of course, as the observer moves through a scene, the flow might look different—houses flow past on a city street, and trees on a country road—but flow is still there.

The FOE is another invariant property because it always occurs at the point toward which the observer is moving. If an observer changes direction, the FOE shifts to a new location, but the FOE is still there. Thus, even when specific aspects of a scene change, flow and the FOE continue to provide information about how fast a person is moving and where he or she is heading. When we consider depth perception in Chapter 11, we will see that Gibson proposed other sources of invariant information that indicate an object's size and its distance from the observer.

Self-Produced Information

Another idea of the ecological approach is **self-produced information**: When a person makes a movement, that movement creates information, and this information is, in turn, used to guide further movement (**Figure 7.3**). For example, when a person is driving down the street, movement of the car provides flow information, and the observer then uses this flow information to help steer the car in the right direction. Another example of movement that creates information that is used to guide further movement is provided by somersaulting.

We can appreciate the problem facing a gymnast who wants to execute an airborne backward somersault (or back flip) by realizing that, within 600 ms, the gymnast must execute the somersault and then end in exactly the correct body configuration precisely at the moment that he or she hits the ground (**Figure 7.4**). One way this could be accomplished is to learn to run a predetermined sequence of motions within a specific period of time. In this case, performance should be the same with eyes open or closed. However, Benoit Bardy and Makel Laurent (1998) found that expert gymnasts performed somersaults better with their eyes open. Films showed that

Figure 7.4 "Snapshots" of a somersault, or backflip, starting on the left and finishing on the right. From Bardy, B. G., & Laurent, M. (1998). How is body orientation controlled during somersaulting? *Journal of Experimental Psychology: Human Perception and Performance, 24,* 963–977. Copyright © 1998 by The American Physiological Society. Reprinted by permission.

when their eyes were open, the gymnasts appeared to be making in-the-air corrections to their trajectory. For example, a gymnast who initiated the extension of his or her body a little too late compensated by performing the rest of the movement more rapidly.

Another interesting result was that closing the eyes did not affect the performance of novice somersaulters as much as it affected the performance of experts. Apparently, experts learn to coordinate their movements with their perceptions, but novices have not yet learned to do this. Therefore, when the novices closed their eyes, the loss of visual information had less effect than it did for the experts. Thus, somersaulting, like driving a car or piloting an airplane, involves using information created by movement to guide further movement.

The Senses Do Not Work in Isolation

Gibson also proposed that the senses do not work in isolation. He believed that rather than considering vision, hearing, touch, smell, and taste as separated senses, we should consider how each one provides information for the same behaviors. One example of how a behavior originally thought to be the exclusive responsibility of one sense is also served by another one is provided by the sense of balance.

Your ability to stand up straight and to keep your balance while standing still or walking depends on systems that enable you to sense the position of your body. These systems include the vestibular canals of your inner ear and receptors in the joints and muscles. However, Gibson argued that information provided by vision also plays a role in keeping our balance. One way to illustrate the role of vision in balance is to consider what happens when visual information isn't available, as in the following demonstration.

DEMONSTRATION
Keeping Your Balance

Keeping your balance is something you probably take for granted. Stand up. Raise one foot from the ground and stay balanced on the other. Then close your eyes and notice what happens.

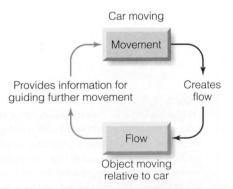

Figure 7.3 The relationship between movement and flow is reciprocal, with movement causing flow and flow guiding movement. This is the basic principle behind much of our interaction with the environment. © Cengage Learning 2014

Did staying balanced become more difficult when you closed your eyes? Vision provides a frame of reference that helps the muscles constantly make adjustments to help maintain balance.

The importance of vision in maintaining balance was demonstrated by David Lee and Eric Aronson (1974). Lee and Aronson placed 13- to 16-month-old toddlers in a "swinging room" (**Figure 7.5**). In this room, the floor was stationary, but the walls and ceiling could swing toward and away from the toddler. **Figure 7.5a** shows the room swaying toward the toddler. This movement of the wall creates the optic flow pattern on the right. Notice that this pattern is similar to the optic flow that occurs when moving forward, as when you are driving through a tunnel.

The flow pattern that the toddler observes creates the impression that he or she is swaying forward. This causes the toddler to sway back to compensate (**Figure 7.5b**). When the room moves back, as in **Figure 7.5c**, the flow pattern creates the impression of swaying backward, so the toddler sways forward to compensate. Although a few of the toddlers were unaffected by the sway, 26 percent swayed, 23 percent staggered, and 33 percent fell down, even though the floor remained stationary throughout the entire experiment!

Adults were also affected by the swinging room. Some of them braced themselves so they just swayed back and forth rather than staggering or falling down. Lee describes their behavior as follows: "oscillating the experimental room through as little as 6 mm caused adult subjects to sway approximately in phase with this movement. The subjects were like puppets visually hooked to their surroundings and were unaware of the real cause of their disturbance" (p. 173). Adults who didn't brace themselves could, like the toddlers, be knocked over by their perception of the moving room.

The swinging room experiments show that vision is such a powerful determinant of balance that it can override the traditional sources of balance information provided by the inner ear and the receptors in the muscles and joints (see also Fox, 1990). In a developmental study, Bennett Berthenthal and coworkers (1997) showed that infants as young as 4 months old sway back and forth in response to movements of a room,

(a) Room swings toward person.   Floor remains stationary

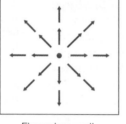
Flow when wall
is moving
toward person

(b) Person sways back to compensate.

(c) When room swings away, person sways forward to compensate.

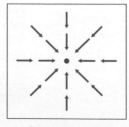
Flow when wall
is moving
away from person

Figure 7.5 Lee and Aronson's swinging room. (a) Moving the wall toward the observer creates an optic flow pattern associated with moving forward, so (b) the observer sways backward to compensate. (c) As the wall moves away from the observer, flow corresponds to moving backward, so the person leans forward to compensate and may even lose his or her balance. Based on Lee, D. N., & Aronson, E. (1974). Visual proprioceptive control of standing in human infants. *Perception and Psychophysics, 15,* 529–532, Figure 2.

and that the coupling of the room's movement and the swaying becomes closer with age. (See also Stoffregen et al., 1999, for more evidence that flow information can influence posture while standing still; and Warren et al., 1996, for evidence that flow is involved in maintaining posture while walking.)

Gibson's emphasis on (1) the moving observer, (2) identifying invariant information in the environment that observers use for perception, and (3) considering the senses as working together was revolutionary for its time. But even though perception researchers were aware of Gibson's ideas, most research continued in the traditional way—testing stationary subjects looking at stimuli in laboratory settings. Of course, there is nothing wrong with testing stationary observers in the laboratory, and much of the research described in this book takes this approach. However, Gibson's idea that perception should also be studied as it is often experienced (by observers who are moving and in more naturalistic settings) finally began to take hold in the 1980s, and today perception in naturalistic settings is one of the major themes of perception research.

In the remainder of this chapter we will consider the following ways that perception and action occur together in the environment: (1) navigating through the environment by walking or driving; (2) interacting with objects in the environment by reaching out and grasping them; and (3) watching other people take action in the environment.

Navigating Through the Environment

Gibson proposed that optic flow provides information about where a moving observer is heading. But can observers actually use this information? We consider this question next and then consider sources of information in addition to optic flow that help people navigate through the environment.

Do Observers Use Optic Flow Information?

Research on whether people use flow information has asked observers to make judgments regarding where they are heading based on computer-generated displays of moving dots that create optic flow stimuli. The observer's task is to judge, based on optic flow stimuli, where he or she would be heading relative to a reference point such as the vertical line in **Figures 7.6a** and **b**. The flow in Figure 7.6a indicates movement directly toward the line, and the flow in Figure 7.6b indicates movement to the right of the line. Observers viewing stimuli such as this can judge where they are heading relative to the vertical line to within about 0.5 to 1 degree (Warren, 1995, 2004; also see Fortenbaugh et al., 2006; Li, 2006). **VL**

Psychophysical results such as these support Gibson's idea that optic flow provides information about where a person is heading. Researchers have also identified neurons

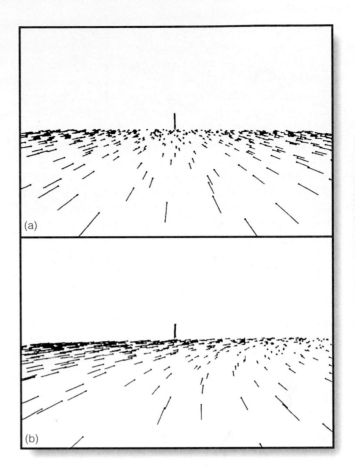

Figure 7.6 (a) Optic flow generated by a person moving straight ahead toward the vertical line on the horizon. The lengths of the lines indicate the person's speed. (b) Optic flow generated by a person moving in a curved path that is headed to the right of the vertical line.

From Warren, W. H. (1995). Self-motion: Visual perception and visual control. In W. Epstein & S. Rogers (Eds.), *Handbook of perception and cognition: Perception of space and motion* (pp. 263–323). Copyright © 1965, with permission from Elsevier.

in the brain that respond to flow patterns. One place where these neurons are found is in the medial superior temporal area (MST), which we will see in Chapter 8 is important for perceiving movement (**Figure 7.7**).

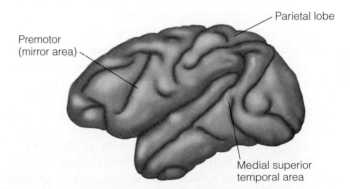

Figure 7.7 The human brain, showing the medial superior temporal area (MST), which responds to optic flow, as discussed here. Other areas, which will be discussed later, are the parietal reach region (PRR) in the parietal lobe, which is involved in reaching and grasping, and the premotor cortex (PM), which is involved in observing other people's actions. © Cengage Learning 2014

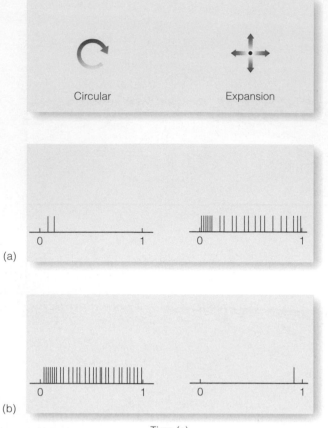

(a)

(b)

Time (s)

Figure 7.8 (a) Response of a neuron in the monkey's MST that responds to an expanding stimulus, but hardly responds to a stimulus that moves in a circular motion. (b) A neuron that responds to circular movement, but doesn't respond to expansion. Based on Graziano, M. S. A., Andersen, R. A., & Snowden, R. J. (1994). Tuning of MST neurons to spiral motions. *Journal of Neuroscience, 14,* 54-67.

Figure 7.8 shows the response of a neuron in a monkey's MST that responds best as the monkey observes a pattern of dots that are expanding outward, as would occur if the monkey were moving forward (**Figure 7.8a**), and another neuron that responds best to circular motions, as would occur if the monkey were swinging through the trees (**Figure 7.8b**; see also Duffy & Wurtz, 1991; Orban et al., 1992; Raffi et al., 2002; Regan & Cynader, 1979). What does the existence of these optic flow neurons mean? We know from previous discussions that finding a neuron that responds to a specific stimulus is only the first step in determining whether this neuron has anything to do with perceiving that stimulus (see Chapter 3, page 66). The next step is to demonstrate a connection between the neuron's response and behavior.

Kenneth Britten and Richard van Wezel (2002) demonstrated a connection between the response of neurons in MST and behavior by first training monkeys to indicate whether the flow of dots on a computer screen indicated movement to the left or right of straight ahead. For example, **Figure 7.9** shows a monkey viewing a flow that would occur if the monkey were moving slightly to the left.

The left bar in **Figure 7.9b** shows that the monkey responded to a stimulus like this by judging the movement as

(a)

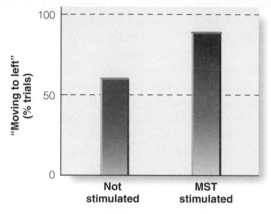

(b)

Figure 7.9 (a) A monkey watches a display of moving dots on a computer monitor. The dots indicate the flow pattern for movement slightly to the left of straight ahead. (b) Effect of microstimulation of the monkey's MST neurons that were tuned to respond to leftward movement. Stimulation (red bar) increases the monkey's judgment of leftward movement. Based on data from Britten, K. H., & van Wezel, R. J. A. (2002). Area MST and heading perception in macaque monkeys. *Cerebral Cortex, 12,* 692–701.

being to the left on 60 percent of the trials. But if, as the monkey was making its judgment, Britten and van Wezel electrically stimulated MST neurons that were tuned to respond to flow associated with movement to the left, the monkey's judgment was shifted even more to the left, increasing from 60 percent to 80 percent of the trials. This demonstration that stimulating flow neurons can influence the monkey's judgment of the direction of movement supports the idea that flow neurons can, in fact, help determine the direction of perceived movement.

Driving a Car

The experiments described above show that observers and neurons can respond to the flow indicated by computer-generated patterns of moving dots. But what about the flow that occurs in an actual environmental situation such as driving? To study information people use to stay on course when driving, Michael Land and David Lee (1994) fitted an automobile with instruments to record the angle of the

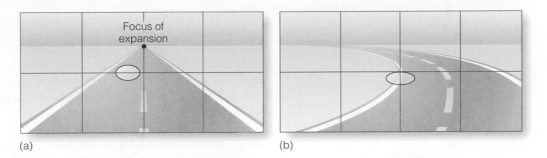

(a)

(b)

Figure 7.10 Results of Land and Lee's (1994) experiment. The ellipses indicate the place where the drivers were most likely to look while driving down (a) a straight road and (b) a curve to the left. From Land, M. F., & Lee, D. N. (1994). Where we look when we steer. *Nature, 377,* 742–744..

steering wheel and the speed, and measured where the driver was looking with a video eye tracker. According to Gibson, the focus of expansion (FOE) provides information about the place toward which a moving observer is headed. However, Land and Lee found that although drivers look straight ahead while driving, they tend to look at a spot in front of the car rather than looking directly at the FOE (**Figure 7.10a**).

Land and Lee also studied where drivers look as they are negotiating a curve. This task poses a problem for the idea of FOE because the driver's destination keeps changing as the car rounds the curve. Land and Lee found that when going around a curve, drivers don't look directly at the road, but instead look at the tangent point of the curve on the side of the road, as shown in **Figure 7.10b**. Because drivers don't look at the FOE, which would be in the road directly ahead, Land and Lee suggested that drivers probably use information in addition to optic flow to determine the direction they are heading. An example of this additional information would be noting the position of the car relative to the lines in the center of the road or relative to the side of the road. (See also Kandil et al., 2009; Land & Horwood, 1995; Rushton & Salvucci, 2001; Wann & Land, 2000; Wilkie & Wann, 2003, for more research on the information drivers use to stay on the road.) **VL**

Walking

How do people navigate on foot? Apparently, an important strategy used by walkers (and perhaps drivers as well) that does not involve optic flow is the **visual direction strategy**, in which observers keep their body pointed toward a target. If they go off course, the target will drift to the left or right (**Figure 7.11**). When this happens, the walker can correct course by recentering the target (Fajen & Warren, 2003; Rushton et al., 1998).

Another indication that flow information is not always necessary for navigation is that we can find our way even when flow information is minimal, such as at night or in a snowstorm (Harris & Rogers, 1999). Jack Loomis and coworkers (Loomis et al., 1992; Philbeck, Loomis, & Beall, 1997) have demonstrated this by eliminating flow altogether, with a "blind walking" procedure in which people observe a target object located up to 12 meters away, then walk to the target with their eyes closed. **VL**

These experiments show that people are able to walk directly toward the target and stop within a fraction of a meter of it (red lines in **Figure 7.12**). In fact, people can do this even when they are asked to walk off to the side first and then make a turn and walk to the target, while keeping their eyes closed. Some records from these "angled" walks are shown by the blue lines in Figure 7.12, which depict the paths taken

(a)

(b)

(c)

(d)

Figure 7.11 (a) As long as a person is moving toward the tree, it remains in the center of the person's field of view. (b) When the person walks off course, the tree drifts to the side. (c) When the person corrects course, the tree moves back to the center of the field of view, until (d) the person arrives at the tree.

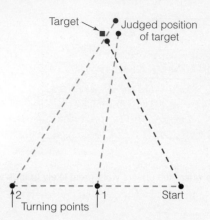

Figure 7.12 The results of a "blind walking" experiment (Philbeck et al., 1997). Participants looked at the target, which was 6 meters from the starting point, then closed their eyes and begin walking to the left. They turned either at point 1 or 2, keeping their eyes closed the whole time, and continued walking until they thought they had reached the target. © Cengage Learning 2014

when a person first walked to the left from the "start" position and then was told to turn either at turning point 1 or 2 and walk to a target that was 6 meters away. The fact that the person generally stopped close to the target shows that we are able to accurately navigate short distances in the absence of any visual stimulation at all (also see Sun et al., 2004).

Wayfinding

So far we have been considering information that observers might use to travel toward a destination they can see. But we often travel to destinations we can't see from the starting point, such as when we walk across campus from one class to another or drive to a destination several miles away. This kind of navigation, in which we take a route that involves making turns, is called **wayfinding**.

Our ability to get from one place to another may seem simple, especially for routes you have traveled many times. But just as there is nothing simple about perception, there is nothing simple about wayfinding. It is a complex process that involves perceiving objects in the environment, remembering objects and their relation to the overall scene, and knowing when to turn and in what direction.

The Importance of Landmarks One important source of information for wayfinding is **landmarks**—objects on the route that serve as cues to indicate where to turn. Sahar Hamid and coworkers (2010) studied how subjects used landmarks as they learned to navigate through a mazelike environment displayed on a computer screen in which pictures of common objects served as landmarks. Subjects first navigated through the maze until they learned its layout (training phase) and then were told to travel from one location in the maze to another (testing phase). During both the training and testing phases, subjects' eye movements were measured using a head-mounted eye tracker like the one used in the

experiment described in Chapter 6 in which eye movements were measured as a subject made a peanut butter and jelly sandwich (see page 132). This maze contained both *decision-point landmarks*—objects at corners where the subject had to decide which direction to turn—and *non-decision-point landmarks*—objects located in the middle of corridors that provided no information about how to navigate.

The eye-tracking measurements showed that subjects spent more time looking at decision-point landmarks than at non-decision-point landmarks, probably because the decision-point landmarks were more important for navigating the maze. In fact, when maze performance was tested with half of the landmarks removed, removing landmarks that had been viewed less (and were likely to be in the middle of the corridors) had little effect on performance (**Figure 7.13a**). However, removing landmarks that observers had looked at longer caused a substantial drop in performance (**Figure 7.13b**).

It makes sense that landmarks that are looked at the most would be the ones that are used to guide navigation. Another study, in which subjects learned a walking route through the University of Pennsylvania campus, showed that after subjects had learned the route, they were more likely to recognize pictures of buildings that were located at decision points than those located in the middle of the block (Schinazi & Epstein, 2010).

The studies we have described have measured eye movements, maze performance, and recognition, all of which are behaviors related to landmarks. But what is happening in the brain? When subjects in the University of Pennsylvania study were shown pictures of buildings when in an fMRI scanner, the brain response in areas of the brain known to be associated with navigation, such as the parahippocampal gyrus

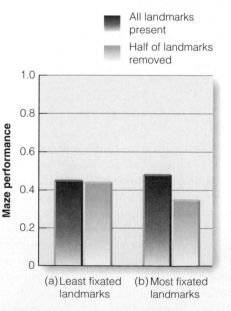

Figure 7.13 Effect of removing landmarks on maze performance. Red = all landmarks are present; green = half have been removed. (a) Removing half of the least fixated landmarks has no effect on performance. (b) Removing half of the most fixated landmarks causes a decrease in performance. Based on Hamid, S. N., Stankiewicz, B., & Hayhoe, M. (2010). Gaze patterns in navigation: Encoding information in large-scale environments. *Journal of Vision, 10*(12):18, 1–11. Figure 4.

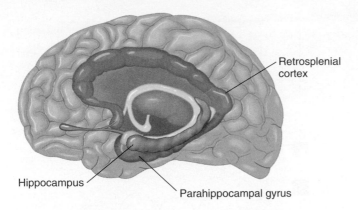

Figure 7.14 The human brain, showing three structures important to navigation: the parahippocampal gyrus, the hippocampus, and the retrosplenial cortex. © Cengage Learning 2014

(see **Figure 7.14**), was larger than the response to non-decision-point buildings. Thus, decision-point landmarks are not only more likely to be recognized than non-decision-point landmarks, but they generate greater levels of brain activity.

In another brain scanning experiment, Janzen and van Turennout (2004) had observers first study a film sequence that moved through a "virtual museum" (**Figure 7.15**). Observers were told that they needed to learn their way around the museum well enough to be able to guide a tour

through it. Objects ("exhibits") were located along the hallway of this museum. Decision-point objects, like the object at (a), marked a place where it was necessary to make a turn. Non-decision-point objects, like the one at (b), were located at a place where a decision was not required.

After studying the museum's layout in the film, observers were given a recognition test while in an fMRI scanner. They saw objects that had been in the hallway and some objects they had never seen. Their brain activation was measured in the scanner as they indicated whether they remembered seeing each object. **Figure 7.15c** indicates activity in the right parahippocampal gyrus for objects the observers had seen as they learned their way through the museum. The left pair of bars indicates, as we might expect, that for objects that the observers remembered, activation was greater for decision-point objects than for non-decision-point objects. But the most interesting result, indicated by the right pair of bars, was that the advantage for decision-point objects also occurred for objects that were not remembered during the recognition test.

Janzen and van Turennout concluded that the brain automatically distinguishes objects that are used as landmarks to guide navigation. The brain therefore responds not just to the object but also to how relevant that object is for guiding navigation. This means that the next time you are trying to find your way along a route that you have traveled before but aren't totally confident about, activity in your

(a) Toy at decision point

(b) Toy at nondecision point

Nondecision points
Decision points

(c)

Figure 7.15 (a & b) Two locations in the "virtual museum" viewed by Janzen and van Turennout's (2004) observers. (c) Brain activation during the recognition test for objects that had been located at decision points (red bars) and non-decision points (blue bars). Notice that brain activation was greater for decision-point objects even if they weren't remembered. Adapted by permission from Macmillan Publishers Ltd., from Janzen, G., & van Turennout, M., Selective neural representation of objects relevant for navigation, *Nature Neuroscience, 7,* 673–677. Copyright 2004.

parahippocampal gyrus may automatically be "highlighting" landmarks that indicate when you should continue going straight, or make a right turn or a left turn, even in cases when you may not remember having seen these landmarks before.

From both the behavioral and physiological experiments we have described, it is apparent that landmarks play an important role in wayfinding. But there is more to wayfinding than landmarks. Before you begin a trip, you need to know which direction to go, and you probably also have a mental "map" of your route and the surrounding area in your mind. You may not think of route planning as involving a map, especially for routes that are very familiar, but research studying people who have lost the ability to find their way because of damage to the brain shows that identifying landmarks is just one of the abilities needed to find one's way.

The Effect of Brain Damage on Wayfinding A large amount of research shows how the ability to navigate through the environment is affected by damage to various brain structures. We will describe cases that involved damage to two structures that have been shown to be involved in navigation, the retrosplenial cortex and the hippocampus (see Figure 7.14).

Retrosplenial Cortex Damage On the evening of December 11, 2000, a 55-year-old taxi driver was suddenly unable to find his way home from work. He was able to recognize buildings, so he knew where he was, but he couldn't figure out which direction to turn to get home. He called his wife and got home by following her directions (Ino et al., 2007). When this patient was tested at the hospital, it was found that he had damage to his retrosplenial cortex. Behavioral testing revealed that he could identify buildings and other common objects and was able to remember the positions of objects in a room, but he couldn't describe or draw routes between his house and familiar places or draw the layout of his house. Results such as these led to the conclusion that this patient had lost his *directional ability*—he couldn't determine the direction of any familiar destination with respect to his current position, and wasn't able to use directional information provided by familiar landmarks.

This problem in determining direction is illustrated by another case of retrosplenial cortex damage, a 70-year-old retired schoolteacher who was unable to determine the viewpoints from which photographs of familiar places were taken. For example, the three red arrows in **Figure 7.16** show her judgments of the viewpoint from which she thought a photograph of her garden was taken. These responses were, however, completely different from the correct viewpoint, shown by the green arrow (Suzuki, 1998).

Hippocampus Damage Patient T.T. had been a London taxi driver for 37 years when he contracted a severe case of encephalitis that damaged his hippocampus (Maguire et al., 2006). After the damage, he was unable to find his way around his own neighborhood. T.T. was tested on his ability to drive from one place to another in London by navigating a car in an interactive computer game called "The Getaway," which accurately depicted

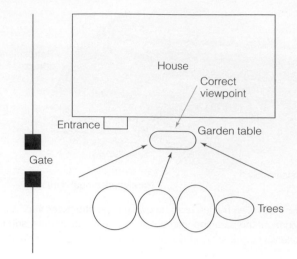

Figure 7.16 Responses of a patient with retrosplenial cortex damage when she was asked to identify the viewpoint of a photograph of her garden. The green arrow indicates the correct viewpoint of the photograph. The three red arrows are the patient's indications of the viewpoints. She was able to identify the garden table, but she could not indicate the direction from which it was seen.

From Suzuki, K., Yamadori, A., Hayakawa, Y., & Fujii, T. (1998). Pure topographical disorientation related to dysfunction of the viewpoint dependent visual system. *Cortex, 34*, 589–599. Reproduced by permission.

the streets of central London as seen through the front window of a car, including all the buildings and landmarks along the road and some pedestrians as well (**Figure 7.17**).

T.T. was able to do this as well as control subjects, a group of retired London taxi drivers, but only if the route involved just main roads. As soon as it was necessary to navigate along side streets, T.T. became lost, even though he had been taking people on taxi rides though the same side streets for 37 years. Eleanor Maguire and coworkers (2006) concluded that the hippocampus is important for accessing details of routes that were learned long ago.

The research we have described on how the brain is involved in wayfinding has focused on three structures: the parahippocampal gyrus, the retrosplenial cortex, and the hippocampus. Physiological research studying the behavior of patients with

Figure 7.17 A view similar to the one in the video game *The Getaway* (© Sony Computer Entertainment Europe), which duplicates the roadways and buildings of downtown London.

brain damage and analysis of the results of brain scanning experiments have also identified a number of other brain areas involved in various components of wayfinding (Schinazi & Epstein, 2010). The important message of all of these studies, taken together, is that wayfinding is distributed throughout many structures in the brain. This isn't surprising when we consider that wayfinding involves seeing and recognizing objects along a route (perception), paying attention to specific objects (attention), using information stored from past trips through the environment (memory), and combining all this information to create maps that help us relate what we are perceiving to where we are now and where we need to go next.

TEST YOURSELF 7.1

1. What two factors does the ecological approach to perception emphasize?

2. What is optic flow? What are two characteristics of optic flow?

3. What is invariant information? How is invariance related to optic flow?

4. What is observer-produced information? Describe its role in somersaulting and why there is a difference between novices and experts when they close their eyes.

5. Describe the swinging room experiments. What principles do they illustrate?

6. What is the evidence (a) that optic flow provides information for the direction someone is heading and (b) that there are neurons that respond to optic flow?

7. What does research on driving a car and walking tell us about how optic flow may (or may not) be used in navigation? What are some other sources of information for navigation?

8. What is wayfinding? Describe the research of Hamid et al. (computer maze) and Schinazi and Epstein (walking on the Penn campus) that investigated the role of landmarks in wayfinding.

9. What do the brain scanning experiments of Schinazi and Epstein (measuring responses to buildings on the Penn campus) and Janzen and van Turennout (measuring activation when navigating a virtual museum) indicate about brain activity and landmarks?

10. Describe the case studies of patients with damage to their RSP and hippocampus. What conclusions about the function of these structures were reached from these observations?

11. What does it mean to say that wayfinding is "multifaceted"?

Acting on Objects

So far, we have been describing how we move around in the environment. But our actions go beyond walking or driving. One of the major actions we take is reaching to pick something up, as Serena did on her bike ride when she reached down, grabbed her water bottle, and raised it to her mouth. One of the characteristics of reaching and grasping is that it is usually directed toward a specific object, to accomplish a specific goal. We reach for and grasp a doorknob to open a door; we reach for a hammer to pound a nail. An important concept related to reaching and grasping is *affordances*, which we describe next.

Affordances: What Objects Are Used For

Remember that Gibson's ecological approach involves identifying information in the environment that is useful for perception. Earlier in the chapter we described optic flow, which is created by movement of the observer. Another type of information that Gibson specified is **affordances**—information that indicates what an object is used for. In Gibson's (1979) words, "The affordances of the environment are what it *offers* the animal, what it *provides for* or *furnishes*." A chair, or anything that is sit-on-able, affords sitting; an object of the right size and shape to be grabbed by a person's hand affords grasping; and so on.

What this means is that perception of an object not only includes physical properties, such as shape, size, color, and orientation, that might enable us to recognize the object; our perception also includes information about how the object is used. For example, when you look at a cup, you might receive information indicating that it is "a round white coffee cup, about 5 inches high, with a handle," but your perceptual system would also respond with information indicating "you can pick the cup up" and "you can pour liquid into it." Information such as this goes beyond simply seeing or recognizing the cup; it provides information that can guide our actions toward it. Another way of saying this is that "potential for action" is part of our perception of an object.

One way that affordances have been studied is by looking at the behavior of people with brain damage. Glyn Humphreys and Jane Riddoch (2001) studied affordances by testing patient M.P., who had damage to his temporal lobe that impaired his ability to name objects. M.P. was given a cue, either (1) the name of an object ("cup") or (2) an indication of the object's function ("an item you could drink from"). He was then shown 10 different objects and was told to press a key as soon as he found the object. The results of this testing showed that M.P. identified the object more accurately and rapidly when given the cue that referred to the object's function. Humphreys and Riddoch concluded from this result that M.P. was using his knowledge of an object's affordances to help find it.

Although M.P. wasn't reaching for these objects, it is likely that he would be able to use the information about an object's function to help him take action with respect to the object. In line with this idea, there are other patients with temporal lobe damage who cannot name objects, or even describe how they can be used, but who can pick them up and use them nonetheless.

The Physiology of Reaching and Grasping

An important breakthrough in the study of the physiology of reaching and grasping came with the discovery of ventral (or *what*) and dorsal (or *where/how*) pathways that we described in Chapter 4 (see Figure 4.14).

The Dorsal and Ventral Pathways Remember that D.F., who had damage to her ventral pathway, had difficulty recognizing objects or judging their orientation, but she could "mail" an object by placing it through an oriented opening. The idea that there is one processing stream for perceiving objects and another for acting on them helps us understand what is happening when Serena, sitting at the coffee shop after her ride, reaches for her cup of coffee (**Figure 7.18**). She first identifies the coffee cup among the flowers and other objects on the table (ventral pathway). Once the coffee cup is perceived, she reaches for it, taking into account its location on the table (dorsal pathway). As she reaches, avoiding the flowers, she positions her hand and fingers to grasp the cup (dorsal), taking into account her perception of the cup's handle (ventral). She then lifts the cup with just the right amount of force (dorsal), taking into account her estimate of how heavy it is based on her perception of its fullness (ventral).

Thus, reaching and picking up a cup involves continually perceiving the position of the cup, shaping the hand and fingers relative to the cup, and calibrating actions in order to accurately grasp the cup and pick it up without spilling any coffee (Goodale, 2011). Even a seemingly simple action like picking up a coffee cup involves a number of areas of the brain, which coordinate their activity to create perceptions and behaviors.

The Parietal Reach Region One of the most important areas of the brain for reaching and grasping is the parietal lobe at the end of the dorsal pathway (Figure 7.7). The areas in the monkey and human parietal cortex that are involved in reaching for objects have been called the **parietal reach region (PRR)**. This region contains neurons that control not only grasping but also reaching (Connolly et al., 2003). Recently, evidence has been presented suggesting that there are a number of different parietal reach regions in the human parietal lobe (Filimon et al., 2009), and recording from single neurons in a monkey's parietal lobe has revealed neurons in an area next to the parietal reach region that respond to specific types of hand grips (Fattori et al., 2010).

The procedure for the monkey hand grip experiment, which was carried out by Patrizia Fattori and coworkers (2010), is shown in **Figure 7.19**: (1) The monkey observes a small fixation light in the dark; (2) lights are turned on for half a second to reveal the object to be grasped; (3) the lights go out and then, after a brief pause, the fixation light changes color, signaling that the monkey should reach for the object.

The key part of this sequence occurs when the monkey reaches for the object in the dark. The monkey knows what the object is from seeing it when the lights were on (a round ball in this example), so while it is reaching for the object in the dark, it adjusts its grip to match the object. A number of different objects were used, as shown in **Figure 7.19b**, each of which required a different grip. **VL**

The key result of the experiment is that there are neurons that respond best to specific grips. For example, neuron A in **Figure 7.20** responds best to "whole hand prehension" whereas neuron B responds best to "advanced precision grip." There are also neurons, like C, that respond to a number of different grips. Remember that when these neurons were firing, the monkey was reaching for the object in the dark, so the firing reflected not perception but the monkey's actions.

In a follow-up experiment on the same monkeys, Fattori and coworkers (2012) discovered neurons that responded not only when a monkey was preparing to grasp a specific object, but also when the monkey *viewed* that specific object. An example of this type of neuron, which Fattori calls **visuomotor grip cells**, is a neuron that initially responds when the monkey sees a specific object, and then also responds as the monkey is

(a) Perceive cup   (b) Reach for cup   (c) Grasp cup

Figure 7.18 Picking up a cup of coffee: (a) perceiving and recognizing the cup, (b) reaching for it, and (c) grasping and picking it up. This action involves coordination between perceiving and action that is carried out by two separate streams in the brain, as described in the text. From Goldstein, E. B., *Cognitive Psychology*, 3rd ed. © 2011 Wadsworth, a part of Cengage Learning, Inc. Reproduced by permission. www.cengage.com/permissions.

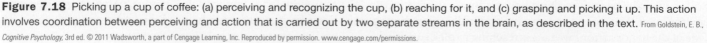

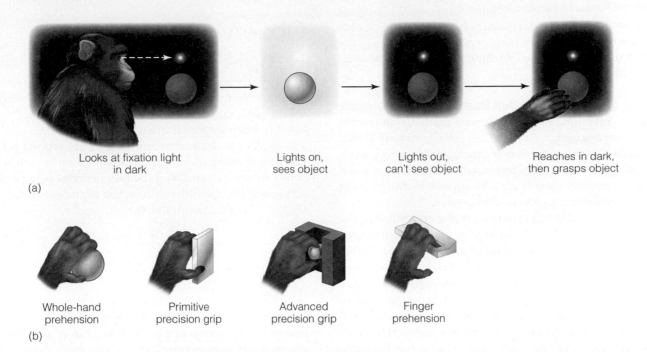

(a)

Looks at fixation light in dark → Lights on, sees object → Lights out, can't see object → Reaches in dark, then grasps object

Whole-hand prehension   Primitive precision grip   Advanced precision grip   Finger prehension

(b)

Figure 7.19 (a) The monkey's task in Fattori and coworkers' (2010) experiment. The monkey always looks at the small light above the sphere. The monkey sees the object to be grasped when the lights go on, then reaches for and grasps the object once the lights go off and the fixation light changes color. (b) Four of the objects used in the task. Each one involves a different type of grasping movement. Based on Fattori, P., Raos, V., Breveglieri, R, Bosco, A., Marzocchi, N., & Galleti, C. (2010). The dorsomedial pathway is not just for reaching: Grasping neurons in the medial parieto-occipital cortex of the Macaque monkey. *Journal of Neuroscience, 30,* 342–349. Figure 2b, c.

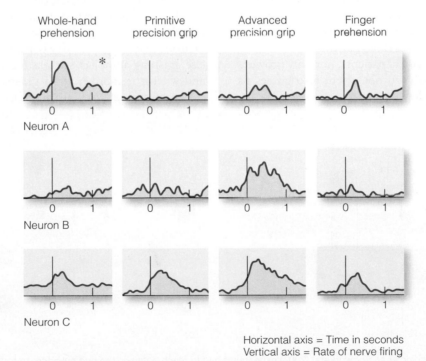

Horizontal axis = Time in seconds
Vertical axis = Rate of nerve firing

Figure 7.20 Results of Fattori and coworkers' (2010) experiment showing how three different neurons respond to reaching and grasping each of the objects. Neuron A responds best to "whole hand prehension" (starred record). Neuron B responds to "advanced precision grip." Neuron C responds to all of the grips. Based on Fattori, P., Raos, V., Breveglieri, R, Bosco, A., Marzocchi, N., & Galleti, C. (2010). The dorsomedial pathway is not just for reaching: Grasping neurons in the medial parieto-occipital cortex of the Macaque monkey. *Journal of Neuroscience, 30,* 342–349. Figure 2.

forming its hand to grasp the same object. This type of neuron is therefore involved in both perception (identifying the object by seeing) and action (reaching for the object and gripping it with the hand).

Avoiding Other Objects When Reaching When we reach, we have to take into account not only the location toward which we are reaching, so we can direct our hand toward that location, but also the location of other nearby objects, so we can avoid them as we reach. Serena faced this problem when she had to reach toward her coffee cup while avoiding the vase of flowers and the glass of orange juice.

The fact that obstacle avoidance is also controlled by the parietal regions responsible for reaching was demonstrated in an experiment by Igor Schindler and coworkers (2004), who tested two patients with parietal lobe damage who had trouble pointing to visual stimuli, a condition called **optic ataxia**. These ataxia patients and a group of normal control subjects were presented with two cylinders, separated by 8 to 10 inches (**Figure 7.21a**). Their task was to reach between the two cylinders and touch anywhere on a gray strip located 20 cm behind the cylinders. The cylinders were moved to different positions, as shown by the top views of pairs of cylinders in **Figure 7.21b**.

The arrows indicate where the subject's hand passed between the cylinders as he or she reached to touch the strip. Notice that the control subjects (red arrows) changed their reach in response to changes in the cylinders' position, shifting their reach to the left when the cylinders were shifted to the left. In contrast, the reach of the ataxia patients was the same for all arrangements of the cylinders, as shown for one of the patients by the blue arrows. In other words, they didn't take account of the varying locations of the obstacles. Schindler concludes from this result that the dorsal stream, which was damaged in the ataxia patients, not only provides guidance as we reach toward an object but also guides us away from potential obstacles.

Observing Other People's Actions

We not only take action ourselves, but we regularly watch other people take action. This "watching others act" is most obvious when we watch other people's actions on TV or in a movie, but it also occurs any time we are around someone else who is doing something. One of the most exciting outcomes of research studying the link between perception and action was the discovery of neurons in the premotor cortex (Figure 7.7) called *mirror neurons*.

Mirroring Others' Actions in the Brain

In the early 1990s, Giacomo Rizzolatti and coworkers (2006; also see di Pelligrino et al., 1992; Gallese et al., 1996) were investigating how neurons in the monkey's premotor cortex fired as the monkey performed actions like picking up a toy or a piece of food. Their goal was to determine how neurons fired as the monkey carried out specific actions. But as sometimes happens in science, they observed something they didn't expect. When one of the experimenters picked up a piece of food while the monkey was watching, neurons in the monkey's cortex fired. What was so unexpected was that the neurons that fired to observing the experimenter pick up the food were the same ones that had fired earlier when the monkey had itself picked up the food.

This initial observation, followed by many additional experiments, led to the discovery of **mirror neurons**—neurons that respond both when a monkey observes someone else grasping an object such as food on a tray (**Figure 7.22a**) and when the monkey itself grasps the food (**Figure 7.22b**; Rizzolatti et al., 2006). They are called mirror neurons because

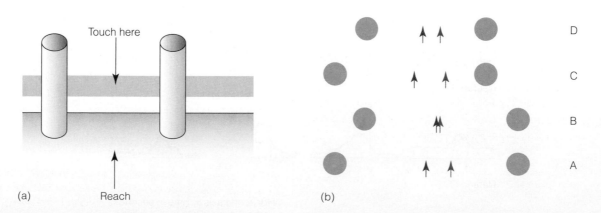

(a) Touch here / Reach

(b) D C B A

Figure 7.21 (a) Subjects in Schindler and coworkers' (2004) experiment had to reach between the two cylinders to touch a gray strip located behind the cylinders. (b) The pairs of cylinders in Schindler and coworkers' (2004) experiment were located in different positions on different trials, as shown in this top view. The red arrows show that control subjects adjusted their reach to compensate for the different locations of the cylinders. The blue arrows, which show the data for one of the ataxia patients, indicate that the patients' reach stayed the same for all arrangements of the cylinders. Based on Schindler, I., Rice, N. J., McIntosh, R. D., Rossetti, Y., Vighetto, A., & Milner, D.A. (2004). Automatic avoidance of obstacles is a dorsal stream function: Evidence from optic ataxia. *Nature Neuroscience, 7*, 779–784.

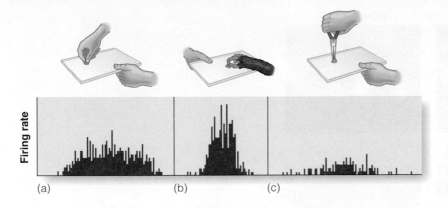

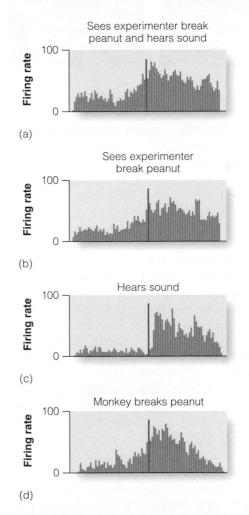

Figure 7.22 Response of a mirror neuron. (a) Response to watching the experimenter grasp food on the tray. (b) Response when the monkey grasps the food. (c) Response to watching the experimenter pick up food with a pair of pliers. Reprinted from Rizzolatti, G., et al., Premotor cortex and the recognition of motor actions, *Cognitive Brain Research, 3,* 131–141. Copyright 2000, with permission from Elsevier.

the neuron's response to watching the experimenter grasp an object is similar to the response that would occur if the monkey were performing the same action. Just looking at the food causes no response, and watching the experimenter grasp the food with a pair of pliers, as in **Figure 7.22c**, causes only a small response (Gallese et al., 1996; Rizzolatti et al., 2000).

Most mirror neurons are specialized to respond to only one type of action, such as grasping or placing an object somewhere. Although you might think that the monkey may have been responding to the anticipation of receiving food, the type of object made little difference. The neurons responded just as well when the monkey observed the experimenter pick up an object that was not food. **VL**

But could the mirror neurons simply be responding to the pattern of motion? The fact that the neuron does not respond when watching the experimenter pick up the food with pliers argues against this idea. Further evidence that mirror neurons are doing more than just responding to a particular pattern of motion is the discovery of neurons that respond to sounds that are *associated with* actions. These neurons in the premotor cortex, called **audiovisual mirror neurons**, respond when a monkey performs a hand action *and* when it hears the sound associated with this action (Kohler et al., 2002). For example, the results in **Figure 7.23** show the response of a neuron that fires (a) when the monkey sees and hears the experimenter break a peanut, (b) when the monkey just sees the experimenter break the peanut, (c) when the monkey just hears the sound of the breaking peanut, and (d) when the *monkey* breaks the peanut. What this means is that just *hearing* a peanut breaking or just *seeing* a peanut being broken causes activity that is also associated with the perceiver's *action* of breaking a peanut. These neurons are responding, therefore, to what is "happening"—breaking a peanut—rather than to a specific pattern of movement.

Predicting People's Intentions

Some researchers have proposed that there are mirror neurons that respond not just to *what* is happening but to *why* something is happening, or more specifically, to the *intention* behind what is happening. To understand what this means, let's return to Serena in the coffee shop. As we see her reach

Figure 7.23 Response of an audiovisual mirror neuron to four different stimuli. From Kohler, E., et al., 2002, Hearing sounds, understanding actions: Action representation in mirror neurons. *Science, 297,* 846–848. Copyright © 2002 by AAAS. Reprinted with permission from AAAS.

for her coffee cup, we might wonder why she is reaching for it. One obvious answer is that she intends to drink some coffee, although if we notice that the cup is empty, we might instead decide that she is going to take the cup back to the counter to get a refill, or if we know that she never drinks more than one cup, we might decide that she is going to place the cup in the used cup bin. Thus, there are a number of different intentions that may be associated with the same action.

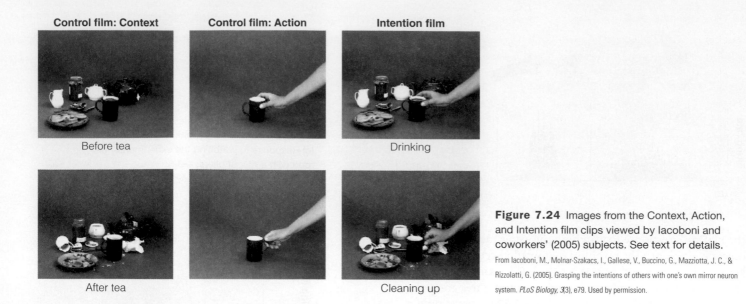

Control film: Context   Control film: Action   Intention film

Before tea

After tea

Drinking

Cleaning up

Figure 7.24 Images from the Context, Action, and Intention film clips viewed by Iacoboni and coworkers' (2005) subjects. See text for details.

From Iacoboni, M., Molnar-Szakacs, I., Gallese, V., Buccino, G., Mazziotta, J. C., & Rizzolatti, G. (2005). Grasping the intentions of others with one's own mirror neuron system. *PLoS Biology, 3*(3), e79. Used by permission.

What is the evidence that the response of mirror neurons can be influenced by different intentions? Mario Iacoboni and coworkers (2005) provide this evidence in an experiment in which they measured subjects' brain activity as they watched short film clips represented by the stills in **Figure 7.24.** Stills for the two Intention films, on the right, show a hand reaching in to pick up a cup, but there is an important difference between the two scenes. In the top panel, the table is neatly set up, the food is untouched, and the cup is full of tea. In the bottom panel, the table is a mess, the food has been eaten, and the cup appears to be empty. Iacoboni hypothesizes that it is likely that viewing the top film would lead the viewer to infer that the person picking up the cup intends to drink from it, and that viewing the bottom film would lead the viewer to infer that the person is cleaning up.

Iacoboni's subjects also viewed the control films shown in the other panels. The Context film showed the table setting, and the Action film showed the hand reaching in to pick up an isolated cup. The reason these two types of films were presented was that they contained the visual elements of the intention films, but didn't suggest a particular intention.

When Iacoboni compared the brain activity in the Intention films to the activity in the Context and Action films, he found that the Intention films caused greater activity than the control films in areas of the brain known to have mirror neuron properties. **Figure 7.25** shows that the amount of activity was least in the Action condition, was higher for the Cleaning Up condition, and was highest for the Drinking condition. Based on the increased activity for the two Intention conditions, Iacoboni concluded that the mirror neuron area is involved with understanding the intentions behind the actions shown in the films. He reasoned that if the mirror neurons were just signaling the action of picking up the cup, then a similar response would occur regardless of whether a context surrounding the cup was present. Mirror neurons,

according to Iacoboni, code the "why" of actions and respond differently to different intentions.

If mirror neurons do, in fact, signal intentions, how do they do it? One possibility is that the response of these neurons is determined by the chain of motor activities that could be *expected* to happen in a particular context (Fogassi et al., 2005; Gallese, 2007). For example, when a person picks up a cup with the intention of drinking, the next expected actions would be to bring the cup to the mouth and then to drink some coffee. However, if the intention is to clean up, the expected action might be to carry the cup over to the sink. According to this idea, mirror neurons that respond to different intentions are responding to the action that is happening *plus* the sequence of actions that is most likely to follow, given the context.

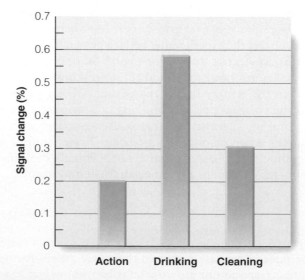

Figure 7.25 Iacoboni and coworkers' (2005) results, showing the brain response for the Action, Drinking, and Cleaning conditions.
© Cengage Learning 2014

The exact functions of mirror neurons in humans are still being actively researched (Caggiano et al., 2011; de Lange et al., 2008; Gazzola et al., 2007; Kilner, 2011). In addition to proposing that mirror neurons signal what is happening as well as the intentions behind various actions, researchers have also proposed that mirror neurons help us understand (1) communications based on facial expressions (Buccino et al., 2004; Ferrari et al., 2003); (2) gestures used while speaking (Gallese, 2007); (3) the meanings of sentences (Gallese, 2007); and (4) differences between ourselves and others (Uddin et al., 2007). As might be expected from this list, it has also been proposed that mirror neurons play an important role in guiding social interactions (Rizzolatti & Sinigaglia, 2010; Yoshida et al., 2011).

As with any newly discovered phenomenon, more research is needed before we can state with more certainty exactly what the function of mirror neurons is. Consider that when feature detectors that respond to oriented moving lines were discovered in the 1960s, some researchers proposed that these feature detectors could explain how we perceive objects. With the information available at the time, this was a reasonable proposal. However, later, when neurons that respond to faces, places, and bodies were discovered, researchers revised their initial proposals to take these new findings into account. In all likelihood, a similar process will occur for mirror neurons. Some of the proposed functions will be confirmed, but others may need to be revised. This evolution of thinking about what research results mean is a basic property not only of research in perception but of scientific research in general.

SOMETHING TO CONSIDER:
Action-Based Accounts of Perception

The traditional approach to perception has focused on how the environment is *represented* in the nervous system and in the perceiver's mind. According to this idea, the purpose of visual perception is to create a representation in the mind of whatever we are looking at. Thus, if you look at a scene and see buildings, trees, grass, and some people, your perception of the buildings, trees, grass, and people is representing what is "out there," and so accomplishes vision's purpose of representing the environment.

But as you might have suspected after reading this chapter, many researchers believe that the purpose of vision is not to create a representation of what is out there but to guide our actions. We can appreciate the reasoning behind this idea by imagining a situation in which action is important for survival. Consider a monkey foraging for food in the forest. The monkey's color perception enables it to see some orange fruit that stands out against green leaves. The monkey reaches for the fruit and eats it. Of course, seeing (and perhaps smelling) the fruit is crucial, because it makes the monkey aware that the fruit is present. But the second step—reaching for the fruit—is just as important, because the monkey can't live on visual experiences alone. It has to reach for and grab the fruit in order to survive.

Although there may be situations—such as looking at paintings in an art gallery or looking out at a misty lake in the morning—when seeing what is out there is an end in itself, the vast majority of our experience involves a two-step process: first *perceiving* an object or scene and then *taking action* toward the objects or within the scene.

The idea that action is crucial for survival has been described by Mel Goodale (2011) as follows: "Many researchers now understand that brains evolved not to enable us to think (or perceive), but to enable us to move and interact with the world" (p. 17). According to this idea, perception may provide valuable information about the environment, but taking a step beyond perception and acting on this information enables us to survive so we can perceive another day (Milner & Goodale, 2006).

The idea that the purpose of perception is to enable us to interact with the environment has been taken a step further by researchers who have turned the equation around from "action depends on perception" to "perception depends on action" or "people perceive their environment in terms of their ability to act on it." This last statement, by Jessica Witt (2011), is based on the results of many experiments, some of which involve sports. For example, Witt and Dennis Proffitt (2005) presented a series of circles to softball players just after they had finished a game and asked them to pick the circle that best corresponded to the size of a softball. When they compared the players' estimates to their batting averages from the just-completed game, they found that batters who hit well perceived the ball to be bigger than batters who were less successful. **VL**

Other experiments that have focused on sports have shown that tennis players who have recently won report that the net is lower (Witt & Sugovic, 2010), and that subjects who were most successful at kicking football field goals estimated the goal posts to be farther apart (Witt & Dorsch, 2009). The field goal experiment is especially interesting because the effect occurred only after they had attempted 10 field goals. Before they began, the estimates of the poor kickers and the good kickers were the same.

The sports examples all involved making judgments after doing either well or poorly. This supports the idea that perception can be affected by performance. What about situations in which the person hasn't carried out any action but has an expectation about how difficult it would be to perform that action? For example, what if people who were physically fit and people who were not physically fit were asked to estimate the steepness of a hill? When Mukul Bhalla and Dennis Proffitt (1999) asked people ranging from varsity athletes to people who didn't work out regularly to estimate the slant of steep hills, they found that the least fit people (as measured by heart rate and oxygen consumption during and after exercise) judged the hills as being steeper. The reason for this, according to Bhalla and Proffitt, is that over time people's general fitness level affects their perception of how difficult it will be to carry out various types of physical activity, and this in turn affects their perception of these activities. Thus, a person who isn't very fit experiences steep hills as being difficult to climb, and this causes them to perceive the hills as being steeper even if they are just looking at them (Proffitt, 2009).

The idea that the expected difficulty of carrying out an action can influence a person's judgment of an object's properties was also studied by Adam Doerrfeld and coworkers (2011), who asked subjects to estimate the weight of a basket of golf balls before and after lifting the basket. Subjects made this estimate under two conditions: (1) solo, in which the subject expected that he or she would be lifting the basket alone, and (2) joint, in which the subject expected that he or she would be lifting the basket with another person. The actual weight of the basket of golf balls was 20 pounds. Before lifting the basket, the subjects estimated that the basket weighed 21 pounds if they thought they would be lifting it alone, and 17.5 pounds if they thought they would be lifting it with another person. After lifting the basket, the average estimate was about 20 pounds for both conditions. Doerrfeld and coworkers conclude from this result that anticipation of how difficult a task will be can influence the perception of an object's properties.

There are, however, researchers who question whether the perceptual judgments measured in some of the experiments we have described are actually measuring perception. Subjects might be affected, they suggest, by "judgmental bias," caused by their expectations about what they think will happen in a particular situation. For example, Bhalla and Proffitt (1999), who found that people who were not in good physical condition judged hills as being steeper, also found that people who were wearing a heavy backpack judged hills to be steeper. Bhalla and Proffitt interpreted this result as showing that wearing the heavy backpack influenced the person's perception of steepness. An alternative interpretation is that perhaps the subjects' *expectation* that hills could appear steeper when carrying something heavy might cause them to *say* a hill appears steeper when they are wearing a heavy backpack, even though their *perception* of the hill's steepness was actually not affected (Durgin et al., 2010; Loomis & Philbeck, 2008; Woods et al., 2009).

This explanation highlights a basic problem in measuring perception in general: Our measurement of perception is based on people's responses, and there is no guarantee that these responses accurately reflect what a person is perceiving. Thus, as pointed out above, there may be some instances in which subjects' responses may reflect not what they are perceiving, but what they think they should be perceiving. Even though some experiments may be open to criticism (Durgin et al., 2010; Proffitt, 2009), it is important to note that there are some experiments that do demonstrate a relationship between a person's ability to act and perception (Creem-Regehr & Kunz, 2010).

The results of the experiments demonstrating this relationship between ability to act and perception are consistent with J. J. Gibson's idea of affordances, described earlier (page 163). Affordances, according to Gibson, are an object's "possibilities for action." Thus, perception of a particular object is determined both by what the object looks like and by the way we might interact with it.

This brings us to the following statement by J. J. Gibson, from his final book, *The Ecological Approach to Perception* (1979): "Perceiving is an achievement of the individual, not an appearance in the theater of his consciousness. It is a keeping-in-touch with the world, an experiencing of things, rather than a having of experiences" (p. 239). This statement did not lead to much research when it was proposed, but years later many researchers have embraced the idea that perception is not just "an appearance in the theater of consciousness," but is the first step toward taking action in the environment. In addition, some researchers have gone a step farther and suggested that action, or the potential for action, may affect perception.

TEST YOURSELF 7.2

1. What is an affordance? Describe the results of the experiments on patient M.P. that illustrates the operation of affordances.

2. Describe the early experiments that showed that there are neurons in the parietal cortex that respond to goal-directed reaching.

3. How does the idea of *what* (ventral) and *how* (dorsal) streams help us describe an action such as reaching for a coffee cup?

4. Describe Fattori et al.'s experiments on "grasping neurons" and "visuomotor grip cells."

5. What is the parietal reach region?

6. Describe the experiment on optic ataxia patients that shows that the dorsal stream is involved in helping to avoid obstacles.

7. What are mirror neurons? What is the evidence that mirror neurons aren't just responding to a specific pattern of motion?

8. Describe Iacoboni's experiment that suggested that there are mirror neurons that respond to intentions.

9. What is a possible mechanism that might be involved in mirror neurons that respond to intentions?

10. What are some of the proposed functions of mirror neurons? What is the scientific status of these functions?

11. Describe the action-based account of perception. In your discussion, indicate (a) why some researchers think the brain evolved to enable us to take action; (b) how experiments have demonstrated a link between perception and "ability to act."

THINK ABOUT IT

1. It is a common observation that people tend to slow down as they are driving through long tunnels. Explain the possible role of optic flow in this situation. (p. 154)

2. We have seen that gymnasts appear to take visual information into account as they are in the act of executing a somersault. In the sport of synchronized diving, two people execute a dive simultaneously from two side-by-side diving boards. They are judged based on how well they execute the dive and how well the two divers are synchronized with each other. What environmental stimuli do you think synchronized divers need to take into account in order to be successful? (p. 155)

3. Can you identify specific environmental information that you use to help you carry out actions in the environment? This question is often particularly relevant to athletes.

4. If mirror neurons do signal intentions, what does that say about the role of top-down and bottom-up processing in determining the response of mirror neurons? (p. 166)

5. How do you think the response of your mirror neurons might be affected by how well you know a person whose actions you were observing? (p. 166)

6. How does your experience in interacting with the environment (climbing hills, playing sports) correspond or not correspond to the findings of the "potential for action" experiments described in the Something to Consider section? (p. 169)

KEY TERMS

Affordance (p. 163)
Audiovisual mirror neuron (p. 167)
Ecological approach to perception (p. 154)
Focus of expansion (FOE) (p. 154)
Gradient of flow (p. 154)

Invariant information (p. 155)
Landmarks (p. 160)
Mirror neuron (p. 166)
Optic ataxia (p. 166)
Optic flow (p. 154)

Parietal reach region (PRR) (p. 164)
Self-produced information (p. 155)
Visual direction strategy (p. 159)
Visuomotor grip cells (p. 164)
Wayfinding (p. 160)

MEDIA RESOURCES

CourseMate

Go to CengageBrain.com to access Psychology CourseMate, where you will find the Virtual Labs plus an interactive eBook, flashcards, quizzes, videos, and more.

Virtual Labs **VL**

The Virtual Labs are designed to help you get the most out of this course. The Virtual Lab icons direct you to specific media demonstrations and experiments designed to help you visualize what you are reading about. The numbers below indicate the number of the Virtual Lab you can access through Psychology CourseMate.

7.1 Flow From Moving Down a Hallway (p. 154)
A computer-generated program showing the optic flow that occurs when moving through a patterned hallway. (Courtesy of William Warren)

7.2 Optic Flow Over Surface (p. 154)
Flow from moving across a texture field. (Courtesy of Zhi Li and Frank Durgin)

7.3 Stimuli Used in Warren's Experiment (p. 157)
Moving stimulus pattern seen by observers in William Warren's experiment. (Courtesy of William Warren)

7.4 Eye Movements While Driving (p. 159)
Eye tracking while driving under different conditions. (Courtesy of Farid Kandil)

7.5 Optic Flow and the Visual Control of Locomotion (p. 159)
A review of optic flow and visual direction as sources of information for locomotion, and description of ongoing research. (Courtesy of William Warren)

7.6 Blind Walking Experiment (p. 159)
Subjects carrying out instructions in a blind walking experiment. (Courtesy of John Philbeck)

7.7 Monkey Grasping (p. 164)
Shows how monkeys grasped objects in the Fattori and colleagues' (2010) experiment. (Courtesy of Patrizia Fattori)

Perceiving Motion

◀ Our perception of motion depends on the movement of images across our retina, as would occur if these birds flew across our field of view; on signals generated by movement of our eyes, which would occur if we followed the birds' movement; and on cognitive mechanisms based on what we have learned by observing our environment. Our perception of this picture as birds in motion is based on our general knowledge of birds and on cues to motion such as the blurred images of some of the birds.

VL The Virtual Lab icons direct you to specific animations and videos designed to help you visualize what you are reading about. Virtual Labs are listed at the end of the chapter, keyed to the page on which they appear, and can be accessed through Psychology CourseMate.

Some Questions We Will Consider:

- Why do some animals freeze in place when they sense danger? (p. 177)
- When we scan or walk through a room, the image of the room moves across the retina, but we perceive the room and the objects in it as remaining stationary. Why does this occur? (p. 182)
- Why is motion of the human body "special"? (p. 190)

We are always taking action, either dramatically—as in Serena's bike ride in Chapter 7 (page 153)—or routinely, as in reaching for a coffee cup or walking across a room. Whatever form action takes, it involves motion, and one of the things that makes the study of motion perception both fascinating and challenging is that we are not simply passive observers of the motion of others. We are often moving ourselves. Thus, we perceive motion when we are stationary, as when we are watching other people cross the street (**Figure 8.1a**), and we also perceive motion as we ourselves are moving, as might happen when playing basketball (**Figure 8.1b**). We will see in this chapter that both the "simple" case of a stationary observer perceiving motion and the more complicated case of a moving observer perceiving motion involve complex "behind-the-scenes" mechanisms.

(a)

(b)

Figure 8.1 Motion perception occurs (a) when a stationary observer perceives moving stimuli, such as this couple crossing the street; and (b) when a moving observer, like this basketball player, perceives moving stimuli, such as the other players on the court.

Functions of Motion Perception

Motion perception has a number of different functions, ranging from providing us with updates about what is happening to helping us perceive things such as the shapes of objects and people's moods. Perhaps most important of all, especially for animals, the perception of motion is intimately linked to survival.

Motion Helps Us Understand Events in Our Environment

As you walk through a shopping mall, looking at the displays in the store windows, you are also observing other actions— a group of people engaged in an animated conversation, a salesperson rearranging piles of clothing and then walking over to the cash register to help a customer, a TV program in a restaurant that you recognize as a dramatic moment in a soap opera.

Much of what you observe involves information provided by motion. The gestures of the people in the group indicate the intensity of their conversation; the motions of the salesperson indicate what she is doing and changes in motion indicate when she has shifted to a new task; and motion indicates, even in the absence of sound, that something

important is happening in the soap opera (Zacks, 2004; Zacks & Swallow, 2007).

A particularly compelling demonstration of motion's power to indicate what is happening was provided by Fritz Heider and Marianne Simmel (1944), who showed a 2½-minute animated film to subjects and asked them to describe what was happening in the movie. The movie consisted of a "house" and three "characters"—a small circle, a small triangle, and a large triangle. These three geometric objects moved around both inside and outside the house, and sometimes interacted with each other (**Figure 8.2**).

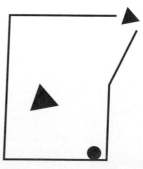

Figure 8.2 One image from the film used by Heider and Simmel (1944). The objects moved in various ways, going in and out of the "house" and sometimes interacting with each other. The nature of the movements led subjects to make up stories that often described the objects as having feelings, motivations, and personalities. Adapted from Heider, F., & Simmel, M. (1944). An experimental study of apparent behavior. *American Journal of Psychology*, 13, 243–259.

Although the characters were geometric objects, the subjects created stories to explain the objects' actions, and often gave them humanlike characteristics and personalities. For example, one account described the small triangle and circle as a couple who were trying to be alone in the house when the big triangle ("a bully") entered the house and interrupted them. The small triangle didn't appreciate this intrusion and attacked the big triangle. Who would have thought the world of geometric objects could be so exciting?

Returning to the world of people, motion perception is essential for our ability to move through the environment. As we saw in Chapter 7 when we described how people navigate (see page 157), one source of information about where we are going and how fast we are moving is the way objects in the environment flow past us as we move. As a person moves forward, objects move relative to the person in the opposite direction. This movement, called *optic flow* (Figures 7.1 and 7.2, page 154), provides information about the walker's direction and speed. In Chapter 7 we discussed how we can use this information to help us stay on course.

While motion provides information about what is going on and where we are moving, it provides information for more subtle actions as well. Consider, for example, the action of pouring water into a glass. As we pour the water, we watch the level rise, and this helps us know when to stop pouring. We can appreciate the importance of this ability by considering the case of a 43-year-old woman who lost the ability to perceive motion when she suffered a stroke that damaged an area of her cortex involved in motion perception. Her condition, called **akinetopsia** (blindness to motion), made it difficult for her to pour tea or coffee into a cup because the liquid appeared frozen, so she couldn't perceive the fluid rising in the cup and had trouble knowing when to stop pouring. It was also difficult for her to follow dialogue because she couldn't see the motions of a speaker's face and mouth (Zihl et al., 1983, 1991).

But the most disturbing effect of her brain damage occurred when people suddenly appeared or disappeared, because she couldn't see them approaching. Crossing the street presented serious problems because at first a car might seem far away, but then suddenly, without warning, it would appear very near. This disability was not just a social inconvenience but enough of a threat to the woman's well-being that she rarely ventured outside into the world of moving— and sometimes dangerous—objects. This case of a breakdown in the ability to perceive motion provides a dramatic demonstration of the importance of motion perception in day-to-day life.

Motion Attracts Attention

As you try to find your friend among the sea of faces in the student section of the stadium, you realize that you have no idea where to look. But you suddenly see a person waving and recognize that it is your friend. The ability of motion to attract attention is called **attentional capture**. This effect occurs not only when you are consciously looking for something but also while you are paying attention to something else. For example, as you are having a conversation, your attention may suddenly be captured by something moving in your peripheral vision.

The fact that movement can attract attention plays an important role in animal survival. You have probably seen animals freeze in place when they sense danger. If a mouse's goal is to avoid being detected by a cat, one thing it can do is to stop moving. Freezing in place not only eliminates the attention-attracting effects of movement, it also makes it harder for the cat to differentiate between the mouse and its surroundings.

Motion Provides Information About Objects

The idea that not moving can help an animal blend into the background is illustrated by the following demonstration. ▣

DEMONSTRATION

Perceiving a Camouflaged Bird

For this demonstration, you will need to prepare stimuli by photocopying the bird and the hatched-line pattern in **Figure 8.3**. Then cut out the bird and the hatched pattern so

Figure 8.3 The bird becomes camouflaged when the random lines are superimposed on it. When the bird is moved relative to the lines, it becomes visible, an example of how movement enhances the perception of form. From Regan, D. (1986). Luminance contrast: Vernier discrimination. *Spatial Vision, 1,* 305–318. Reprinted by permission of David Regan.

they are separated. Hold the picture of the bird up against a window during the day. Turn the copy of the hatched pattern over so the pattern is facing out the window (the white side of the paper should be facing you) and place it over the bird. If the window is adequately illuminated by daylight, you should be able to see the hatched pattern. Notice how the presence of the hatched pattern makes it more difficult to see the bird. Then, slide the bird back and forth under the pattern, and notice what happens to your perception of the bird (from Regan, 1986).

The stationary bird is difficult to see when it is covered by the pattern because the bird and the pattern are made up of similar lines. But as soon as all the elements of the bird begin moving in the same direction, the bird becomes visible. Movement has perceptually organized all the elements of the bird, so they create a figure that is separated from the background. Returning to our mouse hiding from the cat, we can say that it is to the mouse's advantage to freeze because this decreases the chances that the mouse will become perceptually separated from its surroundings in the cat's mind. **VL**

You might say, in reaction to the camouflaged bird demonstration, that although motion does make the bird easy to perceive amid the tangle of obscuring lines, this seems like a special case because most of the objects we see are not camouflaged. But if you remember our discussion from Chapter 5 (page 97) about how even clearly visible objects may be ambiguous, you can appreciate how motion of an object can reveal characteristics of the object that might not be obvious from a single, stationary view (**Figure 8.4a**). Movement of an observer around an object causes a similar effect: viewing the "horse" in **Figure 8.4b**

from different perspectives reveals that its shape is not exactly what you may have expected based on your initial view. Thus, our own motion relative to objects is constantly adding to the information we have about the objects, and most relevant to this chapter, we receive similar information when objects move relative to us. Observers perceive shapes more rapidly and accurately when an object is moving (Wexler et al., 2001).

Studying Motion Perception

To describe how motion perception is studied, the first question we will consider is: When do we perceive motion?

When Do We Perceive Motion?

The answer to this question may seem obvious: We perceive motion when something moves across our field of view. Actual motion of an object is called **real motion**. Perceiving a car driving by, people walking, or a bug scurrying across a tabletop are all examples of the perception of real motion.

There are also a number of ways to produce the perception of motion that involve stimuli that are not moving. Perception of motion when there actually is none is called **illusory motion**. The most famous, and best studied, type of illusory motion is called **apparent motion**. We introduced apparent motion in Chapter 5 when we told the story of Max Wertheimer's observation that when two stimuli in

(a)

(b)

© Cengage Learning 2014

Bruce Goldstein

Figure 8.4 (a) The shape and features of this car are revealed as different aspects of it become visible as it moves. (b) Moving around this "horse" reveals its true shape.

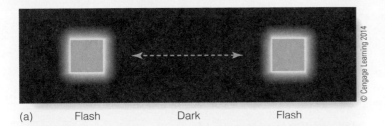

(a)   Flash   Dark   Flash

© Cengage Learning 2014

(b)

Bruce Goldstein

Figure 8.5 Apparent motion (a) between two dots when they are flashed one after the other; (b) on a moving sign. Our perception of words moving across a lighted display is so compelling that it is often difficult to realize that signs like this one are simply dots flashing on and off.

slightly different locations are alternated with the correct timing, an observer perceives one stimulus moving back and forth smoothly between the two locations (**Figure 8.5a**). This perception is called apparent motion because there is no actual (or real) motion between the stimuli. This is the basis for the motion we perceive in movies, on television, and in moving signs that are used for advertising and entertainment (**Figure 8.5b**). (Also see Figure 5.15, page 101.)

Induced motion occurs when motion of one object (usually a large one) causes a nearby stationary object (usually smaller) to appear to move. For example, the moon usually appears stationary in the sky. However, if clouds are moving past the moon on a windy night, the moon may appear to be racing through the clouds. In this case, movement of the larger object (clouds covering a large area) makes the smaller, but actually stationary, moon appear to be moving.

Motion aftereffects occur when viewing a moving stimulus for 30 to 60 seconds causes a stationary stimulus to appear to move. One example of a motion aftereffect is the **waterfall illusion** (Addams, 1834) (**Figure 8.6a**). If you look at a waterfall for 30 to 60 seconds (be sure it fills up only part of your field of view) and then look off to the side at part of the scene that is stationary, you will see everything you are looking at—rocks, trees, grass—appear to move up for a few seconds (**Figure 8.6b**).

Researchers studying motion perception have investigated all the types of perceived motion described above—and a number of others as well (Blaser & Sperling, 2008; Cavanagh, 2011). Our purpose, however, is not

Figure 8.6 The waterfall movement aftereffect. (a) Observation of motion in one direction, such as occurs when viewing a waterfall, can cause (b) the perception of motion in the opposite direction, indicated by the arrows, when viewing stationary objects in the environment.

(a)   (b)

Bruce Goldstein

to understand every type of motion perception but to understand some of the principles governing motion perception in general. To do this, we will focus on real and apparent motion.

Comparing Real and Apparent Motion

For many years, researchers treated the apparent motion created by flashing stationary objects or pictures and the real motion created by actual motion through space as though they were separate phenomena, governed by different mechanisms. However, there is ample evidence that these two types of motion have much in common. For example, Axel Larsen and coworkers (2006) presented three types of displays to a person in an fMRI scanner: (1) a *control condition*, in which two dots in slightly different positions were flashed simultaneously (**Figure 8.7a**); (2) a *real motion display*, in which a small dot moved back and forth (**Figure 8.7b**); and (3) an *apparent motion display*, in which dots were flashed one after another so that they appeared to move back and forth (**Figure 8.7c**). **VL**

Larsen's results are shown below the dot displays. The blue-colored area in Figure 8.7a is the area of visual cortex activated by the control dots, which are perceived as two dots simultaneously flashing on and off with no motion between them. Each dot activates a separate area of the cortex. In Figure 8.7b, the red indicates the area of cortex activated by real movement of the dot. In Figure 8.7c, the yellow indicates the area of cortex activated by the apparent motion display. Notice that the activation associated with apparent motion is similar to the activation for the real motion display. Two flashed dots that result in apparent motion activate the area of brain representing the space between the positions of the flashing dots even though no stimulus was presented there.

Because of the similarities between the neural responses to real and apparent motion, researchers study both types of motion together and concentrate on discovering general mechanisms that apply to both. In this chapter, we will follow this approach as we look for general mechanisms of motion perception.

What We Want to Explain

Our goal is to understand how we perceive things that are moving. At first this may seem like an easy problem. For example, **Figure 8.8a** shows what Maria sees when she looks straight ahead as Jeremy walks by. Because she doesn't move her eyes, Jeremy's image sweeps across her retina. Explaining motion perception in this case seems straightforward because as Jeremy's image moves across Maria's retina, it stimulates a series of receptors one after another, and this stimulation signals Jeremy's motion.

Figure 8.8b shows what Maria sees when she follows Jeremy's motion with her eyes. In this case, Jeremy's image remains stationary on Maria's foveas as he walks by. This adds an interesting complication to explaining motion perception, because although Jeremy's image remains stationary on her retina, Maria perceives Jeremy as moving. This means that motion perception can't be explained just by the motion of an image across the retina.

Let's consider what happens if Jeremy isn't present, and Maria scans the room by moving her eyes from left to right. When Maria does this, the images of the walls and objects in the room move to the left across her retina (**Figure 8.8c**), but Maria doesn't see the room or its contents as moving. In this case, there is motion across the retina but no perception that objects are moving. This is another example of why we can't simply consider what is happening on the retina. **Table 8.1** summarizes the three situations in Figure 8.8.

In the sections that follow, we will consider a number of different approaches to explaining motion perception, with the goal being to explain each of the situations in Figure 8.8 and Table 8.1. We begin by considering an approach that focuses on how information in the environment signals motion.

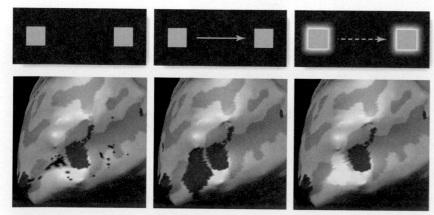

(a) Control   (b) Real   (c) Apparent

Figure 8.7 Three conditions in Larsen's (2006) experiment: (a) control condition; (b) real motion; (c) apparent motion (flashing dots). Stimuli are shown on top, and the resulting brain activation is shown below. In (c), the brain is activated in the space that represents the area between the two dots, where movement was perceived but no stimuli were present. From Larsen, A., Madsen, K. H., Lund, T. E., & Bundesen, C., Images of illusory motion in primary visual cortex. *Journal of Cognitive Neuroscience, 18,* 1174–1180. © 2006 by the Massachusetts Institute of Technology.

(a) Jeremy walks past Maria; Maria's eyes are stationary
(creates local disturbance in optic array)

(b) Jeremy walks past Maria; Maria follows him with her eyes
(creates local disturbance in optic array)

(c) Scans scene by moving her eyes from left to right
(creates global optic flow)

Figure 8.8 Three motion situations: (a) Maria is stationary and looks straight ahead as Jeremy walks past; (b) Maria follows Jeremy's movement with her eyes; (c) Maria scans the room by moving her eyes to the right. (The optic array and optic flow are described in the next section.)
© Cengage Learning

TABLE 8.1 Conditions for Perceiving and Not Perceiving Motion Depicted in Figure 8.8

	SITUATION	OBJECT	EYES	IMAGE ON OBSERVER'S RETINA	OBJECT MOVEMENT PERCEIVED?
1	Look straight as an object moves past	Moves	Stationary	Moves	YES
2	Follow a moving object with eyes	Moves	Move	Stationary	YES
3	Look around the room	Stationary	Move	Moves	NO

© Cengage Learning

Motion Perception: Information in the Environment

From the three situations in Figure 8.8, we saw that motion perception can't be explained by considering just what is happening on the retina. A solution to this problem was suggested by J. J. Gibson, who founded the ecological approach to perception. In Chapter 7 we noted that Gibson's approach (1950, 1966, 1979) involves looking for information in the environment that is useful for perception (see page 154). This information for perception, according to Gibson, is located not on the retina but "out there" in the environment. He thought about information in the environment in terms of the **optic array**—the structure created by the surfaces, textures, and contours of the environment—and he focused on how movement of the observer causes changes in the optic array. Let's see how this works by returning to Jeremy and Maria in Figure 8.8.

In Figure 8.8a, when Jeremy walks across Maria's field of view, portions of the optic array become covered as he walks by and then are uncovered as he moves on. This result is called a **local disturbance in the optic array**. This local disturbance in the optic array occurs when Jeremy moves relative to the environment, covering and uncovering the stationary background. According to Gibson, this local disturbance in the optic array provides information that Jeremy is moving relative to the environment.

In Figure 8.8b, Maria follows Jeremy with her eyes. Remember that Gibson doesn't care what is happening on the retina. Even though Jeremy's image is stationary on the retina, the same local disturbance information that was available when Maria was keeping her eyes still—Jeremy covering and uncovering parts of the array—remains available when she is moving her eyes, and this local disturbance information indicates that Jeremy is moving.

However, when Maria scans the scene in Figure 8.8c, something different happens: As her eyes move across the scene from left to right, everything around her—the walls, the window, the trash can, the clock, and the furniture—moves to the left of her field of view. A similar situation would occur if Maria were to walk through the scene. The fact that everything moves at once in response to movement of the observer's eyes or body is called **global optic flow**; this signals that the environment is stationary. Thus, according to Gibson, motion is perceived when one part of the visual scene moves relative to the rest of the scene, and no motion is perceived when the entire field moves, or remains stationary.

Motion Perception: Retina/Eye Information

Gibson's approach focuses on information that is "out there" in the environment. Another approach to explaining the various movement situations in Figure 8.8 is to consider the neural signals that travel from the eye to the brain.

The Reichardt Detector

An early neural explanation for motion perception is a neural circuit proposed by Werner Reichardt (1969) called the **Reichardt detector**, which results in neurons that fire to movement in one direction. **Figure 8.9** illustrates the basic principle of the Reichardt detector. Excitation and inhibition are arranged so that movement in one direction creates inhibition that eliminates neural responding, whereas movement in the opposite direction creates excitation that enhances neural responding.

We can understand how this works by following what happens as a spot of light moves across the retinal receptors. Figures 8.9a and b show what happens when the light is moving from left to right. Receptor A is stimulated first. The synapse between receptor A and E is excitatory (indicated by the Y), so stimulation of A excites E (indicated by green). Receptor E makes an inhibitory synapse with F (indicated by the vertical line), so F is inhibited (indicated by orange). While this is occurring, the light has moved to the right to receptor B and causes it to respond and to send an excitatory signal to F, but since F has already been inhibited by E, it does not fire (**Figure 8.9b**). Thus, when the light is moving to the right, the

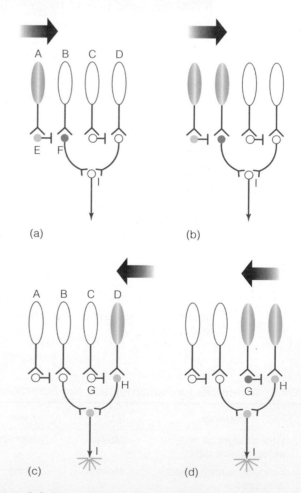

Figure 8.9 Reichardt circuit. Green indicates excitation; orange indicates inhibition. (a) and (b) When the receptors are stimulated from left to right, neuron I does not fire. (c) and (d) When the receptors are stimulated from right to left, neuron I fires. © Cengage Learning 2014

signals from receptors A and B do not get past F and therefore never reach I, the neuron at the end of the circuit. This process is repeated as the stimulus moves across the remaining receptors. The net result is that when the light is moving across the receptors from left to right, neuron I does not respond.

The outcome is different, however, when the light starts at receptor D and moves to the left. Receptor D sends a signal to H, which causes it to fire (**Figure 8.9c**) and to excite neuron I. When the light moves to the left and stimulates receptor C, it activates neuron G, which sends inhibition back to H. This inhibition, however, arrives too late, because H has already fired and has stimulated neuron I (**Figure 8.9d**). This process is repeated as the stimulus moves across the remaining receptors. Thus, when the light is moving to the left, the inhibition arrives too late to stop the signal from getting to neuron I, so neuron I fires. Neuron I, therefore, does not fire to movement to the right (Figure 8.9a and b) but does fire to movement to the left (Figure 8.9c and d).

Corollary Discharge Theory

Reichardt detectors can detect motion in a specific direction, but they can only explain the situation in Figure 8.8a, when an image (in this case, the image of Jeremy) sweeps across the receptors. In order to explain situations like those in Figure 8.8b (when Maria moves her eyes to follow Jeremy's movements) and Figure 8.8c (when Maria scans the room), we need to take into account not only how the image is moving on the retina but also how the eye is moving. **Corollary discharge theory** takes eye movements into account. The first step in understanding corollary discharge theory is to consider how neural signals associated with the retina and with the eye muscles are related to the three situations in Figure 8.8.

Signals From the Retina and the Eye Muscles Corollary discharge theory explains motion perception by taking into account the following signals, which are generated by movement of a stimulus on the retina and by movement of the eyes.

1. An **image displacement signal (IDS)** (**Figure 8.10a**) occurs when an image moves across receptors in the retina, as when Jeremy walks across Maria's field of view while she stares straight ahead.
2. A **motor signal (MS)** (**Figure 8.10b**) occurs when a signal is sent from the brain to the eye muscles. This signal occurs when Maria moves her eyes to follow Jeremy as he walks across the room.
3. A **corollary discharge signal (CDS)** is a copy of the motor signal that, instead of going to the eye muscles, is sent to a different place in the brain (Figure 8.10b). This is analogous to using the "cc" (copy) function when sending an email message. The email goes to the person it is addressed to, and a copy of the email is simultaneously sent to someone else at another address.

Now that we have introduced these signals, we can see a solution to our problem by asking what situations 1 and 2,

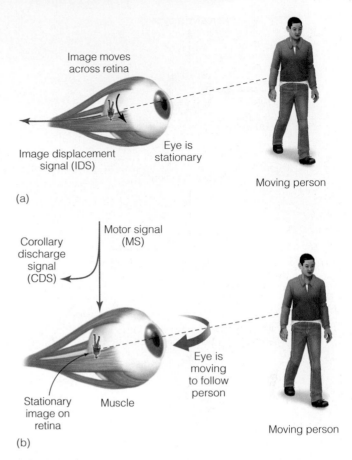

(a)

(b)

Figure 8.10 (a) When the image of an object moves across the retina, movement of the image across the retina creates an image displacement signal (IDS). (b) When a motor signal (MS) to move the eyes is sent to the eye muscles, so the eye can follow a moving object, there is a corollary discharge signal (CDS), which splits off from the motor signal. © Cengage Learning

in which the object is perceived to move, have in common. We can answer that question by focusing on the two signals that are transmitted toward the brain: the image displacement signal (IDS) and the corollary discharge signal (CDS). In situation 1, when Maria keeps her eyes stationary and Jeremy's image moves across her retina, only an IDS occurs. In situation 2, in which Maria moves her eyes to follow Jeremy so Jeremy's image doesn't move across her retina, only a CDS occurs. So perhaps the solution is this: When only one type of signal, either the IDS or the CDS, is sent to the brain, motion is perceived. Furthermore, if both signals occur, as happens in situation 3, when an observer scans the room as in Figure 8.8c, then no motion is perceived. This solution is, in fact, the basis of corollary discharge theory.

According to corollary discharge theory, the brain contains a structure or mechanism called the **comparator** that receives both the IDS and the CDS. The operation of the comparator is governed by the rules illustrated in **Figure 8.11**. If just one type of signal reaches the comparator—either the IDS (**Figure 8.11a**) or the CDS (**Figure 8.11b**)—it relays a message to the brain that "movement has occurred," and motion is perceived. But if both the CDS and IDS reach the comparator at the same time (**Figure 8.11c**), they cancel each

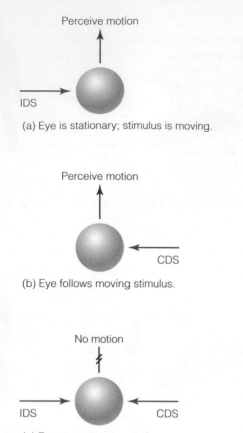

(a) Eye is stationary; stimulus is moving.

(b) Eye follows moving stimulus.

(c) Eye moves across stationary scene.

Figure 8.11 According to corollary discharge theory, (a) when the IDS reaches the comparator alone, a signal is sent to the brain and motion is perceived; (b) when the CDS reaches the comparator alone, a signal is sent to the brain and motion is perceived; (c) if both a CDS and an IDS reach the comparator simultaneously, they cancel each other, so no signals are sent to the brain and no motion is perceived. © Cengage Learning

other, so no signal is sent to the area of the brain responsible for motion perception. This handles our problem, because motion is perceived in situations 1 and 2, in which only one type of signal is present, but isn't perceived in situation 3, when both types of signal are present. **VL**

Upon hearing this explanation, students often ask where the comparator is located. The answer is that the comparator is most likely not located in one specific place in the brain but may involve a number of different structures. Similarly, the CDS probably originates from a number of different places in the brain (Sommer & Crapse, 2010; Sommer & Wurtz, 2008). The important thing for our purposes is that corollary discharge theory proposes that the visual system takes into account both information about stimulation of the receptors and information about movement of the eyes. And although we can't pinpoint exactly where the CDS and comparator are located, there is evidence that supports the theory. Here is some of the behavioral and physiological evidence.

Behavioral Evidence for Corollary Discharge Theory

These two demonstrations create a perception of motion even though there is no motion across the retina.

Figure 8.12 Afterimage stimulus. © Cengage Learning

Eliminating the Image Displacement Signal With an Afterimage

Illuminate the circle in **Figure 8.12** with your desk lamp and look at it for about 60 seconds. Then go into your closet (or a completely dark room) and observe what happens to the circle's afterimage (blink to make it come back if it fades) as you look around. Notice that the afterimage moves in synchrony with your eye motions (**Figure 8.13**).

Eye moves in dark

Bleached patch stays stationary on retina as eye moves

Figure 8.13 Afterimage demonstration. When the eye moves in the dark, the image remains stationary (the bleached area on the retina indicated by the red oval), but a CDS is sent to the comparator, so the afterimage appears to move. © Cengage Learning

Why does the afterimage appear to move when you move your eyes? The answer cannot be that an image is moving across your retina because the circle's image always remains at the same place on the retina. (The circle's image on the retina has created a circular area of bleached visual pigment, which remains in the same place no matter where the eye is looking.) Without motion of the stimulus across the retina, there is no image displacement signal. However, the motor signals sent to move your eyes are creating a corollary discharge signal, which reaches the comparator alone, so the afterimage appears to move (Figure 8.11b).

Seeing Motion by Pushing on Your Eyelid

Pick a point in the environment and keep looking at it while *very gently* pushing back and forth on the side of your eyelid, as shown in **Figure 8.14**. As you do this, you will see the scene move.

Figure 8.14 Why is this woman smiling? Because when she pushes on her eyelid, while keeping her eye fixed on one place, she sees the world jiggle.

Bruce Goldstein

Why do you see motion when you push on your eyelid? Lawrence Stark and Bruce Bridgeman (1983) did an experiment in which they instructed observers to keep looking at a particular point while pushing on their eyelid. Because the observers were paying strict attention to the instructions ("Keep looking at that point!"), the push in their eyelid didn't cause their eyes to move. This lack of movement occurred because the observer's eye muscles were pushing back against the force of the finger to keep the eye in place. According to corollary discharge theory, the motor signal sent to the eye muscles to hold the eye in place created a corollary discharge signal, which reached the comparator alone, as in Figure 8.11b, so Stark and Bridgeman's observers saw the scene move (also see Bridgeman

& Stark, 1991; Ilg, Bridgeman, & Hoffmann, 1989). (See "Think About It" #3 on page 196 for a question related to this explanation.)

These demonstrations support the central idea proposed by corollary discharge theory that there is a signal (the corollary discharge) that indicates when the observer moves, or tries to move, his or her eyes. When the theory was first proposed, there was little physiological evidence to support it, but now there is a great deal of physiological evidence for the theory.

Physiological Evidence for Corollary Discharge Theory

In both of our demonstrations, there was a corollary discharge signal but no image displacement signal. What would happen if there were no corollary discharge signal but there *was* an image displacement signal? That is apparently what happened to R.W., a 35-year-old male who experienced vertigo (dizziness) anytime he moved his eyes or experienced motion when he looked out the window of a moving car.

A brain scan revealed that R.W. had lesions in an area of his cortex called the medial superior temporal (MST) area (refer back to Figure 7.7). Behavioral testing of R.W. also revealed that as he moved his eyes, the stationary environment appeared to move with a velocity that matched the velocity with which he was moving his eyes (Haarmeier et al., 1997). Thus, when he moved his eyes to the left, there was an IDS, because images were moving across his retina to the right but the damage to his brain had apparently eliminated the CDS. Because only the IDS reached the comparator, R.W. saw motion when there actually was none.

Other physiological evidence for the theory comes from experiments that involve recording from neurons in the monkey's cortex. **Figure 8.15** shows the response recorded from a motion-sensitive neuron in the monkey's extrastriate cortex.

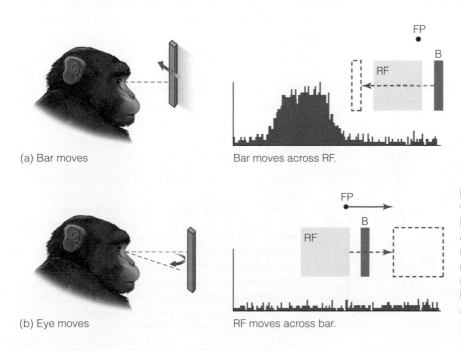

(a) Bar moves — Bar moves across RF.

(b) Eye moves — RF moves across bar.

Figure 8.15 Responses of a real-motion neuron in the extrastriate cortex of a monkey. In both cases, a bar (B) sweeps across the neuron's receptive field (RF) as the monkey looks at a fixation point (FP). (a) The neuron fires when the bar moves to the left across the receptive field. (b) The neuron doesn't fire when the eye moves to the right even though this also causes the bar to move across the receptive field. Adapted from Galletti, C., & Fattori, P. (2003). Neuronal mechanisms for detection of motion in the field of view. *Neuropsychologia, 41,* 1717–1727.

This neuron responds strongly when the monkey looks steadily at the fixation point (FP) as a moving bar sweeps across the neuron's receptive field (RF) (**Figure 8.15a**). But what if the monkey moves its eyes to follow a moving fixation point so its eyes sweep across a stationary bar (**Figure 8.15b**)? In this case, the bar's image will sweep across the neuron's receptive field, just as it did in Figure 8.15a. Even though the bar is sweeping across the receptive field, just as before, the neuron doesn't fire (Galletti & Fattori, 2003).

This neuron is called a **real-motion neuron** because it responds only when the stimulus moves and doesn't respond when the eye moves, even though the stimulus on the retina—a bar sweeping across the cell's receptive field—is the same in both situations. This real-motion neuron must be receiving information like the corollary discharge signal, which tells the neuron when the eye is moving. Real-motion neurons have also been observed in many other areas of the cortex (Battaglini et al., 1996; Robinson & Wurtz, 1976), and more recent research has begun to determine where the corollary discharge signal is acting in the brain (Sommer & Wurtz, 2006; Wang et al., 2007).

TEST YOURSELF 8.1

1. Describe four different functions of motion perception.

2. Describe four different situations that can result in motion perception. Which of these situations involve real motion, and which involve illusions of motion?

3. What is the evidence for similar neural responding to real motion and apparent motion?

4. Describe Gibson's ecological approach to motion perception. What is the advantage of this approach? (Give a specific example of how the ecological approach can explain the situations in Figure 8.8b and c.)

5. Describe the operation of the neural circuit that creates the Reichardt detector.

6. Describe the corollary discharge model. In your description, indicate (1) what the model is designed to explain; (2) the three types of signals—image displacement signal, motor signal, corollary discharge signal; and (3) when these signals do and do not cause motion perception when reaching the comparator.

Motion Perception and the Brain

In this section we will focus on the brain, and specifically on the middle temporal (MT) area, and the medial superior temporal (MST) area, both of which play important roles in the perception of motion.

The Movement Area of the Brain

When we described Hubel and Wiesel's (1959, 1965) pioneering work on receptive fields, we saw that they recorded from neurons in the visual receiving area that responded to bars that moved in a specific direction (see Figure 3.29). Another area that contains many directionally sensitive cells is the middle temporal (MT) area. Evidence that the MT cortex is specialized for processing information about motion is provided by experiments that have used moving dot displays in which the direction of motion of individual dots can be varied.

Figure 8.16a represents a display in which all of the dots are moving in random directions. William Newsome and coworkers (1995) used the term **coherence** to indicate the degree to which the dots move in the same direction. When the dots are all moving in random directions, coherence is 0 percent. **Figure 8.16b** represents a coherence of 50 percent, as indicated by the darkened dots, which means that at any point in time half of the dots are moving in the same direction. **Figure 8.16c** represents 100 percent coherence, which means that all of the dots are moving in the same direction.

Newsome and coworkers used these moving dot stimuli to determine the relationship between (1) a monkey's ability to judge the direction in which dots were moving and (2) the response of a neuron in the monkey's MT cortex. They found that as the dots' coherence increased, two things happened: (1) the monkey judged the direction of motion more accurately, and (2) the MT neuron fired more rapidly. The monkey's behavior and the firing of the MT neurons were so closely related that the researchers could predict one from the other. For example, when the dots' coherence was

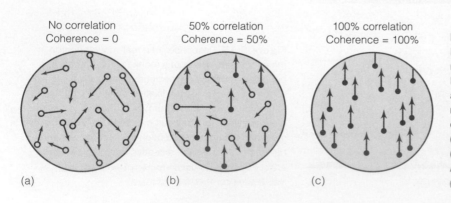

No correlation
Coherence = 0

50% correlation
Coherence = 50%

100% correlation
Coherence = 100%

(a)   (b)   (c)

Figure 8.16 Moving dot displays used by Newsome, Britten, and Movshon (1989). These pictures represent moving dot displays that were created by a computer. Each dot survives for a brief interval (20–30 microseconds), after which it disappears and is replaced by another randomly placed dot. Coherence is the percentage of dots moving in the same direction at any point in time. (a) Coherence = 0 percent; (b) Coherence = 50 percent; (c) Coherence = 100 percent. From Newsome, W. T., & Paré, E. B. (1988). A selective impairment of motion perception following lesions of the middle temporal visual area (MT). *Journal of Neuroscience, 8*, 2201–2211. Reproduced by permission.

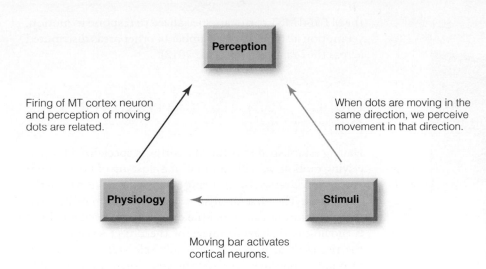

Firing of MT cortex neuron and perception of moving dots are related.

When dots are moving in the same direction, we perceive movement in that direction.

Moving bar activates cortical neurons.

Figure 8.17 The perceptual cycle from Chapter 1. Newsome measured the physiology–perception relationship by simultaneously recording from neurons and measuring the monkey's behavioral response. Other research we have discussed, such as Hubel and Wiesel's receptive field studies, have measured the stimulus–physiology relationship.
© Cengage Learning 2014

0.8 percent, the monkey was not able to judge the direction of the dots' motion and the neuron's response did not differ appreciably from its baseline firing rate. But at a coherence of 12.8 percent—so, out of 200 moving dots, about 25 were moving in the same direction—the monkey judged the direction of the dots that were moving together correctly on virtually every trial, and the MT neuron always fired faster than its baseline rate.

We can appreciate the importance of Newsome's experiments by considering the following three basic relationships in **Figure 8.17**, which we introduced in Chapter 1 (see Figure 1.10):

- *The stimulus–perception relationship (green arrow)*: Presenting a stimulus and determining whether motion is perceived. For example, when an object moves fast enough, we perceive movement; when an array of dots are moving in the same direction, we perceive movement in that direction.

- *The stimulus–physiology relationship (orange arrow)*: Presenting a movement stimulus and measuring neural responding. For example, in the experiment shown in Figure 8.15a, a moving bar caused a response in a monkey's cortex.

- *The physiology–perception relationship (red arrow):* Measuring the relationship between physiological responding and perception. This is the relationship measured by Newsome and coworkers because they measured the response of the MT neurons to the moving dots and also measured the monkey's perception of the moving dots.

The simultaneous measurement of neural firing and perception indicated by the red arrow is extremely difficult because before the recording experiments can begin, monkeys must be trained for months to indicate the direction in which they perceive the dots moving. (They are given a reward when they correctly signal the direction of movement.) Only after this extensive behavioral training can the monkey's perception and neural firing be measured simultaneously. The payoff, however, is that the relationship between physiology and perception is measured *directly*, thereby completing the triangle by providing the third relationship in Figure 8.17.

Effect of Lesioning and Microstimulation

Measuring perception and the firing of neurons in the monkey's MT cortex simultaneously is one way of showing that the MT cortex is important for motion perception. The role of the MT cortex has also been studied by determining how the perception of motion is affected by (1) lesioning (destroying or deactivating) some or all of the MT cortex or (2) electrically stimulating neurons in the MT cortex.

A monkey with an intact MT cortex can begin detecting the direction dots are moving when coherence is as low as 1 to 2 percent. However, after the MT is lesioned, the coherence must be 10 to 20 percent before monkeys can begin detecting the direction of motion (Newsome & Paré, 1988; also see Movshon & Newsome, 1992, Newsome et al., 1995; Pasternak & Merigan, 1994). This example of the physiology–perception relationship provides further evidence linking the firing of MT neurons to the perception of the direction of motion.

Another way this link between the MT cortex and motion perception has been studied is by electrically stimulating neurons in the MT cortex using a technique called *microstimulation*.

METHOD
Microstimulation

Microstimulation is achieved by lowering a small wire electrode into the cortex and passing a weak electrical charge through the tip of the electrode. This weak shock stimulates neurons that are near the electrode tip and causes them to fire, just as they would if they were being stimulated by chemical neurotransmitters released from other neurons.

Remember from Chapter 4 that neurons are organized in columns in the cortex, with neurons in the same column responding best to one orientation (page 80). Because neurons that respond to a specific direction of movement are also organized into columns, it is possible to activate neurons that respond to a specific direction of motion by applying microstimulation to a particular column.

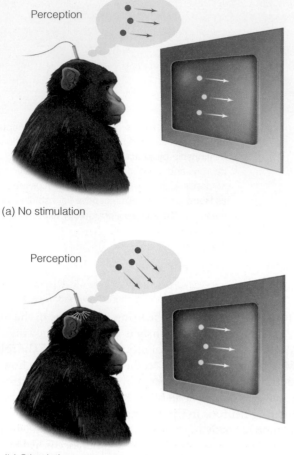

(a) No stimulation

(b) Stimulation

Figure 8.18 (a) A monkey judges the motion of dots moving horizontally to the right. (b) When a column of neurons that prefer downward motion is stimulated, the monkey judges the same motion as being downward and to the right. © Cengage Learning

Anthony Movshon and William Newsome (1992) used this microstimulation procedure in an experiment in which a monkey was looking at dots moving in a particular direction while indicating the direction of motion it was perceiving. For example, **Figure 8.18a** shows that as the monkey observed dots moving to the right, it reported that the dots were moving to the right. But **Figure 8.18b** shows that when Movshon and Newsome stimulated a column of MT neurons that preferred downward motion, the monkey began responding as though the dots were moving downward and to the right. The fact that stimulating the MT neurons shifted the monkey's perception of the direction of movement provides more evidence linking MT neurons and motion perception.

In addition to the MT cortex, another area involved in motion perception is the nearby medial superior temporal (MST) area (see Figure 7.7). But motion activates other areas as well. Remember from Chapter 4 that there are areas specialized to respond to faces (the fusiform face area) and bodies (the extrastriate body area), yet these objects also activate many other areas of the brain (Figure 4.22). Similarly,

the MT and MST cortex are specialized to respond to motion, yet motion also activates a number of other areas distributed across the brain (Fischer et al., 2012).

Motion From a Single Neuron's Point of View

Having established that the MT cortex is specialized for perceiving motion, we will now look at a close-up of how motion perception is served by the firing of single neurons within the MT cortex. The obvious answer to the question of how the firing of neurons can signal the direction in which an object is moving is that as an image of the object sweeps across the retina, it activates directionally selective neurons that respond to movement in a specific direction (see Figure 3.29).

Although this appears to be a straightforward solution to signaling the direction an object is moving, it turns out that the response of individual directionally selective neurons does not provide sufficient information to indicate the direction of movement. We can understand why this is so by considering how a directionally selective neuron would respond to movement of a vertically oriented pole like the one being carried by the woman in **Figure 8.19**.

Figure 8.19 The pole's overall motion is horizontally to the right (blue arrows). The ellipse represents the area in an observer's field of view that corresponds to the receptive field of a cortical neuron on the observer's retina. The pole's motion across the receptive field is also horizontal to the right (red arrows). © Cengage Learning

We are going to focus on the pole, which is essentially a vertical bar. The ellipse represents the area of the receptive field of a neuron in the cortex that responds when a vertical bar moves to the right across the neuron's receptive field. Figure 8.19 shows the pole entering the receptive field on the left. As the pole moves to the right, it moves across the receptive field in the direction indicated by the red arrow, and the neuron fires.

But what happens if the woman climbs some steps? **Figure 8.20** shows that as she walks up the steps, she and the pole are now moving up and to the right (blue arrow). We know this because we can see the woman and the flag moving up. But the neuron, which only sees movement through the narrow view of its receptive field, only receives information about the rightward movement. You can demonstrate this for yourself by doing the following demonstration.

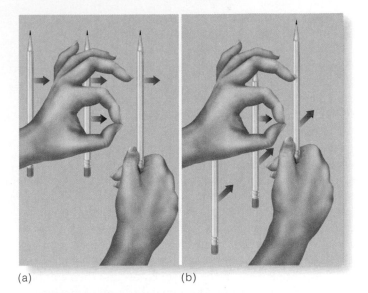

(a)   (b)

Figure 8.21 Moving a pencil behind an aperture in the "Movement of a Bar Across an Aperture" demonstration. See text for details.
© Cengage Learning

DEMONSTRATION
Movement of a Bar Across an Aperture

Make a small aperture, about 1 inch in diameter, by creating a circle with the fingers of your left hand, as shown in **Figure 8.21** (or you can create a circle by cutting a hole in a piece of paper). Then orient a pencil vertically, and move the pencil from left to right behind the circle, as in **Figure 8.21a**. As you do this, focus on the direction that the *front edge* of the pencil appears to be moving across the aperture. Now, again holding the pencil vertically, position the pencil below the circle, as shown in **Figure 8.21b**, and move it up behind the aperture at a 45-degree angle (being careful to keep its orientation vertical). Again, notice the direction in which the *front edge* of the pencil appears to be moving across the aperture.

Figure 8.20 In this situation, the pole's overall motion is up and to the right (blue arrows). However, the pole's motion across the receptive field is horizontal to the right (red arrows), as in Figure 8.19. Thus, the receptive field "sees" the same motion for motion that is horizontal and motion that is up and to the right. © Cengage Learning

If you were able to focus only on what was happening inside the aperture, you probably noticed that the direction that the front edge of the pencil was moving appeared the same whether the pencil was moving (a) horizontally to the right or (b) up and to the right. In both cases, the front edge of the pencil moves across the aperture horizontally, as indicated by the red arrow. Another way to state this is that the movement of an edge across an aperture occurs *perpendicular to the direction in which the edge is oriented*. Because the pencil in our demonstration was oriented vertically, motion through the aperture was horizontal.

Because the motion of the edge was the same in both situations, a single directionally selective neuron would fire similarly in (a) and (b), so based just on the activity of this neuron, it isn't possible to tell whether the pencil is moving horizontally to the right or upward at an angle. The fact that viewing only a small portion of a larger stimulus can result in misleading information about the direction in which the stimulus is moving is called the **aperture problem**.

The visual system appears to solve the aperture problem by pooling the responses of a number of neurons. Evidence that the MT cortex may be involved in pooling the responses from a number of neurons was provided by an experiment by Christopher Pack and Richard Born (2001), in which they determined how neurons in the monkey's MT cortex responded to moving oriented lines like the pole or our pencil. They found that the MT neurons' initial response to the stimulus, about 70 msec after the stimulus was presented, was determined by the orientation of the bar. Thus the neurons responded in the same way to a vertical bar moving horizontally to the right and a vertical bar moving up and to the right (red arrows in Figure 8.21). However, 140 ms after presentation of the moving bars, the neurons began responding to the *actual* direction in which the bars were moving (blue arrows in Figure 8.21). Apparently, MT neurons receive signals from a number of neurons in the striate cortex and then combine these signals to determine the actual direction of motion.

Can you think of another way a neuron might indicate that the pole in Figure 8.20 is moving up and to the right? One of my students tried the demonstration in Figure 8.21 and noticed that when he followed the directions for the demonstration, the edge of the pencil did appear to be moving horizontally across the aperture, whether the pencil was moving horizontally or up at an angle. However, when he moved the pencil so that he could see its tip moving through the aperture, as in **Figure 8.22**, he could tell that the pencil was moving up. Thus, a neuron could use information about the end of a moving object (such as the tip of the pencil) to determine its direction of motion. As it turns out, neurons that could signal this information, because they respond to the ends of moving objects, have been found in the striate cortex (Pack et al., 2003).

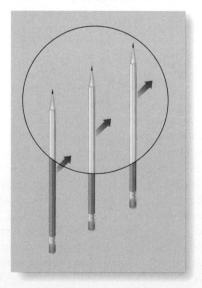

Figure 8.22 The circle represents a neuron's receptive field. When the pencil is moved up and to the right, as shown, movement of the tip of the pencil provides information indicating that the pencil is moving up and to the right. © Cengage Learning

What all of this means is that the "simple" situation of an object moving across the visual field as an observer looks straight ahead is not so simple because of the aperture problem. The visual system apparently solves this problem (1) by using information from neurons in the MT cortex that pool the responses of a number of directionally selective neurons, and (2) by using information from neurons in the striate cortex that respond to the movement of the ends of objects (also see Rust et al., 2006; Smith et al., 2005; Zhang & Britten, 2006). **VL**

Motion and the Human Body

We have just seen that experiments using dots and lines as stimuli have taught us a great deal about the mechanisms of motion perception. But what about the more complex stimuli created by moving humans and animals that are so prevalent in our environment? We will now consider two examples of the ways in which researchers have studied how we perceive movement of the human body.

Apparent Motion of the Body

Earlier in this chapter we described *apparent motion* as the perception of motion that occurs when two stimuli that are in slightly different locations are presented one after the other. Even though these stimuli are stationary, movement is perceived back and forth between them if they are alternated with the correct timing. Generally, this movement follows a principle called the **shortest path constraint**—apparent movement tends to occur along the shortest path between two stimuli.

Maggie Shiffrar and Jennifer Freyd (1990, 1993) had observers view photographs like the ones in **Figure 8.23a**, with the photographs alternating rapidly. Notice that in the first picture, the woman's hand is in front of her head, and in the second, it is behind her head. According to the shortest path constraint, motion should be perceived in a straight line between the hands in the alternating photos, which means observers would see the woman's hand as moving through her head, as shown in **Figure 8.23b**. This is, in fact, exactly what happens when the pictures are alternated very rapidly (five or more times a second), even though motion through the head is physically impossible. **VL**

While the straight-line motion of the hand through the head is an interesting result, the most important result occurred when the rate of alternation was slowed. When the pictures were alternated less than five times per second, observers began perceiving the motion as shown in **Figure 8.23c**, so the hand appeared to move around the woman's head. These results are interesting for two reasons: (1) They show that the visual system needs time to process information in order to

Apparent motion stimulus (pictures alternate)   **Two possible perceptions (as seen from above)**

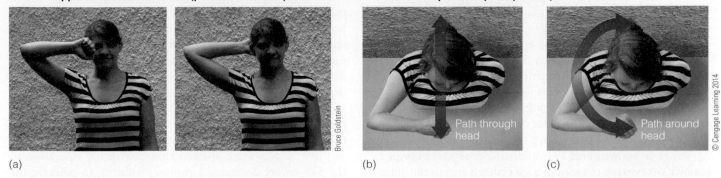

(a)   (b)   (c)

Figure 8.23 The two pictures in (a) are photographs similar to those used in Shiffrar and Freyd's (1993) experiment. The pictures were alternated either rapidly or more slowly. (b) When alternated rapidly, observers perceived the hand as moving through the head. (c) When alternated more slowly, the hand was seen as moving around the head.

perceive the movement of complex meaningful stimuli; and (2) they suggest that there may be something special about the meaning of the stimulus—in this case, the human body—that influences the way movement is perceived. To test the idea that the human body is special, Shiffrar and coworkers showed that when objects such as boards are used as stimuli, the likelihood of perceiving movement along the longer path doesn't increase at lower rates of alternation, as it does for pictures of humans (Chatterjee, Freyd, & Shiffrar, 1996).

What is happening in the cortex when observers view apparent motion generated by pictures like the one in Figure 8.23? To find out, Jennifer Stevens and coworkers (2000) measured brain activation using the PET scan technique. They found that both movement through the head and movement around the head activated areas in the parietal cortex associated with movement. However, when the observers saw movement as occurring around the head, the motor cortex was activated as well. Thus, the motor cortex is activated when the perceived movements are humanly possible but isn't activated when the perceived movements are not possible. This connection between the brain area associated with perceiving movement and the motor area reflects the close connection between perception and taking action that we discussed in Chapter 7.

Motion of Point-Light Walkers

Another approach to studying motion of the human body involves stimuli called **point-light walkers** that are created by placing small lights on people's joints and then filming the patterns created by these lights when people walk and carry out other actions in the dark (Johansson, 1973, 1975) (**Figure 8.24**).

Perceptual Organization At the beginning of the chapter, we showed how movement can cause individual elements to become perceptually organized (see the camouflaged bird demonstration, page 177). Similarly, motion creates organization for point-light walkers. When the person wearing

Figure 8.24 A point-light walker is created by placing lights on a person's joints and having the person walk in the dark so only the lights can be seen. © Cengage Learning

the lights is stationary, the lights look like a meaningless pattern. However, as soon as the person starts walking, with arms and legs swinging back and forth and feet moving in flattened arcs, first one leaving the ground and touching down, and then the other, the motion of the lights is immediately perceived as being caused by a walking person. This self-produced motion of a person or other living organism is called **biological motion.** **VL**

One reason we are particularly good at perceptually organizing the complex motion of an array of moving dots into the perception of a walking person is that we see biological motion all the time. Every time you see a person walking, running, or behaving in any way that involves movement, you are seeing biological motion.

Brain Mechanisms Our ability to easily organize biological motions into meaningful perceptions led some researchers to suspect that there may be an area in the brain that responds to biological motion, just as there are areas such as the extrastriate body area (EBA) and fusiform face area (FFA) that are specialized to respond to bodies and faces, respectively.

Emily Grossman and Randolph Blake (2001) provided evidence supporting the idea of a specialized area in the brain for biological motion by measuring observers' brain activity as they viewed the moving dots created by a point-light walker (**Figure 8.25a**) and as they viewed dots that moved similarly to the point-light walker dots, but were scrambled so they did not result in the impression of a person walking (**Figure 8.25b**). They found that a small area in the superior temporal sulcus (STS) was more active when viewing biological motion than viewing scrambled motion in all eight of their observers. In another experiment, Grossman and Blake (2002) showed that other regions, such as the FFA, were activated more by biological motion than by scrambled motion, but that activity in the EBA did not distinguish between biological and scrambled motion. Based on these results, they concluded that there is a network of areas, which includes the STS and FFA, that is specialized for the perception of biological motion (also see Pelphrey et al., 2003).

One of the principles we have discussed in this book is that just showing that a structure responds to a specific type of stimulus does not prove that the structure is involved in *perceiving* that stimulus. Earlier in the chapter we described how Newsome used a number of different methods to show that the MT cortex is specialized for the perception of motion. In addition to showing that the MT cortex is *activated* by motion, he also showed that *perception* of motion is decreased by lesioning the MT cortex and is influenced by stimulating neurons in the MT cortex. Directly linking brain processes and perception enabled Newsome to conclude that the MT cortex is important for the perception of motion.

Just as Newsome showed that disrupting operation of the MT cortex decreases a monkey's ability to perceive the direction of moving dots, Emily Grossman and coworkers (2005) showed that disrupting operation of the STS in humans decreases the ability to perceive biological motion. Grossman accomplished this using a procedure called *transcranial magnetic stimulation*.

METHOD
Transcranial Magnetic Stimulation (TMS)

One way to investigate whether an area of the brain is involved in determining a particular function is to remove that part of the brain, as Newsome did in his studies of the MT cortex in monkeys. Of course, we cannot purposely remove a portion of a person's brain, but it is possible to temporarily disrupt the functioning of a particular area by applying a pulsating magnetic field using a stimulating coil placed over the person's skull (**Figure 8.26**). A series of pulses presented to a particular area of the brain for a few seconds interferes with brain functioning in that area for seconds or minutes. If a particular behavior is disrupted by the pulses, researchers conclude that the disrupted area of the brain is involved in that behavior.

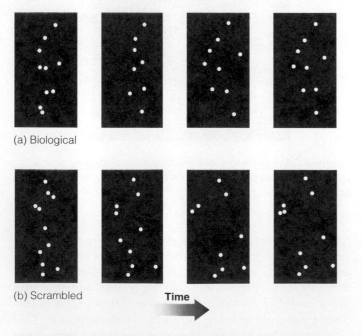

(a) Biological

(b) Scrambled   **Time**

Figure 8.25 Frames from the stimuli used by Grossman and Blake (2001). (a) Sequence from the point-light walker stimulus. (b) Sequence from the scrambled point-light stimulus. From Grossman, E. D., & Blake, R. (2001). Brain activity evoked by inverted and imagined biological motion. *Vision Research, 41*, 1475–1482. With permission from Elsevier.

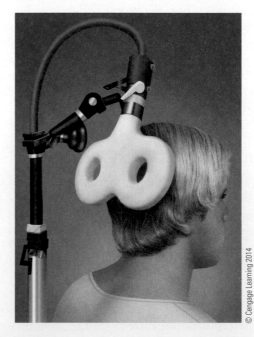

Figure 8.26 TMS coil positioned to present a magnetic field to the back of the person's head.

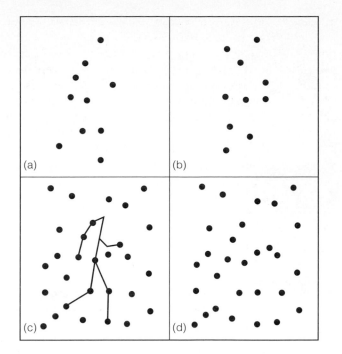

Figure 8.27 (a) Biological motion stimulus. (b) Scrambled stimulus. (c) Biological motion stimulus with noise added. The dots corresponding to the walker are indicated by lines (which were not seen by the observer). (d) How the stimulus appears to the observer.

From Grossman, E. D., Batelli, L., & Pascual-Leone, A. (2005). Repetitive TMS over posterior STS disrupts perception of biological motion. *Vision Research, 45,* 2847–2853. With permission from Elsevier.

The observers in Grossman's (2005) experiment viewed point-light stimuli for activities such as walking, kicking, and throwing (**Figure 8.27a**), and they also viewed scrambled point-light displays (**Figure 8.27b**). Their task was to determine whether a display was biological motion or scrambled motion. This is normally an extremely easy task, but Grossman made it more difficult by adding extra dots to create "noise" (**Figure 8.27c** and **d**). The amount of noise was adjusted for each observer so that they could distinguish between biological and scrambled motion with 71 percent accuracy.

The key result of this experiment was that presenting transcranial magnetic stimulation to the area of the STS that is activated by biological motion caused a significant decrease in the observers' ability to perceive biological motion. Such magnetic stimulation of other motion-sensitive areas, such as the MT cortex, had no effect on the perception of biological motion. From this result, Grossman concluded that normal functioning of the "biological motion" area, STS, is necessary for perceiving biological motion. This conclusion is also supported by studies showing that people who have suffered damage to this area have trouble perceiving biological motion (Battelli et al., 2003). What all of this means is that biological motion is more than just "motion"; it is a special type of motion that is served by specialized areas of the brain.

Representational Momentum: Motion Responses to Still Pictures

Look at the picture in **Figure 8.28**. Most people perceive this picture as a "freeze frame" of an action—skiing—that involves motion. It is not hard to imagine the person moving to a different location immediately after this picture was taken.

Figure 8.28 A picture that creates implied motion.

Ales Fevzer/CORBIS

(a) First picture (b) Forward in time (c) Backward in time

Figure 8.29 Stimuli like those used by Freyd (1983). See text for details. © Cengage Learning 2014

A situation such as this, in which a still picture depicts an action involving motion, is called **implied motion**.

Jennifer Freyd (1983) did an experiment involving implied motion by briefly showing observers pictures that depicted a situation involving motion, such as a person jumping off a low wall (**Figure 8.29a**). Freyd predicted that subjects looking at this picture would "unfreeze" the implied motion depicted in the picture and anticipate the motion that was about to happen. If this occurred, observers might "remember" the picture as depicting a situation that occurred slightly later in time. For the picture of the person jumping off the wall, that would mean the observers might remember the person as being closer to the ground (as in **Figure 8.29b**) than he was in the initial picture.

To test this idea, Freyd showed subjects a picture of a person in midair, like Figure 8.29a, and then after a pause, she showed her observers either (1) the same picture; (2) a picture slightly forward in time (the person who had jumped off the wall was closer to the ground, as in Figure 8.29b); or (3) a picture slightly backward in time (the person was farther from the ground, as in **Figure 8.29c**). The observers' task was to indicate, as quickly as possible, whether the second picture was the same as or different from the first picture.

When Freyd compared the time it took for subjects to decide if the "time-forward" and "time-backward" pictures were different from the first picture they had seen, she found that subjects took longer to decide if the time-forward picture was the same or different. She concluded from this that the time-forward judgment was more difficult because her subjects had anticipated the downward motion that was about to happen and so confused the time-forward picture with what they had actually seen.

The idea that the motion depicted in a picture tends to continue in the observer's mind is called **representational momentum** (David & Senior, 2000; Freyd, 1983). Representational momentum is an example of experience

influencing perception because it depends on our knowledge of the way situations involving motion typically unfold.

If implied motion causes an object to continue moving in a person's mind, then it would seem reasonable that this continued motion might be reflected by activity in the brain. When Zoe Kourtzi and Nancy Kanwisher (2000) measured the fMRI response in the MT and MST cortex to pictures like the ones in **Figure 8.30**, they found that the area of the brain that responds to actual motion also responds to *pictures* of motion, and that implied-motion (IM) pictures caused a greater response than no-implied-motion (no-IM) pictures, at rest (R) pictures, or house (H) pictures. Thus, activity

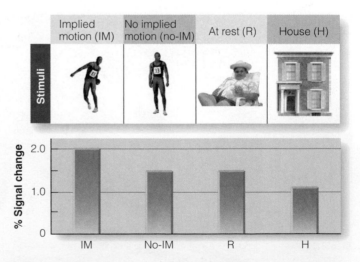

Figure 8.30 Examples of pictures used by Kourtzi and Kanwisher (2000) to depict implied motion (IM), no implied motion (no-IM), at rest (R), and a house (H). The height of the bars below each picture indicates the average fMRI response of the MT cortex to that type of picture. From Kourtzi, Z., & Kanwisher, N., Activation in human MT/MST by static images with implied motion, *Journal of Cognitive Neuroscience, 12,* 1, January 2000, 48–55. © 2000 by Massachusetts Institute of Technology. All rights reserved. Reproduced by permission.

occurs in the brain that corresponds to the continued motion that implied-motion pictures create in a person's mind (also see Lorteije et al., 2006; Senior et al., 2000).

Building on the idea that the brain responds to implied motion, Jonathan Winawer and coworkers (2008) wondered whether still pictures that implied motion, like the one in Figure 8.28, would elicit a motion aftereffect (MAE). To test this, they did a psychophysical experiment in which they asked whether viewing still pictures showing implied motion in a particular direction can cause a motion aftereffect (MAE) in the opposite direction. We described one type of motion aftereffect at the beginning of the chapter by noting that after viewing the downward movement of a waterfall, nearby stationary objects appear to move upward. There is evidence that this occurs because prolonged viewing of the waterfall's downward motion decreases the activity of neurons that respond to downward motion, so more upward-motion neuronal activity remains (Barlow & Hill, 1963; Mather et al., 1998).

To determine whether implied motion stimuli would have the same effect, Winawer had his subjects observe a series of pictures showing implied motion. For a particular trial, subjects saw either a series of pictures that all showed movement to the right or a series of pictures that all showed movement to the left. After adapting to this series of pictures for 60 seconds, the subjects' task was to indicate the direction of movement of arrays of moving dots like the ones we described earlier (see Figure 8.16).

The key result of this experiment was that before observing the implied-motion stimuli, subjects were equally likely to perceive dot stimuli with zero coherence (all the dots moving in random directions) as moving to the left or to the right. However, after viewing photographs showing rightward implied motion, subjects were more likely to see the dots as moving to the left. After viewing leftward-implied motion, subjects were more likely to see the dots as moving to the right. Because this is the same result that would occur for adapting to real movement to the left or right, Winawer concluded that viewing implied motion in pictures decreases the activity of neurons selective to that direction of motion.

SOMETHING TO CONSIDER:
Event Perception

When you look out at a scene, you don't see an abstract arrangement of light, dark, and color. You see individual objects arranged relative to each other in space. This is the result of perceptual organization and perceptual segmentation, which we described in Chapter 5. When I see the papers, a coffee cup, keys, and a pen on the surface of the table in front of me, I am perceptually segregating this tabletop scene into separated objects.

But what does this have to do with perceiving movement? I'll answer that question by describing what I see when I look up from the array of objects on the table. A person enters the coffee shop where I'm sitting, stops at the counter, has a brief conversation with the coffee barista behind the counter, who leaves and returns with coffee in a paper cup. The customer pushes down on the lid to make sure it is secure, pays for the coffee, drops a tip into the tip jar, turns around, and walks out the door. This short description, which represents only a small fraction of what is happening in the coffee shop, is a sequence of events unfolding in time. Just as we can segment a static scene into individual objects, we can segment ongoing behavior into a sequence of events, where an **event** is defined as a segment of time at a particular location that is perceived by observers to have a beginning and an ending (Zacks & Tversky, 2001; Zacks et al., 2009). An **event boundary** is the point in time when one event ends and another begins.

In our coffee shop scenario, placing an order with the coffee barista is an event; reaching out to accept the cup of coffee is an event; dropping change in the tip jar is an event; and so on. Our everyday life is a cascade of events, which can include our own behavior as well as our observations of the behaviors of others. The connection of events to motion perception becomes obvious when we consider that events almost always involve motion, and that changes in the nature of motion are often associated with event boundaries. One pattern of motion occurs when placing the order, another when reaching out for the coffee cup, and so on.

Jeffrey Zacks and coworkers (2009) have measured the connection between events and motion perception by having subjects watch films of common activities such as paying bills or washing dishes, and asking them to press a button when they believe one unit of meaningful activity ends and another begins (Newtson & Engquist, 1976; Zacks et al., 2001). When Zacks compared event boundaries to the actor's body movements measured with a motion tracking system, he found that event boundaries were more likely to occur when there was a change in the speed or acceleration of the actor's hands. From the results of this and other experiments, Zacks concluded that the perception of movement plays an important role in separating activities into meaningful events.

This brings us back to our example at the beginning of the chapter, in which we described the motions of a salesperson in a clothing store and noted that the person's motions indicated not only what she was doing (rearranging clothes) but also indicated when a new task began (helping a customer). Events, which are often defined by motion, follow one after the other to create our understanding of what is happening. **VL**

TEST YOURSELF 8.2

1. What is the evidence that the MT cortex is specialized for processing movement? Describe the series of experiments that used moving dots as stimuli and (a) recorded from neurons in the MT cortex, (b) lesioned the MT cortex, and (c) stimulated neurons in the MT cortex. What do the results of these experiments enable us to conclude about the role of the MT cortex in motion perception?

2. Describe the aperture problem—why the response of individual directionally selective neurons does not provide sufficient information to indicate the direction of motion. Also describe two ways that the brain might solve the aperture problem.

3. What is biological motion, and how has it been studied using point-light displays?

4. Describe experiments on apparent motion of a person's arm. How do the results differ for slow and fast presentations of the stimuli? How is the brain activated by slow and fast presentations?

5. Describe the experiments that have shown that an area in the STS is specialized for perceiving biological motion.

6. What is implied motion? Representational momentum? Describe behavioral evidence demonstrating representational momentum, physiological experiments that investigated how the brain responds to implied motion stimuli, and the experiment that used photographs to generate a motion aftereffect.

7. What is an event? What is the evidence that motion helps determine the location of event boundaries? What is the relation between events and our ability to predict what is going to happen next?

THINK ABOUT IT

1. We perceive real motion when we see things that are physically moving, such as cars on the road and people on the sidewalk. But we also see motion on TV, in movies, on our computer screens, and in electronic displays such as those in Las Vegas or Times Square. How are images presented in these situations in order to result in the perception of motion? (This may require some research.)

2. In the present chapter we have described a number of principles that also hold for object perception (Chapter 5). Find examples from Chapter 5 of the following (page numbers are for this chapter).

- There are neurons that are specialized to respond to specific stimuli (182).

- There are parallels between physiology and perception (187).

- More complex stimuli are processed in higher areas of the cortex (192).

- Experience can affect perception (190, 194).

3. Stark and Bridgeman explained the perception of movement that occurs when pushing gently on the eyelid by a corollary discharge signal generated when muscles are pushing back to counteract the push on the side of the eye. What if the push on the eyelid causes the eye to move, and the person sees the scene move? How would perception of the scene's movement in this situation be explained by corollary discharge theory? (p. 185)

4. We described how the representational momentum effect shows how knowledge can affect perception. Why could we also say that representational momentum illustrates an interaction between perception and memory? (p. 194)

KEY TERMS

Akinetopsia (p. 177)
Aperture problem (p. 189)
Apparent motion (p. 178)
Attentional capture (p. 177)
Biological motion (p. 191)
Coherence (p. 186)
Comparator (p. 183)
Corollary discharge signal (CDS) (p. 183)
Corollary discharge theory (p. 183)

Event (p. 195)
Event boundary (p. 195)
Global optic flow (p. 182)
Illusory motion (p. 178)
Image displacement signal (IDS) (p. 183)
Implied motion (p. 194)
Induced motion (p. 179)
Local disturbance in the optic array (p. 182)
Microstimulation (p. 187)

Motion aftereffect (p. 179)
Motor signal (MS) (p. 183)
Optic array (p. 182)
Point-light walker (p. 191)
Real motion (p. 178)
Real-motion neuron (p. 186)
Reichardt detector (p. 182)
Representational momentum (p. 194)
Shortest path constraint (p. 190)
Waterfall illusion (p. 179)

MEDIA RESOURCES

CourseMate

Go to CengageBrain.com to access Psychology CourseMate, where you will find the Virtual Labs plus an interactive eBook, flashcards, quizzes, videos, and more.

Virtual Labs **VL**

The Virtual Labs are designed to help you get the most out of this course. The Virtual Lab icons direct you to specific media demonstrations and experiments designed to help you visualize what you are reading about. The numbers below indicate the number of the Virtual Lab you can access through Psychology CourseMate.

8.1 Motion Providing Organization: The Hidden Bird (p. 177)
How movement can cause an image to stand out from a complex background. (Courtesy of Michael Bach and David Regan)

8.2 Perceptual Organization: The Dalmatian (p. 178)
How a black and white pattern can be perceived as a Dalmatian. (Courtesy of Michael Bach)

8.3 Shape From Movement (p. 178)
How movement can create shape in an array of dots.

8.4 Larsen Experiment (p. 180)
Shows stimulus presentation for Larsen and colleagues' (2006) experiment. (Courtesy of Axel Larsen)

8.5 Corollary Discharge Model (p. 184)
A demonstration of how components of the model affect firing.

8.6 Motion Binding (p. 190)
Illustrates how adding an object to a display of four moving lines can influence how we perceive the motion of the lines. (Courtesy of Michael Bach)

8.7 Motion Perception in Depth (p. 190)
Narrated animation describing how conflicting right and left eye information creates perception of motion in depth. (Courtesy of Alex Huk)

8.8 Apparent Movement of the Human Body (p. 190)
Demonstration of possible and impossible apparent motion. (Courtesy of Maggie Shiffrar)

8.9 Biological Motion 1 (p. 191)
Illustrates how biological motion stimuli for a human walker change when gender, weight, and mood are varied. (Courtesy of Nikolaus Troje)

8.10 Biological Motion 2 (p. 191)
Illustrates biological motion stimuli for humans, cats, and pigeons and what happens when these stimuli are inverted, scrambled, and masked. (Courtesy of Nikolaus Troje)

8.11 Event Perception: Paying Bills (p. 195)
Shows person paying bills. Record below shows event segmentation and movement. (Courtesy of Jeffrey Zacks)

8.12 Event Perception: Working in Kitchen (p. 195)
Film of person working in kitchen. Record below shows coarse and fine event segmentation. (Courtesy of Jeffrey Zacks)

Perceiving Color

◄ The colors in this section of a stained glass window in the Cathedral de Notre Dame Montreal are beautiful and a source of inspiration. But the most amazing thing about color is that it doesn't exist within the colored object, but is created by the brain. As we will see in this chapter, the perception of the *blue*, *orange*, *red*, and *green* in this image is the end result of a process that begins when different wavelengths of light activate cone receptors in the retina and culminates in the firing of neurons in the brain that somehow creates the experience of color.

SOMETHING TO CONSIDER: **Color Is a Construction of the Nervous System**

DEVELOPMENTAL DIMENSION: **Infant Color Vision**

Think About It

VL The Virtual Lab icons direct you to specific animations and videos designed to help you visualize what you are reading about. Virtual Labs are listed at the end of the chapter, keyed to the page on which they appear, and can be accessed through Psychology CourseMate.

Some Questions We Will Consider:

- What does someone who is "color-blind" see? (p. 209)
- Why do we perceive blue dots when a yellow flash bulb goes off? (p. 210)
- What colors does a honeybee perceive? (p. 221)

olor is one of the most obvious and pervasive qualities in our environment. We interact with it every time we note the color of a traffic light, choose clothes that are color coordinated, or appreciate the colors of a painting. We pick favorite colors (blue is the most favored; Terwogt & Hoeksma, 1994), we associate colors with emotions (we turn purple with rage, red with embarrassment, green with envy, and feel blue; Terwogt & Hoeksma, 1994; Valdez & Mehribian, 1994), and we imbue colors with special meanings (for example, red signifies danger; purple, royalty; green, ecology). But for all of our involvement with color, we sometimes take it for granted, and—just as with our other perceptual abilities—we may not fully appreciate color unless we lose our ability to experience it. The depth of this loss is illustrated by the case of Mr. I., a painter who became color-blind at the age of 65 after suffering a concussion in an automobile accident.

In March 1986, the neurologist Oliver Sacks received an anguished letter from Mr. I., who, identifying himself as a "rather successful artist," described how ever since he had been involved in an automobile accident, he had lost his ability to experience colors. He exclaimed with some anguish, "My dog is gray. Tomato juice is black. Color TV is a hodge-podge. . . ." In the days following his accident, Mr. I. became more and more depressed. His studio, normally awash with the brilliant colors of his abstract paintings, appeared drab to him, and his paintings, meaningless. Food, now gray, became difficult for him to look at while eating; and sunsets, once seen as rays of red, had become streaks of black against the sky (Sacks, 1995).

Mr. I.'s color blindness was caused by cortical injury after a lifetime of experiencing color, whereas most cases of total color blindness or of color deficiency (partial color blindness, which we'll discuss in more detail later in this chapter) occur at birth because of the genetic absence of one or more types of cone receptors. Most people who are born partially color-blind are not disturbed by their decreased color perception compared to "normal," because they have never experienced color. However, some of their reports, such as the darkening of reds, are similar to Mr. I.'s. People with total color blindness often echo Mr. I.'s complaint that it is sometimes difficult to distinguish one object from another, as when his brown dog, which he could easily see silhouetted against a light-colored road, became very difficult to perceive when seen against irregular foliage.

Eventually, Mr. I. overcame his strong psychological reaction and began creating striking black-and-white pictures. But his account of his color-blind experiences provides an impressive testament to the central place of color in our everyday lives. (See Heywood et al., 1991; Nordby, 1990; Young et al., 1980; and Zeki, 1990, for additional descriptions of cases of complete color blindness.)

In this chapter, we consider color perception in three parts. (1) We consider some basic facts about color perception. Then we ask, (2) What is the connection between color perception and the firing of neurons? and (3) How do we perceive the colors and lightness of objects in the environment under changing illumination?

Introduction to Color

Why do we perceive different colors? We will begin answering this question by first speculating about some of the functions that color serves in our lives. We will then look at how we describe our experience of color and how this experience is linked to the properties of light.

What Are Some Functions of Color Vision?

Color adds beauty to our lives, but it does more than that. Color serves important signaling functions, both natural and contrived by humans. The natural and human-made world provides many color signals that help us identify and classify

things. I know the rock on my desk contains copper by the rich blue vein that runs through it; I know a banana is ripe when it has turned yellow; and I know to stop when the traffic light turns red.

In addition to its signaling function, color helps facilitate perceptual organization, the process we discussed in Chapter 5 (page 100) by which small elements become grouped perceptually into larger objects. Color perception greatly facilitates the ability to tell one object from another and especially to pick out objects within scenes, an ability crucial to the survival of many species. Consider, for example, a monkey foraging for fruit in the forest or jungle. A monkey with good color vision easily detects red fruit against a green background (**Figure 9.1a**), but a color-blind monkey would find it more difficult to find the fruit (**Figure 9.1b**). Color vision thus enhances the contrast of objects that, if they didn't appear colored, would appear more similar.

This link between good color vision and the ability to detect colored food has led to the proposal that monkey and human color vision may have evolved for the express purpose of detecting fruit (Mollon, 1989, 1997; Sumner & Mollon, 2000; Walls, 1942). This suggestion sounds reasonable when we consider the difficulty color-blind human observers have when confronted with the seemingly simple task of picking berries. Knut Nordby (1990), a totally color-blind visual scientist who sees the world in shades of gray, described his experience as follows: "Picking berries has always been a big problem. I often have to grope around among the leaves with my fingers, feeling for the berries by their shape" (p. 308).

Our ability to perceive color not only helps us detect objects that might otherwise be obscured by their surroundings, it also helps us recognize and identify things we can see easily. James W. Tanaka and L. M. Presnell (1999) demonstrated this by asking observers to identify objects like the ones in **Figure 9.2**, which appeared either in their normal colors, like the yellow banana, or in inappropriate colors, like the purple banana. The result was that observers recognized the appropriately colored objects more rapidly and accurately. Thus, knowing the colors of familiar objects helps us to recognize these objects (Tanaka et al., 2001). (Remember from Chapter 5, page 110, that color also helps us process complex scenes.)

(a)   (b)

Figure 9.1 (a) Red berries in green foliage. (b) These berries become more difficult to detect without color vision.

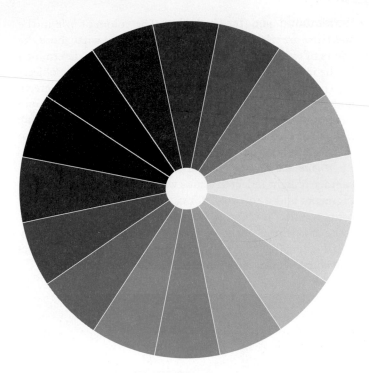

Figure 9.2 Subjects in Tanaka and Presnell's (1999) experiment were able to recognize appropriately colored objects like the fruits on the left more rapidly than inappropriately colored objects like the fruits on the right. From Tanaka, J. W., Weiskopf, D., & Williams, P. The role of color in high-level vision. *Trends in Cognitive Sciences, 5,* 211–215. Copyright 2001, with permission from Elsevier.

What Colors Do We Perceive?

We can describe all the colors we can perceive by using the terms *blue, green, yellow, red,* and combinations of these terms (such as "bluish green") (Abramov & Gordon, 1994; Hurvich, 1981). When people are presented with many different colors and are asked to describe them, they can describe all of them when they are allowed to use all four of these terms, but they can't when one of these terms is omitted. Other colors, such as orange, violet, purple, and brown, are not needed to achieve these descriptions (Fuld et al., 1981; Quinn et al., 1988). Color researchers therefore consider red, yellow, green, and blue to be *pure* or *unique* colors (Backhaus, 1998).

Figure 9.3 shows the colors arranged in a circle. The order of the four basic colors in the color circle—blue, green, yellow, and red—matches the order of the colors in the visible spectrum, shown in **Figure 9.4**, in which the short-wavelength end of the spectrum is blue, green is in the middle of the spectrum, and yellow and red are at the long-wavelength end of the spectrum.

Although the color circle is based on four colors, there are more than four colors in the circle. In fact, people can discriminate between about 200 different colors across the length of the visible spectrum (Gouras, 1991). We can create even more colors by changing the intensity of the light to make colors brighter or dimmer, or by adding white to change a color's **saturation**. For example, adding white to the deep red at the top of the color circle makes it become pink, which is a less saturated (or **desaturated**) form of red.

By changing the wavelength (which we discuss next), the intensity, and the saturation, we can create about a million or more different colors (Backhaus, 1998; Gouras, 1991). This is far more than we can discriminate, but it is the number of

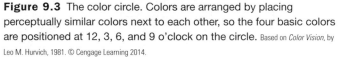

Figure 9.3 The color circle. Colors are arranged by placing perceptually similar colors next to each other, so the four basic colors are positioned at 12, 3, 6, and 9 o'clock on the circle. Based on *Color Vision*, by Leo M. Hurvich, 1981. © Cengage Learning 2014.

colors on a high-quality color monitor that is capable of accurately representing our everyday experience of color.

Having described the different colors we can perceive, we now turn to the question of how these colors come about. What causes us to perceive a tomato as red or a banana as yellow? Our first answer to this question is that these colors are related to the wavelength of light.

Color and Wavelength

The first step in understanding how our nervous system creates our perception of color is to consider the visible spectrum in Figure 9.4. When we introduced this spectrum in Chapter 2 (page 22), we saw that the perception of color is associated with the physical property of wavelength. The spectrum stretches from short wavelengths (400 nm) to long wavelengths (700 nm), and bands of wavelengths within this range are associated with different colors. Wavelengths from about 400 to 450 nm appear violet; 450 to 490 nm, blue; 500 to 575 nm, green; 575 to 590 nm, yellow; 590 to 620 nm, orange; and 620 to 700 nm, red.

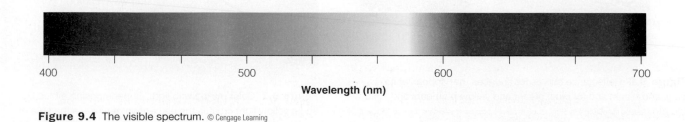

Figure 9.4 The visible spectrum. © Cengage Learning

Reflectance and Transmission The colors of *light* in the spectrum are related to their wavelengths, but what about the colors of *objects*? The colors of objects are largely determined by the wavelengths of light that are *reflected* from the objects into our eyes. **Chromatic colors** or **hues,** such as blue, green, and red, occur when some wavelengths are reflected more than others, a process called **selective reflection (Figure 9.5a).** **Achromatic colors,** such as white, gray, or black, occur when light is reflected equally across the spectrum.

Figure 9.6 shows **reflectance curves**—plots of the percentage of light reflected versus wavelength—for a number of pigments and a tomato. Notice that the pigments and the tomato reflect a range of wavelengths but selectively reflect more in one part of the spectrum. The curves for the achromatic colors (black, gray, and white) are flat, indicating equal reflectance across the spectrum.

Most colors in the environment are created by the way objects selectively reflect some wavelengths. But in the case of things that are transparent, such as liquids, plastics, and glass, chromatic color is created by **selective transmission,** meaning that only some wavelengths pass through the object or substance (**Figure 9.5b**). For example, cranberry juice selectively transmits long-wavelength light and appears red, whereas limeade selectively transmits medium-wavelength light and appears green. **Transmission curves**—plots of the percentage of light transmitted versus wavelength—look similar to the reflectance curves in Figure 9.6. Table 9.1 indicates the relationship between the wavelengths reflected or transmitted and the color perceived.

The idea that the color we perceive depends largely on the wavelengths of the light that reaches our eyes provides a way to explain what happens when we mix different colors together. We will describe two ways of mixing colors: mixing lights and mixing paints.

Mixing Lights If a light that appears blue is projected onto a white surface and a light that appears yellow is superimposed onto the blue, the area that is superimposed is perceived as white (**Figure 9.7**). Although this result may surprise

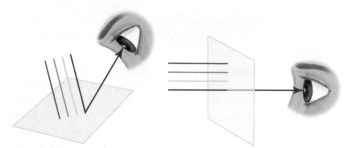

(a) Selective reflection   (b) Selective transmission

Figure 9.5 Examples of (a) selective reflection and (b) selective transmission. When white light, containing all of the wavelengths in the spectrum, hits the surface, only the long-wavelength light is reflected in this example. The rest of the wavelengths are absorbed. For selective transmission, only the long-wavelength light is transmitted. © Cengage Learning 2014

TABLE 9.1   Relationship Between Predominant Wavelengths Reflected and Color Perceived

WAVELENGTHS REFLECTED OR TRANSMITTED	PERCEIVED COLOR
Short	Blue
Medium	Green
Long and medium	Yellow
Long	Red
Long, medium, and short	White

© Cengage Learning

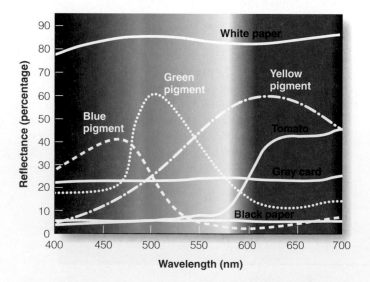

Figure 9.6 Reflectance curves for surfaces that appear white, gray, and black, and for blue, green, and yellow pigments and a red tomato. Adapted from Clulow, F. W. (1972). *Color: Its principles and their applications.* New York: Morgan & Morgan. Adapted by permission of the author.

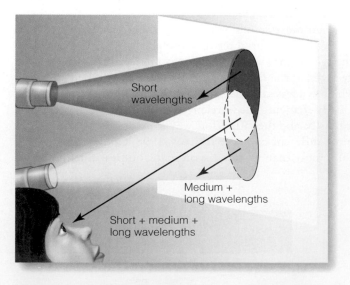

Figure 9.7 Color mixing with light. Superimposing a blue light and a yellow light creates the perception of white in the area of overlap. This is additive color mixing. © Cengage Learning

you if you have ever mixed blue and yellow paints to create green, you can understand why this occurs by considering the wavelengths that the mixture of blue and yellow lights reflect into the eye. Because the two spots of light are projected onto a white surface, which reflects all wavelengths, all of the wavelengths that hit the surface are reflected into an observer's eyes (see the reflectance curve for white paper in Figure 9.6). The blue spot consists of a band of short wavelengths, so when it is projected alone, the short-wavelength light is reflected into the observer's eyes (Table 9.2). Similarly, the yellow spot consists of medium and long wavelengths, so when presented alone, these wavelengths are reflected into the observer's eyes.

The key to understanding what happens when colored lights are superimposed is that *all of the light that is reflected from the surface by each light when alone is also reflected when the lights are superimposed*. Thus, where the two spots are superimposed, the light from the blue spot and the light from the yellow spot are both reflected into the observer's eye. The added-together light therefore contains short, medium, and long wavelengths, which results in the perception of white. Because mixing lights involves adding up the wavelengths of each light in the mixture, mixing lights is called **additive color mixture**.

Mixing Paints We can appreciate why we see different colors when mixing paints than when mixing lights by considering the blobs of paint in **Figure 9.8**. The blue blob absorbs long-wavelength light and reflects some short-wavelength light and some medium-wavelength light (see the reflectance curve for "blue pigment" in Figure 9.6). The yellow blob absorbs short-wavelength light and reflects some medium- and long-wavelength light (see the reflectance curve for "yellow pigment" in Figure 9.6).

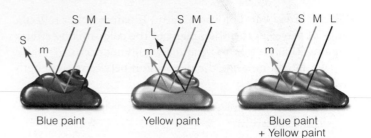

Figure 9.8 Color mixing with paint. Mixing blue paint and yellow paint creates a paint that appears green. This is subtractive color mixture. © Cengage Learning

The key to understanding what happens when colored paints are mixed together is that when mixed, *both paints still absorb the same wavelengths they absorbed when alone, so the only wavelengths reflected are those that are reflected by both paints in common*. Because medium wavelengths are the only ones reflected by both paints in common, a mixture of blue and yellow paints appears green (Table 9.3). Because each blob of paint absorbs wavelengths and these wavelengths are still absorbed by the mixture, mixing paints is called **subtractive color mixture**. The blue and yellow blobs subtract all of the wavelengths except some that are associated with green.

The reason that mixing blue and yellow paints results in green is that both paints reflect some light in the green part of the spectrum (see the overlap between the blue and yellow pigment curves in Figure 9.6). If our blue paint had reflected only short wavelengths and our yellow paint had reflected only medium and long wavelengths, these paints would reflect no color in common, so mixing them would result in little or no reflection across the spectrum, and the mixture would appear black. It is rare, however, for paints to reflect light in only one region of the spectrum. Most paints

TABLE 9.2   Mixing Blue and Yellow Lights (Additive Color Mixture)

Parts of the spectrum that are reflected from a white surface for blue and yellow spots of light projected onto the surface. Wavelengths that are reflected from the mixture are highlighted.

	WAVELENGTHS		
	SHORT	MEDIUM	LONG
Spot of blue light	Reflected	No Reflection	No Reflection
Spot of yellow light	No Reflection	Reflected	Reflected
Overlapping blue and yellow spots	**Reflected**	**Reflected**	**Reflected**

© Cengage Learning

TABLE 9.3   Mixing Blue and Yellow Paints (Subtractive Color Mixture)

Parts of the spectrum that are absorbed and reflected by blue and yellow paint. Wavelengths that are reflected from the mixture are highlighted. Light that is usually seen as green is the only light that is reflected in common by both paints.

	WAVELENGTHS		
	SHORT	MEDIUM	LONG
Blob of blue paint	Reflects all	Reflects some	Absorbs all
Blob of yellow paint	Absorbs all	Reflects some	Reflects some
Mixture of blue and yellow blobs	Absorbs all	**Reflects some**	Absorbs all

© Cengage Learning

reflect a broad band of wavelengths. If paints didn't reflect a range of wavelengths, then many of the color-mixing effects of paints that we take for granted would not occur.

We can summarize the connection between wavelength and color as follows:

- Colors of light are associated with wavelengths in the visible spectrum.

- The colors of objects are associated with which wavelengths are *reflected* (for opaque objects) or *transmitted* (for transparent objects).

- The colors that occur when we mix colors are also associated with which wavelengths are reflected into the eye. Mixing *lights* causes more wavelengths to be reflected (each light *adds* wavelengths to the mixture); mixing *paints* causes fewer wavelengths to be reflected (each paint *subtracts* wavelengths from the mixture).

We will see later in the chapter that things other than the wavelengths reflected into our eye can influence color perception. For example, our perception of an object's color can be influenced by the background on which the object is seen. But for now our main focus is on the connection between wavelength and color.

The connection between wavelength and color has formed the basis of two theories of color vision, both of which describe how the visual system analyzes light to signal the wavelengths that are present. We will consider each of the theories in turn, first describing the behavioral evidence on which the theory was based and then describing the physiological evidence that became available later.

Trichromatic Theory of Color Vision

The **trichromatic theory of color vision**, which states that color vision depends on the activity of three different receptor mechanisms, was proposed by two eminent 19th-century researchers, Thomas Young (1773–1829) and Hermann von Helmholtz (1821–1894). They based their theory on the results of a psychophysical procedure called *color matching*.

Behavioral Evidence for the Theory

In Helmholtz's **color-matching experiments**, observers adjusted the amounts of three different wavelengths of light mixed together in a "comparison field" until the color of this mixture matched the color of a single wavelength in a "test field." For example, an observer might be asked to adjust the amount of 420-nm, 560-nm, and 640-nm light in a comparison field until the field matched the color of a 500-nm light presented in the test field (**Figure 9.9**). (Any three wavelengths

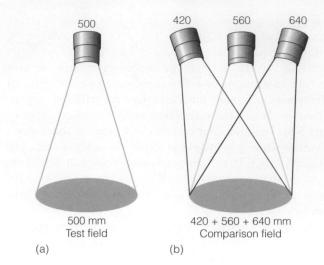

Figure 9.9 In a color-matching experiment, the observer adjusts the amount of three wavelengths in one field (right) so that it matches the color of the single wavelength in the other field (left). © Cengage Learning 2014

can be used, as long as any of them can't be matched by mixing the other two.) The key findings of these color-matching experiments were as follows:

1. By correctly adjusting the proportions of *three* wavelengths in the comparison field, it was possible to match any wavelength in the test field.

2. People cannot match all wavelengths in the spectrum with only two wavelengths. For example, if they were given only the 420-nm and 640-nm lights to mix, they would be unable to match certain colors.

Thomas Young (1802) proposed the trichromatic theory of color vision based on the finding that people with normal color vision need at least three wavelengths to match any other wavelength. This theory was later championed and refined by Helmholtz (1852) and is therefore also called the **Young-Helmholtz theory of color vision**. The central idea of the theory is that color vision depends on three receptor mechanisms, each with different spectral sensitivities. (Remember from Chapter 2 that spectral sensitivity indicates the sensitivity to wavelengths in the visible spectrum, as shown in Figure 2.18b.)

According to this theory, light of a particular wavelength stimulates each receptor mechanism to different degrees, and the pattern of activity in the three mechanisms results in the perception of a color. Each wavelength is therefore represented in the nervous system by its own pattern of activity in the three receptor mechanisms.

Physiological Evidence for the Theory

More than a century after the trichromatic theory was first proposed, physiological research identified the three receptor mechanisms proposed by the theory.

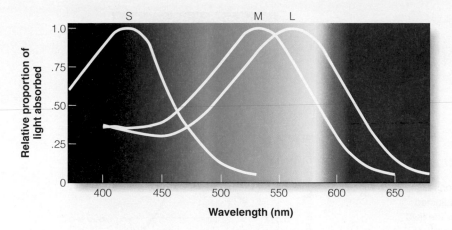

Figure 9.10 Absorption spectra of the three cone pigments. From Dartnall, H. J. A., Bowmaker, J. K., & Mollon, J. D. (1983). Human visual pigments: Microspectrophotometric results from the eyes of seven persons. *Proceedings of the Royal Society of London B, 220,* 115–130, by permission of the Royal Society.

Cone Pigments Physiological researchers who were working to identify the receptor mechanisms proposed by trichromatic theory asked the following question: Are there three mechanisms, and if so, what are their physiological properties? This question was answered in the 1960s, when researchers were able to determine that there were three different cone pigments, the short-wavelength pigment (S), with maximum absorption at 419-nm; the middle-wavelength pigment (M), with maximum absorption at 531-nm; and long-wavelength pigment (L), with maximum absorption at 558-nm (S, M, and L in **Figure 9.10**) (Brown & Wald, 1964; Dartnall et al., 1983; Schnapf et al., 1987). As you recall from Chapter 2 (page 27), all visual pigments are made up of a large protein component called *opsin* and a small light-sensitive component called *retinal*. Differences in the structure of the long opsin part of the pigments are responsible for the three different absorption spectra (Nathans et al., 1986). (See Chapter 2, page 34 to review pigments and absorption spectra.)

Cone Responding and Color Perception If color perception is based on the pattern of activity of these three cone receptor mechanisms, we should be able to determine which colors will be perceived if we know the response of each of the receptor mechanisms. **Figure 9.11** shows the relationship between the responses of the three kinds of receptors and our perception of color. In this figure, the responses in the S, M, and L receptors are indicated by the size of the receptors. For example, blue is signaled by a large response in the S receptor, a smaller response in the M receptor, and an even smaller response in the L receptor. Yellow is signaled by a very small response in the S receptor and large, approximately equal responses in the M and L receptors. White is signaled by equal activity in all the receptors.

Thinking of wavelengths as causing certain patterns of receptor responding helps us to predict which colors should result when we combine lights of different colors. We have already seen that combining blue and yellow lights on a white background results in white. The patterns of receptor activity in Figure 9.11 show that blue light causes high activity in the S receptors and that yellow light causes high activity in the M and L receptors. Thus, combining both lights should

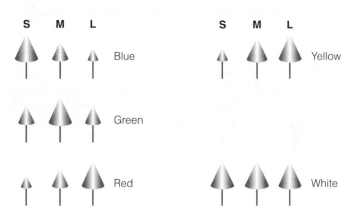

Figure 9.11 Patterns of firing of the three types of cones to different colors. The size of the cone symbolizes the size of the receptor's response. © Cengage Learning

stimulate all three receptors equally, which is associated with the perception of white.

Now that we know that our perception of colors is determined by the pattern of activity in different kinds of receptors, we can explain the physiological basis behind the color-matching results that led to the proposal of trichromatic theory. Remember that in a color-matching experiment, a wavelength in one field is matched by adjusting the proportions of three different wavelengths in another field (Figure 9.9). This result is interesting because the lights in the two fields are physically different (they contain different wavelengths) but they are perceptually identical (they look the same). This situation, in which two physically different stimuli are perceptually identical, is called **metamerism**, and the two identical fields in a color-matching experiment are called **metamers**.

The reason metamers look alike is that they both result in the same pattern of response in the three cone receptors. For example, when the proportions of a 620-nm red light and a 530-nm green light are adjusted so the mixture matches the color of a 580-nm light, which looks yellow, the two mixed wavelengths create the same pattern of activity in the cone receptors as the single 580-nm light (**Figure 9.12**). The 530-nm

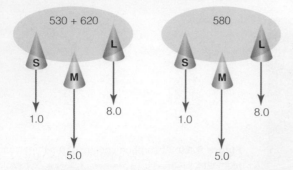

Figure 9.12 Principle behind metamerism. The proportions of 530- and 620-nm lights in the field on the left have been adjusted so that the mixture appears identical to the 580-nm light in the field on the right. The numbers indicate the responses of the short-, medium-, and long-wavelength receptors. There is no difference in the responses of the two sets of receptors, so the two fields are perceptually indistinguishable. © Cengage Learning

green light causes a large response in the M receptor, and the 620-nm red light causes a large response in the L receptor. Together, they result in a large response in the M and L receptors and a much smaller response in the S receptor. This is the pattern for yellow and is the same as the pattern generated by the 580-nm light. Thus, even though the lights in these two fields are *physically different*, the two lights result in identical patterns of physiological responses, so are identical as far as the brain is concerned, and are therefore perceived as being the same.

Are Three Receptor Mechanisms Necessary for Color Vision? According to trichromatic theory, a light's wavelength is signaled by the pattern of activity of *three* receptor mechanisms. But do we need three different mechanisms to see colors? Let's first consider why color vision does not occur in individuals who have just one receptor type (so they have only one pigment).

We can understand why color vision is not possible in a person with just one receptor type by considering how a person with just one pigment would perceive two lights, one 480 nm and one 600 nm (**Figure 9.13a**), which a person with normal color vision sees as blue and red, respectively. The absorption spectrum for the single pigment, shown in **Figure 9.13b**, indicates that the pigment absorbs 10 percent of 480-nm light and 5 percent of 600-nm light.

To discuss what happens when our one-pigment observer looks at the two lights, we have to return to our description of visual pigments in Chapter 2 (see page 26). Remember that when light is absorbed by the *retinal* part of the visual pigment molecule, the retinal changes shape, a process called *isomerization*. (Although we will usually specify light in terms of its wavelength, light can also be described as consisting of small packets of energy called *photons*, with one photon being the smallest possible packet of light energy.) The visual pigment molecule isomerizes when the molecule absorbs one photon of light. This isomerization activates the molecule and triggers the process that activates the visual receptor and leads to seeing the light.

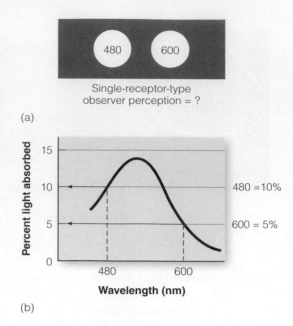

Single-receptor-type observer perception = ?

(a)

(b)

Figure 9.13 (a) Two lights, 480 nm on the left and 600 nm on the right. (b) Absorption spectrum of a visual pigment that absorbs 10 percent of 480-nm light and 5 percent of 600-nm light. © Cengage Learning 2014

If the intensity of each light is adjusted so 1,000 photons of each light enters our one-pigment observer's eyes, we can see from **Figure 9.14a** that the 480-nm light isomerizes 1,000 × 0.10 = 100 visual pigment molecules and the 600-nm light isomerizes 1,000 × 0.05 = 50 molecules. Because the 480-nm light isomerizes twice as many visual pigment molecules as the 600-nm light, it will cause a larger response in the receptor, resulting in perception of a brighter light. But if we increase the intensity of the 600-nm light to 2,000 photons, as shown in **Figure 9.14b**, then this light will also isomerize 100 visual pigment molecules.

When the 1,000 photon 480-nm light and the 2,000 photon 600-nm light both isomerize the same number of molecules, the result will be that the two spots of light will appear identical. The fact that the wavelengths of light are different doesn't matter, because of the **principle of univariance**, which states that once a photon of light is absorbed by a visual pigment molecule, the identity of the light's wavelength is lost. An isomerization is an isomerization no matter what wavelength caused it. Univariance means that the receptor does not know the *wavelength* of light it has absorbed, only the *total amount* it has absorbed. Thus, by adjusting the intensities of the two lights, we can cause the single pigment to result in identical responses, so the lights will appear the same even though their wavelengths are different.

What this means is that a person with only one visual pigment can match any wavelength in the spectrum by adjusting the *intensity* of any other wavelength, and sees all of the wavelengths as shades of gray. Thus, adjusting the intensity appropriately can make the 480-nm and 600-nm lights (or any other wavelengths) look identical.

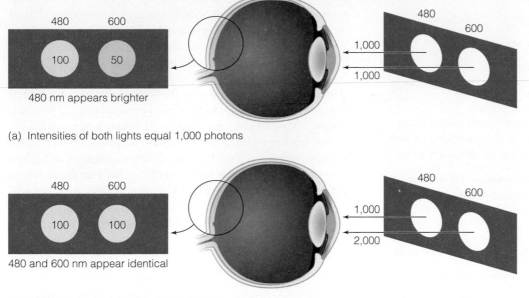

(a) Intensities of both lights equal 1,000 photons

480 nm appears brighter

(b) 600-nm light increased to 2,000 photons

480 and 600 nm appear identical

Figure 9.14 Calculation of how many molecules of the visual pigment in Figure 9.13 are isomerized. (a) When the intensity of both is 1,000 photons, the 480-nm light isomerizes 100 molecules and the 600-nm light isomerizes 50 molecules, so the 480-nm light looks brighter. (b) When the intensity of the 600-nm light is increased to 2,000, both wavelengths isomerize the same number of molecules, so the two wavelengths are perceived as identical. © Cengage Learning 2014

How can the nervous system tell the difference between the two wavelengths, no matter what the light intensity? The answer to this question is that adding a second pigment makes it possible to distinguish between wavelengths *independent of light intensity*. We can see why this is so by considering what happens when we add a second pigment, with an absorption spectrum shown by the dashed curve in **Figure 9.15**. This pigment absorbs more 600-nm light than 480-nm light, so the intensity that causes pigment 1 to generate the same response to the two wavelengths causes pigment 2 to generate a much larger response to the 600-nm light. Thus, the responses created by both pigments together could indicate a difference between the two different wavelengths.

Another way to look at this two-pigment situation is to consider the *ratios* of responses of the two pigments to the two wavelengths. From Figure 9.15 we can see that the 480-nm light causes a large response from pigment 1 and a smaller response from pigment 2, and that the 600-nm light

causes a larger response in pigment 2 and a smaller response in pigment 1. These ratios remain the same no matter what the light intensities. The ratio of the response of pigment 1 to pigment 2 is always 10 to 2 for the 480-nm light, and 5 to 10 for the 600-nm light. Thus, the visual system can use ratio information such as this to identify the wavelength of any light. This same constancy of the ratio information also occurs when there are three pigments, which is the basis of trichromatic theory's proposal that color perception depends on the *pattern of activity* in three receptor mechanisms.

As we will see when we consider color deficiency in the next section, there are people with just two types of cone pigment. These people, called *dichromats*, do see colors, just as our calculations predict, but they see fewer colors than people with three visual pigments, who are called **trichromats**. The addition of a third pigment, although not necessary for creating color vision, increases the number of colors that can be seen across the visual spectrum.

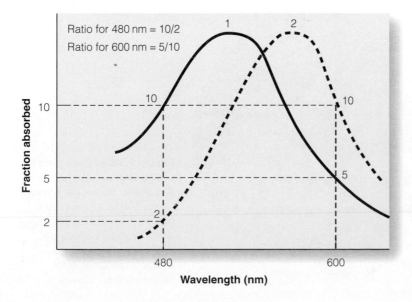

Figure 9.15 Adding a second pigment (dashed curve) to the one in Figure 9.13. Now the 480-nm and 600-nm lights can be identified by the ratio of response in the two pigments. The ratio for the 480-nm light is 10/2 (blue-dashed line). The ratio for the 600-nm light is 5/10 (red-dashed line). These ratios occur no matter what the intensity of the light. © Cengage Learning 2014

1. What are the various functions of color vision?

2. What physical characteristic is most closely associated with color perception? How is this demonstrated by differences in reflection of different objects?

3. Describe additive color mixture and subtractive color mixture. How can the results of these two types of color mixing be related to the wavelengths that are reflected into an observer's eyes?

4. Describe trichromatic theory and the experiments on which it was based. How does this theory explain the results of color-matching experiments?

5. Describe how trichromatic theory is based on cone pigments and how the wavelengths are indicated by the activity of the cones.

6. What are metamers, and how can our perception of metamers be explained by the activity of the cones as described above?

7. Why is color vision possible when there are only two different pigments but not possible when there is just one pigment? What is the effect on color vision of having three pigments rather than just two?

Color Deficiency

It has long been known that some people have difficulty perceiving certain colors. At the beginning of the chapter, we described the case of Mr. I., who lost his ability to see color after a concussion. However, most problems with color vision involve only a partial loss of color perception, called **color deficiency**, and are associated with problems with the receptors in the retina that are present at birth.

In a famous early report of color deficiency, the well-known 18th-century chemist John Dalton (1798/1948) described his own color perceptions as follows: "All crimsons appear to me to consist chiefly of dark blue: but many of them seem to have a tinge of dark brown. I have seen specimens of crimson, claret, and mud, which were very nearly alike" (p. 102).

Dalton's descriptions of his abnormal color perceptions led to the early use of the term *Daltonism* to describe color deficiency. We now know that there are a number of different types of color deficiency. This has been determined by color vision tests like the ones shown in **Figure 9.16a**, which are called **Ishihara plates**. In this example, people with normal color vision see a "74," but people with a form of red–green color deficiency might see something like the depiction in **Figure 9.16b**, in which the "74" is not visible. Another way to determine the presence of color deficiency is by using the color-matching procedure to determine the minimum number of wavelengths needed to match any other wavelength in the spectrum. This procedure has revealed the following three types of color deficiency:

1. A **monochromat** can match any wavelength in the spectrum by adjusting the intensity of any other wavelength. Thus, a monochromat needs only one wavelength to match any color in the spectrum and sees only in shades of gray. Our one-pigment observer from Figure 9.13 is a monochromat.

2. A **dichromat** needs only two wavelengths to match all other wavelengths in the spectrum. Our two-pigment observer from Figure 9.15 is a dichromat.

3. An **anomalous trichromat** needs three wavelengths to match any wavelength, just as a normal trichromat does. However, the anomalous trichromat mixes these wavelengths in different proportions from a trichromat, and an anomalous trichromat is not as good as a trichromat at discriminating between wavelengths that are close together.

Once we have determined whether a person's vision is color deficient, we are still left with the question: What colors

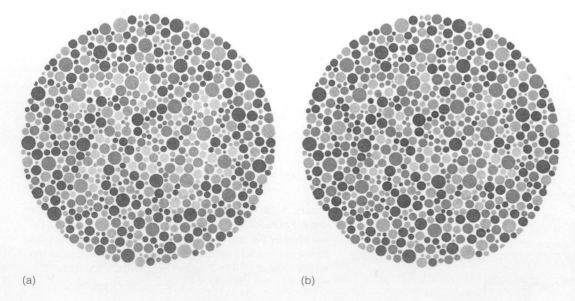

(a)   (b)

Figure 9.16 Ishihara plate for testing color deficiency. (a) A person with normal color vision sees a "74" when the plate is viewed under standardized illumination. (b) Ishihara plate as perceived by a person with a form of red–green color deficiency. © Cengage Learning

does a person with color deficiency see? When I pose this question in my class, a few students suggest that we can answer it by pointing to objects of various colors and asking a color deficient person what he sees. (Most color deficient people are male; see below) This method does not really tell us what the person perceives, however, because a color deficient person may say "red" when we point to a strawberry simply because he has learned that people call strawberries "red." It is quite likely that the color deficient person's experience of "red" is very different from the experience of the person without color deficiency. For all we know, he may be having an experience similar to what a person without deficient color vision would call "yellow."

To determine what a dichromat perceives, we need to locate a **unilateral dichromat**—a person with trichromatic vision in one eye and dichromatic vision in the other. Both of the unilateral dichromat's eyes are connected to the same brain, so this person can look at a color with his dichromatic eye and then determine which color it corresponds to in his trichromatic eye. Although unilateral dichromats are extremely rare, the few who have been tested have helped us determine the nature of a dichromat's color experience (Alpern et al., 1983; Graham et al., 1961; Sloan & Wollach, 1948). Let's now look at the nature of the color experience of both monochromats and dichromats.

Monochromatism

Monochromatism is a rare form of color blindness that is usually hereditary and occurs in only about 10 people out of 1 million (LeGrand, 1957). Monochromats usually have no functioning cones; therefore, their vision has the characteristics of rod vision in both dim and bright lights. Monochromats see everything in shades of lightness (white, gray, and black) and can therefore be called **color-blind** (as opposed to dichromats, who see some chromatic colors and therefore should be called *color deficient*).

In addition to a loss of color vision, people with hereditary monochromatism have poor visual acuity and are so sensitive to bright lights that they often must protect their eyes with dark glasses during the day. The rod system is not designed to function in bright light and so becomes overloaded in strong illumination, creating a perception of glare.

Dichromatism

Dichromats experience some colors, though a lesser range than trichromats. There are three major forms of dichromatism: *protanopia*, *deuteranopia*, and *tritanopia*. The two most common kinds, protanopia and deuteranopia, are inherited through a gene located on the X chromosome (Nathans et al., 1986).

Males (XY) have only one X chromosome, so a defect in the visual pigment gene on this chromosome causes color deficiency. Females (XX), on the other hand, with their two X chromosomes, are less likely to become color deficient because only one normal gene is required for normal color vision. These forms of color vision are therefore called sex-linked because

women can carry the gene for color deficiency without being color deficient themselves, and they can pass the condition on to their male offspring. Thus, many more men than women are dichromats. As we describe what the three types of dichromats perceive, we use as our reference points Figures 9.17d and 9.18d, which show how a trichromat perceives a bunch of colored paper flowers and the visible spectrum, respectively.

- **Protanopia** affects 1 percent of males and 0.02 percent of females and results in the perception of colors shown in **Figure 9.17a**. A protanope perceives short-wavelength light as blue, and as the wavelength is increased, the blue becomes less and less saturated until, at 492 nm, the protanope perceives gray (**Figure 9.18a**). The wavelength at which the protanope perceives gray is called the **neutral point**. At wavelengths above the neutral point, the protanope perceives yellow, which becomes less intense at the long-wavelength end of the spectrum.

- **Deuteranopia** affects about 1 percent of males and 0.01 percent of females and results in the perception of color in **Figure 9.17b**. A deuteranope perceives blue at short wavelengths, sees yellow at long wavelengths, and has a neutral point at about 498 nm (**Figure 9.18b**) (Boynton, 1979).

- **Tritanopia** is very rare, affecting only about 0.002 percent of males and 0.001 percent of females. A tritanope sees colors as in **Figure 9.17c**, and sees the spectrum as in **Figure 9.18c**—blue at short wavelengths, red at long wavelengths, and a neutral point at 570 nm (Alpern et al., 1983).

(a) (b)

(c) (d)

Bruce Goldstein

Figure 9.17 How colored paper flowers appear to (a) protanopes; (b) deuteranopes; (c) tritanopes; and (d) trichromats. *Color processing courtesy of Jay Neitz and John Carroll.*

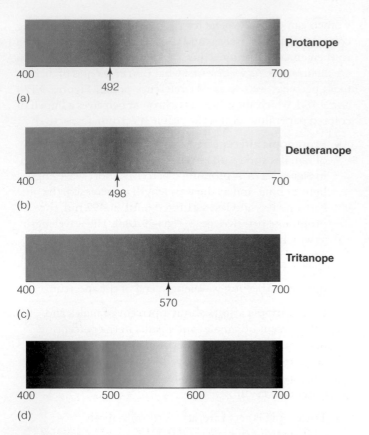

Protanope

400   492   700

(a)

Deuteranope

400   498   700

(b)

Tritanope

400   570   700

(c)

400   500   600   700

(d)

Figure 9.18 How the visible spectrum appears to (a) protanopes; (b) deuteranopes; (c) tritanopes; and (d) trichromats. The number indicates the wavelength of the neutral point. Spectra courtesy of Jay Neitz and John Carroll. © Cengage Learning

Physiological Mechanisms of Receptor-Based Color Deficiency

What are the physiological mechanisms of color deficiency? Most monochromats have no color vision because they have just one type of cone or no cones. Dichromats are missing one visual pigment—in protanopes, the long-wavelength pigment (which is why color becomes less intense at long wavelengths for protanopes); in deuteranopes, the medium-wavelength pigment; and in tritanopes, the short-wavelength pigment.

Genetic research has identified differences in the genes that determine visual pigment structure in trichromats and dichromats (Nathans et al., 1986). Based on this research, it has been shown that anomalous trichromats match colors differently from normal trichromats and have more difficulty discriminating between some wavelengths because their M and L pigment spectra have been shifted so they are closer together (Neitz et al., 1991).

While the signals from the S, M, and L receptors are the basis of trichromatic vision, the *relative sizes* of the S, M, and L signals are not transmitted to the brain. Instead, information about the *difference* between pairs of receptor signals is sent to the brain. The difference between pairs of signals is central

to the *opponent-process theory of color vision* proposed by Ewald Hering (1834–1918), an eminent physiologist who was working at about the same time as Helmholtz. **VL**

Opponent-Process Theory of Color Vision

We have seen that the trichromatic theory was originally proposed based on the results of psychophysical experiments. The **opponent-process theory of color vision** was also originally proposed based on behavioral observations, but instead of the precise psychophysical color-matching experiments that led to trichromatic theory, opponent-process theory was based on the results of phenomenological observations, in which stimuli were presented and observers described what they perceived. The results of these observations led Ewald Hering to propose the opponent-process theory, which states that color vision is caused by opposing responses generated by blue and yellow and by red and green.

Behavioral Evidence for the Theory

You can make some phenomenological observations similar to Hering's by doing the following demonstrations.

DEMONSTRATION
The Colors of the Flag

Look at the cross at the center of the strangely colored American flag in **Figure 9.19** for about 30 seconds. If you then look at a piece of white paper and blink, the image you see, which is called an *afterimage*, has colors that probably match the red, white, and blue of the American flag. Notice that the green area of the flag in Figure 9.19 created a red afterimage, and the yellow area created a blue afterimage.

Although Hering didn't use a strangely colored flag to create afterimages, he did observe that viewing a green field

Figure 9.19 Stimulus for afterimage demonstration. © Cengage Learning

generates a red afterimage, and viewing a yellow field creates a blue afterimage. He also observed the opposite—viewing green causes a red afterimage, and viewing blue causes a yellow afterimage. You can demonstrate that this works both ways by looking at the center of **Figure 9.20** for 30 seconds and then looking at a white surface and noticing how red and green, and blue and yellow, have changed places. (Note that the colors associated with long wavelengths—red and yellow—are on the right in the figure, and switch to the left in the afterimage.) Based on observations such as these, Hering proposed that red and green are paired and blue and yellow are paired. Here is another demonstration that illustrates this pairing.

DEMONSTRATION
Afterimages and Simultaneous Contrast

Cut out a 1/2-inch square of white paper and place it in the center of the green square in Figure 9.20. Cover the other squares with white paper and stare at the center of the white square for about 30 seconds. Then look at a white background and blink to observe the afterimage. What color is the outside area of the afterimage? What color is the small square in the center? Repeat your observations on the red, blue, and yellow squares in Figure 9.20.

When you made your observations using the green square, you probably confirmed your previous observation that green and red are paired because the afterimage corresponding to the green area of the original square is red. But the color of the small square in the center also shows that green and red are paired: Most people see a green square inside the red afterimage. This green afterimage is due to **simultaneous color contrast**, an effect that occurs when surrounding an area with a color changes the appearance of the surrounded area. In this case, the red afterimage surrounds a white area and causes the white area to appear green. Table 9.4 summarizes this result and the results that occur when we

Figure 9.20 Color matrix for afterimage and simultaneous contrast demonstrations. © Cengage Learning

TABLE 9.4 Results of Afterimage and Simultaneous Contrast Demonstration

ORIGINAL SQUARE	COLOR OF OUTSIDE AFTERIMAGE	COLOR OF INSIDE AFTERIMAGE
Green	Red	Green
Red	Green	Red
Blue	Yellow	Blue
Yellow	Blue	Yellow

© Cengage Learning

repeat this demonstration on the other squares. All of these results show a clear pairing of red and green and of blue and yellow.

DEMONSTRATION
Visualizing Colors

This demonstration involves visualizing colors. Start by visualizing the color red, with your eyes either open or closed, whichever works best for you. Attach this color to a specific object such as a fire engine, if that makes your visualizing easier. Now visualize a reddish-yellow and then a reddish-green. Which of these two combinations is easier to visualize? Now do the same thing for blue. Visualize a pure blue, then a bluish-green and a bluish-yellow. Again, which of these combinations is easier to visualize?

Most people find it easy to visualize a bluish-green or a reddish-yellow, but find it difficult (or impossible) to visualize a reddish-green or a bluish-yellow. In other experiments, in which observers were shown patches of color and were asked to estimate the percentages of blue, green, yellow, and red in each patch, they rarely reported seeing blue and yellow or red and green at the same time (Abramov & Gordon, 1994), just as the results of the visualization demonstration would predict.

The above observations, plus Hering's observation that people who are color-blind to red are also color-blind to green, and that people who can't see blue also can't see yellow, led to the conclusion that red and green are paired and that blue and yellow are paired. Based on this conclusion, Hering proposed the opponent-process theory of color vision (Hering, 1878, 1905, 1964).

The basic idea underlying Hering's theory is shown in **Figure 9.21**. He proposed three mechanisms, each of which responds in opposite ways to different intensities or

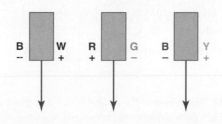

Figure 9.21 The three opponent mechanisms proposed by Hering. © Cengage Learning

wavelengths of light. The Black (−) White (+) mechanism responds positively to white light and negatively to the absence of light. Red (+) Green (−) responds positively to red and negatively to green, and Blue (−) Yellow (+) responds negatively to blue and positively to yellow. Although Hering's phenomenological observations supported his theory, it wasn't until many years later that modern physiological research showed that these colors do cause physiologically opposite responses.

Physiological Evidence for the Theory

Modern physiological research has measured the response of single neurons to different wavelengths to provide physiological evidence for neurons that respond in opposite ways to blue and yellow and to red and green.

Opponent Neurons In the 1950s and 1960s, researchers began finding **opponent neurons** in the retina and lateral geniculate nucleus that responded with an excitatory response to light from one part of the spectrum and with an inhibitory response to light from another part (DeValois, 1960; Svaetichin, 1956). For example, the left column of **Figure 9.22** shows records for a neuron in a monkey's lateral geniculate nucleus that responds to short-wavelength light with an increase in firing and to long-wavelength light with a decrease in firing. (Notice that firing decreases to below the level of spontaneous activity.) This neuron is called a B+ Y− neuron because the wavelengths that cause an increase in firing are in the blue part of the spectrum, and the wavelengths that cause a decrease are in the yellow part of the spectrum.

The right column of Figure 9.22 shows records for an R+ G− neuron, which increases firing to light in the red part of the spectrum and decreases firing to light in the green part of the spectrum. There are also B− Y+ and G+ R− neurons (DeValois et al., 1966).

How Opponent Responding Can Be Created by Three Receptors The discovery of opponent neurons provided physiological evidence for opponent-process theory to go with the three different cone pigments of trichromatic theory. When these two theories were first proposed in the 1800s, they were seen as competitors. The idea at that time was that one or the other was correct, but not both. But the discovery of physiological evidence that supported both theories meant that both theories were correct. How could this be? The answer is that the psychophysical findings on which each theory was based were each reflecting physiological activity at different places in the visual system. This is diagrammed in **Figure 9.23**. The color-matching results, that three wavelengths are needed to match all other wavelengths, come from the cone receptors that are right at the beginning of the visual system, and the perceptual pairing of blue and yellow and red and green that we see in effects like afterimages and simultaneous contrast are created by the opponent neurons that come later in the visual system.

The circuit in **Figure 9.24a** shows how this works. The L-cone sends excitatory input to a bipolar cell (see Chapter 2, page 42), whereas the M-cone sends inhibitory input to the cell. This creates an R+ G− cell that responds with excitation to the long wavelengths that cause the L-cone to fire and with inhibition to the shorter wavelengths that cause the M-cone

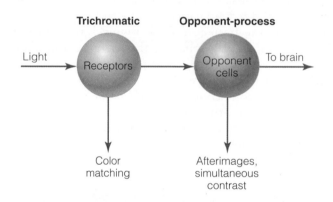

Figure 9.23 Our experience of color is shaped by physiological mechanisms, both in the receptors and in opponent neurons. © Cengage Learning

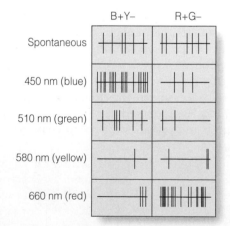

Figure 9.22 Responses of B+ Y− and R+ G− opponent cells in the monkey's lateral geniculate nucleus. From DeValois, R. L., & Jacobs, G. H. (1968). Primate color vision. *Science, 162,* 533–540, Figure 5. Copyright © 1968 by the American Association for the Advancement of Science. Reproduced by permission.

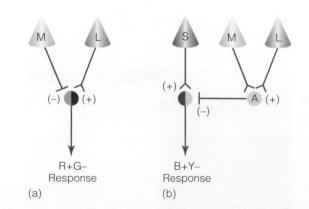

Figure 9.24 Neural circuits showing how (a) the red–green and (b) the blue–yellow mechanisms can be created by excitatory and inhibitory inputs from the cone receptors. © Cengage Learning 2014

to fire. (This is also called an L+ M− cell to indicate the receptors involved.)

Figure 9.24b shows that the B+ Y− cell also receives inputs from the cones. It receives an excitatory input from the S cone and an inhibitory input from cell A, which sums the inputs from the M and L cones. This arrangement makes sense if we remember that we perceive yellow when both the M and the L receptors are stimulated. Thus, cell A, which receives inputs from both of these receptors, causes the "yellow" response of the B+ Y− mechanism.

Although these diagrams are greatly simplified, they illustrate the basic principles of the neural circuitry for color coding in the retina. (See DeValois & DeValois, 1993, for examples of more complex neural circuits that have been proposed to explain opponent responding.) The important thing about these circuits is that their responses are determined both by the wavelengths to which the receptors respond best and by the arrangement of inhibitory and excitatory synapses. Processing in these circuits therefore takes place in two stages: First, the receptors respond with different patterns to different wavelengths (trichromatic theory); then, later, neurons integrate the inhibitory and excitatory signals from the receptors (opponent-process theory).

This description of opponent neurons brings us back to the idea that the signals for color that are sent to the brain indicate the *difference* in responding of pairs of cones. We can understand how this works at a neural level by looking at **Figure 9.25**, which shows how an L+ M− neuron receiving excitation from the L receptor and inhibition from the M receptor responds to 500-nm and 600-nm lights. **Figure 9.25a** shows that the 500-nm light results in an inhibitory signal of −80 and an excitatory signal of +50, so the response of the L+ M− neuron would be −30. **Figure 9.25b** shows that the 600-nm light results in an excitatory signal of +75 and an inhibitory signal of −25, so the response of the L+ M− neuron would be +50. This "difference information" is the type of information sent by the opponent neurons to the brain.

The trichromatic "ratio information" and opponent "difference information" for wavelength originate in the receptors and neural connections in the retina. But what happens to all this information when it reaches the cortex?

Color in the Cortex

What are the cortical mechanisms of color perception? We will consider a number of facets of this question: (1) Is there a single "color center" in the cortex? (2) What types of opponent neurons are found in the cortex, and what is their function? (3) What is the relation between color and form?

Is There a Single Color Center in the Cortex?

Is there one area in the cortex specialized for processing information about color? If there is such an area, that would make

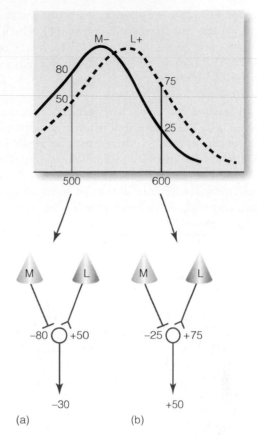

Figure 9.25 How opponent neurons determine the difference between the receptor responses to different wavelengths. (a) The response of the L+ M− neuron to a 500-nm light is negative, because the M receptor results in an inhibitory response that is larger than receptor L's excitatory response. This means the action of the 500-nm light on this neuron will cause a decrease in any ongoing activity. (b) The response to a 600-nm light is positive, so this wavelength causes an increase in the response of this neuron. © Cengage Learning 2014

color similar to faces, bodies, and places, which can claim the fusiform face area (FFA), extrastriate body area (ESB), and parahippocampal place area (PPA) as specialized processing areas (see Chapter 4, page 88). The idea of an area specialized for color was put forth by Semir Zeki (1983a, 1983b, 1990) based on his finding of many neurons in a visual area outside of the monkey's visual receiving area (V1) called V4 that responded to color, and on the phenomenon of **cerebral achromatopsia**. Achromatopsia is a condition caused by damage to the brain like that experienced by Mr. I., the painter described at the beginning of the chapter, who suffered an automobile accident that left his perception of form and motion intact but caused him to lose his ability to see color. The fact that the damage that typically results in achromatopsia is near or identical to areas identified as human color areas supports the idea of a specialized module for color perception.

However, additional evidence has led many researchers to reject the idea of a "color center" in favor of the idea that color processing is distributed across a number of different cortical areas that process information about color and about other types of information as well. One result that has led to this conclusion is that opponent neurons have been found in many areas of the cortex, including the primary visual receiving area, V1; the inferotemporal cortex (IT), which is associated with form perception; and V4, which was originally proposed as the color center (Engel, 2005; Harada et al., 2009; Johnson et al., 2008; Shapley & Hawken, 2011; Tanigawa et al., 2010; Tootell et al., 2004).

In addition, a survey of the effects of brain damage on color perception has shown that when brain damage causes achromatopsia, it causes other effects as well, including prosopagnosia—the inability to recognize faces (Bouvier & Engel, 2006). The results of this survey support the idea that color perception results from activity in many different visual areas that respond not only to color but to other qualities, such as form, as well.

Types of Opponent Neurons in the Cortex

Whether or not there is a "color center" in the cortex, there is no doubt that there are neurons in many areas that respond in an opponent way—increasing firing to wavelengths in one region of the spectrum and decreasing firing to neurons in another region. Two types of opponent neurons in the cortex are **single-opponent neurons** and **double-opponent neurons**.

The receptive field of a single-opponent neuron is shown in **Figure 9.26a**. This M+ L– neuron increases firing to medium wavelengths presented to the center of the receptive field and decreases firing to long wavelengths presented to the surround. Most double-opponent neurons have receptive fields like the one in **Figure 9.26b**, with side-by-side regions, like the simple cortical cells we described in Chapter 3 (see page 64). The neuron with the receptive field in Figure 9.26b responds best to a medium-wavelength vertical bar presented to the left side of the receptive field and to a long-wavelength vertical bar presented to the right side of the receptive field. It has

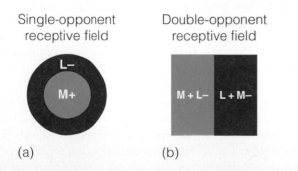

Single-opponent
receptive field

Double-opponent
receptive field

(a) (b)

Figure 9.26 (a) Receptive field of a single-opponent cortical neuron. This M+ L– neuron has a center-surround receptive field. Its firing increases when a medium-wavelength light is presented to the center area and decreases when a long-wavelength light is presented to the surrounding area. (b) Receptive field of a double-opponent cortical neuron. When the M+ L– area is stimulated, firing increases to medium wavelength light and decreases to long-wavelength light. When the L+ M– area is stimulated, firing increases to a long-wavelength light and decreases to a medium-wavelength light. Based on Johnson, E. N., Hawken, M. J., & Shapley, R. (2008). The orientation selectivity of color-responsive neurons in Macaque V1. *Journal of Neuroscience, 28*, 8096–8106, Figure 9. © Cengage Learning 2014.

been suggested that single-opponent cells are important for perceiving the color within regions, and double-opponent cells are important for perceiving boundaries between different colors (Johnson et al., 2008).

The Relation Between Color and Form

One idea about the relation between color and form is that the visual system determines an object's form and then color "fills in" the form. Color, according to this idea, is added after form is determined. However, recent research suggests a close connection between the processing of form and color, and even that color may play a role in determining form. Form and color have been linked physiologically by neurons with side-by-side receptive fields like the ones in Figure 9.26b. These neurons can fire to oriented colored bars even when the intensity of the side-by-side bars is adjusted so they appear to be equally bright. In other words, these cells fire when the bar's form is determined only by differences in color. Evidence such as this has been used to support the idea of a close bridge between the processing of color and the processing of form in the cortex (Friedman et al., 2003; Johnson et al., 2008). Thus, when you look out at a colorful scene, the colors you see are not only "filling in" the objects and areas in the scene but may also be helping define the edges and shapes of these objects and areas.

TEST YOURSELF 9.2

1. What is color deficiency? How can it be detected using the procedure of color mixing? How can we determine how a color-deficient person perceives different wavelengths?

2. How is color deficiency caused by (a) problems with the receptors? (b) damage to the cortex?

3. Describe opponent-process theory, including the observations on which it is based and the physiological basis of this theory.

4. What is the purpose of opponent neurons?

5. What is the evidence for and against the idea of a specialized "color center" in the cortex?

6. Describe the opponent neurons in the cortex, including their receptive fields and possible functions.

7. How is the processing of color related to the processing of form in the cortex?

Color Constancy

It is midday, with the sun high in the sky, and as you are walking to class you notice a classmate who is wearing a green sweater. Then, as you are sitting in class a few minutes later, you again notice the same green sweater. The fact that the sweater appears green both outside under sunlight illumination and inside under artificial indoor illumination may not seem particularly remarkable. After all, the sweater *is* green, isn't it? However, when we consider the interaction between the illumination and the properties of the sweater, we can appreciate that your perception of the sweater as green, both outside and inside, represents a remarkable achievement of the visual system. This achievement is called **color constancy**—we perceive the colors of objects as being relatively constant even under changing illumination.

We can appreciate why color constancy is an impressive achievement by considering the interaction between illumination, such as sunlight or lightbulbs, and the reflection properties of an object, such as the green sweater. First, let's consider the illumination. **Figure 9.27** shows the wavelengths from sunlight and the wavelengths from a lightbulb. The sunlight contains approximately equal amounts of energy at all wavelengths, which is a characteristic of white light. The bulb contains much more energy at long wavelengths. This wavelength distribution is sometimes called "tungsten" light because it is produced by the tungsten filament inside old-style lightbulbs (which are in the process of being replaced with screw-in "twisty" fluorescent lightbulbs). This large amount of long-wavelength light is why the tungsten bulb looks slightly yellow.

Now consider the interaction between the wavelengths produced by the illumination and the wavelengths reflected from the green sweater. The reflectance curve of the sweater is indicated by the green line in **Figure 9.28**. It reflects mostly medium-wavelength light, as we would expect of something that is green.

The actual light that is reflected from the sweater depends on both its reflectance curve and the illumination that reaches the sweater and is then reflected from it. To determine the wavelengths that are actually reflected from the sweater, we multiply the sweater's reflectance curve at each wavelength by the amount of illumination at each wavelength. This calculation indicates that the sweater reflects more

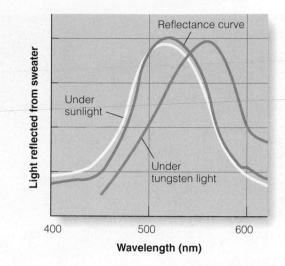

Figure 9.28 Reflectance curve of a sweater, and light reflected from the sweater when illuminated by sunlight and by tungsten light.
© Cengage Learning

long-wavelength light when it is illuminated by tungsten light (the orange line in Figure 9.28) than when it is illuminated by sunlight (the white line in Figure 9.28). The fact that we still see the sweater as green even though the wavelength composition of the reflected light differs under different illuminations is color constancy. Without color constancy, the color we see would depend on how the sweater was being illuminated (Delahunt & Brainard, 2004; Olkkonen et al., 2010).

Why does a green sweater look green even when viewed under different illuminations? The answer to this question involves a number of different mechanisms. We begin by considering how the eye's sensitivity is affected by the color of the illumination of the overall scene, a process called *chromatic adaptation*.

Chromatic Adaptation

One reason why color constancy occurs lies in the results of the following demonstration.

DEMONSTRATION
Adapting to Red

Illuminate **Figure 9.29** with a bright light from your desk lamp. With your left eye near the page and your right eye closed, look at the field with your left eye for about 30 to 45 seconds. Then look at various colored objects in your environment, first with your left eye and then with your right.

This demonstration shows that color perception can be changed by **chromatic adaptation**—prolonged exposure to chromatic color. Adaptation to the red light selectively bleaches your long-wavelength cone pigment, which decreases your sensitivity to red light and causes you to see the reds and oranges viewed with your left (adapted) eye as less saturated and bright than those viewed with the right eye.

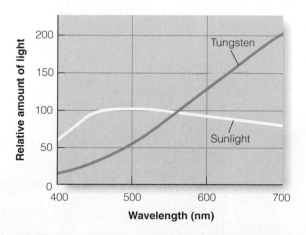

Figure 9.27 The wavelength distribution of sunlight and of light from a tungsten lightbulb. From Judd, D. B., MacAdam, D. L., & Wyszecki, G. (1964). Spectral distribution of typical daylight as a function of correlated color temperature. *Journal of the Optical Society of America, 54,* 1031–1040. Reproduced by permission.

Figure 9.29 Red adapting field. © Cengage Learning

The idea that chromatic adaptation is responsible for color constancy has been tested in an experiment by Keiji Uchikawa and coworkers (1989). Observers viewed isolated patches of colored paper under three different conditions (**Figure 9.30**): (a) *baseline*—paper and observer illuminated by white light; (b) *observer not adapted*—paper illuminated by red light, observer by white (the observer is not chromatically adapted); and (c) *observer adapted to red*—both paper and observer illuminated by red light (the observer is chromatically adapted).

The results from these three conditions are shown above each condition. In the *baseline* condition, a green paper is perceived as green. In the *observer not adapted* condition, the observer perceives the paper's color as being shifted toward the red. Color constancy does not occur in this condition because the observer is not adapted to the red light that is illuminating the paper. But in the *observer adapted to red* condition, perception is shifted only slightly to the red, so it appears more yellowish. Thus, the chromatic adaptation has

created **partial color constancy**—the perception of the object is shifted after adaptation, but not as much as when there was no adaptation. This means that the eye can adjust its sensitivity to different wavelengths to keep color perception approximately constant as illumination changes.

This principle operates when you walk into a room illuminated with yellowish tungsten light. The eye adapts to the long-wavelength-rich light, which decreases your eye's sensitivity to long wavelengths. This decreased sensitivity causes the long-wavelength light reflected from objects to have less effect than before adaptation, and this compensates for the greater amount of long-wavelength tungsten light that is reflected from everything in the room. Because of this adaptation, the yellowish tungsten illumination has only a small effect on your perception of color.

A similar effect also occurs in environmental scenes, which can have different dominant colors in different seasons. For example, the same scene can be "lush" in summer, with a lot of green (**Figure 9.31a**) and "arid" in winter, with more yellows (**Figure 9.31b**). Based on calculations taking into account how this "greenness" and "yellowness" would affect the cone receptors, Michael Webster (2011) determined that adaptation to the green in the lush scene would decrease the perception of green in that scene (**Figure 9.31c**), and adaptation to the yellow of the arid scene would decrease the perception of yellow of the arid scene (**Figure 9.31d**). Thus, adaptation "tones down" the dominant colors in a scene, so if we compare the *perceived* color of the lush and arid scenes in (c) and (d), we see that the colors are more similar than before the chromatic adaptation. This adaptation also causes novel colors to stand out, so yellow becomes more obvious in the lush scene and the green stands out in the arid scene.

The Effect of the Surroundings

An object's perceived color is affected not only by the observer's state of adaptation but also by the object's surroundings, as shown by the following demonstration.

Perception: Paper is green

Perception: Paper shifted toward red

Perception: Paper shifted only slightly toward red so it appears more yellowish

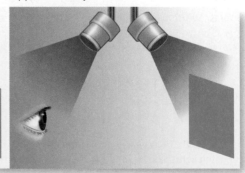

(a) Baseline   (b) Observer not adapted   (c) Observer adapted to red

Figure 9.30 The three conditions in Uchikawa et al.'s (1989) experiment. See text for details. © Cengage Learning

Lush (summer) Arid (winter)

(a)

(b)

(c) (d)

After adapting to lush scenes After adapting to arid scenes

Figure 9.31 How chromatic adaptation to the dominant colors of the environment can influence perception of the colors of a scene. The dominant color of the scene in (a) is green. Looking at this scene causes adaptation to green and decreases the perception of green in the scene, as shown in (c). The dominant color of the arid scene in (b) is yellow. Adapting to this scene causes a decreased perception of yellow in the scene, as shown in (d). Photos courtesy of Michael Webster, University of Nevada.

DEMONSTRATION
Color and the Surroundings

Illuminate the green quadrant of Figure 9.20 with tungsten light, and then look at the square through a small hole punched in a piece of paper so that all you see through the hole is part of the green area. Now repeat this observation while illuminating the same area with daylight from your window.

When the surroundings are masked, most people perceive the green area to be slightly more yellow under the tungsten light than in daylight, which shows that color constancy works less well when an object is seen in isolation. A number of investigators have shown that color constancy works best when an object is surrounded by objects of many different colors, a situation that often occurs when viewing objects in the environment (Foster, 2011; Land, 1983, 1986; Land & McCann, 1971).

The surroundings help us achieve color constancy because the visual system—in ways that are still not completely understood—uses the information provided by the way objects in a scene are illuminated to estimate the characteristics of the illumination and to make appropriate corrections. (For some theories about exactly how the presence of the surroundings enhances color constancy, see Brainard & Wandell, 1986; Land, 1983, 1986; Pokorny et al., 1991.)

Memory and Color

Another thing that helps achieve color constancy is our knowledge about the usual colors of objects in the environment. This effect on perception of prior knowledge of the typical colors of objects is called **memory color**. Research has shown that because people know the colors of familiar objects, like a red stop sign or a green tree, they judge these familiar objects as having richer, more saturated colors than unfamiliar objects that reflect the same wavelengths (Ratner & McCarthy, 1990).

Thorsten Hansen and coworkers (2006) demonstrated an effect of memory color by presenting observers with pictures of fruits with characteristic colors, such as lemons, oranges, and bananas, against a gray background. Observers also viewed a spot of light against the same gray background. When the intensity and wavelength of the spot of light were adjusted so the spot was physically the same as the background, observers reported that the spot appeared the same gray as the background. But when the intensity and wavelength of the fruits were set to be physically the same as the background, observers reported that the fruits appeared slightly colored. For example, a banana that was physically the same as the gray background appeared slightly yellowish, and an orange looked slightly orange. This led Hansen to conclude that the observer's knowledge of the fruit's characteristic colors actually changed the colors they were experiencing. The effect of memory on our experience of color is a small one, but nonetheless may make a small contribution to our ability to accurately perceive the colors of familiar objects under different illuminations.

Lightness Constancy

Just as our perception of chromatic colors like red and green as remaining relatively constant even when the illumination changes, we also perceive achromatic colors—white, gray, and black—as remaining about the same when the illumination changes. Picture, for example, a black Labrador retriever lying on a living room rug illuminated by a 100-watt lightbulb. A small percentage of the light that hits the retriever's coat is reflected, and we see it as black. But when the retriever runs outside into bright sunlight, its coat still appears black. Even though more light is reflected in the sunlight, the perception of the shade of achromatic color (white, gray, and black), which we call **lightness**, remains the same. The fact that we see whites, grays, and blacks as staying about the same shade under different illuminations is called **lightness constancy**.

The visual system's problem is that the amount of light reaching the eye from an object depends on two things: (1) the illumination—the *total amount of light* that is striking the object's surface—and (2) the object's **reflectance**—the *proportion of this light* that the object reflects into our eyes. When lightness constancy occurs, our perception of lightness is determined not by the *intensity of the illumination* hitting an object, but by the object's *reflectance*. Objects that look black reflect about 5 percent of the light. Objects that look gray reflect about 10 to 70 percent of the light (depending on the shade of gray); and objects that look white, like the paper in this book, reflect 80 to 95 percent of the light. Thus, our perception of an object's lightness is related not to the *amount* of light that is reflected from the object, which can change depending on the illumination, but to the *percentage* of light reflected from the object, which remains the same no matter what the illumination.

You can appreciate the existence of lightness constancy by imagining a checkerboard, like the one in **Figure 9.32**, illuminated by room light. Let's assume that the white squares have a reflectance of 90 percent, and the black squares have a reflectance of 9 percent. If the light intensity inside the room is 100 units, the white squares reflect 90 units and the black squares reflect 9 units. Now, if we take the checkerboard outside into bright sunlight, where the intensity is 10,000 units, the white squares reflect 9,000 units of light, and the black squares reflect 900 units. But even though the black squares when outside reflect much more light than the white squares did when the checkerboard was inside, the black squares still look black. Your perception is determined by the reflectance, not the amount of light reflected. What is responsible for lightness constancy? There are a number of possible causes.

Intensity Relationships: The Ratio Principle

One observation about our perception of lightness is that when an object is illuminated evenly—that is, when the illumination is the same over the whole object, as in our checkerboard example—then lightness is determined by the *ratio* of reflectance of the object to the reflectance of surrounding objects. According to the **ratio principle**, as long as this ratio remains the same, the perceived lightness will remain the same (Jacobson & Gilchrist, 1988; Wallach, 1963). For example, consider one of the black squares in the checkerboard. The ratio of a black square to the surrounding white squares is 9/90 = 0.10 under low illuminations and 900/9,000 = 0.10 under high illuminations. Because the ratio of the reflectances is the same, our perception of the lightness remains the same.

The ratio principle works well for flat, evenly illuminated objects like our checkerboard. However, things get more complicated in three-dimensional scenes, which are usually illuminated unevenly.

Lightness Perception Under Uneven Illumination

If you look around, you will probably notice that the illumination is not even over the entire scene, as was the case for our two-dimensional checkerboard. The illumination in three-dimensional scenes is usually uneven because of shadows cast by one object onto another or because one part of an object faces the light and another part faces away from the light. For example, in **Figure 9.33**, in which a shadow is cast across a wall, we need to determine whether the changes in appearance we see across the wall are due to differences in the properties of different parts of the wall or to differences in the way the wall is illuminated.

The problem for the perceptual system is that it has to somehow take the uneven illumination into account. One way to state this problem is that the perceptual system needs to distinguish between *reflectance edges* and *illumination edges*. A **reflectance edge** is an edge where the reflectance of two surfaces changes. The border between areas *a* and *c* in Figure 9.33 is a reflectance edge because it is made of

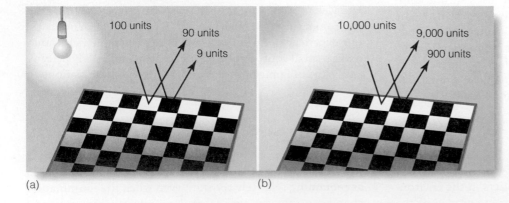

(a)   (b)

Figure 9.32 A black-and-white checkerboard illuminated by (a) tungsten light and (b) sunlight. © Cengage Learning

Figure 9.33 This unevenly illuminated wall contains both reflectance edges (between *a* and *c*) and illumination edges (between *a* and *b*). The perceptual system must distinguish between these two types of edges to accurately perceive the actual properties of the wall, as well as other parts of the scene.

different materials that reflect different amounts of light. An **illumination edge** is an edge where the lighting changes. The border between *a* and *b* is an illumination edge because area *a* is receiving more light than area *b*, which is in shadow.

Some explanations for how the visual system distinguishes between these two types of edges have been proposed (see Adelson, 1999; Gilchrist, 1994; and Gilchrist et al., 1999, for details). The basic idea behind these explanations is that the perceptual system uses a number of sources of information to take the illumination into account.

The Information in Shadows In order for lightness constancy to work, the visual system needs to be able to take the uneven illumination created by shadows into account. It must determine that this change in illumination caused by a shadow is due to an illumination edge and not to a reflectance edge. Obviously, the visual system usually succeeds in doing this because although the light intensity is reduced by shadows, you don't usually see shadowed areas as gray or black. For example, in the case of the wall in **Figure 9.34**, you assume that the shadowed and unshadowed areas are bricks with the same lightness, but that less light falls on some areas than on others.

How does the visual system know that the change in intensity caused by the shadow is an illumination edge and not a reflectance edge? One thing the visual system may take into account is the shadow's meaningful shape. In this particular example, we know that the shadow was cast by a tree, so we know it is the illumination that is changing, not the color of the bricks on the wall. Another clue is provided by the nature of the shadow's contour, as illustrated by the following demonstration.

Figure 9.34 In this photo, you assume that the shadowed and unshadowed areas are bricks with the same lightness, but that less light falls on some areas than on others because of the shadow cast by the tree.

(a)

(b)

Figure 9.35 (a) A cup and its shadow. (b) The same cup and shadow with the penumbra covered by a black border.

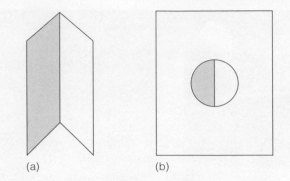
(a)   (b)

Figure 9.36 Viewing a shaded corner. (a) Illuminate the card so one side is illuminated and the other is in shadow. (b) View the card through a small hole so the two sides of the corner are visible, as shown. © Cengage Learning

---

DEMONSTRATION

The Penumbra and Lightness Perception

Place an object, such as a cup, on a white piece of paper on your desk. Then illuminate the cup at an angle with your desk lamp and adjust the lamp's position to produce a shadow with a slightly fuzzy border, as in **Figure 9.35a**. (Generally, moving the lamp closer to the cup makes the border get fuzzier.) The fuzzy border at the edge of the shadow is called the shadow's **penumbra**. Now take a marker and draw a thick line, as shown in **Figure 9.35b**, so you can no longer see the penumbra. What happens to your perception of the shadowed area inside the black line?

Covering the penumbra causes most people to perceive a change in the appearance of the shadowed area. Apparently, the penumbra provides information to the visual system that the dark area next to the cup is a shadow, so the edge between the shadow and the paper is an illumination edge. However, masking off the penumbra eliminates that information, so the area covered by the shadow is seen as a change in reflectance. In this demonstration, lightness constancy occurs when the penumbra is present, but does not occur when it is masked.

The Orientation of Surfaces The following demonstration provides an example of how information about the orientation of a surface affects our perception of lightness.

DEMONSTRATION

Perceiving Lightness at a Corner

Stand a folded index card on end so that it resembles the outside corner of a room, and illuminate it so that one side is illuminated and the other is in shadow. When you look at the corner, you can easily tell that both sides of the corner are made of the same white material but that the nonilluminated side is shadowed (**Figure 9.36a**). In other words, you perceive the edge between the illuminated and shadowed "walls" as an illumination edge.

Now create a hole in another card and, with the hole a few inches from the corner of the folded card, view the corner with

one eye about a foot from the hole (**Figure 9.36b**). If, when viewing the corner through the hole, you perceive the corner as a flat surface, your perception of the left and right surfaces will change.

In this demonstration, the illumination edge you perceived at first became transformed into an erroneous perception of a reflectance edge, so you saw the shadowed white paper as being gray paper. The erroneous perception occurs because viewing the shaded corner through a small hole eliminated information about the conditions of illumination and the orientation of the corner. In order for lightness constancy to occur, it is important that the visual system have adequate information about the conditions of illumination. Without this information, lightness constancy can break down and a shadow can be seen as a darkly pigmented area. **Figure 9.37** shows the opposite situation. There appear to be many shadows on the hillside in **Figure 9.37a** when it is viewed from far away. But a closer view (**Figure 9.37b**) reveals that the "shadows" are, in fact, dirt. As with color perception, we sometimes are fooled by conditions of illumination or by ambiguous information, but most of the time we perceive lightness accurately. **VL**

(a)   (b)

Figure 9.37 (a) Observed from a distance, this hillside appears to have shadows, caused by the contours of the hill. (b) Closer inspection reveals that the "shadows" are actually dirt.

SOMETHING TO CONSIDER:
Color Is a Construction of the Nervous System

Our discussion so far has been dominated by the idea that there is a connection between wavelength and color. This idea is most strongly demonstrated by the visual spectrum in which each wavelength is associated with a specific color (**Figure 9.38a**). But this connection between wavelength and color can be misleading, because it might lead you to believe that wavelengths are colored—450-nm light is blue, 520-nm light is green, and so on. As it turns out, however, wavelengths are completely colorless. This is demonstrated by considering what happens to our perception of color under dim illumination, as happens at dusk. As illumination decreases, hues such as blue, green, and red become less distinct and eventually disappear altogether, until the spectrum, once lushly colored, has become a series of different shades of gray (**Figure 9.38b**).

What has caused this transformation from chromatic to achromatic color? The wavelengths are essentially the same in both cases, and it is unlikely that wavelengths somehow lose their color at low intensities. The shift in perception can be explained by noting that different visual receptors are responsible for perception in high and low illumination. Under high illumination, the three cones of trichromatic vision (or two cones for dichromats) control perception, but under dim illumination, only the rods control perception. We know from our earlier discussion that just one visual pigment can't distinguish between different wavelengths, so when only the rods are active, there is no color perception.

The idea that color is not a property of wavelengths was asserted by Isaac Newton in his statement that "the Rays . . . are not coloured."

The Rays to speak properly are not coloured. In them there is nothing else than a certain Power and Disposition to stir up a Sensation of this or that Colour. . . . So Colours in the Object are nothing but a Disposition to reflect this or that sort of Rays more copiously than the rest. (*Optiks*, 1704)

Newton's idea is that the colors that we see in response to different wavelengths are not contained in the rays of light themselves, but that the rays "stir up a sensation of that color." Stating this idea in modern-day physiological terms, we would say that light rays are simply energy, so there is nothing intrinsically "blue" about short wavelengths or "red" about long wavelengths, and that we perceive color because of the way our nervous system responds to this energy.

We can appreciate the role of the nervous system in creating color experience by considering not only what happens when vision shifts from cone to rod receptors but also the fact that people like Mr. I., the artist who lost his ability to see color in a car accident, see no colors, even though they are receiving the same stimuli as people with normal color vision. Also, many animals perceive either no color or a greatly reduced palette of colors compared to humans, and others sense a wider range of colors than humans, depending on the nature of their visual systems.

For example, **Figure 9.39** shows the absorption spectra of a honeybee's visual pigments. The pigment that absorbs short-wavelength light enables the honeybee to see short wavelengths that can't be detected by humans (Menzel & Backhaus, 1989; Menzel et al., 1986). What "color" do you think bees perceive at 350 nm, which you can't see? You might be tempted to say "blue" because humans see blue at the short-wavelength end of the spectrum, but you really have no way of knowing what the honeybee is seeing, because, as Newton stated, "The Rays . . . are not coloured." There is no color in the wavelengths, so the bee's nervous system creates the bee's experience of color. For all we know, the honeybee's experience of color at short wavelengths is quite different from ours, and may also be different for wavelengths in the middle of the spectrum that humans and honeybees can both see.

The idea that the nervous system is responsible for the quality of our experience also holds for other senses.

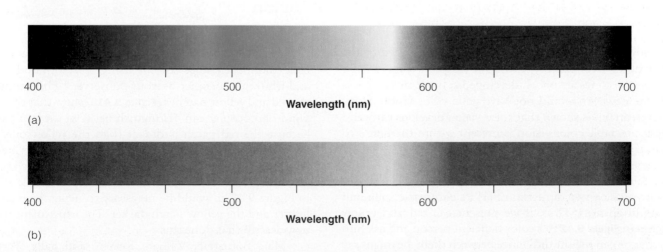

Figure 9.38 (a) Visible spectrum. (b) At low intensities, maximum sensitivity is shifted to shorter wavelengths, and color is lost. © Cengage Learning

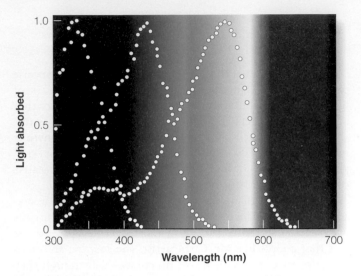

Figure 9.39 Absorption spectra of honeybee visual pigments.
© Cengage Learning

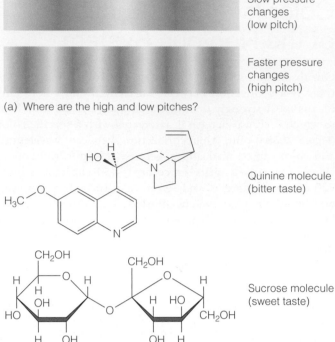

(a) Where are the high and low pitches?

(b) Where are the bitter and sweet tastes?

Figure 9.40 (a) Low and high pitches are associated with slow and fast pressure waves, but pressure waves don't have "pitch." The pitch is created by how the auditory system responds to the pressure waves. (b) Molecules don't have taste. The nervous system creates different tastes in response to the action of the molecules on the taste system. © Cengage Learning 2014

For example, we will see in Chapter 11 that our experience of hearing is caused by pressure changes in the air. But why do we perceive slow pressure changes as low pitches (like the sound of a tuba) and rapid pressure changes as high pitches (like a piccolo)? Is there anything intrinsically "high-pitched" about rapid pressure changes (**Figure 9.40a**)? Or consider the sense of taste. We perceive some substances as "bitter" and others as "sweet," but where is the "bitterness" or "sweetness" in the molecular structure of the substances that enter the mouth? Again, the answer is that these perceptions are not in the molecular structures. They are created by the action of the molecular structures on the nervous system (**Figure 9.40b**).

One of the themes of this book has been that our experience is filtered through our nervous system, so the properties of the nervous system can affect what we experience. We know, for example, that our ability to detect dim lights and fine details is affected by the way the rod and cone receptors converge onto other neurons in the retina (see Chapter 2, page 40). The idea we have introduced here is that our perceptual experience is not only *shaped* by the nervous system, as in the example of rod and cone vision, but—in cases such as color vision, hearing, taste, and smell—the very essence of our experience is *created* by the nervous system.

DEVELOPMENTAL DIMENSION: Infant Color Vision

We know that our perception of color is determined by the action of three different types of cone receptors (Figure 9.10). Because the cones are poorly developed at birth, we can guess that the newborn would not have good color vision. However, research has shown that color vision develops early and that appreciable color vision is present within the first 3 to 4 months of life.

One of the challenges in determining whether infants have color vision is that perception of a light stimulus can vary on at least two dimensions: (1) its chromatic color and (2) its brightness. Thus, if we present the red and yellow patches in **Figure 9.41** to a color-deficient person and ask him whether he can tell the difference between them, he might say yes, because the yellow patch looks brighter than the red one.

You can make this observation, if you don't have access to a color-deficient person, by using a "color-blind" black-and-white photocopier as your "observer." Photocopies of the red and yellow patches (**Figure 9.41b**) show that the color-blind photocopier can distinguish between the two patches because the red patch is darker than the yellow one. This means that when stimuli with different wavelengths are used to test color vision, their intensity should be adjusted so that they have the same brightness. For example, for the stimuli in Figure 9.41, it would be necessary to make the red patch lighter and the yellow patch darker. The experiment we will now describe has done this.

Marc Bornstein, William Kessen, and Sally Weiskopf (1976) assessed the color vision of 4-month-old infants by

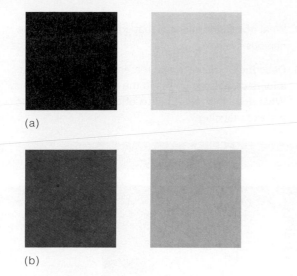

(a)

(b)

Figure 9.41 (a) Two color patches. (b) The same two patches as "seen" by a photocopy machine. © Cengage Learning

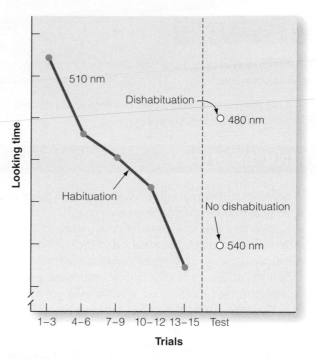

Figure 9.43 Results of Bornstein, Kessen, and Weiskopf's (1976) experiment. Looking time decreases over the first 15 trials as the infant habituates to repeated presentations of a 510-nm stimulus. Looking times for presentation of 480-nm and 540-nm stimuli presented on trial 16 are indicated by the dots on the right. © Cengage Learning

determining whether they perceive the same color categories in the spectrum as adults. People with normal trichromatic vision see the spectrum as a sequence of color categories, starting with blue at the short-wavelength end, followed by green, yellow, orange, and red, with fairly abrupt transitions between one color and the next (see the spectrum in Figure 9.38).

Bornstein and coworkers used the method of habituation, which was described in Chapter 6 (see page 147). They habituated infants to a 510-nm light—a wavelength that appears green to an adult with normal color vision (**Figure 9.42**), by presenting the light a number of times and measuring how long the infant looked at it (**Figure 9.43**). The decrease in looking time (green dots) indicates that habituation is occurring.

After trial 15 of habituation, a 480-nm light (Figure 9.42) is presented. This wavelength appears blue to an adult observer and is therefore in a different category than the 510-nm light for adults. The infant's increase in looking time, which is called dishabituation, indicates that the perception caused by the 480-nm light is also in a different category for the infants. However, when this procedure is repeated, first presenting the 510-nm light and then a 540-nm light (which is

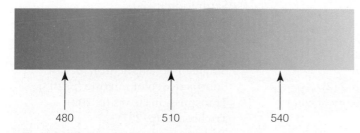

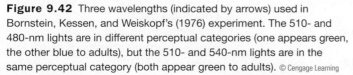

Figure 9.42 Three wavelengths (indicated by arrows) used in Bornstein, Kessen, and Weiskopf's (1976) experiment. The 510- and 480-nm lights are in different perceptual categories (one appears green, the other blue to adults), but the 510- and 540-nm lights are in the same perceptual category (both appear green to adults). © Cengage Learning

also perceived as green by adults and so is in the same category; see Figure 9.42), dishabituation does not occur, indicating that the 540-nm light is in the same category for the infants. From this result and the results of other experiments, Bornstein concluded that 4-month-old infants categorize colors the same way adult trichromats do.

Bornstein and coworkers dealt with the problem of equating brightness by setting the intensity at each wavelength so each stimulus looked equally bright to adults. This is not an ideal procedure because infants may perceive brightness differently from adults. However, as it turns out, Bornstein's result appears to be correct, because later research has confirmed Bornstein's conclusion that young infants have color vision (see Franklin & Davies, 2004; Hamer et al., 1982; Varner et al., 1985).

As with all research in which we are drawing conclusions about how things appear to subjects, it is important to realize that research that indicates that infants categorize colors in the same way as adults doesn't tell us how those colors appear to the infants (Dannemiller, 2009). Just as it is not possible to know whether two adults who call a light "red" are having exactly the same experience, it is also not possible to know exactly what the infants are experiencing when their looking behavior indicates that they can tell the difference between two wavelengths. In addition, there is evidence that color vision continues to develop into the teenage years (Teller, 1997). It is safe to say, however, that the foundations of trichromatic vision are present at about 4 months of age.

1. What is color constancy? Describe three factors that help us achieve color constancy.

2. What is lightness constancy? Describe the factors that are responsible for lightness constancy.

3. What does it mean to say that color is created by the nervous system?

4. Describe Bornstein's experiment that showed that infants categorize colors in the same way as adults. What does this result tell us about what the infants are experiencing?

THINK ABOUT IT

1. A person with normal color vision is called a trichromat. This person needs to mix three wavelengths to match all other wavelengths and has three cone pigments. A person who is color deficient is called a dichromat. This person needs only two wavelengths to match all other wavelengths and has only two operational cone pigments. A tetrachromat needs four wavelengths to match all other wavelengths and has four cone pigments. If a tetrachromat were to meet a trichromat, would the tetrachromat think that the trichromat was color deficient? How would the tetrachromat's color vision be "better than" the trichromat's? (p. 204)

2. When we discussed color deficiency, we noted the difficulty in determining the nature of a color-deficient person's color experience. Discuss how this is related to the idea that color experience is a creation of our nervous system. (p. 208)

3. When you walk from outside, which is illuminated by sunlight, to inside, which is illuminated by tungsten illumination, your perception of colors remains fairly constant. But under some illuminations, such as streetlights called "sodium-vapor" lights that sometimes illuminate highways or parking lots, colors do seem to change. Why do you think color constancy would hold under some illuminations but not others? (p. 215)

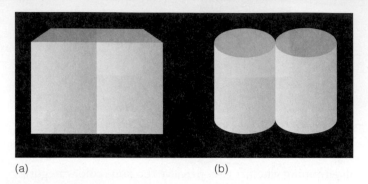

(a)   (b)

Figure 9.44 The light distribution is identical for (a) and (b), though it appears to be different. Figure courtesy of David Knill and Daniel Kersten.

4. **Figure 9.44** shows two displays. The display in (b) was created by changing the top and bottom of the display in (a), while keeping the intensity distributions across the centers of the displays constant. (You can convince yourself that this is true by masking off the top and bottom of the displays.) But even though the intensities are the same, the display in (a) looks like a dark surface on the left and a light surface on the right, whereas the display in (b) looks like two curved cylinders with a slight shadow on the left one. How would you explain this, based on what we know about the causes of lightness constancy? (p. 218) **VL**

KEY TERMS

MEDIA RESOURCES

CourseMate ⬛

Go to CengageBrain.com to access Psychology CourseMate, where you will find the Virtual Labs plus an interactive eBook, flashcards, quizzes, videos, and more.

Virtual Labs VL

The Virtual Labs are designed to help you get the most out of this course. The Virtual Lab icons direct you to specific media demonstrations and experiments designed to help you visualize what you are reading about. The numbers below indicate the number of the Virtual Lab you can access through Psychology CourseMate.

9.1 Monkey See (p. 210)
Film describing the genetic basis of color deficiency in monkeys and the principle behind gene therapy. (Courtesy of Nathan Dappen)

9.2 Checker-Shadow Illusion (p. 220)
Illustrates how interpretation of a display as a three-dimensional scene can affect judgment of the lightness of a surface. (Courtesy of Michael Bach and Edward Adelson)

9.3 Corrugated Plaid Illusion 1 (p. 220)
Demonstration of how interpretation of a display as three-dimensional can affect the perception of lightness. (Courtesy of Edward Adelson)

9.4 Corrugated Plaid Illusion 2 (p. 220)
Another demonstration of how interpretation of a display as three-dimensional can affect the perception of lightness. (Courtesy of Michael Bach)

9.5 Impossible Steps (p. 220)
Illustrates how the three-dimensional interpretation of a display can change a reflectance edge into an illumination edge. (Courtesy of Edward Adelson)

9.6 Knill and Kersten's Illusion (p. 224)
An illustration of how perception of shading caused by curvature can affect lightness perception. (Courtesy of Edward Adelson)

Perceiving Depth and Size

◀ Our perception of depth is created by many sources of information in the environment. In this picture, the perception of depth is created by perspective convergence—the way parallel lines come together in the distance—and by a texture gradient—the way the brown and white structural elements of the building become more closely spaced farther in the distance. In this chapter we will consider many other sources of depth information and also the perception of size.

VL The Virtual Lab icons direct you to specific animations and videos designed to help you visualize what you are reading about. Virtual Labs are listed at the end of the chapter, keyed to the page on which they appear, and can be accessed through Psychology CourseMate.

Some Questions We Will Consider:

■ How can we see far into the distance based on the flat image on the retina? (p. 231)

■ Why do we see depth better with two eyes than with one eye? (p. 236)

■ Why don't people appear to shrink in size when they walk away? (p. 248)

You can easily tell that this book is about 12 to 18 inches away and, when you look up at the scene around you, that other objects are located at distances ranging from your nose (very close!) to across the room, down the street, or even as far as the horizon, depending on where you are. What's amazing about this ability to see the distances of objects in your environment is that your perception of these objects, and the scene as a whole, is based on the flat two-dimensional image on your retina.

We can begin to appreciate the problem of perceiving depth based on two-dimensional information on the retina by considering two points on the scene in **Figure 10.1a**. Light is reflected from point T on the tree and from point H on the house onto points T and H on the retina at the back of the eye. Looking just at these points on the flat surface of the retina (**Figure 10.1b**), we have no way of knowing how far the light has traveled to reach each point. For all we know, the light stimulating either point on the retina could have come from 1 foot away or from a distant star. Clearly, we need to expand our view beyond single points on the retina to determine where objects are located in space.

(a) Eye and scene

(b) Image of scene on retina

Figure 10.1 (a) In the scene, the house is farther away than the tree, but images of points H on the house and T on the tree both fall on the two-dimensional surface of the retina on the back of the eye. (b) These two points on the retinal image, considered by themselves, do not tell us the distances of the house and the tree.
© Cengage Learning

When we expand our view from two isolated points to the entire retinal image, we increase the amount of information available to us because now we can see the images of the house and the tree. However, because this image is two-dimensional, we still need to explain how we get from the flat image on the retina to the three-dimensional perception of the scene.

One way researchers have approached this problem is by the **cue approach to depth perception**, which focuses on identifying information in the retinal image that is correlated with depth in the scene. For example, when one object partially covers another object, as the tree in the foreground in Figure 10.1a covers part of the house, the object that is partially covered must be farther than the object that is covering it. This situation, which is called **occlusion**, is a cue that one object is in front of another. According to cue theory, we learn the connection between this cue and depth through our previous experience with the environment. After this learning has occurred, the association between particular cues and depth becomes automatic, and when these depth cues are present, we experience the world in three dimensions. A number of different types of cues that signal depth in a scene have been identified. We can divide these cues into three major groups:

1. *Oculomotor.* Cues based on our ability to sense the position of our eyes and the tension in our eye muscles.

2. *Monocular.* Cues that work with one eye.

3. *Binocular.* Cues that depend on two eyes.

Oculomotor Cues

The **oculomotor cues** are created by (1) convergence, the inward movement of the eyes that occurs when we look at nearby objects, and (2) accommodation, the change in the shape of the lens that occurs when we focus on objects at various distances. The idea behind these cues is that we can *feel* the inward movement of the eyes that occurs when the eyes converge to look at nearby objects, and we feel the tightening of eye muscles that change the shape of the lens to focus on a nearby object. You can experience the feelings in your eyes associated with convergence and accommodation by doing the following demonstration. **VL**

DEMONSTRATION
Feelings in Your Eyes

Look at your finger as you hold it at arm's length. Then, as you slowly move your finger toward your nose, notice how you feel your eyes looking inward and become aware of the increasing tension inside your eyes.

The feelings you experience as you move your finger closer are caused by (1) the change in convergence angle as your eye muscles cause your eyes to look inward, as in **Figure 10.2a,** and (2) the change in the shape of the lens as the eye accommodates to focus on a near object (Figure 2.4). If you move your finger farther away, the lens flattens, and your eyes move away from the nose until they are both looking straight ahead, as in **Figure 10.2b**. Convergence and accommodation indicate when an object is close and are useful up to a distance of about arm's length, with convergence being the more effective of the two (Cutting & Vishton, 1995; Mon-Williams & Tresilian, 1999; Tresilian et al., 1999).

Monocular Cues

Monocular cues work with only one eye. They include *accommodation*, which we have described under oculomotor cues; *pictorial cues*, which are sources of depth information in a

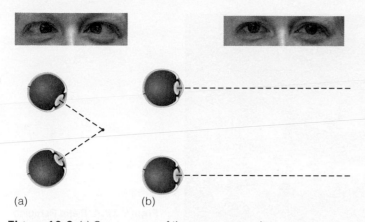

Figure 10.2 (a) Convergence of the eyes occurs when a person looks at something that is very close. (b) The eyes look straight ahead when the person observes something that is far away. © Cengage Learning 2014

two-dimensional picture; and *movement-based cues*, which are sources of depth information created by movement.

Pictorial Cues

Pictorial cues are sources of depth information that can be depicted in a picture, such as the illustrations in this book or an image on the retina (Goldstein, 2001b).

Occlusion We have already described the depth cue of occlusion. Occlusion occurs when one object hides or partially hides another from view. The partially hidden object is seen as being farther away, so the mountains in **Figure 10.3** are perceived as being farther away than the cactus and the

hill. Note that occlusion does not provide information about an object's distance. It indicates that the object that is partially covered is farther away than another object, but from occlusion alone we can't tell how much farther.

Relative Height In the photograph of the scene in **Figure 10.3a**, some objects are near the bottom of the frame and others nearer the top. The height in the frame of the photo corresponds to the height in our field of view, and objects that are higher in the field of view are usually farther away. This is illustrated in **Figure 10.3b**, in which dashed lines 1, 2, and 3 have been added under the front motorcycle, the rear motorcycle, and one of the telephone poles. Notice that dashed lines higher in the picture are under objects that are farther away. You can demonstrate this by looking out at a scene and placing your finger at the places where objects contact the ground. When you do this, you will notice that your finger is higher for farther objects. According to the cue of **relative height**, objects with their bases closer to the horizon are usually seen as being more distant. This means that being *higher* in the field of view causes objects on the *ground* to appear farther away (see lines 1, 2, and 3 in Figure 10.3b), whereas being *lower* in the field of view causes objects in the *sky* to appear farther away (see lines 4 and 5).

Relative Size According to the cue of **relative size**, when two objects are of equal size, the one that is farther away will take up less of your field of view than the one that is closer. This cue depends, to some extent, on a person's knowledge of physical sizes—for example, that the two telephone poles in Figure 10.3 are about the same size, as are the two motorcycles.

Figure 10.3 (a) A scene in Tucson, Arizona, containing a number of depth cues: occlusion (the cactus on the right occludes the hill, which occludes the mountain); relative height (the far motorcycle is higher in the field of view than the closer motorcycle); relative size (the far motorcycle and telephone pole are smaller than the near ones); and perspective convergence (the sides of the road converge in the distance). (b) 1, 2, and 3 indicate the increasing height in the field of view of the bases of the motorcycles and the far telephone pole, which reveals that being higher in the field of view causes objects on the ground to appear farther away; 4 and 5 reveal that being *lower* in the field of view causes objects in the *sky* to appear farther away.

Perugino,Pietro/The Art Gallery Collection/Alamy

Figure 10.4 Pietro Perugino. *Christ Handing the Keys to St. Peter* (Sistine Chapel). The convergence of lines on the plaza illustrates perspective convergence. The sizes of the people in the foreground and middle ground illustrate relative size.

Perspective Convergence When you look down parallel railroad tracks that appear to converge in the distance, you are experiencing **perspective convergence**. This cue was often used by Renaissance artists to add to the impression of depth in their paintings, as in Pietro Perguno's painting in **Figure 10.4**. Notice that in addition to the perspective convergence provide by the lines on the plaza, Perugino has included people in the middle ground, enhancing the perception of depth further through the cue of relative size. Figure 10.3 illustrates both perspective convergence (the road) and relative size (the motorcycles) in our Tucson mountain scene.

Familiar Size We use the cue of **familiar size** when we judge distance based on our prior knowledge of the sizes of objects. We can apply this idea to the coins in **Figure 10.5**. If you are influenced by your knowledge of the actual size of dimes, quarters, and half-dollars, you would probably say that the dime is closer than the quarter. An experiment by William Epstein (1965) shows that under certain conditions, our knowledge of an object's size influences our perception of that object's distance. The stimuli in Epstein's experiment were equal-sized photographs of a dime, a quarter, and a

half-dollar, which were positioned the same distance from an observer. By placing these photographs in a darkened room, illuminating them with a spot of light, and having subjects view them with one eye, Epstein created the illusion that these pictures were real coins.

When the observers judged the distance of each of the coin photographs, they estimated that the dime was closest, the quarter was farther than the dime, and the half-dollar was the farthest of all. The observers' judgments were influenced by their knowledge of the sizes of real dimes (small), quarters (larger), and half-dollars (largest). This result does not occur, however, when observers view the scene with both eyes, because, as we will see when we discuss binocular (two-eyed) vision, the use of two eyes provides information indicating the coins are at the same distance. The cue of familiar size is therefore most effective when other information about depth is absent (see also Coltheart, 1970; Schiffman, 1967).

Atmospheric Perspective **Atmospheric perspective** occurs when distant objects appear less sharp than nearer objects and often have a slight blue tint. **Figure 10.6** illustrates atmospheric perspective. The details in the foreground are sharp and well defined, but details become less and less visible as we look farther into the distance.

The farther away an object is, the more air and particles (dust, water droplets, airborne pollution) we have to look through, making objects that are farther away look less sharp and bluer than close objects.

The reason that farther objects look bluer is related to the reason the sky appears blue. Sunlight contains a distribution of all of the wavelengths in the spectrum, but the atmosphere preferentially scatters short-wavelength light (see Figure 9.4), which appears blue. This scattered light gives the sky its blue tint and also creates a veil of scattered light between us and objects we are looking at, although the blueness becomes obvious only

Dime   Quarter   Half-dollar

Figure 10.5 Drawings of the stimuli used in Epstein's (1965) familiar-size experiment. The actual stimuli were photographs that were all the same size as a real quarter. © Cengage Learning

Figure 10.6 A scene on the coast of Maine showing the effect of atmospheric perspective.

when we are looking through a large distance or when there are more particles in the atmosphere to scatter the light.

If, instead of viewing this cliff along the coast of Maine, you were standing on the moon, where there is no atmosphere and hence no atmospheric perspective, far craters would not look blue and would look just as clear as near ones. But on Earth, there is atmospheric perspective, with the exact amount depending on the nature of the atmosphere.

Texture Gradient Another source of depth information is the **texture gradient**: Elements that are equally spaced in a scene appear to be more closely packed as distance increases, as in the scenes in **Figure 10.7**. Whether the closer packing

occurs for marathon runners, flowers, or any other repeating elements seen in depth, the increasing fineness of texture as distance increases enhances the perception of depth.

Shadows Shadows—decreases in light intensity caused by the blockage of light—can provide information regarding the locations of these objects. Consider, for example, **Figure 10.8a**, which shows seven spheres and a checkerboard. In this picture, the location of the spheres relative to the checkerboard is unclear. They could be resting on the surface of the checkerboard or floating above it. But adding shadows, as shown in **Figure 10.8b**, makes the spheres' locations clearer— the ones on the left are resting on the checkerboard, and the

(a)

(b)

Figure 10.8 (a) Where are the spheres located in relation to the checkerboard? (b) Adding shadows makes their location clearer. Courtesy of Pascal Mamassian.

(a)

(b)

Figure 10.7 Texture gradients created by marathon runners and flowers. The increasing fineness of texture as distance increases enhances the perception of depth.

(a)   (b)

Figure 10.9 (a) Early morning shadows emphasize the mountain's contours. (b) When the sun is overhead, the shadows vanish, and it becomes more difficult to see the mountain's contours.

ones on the right are floating above it. This illustrates how shadows can help determine the location of objects (Mamassian et al., 1998).

Shadows also enhance the three-dimensionality of objects. For example, shadows make the circles in Figure 10.8 appear spherical and help define some of the contours in the mountains in **Figure 10.9**, which appear three-dimensional in the early morning when there are shadows **(Figure 10.9a)**, but flat in the middle of the day when the sun is directly overhead and there are no shadows **(Figure 10.9b)**. **VL**

Motion-Produced Cues

All of the cues we have described so far work if the observer is stationary. But once we start moving, new cues emerge that further enhance our perception of depth. We will describe two motion-produced cues: (1) motion parallax and (2) deletion and accretion.

Motion Parallax Motion parallax occurs when, as we move, nearby objects appear to glide rapidly past us, but more distant objects appear to move more slowly. Thus, when you look out the side window of a moving car or train, nearby objects appear to speed by in a blur, whereas objects that are farther away may appear to be moving only slightly.[1] We can understand why motion parallax occurs by noting how the image of a near object (the tree in **Figure 10.10a**) and a far object (the house in **Figure 10.10b**) move across the retina as an eye moves from position 1 to position 2 without rotating. First let's consider the tree: Figure 10.10a shows

one eye that moves from 1 to 2, so the tree's image moves all the way across the retina from T_1 to T_2, as indicated by the dashed arrow. Figure 10.8b shows that the house's image moves a shorter distance, from H_1 to H_2. Because the image of the tree travels a larger distance across the retina than the house, in the same amount of time, it appears to move more rapidly.

Motion parallax is one of the most important sources of depth information for many animals. The information provided by motion parallax has been used to enable human-designed mechanical robots to determine how far they are from obstacles as they navigate through the environment (Srinivasan & Venkatesh, 1997). Motion parallax is also widely used to create an impression of depth in cartoons and video games.

Deletion and Accretion As an observer moves sideways, some things become covered, and others become uncovered. Try the following demonstration.

DEMONSTRATION
Deletion and Accretion

Close one eye. Position your hands as shown in **Figure 10.11**, so your right hand is at arm's length and your left hand at about half that distance, just to the left of the right hand. Then as you look at your right hand, move your head sideways to the left, being sure to keep your hands still. As you move your head, your left hand appears to cover your right hand. This covering of the farther right hand is **deletion**. If you then move your head back to the right, the nearer hand moves back and uncovers the right hand. This uncovering of the far hand is **accretion**. Deletion and accretion occur all the time as we move through the environment and create information that the object or surface being covered and uncovered is farther away (Kaplan, 1969).

---

[1] If, when looking out the window, you keep your eyes fixed on one object, objects farther and closer than the object you are looking at appear to move in opposite directions.

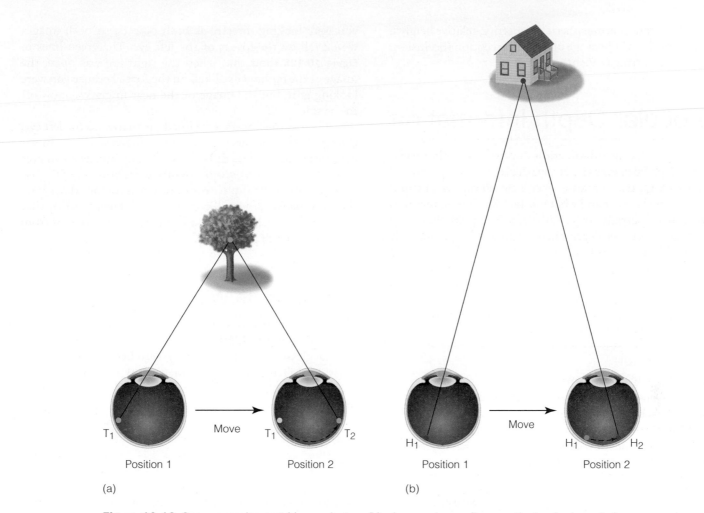

(a)

(b)

Figure 10.10 One eye moving past (a) a nearby tree; (b) a far-away house. Because the tree is closer, its image moves farther across the retina than the image of the house. © Cengage Learning

Bruce Goldstein

Figure 10.11 Position of the hands for "Deletion and Accretion" demonstration.

Our discussion so far has described a number of the cues that contribute to our perception of depth. As shown in **Table 10.1**, these cues work over different distances: some only at close range (accommodation, convergence); some at close and medium ranges (motion parallax, deletion and accretion);

TABLE 10.1 Range of Effectiveness of Different Depth Cues

DEPTH INFORMATION	0–2 METERS	2–20 METERS	ABOVE 30 METERS
Deletion and accretion	✓	✓	
Occlusion	✓	✓	✓
Relative size	✓	✓	✓
Accommodation and convergence	✓		
Motion parallax	✓	✓	
Relative height		✓	✓
Atmospheric perspective			✓

Source: Based on Cutting & Vishton, 1995.

some at long range (atmospheric perspective, relative height); and some at the whole range of depth perception (occlusion, relative size; Cutting & Vishton, 1995).

Binocular Depth Information

One of the myths I heard sometime during my childhood was that you need both eyes to perceive depth. I soon figured out that this wasn't true, because when I closed one eye, I could still tell what was near and what was far away. But sometimes myths can be partially true. Although it is possible to use monocular cues to see depth, there is something qualitatively different about the depth perception experienced when using both eyes. Two-eyed depth perception, called **stereoscopic vision**, involves mechanisms that take into account differences in the images formed on the left and right eyes. The following demonstration illustrates these differences.

DEMONSTRATION
Two Eyes: Two Viewpoints

Close your right eye. Hold a finger on your left hand at arm's length. Position a right-hand finger about a foot away, so it covers the other finger. Then open the right eye and close the left. When you switch eyes, how does the position of your front finger change relative to the rear finger?

When you switched from looking with your left eye to your right, you probably noticed that the front finger appeared to move to the left relative to the far finger. **Figure 10.12** diagrams what happened on your retinas. The green line in **Figure 10.12a** shows that when the left eye was open, the images of the near and far fingers were lined up with the same place on the retina. This occurred because

you were looking directly at both objects, so both images would fall on the foveas of the left eye. The green lines in **Figure 10.12b** show that when the right eye was open, the image of the far finger still fell on the fovea because you were looking at it, but the image of the near finger was now off to the side.

Whereas the fingers were lined up relative to the left eye, the right eye "looks around" the near finger, so the far finger becomes visible. These different viewpoints for the two eyes is the basis of **stereoscopic depth perception**—depth perception created by input from both eyes. Before describing these mechanisms, we will consider what it means to say that stereoscopic depth perception is qualitatively different from monocular depth perception.

Seeing Depth With Two Eyes

Three-dimensional movies were introduced to the public on a large scale in the 1950s, when audiences were introduced to 3-D glasses, and *The House of Wax* became the highest grossing 3-D movie. Three-dimensional movies soon lost their allure, both because of the quality of the stories and the inconvenience of wearing 3-D glasses, and were relegated mainly to short features shown in theme parks. But recently, with the development of better 3-D technology and films like *Avatar* (2009) and *Hugo* (2011), 3-D movies have become a standard fixture of moviegoing, with 3-D TV sets not far behind (more on this later). If you have seen a 3-D movie, it is easy to appreciate the added dimension provided by stereoscopic depth. Scenes seen in 3-D appear to have added depth compared to 2-D, with objects sometimes appearing to jut far out from the screen.

The main reason for the difference between our perception of 2-D and 3-D movies is shown in **Figure 10.13**. Even though we view a 2-D movie with both eyes, the screen

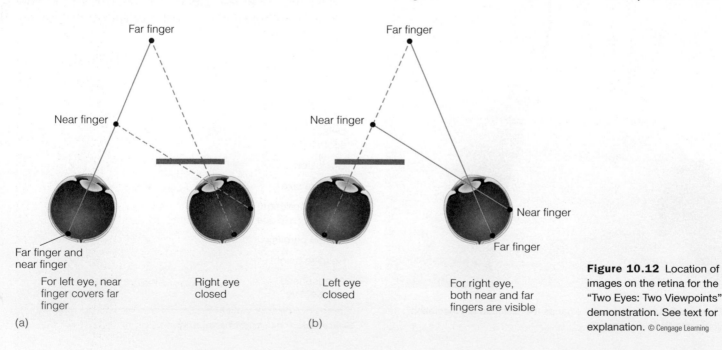

Far finger

Near finger

Far finger and near finger

For left eye, near finger covers far finger

Right eye closed

(a)

Far finger

Near finger

Left eye closed

For right eye, both near and far fingers are visible

Near finger

Far finger

(b)

Figure 10.12 Location of images on the retina for the "Two Eyes: Two Viewpoints" demonstration. See text for explanation. © Cengage Learning

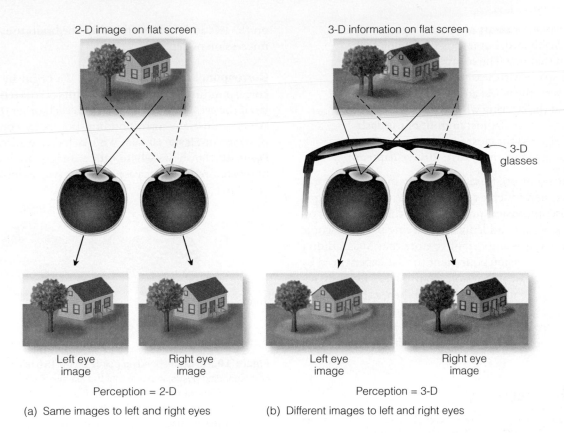

2-D image on flat screen

3-D information on flat screen

3-D glasses

Left eye image   Right eye image

Perception = 2-D

(a) Same images to left and right eyes

Left eye image   Right eye image

Perception = 3-D

(b) Different images to left and right eyes

Figure 10.13 (a) When we view a two-dimensional movie, the left and right eyes receive essentially the same images, so depth is indicated only by monocular pictorial depth cues. (b) When viewing a 3-D movie, the left and right eyes receive different images, so stereoscopic depth perception occurs.
© Cengage Learning 2014

is flat, so both eyes receive essentially the same images (**Figure 10.13a**). Thus any depth perceived in these movies results from monocular or pictorial depth cues.

The situation for 3-D movies is different, because 3-D technology causes the left and right eyes to receive slightly different images, as shown in **Figure 10.13b**. These different views duplicate what happens in the real 3-D world, which we see from two viewing positions, as illustrated in the finger demonstration.

Another way to appreciate the qualitative difference between monocular depth perception and stereoscopic depth perception is to consider the story of Susan Barry, a neuroscientist at Mt. Holyoke College. Her story—first described by neurologist Oliver Sacks, who dubbed her "Stereo Sue" (Sachs, 2006, 2010), and then in her own book, *Fixing My Gaze* (Barry, 2011)—begins with Susan's childhood eye problems. She was cross-eyed, so when she looked at something with one eye, the other eye would be looking somewhere else. For most people, both eyes aim at the same place and work in coordination with each other, but in Susan's case, the input was uncoordinated. Situations such as this, along with a condition called "walleye" in which the eyes look out, are forms of **strabismus**, or misalignment of the eyes. When this occurs, the visual system suppresses vision in one of the eyes to avoid double vision, so the person sees the world with only one eye at a time.

Susan had a number of operations as a child, which made it more difficult to detect her strabismus, but her vision was still dominated by one eye. Although her perception of depth was achieved through monocular cues, she was able to get along quite well. She could drive, play softball, and do most of the things people with stereoscopic vision can do. For example, she describes her vision in a college classroom as follows:

> I looked around. The classroom didn't seem entirely flat to me. I knew that the student sitting in front of me was located between me and the blackboard because the student blocked my view of the blackboard. When I looked outside the classroom window, I knew which trees were located further away because they looked smaller than the closer ones. (Barry, 2011, Chapter 1)

Although Susan could use the monocular cues she describes above to perceive depth, her knowledge of the neuroscience literature and various other experiences she describes in her book led her to realize that she was still seeing with one eye despite her childhood operations. She therefore consulted an optometrist, who confirmed her one-eyed vision and assigned eye exercises designed to improve the coordination between her two eyes. These exercises enabled Susan to coordinate her eyes, and one day after leaving the optometrist's office, she had her first experience with stereoscopic depth perception, which she describes as follows:

> I got into my car, sat down in the driver's seat, placed the key in the ignition, and glanced at the steering

wheel. It was an ordinary steering wheel against an ordinary dashboard, but it took on a whole new dimension that day. The steering wheel was floating in its own space, with a palpable volume of empty space between the wheel and the dashboard. I closed one eye and the steering wheel looked "normal" again; that is, it lay flat just in front of the dashboard. I reopened the closed eye, and the steering wheel floated before me. (Barry, 2011, Chapter 6)

From that point on, Susan had many more experiences that astounded her, much as someone who had never experienced stereoscopic vision might react if they could put on 3-D movie glasses and suddenly begin seeing in stereoscopic three dimensions. It is important to note that Susan didn't suddenly gain stereovision equivalent to that experienced by a person with stereoscopic vision from birth. Her stereovision occurred first for nearby objects and then, as her training progressed, was extended to farther distances. But what she did experience dramatically illustrates the richness that stereoscopic vision adds to the experience of depth perception.

Binocular Disparity

Binocular disparity, the differences in the images on the left and right retinas, is the basis of the stereoscopic vision Susan experienced. We now look more closely at the information

on the left and right retinas that the brain uses to create an impression of depth.

Corresponding Retinal Points We begin by introducing **corresponding retinal points**—points on the retina that overlap if the eyes are superimposed on each other (**Figure 10.14**). We can illustrate corresponding points by considering the observer in **Figure 10.15a**, who is looking directly at Julie. **Figure 10.15b** shows where Julie's images are located on the observer's retinas. Because the observer is looking directly

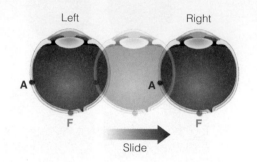

Figure 10.14 Corresponding points on the two retinas. To determine corresponding points, imagine that the left eye is slid on top of the right eye. F indicates the fovea, where the image of an object occurs when an observer looks directly at the object, and A is a point in the peripheral retina. Images on the fovea always fall on corresponding points. Notice that the A's, which also fall on corresponding points, are the same distance from the fovea in the left and right eyes. © Cengage Learning

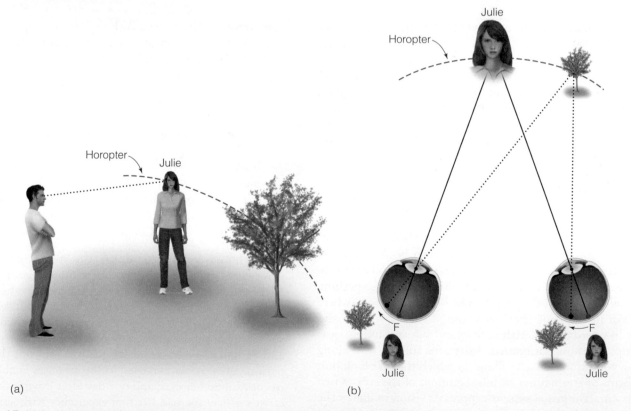

Figure 10.15 (a) An observer looking at Julie's face, with a tree off to the side. (b) The observer's eyes, showing where the images of Julie and the tree fall on each eye. Julie's images fall on the fovea, so they are on corresponding points. The arrows indicate that the tree's images are located the same distances from the fovea in the two eyes, so they are also on corresponding points. The dashed blue line is the horopter. The images of objects that are on the horopter fall on corresponding points. © Cengage Learning 2014

at Julie, her images fall on the observer's foveas on both eyes, indicated by the green dots. The two foveas are corresponding points, so Julie's images fall on corresponding points.

In addition, the images of other objects also fall on corresponding points. Consider, for example, the tree in Figure 10.15b. The tree's images are on the same place relative to the foveas—to the left and at the same distance (indicated by the arrows). This means that the tree's images are on corresponding points. (If you were to slide the eyes on top of each other, Julie's images would overlap, and the tree's images would overlap.) Thus, whatever a person is looking at directly (like Julie) falls on corresponding points, and some other objects (like the tree) fall on corresponding points as well. Julie, the tree, and any other objects that fall on corresponding points are located on a surface called the **horopter**. The blue dashed lines in Figure 10.15a and 10.15b show part of the horopter.

Absolute Disparity Indicates Distance From the Horopter

The images of objects that are *not* on the horopter fall on **noncorresponding points**. The degree to which these objects *deviate* from falling on corresponding points is called **absolute disparity**. This is illustrated in **Figure 10.16a**, which shows Julie again, with her images on corresponding points, and a new character, Bill, whose images are on noncorresponding points. The amount of absolute disparity, which is called the **angle of disparity**, is indicated by the red arrow, which shows the angle between the corresponding point for the left-eye image of Bill (red dot) and where the image is actually located.

Figure 10.16b shows that the angle of disparity is greater for objects at greater distances from the horopter. The observer is still looking at Julie, and Bill is where he was before, but now we have added Dave, who is located even farther from the horopter than Bill. When we compare Dave's angle of disparity in this figure (blue arrow) to Bill's in Figure 10.16a (red arrow), we see that Dave's disparity is greater. (The same thing also happens for objects farther away than the horopter, with greater distance also associated with greater disparity.) The angle of disparity therefore provides information about an object's distance from the horopter, with greater angles of disparity indicating greater distances from the horopter.

Relative Disparity Is Related to Objects' Positions Relative to Each Other

Let's now consider what happens when the observer shifts his gaze from one object to another. When the observer is looking at Julie (**Figure 10.17a**), Julie's images fall on the observer's foveas (so Julie's disparity is zero), but the images of Bill fall on noncorresponding points (so there is disparity). But when the observer shifts his gaze to Bill (**Figure 10.17b**), Bill's images fall on the foveas (so Bill's disparity is now zero) and Julie's images fall on noncorresponding points (so there is disparity).

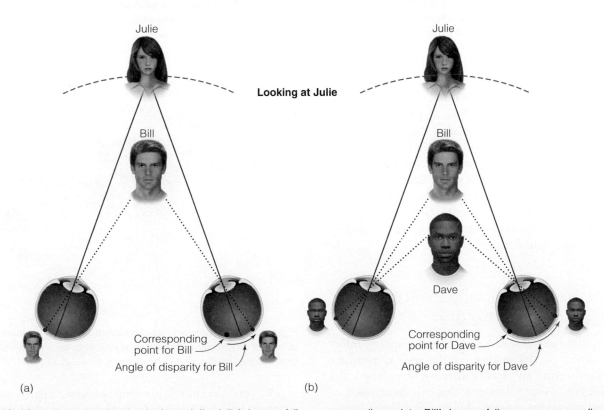

Figure 10.16 (a) When the observer looks at Julie, Julie's images fall on corresponding points. Bill's images fall on noncorresponding points. The angle of disparity, indicated by the red arrow, is determined by measuring the angle between where the corresponding point for Bill's image would be located (black dot) and where Bill's image is actually located (red dot). (b) Dave has been added to Figure 10.16a. Dave's angle of disparity (blue arrow) is greater than Bill's, because Dave is located farther from the horopter. © Cengage Learning 2014

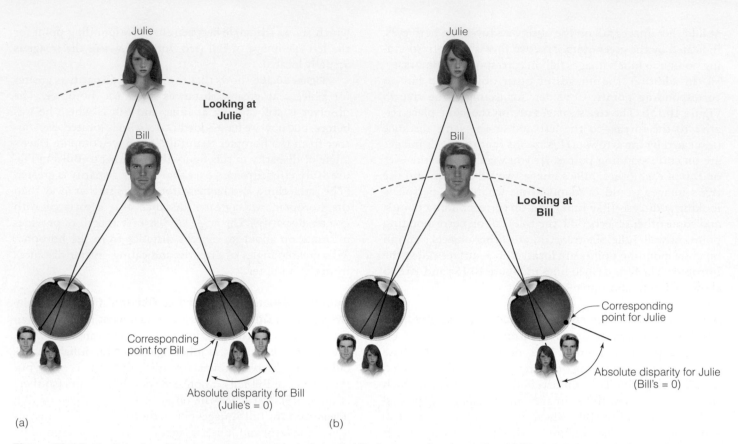

Julie

Looking at
Julie

Bill

Corresponding
point for Bill

Absolute disparity for Bill
(Julie's = 0)

(a)

Julie

Looking at
Bill

Bill

Corresponding
point for Julie

Absolute disparity for Julie
(Bill's = 0)

(b)

Figure 10.17 Absolute disparities change when an observer's gaze shifts from one place to another. (a) When the observer looks at Julie, the disparity of her images is zero. Bill's angle of disparity is indicated by the arrow. (b) When the observer looks at Bill, the disparity of Bill's images becomes zero. Julie's angle of disparity is indicated by the arrow. Because one of the disparities in each pair is zero, the arrows indicate the *difference in disparity* between Julie's and Bill's images. Note that the difference in disparity is the same in (a) and (b). This means that the *relative disparity* of Julie and Bill remains the same as the observer looks at different places. © Cengage Learning 2014

If we compare the two situations in 10.17a and b, we notice that the difference in absolute disparities between Julie and Bill (indicated by the lengths of the arrows) is the same in both situations. The *difference* in absolute disparities of objects in a scene, called **relative disparity**, remains the same as an observer looks around a scene. Relative disparity helps indicate where objects in a scene are located relative to one another. As we will see below, there is evidence that both absolute and relative disparity information is represented by neural activity in the visual system.

Disparity (Geometrical) Creates Stereopsis (Perceptual)

We have seen that both absolute and relative disparity information contained in the images on the retinas provides information indicating an object's distance from where the observer is looking. Notice, however, that our description of disparity has focused on *geometry*—looking at where objects' images fall on the retina—but has not mentioned *perception*, the observer's experience of an object's depth or its relation to other objects in the environment (**Figure 10.18**).

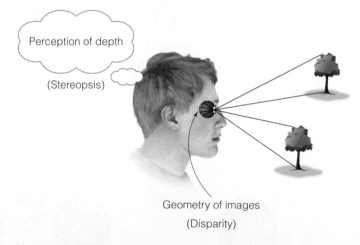

Perception of depth

(Stereopsis)

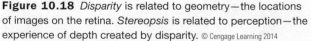

Geometry of images

(Disparity)

Figure 10.18 *Disparity* is related to geometry—the locations of images on the retina. *Stereopsis* is related to perception—the experience of depth created by disparity. © Cengage Learning 2014

We consider the relationship between disparity and what observers perceive by introducing **stereopsis**—the impression of depth that results from information provided by binocular disparity. An example of stereopsis is provided by the depth effect achieved by the **stereoscope**, a device introduced by the

(a) Left eye image

(b) Right eye image

Bruce Goldstein

Figure 10.19 The two images of a stereoscopic photograph. The difference between the two images, such as the distances between the front cactus and the window in the two views, creates retinal disparity. This creates a perception of depth when the left image is viewed by the left eye and the right image is viewed by the right eye.

physicist Charles Wheatstone (1802–1875), which produces a convincing illusion of depth by using two slightly different pictures. This device, extremely popular in the 1800s and reintroduced as the View Master in the 1940s, presents two photographs made with a camera with two lenses separated by the same distance as the eyes. The result is two slightly different views, like those shown in **Figure 10.19**. The stereoscope presents the left picture to the left eye and the right picture to the right eye. This creates the same binocular disparity that occurs when a person views the scene naturally, so that slightly different images appear in the left and right eyes.

The principle behind the stereoscope is also used in 3-D movies. The left-eye and right-eye images are presented superimposed on the screen, slightly displaced from one another, to create disparity. There are a number of ways of achieving this. One way is to color one image red and the other green and to view the film through glasses with a red filter for one eye and a green filter for the other eye. Another way of separating the left and right images, which has been

used in movies like *Avatar* and *Hugo*, is to create the left and right images from polarized light—light waves that vibrate in only one orientation. One image is polarized so its vibration is vertical, and the other is polarized so its vibration is horizontal. Viewing the film through polarizing lenses, which let vertically polarized light into one eye and horizontally polarized light into the other eye, creates the disparity that results in three-dimensional perception. This method creates better color than the red–green method, which results in little or no variation in color.

Similar techniques are used to create 3-D perception of TV images, but with some variations based on the way TV images are created. The main methods are illustrated in **Figure 10.20**. The **passive method** works according to the principles we have described for 3-D movies, with two superimposed polarized images viewed through polarizing glasses (**Figure 10.20a**). The **active method** alternates the left-eye and right-eye images on the screen 30 or more times a second. This method is called active because the viewing glasses

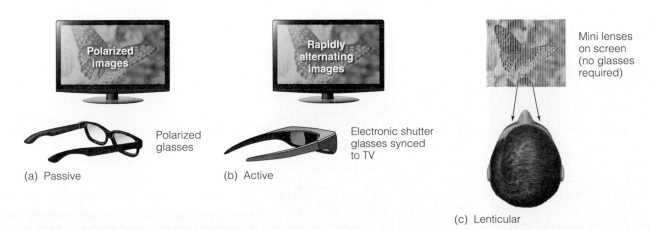

(a) Passive — Polarized glasses

(b) Active — Electronic shutter glasses synced to TV

(c) Lenticular — Mini lenses on screen (no glasses required)

Figure 10.20 Three types of 3-D TV. See text for details. © Cengage Learning 2014

have a shutter system that is synchronized with the alternation of images occurring on the TV screen, so the shutter for the left eye opens when the left-eye image is present on the screen, and the shutter for the right eye opens when the right-eye image is present (**Figure 10.20b**). A disadvantage of this method is that the glasses are expensive, and some people report headaches after extended viewing; an advantage is that better image quality may be possible than with passive viewing.

In a third method, called **lenticular projection**, the screen is coated with a film that contains two sets of lenses that direct different images to the left and right eyes (**Figure 10.20c**). You may have experienced lenticular images in postcards that show different images when viewed at different angles or that create a 3-D impression when viewed from one viewing point. An advantage of this method is that glasses are not required. Disadvantages are that the effect works best when viewed from a particular viewpoint, and viewing the images causes motion sickness in some people. The technology of 3-D television is developing so rapidly that some of the disadvantages described here may have become less important by the time you are reading this book!

Returning to our consideration of whether disparity creates stereopsis, we can point out that all of the methods we have been describing use disparity to create 3-D perception. However, these examples don't conclusively prove that disparity creates stereopsis, because images such as those in Figure 10.19 also contain potential depth cues, such as occlusion and relative height, which could contribute to our perception of depth. In order to show that disparity alone can result in depth perception, Bela Julesz (1971) created a stimulus called the *random-dot stereogram*, which contains no pictorial cues.

By creating stereoscopic images of random-dot patterns, Julesz showed that observers can perceive depth in displays that contain no depth information other than disparity. Two such random-dot patterns, which together constitute a **random-dot stereogram**, are shown in **Figure 10.21**. These patterns were constructed by first generating two identical random-dot patterns on a computer and then shifting a square-shaped section of the dots one or more units to the side.

In the stereogram in **Figure 10.21a**, a section of dots from the pattern on the left has been shifted one unit to the right to form the pattern on the right. This shift is too subtle to be seen in the dot patterns, but we can understand how it is accomplished by looking at the diagrams below the dot patterns (**Figure 10.21b**). In these diagrams, the black dots are indicated by 0's, A's, and X's and the white dots by 1's, B's, and Y's. The A's and B's indicate the square-shaped section where the shift is made in the pattern. Notice that the A's and B's are shifted one unit to the right in the right-hand pattern. The X's and Y's indicate areas uncovered by the shift that must be filled in with new black dots and white dots to complete the pattern.

(a)

1	0	1	0	1	0	0	1	0	1
1	0	0	1	0	1	0	1	0	0
0	0	1	1	0	1	1	0	1	0
0	1	0	A	A	B	B	1	0	1
1	1	1	B	A	B	A	0	0	1
0	0	1	A	A	B	A	0	1	0
1	1	1	B	B	A	B	1	0	1
1	0	0	1	1	0	1	1	0	1
1	1	0	0	1	1	0	1	1	1
0	1	0	0	0	1	1	1	1	0

1	0	1	0	1	0	0	1	0	1
1	0	0	1	0	1	0	1	0	0
0	0	1	1	0	1	1	0	1	0
0	1	0	Y	A	A	B	B	0	1
1	1	1	X	B	A	B	A	0	1
0	0	1	X	A	A	B	A	1	0
1	1	1	Y	B	B	A	B	0	1
1	0	0	1	1	0	1	1	0	1
1	1	0	0	1	1	0	1	1	1
0	1	0	0	0	1	1	1	1	0

(b)

Figure 10.21 (a) A random-dot stereogram. (b) The principle for constructing the stereogram. See text for an explanation. © Cengage Learning

Even though it is not possible to tell that the dots have been shifted when looking at Figure 10.21a, the visual system detects a difference when the left image is presented to the left eye and the right image to the right eye. The disparity created by the shifted section results in perception of a small square floating above the background. Because binocular disparity is the only depth information present in these stereograms, disparity alone must be causing the perception of depth.

Psychophysical experiments, particularly those using Julesz's random-dot stereograms, show that retinal disparity creates a perception of depth. But before we can fully understand the mechanisms responsible for depth perception, we must answer one more question: How does the visual system match the parts of the images in the left and right eyes that correspond to one another? This is called the **correspondence problem**, and as we will see, it has still not been fully explained.

The Correspondence Problem

Let's return to the stereoscopic images of Figure 10.19. When we view this image in a stereoscope, we see different parts of the image at different depths because of the disparity between images on the left and right retinas. Thus, the cactus and the window appear to be at different distances when viewed through the stereoscope because they create different amounts of disparity. But in order for the visual system to calculate this disparity, it must compare the images of the cactus on the left and right retinas and the images of the window on the left and right retinas. This is the correspondence problem. How does the visual system match up the images in the two eyes?

A possible answer to this question is that the visual system may match the images on the left and right retinas on the basis of the specific features of the objects. For example, the upper-left windowpane on the left could be matched with the upper-left pane on the right, and so on. Explained in this way, the solution seems simple: Most things in the world are quite discriminable from one another, so it is easy to match an image on the left retina with the image of the same thing on the right retina. But what about images in which matching similar points would be extremely difficult, as with Julesz's random-dot stereogram?

You can appreciate the problem involved in matching similar parts of a stereogram by trying to match up the points in the left and right images of the stereogram in Figure 10.21. Most people find this to be an extremely difficult task, involving switching their gaze back and forth between the two pictures and comparing small areas of the pictures one after another. But even though matching similar features on a random-dot stereogram is much more difficult and time-consuming than matching features in the real world, the visual system somehow matches similar parts of the two stereogram images, calculates their disparities, and creates a perception of depth. A number of proposals, all too complex to describe here, have been put forth to explain

how the visual system solves the correspondence problem, but a totally satisfactory answer has yet to be proposed (see Blake & Wilson, 1991; Menz & Freeman, 2003; Ohzawa, 1998; Ringbach, 2003).

The Physiology of Binocular Depth Perception

The idea that binocular disparity provides information for the positions of objects in space implies that there should be neurons that signal different amounts of disparity. Research beginning in the 1960s and 1970s revealed neurons that respond to absolute disparity (Barlow et al., 1967; Hubel & Wiesel, 1970). These neurons are called **binocular depth cells** or **disparity-selective cells**. A given cell responds best when stimuli presented to the left and right eyes create a specific amount of absolute disparity (Uka & DeAngelis, 2003). **Figure 10.22** shows a **disparity tuning curve** for one of these neurons. This particular neuron responds best when the left and right eyes are stimulated to create an absolute disparity of about 1 degree. Further research has shown that there are also neurons higher up in the visual system that respond to relative disparity (Parker, 2007).

Brain-imaging experiments on humans show that a number of different areas are activated by stimuli that create binocular disparity (Backus et al., 2001; Kwee et al., 1999; Ts'o et al., 2001). Experiments on monkeys have determined that neurons sensitive to absolute disparity are found in the primary visual receiving area, and neurons sensitive to relative disparity are found in the temporal lobe and other areas. Apparently, depth perception involves a number of stages of processing, beginning in the primary visual cortex and extending to many different areas in both the ventral and dorsal streams (Parker, 2007).

The relationship between binocular disparity and the firing of binocular depth cells is an example of the stimulus–physiology relationship in the diagram of the perceptual process in **Figure 10.23** (orange arrow). This diagram, which we introduced in Chapter 1 (see Figure 1.10) and repeated

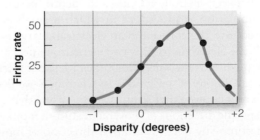

Figure 10.22 Disparity tuning curve for a neuron sensitive to absolute disparity. This curve indicates the neural response that occurs when stimuli presented to the left and right eyes create different amounts of disparity. © Cengage Learning 2014

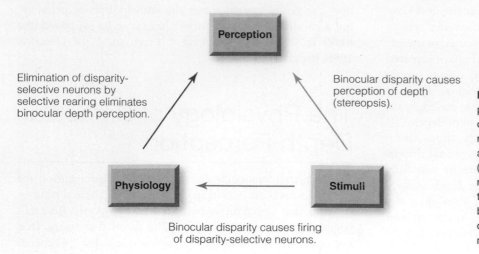

Figure 10.23 The three relationships in the perceptual process, as applied to binocular disparity. We have described experiments relating disparity to perception (green arrow) and relating disparity to physiological responding (orange arrow). The final step is to determine the relationship between physiological responses to disparity and perception (red arrow). This has been studied by selective rearing, which eliminates disparity-selective neurons, as well as by other methods described in the text. © Cengage Learning 2014

in Chapter 8 (see Figure 8.17), also depicts two other relationships. The stimulus–perception relationship (green arrow) is the relationship between binocular disparity and the perception of depth. The final relationship, between physiology and perception (red arrow), involves demonstrating a connection between disparity-selective neurons and depth perception. This has been achieved in a number of ways.

An early demonstration of a connection between binocular neurons and perception involved the selective rearing procedure we described in our discussion of the relationship between feature detectors and perception in Chapter 3 (see page 66). Applying this procedure to depth perception, Randolph Blake and Helmut Hirsch (1975) reared cats so that their vision was alternated between the left and right eyes every other day during the first 6 months of their lives. After this 6-month period of presenting stimuli to just one eye at a time, Blake and Hirsch recorded from neurons in the cat's cortex and found that (1) these cats had few binocular neurons, and (2) they were not able to use binocular disparity to perceive depth. Thus, eliminating binocular neurons eliminates stereopsis and confirms what everyone suspected all along—that disparity-selective neurons are responsible for stereopsis (also see Olson & Freeman, 1980).

Another technique that has been used to demonstrate a link between neural activity and depth perception is microstimulation, a procedure in which a small electrode is inserted into the cortex and an electrical charge is passed through the electrode to activate the neurons near the electrode (Cohen & Newsome, 2004). (See Method: Microstimulation in Chapter 8, page 187) In Chapter 8 we described research that showed that stimulating neurons that respond best to specific directions of movement shifts a monkey's perception of moving dots toward that direction of movement. Gregory DeAngelis and coworkers (1998) demonstrated the same effect for depth perception by training monkeys to indicate the depth created by presenting images with different absolute disparities. Presumably, the monkey perceived

depth because the disparate images on the monkey's retinas activated disparity-selective neurons in the cortex. But what would happen if microstimulation were used to activate a different group of disparity-selective neurons?

Neurons that are sensitive to the same disparities tend to be organized in clusters, so stimulating one of these clusters activates a group of neurons that respond best to a specific disparity. When DeAngelis and coworkers stimulated neurons that were tuned to a disparity different from what was indicated by the images on the retina, the monkey shifted its depth judgment toward the disparity signaled by the stimulated neurons (**Figure 10.24**). The results of the selective rearing and the microstimulation experiments indicate that binocular depth cells are a physiological mechanism responsible for depth perception, thus providing the physiology–perception relationship of the perceptual process in Figure 10.23.

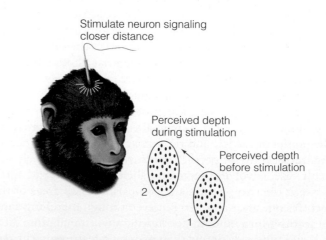

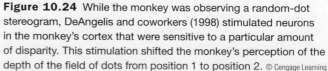

Figure 10.24 While the monkey was observing a random-dot stereogram, DeAngelis and coworkers (1998) stimulated neurons in the monkey's cortex that were sensitive to a particular amount of disparity. This stimulation shifted the monkey's perception of the depth of the field of dots from position 1 to position 2. © Cengage Learning

1. What is the basic problem of depth perception, and how does the cue approach deal with this problem?

2. What monocular cues provide information about depth in the environment?

3. What do comparing the experience of viewing 3-D and 2-D movies and the experiences of "Stereo Sue" tell us about what binocular vision adds to our perception of depth?

4. What is binocular disparity? What is the difference between absolute disparity and relative disparity? How are absolute and relative disparity related to the depths of objects in a scene?

5. What is stereopsis? What is the evidence that disparity creates stereopsis?

6. What does perception of depth from a random-dot stereogram demonstrate?

7. What is the correspondence problem? Has this problem been solved?

8. Describe each of the relationships in the perceptual process of Figure 10.23, and provide examples for each relationship that has been determined by psychophysical and physiological research on depth perception.

Perceiving Size

We discuss size perception in this chapter because our perception of size can be affected by our perception of depth. This link between size perception and depth perception is graphically illustrated by the example of whiteout, a treacherous weather condition faced by helicopter pilots flying across snow-covered terrain. The following description, based on an actual incident at an Antarctic research facility, illustrates the effect of whiteout on size perception:

> As Frank pilots his helicopter across the Antarctic wastes, blinding light, reflected down from thick cloud cover above and up from the pure white blanket of snow below, makes it difficult to see the horizon, details on the surface of the snow, or even up from down. He is aware of the danger because he has known pilots dealing with similar conditions who flew at full power directly into the ice. He thinks he can make out a vehicle on the snow far below, and he drops a smoke grenade to check his altitude. To his horror, the grenade falls only three feet before hitting the ground. Realizing that what he thought was a truck was actually a small box, Frank pulls back on the controls and soars up, his face drenched in sweat, as he comprehends how close he just came to becoming another whiteout fatality.

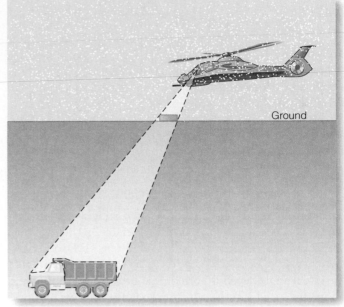

Figure 10.25 When a helicopter pilot loses the ability to perceive distance in a "whiteout," a small box that is close can be mistaken for a truck that is far away.

This account illustrates that our ability to perceive an object's size can sometimes be drastically affected by our ability to perceive the object's distance. A small box seen close up can, in the absence of accurate information about its distance, be misperceived as a large truck seen from far away (**Figure 10.25**). The idea that we can misperceive size when accurate depth information is not present was demonstrated in a classic experiment by A. H. Holway and Edwin Boring (1941).

The Holway and Boring Experiment

Observers in Holway and Boring's experiment sat at the intersection of two hallways and saw a luminous *test circle* when looking down the right hallway and a luminous *comparison circle* when looking down the left hallway (**Figure 10.26**).

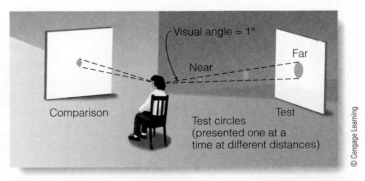

Figure 10.26 Setup of Holway and Boring's (1941) experiment. The observer changes the diameter of the comparison circle in the left corridor to match his or her perception of the size of test circles presented in the right corridor. Each test circle has a visual angle of 1 degree and is presented separately. This diagram is not drawn to scale. The actual distance of the far test circle was 100 feet.

The comparison circle was always 10 feet from the observer, but the test circles were presented at distances ranging from 10 feet to 120 feet. An important property of the fixed-in-place comparison circle was that its size could be adjusted. The observer's task on each trial was to adjust the diameter of the comparison circle in the left corridor to match his or her perception of the sizes of the various test circles presented in the right corridor.

An important feature of the test stimuli in the right corridor was that they all cast exactly the same-sized image on the retina. We can understand how this was accomplished by introducing the concept of visual angle.

What Is Visual Angle?
Visual angle is the angle of an object relative to the observer's eye. **Figure 10.27a** shows how we determine the visual angle of a stimulus (a person, in this example) by extending lines from the person to the lens of the observer's eye. The angle between the lines is the visual angle. Notice that the visual angle depends both on the size of the stimulus and on its distance from the observer, so when the person moves closer, as in **Figure 10.27b**, the visual angle becomes larger.

The visual angle tells us how large the object will be on the back of the eye. There are 360 degrees around the entire circumference of the eyeball, so an object with a visual angle of 1 degree would take up 1/360 of this circumference—about 0.3 mm in an average-sized adult eye. One way to get a feel for visual angle is to fully extend your arm and look at your thumb, as the woman in **Figure 10.28** is doing. The approximate visual angle of the *width* of the thumb at arm's length is 2 degrees. Thus, an object that is exactly covered by the thumb held at arm's length, such as the phone in Figure 10.28, has a visual angle of approximately 2 degrees.

This "thumb technique" provides a way to determine the approximate visual angle of any object in the environment. It also illustrates an important property of visual angle: A small object that is near (like the thumb) and a larger object that is far (like the phone) can have the same visual angle. An extreme example of this is illustrated in **Figure 10.29**, which shows a photograph taken by Jennifer, a student in my sensation and perception class. To take this picture, Jennifer adjusted the distance between her fingers so that the Eiffel Tower just fit between them. When she did this,

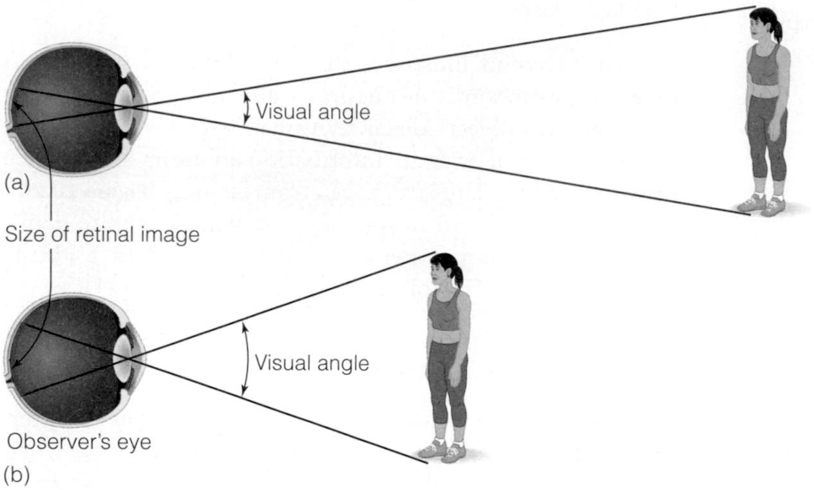

Visual angle

(a)

Size of retinal image

Visual angle

Observer's eye

(b)

Figure 10.27 (a) The visual angle depends on the size of the stimulus (the woman in this example) and its distance from the observer. (b) When the woman moves closer to the observer, the visual angle and the size of the image on the retina increase. This example shows that halving the distance between the stimulus and observer doubles the size of the image on the retina. © Cengage Learning

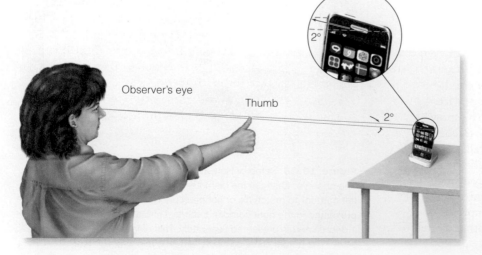

Observer's eye

Thumb

2°

2°

Figure 10.28 The "thumb" method of determining the visual angle of an object. When the thumb is at arm's length, it has a visual angle of about 2 degrees. The woman's thumb covers the width of her phone, so the visual angle of the phone, from the woman's point of view, is 2 degrees. Note that the visual angle will change if the distance between the woman and the phone changes. © Cengage Learning

Figure 10.29 The visual angle between the two fingers is the same as the visual angle of the Eiffel tower.

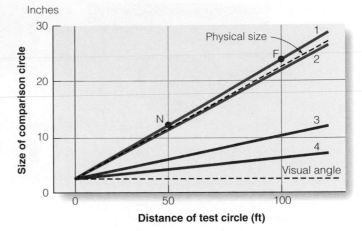

Figure 10.30 Results of Holway and Boring's experiment. The dashed line labeled "physical size" is the result that would be expected if the observers adjusted the diameter of the comparison circle to match the actual diameter of each test circle. The line labeled "visual angle" is the result that would be expected if the observers adjusted the diameter of the comparison circle to match the visual angle of each test circle. © Cengage Learning

the space between her fingers, which were about a foot away, had the same visual angle as the Eiffel Tower, which was miles away.

How Holway and Boring Tested Size Perception in a Hallway

The idea that objects with different sizes can have the same visual angle was used in the creation of the test circles in Holway and Boring's experiment. As shown in Figure 10.26, small circles that were positioned close to the observer and larger circles that were positioned farther away all had visual angles of 1 degree. Because objects with the same visual angle create the same-sized image on the retina, all of the test circles had the same-sized image on the observers' retinas, no matter where in the hallway they were located.

In the first part of Holway and Boring's experiment, many depth cues were available, including binocular disparity, motion parallax, and shading, so the observer could easily judge the distance of the test circles. The results, plotted in **Figure 10.30**, show that when the observers viewed a large test circle that was located far away (far circle in Figure 10.26), they made the comparison circle large (point F in Figure 10.30); when they viewed a small test circle that was located nearby (near circle in Figure 10.26), they made the comparison circle small (point N in Figure 10.30). Thus, when good depth cues were present, the observer's judgments of the size of the circles matched the physical sizes of the circles.

Holway and Boring then determined how eliminating depth information would affect the observer's judgments

of size. They did this by having the observer view the test circles with one eye, which eliminated binocular disparity (line 2 in Figure 10.30); then by having the observer view the test circles through a peephole, which eliminated motion parallax (line 3); and finally by adding drapes to the hallway to eliminate shadows and reflections (line 4). Each time some depth information was eliminated, the observer's judgments of the sizes of the test circles became less accurate. When all depth information was eliminated, the observer's perception of size was determined not by the actual size of the test circles but by the relative sizes of the circle's images on the observer's retinas.

Because all of the test circles in Holway and Boring's experiment had the same retinal size, eliminating depth information caused them to be perceived as being about the same size. Thus, the results of this experiment indicate that size estimation is based on the actual sizes of objects when there is good depth information (blue lines), but that size estimation is strongly influenced by the object's visual angle when depth information is eliminated (red lines).

An example of size perception that is determined by visual angle is our perception of the sizes of the sun and the moon, which, by cosmic coincidence, have the same visual angle. The fact that they have identical visual angles becomes most obvious during an eclipse of the sun. Although we can see the flaming corona of the sun surrounding the moon, as shown in **Figure 10.31**, the moon's disk almost exactly covers the disk of the sun.

If we calculate the visual angles of the sun and the moon, the result is 0.5 degrees for both. As you can see in Figure 10.31, the moon is small (diameter 2,200 miles) but close (245,000 miles from Earth), whereas the sun is large (diameter 865,400 miles) but far away (93 million miles

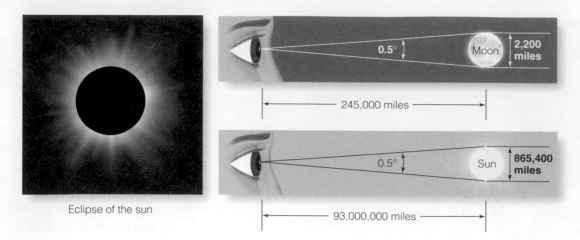

Eclipse of the sun

Figure 10.31 The moon's disk almost exactly covers the sun during an eclipse because the sun and the moon have the same visual angles. © Cengage Learning

from Earth). Even though these two celestial bodies are vastly different in size, we perceive them to be the same size because, as we are unable to perceive their distance, we base our judgment on their visual angles.

In yet another example, we perceive objects viewed from a high-flying airplane as very small. Because we have no way of accurately estimating the distance from the airplane to the ground, we perceive size based on objects' visual angles, which are very small because we are so high up.

Size Constancy

One of the most obvious features of the scene in **Figure 10.32**, on the campus of the University of Arizona, is that looking down the row of palm trees, each more distant tree becomes smaller in the picture. If you were standing on campus observing this scene, the more distant trees would appear to take up

Figure 10.32 All of the palm trees appear to be the same size when viewed in the environment, even though the farther ones have a smaller visual angle.

less of your field of view, as in the picture, but at the same time you would not perceive the farther tree as shorter than the near trees. Even though the far trees take up less of your field of view (or to put it another way, have a smaller *visual angle*), they appear constant in size. The fact that our perception of an object's size is relatively constant even when we view the object from different distances is called **size constancy**.

To introduce the idea of size constancy to my perception class, I ask someone in the front row to estimate my height when I am standing about 3 feet away. Their guess is usually accurate, around 5 feet 9 inches. I then take one large step back so I am now twice as far away and ask the person to estimate my height again. It probably doesn't surprise you that the second estimate of my height is about the same as the first. The point of this demonstration is that even though my image on the person's retina becomes half as large when I double my distance (compare Figures 10.27a and b), I do not appear to shrink to less than 3 feet tall, but still appear to be my normal size. The following demonstration illustrates size constancy in another way.

DEMONSTRATION
Perceiving Size at a Distance

Hold a quarter between the fingertips of each hand so you can see the faces of both coins. Hold one coin about a foot from you and the other at arm's length. Observe the coins with both of your eyes open and note their sizes. Under these conditions, most people perceive the near and far coins as being approximately the same size. Now close one eye, and holding the coins so they appear side-by-side, notice how your perception of the size of the far coin changes so that it now appears smaller than the near coin. This demonstrates how size constancy is decreased under conditions of poor depth information.

Although students often propose that size constancy works because we are familiar with the sizes of objects, research has shown that observers can accurately estimate the sizes of unfamiliar objects viewed at different distances (Haber & Levin, 2001).

Size Constancy as a Calculation The link between size constancy and depth perception has led to the proposal that size constancy is based on a mechanism called **size–distance scaling** that takes an object's distance into account (Gregory, 1966). Size-distance scaling operates according to the equation $S = K(R \times D)$, where S is the object's perceived size, K is a constant, R is the size of the retinal image, and D is the perceived distance of the object. (Since we are mainly interested in R and D, and K is a scaling factor that is always the same, we will omit K in the rest of our discussion).

According to the size-distance equation, as a person walks away from you, the size of the person's image on your retina (R) gets smaller, but your perception of the person's distance (D) gets larger. These two changes balance each other, and the net result is that you perceive the person's size (S) as staying the same.

DEMONSTRATION
Size–Distance Scaling and Emmert's Law

You can demonstrate size–distance scaling to yourself by looking back at Figure 8.12 in Chapter 8 (page 184). Look at the center of the circle for about 60 seconds. Then look at the white space to the side of the circle. If you blink, you should see the circle's afterimage floating in front of the page. Before the afterimage fades, also look at a wall far across the room. You should see that the size of the afterimage depends on where you look. If you look at a distant surface, such as the far wall of the room, you see a large afterimage that appears to be far away. If you look at a near surface, such as the page of this book, you see a small afterimage that appears to be close.

Figure 10.33 illustrates the principle underlying the effect you just experienced, which was first described by Emmert in 1881. Staring at the circle bleached a small circular area of visual pigment on your retina. This bleached area of the retina determined the retinal size of the afterimage and remained constant no matter where you were looking.

The perceived size of the afterimage, as shown in Figure 10.33, is determined by the distance of the surface against which the afterimage is viewed. This relationship between the apparent distance of an afterimage and its perceived size is known as **Emmert's law**: The farther away an afterimage appears, the larger it will seem. This result follows from our size-distance scaling equation, $S = R \times D$. The size of the bleached area of pigment on the retina (R) always stays the same, so that increasing the afterimage's distance (D) increases the magnitude of $R \times D$. We therefore perceive the size of the afterimage (S) as larger when it is viewed against the far wall.

The size–distance scaling effect demonstrated by the afterimage demonstration is working constantly when we look at objects in the environment, with the visual system taking both an object's size in the field of view (which determines retinal size) and its distance into account to determine our perception of its size. This process, which is happening constantly without any effort on our part, helps us perceive a stable environment. Just think of how confusing it would be if objects appeared to shrink or expand just because we happen to be viewing them from different distances. Luckily, because of size constancy, this doesn't happen.

Other Information for Size Perception Although we have been stressing the link between size constancy and depth perception and how size–distance scaling works, other sources of information in the environment also help us achieve size

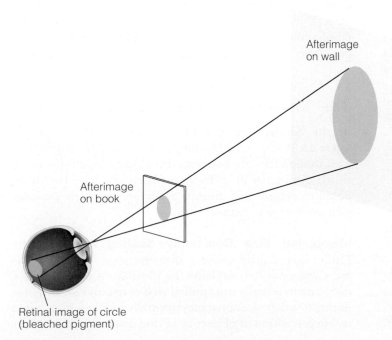

Afterimage on wall

Afterimage on book

Retinal image of circle (bleached pigment)

Figure 10.33 The principle behind the observation that the size of an afterimage increases as the afterimage is viewed against more distant surfaces. © Cengage Learning

Figure 10.34 The size of this wheel becomes apparent when it is compared to the person. If the wheel were seen in isolation, it would be difficult to know that it is so large.

Figure 10.35 Two cylinders resting on a texture gradient. The fact that the bases of both cylinders cover the same portion of a paving stone indicates that the two cylinders are the same size.

constancy. One source of information for size perception is relative size. We often use the sizes of familiar objects as a yardstick to judge the size of other objects, as in **Figure 10.34**, in which the size of the woman indicates that the wheel is very large. This idea that our perception of the sizes of objects can be influenced by the sizes of nearby objects explains why we often fail to appreciate how tall basketball players are, when all we see for comparison are other basketball players. But as soon as a person of average height stands next to one of these players, the player's true height becomes evident.

Another source of information for size perception is the relationship between objects and texture information on the ground. We saw that a texture gradient occurs when elements that are equally spaced in a scene appear to be more closely packed as distance increases (Figure 10.7). **Figure 10.35** shows two cylinders sitting on a texture gradient formed by a cobblestone road. Even if we have trouble perceiving the depth of the near and far cylinders, we can tell that they are the same size because their bases both cover the same portion of a paving stone.

Visual Illusions

Visual illusions fascinate people because they demonstrate how our visual system can be "tricked" into seeing inaccurately (Bach & Poloschek, 2006). We have already described a number of types of illusions. Illusions of lightness include Mach bands (page 56), in which small changes in lightness are seen near a border even though no changes are present in the physical pattern of light; simultaneous contrast (page 58)

and White's illusion (page 59), in which two physically identical fields can appear different; and the Hermann grid (page 56), in which small gray spots are seen that aren't there in the light. Attentional effects include change blindness (page 139), in which two alternating scenes appear similar even though there are differences between them. Illusions of motion are those in which stationary stimuli are perceived as moving (page 178).

We will now describe some illusions of size—situations that lead us to misperceive the size of an object. We will see that some explanations of these illusions involve the connection we have described between the perception of size and the perception of depth. We will also see that some of the most familiar illusions have yet to be fully explained. A good example of this situation is provided by the Müller-Lyer illusion.

The Müller-Lyer Illusion

In the **Müller-Lyer illusion**, the right vertical line in **Figure 10.36** appears to be longer than the left vertical line, even though they are both exactly the same length (measure them). A number of different explanations have been proposed to explain this illusion. An influential early explanation involves size–distance scaling.

Misapplied Size Constancy Scaling Why does the Müller-Lyer display cause a misperception of size? Richard Gregory (1966) explains the illusion on the basis of a mechanism he calls **misapplied size constancy scaling**. He points out that size constancy normally helps us maintain a stable perception of objects by taking distance into account

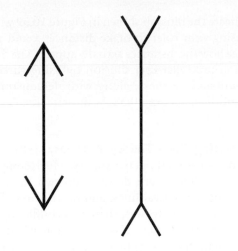

Figure 10.36 The Müller-Lyer illusion. Both lines are actually the same length. © Cengage Learning

(as expressed in the size–distance scaling equation). Thus, size constancy scaling causes a 6-foot-tall person to appear 6 feet tall no matter what his distance. Gregory proposes, however, that the very mechanisms that help us maintain stable perceptions in the three-dimensional world sometimes create illusions when applied to objects drawn on a two-dimensional surface.

We can see how misapplied size constancy scaling works by comparing the left and right lines in Figure 10.36 to the left and right lines that have been superimposed on the corners in **Figure 10.37**. Both lines are the same size, but according to Gregory the lines appear to be at different distances because the fins on the right line in Figure 10.37 make this line look like part of an inside corner of a room, and the fins on the left line make this line look like part of a corner viewed from outside. Because inside corners appear to "recede" and outside corners "jut out," our size–distance scaling mechanism treats the inside corner as if it is farther away, so the term D in the equation $S = R \times D$ is larger and this line therefore appears longer. (Remember that the retinal sizes, R, of the two lines are the same, so perceived size, S, is determined by the perceived distance, D.)

At this point, you could say that although the Müller-Lyer figures may remind Gregory of inside and outside corners, they don't look that way to you (or at least they didn't until Gregory told you to see them that way). But according to Gregory, it is not necessary that you be consciously aware that these lines can represent three-dimensional structures; your perceptual system unconsciously takes the depth information contained in the Müller-Lyer figures into account, and your size–distance scaling mechanism adjusts the perceived sizes of the lines accordingly.

Gregory's theory of visual illusions has not, however, gone unchallenged. For example, figures like the dumbbells in

Figure 10.37 According to Gregory (1966), the Müller-Lyer line on the left corresponds to an outside corner, and the line on the right corresponds to an inside corner. Note that the two vertical lines are the same length (measure them!).

Figure 10.38, which contain no obvious perspective or depth, still result in an illusion. And Patricia DeLucia and Julian Hochberg (1985, 1986, 1991; Hochberg, 1987) have shown that the Müller-Lyer illusion occurs for a three-dimensional display like the one in **Figure 10.39**, in which it is obvious that the spaces between the two sets of fins are not at different depths. (Measure distances *x* and *y* to convince yourself that they are the same.) You can experience this effect for yourself by doing the following demonstration.

DEMONSTRATION
The Müller-Lyer Illusion With Books

Pick three books that are the same size and arrange two of them with their corners making a 90-degree angle and standing in positions A and B, as shown in Figure 10.39. Then, without using a ruler, position the third book at position C, so that distance *x* appears to be equal to distance *y*. Check your placement, looking down at the books from the top and from other angles as well. When you are satisfied that distances *x* and *y* appear about equal, measure the distances with a ruler. How do they compare?

If you set distance *y* so that it was smaller than distance *x*, this is exactly the result you would expect from the two-dimensional Müller-Lyer illusion, in which the distance between the outward-facing fins appears enlarged compared to the distance between the inward-facing fins. You can also

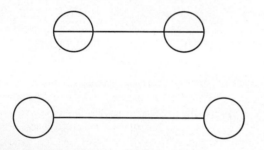

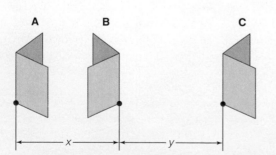

Figure 10.38 The "dumbbell" version of the Müller-Lyer illusion. As in the original Müller-Lyer illusion, the two straight lines are actually the same length. © Cengage Learning

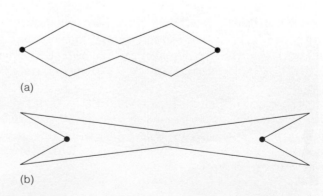

Figure 10.39 A three-dimensional Müller-Lyer illusion. The 2-foot-high wooden "fins" stand on the floor. Although the distances *x* and *y* are the same, distance *y* appears larger, just as in the two-dimensional Müller-Lyer illusion. © Cengage Learning

duplicate the illusion shown in Figure 10.39 with your books by using your ruler to make distances *x* and *y* equal. Then, notice how the distances actually appear. The fact that we can create the Müller-Lyer illusion by using three-dimensional stimuli such as these, along with demonstrations like the dumbbell in Figure 10.38, is difficult for Gregory's theory to explain.

Conflicting Cues Theory R. H. Day (1989, 1990) has proposed the **conflicting cues theory**, which states that our perception of line length depends on two cues: (1) the actual length of the vertical lines, and (2) the overall length of the figure. According to Day, these two conflicting cues are integrated to form a compromise perception of length. Because the overall length of the right figure in Figure 10.36 is larger due to its outward-oriented fins, the vertical line appears larger.

Another version of the Müller-Lyer illusion, shown in **Figure 10.40**, results in the perception that the space between the dots is greater in the lower figure than in the upper figure, even though the distances are actually the same. According to Day's conflicting cues theory, the space in the lower figure appears greater because the overall extent of the figure is greater. Notice that conflicting cues theory can also be applied to the dumbbell display in Figure 10.38. Thus, although Gregory believes that depth information is involved in determining illusions, Day rejects this idea and proposes that cues for length are what is important. Let's now look at some more examples of illusions and the mechanisms that have been proposed to explain them.

The Ponzo Illusion

In the **Ponzo** (or railroad track) **illusion**, shown in **Figure 10.41**, both animals are the same size on the page, and so have the same visual angle, but the one on top appears longer. According to Gregory's misapplied scaling explanation, the top animal appears bigger because of depth information provided by the converging railroad tracks that make

(a)

(b)

Figure 10.40 An alternate version of the Müller-Lyer illusion. We perceive that the distance between the dots in (a) is less than the distance in (b), even though the distances are the same. (From Day, 1989.) © Cengage Learning

Figure 10.41 The Ponzo (or railroad track) illusion. The two animals are the same length on the page (measure them), but the upper one appears larger. Courtesy of Mary Bravo

Figure 10.42 The Ames room. Both women are actually the same height, but the woman on the right appears taller because of the distorted shape of the room. (The Exploratorium/S. Schwartzenberg.)

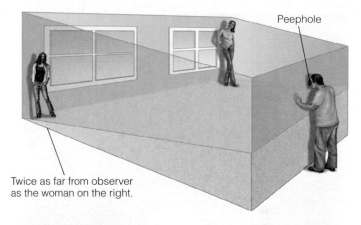

Peephole

Twice as far from observer
as the woman on the right.

Figure 10.43 The Ames room, showing its true shape. The person on the left is actually almost twice as far away from the observer as the person on the right; however, when the room is viewed through the peephole, this difference in distance is not seen. In order for the room to look normal when viewed through the peephole, it is necessary to enlarge the left side of the room. © Cengage Learning

the top animal appear farther away. Thus, just as in the Müller-Lyer illusion, the scaling mechanism corrects for this apparently increased depth (even though there really isn't any, because the illusion is on a flat page), and we perceive the top animal to be larger. (Also see Prinzmetal et al., 2001; Shimamura & Prinzmetal, 1999, for another explanation of the Ponzo illusion.) **VL**

The Ames Room

The **Ames room** causes two people of equal size to appear very different in size (Ittelson, 1952). In **Figure 10.42**, you can see that the woman on the right looks much taller than the woman on the left. This perception occurs even though both women are actually about the same height. The reason for this erroneous perception of size lies in the construction of the room. The shapes of the wall and the windows at the rear of the room make it look like a normal rectangular room when viewed from a particular observation point; however, as shown in the diagram in **Figure 10.43**, the Ames room is actually shaped so that the left corner of the room is almost twice as far from the observer as the right corner.

What's happening in the Ames room? The construction of the room causes the woman on the left to have a much smaller visual angle than the one on the right. We think that we are looking into a normal rectangular room at two women who appear to be at the same distance, so we perceive the

one with the smaller visual angle as shorter. We can understand why this occurs by returning to our size–distance scaling equation, $S = R \times D$. Because the *perceived* distance (D) is the same for the two women, but the size of the retinal image (R) is smaller for the woman on the left, her perceived size (S) is smaller.

Another explanation for the Ames room is based not on size–distance scaling but on relative size. The relative size explanation states that our perception of the size of the two women is determined by how they fill the distance between the bottom and top of the room. Because the woman on the right fills the entire space and the woman on the left occupies only a little of it, we perceive the woman on the right as taller (Sedgwick, 2001).

The Moon Illusion

You may have noticed that when the moon is on the horizon, it appears much larger than when it is higher in the sky. This enlargement of the horizon moon compared to the elevated moon, shown in **Figure 10.44**, is called the **moon illusion**. When I discuss this in class, I first explain that visual angles of the horizon moon and elevated moon are the same. This must be so because the moon's physical size (2,200 miles in diameter) stays the same (obviously) and it remains the same distance from Earth (245,000 miles) throughout the night; therefore, the moon's visual angle must be constant. (If you are still skeptical, photograph the horizon moon and the elevated moon with a digital camera. When you compare the two images, you will find that the diameters in the resulting two pictures are identical. Or you can view the moon through a quarter-inch-diameter hole held at about arm's length. For most people, the moon just fits inside this hole, wherever it is in the sky.)

Figure 10.44 An artist's conception of how the moon is perceived when it is on the horizon and when it is high in the sky. Note that the visual angle of the horizon moon is depicted as larger than the visual angle of the moon high in the sky. This is because the picture is simulating the illusion. In the environment, the visual angles of the two moons are the same. © Cengage Learning

Once students are convinced that the moon's visual angle remains the same throughout the night, I ask why they think the moon appears larger on the horizon. One common response is "When the moon is on the horizon, it appears closer, and that is why it appears larger." When I ask why it appears closer, I often receive the explanation "Because it appears larger." But saying "It appears larger because it appears closer, and it appears closer because it appears larger" is clearly a case of circular reasoning that doesn't really explain the moon illusion.

One explanation that isn't circular is called the **apparent distance theory**. This theory does take distance into account, but in a way opposite to our hypothetical student's explanation. According to apparent distance theory, the moon on the horizon appears more distant because it is viewed across the filled space of the terrain, which contains depth information; but when the moon is higher in the sky, it appears less distant because it is viewed through empty space, which contains little depth information.

The idea that the horizon is perceived as farther away than the sky overhead is supported by the fact that when people estimate the distance to the horizon and the distance to the sky directly overhead, they report that the horizon appears to be farther away. That is, the heavens appear "flattened" (**Figure 10.45**).

The key to the moon illusion, according to apparent distance theory, is that the horizon moon and the elevated moon have the same visual angle, but because the horizon moon is seen against the horizon, which appears farther than the zenith sky, it appears larger. This follows from the size–distance scaling equation, $S = R \times D$. Retinal size, R, is the same for both locations of the moon (remember that the visual angle is always the same no matter where the moon appears in the sky), so the moon that appears farther away will appear larger. This is the principle we invoked in the Emmert's law demonstration to explain why an afterimage appears larger if it is viewed against a faraway surface.

Just as the near and far afterimages in the Emmert's law demonstration have the same visual angles, so do the horizon and elevated moons. The afterimage that appears on the far wall simulates the horizon moon; the circle appears farther away, so your size–distance scaling mechanism makes it appear larger. The afterimage that is viewed on a close surface simulates the elevated moon; the circle appears closer,

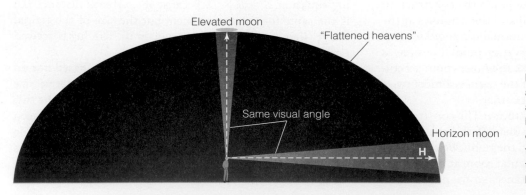

Figure 10.45 When observers are asked to consider the sky as a surface and to compare the distance to the horizon (H) and the distance to the top of the sky on a clear moonless night, they usually say that the horizon appears farther away. This results in the "flattened heavens" shown here. © Cengage Learning

so your scaling mechanism makes it appear smaller (King & Gruber, 1962).

Lloyd Kaufman and Irvin Rock (1962a, 1962b) have done a number of experiments that support the apparent distance theory. In one of their experiments, they showed that when the horizon moon was viewed over the terrain, which made it seem farther away, it appeared 1.3 times larger than the elevated moon; however, when the terrain was masked off so that the horizon moon was viewed through a hole in a sheet of cardboard, the illusion vanished (Kaufman & Rock, 1962a, 1962b; Rock & Kaufman, 1962).

Some researchers, however, are skeptical of the apparent distance theory. They question the idea that the horizon moon appears farther, as shown in the flattened heavens effect in Figure 10.45, because some observers see the horizon moon as floating in space in front of the sky (Plug & Ross, 1994).

Another theory of the moon illusion is the **angular size contrast theory**, which states that the moon appears smaller when it is surrounded by larger objects. Thus, when the moon is elevated, the large expanse of sky surrounding it makes it appear smaller. However, when the moon is on the horizon, less sky surrounds it, so it appears larger (Baird et al., 1990).

Even though scientists have been proposing theories to explain the moon illusion for hundreds of years, there is still no agreement on an explanation (Hershenson, 1989). Apparently a number of factors are involved, in addition to the ones we have considered here, including atmospheric perspective (looking through haze on the horizon can increase size perception), color (redness increases perceived size), and oculomotor factors (convergence of the eyes, which tends to occur when we look toward the horizon and can cause an increase in perceived size; Plug & Ross, 1994). Just as many different sources of depth information work together to create our impression of depth, many different factors may work together to create the moon illusion, and perhaps the other illusions as well.

SOMETHING TO CONSIDER:
Depth Information Across Species

Humans make use of a number of different sources of depth information in the environment. But what about other species? Many animals have excellent depth perception. Cats leap on their prey; monkeys swing from one branch to the next; and a male housefly maintains a constant distance of about 10 cm as it follows a flying female. There is no doubt that many animals are able to judge distances in their environment, but what depth information do they use? Considering the information used by different animals, we find that animals use the entire range of cues described in this chapter. Some animals use many cues, and others rely on just one or two.

To make use of binocular disparity, an animal must have eyes that have overlapping visual fields. Thus, animals such as cats, monkeys, and humans that have **frontal eyes** (**Figure 10.46a**), which result in overlapping fields of view, can use disparity to perceive depth. Animals with **lateral eyes**, such as the rabbit (**Figure 10.46b**), do not have overlapping visual fields and therefore cannot use disparity to perceive depth. Note, however, that in sacrificing binocular disparity, animals with lateral eyes gain a wider field of view—something that is extremely important for animals that need to constantly be on the lookout for predators.

The pigeon is an example of an animal with lateral eyes that are placed so that the visual fields of the left and right eyes overlap only in a 35-degree area surrounding the pigeon's beak. This overlapping area, however, happens to be exactly where pieces of grain would be located when the pigeon is

(a)

(b)

Figure 10.46 (a) Frontal eyes, such as those of the cat, have overlapping fields of view that provide good depth perception. (b) Lateral eyes, such as those of the rabbit, provide a panoramic view but poorer depth perception.

pecking at them, and psychophysical experiments have shown that the pigeon does have a small area of binocular depth perception right in front of its beak (McFadden, 1987; McFadden & Wild, 1986).

Movement parallax is probably insects' most important method of judging distance, and they use it in a number of different ways (Collett, 1978; Srinivasan & Venkatesh, 1997). For example, the locust uses a "peering" response—moving its body from side to side to create movement of its head—as it observes potential prey. T. S. Collett (1978) measured a locust's "peering amplitude"—the distance of this side-to-side sway—as it observed prey at different distances, and found that the locust swayed more when targets were farther away. Since more distant objects move less across the retina than nearer objects for a given amount of observer movement (Figure 10.10), a larger sway would be needed to cause the image of a far object to move the same distance across the retina as the image of a near object. The locust may therefore be judging distance by noting how much sway is needed to cause the image to move a certain distance across its retina (also see Sobel, 1990).

These examples show how depth can be determined from different sources of information in light. But bats, some of which are blind to light, use a form of energy we usually associate with sound to sense depth. Bats sense objects by using a method similar to the sonar system used in World War II to detect underwater objects such as submarines and mines. Sonar, which stands for **so**und **na**vigation and **r**anging, works by sending out pulses of sound and using information contained in the echoes of this sound to determine the location of objects. Donald Griffin (1944) coined the term **echolocation** to describe the biological sonar system used by bats to avoid objects in the dark.

Bats emit pulsed sounds that are far above the upper limit of human hearing, and they sense objects' distances by noting the interval between when they send out the pulse and when they receive the echo (**Figure 10.47**). Since they use sound echoes to sense objects, they can avoid obstacles even when it is totally dark (Suga, 1990). Although we don't have any way of knowing what the bat experiences when these

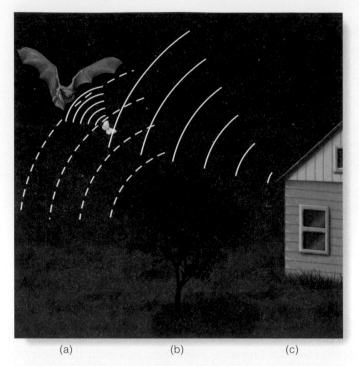

(a) (b) (c)

Figure 10.47 When a bat sends out its pulses, it receives echoes from a number of objects in the environment. This figure shows the echoes received by the bat from (a) a nearby moth; (b) a tree located about 2 meters away; and (c) a house located about 4 meters away. The echoes from more distant objects take longer to return. The bat locates the positions of objects in the environment by sensing how long it takes the echoes to return. © Cengage Learning

echoes return, we do know that the timing of these echoes provides the information the bat needs to locate objects in its environment. (Also see von der Emde et al., 1998, for a description of how electric fish sense depth based on "electrolocation.") From these examples, we can see that animals use a number of different types of information to determine depth, with the type of information used depending on the animal's specific needs and on its anatomy and physiological makeup.

DEVELOPMENTAL DIMENSION: Infant Depth Perception

At what age are infants able to use different kinds of depth information? The answer to this question is that different types of information become operative at different times. Binocular disparity becomes functional early, and pictorial depth cues become functional later.

Using Binocular Disparity

One requirement for the operation of binocular disparity is that the eyes must be able to **binocularly fixate**, so that the two eyes are both looking directly at the object and the two

foveas are directed to exactly the same place. Newborns have only a rudimentary, imprecise ability to fixate binocularly, especially on objects that are changing in depth (Slater & Findlay, 1975).

Richard Aslin (1977) determined when binocular fixation develops by making some simple observations. He filmed infants' eyes while he moved a target back and forth between 12 cm and 57 cm from the infant. When the infant is directing both eyes at a target, the eyes should diverge (rotate outward) as the target moves away and should converge (rotate inward) as the target moves closer. Aslin's films indicate that although some divergence and convergence do occur in 1- and 2-month-old infants, these eye movements do not reliably direct both eyes toward the target until about 3 months of age.

Although binocular fixation may be present by 3 months of age, this does not guarantee that the infant can use the resulting disparity information to perceive depth. To determine when infants can use this information to perceive depth, Robert Fox and coworkers (1980) presented random-dot stereograms to infants ranging in age from 2 to 6 months (see page 242 to review random-dot stereograms).

The beauty of random-dot stereograms is that the binocular disparity information in the stereograms results in stereopsis. This occurs only (1) if the stereogram is observed with a device that presents one picture to the left eye and the other picture to the right eye and (2) if the observer's visual system can convert this disparity information into the perception of depth. Thus, if we present a random-dot stereogram to an infant whose visual system cannot yet use disparity information, all he or she sees is a random collection of dots.

In Fox's experiment, an infant wearing special viewing glasses was seated in his or her mother's lap in front of a television screen (**Figure 10.48**). The child viewed a random-dot stereogram that appeared, to an observer sensitive to disparity information, as a rectangle-in-depth, moving either to the left or to the right. Fox's premise was that an infant sensitive to disparity will move his or her eyes to follow the moving rectangle. He found that infants younger than about 3 months of age would not follow the rectangle, but that infants between 3 and 6 months of age would follow it. He therefore concluded that the ability to use disparity information to perceive depth emerges sometime between 3½ and 6 months of age. This time for the emergence of binocular depth perception has been confirmed by other research using a variety of different methods (Held, Birch, & Gwiazda, 1980; Shimojo et al., 1986; Teller, 1997).

Another type of depth information is provided by pictorial cues. These cues develop later than disparity, presumably because they depend on experience with the environment and the development of cognitive capabilities. In general, infants begin to use pictorial cues such as overlap, familiar size, relative size, shading, linear perspective, and texture gradients sometime between about 5 and 7 months of age (Kavšek, Granrud, & Yonas (2009); Yonas et al., 1982). We will describe research on two of these cues: familiar size and cast shadows.

Depth From Familiar Size

Granrud, Haake, and Yonas (1985) conducted a two-part experiment to see whether infants can use their knowledge of the sizes of objects to help them perceive depth. In the *familiarization period*, 5- and 7-month-old infants played with a pair of wooden objects for 10 minutes. One of these objects was large (**Figure 10.49a**), and one was small (**Figure 10.49b**). In the *test period*, which occurred about a minute after the familiarization period, objects (c) and (d) were presented at the same distance from the infant. The prediction was that infants sensitive to familiar size would perceive the object at (c) to be closer if they remembered, from the familiarization period, that this shape was smaller than the other one. In other words, if the infant remembered the green object as being small, then seeing it as big in their field of view could lead the infant to think it was the same small object, but located much closer. How can we determine whether an infant perceives one object as closer than another? The most widely used method is observing an infant's reaching behavior.

METHOD
Preferential Reaching

The preferential reaching procedure is based on observations that infants as young as 2 months old will reach for nearby objects and that 5-month-old infants are extremely likely to reach for an object that is placed within their reach and unlikely to reach for an

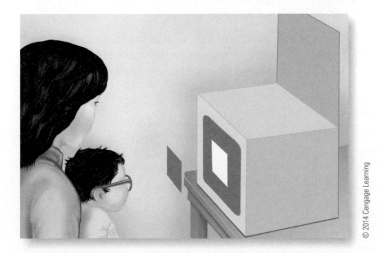

Figure 10.48 The setup used by Fox et al. (1980) to test infants' ability to use binocular disparity information. If the infant can use disparity information to see depth, he or she sees a rectangle moving back and forth in front of the screen. Adapted from "Assessment of Stereopsis in Human Infants," by S. L. Shea, R. Fox, R. Aslin, & S. T. Dumais, 1980, *Investigative Ophthalmology and Visual Science, 19*, 1440–1404, figure 1. Copyright © 1980, with permission from Elsevier.

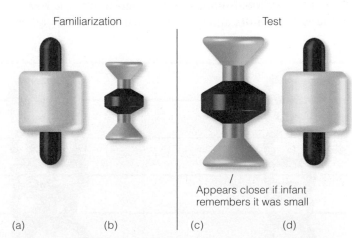

Familiarization   Test

Appears closer if infant remembers it was small

(a)   (b)   (c)   (d)

Figure 10.49 Stimuli for Granrud, Haake, and Yonas's (1985) familiar size experiment. See text for details. From "Infants' Sensitivity to Familiar Size: The Effect of Memory on Spatial Perception," by C. E. Granrud, R. J. Haake, & A. Yonas, 1985, *Perception and Psychophysics, 37*, 459–466. Copyright © 1985 by Psychonomic Society Publications. Reprinted by permission.

object that is beyond their reach (Yonas & Hartman, 1993). Infant's sensitivity to depth has therefore been measured by presenting two objects side by side. As with the preferential looking procedure (Chapter 2, page 46), the left–right position of the objects is changed across trials. The ability to perceive depth is inferred when the infant consistently reaches more for the object that contains information indicating it is closer. When a real depth difference is presented, infants use binocular information and reach for the closer object almost 100 percent of the time. To test infants' use of pictorial depth information only, an eye patch is placed on one eye (this eliminates the availability of binocular information, which overrides pictorial depth cues). If infants are sensitive to the pictorial depth information, they reach for the apparently closer object approximately 60 percent of the time.

When Granrud and coworkers presented the objects to infants, 7-month-old infants reached for object (c), as would be predicted if they perceived it as being closer than object (d). The 5-month-olds, however, did not reach for object (c), which indicated that these infants did not use familiar size as information for depth. Thus, the ability to use familiar size to perceive depth appears to develop sometime between 5 and 7 months.

This experiment is interesting not only because it indicates when the ability to use familiar size develops, but also because the infant's response in the test phase depends on a cognitive ability—the ability to remember the sizes of the objects that he or she played with in the familiarization phase. The 7-month-old infant's depth response in this situation is therefore based on both what is perceived and what is remembered.

Depth From Cast Shadows

We know that shadows provide information indicating an object's position relative to a surface, as occurred in Figure 10.8. To determine when this ability is present in infants, Albert Yonas and Carl Granrud (2006) presented 5- and 7-month-old infants with a display like the one in **Figure 10.50**. Adults and older children consistently report that the object on the right appears nearer than the object on the left. When the infants viewed this display monocularly (to eliminate binocular depth information that would indicate that the objects were actually flat), the 5-month-old infants reached for both the right and left objects on 50 percent of the trials, indicating no preference for the right object. However, the 7-month-old infants reached for the right object on 59 percent of the trials. Yonas and Granrud concluded from this result that 7-month-old infants perceive depth information provided by cast shadows.

This finding fits with other research that indicates that sensitivity to pictorial depth cues develops between 5 and 7 months. But what makes these results especially interesting is that they imply that the infants were able to tell that the dark areas under the toy were shadows and not dark markings on the wall. It is likely that this ability, like the other pictorial depth cues, is based largely on learning from interacting with objects in the environment. In this case, infants need to know something about shadows, including an understanding that most light comes from above (see page 111). **VL**

| **TEST YOURSELF** 10.2 |

1. Describe the Holway and Boring experiment. What do the results of this experiment tell us about how size perception is influenced by depth perception?

2. What are some examples of situations in which our perception of an object's size is determined by the object's visual angle? Under what conditions does this occur?

3. What is size constancy, and under what conditions does it occur?

4. What is size–distance scaling? How does it explain size constancy?

5. Describe two types of information (other than depth) that can influence our perception of size.

6. Describe how illusions of size, such as the Müller-Lyer illusion, the Ponzo illusion, the Ames room, and the moon illusion, can be explained in terms of size–distance scaling.

Figure 10.50 Stimuli presented to 5- and 7-month-old children in Yonas and Granrud's (2006) cast shadow experiment. From Yonas, A., & Granrud, C. E. (2006). Infants' perception of depth from cast shadows. *Perception and Psychophysics, 68,* 154–160. Reproduced by permission.

7. What are some problems with the size–distance scaling explanation of (a) the Müller-Lyer illusion and (b) the moon illusion? What alternative explanations have been proposed?

8. Describe experiments that showed when infants can perceive depth using binocular disparity and using pictorial (monocular) cues. Which develops first? What methods were used?

THINK ABOUT IT

1. One of the triumphs of art is creating the impression of depth on a two-dimensional canvas. Go to a museum or look at pictures in an art book, and identify the depth information that helps increase the perception of depth in these pictures. You may also notice that you perceive less depth in some pictures, especially abstract ones. In fact, some artists purposely create pictures that are perceived as "flat." What steps do these artists have to take to accomplish this? (p. 231)

2. Texture gradients are said to provide information for depth perception because elements in a scene become more densely packed as distance increases. The examples of texture gradients in Figures 10.4 and 10.7 contain regularly spaced elements that extend over large distances. But regularly spaced elements are more the exception than the rule in the environment. Make an informal survey of your environment, both inside and outside, and decide (a) whether texture gradients are present in your environment and (b) if you think the principle behind texture gradients could contribute to the perception of depth even if the texture information in the environment is not as obvious as the examples in this chapter. (p. 233)

3. How could you determine the contribution of binocular vision to depth perception? One way would be to close one eye and notice how this affects your perception. Try this, and describe any changes you notice. Then devise a way to quantitatively measure the accuracy of depth perception that is possible with two-eyed and one-eyed vision. (p. 236)

KEY TERMS

Absolute disparity (p. 237)
Accretion (p. 232)
Active method (3-D TV) (p. 239)
Ames room (p. 251)
Angle of disparity (p. 237)
Angular size contrast theory (p. 253)
Apparent distance theory (p. 252)
Atmospheric perspective (p. 230)
Binocular depth cell (p. 241)
Binocular disparity (p. 236)
Binocularly fixate (p. 254)
Conflicting cues theory (p. 250)
Correspondence problem (p. 241)
Corresponding retinal points (p. 236)
Cue approach to depth perception (p. 228)
Deletion (p. 232)
Disparity-selective cell (p. 241)

Disparity tuning curve (p. 241)
Echolocation (p. 254)
Emmert's law (p. 247)
Familiar size (p. 230)
Frontal eyes (p. 253)
Horopter (p. 237)
Lateral eyes (p. 253)
Lenticular projection (p. 240)
Misapplied size constancy scaling (p. 248)
Monocular cue (p. 228)
Moon illusion (p. 252)
Motion parallax (p. 232)
Müller-Lyer illusion (p. 248)
Noncorresponding points (p. 237)
Occlusion (p. 228)
Oculomotor cue (p. 228)
Passive method (3-D TV) (p. 239)

Perspective convergence (p. 230)
Pictorial cue (p. 229)
Ponzo illusion (p. 250)
Random-dot stereogram (p. 240)
Relative disparity (p. 238)
Relative height (p. 229)
Relative size (p. 229)
Size constancy (p. 246)
Size–distance scaling (p. 247)
Stereopsis (p. 238)
Stereoscope (p. 238)
Stereoscopic depth perception (p. 234)
Stereoscopic vision (p. 234)
Strabismus (p. 235)
Texture gradient (p. 231)
Visual angle (p. 244)

CourseMate ▣

Go to CengageBrain.com to access Psychology CourseMate, where you will find the Virtual Labs plus an interactive eBook, flashcards, quizzes, videos, and more.

Virtual Labs **VL**

The Virtual Labs are designed to help you get the most out of this course. The Virtual Lab icons direct you to specific media demonstrations and experiments designed to help you visualize what you are reading about. The numbers below indicate the number of the Virtual Lab you can access through Psychology CourseMate.

10.1 Convergence (p. 228)
Description of how the eyes converge when looking at near objects.

10.2 Shape From Shading (p. 232)
Description of how shading facilitates perception for a three-dimensional object.

10.3 Ball in a Box (p. 232)
Computer animation showing how shadows affect perception of the location of a ball rolling in a box. (Courtesy of Daniel Kersten)

10.4 Illusory Motion in Depth (p. 232)
How a moving shadow can make a square appear to move in depth. (Courtesy of Daniel Kersten)

10.5 Size Perception and Depth (p. 251)
How perspective cues influence size perception.

10.6 Size Constancy in Infants (p. 256)
Albert Yonas's research on depth perception in infants.

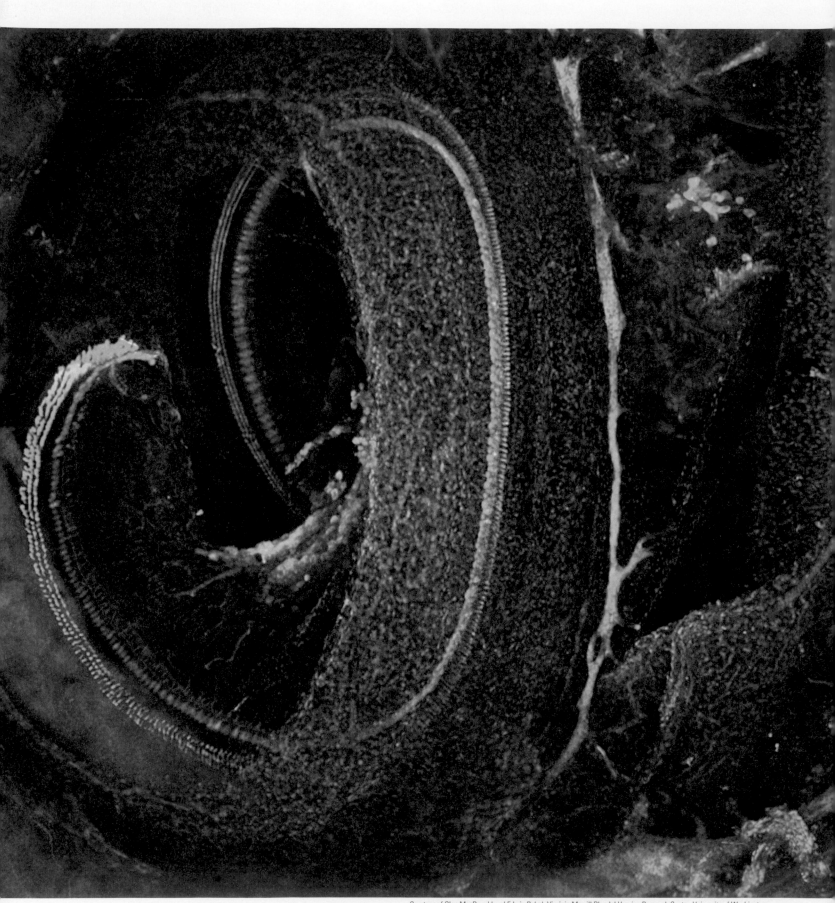

CHAPTER 11

Hearing

by Bruce Goldstein and Christopher Plack

◀ This is a picture of the cochlea of a guinea pig. The cochlea is the structure within the ear that contains the hair cells, which are the receptors for hearing. These hair cells, which are shown in green on the spiral, bend in response to the small pressure changes associated with sound stimuli. This bending generates electrical signals that are sent in nerve fibers, shown in red, to the auditory nerve, where they begin their journey to the auditory areas of the brain.

VL The Virtual Lab icons direct you to specific animations and videos designed to help you visualize what you are reading about. Virtual Labs are listed at the end of the chapter, keyed to the page on which they appear, and can be accessed through Psychology CourseMate.

Some Questions We Will Consider:

- If a tree falls in the forest and no one is there to hear it, is there a sound? (p. 262)

- How do sound vibrations inside the ear lead to the perception of different pitches? (p. 280)

- How can sound damage the auditory receptors? (p. 282)

A student in my class wrote the following about the importance of hearing in her life:

Hearing has an extremely important function in my life. I was born legally blind, so although I can see, my vision is highly impaired and is not correctable. Even though I am not usually shy or embarrassed, sometimes I do not want to call attention to myself and my disability. . . . There are many methods that I can use to improve my sight in class, like sitting close to the board or copying from a friend, but sometimes these things are impossible. Then I use my hearing to take notes. . . . My hearing is very strong. While I do not need my hearing to identify people who are very close to me, it is definitely necessary when someone is calling my name from a distance. I can recognize their voice, even if I cannot see them. (Jill Robbins)

The following statement illustrates another student's reaction to temporarily losing her ability to hear.

> In an experiment I did for my sign language class, I bandaged up my ears so I couldn't hear a sound. I had a signing interpreter with me to translate spoken language. The two hours that I was "deaf" gave me a great appreciation for deaf people and their culture. I found it extremely difficult to communicate, because even though I could read the signing, I couldn't keep up with the pace of the conversation. . . . Also, it was uncomfortable for me to be in that much silence. Knowing what a crowded cafeteria sounds like and not being able to hear the background noise was an uncomfortable feeling. I couldn't hear the buzzing of the fluorescent light, the murmur of the crowd, or the slurping of my friend's Coke (which I usually object to, but which I missed when I couldn't hear it). I saw a man drop his tray, and I heard nothing. I could handle the signing, but not the silence. (Eileen Lusk)

You don't have to bandage up your ears for two hours to appreciate what hearing adds to your life. Just close your eyes for a few minutes and notice what sounds you hear. You may find that by listening closely, you become aware of many events that without hearing you would not be aware of at all. For example, in my office in the psychology department, I hear things that I would be unaware of if I had to rely only on my sense of vision: people talking in the hall; a car passing by on the street below; an ambulance, siren blaring, heading up the hill toward the hospital. If it weren't for hearing, my world at this particular moment would be limited to what I can see in my office and the scene directly outside my window. Although the silence might make it easier to concentrate on writing this book, without hearing I would be unaware of many of the events in my environment.

Our ability to hear events that we can't see serves an important signaling function for both animals and humans. For an animal living in the forest, the rustle of leaves or the snap of a twig may signal the approach of a predator. For humans, hearing provides signals such as the warning sound of a smoke alarm or an ambulance siren, the distinctive high-pitched cry of a baby who is distressed, or telltale noises that indicate problems in a car engine.

But hearing has other functions, too. Ask yourself: If you had to pick between losing hearing or vision, which would you choose? Two of the strongest arguments for keeping hearing instead of vision are music and speech. Many people wouldn't want to give up hearing because of the pleasure they derive from listening to music, and they also realize that speech is important because it facilitates communication between people.

Helen Keller, who was both deaf and blind, stated that she felt being deaf was worse than being blind because blindness isolated her from things, but deafness isolated her from people. Being unable to hear people talking creates an isolation that makes it difficult to relate to people who can hear and sometimes makes it difficult even to know what is going on. To appreciate this last point, try watching a dramatic program on television with the sound turned off. You may be surprised at how little, beyond physical actions and perhaps some intense emotions, you can understand about the story.

So, sound provides useful information while at the same time adding a richness to our experience. But what exactly is sound, and how does it result in experience? The starting point for answering that question is the perceptual process that we introduced in Chapter 1.

The Perceptual Process for Hearing

The first step in the perceptual process for hearing is to identify the environmental stimulus. The environmental stimulus for vision was a tree, which our observer was able to see because light was reflected from the tree into his eyes. Information about the tree, transmitted by the light, then created a representation on the visual receptors.

But what happens when a bird, perched on the tree, sings? The action of the bird's vocal organ is transformed into a sound stimulus—pressure changes in the air. These pressure changes trigger a sequence of events that results in a representation of the bird's song within the ears, neural signals are sent to the brain, and these signals eventually lead to perception of the bird's song.

The road from vibration of the bird's vocal organ to a listener's perception of the bird's song is a long, complex one. We will describe this process as a story with a number of chapters. The main characters in the story are the stimuli for hearing—air pressure changes in the environment—and the structures that receive these stimuli— receptors within the ear.

We will see that sound stimuli can be simple repeating pressure changes, like those often used in laboratory research, or more complex pressure changes such as those produced by musical instruments or a person talking. The properties of these air pressure changes are translated into various perceptions, including whether a sound can be heard or not, whether it sounds soft or loud, low-pitched or high-pitched. Once we have described sound stimuli and their perceptual effects, we will be ready to begin describing the drama that unfolds as sound enters the ear. But first let's set the stage by describing sound stimuli and their effects.

Physical Aspects of Sound

The first step in understanding hearing is to define what we mean by *sound* and to describe the characteristics of sound. One way to answer the question "What is sound?" is to consider the following question: *If a tree falls in the forest and no one is there to hear it, is there a sound?*

This question is useful because it shows that we can use the word **sound** in two different ways. Sometimes *sound* refers to a physical stimulus, and sometimes it refers to a perceptual response. The answer to the question about the tree depends on which of the following definitions of sound we use.

- *Physical definition:* Sound is *pressure changes* in the air or other medium.

- *Perceptual definition:* Sound is the *experience* we have when we hear.

The answer to the question is "yes" if we are using the physical definition, because the falling tree causes pressure changes whether or not someone is there to hear them. The answer to the question is "no" if we are using the perceptual definition, because if no one is in the forest, there will be no experience.

This difference between physical and perceptual is important to be aware of as we discuss hearing in this chapter and the next two. Luckily, it is usually easy to tell from the context in which the terms are used whether "sound" refers to the physical stimulus or to the experience of hearing. For example, "the piercing sound of the trumpet filled the room" refers to the *experience of sound*, but "the sound had a frequency of 1,000 Hz" refers to sound as a *physical stimulus*. In general, we will use the term "sound" or "sound stimulus" to refer to the physical stimulus and "sound perception" to refer to the experience of sound. We begin by describing sound as a physical stimulus.

Sound as Pressure Changes

A sound stimulus occurs when the movements or vibrations of an object cause pressure changes in air, water, or any other elastic medium that surrounds the object. Let's begin by considering a loudspeaker, which is really a device for producing vibrations to be transmitted to the surrounding air. People have been known to turn up the volume on their stereos so high that vibrations can be felt through a neighbor's wall, but even at lower levels, the vibrations are there.

The speaker's vibrations affect the surrounding air, as shown in **Figure 11.1a**. When the diaphragm of the speaker moves out, it pushes the surrounding air molecules together, a process called *condensation*, which causes a slight increase in the density of molecules near the diaphragm. This increased density results in a local increase in the air pressure above atmospheric pressure. When the speaker diaphragm moves back in, air molecules spread out to fill in the increased space, a process called *rarefaction*. The decreased density of air molecules caused by rarefaction causes a slight decrease in air pressure. By repeating this process many hundreds or thousands of times a second, the speaker creates a pattern of alternating high- and low-pressure regions in the air as neighboring air molecules affect each other. This pattern of air pressure changes, which travels through air at 340 meters per second (and through water at 1,500 meters per second), is called a **sound wave**.

You might get the impression from Figure 11.1a that this traveling sound wave causes air to move outward from the speaker into the environment. However, although *air pressure changes* move outward from the speaker, the *air molecules* at each location move back and forth but stay in about the same place. What is transmitted is the pattern of increases and decreases in pressure that eventually reach the listener's ear. What is actually happening is analogous to the ripples created by a pebble dropped into a still pool of water (**Figure 11.1b**). As the ripples move outward from the pebble, the water at any particular place moves up and down. The fact that the water does not move forward becomes obvious when you realize that the ripples would cause a toy boat to bob up and down—not to move outward.

Pure Tones

To describe the pressure changes associated with sound, we will first focus on a simple kind of sound wave called a pure tone. A **pure tone** occurs when changes in air pressure occur in a pattern described by a mathematical function called

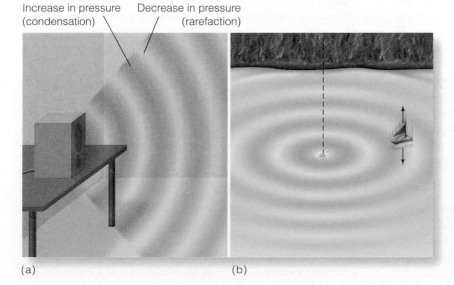

Increase in pressure (condensation)   Decrease in pressure (rarefaction)

(a)   (b)

Figure 11.1 (a) The effect of a vibrating speaker diaphragm on the surrounding air. Dark areas represent regions of high air pressure, and light areas represent areas of low air pressure. (b) When a pebble is dropped into still water, the resulting ripples appear to move outward. However, the water is actually moving up and down, as indicated by movement of the boat. A similar situation exists for the sound waves produced by the speaker in (a). © Cengage Learning

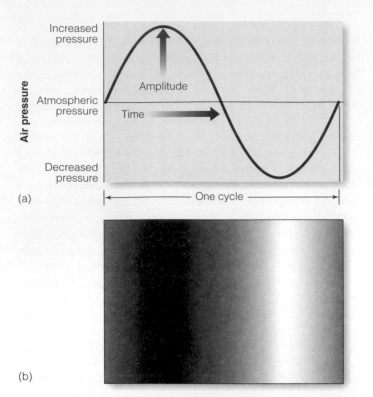

Figure 11.2 (a) Plot of sine-wave pressure changes for a pure tone. (b) Pressure changes are indicated, as in Figure 11.1, by darkening (pressure increased relative to atmospheric pressure) and lightening (pressure decreased relative to atmospheric pressure). © Cengage Learning

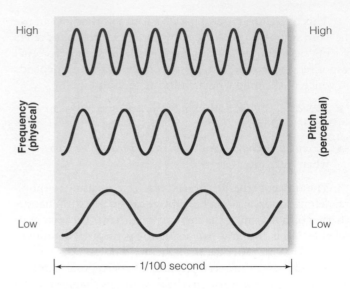

Figure 11.3 Three different frequencies of a pure tone. Higher frequencies are associated with the perception of higher pitches. © Cengage Learning

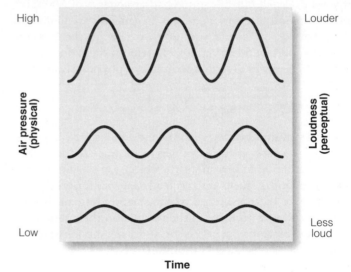

Figure 11.4 Three different amplitudes of a pure tone. Larger amplitude is associated with the perception of greater loudness. © Cengage Learning

a *sine wave*, as shown in **Figure 11.2**. Tones with this pattern of pressure changes are occasionally found in the environment. A person whistling or the high-pitched notes produced by a flute are close to pure tones. Tuning forks, which are designed to vibrate with a sine-wave motion, also produce pure tones. For laboratory studies of hearing, computers generate pure tones that cause a speaker diaphragm to vibrate in and out with a sine-wave motion. This vibration can be described by noting its **frequency**—the number of cycles per second that the pressure changes repeat—and its **amplitude**—the size of the pressure change.

Sound Frequency Frequency, the number of cycles per second that the change in pressure repeats, is measured in units called **hertz (Hz)**, in which 1 Hz is 1 cycle per second. Thus, the middle stimulus in **Figure 11.3**, which repeats five times in 1/100 second, would be a 500-Hz tone. As we will see, humans can perceive frequencies ranging from about 20 Hz to 20,000 Hz. (When we discuss how frequency is perceived, later in the chapter, we will see that higher frequencies are usually associated with higher pitches.)

Sound Amplitude and the Decibel Scale One way to specify a sound's amplitude would be to indicate the difference in pressure between the high and low peaks of the sound wave. **Figure 11.4** shows three pure tones with different amplitudes.

The range of amplitudes we can encounter in the environment is extremely large, as shown in **Table 11.1**, which indicates the relative amplitudes of environmental sounds, ranging from a whisper to a jet taking off. (When we discuss how amplitude is perceived, later in the chapter, we will see that the amplitude of a sound wave is associated with the loudness of a sound.)

We can dramatize the size of the range of amplitudes as follows: If the pressure change plotted in the middle record of Figure 11.4, in which the sine wave is about ½-inch high on the page, represented the amplitude associated with a sound that we can just barely hear, like a whisper, then to plot the graph for a very loud sound, such as music at a rock concert,

TABLE 11.1 Relative Amplitudes and Decibels for Environmental Sounds

SOUND	RELATIVE AMPLITUDE	DECIBELS (DB)
Barely audible (threshold)	1	0
Leaves rustling	10	20
Quiet residential community	100	40
Average speaking voice	1,000	60
Express subway train	100,000	100
Propeller plane at takeoff	1,000,000	120
Jet engine at takeoff (pain threshold)	10,000,000	140

© Cengage Learning

TABLE 11.2 Common Logarithms

NUMBER	POWER OF 10	LOGARITHM
10	10^1	1
100	10^2	2
1,000	10^3	3
10,000	10^4	4

© Cengage Learning

you would need to make the sine wave several miles high! Since this is somewhat impractical, auditory researchers have devised a unit of sound called the **decibel (dB)**, which converts this large range of sound pressures into a more manageable scale.

METHOD
Using Decibels to Shrink Large Ranges of Pressures

The following equation is used for transforming sound pressure level into decibels:

$$dB = 20 \times \text{logarithm}\ (p/p_o)$$

The key term in this equation is "logarithm." Logarithms are often used in situations in which there are extremely large ranges. One example of a large range is provided by a classic animated film by Charles Eames (1977) called *Powers of Ten*. The first scene shows a person lying on a picnic blanket on a beach. The camera then zooms out, as if the person were being filmed from a spaceship taking off. The rate of zoom increases by a factor of 10 every 10 seconds, so the "spaceship's" speed and view increase extremely rapidly. From the 10 × 10 meter scene showing the man on the blanket the scene becomes 100 on a side, so Lake Michigan becomes visible, and as the camera speeds away at faster and faster rates, it reaches 10,000,000 meters, so the Earth is visible, and eventually 1,000 million million meters near the edge of the Milky Way. (The film actually continues to zoom out, until reaching the outer limits of the Universe. But we will stop here!)

When numbers become this huge, they become difficult to deal with, especially if they need to be plotted on a graph. Logarithms come to the rescue by converting numbers into exponents or powers. The logarithm of a number is the exponent to which the base, which is 10 for *common logarithms*, has to be raised to produce that number.[1] This is illustrated

in **Table 11.2**. The logarithm of 10 is 1 because the base, 10, has to be raised to the first power to equal 10. The logarithm of 100 is 2 because 10 has to be raised to the second power to equal 100. The main thing to take away from this table is that multiplying a number by 10 corresponds to an increase of just 1 log unit. A log scale, therefore, converts a huge and unmanageable range of numbers to a smaller range that is easier to deal with. Thus the increase in size from 1 to 1,000 million million that occurs as Charles Eames's spaceship zooms out to the edge of the Milky Way is converted into a more manageable scale of 14 log units. The range of sound pressures encountered in the environment, while not as astronomical as the range in Eames's film, ranges from 1 to 10,000,000, which in powers of 10 is a range of 7 log units.

Let's now return to our equation, $dB = 20 \times \text{logarithm}\ (p/p_o)$. According to this equation, decibels are 20 times the logarithm of a ratio of two pressures: p, the pressure of the sound we are considering; and p_o, the reference pressure, usually set at 20 micropascals, which is the pressure near hearing threshold for a 1,000-Hz tone. Let's consider this calculation for two sound pressures.

If the sound pressure, p, is 2,000 micropascals, then

$$dB = 20 \times \log(2,000/20) = 20 \times \log 100$$

The log of 100 is 2, so

$$dB = 20 \times 2 = 40$$

If the sound pressure, p, is 20,000 micropascals, then

$$dB = 20 \times \log(20,000/20) = 20 \times \log 1,000$$

The log of 1,000 is 3, so

$$dB = 20 \times 3 = 60$$

Notice that multiplying sound pressure by 10 causes an increase of 20 decibels. Thus, looking back at Table 11.1, we can see that when the sound pressure increases from 1 to 10,000,000, the decibels increase only from 0 to 140. This means that we don't have to deal with graphs that are several miles high!

When specifying the sound pressure in decibels, the notation **SPL**, for **sound pressure level**, is added to indicate that decibels were determined using the standard pressure p_o of 20 micropascals. In referring to the decibels or sound pressure of a sound stimulus, the term **level** or **sound level** is usually used.

[1]Other bases are used for different applications. For example, logarithms to the base 2, called binary logarithms, are used in computer science.

Complex Tones and Frequency Spectra

We have been using pure tones to illustrate frequency and amplitude. Pure tones are important because they are the fundamental building blocks of sounds, and pure tones have been used extensively in auditory research. Pure tones are, however, rare in the environment. As noted earlier, sounds in the environment, such as those produced by musical instruments or people speaking, have waveforms that are more complex than the pure tone's sine-wave pattern of pressure changes.

Figure 11.5a shows the pressure changes associated with a complex tone that would be created by a musical instrument. Notice that the waveform repeats (for example, the waveform in Figure 11.5a repeats four times). This property of repetition means that this complex tone, like a pure tone, is a **periodic tone**. From the time scale at the bottom of the figure, we see that the tone repeats four times in 20 msec. Because 20 msec is 20/1,000 sec = 1/50 sec, this means that the pattern for this tone repeats 200 times per second. That repetition rate is called the **fundamental frequency** of the tone.

Complex tones like the one in Figure 11.5a are made up of a number of pure tone (sine-wave) components added together. Each of these components is called a **harmonic** of the tone. The **first harmonic**, a pure tone with frequency equal to the fundamental frequency, is usually called the **fundamental** of the tone. The fundamental of this tone, shown in **Figure 11.5b**, has a frequency of 200 Hz, which matches the repetition rate of the complex tone.

Higher harmonics are pure tones with frequencies that are *whole-number* (2, 3, 4, etc.) multiples of the fundamental frequency. This means that the second harmonic of our complex tone has a frequency of $200 \times 2 = 400$ Hz. (**Figure 11.5c**), the third harmonic has a frequency of $200 \times 3 = 600$ Hz (**Figure 11.5d**), and so on. These additional tones are the higher harmonics of the tone. Adding the fundamental and the higher harmonics results in the waveform of the complex tone (that is, Figure 11.5a).

Another way to represent the harmonic components of a complex tone is by **frequency spectra**, shown on the right of Figure 11.5. Notice that the horizontal axis is *frequency*, not *time*, as is the case for the waveform plot on the left. The position of each line on the horizontal axis indicates the frequency of one of the tone's harmonics, and the height of the line indicates the harmonic's amplitude. Frequency spectra provide a way of indicating a complex tone's fundamental frequency and harmonics that add up to the tone's complex waveform.

Although a repeating sound wave is composed of harmonics with frequencies that are whole-number multiples of the fundamental frequency, not all the harmonics need to be present for the repetition rate to stay the same. **Figure 11.6** shows what happens if we remove the first harmonic of a complex tone. The tone in **Figure 11.6a** is the one from Figure 11.5a,

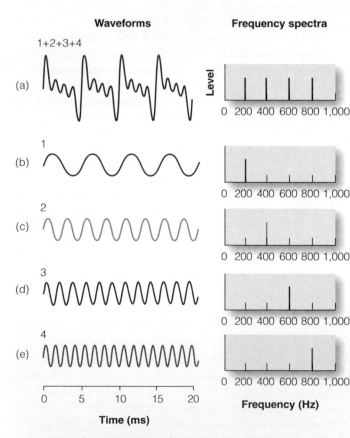

Waveforms   **Frequency spectra**

Figure 11.5 Left: Waveforms of (a) a complex periodic sound with a fundamental frequency of 200 Hz; (b) fundamental (first harmonic) = 200 Hz; (c) second harmonic = 400 Hz; (d) third harmonic = 600 Hz; (e) fourth harmonic = 800 Hz. Right: Frequency spectra for each of the tones on the left. Adapted from Plack, C. J. (2005). *The sense of hearing.* New York: Psychology Press.

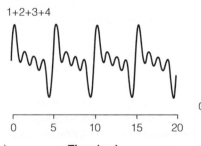

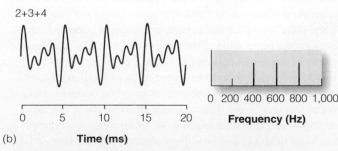

Figure 11.6 (a) The complex tone from Figure 11.5a and its frequency spectrum; (b) the same tone with its first harmonic removed. Adapted from Plack, C. J. (2005). *The sense of hearing.* New York: Psychology Press.

which has a fundamental frequency of 200 Hz. The tone in **Figure 11.6b** is the same tone with the first harmonic (200 Hz) removed, as indicated by the frequency spectrum on the right. Note that removing a harmonic changes the tone's waveform, but that the rate of repetition remains the same. Even though the fundamental is no longer present, the 200-Hz repetition rate corresponds to the frequency of the fundamental. The same effect also occurs when removing higher harmonics. Thus, if the 400-Hz harmonic is removed, the tone's waveform changes, but the repetition rate is still 200.

You may wonder why the repetition rate remains the same even though the fundamental or higher harmonics have been removed. Looking at the frequency spectra on the right, we can see that the spacing between harmonics equals the repetition rate. When the fundamental is removed, this spacing remains, so there is still information in the waveform indicating the frequency of the fundamental. In the next section, we will see that because a tone's pitch (perceiving the tone as "high" or "low") is related to repetition rate, the tone's pitch remains the same even if the fundamental is removed.

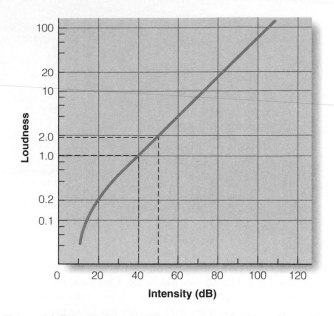

Figure 11.7 Loudness of a 100-Hz tone as a function of intensity, determined using magnitude estimation. Adapted from Gulick, W. L., Gescheider, G. A., & Frisina, R. D. (1989). *Hearing.* New York: Oxford University Press.

Perceptual Aspects of Sound

Our discussion so far has been focused on *physical aspects of the sound stimulus*. Everything we have described so far can be measured by a sound meter that registers pressure changes in the air. A person need not be present, as occurs in our example of a tree falling in the forest when no one is there to hear it. But now let's add a person (or an animal) and consider what people actually *hear*. We begin with thresholds and loudness.

Thresholds and Loudness

Two of the most basic questions about the perception of sound are "Can you hear it?" and "How loud does it sound?" These two questions come under the heading of thresholds (the smallest amount of sound energy that can just barely be detected) and loudness (the perceived intensity of a sound that ranges from "just audible" to "very loud"). **VL**

Loudness and Level Loudness is the perceptual quality most closely related to the *level* or *amplitude* of an auditory stimulus, which is expressed in decibels. Thus, decibels are often associated with loudness, as shown in Table 11.1, which indicates that a sound of 0 dB SPL is just barely detectible and 120 dB SPL is extremely loud (and can cause permanent damage to the receptors inside the ear).

The relationship between level in decibels (physical) and loudness (perceptual) was determined by S. S. Stevens, using the magnitude estimation procedure (see Chapter 1, page 15). **Figure 11.7** shows the relationship between decibels and loudness for a 1,000-Hz pure tone. In this experiment, loudness

was judged relative to a 40 dB SPL tone, which was assigned a value of 1. Thus, a pure tone that sounds 10 times louder than the 40 dB SPL tone would be judged to have a loudness of 10. The dashed lines indicate that increasing the sound level by 10 dB (from 40 to 50) almost doubles the sound's loudness.

It would be tempting to conclude from Table 11.1 and the curve in Figure 11.7 that "higher decibels" equals greater loudness. But it isn't quite that simple, because thresholds and loudness depend not only on decibels but also on frequency. One way to appreciate the importance of frequency in the perception of loudness is to consider the *audibility curve*.

Thresholds Across the Frequency Range: The Audibility Curve A basic fact about hearing is that we only hear within a specific range of frequencies. This means that there are some frequencies we can't hear, and that even within the range of frequencies we can hear, some are easier to hear than others. Some frequencies have low thresholds—it takes very little sound pressure change to hear them—and other frequencies have high thresholds—large changes in sound pressure are needed to make them heard. This is illustrated by the curve in **Figure 11.8**, called the **audibility curve**. This audibility curve, which indicates the threshold for hearing versus frequency, indicates that we can hear sounds between about 20 Hz and 20,000 Hz and that we are most sensitive (the threshold for hearing is lowest) at frequencies between 2,000 and 4,000 Hz, which happens to be the range of frequencies that is most important for understanding speech. **VL**

The light green area above the audibility curve is called the **auditory response area** because we can hear tones that fall within this area. At intensities below the audibility curve, we can't hear a tone. For example, we wouldn't be able to hear a 30-Hz tone at 40 dB SPL (point A). The upper boundary of

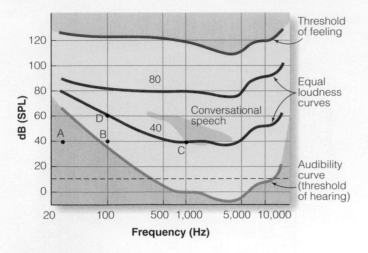

Figure 11.8 The audibility curve and the auditory response area. Hearing occurs in the light green area between the audibility curve (the threshold for hearing) and the upper curve (the threshold for feeling). Tones with combinations of dB and frequency that place them in the light red area below the audibility curve cannot be heard. Tones above the threshold of feeling result in pain. The frequencies between the places where the dashed line at 10 dB crosses the audibility function indicate which frequencies can be heard at 10 dB SPL. From Fletcher, H., & Munson, W. A. (1933). Loudness: Its definition, measurement, and calculation. *Journal of the Acoustical Society of America, 5*, 82–108. Reproduced by permission.

the auditory response area is the curve marked "threshold of feeling." Tones with these high amplitudes are the ones we can "feel"; they can become painful and can cause damage to the auditory system. Although humans hear frequencies between about 20 Hz and 20,000 Hz, other animals can hear frequencies outside the range of human hearing. Elephants can hear stimuli below 20 Hz. Above the high end of the human range, dogs can hear frequencies above 40,000 Hz, cats can hear above 50,000 Hz, and the upper range for dolphins extends as high as 150,000 Hz.

But what happens between the audibility curve and the threshold of feeling? To answer this question, we can pick any frequency and select a point such as point B that is just slightly above the audibility curve. Because that point is just above threshold, it will sound very soft. However, as we increase the level, as we did for the 1,000-Hz tone in Figure 11.7, the loudness increases. Thus, each frequency has a threshold or "baseline"—the decibels at which it can just barely be heard, as indicated by the audibility curve—and loudness increases as we increase the level above this baseline.

Another way to understand the relationship between loudness and frequency is by looking at the red **equal loudness curves** in Figure 11.8. These curves indicate the sound levels that create the same perception of loudness at different frequencies. An equal loudness curve is determined by presenting a standard pure tone of one frequency and level and having a listener adjust the level of pure tones with frequencies across the range of hearing to match the loudness of the standard. For example, the curve marked 40 in Figure 11.8 was determined by matching the loudness of frequencies across the range of hearing to the loudness of a 1,000-Hz

40-dB SPL tone (point C). This means that a 100-Hz tone needs to be played at 60 dB (point D) to sound the same loudness as the 1,000-Hz tone at 40 dB.

Notice that the audibility curve and the equal loudness curve marked 40 bend up at high and low frequencies, but the equal loudness curve marked 80 is almost flat between 30 and 5,000 Hz, meaning that tones at a level of 80 dB SPL are roughly equally loud between these frequencies. Thus, at threshold, the level can be very different for different frequencies, but at some level above threshold, different frequencies can have a similar loudness at the same decibel level.

The difference between the upward-bending curves at threshold and at the lower decibel levels and the relatively flat curves such as the one at 80 dB SL explains something that happens as you adjust the volume control on your music player. If you are playing music at a fairly high level—say, 80 dB SPL—you should be able to easily hear each of the frequencies in the music because, as the equal loudness curve for 80 indicates, all frequencies between about 30 Hz and 5,000 Hz sound equally loud at this level. If, however, you turn the level down to 10 dB SPL, all frequencies don't sound equally loud. In fact, if you look at the horizontal dashed line at 10 dB, you can see that the line is in the red area at frequencies below about 400 Hz, and above about 12,000 Hz. This means that frequencies lower than 400 Hz and higher than 12,000 Hz are not audible at 10 dB SPL.

Being unable to hear very low and very high frequencies at low dB levels means that when you play music softly you won't hear the very low or very high frequencies. To compensate for this, some music players have a setting called "loudness" that boosts the level of very high and very low frequencies when the volume control is turned down. This enables you to hear these frequencies even when the music is soft.

Pitch

Pitch, the perceptual quality we describe as "high" or "low," can be defined as *the property of auditory sensation in terms of which sounds may be ordered on a musical scale* (Bendor & Wang, 2005). While often associated with music, pitch is also a property of speech (low-pitched or high-pitched voice) and other natural sounds.

Pitch is most closely related to the physical property of fundamental frequency (the repetition rate of the sound waveform). Low fundamental frequencies are associated with low pitches (like the sound of a tuba), and high fundamental frequencies are associated with high pitches (like the sound of a piccolo). However, remember that pitch is a psychological, not a physical, property of sound. So pitch can't be measured in a physical way. For example, it isn't correct to say that a sound has a "pitch of 200 Hz." Instead we say that a particular sound has a low pitch or a high pitch, based on how we *perceive* it.

One way to think about pitch is in terms of a piano keyboard. Hitting a key on the left of the keyboard creates

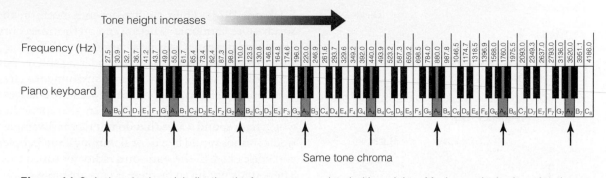

Figure 11.9 A piano keyboard, indicating the frequency associated with each key. Moving up the keyboard to the right increases frequency and tone height. Notes with the same letter, like the A's (arrows), have the same tone chroma.

© Cengage Learning

a low-pitched rumbling "bass" tone; moving up the keyboard creates higher and higher pitches, until tones on the far right are high-pitched and might be described as "tinkly." The *physical* property that is related to this low to high perceptual experience is *frequency*, with the lowest note on the piano having a fundamental frequency of 27.5 Hz and the highest note 4,166 Hz (**Figure 11.9**). The perceptual experience of increasing pitch that accompanies increases in a tone's fundamental frequency is called **tone height**. **VL**

In addition to the increase in tone height that occurs as we move from the low to the high end of the piano keyboard, something else happens: the letters of the notes A, B, C, D, E, F, and G repeat, and we notice that notes with the same letter sound similar. Because of this similarity, we say that notes with the same letter have the same **tone chroma**. Every time we pass the same letter on the keyboard, we have gone up an interval called an **octave**. Tones separated by octaves have the same tone chroma. For example, each of the A's in Figure 11.9, indicated by the arrows, has the same tone chroma.

Notes with the same chroma have fundamental frequencies that are whole-number multiples of one another. Thus, A_1 has a fundamental frequency of 27.5 Hz, A_2's is 55 Hz, A_3's is 110 Hz, and so on. This doubling of frequency for each octave results in similar perceptual experiences. Thus, a male with a low-pitched voice and a female with a high-pitched voice can be regarded as singing "in unison," even when their voices are separated by an octave or more.

While the connection between pitch and fundamental frequency is nicely illustrated by the piano keyboard, there is more to the story than fundamental frequency. As we saw in Figures 11.5 and 11.6a, complex tones like those produced by the piano (or any other instrument) contain a number of harmonics. We also saw that when the fundamental frequency is removed, as in Figure 11.6b, the repetition rate of the tone remains the same. One consequence of this constancy of the repetition rate is that removing the fundamental frequency or a higher-order harmonic from the tone does not affect perception of the tone's pitch.

The constancy of pitch, even when the fundamental or other harmonics are removed, is called the **effect of the missing fundamental**, and the pitch that we perceive in tones that have harmonics removed is called **periodicity pitch**.

The term *periodicity pitch* indicates that pitch is determined by the *period* or *repetition rate* of the sound waveform. Pitch, therefore, is determined not by the *presence* of the fundamental frequency, but by information, such as the spacing of the harmonics and the repetition rate of the waveform, that is related to the fundamental frequency.

The phenomenon of periodicity pitch has practical consequences. Consider, for example, what happens when you listen to someone talking to you on the telephone. Even though the telephone does not reproduce frequencies below about 300 Hz, we can hear the low pitch of a male voice that corresponds to a 100-Hz fundamental frequency because of periodicity pitch created by the higher harmonics (Truax, 1984). **VL**

Timbre

In our discussion of periodicity pitch, we saw that removing harmonics does not affect the perception of pitch. But while pitch stays the same, another perceptual quality, the tone's **timbre** (pronounced TIM-ber or TAM-ber), does change. Timbre is the quality that distinguishes between two tones that have the same loudness, pitch, and duration, but still sound different. For example, when a flute and an oboe play the same note with the same loudness, we can still tell the difference between these two instruments. We might describe the sound of the flute as *clear* and the sound of the oboe as *reedy*. When two tones have the same loudness, pitch, and duration, but sound different, this difference is a difference in timbre.

Timbre is closely related to the harmonic structure of a tone. In **Figure 11.10**, frequency spectra indicate the harmonics of a guitar, a bassoon, and an alto saxophone playing the note G_3 with a fundamental frequency of 196 Hz. Both the relative strengths of the harmonics and the number of harmonics are different in these instruments. For example, the guitar has more high-frequency harmonics than either the bassoon or the alto saxophone. Although the frequencies of the harmonics are always multiples of the fundamental frequency, harmonics may be absent, as is true of some of the high-frequency harmonics of the bassoon and the alto

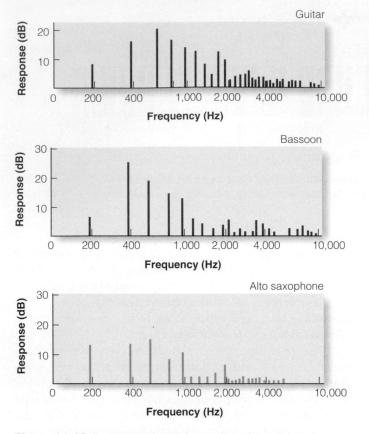

Figure 11.10 Frequency spectra for a guitar, a bassoon, and an alto saxophone playing a tone with a fundamental frequency of 196 Hz. The position of the lines on the horizontal axis indicates the frequencies of the harmonics and their height indicates their intensities. From Olson, H. (1967). *Music, physics, and engineering* (2nd ed.). New York: Dover. Reproduced by permission.

saxophone. It is also easy to notice differences in the timbre of people's voices. When we describe one person's voice as sounding "nasal" and another's as being "mellow," we are referring to the timbres of their voices. **VL**

The difference in the harmonics of different instruments is not the only factor that causes musical instruments to have different timbres. Timbre also depends on the time course of a tone's **attack** (the buildup of sound at the beginning of the tone) and of the tone's **decay** (the decrease in sound at the end of the tone). Thus, it is easy to tell the difference between a tape recording of a high note played on a clarinet and a recording of the same note played on a flute when the attack, the sustained portion, and the decay of the tone are heard. It is difficult, however, to distinguish between the same instruments when the tone's attack and decay are eliminated by erasing the first and last 1/2 second of the recording (Berger, 1964; also see Risset & Mathews, 1969).

Another way to make it difficult to distinguish one instrument from another is to play an instrument's tone backward. Even though this does not affect the tone's harmonic structure, a piano tone played backward sounds more like an organ than a piano because the tone's original decay has become the attack and the attack has become the decay (Berger, 1964;

Erickson, 1975). Thus, timbre depends both on the tone's steady-state harmonic structure and on the time course of the attack and decay of the tone's harmonics. **VL**

The sounds we have been considering so far—pure tones and the tones produced by musical instruments—are all periodic sounds. That is, the pattern of pressure changes repeats, as in the tone in Figure 11.5a. There are also aperiodic sounds, which have sound waves that do not repeat. Examples of aperiodic sounds would be a door slamming shut, people talking, and noises such as the static on a radio not tuned to a station. The sounds produced by these events are more complex than musical tones, but all of these sound stimuli can also be analyzed into a number of simpler frequency components. We will describe how we perceive speech stimuli in Chapter 13. We will focus in this chapter on pure tones and musical tones because these sounds are the ones that have been used in most of the basic research on the operation of the auditory system. In the next section, we will begin considering how the sound stimuli we have been describing are processed by the auditory system so that we can experience sound.

TEST YOURSELF 11.1

1. What are some of the functions of sound? Especially note what information sound provides that is not provided by vision.

2. What are two possible definitions of sound? (Remember the tree falling in the forest.)

3. How is the sound stimulus described in terms of pressure changes in the air? What is a pure tone? sound frequency?

4. What is the amplitude of a sound? Why was the decibel scale developed to measure amplitude? Is decibel "perceptual" or "physical"?

5. What is the relationship between sound level and loudness? Which one is physical, and which one is perceptual?

6. What is the audibility curve, and what does it tell us about the relationship between a tone's physical characteristics (level and frequency) and perceptual characteristics (threshold and loudness)?

7. What are tone height and tone chroma?

8. What is timbre? Describe the characteristics of complex tones and how these characteristics determine timbre.

From Pressure Changes to Electricity

Now that we have described the stimuli and their perceptual effects, we are ready to begin describing what happens inside the ear. What we will be describing in this next part of our story is a journey that begins as sound enters the ear and culminates deep inside the ear at the receptors for hearing.

The auditory system accomplishes three basic tasks during this journey. First, it delivers the sound stimulus to the receptors. Second, it transduces this stimulus from pressure changes into electrical signals. Third, it processes these electrical signals so they can indicate qualities of the sound source such as pitch, loudness, timbre, and location.

As we describe this journey, we will follow the sound stimulus through a complex labyrinth on its way to the receptors. But this is not simply a matter of sound moving through one dark tunnel after another. It is a journey in which sound sets structures along the pathway into vibration and these vibrations are transmitted from one structure to another, starting with the eardrum at the beginning and ending with the vibration of small hairlike receptors for hearing deep within the ear. The ear is divided into three divisions: outer, middle, and inner. We begin with the outer ear.

The Outer Ear

When we talk about ears in everyday conversation, we are usually referring to the **pinnae**, the structures that stick out from the sides of the head. Although this most obvious part of the ear is important in helping us determine the location of sounds and is of great importance for those who wear eyeglasses, it is the part of the ear we could most easily do without. Van Gogh did *not* make himself deaf in his left ear when he attacked his pinna with a razor in 1888. The major workings of the ear are found within the head, hidden from view.

Sound waves first pass through the **outer ear**, which consists of the pinna and the **auditory canal** (**Figure 11.11**). The auditory canal is a tubelike structure, about 3 cm long in adults, that protects the delicate structures of the middle ear from the hazards of the outside world. The auditory canal's 3-cm recess, along with its wax, protects the delicate **tympanic membrane**, or **eardrum**, at the end of the canal and helps keep this membrane and the structures in the middle ear at a relatively constant temperature.

In addition to its protective function, the outer ear has another effect: to enhance the intensities of some sounds by means of the physical principle of resonance. **Resonance** occurs in the auditory canal when sound waves that are reflected back from the closed end of the auditory canal interact with sound waves that are entering the canal. This interaction reinforces some of the sound's frequencies, with the frequency that is reinforced the most being determined by the length of the canal. The frequency reinforced the most is called the **resonant frequency** of the canal.

Measurements of the sound pressures inside the ear indicate that the resonance that occurs in the auditory canal has a slight amplifying effect that increases the sound pressure level of frequencies between about 1,000 and 5,000 Hz, which, as we can see from the audibility curve in Figure 11.8, covers the most sensitive range of human hearing.

The Middle Ear

When airborne sound waves reach the tympanic membrane at the end of the auditory canal, they set it into vibration, and this vibration is transmitted to structures in the middle ear, on the other side of the tympanic membrane. The **middle ear** is a small cavity, about 2 cubic centimeters in volume, that separates the outer and inner ears (**Figure 11.12**). This cavity contains the **ossicles**, the three smallest bones in the body. The first of these bones, the **malleus** (also known as the *hammer*), is set into vibration by the tympanic membrane, to which it is attached, and transmits its vibrations to the **incus** (or *anvil*), which, in turn, transmits its vibrations to the **stapes** (or *stirrup*). The stapes then transmits its vibrations to the inner ear by pushing on the membrane covering the **oval window**.

Why are the ossicles necessary? We can answer this question by noting that both the outer ear and middle ear are filled with air, but the inner ear contains a watery liquid that is much denser than the air (**Figure 11.13**). The mismatch between the low density of the air and the high density of this

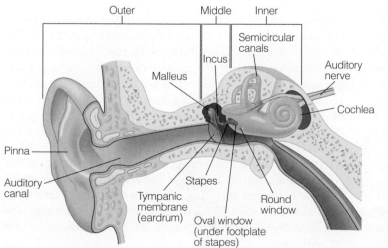

Figure 11.11 The ear, showing its three subdivisions—outer, middle, and inner. From Lindsay, P. H., & Norman, D. A. (1977). *Human information processing* (2nd ed.). New York: Academic Press. Redrawn by permission.

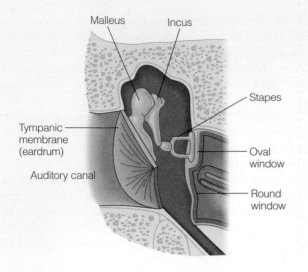

Figure 11.12 The middle ear. The three bones of the middle ear transmit the vibrations of the tympanic membrane to the inner ear.
© Cengage Learning

Air	Air	Cochlear fluid
Outer	Middle	Inner

Figure 11.13 Environments inside the outer, middle, and inner ears. The fact that liquid fills the inner ear poses a problem for the transmission of sound vibrations from the air of the middle ear. © Cengage Learning

liquid creates a problem: pressure changes in the air are transmitted poorly to the much denser liquid. This mismatch is illustrated by the difficulty you would have hearing people talking to you if you were underwater and they were above the surface.

If vibrations had to pass directly from the air in the middle ear to the liquid in the inner ear, less than 1 percent of the vibrations would be transmitted (Durrant & Lovrinic, 1977). The ossicles help solve this problem in two ways: (1) by concentrating the vibration of the large tympanic membrane onto the much smaller stapes, which increases the pressure by a factor of about 20 (**Figure 11.14a**); and (2) by being hinged to create a lever action—an effect similar to what happens when a fulcrum is placed under a board, so that pushing down on the long end of the board makes it possible to lift a heavy weight on the short end (**Figure 11.14b**). We can appreciate the effect of the ossicles by noting that in patients whose ossicles have been damaged beyond surgical repair, it is necessary to increase the sound level by a factor of 10 to 50 to achieve the same hearing as when the ossicles were functioning (Bess & Humes, 2008).

Not all animals require the concentration of pressure and lever effect provided by the ossicles in the human ear. For example, there is only a small mismatch between the density of water, which transmits sound in a fish's environment, and the liquid inside the fish's ear. Thus, fish have no outer or middle ear.

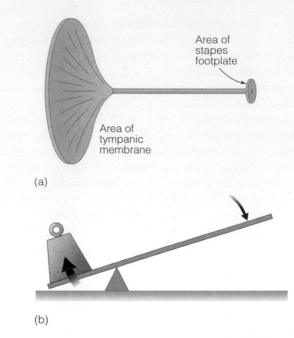

Figure 11.14 (a) A diagrammatic representation of the tympanic membrane and the stapes, showing the difference in size between the two. (b) How lever action can amplify a small force, presented on the right, to lift the large weight on the left. The lever action of the ossicles amplifies the sound vibrations reaching the tympanic inner ear. From Schubert, E. D. (1980). *Hearing: Its function and dysfunction.* Wien: Springer-Verlag. Reproduced by permission.

The middle ear also contains the **middle-ear muscles**, the smallest skeletal muscles in the body. These muscles are attached to the ossicles, and at very high sound levels they contract to dampen the ossicles' vibration. This reduces the transmission of low-frequency sounds and helps to prevent intense low-frequency components from interfering with our perception of high frequencies. In particular, contraction of the muscles may prevent our own vocalizations, and sounds from chewing, from interfering with our perception of speech from other people—an important function in a noisy restaurant!

The Inner Ear

The main structure of the **inner ear** is the liquid-filled **cochlea**, the snail-like structure shown in green in Figure 11.11, and shown partially uncoiled in **Figure 11.15a**. The liquid inside the cochlea is set into vibration by the movement of the stapes against the oval window. **Figure 11.15b** shows the cochlea completely uncoiled to form a long straight tube. The most obvious feature of the uncoiled cochlea is that the upper half, called the *scala vestibuli*, and the lower half, called the *scala tympani*, are separated by a structure called the **cochlear partition**. This partition extends almost the entire length of the cochlea, from its **base** near the stapes to its **apex** at the far end. Note that this diagram is not drawn to scale and so does not show the cochlea's true proportions. In reality, the uncoiled cochlea would be a cylinder 2 mm in diameter and 35 mm long.

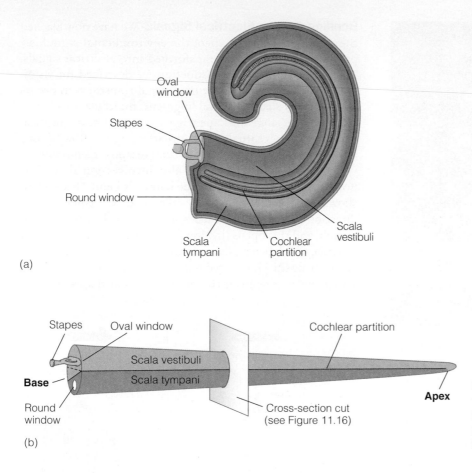

Oval window

Stapes

Round window

Scala tympani

Cochlear partition

Scala vestibuli

(a)

Stapes   Oval window

Cochlear partition

Scala vestibuli

Base   Scala tympani

Round window

Cross-section cut (see Figure 11.16)

Apex

(b)

Figure 11.15 (a) A partially uncoiled cochlea. (b) A fully uncoiled cochlea. The cochlear partition, which is indicated here by a line, actually contains the basilar membrane and the organ of Corti, as shown in Figure 11.16. © Cengage Learning

Although the cochlear partition is indicated by a thin line in Figure 11.15b, it is actually relatively large and contains the structures that transform the vibrations inside the cochlea into electricity. We can see the structures within the cochlear partition by taking a cross section cut of the cochlea, as shown in Figure 11.15b, and looking at the cochlea end-on and in cross section, as in **Figure 11.16a**. When we look at the cochlea in this way, we see the **organ of Corti**, which contains the **hair cells**, the receptors for hearing. In addition,

we see two membranes, the **basilar membrane** and the **tectorial membrane,** which play crucial roles in activating the hair cells.

The Hair Cells and Two Membranes The hair cells are shown in red in **Figure 11.16b**. **Figure 11.17** shows **cilia**, thin processes that protrude from the tops of the hair cells, which bend in response to pressure changes. The two types of hair cells, the **inner hair cells** and the **outer hair cells**, are located

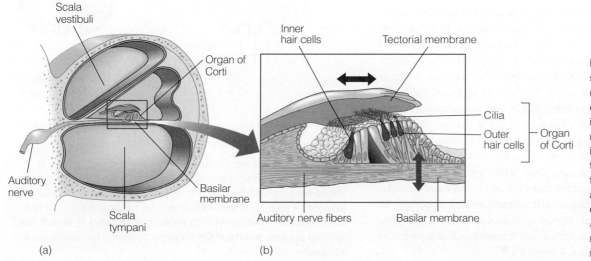

Figure 11.16 (a) Cross-section of the cochlea. (b) Close-up of the organ of Corti, showing how it rests on the basilar membrane. Arrows indicate the motions of the basilar membrane and tectorial membrane that are caused by vibration of the cochlear partition.

Adapted from Denes, P. B., & Pinson, E. N. (1993). *The speech chain* (2nd ed.). New York: Freeman.

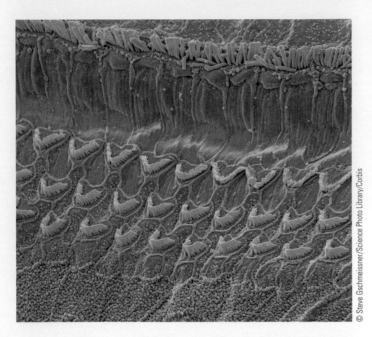

Figure 11.17 Scanning electron micrograph showing inner hair cells (top) and the three rows of outer hair cells (bottom). The hair cells have been colored to stand out.

in different places on the organ of Corti (see Figure 11.16). The human ear contains one row of inner hair cells and about three rows of outer hair cells, with about 3,500 inner hair cells and 12,000 outer hair cells in all (Møller, 2000). It is important to remember that Figures 11.16 and 11.17 are pictures of one place on the organ of Corti, but, as shown in Figure 11.15, the cochlear partition, which contains the organ of Corti, extends the entire length of the cochlea. There are, therefore, hair cells from one end of the cochlea to the other. The tallest row of cilia on the outer hair cells is in contact with the tectorial membrane. The cilia on the inner hair cells, however, are not in contact with the tectorial membrane.

Vibrations Bend the Hair Cells The scene we have described—the organ of Corti sitting on the basilar membrane, with the tectorial membrane arching over the hair cells—is the staging ground for events that occur when vibration of the stapes in the middle ear sets the oval window into motion. The back and forth motion of the oval window transmits vibrations to the liquid inside the cochlea, which sets the basilar membrane into motion (blue arrow in Figure 11.16b). The up-and-down motion of the basilar membrane has two results: (1) it sets the organ of Corti into an up-and-down vibration, and (2) it causes the tectorial membrane to move back and forth, as shown by the red arrow. These two motions mean that the tectorial membrane slides back and forward just above the inner hair cells. The result of this vibration is that the cilia of the hair cells bend—this is because, in the case of the outer hair cells, they are in contact with the tectorial membrane and because, in the case of the inner hair cells, of the pressure waves in the liquid surrounding the cilia (Dallos, 1996). **VL**

Bending Causes Electrical Signals We have now reached the point in our story where the environmental stimulus—pressure waves—become transformed into electrical signals. This is the process of transduction we described for vision in Chapter 2, where we saw that visual transduction occurs when light causes a visual pigment molecule to change shape. This change in shape triggers a sequence of chemical reactions that eventually ends up affecting the flow of ions (charged molecules) across the visual receptor membrane.

Transduction for hearing also involves ion flow. This flow occurs when the cilia of the hair cells bend. **Figure 11.18** shows what happens when the cilia bend. Movement in one direction (**Figure 11.18a**) causes structures called **tip links** to stretch, and this opens tiny ion channels in the membrane of the cilia, which behave like trapdoors. When the ion channels are open, positively charged potassium ions flow into the cell. When the cilia bend in the other direction (**Figure 11.18b**),

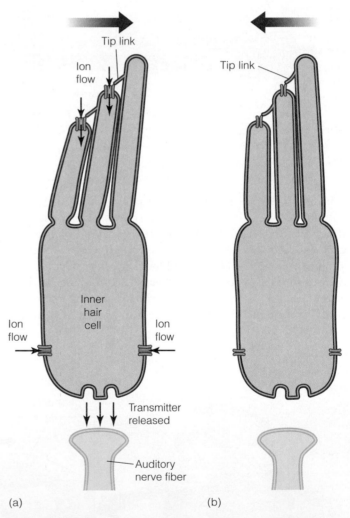

(a)   (b)

Figure 11.18 (a) How movement of the hair cell cilia causes an electrical change in the hair cell. When the cilia are bent to the right, the tip links are stretched and ion channels are opened. Positively charged potassium ions (K+) enter the cell, causing the interior of the cell to become more positive. (b) When the cilia move to the left, the tip links slacken, and the channels close. Based on Plack, C. J. (2005). *The sense of hearing.* New York: Psychology Press.

the tip links slacken and the ion channels close, so electrical signals are not generated. Thus, the back-and-forth bending of the hair cells causes alternating bursts of electrical signals (when the cilia bend in one direction) and no electrical signals (when the cilia bend in the opposite direction). The electrical signals result in the release of neurotransmitters, which diffuse across the synapse separating the inner hair cells from the auditory nerve fibers and cause these auditory nerve fibers to fire.

The Sound's Frequency Determines the Timing of the Electrical Signals

Now that we understand how transduction occurs, we can see how the electrical signals created by the hair cells are related to the frequency of a tone. **Figure 11.19** shows how the bending of the cilia follows the increases and decreases of the pressure of a pure-tone sound stimulus. When the pressure increases, the cilia bend to the right, the hair cell is activated, and attached auditory nerve fibers will tend to fire. When the pressure decreases, the cilia bend to the left, and no firing occurs. This means that auditory nerve fibers fire in synchrony with the rising and falling pressure of the pure tone.

This property of firing at the same place in the sound stimulus is called **phase locking**. For high-frequency tones, a nerve fiber may not fire every time the pressure changes because it needs to rest after it fires (see *refractory period*, Chapter 2, page 37). But when the fiber does fire, it fires at the same time in the sound stimulus, as shown in **Figure 11.20a** and **b**. Since many fibers respond to the tone, it is likely that if some "miss" a particular pressure change, other fibers will be firing at that time. Therefore, when we combine the response of many fibers, each of which fires at the peak of the sound wave, the overall firing matches the frequency of the sound stimulus, as shown in **Figure 11.20c**.

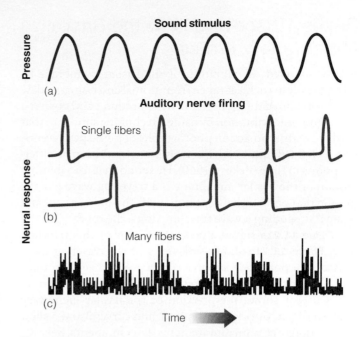

Figure 11.20 (a) Pressure changes for a 250-Hz tone. (b) Pattern of nerve spikes produced by two separate nerve fibers. Notice that the spikes always occur at the peak of the pressure wave. (c) The combined spikes produced by 500 nerve fibers. Although there is some variability in the single neuron response, the response of the large group of neurons represents the periodicity of the 250-Hz tone.

Based on Plack, C. J. (2005). *The sense of hearing.* New York: Psychology Press.

The connection between the frequency of a sound stimulus and the timing of the auditory nerve fiber firing is called **temporal coding**. Measurements of the pattern of firing for auditory nerve fibers indicate that phase locking occurs up to a frequency of about 5,000 Hz.

Now that we have described the connection between frequency and nerve firing, it might seem that the problem of how the auditory stimulus is represented by nerve firing has been solved. But so far we have told only part of the story, because we have confined our view to one place along the organ of Corti. Sitting at this single location, we have seen how the opening and closing of ion channels and the firing of the auditory nerve fibers match the frequency of a sound. But to fully understand the connection between frequency and nerve firing, we need to expand our view to consider how the basilar membrane, and the organ of Corti along with it, vibrates along its entire length, which extends from the base to the apex of the cochlea.

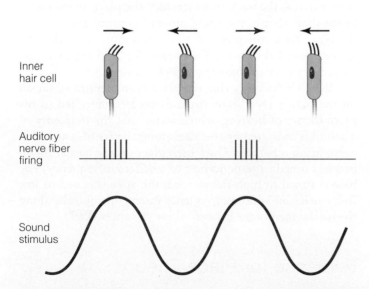

Figure 11.19 How hair cell activation and auditory nerve fiber firing are synchronized with pressure changes of the stimulus. The auditory nerve fiber fires when the cilia are bent to the right. This occurs at the peak of the sine-wave change in pressure. © Cengage Learning

Vibration of the Basilar Membrane

How does the basilar membrane vibrate? This question was answered by Georg von Békésy, who won the Nobel Prize in physiology and medicine in 1961 for his research on the physiology of hearing.

Békésy Discovers How the Basilar Membrane Vibrates

Békésy observed the vibration of the basilar membrane by boring a hole in cochleas taken from animal and human cadavers. He presented different frequencies of sound and observed the membrane's vibration by using a technique similar to that used to create stop-action photographs of high-speed events, which enabled him to see the membrane's position at different points in time (Békésy, 1960). He found that the vibrating motion of the basilar membrane is a **traveling wave** like the motion that occurs when a person holds the end of a rope and "snaps" it, sending a wave traveling down the rope.

Figure 11.21a shows a perspective view of this traveling wave. **Figure 11.21b** shows side views of the traveling wave, caused by a pure tone at three successive moments in time. The solid horizontal line represents the basilar membrane at rest. Curve 1 shows the position of the basilar membrane at one moment during its vibration, and curves 2 and 3 show the positions of the membrane at two later moments. Békésy's measurements showed that most of the membrane vibrates, but that some parts vibrate more than others.

Although the motion takes the form of a traveling wave, the important thing is what happens at particular points along the membrane. If you were at one point, what would you see? You would see the membrane vibrating up and down at the frequency of the tone. This up-and-down vibration occurs all along the membrane. However, the place along the membrane that vibrates the most depends on the frequency of the tone. This relationship between frequency and how different places along the membrane vibrate is shown in **Figure 11.22**. The arrows indicate the extent of the

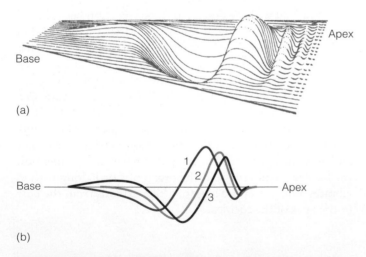

(a)

(b)

Figure 11.21 (a) A traveling wave like the one observed by Békésy. This picture shows what the membrane looks like when the vibration is "frozen" with the wave about two-thirds of the way down the membrane. (b) Side views of the traveling wave caused by a pure tone, showing the position of the membrane at three instants in time as the wave moves from the base to the apex of the cochlear partition. (a) Adapted from Tonndorf, J. (1960). Shearing motion in scalia media of cochlear models. *Journal of the Acoustical Society of America, 32*, 238–244. Reproduced by permission. (b) Adapted from Békésy, G. von (1960). *Experiments in hearing*. New York: McGraw-Hill. Reproduced by permission.

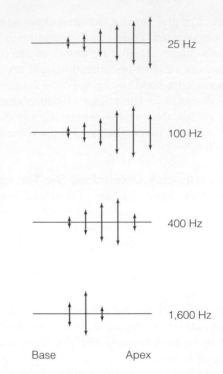

Figure 11.22 The amount of vibration at different locations along the basilar membrane is indicated by the size of the arrows at each location, with the place of maximum vibration indicated in red. When the frequency is 25 Hz, maximum vibration occurs at the apex of the cochlear partition. As the frequency is increased, the location of the maximum vibration moves toward the base of the cochlear partition. Based on data in Békésy, G. von (1960). *Experiments in hearing*. New York: McGraw-Hill.

up-and-down displacement of the membrane at different places on the membrane. The red arrows indicate the place where the membrane vibrates the most for each frequency. Notice that as the frequency increases, the place on the membrane that vibrates the most moves from the apex toward the base. Thus, the place of maximum vibration, which is at the apex of the basilar membrane for a 25-Hz tone, has moved to nearer the base for a 1,600-Hz tone.

Békésy's discovery that the place of maximum vibration on the basilar membrane depends on frequency led to his **place theory of hearing**, which states that the frequency of a sound is indicated by the *place* along the cochlea at which nerve firing is highest. Thus, each place on the basilar membrane is tuned to respond best to a different frequency. The base is tuned to high frequencies, the apex is tuned to low frequencies, and the best frequency varies continuously along the basilar membrane between these extremes. **VL**

Evidence for Place Theory

Békésy's linking of the place on the cochlea with the frequency of a tone has been confirmed by measuring the electrical response at different places along the cochlea. Placing disc electrodes at different places along the length of the cochlea

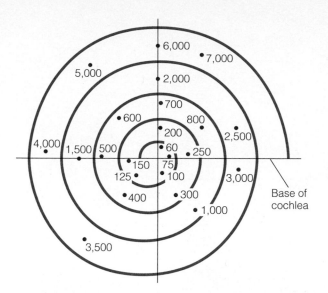

Figure 11.23 Tonotopic map of the guinea pig cochlea. Numbers indicate the location of the maximum electrical response for each frequency. From Culler, E. A., Coakley, J. D., Lowy, K., & Gross, N. A revised frequency map of the Guinea pig cochlea. *American Journal of Psychology, 56,* 1943, 475–500, figure 11. Copyright © 1943 by the Board of Trustees of the University of Illinois. Used with the permission of the author and the University of Illinois.

and measuring the electrical response to different frequencies results in a **tonotopic map**—an orderly map of frequencies along the length of the cochlea (Culler et al., 1943). This result, shown in **Figure 11.23**, confirms the idea that the apex of the cochlea responds best to low frequencies and the base responds best to high frequencies. More precise electrophysiological evidence for place coding is provided by determining neural tuning curves for auditory nerve fibers that signal activity at different places on the cochlea.

METHOD
Neural Frequency Tuning Curves

Each hair cell and auditory nerve fiber responds to a narrow range of frequencies. This range is indicated by each neuron's frequency tuning curve. This curve is determined by presenting pure tones of different frequencies and measuring the sound level necessary to cause the neuron to increase its firing above the baseline or "spontaneous" rate in the absence of sounds. This level is the threshold for that frequency. Plotting the threshold for each frequency results in frequency tuning curves like the ones in **Figure 11.24**. The arrow under each curve indicates the frequency to which the neuron is most sensitive. This frequency is called the **characteristic frequency** of the particular auditory nerve fiber.

The frequency tuning curves in Figure 11.24 were recorded from auditory nerve fibers attached to inner hair cells at different places along the cochlea. As we would expect from Békésy's place theory, the fibers originating near the base of the cochlea have high characteristic frequencies, and those originating near the apex have low characteristic frequencies. Only a small proportion of the total tuning curves are presented in Figure 11.24. In reality, each of the 3,500 inner hair cells has its own tuning curve, so every frequency is represented by a number of neurons that respond best to that frequency.

A Practical Application

An important practical application of Békésy's discovery that each place on the basilar membrane is associated with a particular frequency is the development of a device called a **cochlear implant**, shown in **Figure 11.25**, which is used to create hearing in people with deafness caused by damage to the hair cells in the cochlea. When the hair cells are damaged, hearing aids are ineffective because the damaged hair cells cannot convert the amplified sound provided by the hearing aid into electrical signals. As shown in Figure 11.25, the cochlear implant consists of (1) a microphone that receives sound signals from the environment; (2) a sound processor that divides the sound received by the microphone into a number of frequency bands; (3) a transmitter that sends these signals to (4) an array of 22 electrodes that are implanted along the length of the cochlea. These electrodes stimulate the cochlea at different places along its length, depending

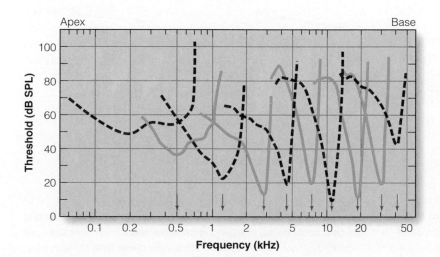

Figure 11.24 Frequency tuning curves of cat auditory nerve fibers. The characteristic frequency of each fiber is indicated by the arrows along the frequency axis. The frequency scale is in kilohertz (kHz), where 1 kHz = 1,000 Hz. From Palmer, A. R. Physiology of the cochlear nerve and cochlear nucleus. *British Medical Bulletin on Hearing, 43,* 1987, 838–855, by permission of Oxford University Press.

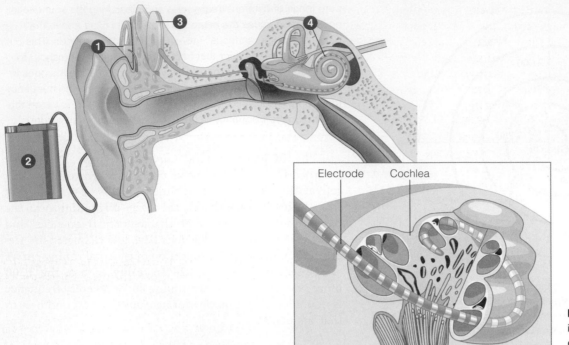

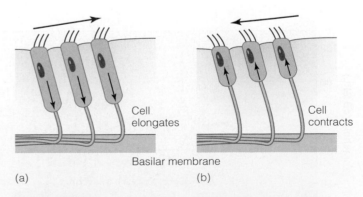

Figure 11.25 Cochlear implant device. See text for details. © Cengage Learning

on the intensities of the frequencies in the stimuli received by the microphone. This stimulation activates auditory nerve fibers along the cochlea, which send signals toward the brain. The hearing that results enables people to recognize everyday sounds such as horns honking, doors closing, water running, and in some cases, speech. **VL**

The development of the cochlear implant is an impressive demonstration of how basic research yields practical benefits. The technology of cochlear implants, which has made it possible to bring deaf adults and children into the world of hearing (Kiefer et al., 1996; Tye-Murray et al., 1995), can be traced directly to the discovery of the tonotopic map along the cochlea.

Updating Békésy: The Cochlear Amplifier

Although the basic idea behind Békésy's place theory has been confirmed by many experiments, when researchers after Békésy made more precise measurements of basilar membrane vibration, they found that vibration for a particular frequency is much more sharply localized than Békésy had observed (Johnstone & Boyle, 1967; Khanna & Leonard, 1982; Narayan et al., 1998). The reason Békésy observed rather "broad" vibration of the membrane, in which a particular frequency caused a large portion of the membrane to vibrate, is that he made his observations on cochleas isolated from animal and human cadavers. Modern researchers have been able to measure the basilar membrane's vibration in live cochleas with techniques more sensitive than the ones available to Békésy.

These new measurements raised the question of why the basilar membrane vibrates more sharply in healthy cochleas than in dead cochleas. The answer is that in healthy cochleas, the outer hair cells expand and contract in response to the vibration of the basilar membrane, and this expansion and contraction amplifies and sharpens the vibration of the basilar membrane. For this reason, the action of the outer hair cells is called the **cochlear amplifier**. **VL**

The operation of the cochlear amplifier is illustrated in **Figure 11.26**. The outer hair cells become elongated when the cilia bend in one direction and contract when they bend in the other direction. This mechanical response of elongation and contraction pushes and pulls on the basilar membrane,

Figure 11.26 The outer hair cell cochlear amplifier mechanism occurs when the cells (a) elongate when cilia bend in one direction and (b) contract when the cilia bend in the other direction. This results in an amplifying effect on the motion of the basilar membrane. © Cengage Learning

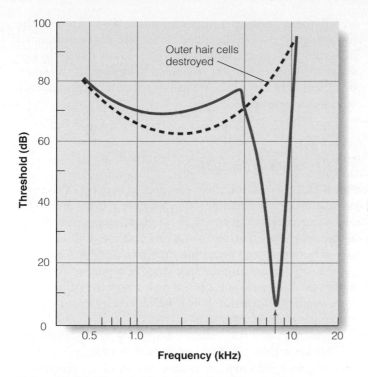

Figure 11.27 Effect of outer hair cell damage on the frequency tuning curve. The solid curve is the frequency tuning curve of a neuron with a characteristic frequency of about 8,000 Hz (arrow). The dashed curve is the frequency tuning curve for the same neuron after the outer hair cells were destroyed by injection of a chemical. Adapted from Fettiplace, R., & Hackney, C. M. (2006). The sensory and motor roles of auditory hair cells. *Nature Reviews Neuroscience, 7,* 19–29.

which increases the motion of the basilar membrane and sharpens its response to specific frequencies.

The importance of the outer hair cells' amplifying effect is illustrated by the frequency tuning curves in **Figure 11.27**. The solid blue curve shows the frequency tuning of a cat's auditory nerve fiber with a characteristic frequency of about 8,000 Hz. The dashed red curve shows what happened when the outer hair cells were destroyed by a chemical that attacked the outer hair cells but left the inner hair cells intact.

Whereas originally the fiber had a low threshold at 8,000 Hz, indicated by the arrow, it now takes much higher intensities to get the auditory nerve fiber to respond to 8,000 Hz and nearby frequencies (Fettiplace & Hackney, 2006; Liberman & Dodds, 1984).

Complex Tones and Vibration of the Basilar Membrane

Up until now we have been focusing on how the basilar membrane vibrates to pure tones. However, most of the sounds in our environment are complex tones, which consist of multiple harmonics. Research that has measured how the basilar membrane responds to complex tones shows that the basilar membrane vibrates to each of the tone's harmonics. There are, therefore, peaks in the membrane's vibration that correspond to the tone's fundamental frequency (the first harmonic) and to each of the other harmonics. Thus, a complex tone with a number of harmonics (**Figure 11.28a**) will cause peak vibration of the basilar membrane at places associated with the frequency of each harmonic (**Figure 11.28b**) (Hudspeth, 1989).

The way the cochlea separates frequencies along its length has been described as an **acoustic prism** (Fettiplace & Hackney, 2006). Just as a prism separates white light, which contains all wavelengths in the visible spectrum, into its components, the cochlea separates frequencies entering the ear into activity at different places along the basilar membrane. This property of the cochlea is particularly important when considering complex tones that contain many frequencies.

All of our descriptions so far have been focused on physical events that occur within the inner ear. Our story has been a purely physical one, limited to describing vibrations, trapdoors opening, ions flowing, nerve firing occurring in synchrony with the sound stimulus, and the traveling wave vibration of the basilar membrane. All of this information is crucial for understanding how the ear functions, but because we are interested in perception, we will now make the jump from physical to perceptual.

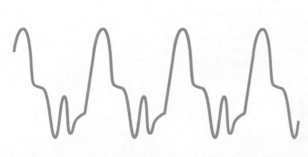

(a) Complex tone
(440, 880, 1,320 Hz harmonics)

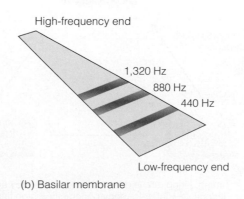

(b) Basilar membrane

Figure 11.28 (a) Waveform of a complex tone consisting of three harmonics. (b) Basilar membrane. The shaded areas indicate locations of peak vibration associated with each harmonic in the complex tone. © Cengage Learning

1. Describe the structure of the ear, focusing on the role that each component plays in transmitting the vibrations that enter the outer ear to the auditory receptors in the inner ear.

2. Focusing on the inner ear, describe (a) what causes the bending of the cilia of the hair cells; (b) what happens when the cilia bend; (c) why we say that the electrical signal follows the timing of the sound stimulus.

3. Describe Békésy's discovery of how the basilar membrane vibrates. Specifically, what is the relationship between sound frequency and basilar membrane vibration?

4. What is a cochlear implant? Why do we say that it is a practical application that can be traced to discoveries of basic research?

5. How do measurements of basilar membrane vibration made by modern researchers compare to Békésy's measurements? What is the reason for the difference? How can the difference be explained by the cochlear amplifier?

6. How does the basilar membrane vibrate to complex tones?

7. Up to this point, how does what we have described about the functioning of the ear apply to the perceptual process? Why can't we say, based on what we have covered so far, that we understand how we *perceive* sound?

The Physiology of Pitch Perception

We have now reached the culmination of our story and are ready to describe what we know about how physiological events are transformed into perceptual experience. In discussing this connection between physical and perceptual,

we will focus on the perception of pitch. We begin with the physiology of the ear, described above, but it is important to note that pitch perception occurs in the brain, not in the ear. What happens in the ear is extremely important, however, because it is here that the frequency content of the auditory stimulus is determined.

Pitch and the Ear

Figure 11.29 shows the three-component version of the perceptual process we introduced in Chapter 1 (see Figure 1.9). From our previous description of the stimulus–perception relationship (green arrow), we know that pitch is related to sound frequency and repetition rate (*periodicity pitch* and *temporal coding*). Increasing the frequency of a pure tone causes higher pitch. For complex tones with a number of harmonics, a similar relationship holds, with increases in periodicity creating higher pitches.

Looking at the stimulus–physiology relationship (orange arrow), we can distinguish the following two types of physiological information related to stimulus frequency: (1) timing information—the firing rate of auditory nerve fibers is related to stimulus frequency and periodicity, with higher frequencies or periodicities causing higher firing rates (phase locking); and (2) place information—the place on the cochlea where the maximum firing occurs is related to frequency, with low frequencies causing greater firing in fibers near the base of the cochlea and high frequencies cause greater firing in fibers near the apex of the cochlea.

With these relationships in mind, we can now consider the connection between physiology and pitch perception. When Békésy was reporting the results of his research, the physiology of pitch perception was explained as follows: A pure tone causes a peak of activity at a specific place on the basilar membrane. The neurons connected to that place respond the most, and this information is carried up the auditory nerve to

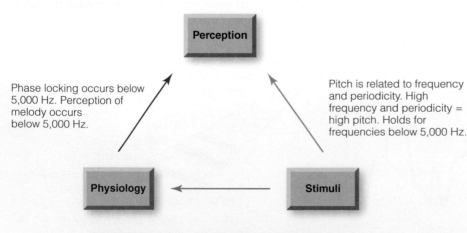

Phase locking occurs below 5,000 Hz. Perception of melody occurs below 5,000 Hz.

Pitch is related to frequency and periodicity. High frequency and periodicity = high pitch. Holds for frequencies below 5,000 Hz.

Timing: Firing rate is determined by frequency and periodicity. High frequency/periodicity = high firing rate.

Place: Place of maximum firing in cochlea is determined by frequency. Low frequency is at apex; high frequency is at base.

Figure 11.29 Perceptual process showing relationships that are related to the perception of pitch. © Cengage Learning 2014

the brain. The brain identifies which neurons are responding the most and uses this information to determine the pitch.

While Békésy's place explanation is straightforward, other evidence indicates that pitch perception cannot be explained by place alone. As it turns out, the timing of nerve firing plays a major role in determining pitch perception. One piece of evidence supporting the idea that timing is important is the relationship between the physiological response of phase locking and perception (red arrow). Phase locking—the firing of bursts of impulses at the peak of the sound stimulus—occurs only at frequencies below 5,000 Hz. When tones are strung together to create a melody, we only perceive a melody if the tones are below 5,000 Hz (Attneave & Olson, 1971). It is probably no coincidence that the highest note on an orchestral instrument (the piccolo) is about 4,500 Hz. Melodies played using frequencies above 5,000 Hz sound rather strange. You can tell that something is changing but it doesn't sound musical. So it seems that our sense of pitch may be limited to those frequencies that create phase locking. Above 5,000 Hz, our ability to discriminate pure tones may be based on the much less accurate information from place cues—the place of peak activity on the basilar membrane—but these cues do not seem to give us a sense of musical pitch.

The evidence that pitch is not determined simply by the place of peak activity on the basilar membrane becomes even clearer when we consider complex tones. Remember that removing the first harmonic changes a tone's waveform but not its repetition rate (Figure 11.6). If the fundamental is gone, there won't be vibration of the basilar membrane at the appropriate place. But after removing the fundamental, the tone's repetition rate and pitch remain the same. This has led to the conclusion that pitch is determined not by the place of vibration associated with the fundamental frequency, but by the tone's periodicity.

The conclusion that pitch is determined largely by periodicity, with place information being important mainly at frequencies above 5,000 Hz, has been based on the vibration of hair cell cilia and firing of auditory nerve fibers. But our perception of pitch doesn't occur in the ear. It occurs when information is transmitted from the ear to the brain.

Pitch and the Brain

How is pitch determined in the auditory cortex? We have seen that the auditory cortex is located in the temporal lobe (see Figure 1.5). In the next chapter, we will look in more detail at the anatomy of the auditory cortex and the structures in the pathway from the cochlea to the cortex. For now, we will focus on the primary auditory receiving area, A1 (**Figure 11.30**).

We have already seen that the frequencies of pure tones are mapped along the length of the cochlea, with low frequencies represented at the apex and higher frequencies at the base (Figure 11.23). This tonotopic map of frequencies also occurs in the structures along the pathway from the cochlea to the cortex and in the primary auditory receiving area, A1. **Figure 11.31** shows the tonotopic map in the monkey cortex, with neurons that respond best to low frequencies located to the left and neurons that respond best to higher frequencies located to the right (Kosaki et al., 1997; also see Reale & Imig, 1980; Schreiner & Mendelson, 1990).

But we know that sensations such as pitch and timbre are not related in a simple way to the place of activation in the

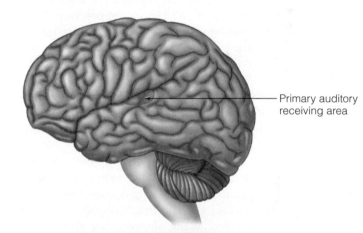

Primary auditory receiving area

Figure 11.30 The human brain, showing the location of the primary auditory receiving area, A1, which also extends inside the temporal lobe. Pulling the temporal lobe back reveals additional auditory areas. These areas will be described in Chapter 12. © Cengage Learning 2014

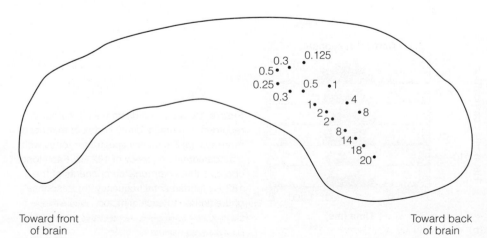

Toward front of brain

Toward back of brain

Figure 11.31 The tonotopic map on the primary auditory receiving area, A1, which is contained within the core area of the auditory cortex, shown in outline. The numbers represent the characteristic frequencies (CF) of neurons in thousands of Hz. Low CFs are on the left, and high CFs are on the right. Adapted from Kosaki, H., Hashikawa, T., He, J., & Jones, E. G. (1997). Tonotopic organization of auditory cortical fields delineated by parvalbumin immunoreactivity in Macaque monkeys. *Journal of Comparative Neurology, 386,* 304–316.

cochlea. How might we determine the physiological mechanisms behind these sensations? The best way to determine a link between physiology and perception is to measure the physiological response and perception simultaneously. In Chapter 8 (page 186), we described how William Newsome and coauthors (1995) achieved this in vision by measuring how neurons in a monkey's MT cortex responded to moving dot stimuli while the monkey was judging the direction the dots were moving. In this experiment, the firing of the MT neurons and the monkey's perception were so closely related that the researchers could predict one from the other.

An experiment by Daniel Bendor and Xiaoqin Wang (2005) did not measure physiological response and perception simultaneously in the same animal but determined how neurons in an area just outside the auditory cortex of a marmoset (a species of New World monkey) responded to complex tones that differed in their harmonic structure but would be perceived by humans as being the same pitch. When they did this, they found neurons that responded similarly to complex tones with the same fundamental frequency but with different harmonic structures. For example, **Figure 11.32a** shows the frequency spectra for a tone with a fundamental frequency of 182 Hz. In the top record, the tone contains the fundamental frequency and the second and third harmonics; in the second record, harmonics 4–6 are present; and so on, until at the bottom, only harmonics 12–14 are present. Even though these stimuli contain different frequencies (for example, 182, 364, and 546 Hz in the top record; 2,184, 2,366, and 2,548 Hz in the bottom record), they are all perceived by humans as having a pitch corresponding to the 182-Hz fundamental.

The corresponding cortical response records (**Figure 11.32b**) show that these stimuli all caused an increase in firing. To demonstrate that this firing occurred only when information about the 182-Hz fundamental frequency was present, Bendor and Wang showed that the neuron responded well to a 182-Hz tone presented alone, but not to any of the harmonics when they were presented alone. These cortical neurons, therefore, responded only to stimuli associated with the 182-Hz tone, which is associated with a specific pitch. For this reason, Bendor and Wang call these neurons **pitch neurons**.

From the research we have described on the ear and the brain, we can conclude that frequency is coded in the cochlea and auditory nerve based both on which fibers are firing (place coding) and on the timing of nerve impulses in auditory nerve fibers (temporal coding). Although pitch perception was originally thought to be determined primarily by place coding, a large amount of evidence points to temporal coding as the most important determinant of pitch perception, especially below 5,000 Hz.

Whereas most of the early research on the auditory system focused on the cochlea and auditory nerve, a great deal of research is now being done on the brain. We will consider more of this research in the next chapter.

SOMETHING TO CONSIDER:
How to Damage Your Hair Cells

Causing damage to your hair cells is a bad idea, because damage to the outer hair cells can have a large effect on the response of auditory nerve fibers, as shown in Figure 11.27. Outer hair cell damage is thought to be the most common cause of hearing loss; it results in a loss of sensitivity (inability to hear quiet sounds) and a loss of the sharp frequency tuning seen in healthy ears (Moore, 1995; Plack et al., 2004). When the outer hair cells are damaged, the response of the basilar membrane becomes similar to the broad response seen for the dead cochleas examined by Békésy. Because of this, it is harder for hearing-impaired people to separate out sounds—for example, to hear speech sounds in noisy environments.

Inner hair cell damage can also cause a large effect, resulting in a loss of sensitivity. For both inner and outer hair cells, hearing loss occurs for the frequencies corresponding to the frequencies detected by the damaged hair cells. Sometimes inner hair cells are lost over an entire region of the cochlea (a "dead region"), and sensitivity to the frequencies that normally excite that region of the cochlea becomes much reduced.

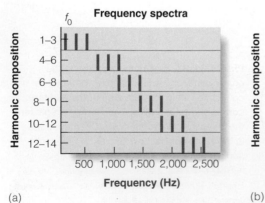

(a)

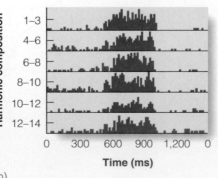

(b)

Figure 11.32 Records from a pitch neuron recorded from the auditory cortex of marmoset monkeys. (a) Frequency spectra for tones with a fundamental frequency of 182 Hz. Each tone contains three harmonic components of the 182-Hz fundamental frequency. (b) Response of the neuron to each stimulus. Adapted from Bendor, D., & Wang, X. (2005). The neuronal representation of pitch in primate auditory cortex. Nature, 436, 1161–1165.

Of course, you wouldn't want to purposely damage your hair cells, but sometimes we expose ourselves to sounds that over the long term do result in hair cell damage. One of the things that contributes to hair cell damage is living in an industrialized environment, which contains sounds that contribute to a type of hearing loss called *presbycusis*.

Presbycusis

Presbycusis is caused by hair cell damage resulting from the cumulative effects over time of noise exposure, the ingestion of drugs that damage the hair cells, and age-related degeneration. The loss of sensitivity associated with presbycusis, which is greatest at high frequencies, affects males more severely than females. **Figure 11.33** shows the progression of loss as a function of age. Unlike the visual problem of presbyopia (see Figure 2.5), which is an inevitable consequence of aging, presbycusis is largely caused by factors in addition to aging; people in preindustrial cultures, who have not been exposed to the noises that accompany industrialization or to drugs that could damage the ear, often do not experience

large decreases in high-frequency hearing in old age. This may be why males, who historically have been exposed to more workplace noise than females, as well as to noises associated with hunting and wartime, experience a greater presbycusis effect.

Although presbycusis may be unavoidable, since most people are exposed over a long period of time to the everyday sounds of our modern environment, there are situations in which people expose their ears to loud sounds that could be avoided. This exposure to particularly loud sounds results in *noise-induced hearing loss*.

Noise-Induced Hearing Loss

Noise-induced hearing loss occurs when loud noises cause degeneration of the hair cells. This degeneration has been observed in examinations of the cochleas of people who have worked in noisy environments and have willed their ear structures to medical research. Damage to the organ of Corti is often observed in these cases. For example, examination of the cochlea of a man who worked in a steel mill indicated that his organ of Corti had collapsed and no receptor cells remained (Miller, 1974). More controlled studies of animals exposed to loud sounds provide further evidence that high-intensity sounds can damage or completely destroy inner hair cells (Liberman & Dodds, 1984). Noise exposure also causes degeneration of auditory nerve fibers (Kujawa & Liberman, 2009). This may not affect sensitivity to quiet sounds but may impair the ability to identify complex sounds, particularly in noisy environments.

Because of the danger to hair cells posed by workplace noise, the United States Occupational Safety and Health Agency (OSHA) has mandated that workers not be exposed to sound levels greater than 85 dB for an 8-hour work shift. In addition to workplace noise, however, other sources of intense sound can cause hair cell damage leading to hearing loss.

If you turn up the volume on your portable music player, you are exposing yourself to what hearing professionals call **leisure noise**. Other sources of leisure noise are activities such as recreational gun use, riding motorcycles, playing musical instruments, and working with power tools. A number of studies have demonstrated hearing loss in people who listen to portable music players (Okamoto et al., 2011; Peng et al., 2007), play in rock/pop bands (Schmuziger et al., 2006), use power tools (Dalton et al., 2001), and attend sports events (Hodgetts & Liu, 2006). The amount of hearing loss depends on the level of sound intensity and the duration of exposure. Given the high levels of sound that occur in these activities, such as the levels above 90 dB SPL that can occur for the 3 hours of a hockey game (**Figure 11.34**) and levels as high as 90 dB SPL while using power tools in woodworking, it isn't surprising that both temporary and permanent hearing losses are associated with these leisure activities. These findings suggest that it might make sense to use ear protection when in particularly noisy environments and to turn down the volume on your portable music player.

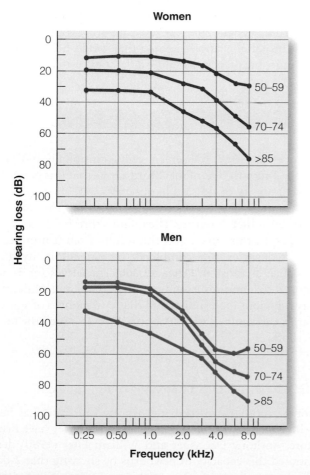

Figure 11.33 Hearing loss in presbycusis as a function of age. All of the curves are plotted relative to the 20-year-old curve, which is taken as the standard. Adapted from Bunch, C. C. (1929). Age variations in auditory acuity. *Archives of Otolaryngology, 9,* 625–636.

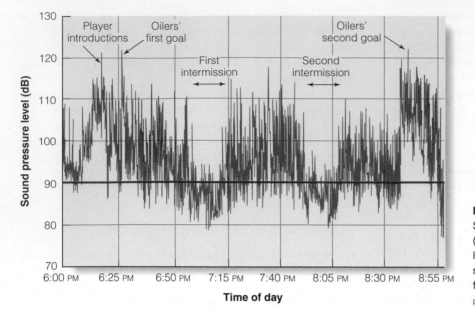

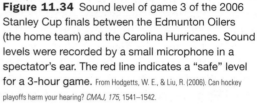

Figure 11.34 Sound level of game 3 of the 2006 Stanley Cup finals between the Edmonton Oilers (the home team) and the Carolina Hurricanes. Sound levels were recorded by a small microphone in a spectator's ear. The red line indicates a "safe" level for a 3-hour game. From Hodgetts, W. E., & Liu, R. (2006). Can hockey playoffs harm your hearing? *CMAJ, 175,* 1541–1542.

The potential for hearing loss from listening to music at high volume for extended periods of time cannot be overemphasized, because at their highest settings, portable music players reach levels of 100 dB SPL or higher—far above OSHA's recommended maximum of 85 dB. This has led Apple Computer to add a setting to iPods that limits the maximum volume, although an informal survey of my students indicates, not surprisingly, that few of them use this feature.

One suggestion for minimizing the potential for hearing damage is to follow this simple rule, proposed by James Battey, Jr., director of the National Institute on Deafness and Other Communication Disorders: If you can't hear someone talking to you at arm's length, turn down the music ("More Noise Than Signal," 2007). If you can't bring yourself to turn down the volume, another thing that would help is to take a 5-minute break from listening at least once an hour!

DEVELOPMENTAL DIMENSION: Infant Hearing

What do newborn infants hear, and how does hearing develop as infants get older? Although some early psychologists believed that newborns were functionally deaf, recent research has shown that newborns do have some auditory capacity and that this capacity improves as the child gets older (Werner & Bargones, 1992). **VL**

Thresholds and the Audibility Curve

What do infant audibility curves look like, and how do their thresholds compare to adults'? Lynne Werner Olsho and coworkers (1988) used the following procedure to determine infants' audibility curves. An infant is fitted with earphones and sits on the parent's lap. An observer, sitting out of view of the infant, watches the infant through a window. A light blinks on, indicating that a trial has begun, and a tone is either presented or not. The observer's task is to decide whether the infant heard a tone (Olsho et al., 1987).

How can observers tell whether the infant has heard a tone? They decide by looking for responses such as eye movements, changes in facial expression, a wide-eyed look, a turn of the head, or changes in activity level. These judgments resulted in the curve in **Figure 11.35a** for a 2,000-Hz tone

(Olsho et al., 1988). Observers only occasionally indicated that the 3-month-old infants heard a tone that was presented at low intensity or not at all; observers were more likely to say that the infant had heard the tone when the tone was presented at high intensity. The infant's threshold was determined from this curve, and the results from a number of other frequencies were combined to create audibility functions such as those in **Figure 11.35b**. The curves for 3- and 6-month-olds and adults indicate that infant and adult audibility functions look similar and that by 6 months of age, the infant's threshold is within about 10 to 15 dB of the adult threshold.

Recognizing Their Mother's Voice

Another approach to studying hearing in infants has been to show that newborns can identify sounds they have heard before. Anthony DeCasper and William Fifer (1980) demonstrated this capacity in newborns by showing that 2-day-old infants will modify their sucking on a nipple in order to hear the sound of their mother's voice. They first observed that infants usually suck on a nipple in bursts separated by pauses. They fitted infants with earphones and let the length

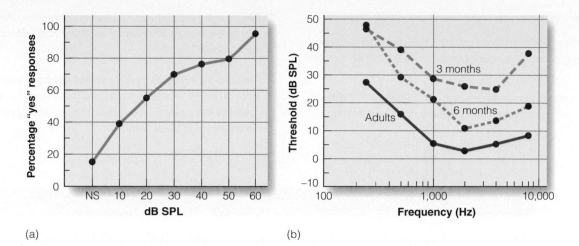

(a)

(b)

Figure 11.35 (a) Data obtained by Olsho et al. (1987), showing the percentage of trials on which the observer indicated that a 3-month-old infant heard 2,000-Hz tones presented at different intensities. NS indicates no sound. (b) Audibility curves for 3- and 6-month-old infants determined from functions like the one in (a). The curve for 12-month-olds, not shown here, is similar to the curve for 6-month-olds. The adult curve is shown for comparison. Adapted from Olsho, L. W., Koch, E. G., Carter, E. A., Halpin, C. F., & Spetner, N. B. (1988). Pure-tone sensitivity of human infants. *Journal of the Acoustical Society of America, 84*, 1316–1324. American Institute of Physics. Reproduced by permission.

of the pause in the infant's sucking determine whether the infant heard a recording of the mother's voice or a recording of a stranger's voice (**Figure 11.36**). For half of the infants, long pauses activated the tape of the mother's voice, and short pauses activated the tape of the stranger's voice. For the other half, these conditions were reversed.

DeCasper and Fifer found that the babies regulated the pauses in their sucking so that they heard their mother's voice more than the stranger's voice. This is a remarkable accomplishment for a 2-day-old, especially because most had been with their mothers for only a few hours between birth and the time they were tested.

Why did the newborns prefer their mother's voice? DeCasper and Fifer suggested that newborns recognize their mother's voice because they heard the mother talking during development in the womb. This suggestion is supported

by the results of another experiment, in which DeCasper and M. J. Spence (1986) had one group of pregnant women read from Dr. Seuss's book *The Cat in the Hat* and another group read the same story with the words *cat* and *hat* replaced with *dog* and *fog*. When the children were born, they regulated the pauses in their sucking in a way that caused them to hear the version of the story their mother had read when they were in the womb. Moon and coworkers (1993) obtained a similar result by showing that 2-day-old infants regulated their sucking to hear a recording of their native language rather than a foreign language (see also DeCasper et al., 1994).

The idea that fetuses become familiar with the sounds they hear in the womb was supported by Barbara Kisilevsky and coworkers (2003), who presented loud (95 dB) recordings of the mother reading a 2-minute passage and a stranger reading a 2-minute passage through a loudspeaker held 10 cm above the abdomen of full-term pregnant women. When they measured the fetus's movement and heart rate as these recordings were being presented, they found that the fetus moved more in response to the mother's voice, and that heart rate increased in response to the mother's voice but decreased in response to the stranger's voice. Kisilevsky concluded from these results that fetal voice processing is influenced by experience, just as the results of earlier experiments had suggested (see also Kisilevsky et al., 2009).

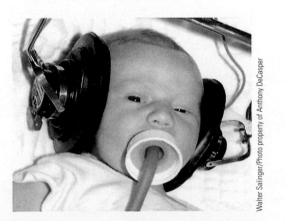

Walter Salinger/Photo property of Anthony DeCasper

Figure 11.36 This baby, from DeCasper and Fifer's (1980) study, could control whether she heard a recording of her mother's voice or a stranger's voice by the way she sucked on the nipple. From DeCasper, A. J., & Fifer, W. P. (1980). Of human bonding: Newborns prefer their mothers' voices. *Science, 208*, 1174–1176.

TEST YOURSELF 11.3

1. Considering what we know about (a) how information about sound frequency is represented in the ear and (b) the relation between frequency, repetition rate, and perception, what can we conclude about the relation between the physiology of the ear and pitch perception? Be sure you consider the roles of both place and timing information.

2. What is the tonotopic map in the brain?

3. Describe the experiment that suggests a relationship between firing of neurons in the auditory cortex and the pitch of complex tones.

4. What is the connection between hair cell damage and hearing loss? exposure to occupational or leisure noise and hearing loss?

5. Describe the procedures for measuring auditory thresholds in infants. How does the infant's audibility curve compare to the adult curve?

6. Describe experiments that show that newborn infants can recognize their mother's voice, and that this capacity can be traced to the infants' having heard the mother talking during development in the womb.

THINK ABOUT IT

1. We saw that decibels are used to compress the large range of sound pressures in the environment into more manageable numbers. Describe how this same principle is used in the Richter scale to compress ranges of earth vibrations from barely perceptible tremors to major earthquakes into a smaller range of numbers.

2. Presbycusis usually begins with loss of high-frequency hearing and gradually involves lower frequencies. From what you know about cochlear function, can you explain why the high frequencies are more vulnerable to damage? (p. 283)

KEY TERMS

Acoustic prism (p. 279)
Amplitude (p. 264)
Apex (of the cochlea or basilar membrane) (p. 272)
Attack (p. 270)
Audibility curve (p. 267)
Auditory canal (p. 271)
Auditory response area (p. 267)
Base (of the cochlea or basilar membrane) (p. 272)
Basilar membrane (p. 273)
Characteristic frequency (p. 277)
Cilia (p. 273)
Cochlea (p. 272)
Cochlear amplifier (p. 278)
Cochlear implant (p. 277)
Cochlear partition (p. 272)
Decay (p. 270)
Decibel (dB) (p. 265)
Eardrum (p. 271)
Effect of the missing fundamental (p. 269)
Equal loudness curve (p. 268)
First harmonic (p. 266)
Frequency (p. 264)

Frequency spectrum (p. 266)
Frequency tuning curve (p. 277)
Fundamental (p. 266)
Fundamental frequency (p. 266)
Hair cells (p. 273)
Harmonic (p. 266)
Hertz (Hz) (p. 264)
Higher harmonics (p. 266)
Incus (p. 271)
Inner ear (p. 272)
Inner hair cells (p. 273)
Leisure noise (p. 283)
Level (p. 265)
Loudness (p. 267)
Malleus (p. 271)
Middle ear (p. 271)
Middle-ear muscles (p. 272)
Noise-induced hearing loss (p. 283)
Octave (p. 269)
Organ of Corti (p. 273)
Ossicles (p. 271)
Outer ear (p. 271)
Outer hair cells (p. 273)
Oval window (p. 271)
Periodic tone (p. 266)

Periodicity pitch (p. 269)
Phase locking (p. 275)
Pinna (p. 271)
Pitch (p. 268)
Pitch neuron (p. 282)
Place theory of hearing (p. 276)
Presbycusis (p. 283)
Pure tone (p. 263)
Resonance (p. 271)
Resonant frequency (p. 271)
Sound (p. 263)
Sound level (p. 265)
Sound pressure level (SPL) (p. 265)
Sound wave (p. 263)
Stapes (p. 271)
Tectorial membrane (p. 273)
Temporal coding (p. 275)
Timbre (p. 269)
Tip links (p. 274)
Tone chroma (p. 269)
Tone height (p. 269)
Tonotopic map (p. 277)
Traveling wave (p. 276)
Tympanic membrane (p. 271)

CourseMate

Go to CengageBrain.com to access Psychology CourseMate, where you will find the Virtual Labs plus an interactive eBook, flashcards, quizzes, videos, and more.

Virtual Labs VL

The Virtual Labs are designed to help you get the most out of this course. The Virtual Lab icons direct you to specific media demonstrations and experiments designed to help you visualize what you are reading about. The numbers below indicate the number of the Virtual Lab you can access through Psychology CourseMate.

11.1 Decibel Scale (p. 267)
Demonstrates how loudness increases for a 10 dB increase in decibels.

11.2 Loudness Scaling (p. 267)
Do a magnitude estimation experiment to determine the relationship between dB and loudness.

11.3 Frequency Response of the Ear (p. 267)
Shows how our ability to hear a tone that is always at the same dB level depends on its frequency.

11.4 Tone Height and Tone Chroma (p. 269)
A demonstration of tone height and tone chroma.

11.5 Periodicity Pitch: Eliminating the Fundamental and Lower Harmonics (p. 269)
How your perception of a tone changes as harmonics are removed.

11.6 Periodicity Pitch: St. Martin Chimes With Harmonics Removed (p. 269)
How your perception of a melody changes as harmonics are removed.

11.7 Harmonics of a Gong (p. 270)
A demonstration that enables you to hear each of the individual harmonics that make up the sound produced by a gong.

11.8 Effect of Harmonics on Timbre (p. 270)
How adding harmonics to a tone changes the quality of the sound.

11.9 Timbre of a Piano Tone Played Backward (p. 270)
How presenting piano tones backward (so the end of the tone comes first and the beginning comes last) affects our perception of the tone's quality.

11.10 Cochlear Mechanics: Cilia Movement (p. 274)
Animation showing how the hair-cell cilia move back and forth in response to a sound stimulus. (Courtesy of Stephen T. Neely)

11.11 Cochlear Mechanics: Traveling Waves (p. 276)
Animation showing how the basilar membrane vibrates in response to two different frequencies. (Courtesy of Stephen T. Neely)

11.12 Cochlear Implant: Environmental Sounds (p. 278)
Illustrates how a person with a cochlear implant perceives some common environmental sounds. Perception that results from different numbers of electrodes is illustrated. (Courtesy of Samantha Goddess/Sensimetrics)

11.13 Cochlear Implant: Music (p. 278)
Illustrates how a person with a cochlear implant perceives music. Perception that results from different numbers of electrodes is illustrated. (Courtesy of Samantha Goddess/Sensimetrics)

11.14 Cochlear Implant: Speech (p. 278)
Illustrates how a person with a cochlear implant perceives speech. Perception that results from different numbers of electrodes is illustrated. (Courtesy of Samantha Goddess/Sensimetrics)

11.15 Cochlear Mechanics: Cochlear Amplifier (p. 278)
Animation showing how changes in the length of the outer hair cells amplify the vibration of the basilar membrane. (Courtesy of Stephen T. Neely)

11.16 Newborn Hearing and Vision (p. 284)
First part of video is on newborn hearing. Second part is on how infants orient toward faces.

Auditory Localization and Organization

◀ As the musicians draw their bows over the strings, vibrations occur, which, as we saw in Chapter 11, create patterns of frequencies that result in perceptual qualities such as pitch and timbre. But there is more to perceiving sound than pitch and timbre. In this chapter we consider how we perceive where a sound is coming from, how our perception is influenced by the acoustics of a room or concert hall, how we are able to separate the sounds of different melodic lines and instruments from one another, and how we perceive music as patterns of sounds in time.

VL The Virtual Lab icons direct you to specific animations and videos designed to help you visualize what you are reading about. Virtual Labs are listed at the end of the chapter, keyed to the page on which they appear, and can be accessed through Psychology CourseMate.

Some Questions We Will Consider:

- What makes it possible to tell where a sound is coming from in space? (p. 290)

- Why does music sound better in some concert halls than in others? (p. 302)

- When we are listening to a number of musical instruments playing at the same time, how can we perceptually separate the sounds coming from the different instruments? (p. 304)

This chapter is about how we make sense of sounds in the environment. It takes us beyond the mechanisms responsible for perceiving the pitch or loudness of pure and complex tones to ask what typically happens in an environment in which we are exposed to sounds coming from a number of different sources, often simultaneously, and also sequences of sounds that create patterns in time.

Consider, for example, the man conversing with the woman in the coffee shop (**Figure 12.1**). He hears her talking from across the table and can tell that music is coming from speakers located behind him. Four things happen that we need to explain: (1) How can he tell where the woman's voice and the music are coming from? This is the *auditory localization problem*. (2) How can he perceive the music clearly, with no "echo," even though some of the sound from the speakers is bouncing off the wall and is arriving at his ears after a slight delay? This is the *problem of reflected sound*. (3) How does he experience the woman's voice as separate from the music and all the other sounds in the room? This is a problem in perceptual organization called the *auditory*

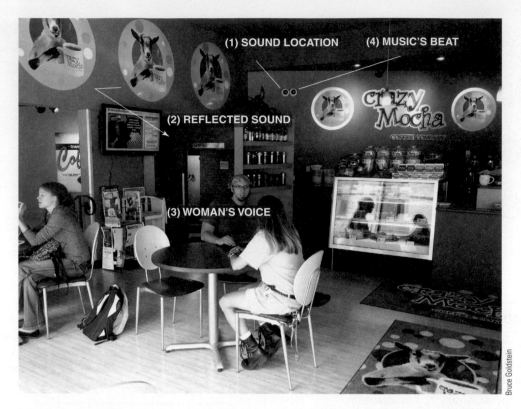

Figure 12.1 Coffee shop scene, which contains multiple sound sources. The most immediate sound source for the man in the middle is the voice of the woman talking to him across the table. Additional sources include speakers on the wall behind him, which are broadcasting music, and all the other people in the room who are speaking. The four problems we will consider in this chapter— (1) auditory localization, (2) sound reflection, (3) analysis of the scene into separate sound sources, and (4) musical patterns that are organized in time—are indicated in this figure.

scene analysis problem. (4) How does he perceive the music's sound as perceptually organized in time, with a regular beat? Perceiving the beat pattern is the *problem of metrical structure*. We will consider each of these four problems in this chapter. We begin by considering localization.

Auditory Localization

After reading this sentence, close your eyes for a moment, listen, and notice what sounds you hear and where they are coming from. When I do this right now, sitting in a coffee shop, I hear the beat and vocals of a song coming from a speaker above my head and slightly behind me, a woman talking somewhere in front of me, and the "fizzy" sound of an espresso maker off to the left. There are other sounds as well, because many people are talking, but let's focus on these three for now.

Each of the sounds—the music, the talking, and the mechanical fizzing sound—are heard as coming from different locations in space. These sounds at different locations

create an **auditory space**, which exists all around, wherever there is sound. This locating of sound sources in auditory space is called **auditory localization**. We can appreciate the problem the auditory system faces in determining these locations by comparing the information for location for vision and hearing. To do this, we substitute a bird in a tree and a cat on the ground in **Figure 12.2** for the sounds in the coffee shop.

Visual information for the relative locations of the bird and the cat is contained in the images of the bird and the cat on the surface of the retina. The ear, however, is different. The bird's "tweet, tweet" and the cat's "meow" stimulate the cochlea based on their sound frequencies, and as we saw in Chapter 11, these frequencies cause patterns of nerve firing that result in our perception of a tone's pitch and timbre. But activation of nerve fibers in the cochlea is based on the tones' frequency components and not on where the tones are coming from. This means that two tones with the same frequency that originate in different locations will activate the same hair cells and nerve fibers in the cochlea. The auditory system must therefore use other information to determine location. The information it uses involves **location cues** that are

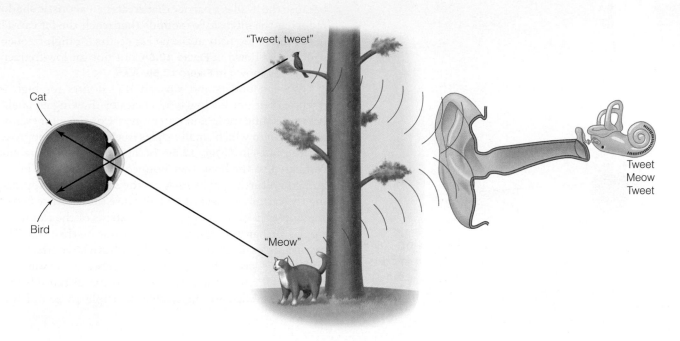

Figure 12.2 Comparing location information for vision and hearing. *Vision:* The bird and the cat, which are located at different places, are imaged on different places on the retina. *Hearing:* The frequencies in the sounds from the bird and cat are spread out over the cochlea, with no regard to the animals' locations. © Cengage Learning

created by the way sound interacts with the listener's head and ears.

There are two kinds of location cues: *binaural cues*, which depend on both ears, and *monaural cues*, which depend on just one ear. Researchers studying these cues have determined how well people can locate the position of a sound in three dimensions: the **azimuth**, which extends from left to right (**Figure 12.3**); **elevation**, which extends up and down; and the **distance** of the sound source from the listener. In this chapter, we will focus on the azimuth and elevation.

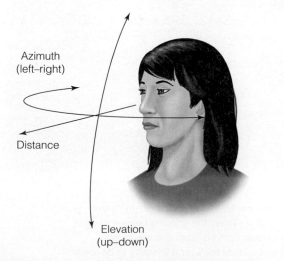

Figure 12.3 The three directions used for studying sound localization: azimuth (left–right), elevation (up–down), and distance.

© Cengage Learning

Binaural Cues for Sound Localization

Binaural cues use information reaching both ears to determine the azimuth (left–right position) of sounds. The two binaural cues are *interaural time difference* and *interaural level difference*. Both are based on a comparison of the sound signals reaching the left and right ears. Sounds that are off to the side reach one ear before the other and are louder at one ear than the other.

Interaural Time Difference The **interaural time difference** (**ITD**) is the difference between when a sound reaches the left ear and when it reaches the right ear (**Figure 12.4**). If the source is located directly in front of the listener, at A, the distance to each ear is the same; the sound reaches the left and right ears simultaneously, so the ITD is zero. However, if a source is located off to the side, at B, the sound reaches the right ear before it reaches the left ear. Because the ITD becomes larger as sound sources are located more to the side, the magnitude of the ITD can be used as a cue to determine a sound's location. Behavioral research, in which listeners judge sound locations as ITD is varied, indicates that ITD is an effective cue for localizing low-frequency sounds (Wightman & Kistler, 1997, 1998).

Interaural Level Difference The other binaural cue, **interaural level difference** (**ILD**), is based on the difference in the sound pressure level (or just "level") of the sound reaching the two ears. A difference in level between the two ears occurs

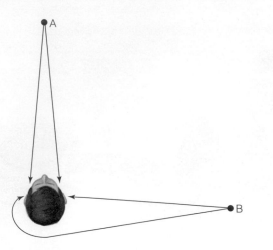

Figure 12.4 The principle behind interaural time difference (ITD). The tone directly in front of the listener, at A, reaches the left and right ears at the same time. However, when the tone is off to the side, at B, it reaches the listener's right ear before it reaches the left ear.

© Cengage Learning

because the head is a barrier that creates an **acoustic shadow**, reducing the intensity of sounds that reach the far ear. This reduction of intensity at the far ear occurs for high-frequency sounds, as shown in **Figure 12.5a**, but not for low-frequency sounds, as shown in **Figure 12.5b**. ▧

We can understand why an ILD occurs for high frequencies but not for low frequencies by drawing an analogy between sound waves and water waves. Consider, for example, a situation in which small ripples in the water are approaching the boat in **Figure 12.5c**. Because the ripples are small compared to the boat, they bounce off the side of the boat and go no further. Now imagine the same ripples approaching the cattails in **Figure 12.5d**. Because the distance between the ripples is large compared to the stems of the cattails, the ripples are hardly disturbed and continue on their way. These two examples illustrate that an object has a large effect on the wave if it is larger than the distance between the waves, but has a small effect if it is smaller than the distance between the waves. When we apply this principle to sound waves

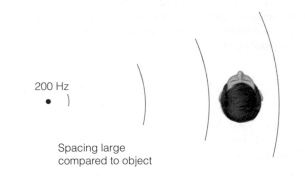

(a)

(b)

(c)

(d)

Figure 12.5 Why interaural level difference (ILD) occurs for high frequencies but not for low frequencies. (a) Person listening to a high-frequency sound; (b) person listening to a low-frequency sound. (c) When the spacing between waves is smaller than the size of the object, illustrated here by water ripples that are smaller than the boat, the waves are stopped by the object. This occurs for the high-frequency sound waves in (a) and causes the sound intensity to be lower on the far side of the listener's head. (d) When the spacing between waves is larger than the size of the object, as occurs for the water ripples and the narrow stalks of the cattails, the object does not interfere with the waves. This occurs for the low-frequency sound waves in (b), so the sound intensity on the far side of the head is not affected. © Cengage Learning

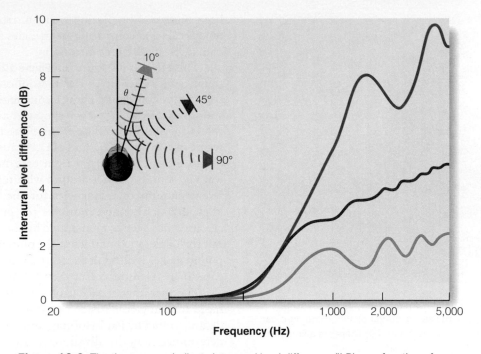

Figure 12.6 The three curves indicate interaural level difference (ILD) as a function of frequency for three different sound-source locations. Note that the difference in ILD for different locations is greater at higher frequencies. Adapted from Hartmann, M. (1999). How we localize sound. *Physics Today on the Web.* www.aip.org/pt/nov99/locsound.html.

interacting with a listener's head, we can understand why high-frequency sound waves (which are small compared to the size of the head) are disrupted by the head and create the acoustic shadow shown in Figure 12.5a, but low-frequency waves do not.

Figure 12.6 illustrates this difference between the ILDs for high and low frequencies. The ILD was measured by using small microphones to record the difference in sound intensity reaching each ear for frequencies ranging from 100 to 5,000 Hz. ILD is plotted against frequency for sound sources located at three different positions relative to the head. Notice that at high frequencies, there is a large difference between the ILD for sounds located at 10 degrees (green curve) and 90 degrees (blue curve). At lower frequencies, however, there is a smaller difference between the ILDs for sounds coming from these two locations until, at very low frequencies, the ILD is a very poor indicator of a sound's location.

The Cone of Confusion When we consider the interaural time difference (ITD) and interaural level difference (ILD) together, we see that they complement each other. The ITD provides information about the location of low-frequency sounds, and the ILD provides information about the location of high-frequency sounds. However, while the time and level differences provide information that enables people to judge location along the azimuth coordinate, they provide ambiguous information about the elevation of a sound source. You can understand why this is so by imagining you are extending your hand directly in front of you at arm's length and

are holding a sound source. Because the source would be equidistant from your left and right ears, the time and level differences would be zero. If you now imagine moving your hand straight up, increasing the sound source's elevation, the source will still be equidistant from the two ears, so both time and level differences are still zero.

Because the time and level differences can be the same at a number of different elevations, they cannot reliably indicate the elevation of the sound source. Similar ambiguous information is provided when the sound source is off to the side. These places of ambiguity are illustrated by the **cone of confusion** shown in **Figure 12.7**. All points on this cone have the same ILD and ITD. For example, points A and B would result in the same ILD and ITD because the distance from A to the left and right ears is the same as the distance from B to the right and left ears. Similar situations occur for other points on the cone, and there are other smaller and larger cones as well. In other words, there are many locations in space where two sounds could result in the same ILD and ITD.

Monaural Cue for Localization

The ambiguous nature of the information provided by ITD and ILD at different elevations means that another source of information is needed to locate sounds along the elevation coordinate. This information is provided by a **monaural cue**—a cue that depends on information from only one ear.

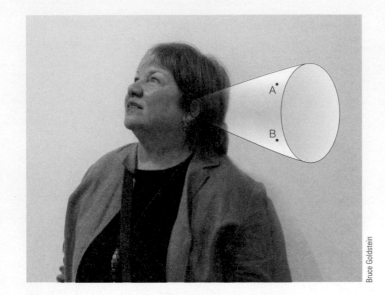

Figure 12.7 The "cone of confusion." There are many pairs of points on this cone that have the same left-ear distance and right-ear distance and so result in the same ILD and ITD. There are also other cones in addition to this one. © Cengage Learning

The primary monaural cue for localization is called a **spectral cue**, because the information for localization is contained in differences in the distribution (or spectrum) of frequencies that reach each ear from different locations. These differences are caused by the fact that before the sound stimulus enters the auditory canal, it is reflected from the head and within the various folds of the pinnae (**Figure 12.8a**). The effect of this interaction with the head and pinnae has

been measured by placing small microphones inside a listener's ears and comparing frequencies from sounds that are coming from different directions.

This effect is illustrated in **Figure 12.8b**, which shows the frequencies picked up by the microphone when a broadband sound (one containing many frequencies) is presented at elevations of 15 degrees above the head and 15 degrees below the head. Sounds coming from these two locations would result in the same ITD and ILD because they are the same distance from the left and right ears, but differences in the way the sounds bounce around within the pinna create different patterns of frequencies for the two locations (King et al., 2001). The importance of the pinna for determining elevation has been demonstrated by showing that smoothing out the nooks and crannies of the pinnae with molding compound makes it difficult to locate sounds along the elevation coordinate (Gardner & Gardner, 1973).

The idea that localization can be affected by using a mold to change the inside contours of the pinnae was also demonstrated by Paul Hofman and coworkers (1998). They determined how localization changes when the mold is worn for several weeks, and then what happens when the mold is removed. The results for one listener's localization performance measured before the mold was inserted are shown in **Figure 12.9a**. Sounds were presented at positions indicated by the intersections of the black grid. Average localization performance is indicated by the blue grid. The overlap between the two grids indicates that localization was fairly accurate.

After measuring initial performance, Hofman fitted his listeners with molds that altered the shape of the pinnae and therefore changed the spectral cue. **Figure 12.9b** shows that

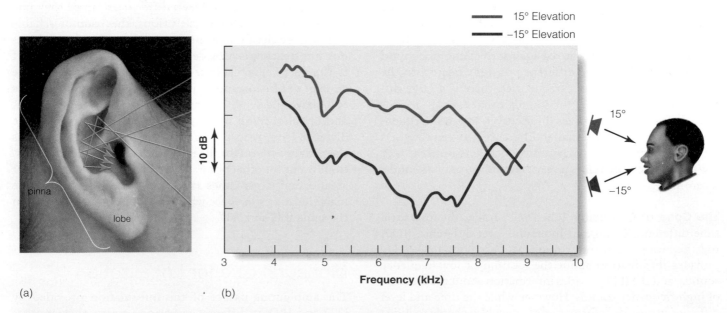

(a)   (b)

Figure 12.8 (a) Pinna showing sound bouncing around in nooks and crannies. (b) Frequency spectra recorded by a small microphone inside the listener's right ear for the same broadband sound coming from two different locations. The difference in the pattern when the sound is 15 degrees above the head (blue curve) and 15 degrees below the head (red curve) is caused by the way different frequencies bounce around within the pinna when entering it from different angles. Adapted from

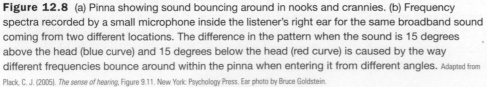

Plack, C. J. (2005). *The sense of hearing*, Figure 9.11. New York: Psychology Press. Ear photo by Bruce Goldstein.

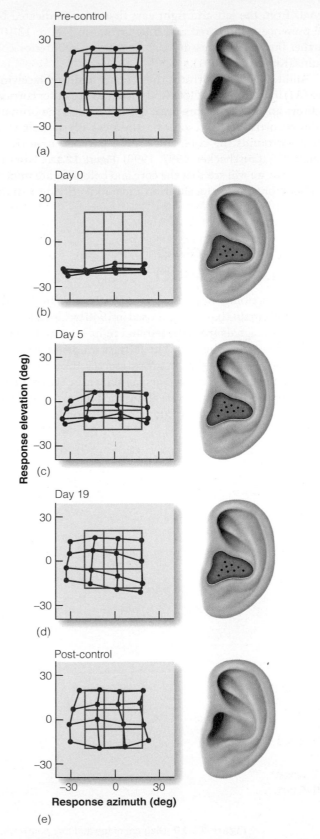

Pre-control

(a)

Day 0

(b)

Day 5

(c)

Day 19

(d)

Post-control

(e)

Response elevation (deg)

Response azimuth (deg)

Figure 12.9 How localization changes when a mold is placed in the ear. See text for explanation. Reprinted from King, A. J., Schnupp, J. W. H., & Doubell, T. P., The shape of ears to come: Dynamic coding of auditory space, *Trends in Cognitive Sciences, 5*, 261–270. Copyright 2001, with permission from Elsevier.

localization performance is poor for the elevation coordinate immediately after the mold is inserted, but locations can still be judged at locations along the azimuth coordinate. This is exactly what we would expect if binaural cues are used for judging azimuth location and spectral cues are responsible for judging elevation locations.

Hofman continued his experiment by retesting localization as his listeners continued to wear the molds. You can see from **Figure 12.9c–d** that localization performance improved, until by 19 days localization had become reasonably accurate. Apparently, the person had learned, over a period of weeks, to associate new spectral cues to different directions in space.

What do you think happened when the molds were removed? It would be logical to expect that once adapted to the new set of spectral cues created by the molds, localization performance would suffer when the molds were removed. However, as shown in **Figure 12.9e**, localization remained excellent immediately after removal of the ear molds. Apparently, training with the molds created a new set of correlations between spectral cues and location, but the old correlation was still there as well. One way this could occur is if different sets of neurons were involved in responding to each set of spectral cues, just as separate brain areas are involved in processing different languages in people who speak more than one language (King et al., 2001; Wightman & Kistler, 1998; also see van Wanrooij & Opstal, 2005).

We have seen that each type of cue works best for different frequencies and different coordinates. ITDs and ILDs work for judging azimuth location, with ITD best for low frequencies and ILD for high frequencies. Spectral cues work best for judging elevation, especially at higher frequencies. These cues work together to help us locate sounds. In real-world listening, we also move our heads, which provides additional ITD, ILD, and spectral information that helps minimize the effect of the cone of confusion and helps locate continuous sounds. Vision also plays a role in sound localization, as when you hear talking and see a person making gestures and lip movements that match what you are hearing. Thus, the richness of the environment and our ability to actively search for information help us zero in on a sound's location.

The Physiology of Auditory Localization

Having identified the cues that are associated with where a sound is coming from, we now ask how the information in these cues is represented in the nervous system. Are there neurons in the auditory system that signal ILD or ITD? To begin answering this question, we will describe the pathway from the cochlea to the cortex, because it is along this pathway that signals from the left and right ears meet, and then continue on to the auditory cortex.

The Auditory Pathway and Cortex

Signals generated in the hair cells of the cochlea are transmitted out of the cochlea in nerve fibers of the auditory nerve (refer back to Figure 11.16). The auditory nerve carries the signals generated by the inner hair cells away from the cochlea and toward the auditory receiving area in the cortex. **Figure 12.10** shows the pathway the auditory signals follow from the cochlea to the auditory cortex. Auditory nerve fibers from the cochlea synapse in a sequence of **subcortical structures**—structures below the cerebral cortex. This sequence begins with the **cochlear nucleus** and continues to the **superior olivary nucleus** in the brain stem, the **inferior colliculus** in the midbrain, and the **medial geniculate nucleus** in the thalamus.

From the medial geniculate nucleus, fibers continue to the **primary auditory cortex** (or **auditory receiving area, A1**), in the temporal lobe of the cortex. If you have trouble remembering this sequence of structures, remember the acronym SONIC MG (a very fast sports car), which represents the three structures between the cochlear nucleus and the auditory cortex, as follows: SON = superior olivary nucleus; IC = inferior colliculus; MG = medial geniculate nucleus.

A great deal of processing occurs as signals travel through the subcortical structures along the pathway from the cochlea to the cortex. Processing in the superior olivary nucleus is important for binaural localization because it is here that signals from the left and right ears first meet (indicated by the presence of both red and blue arrows in Figure 12.10). Further binaural processing also occurs in the inferior colliculus (King et al., 2001).

Auditory signals arrive at the primary auditory receiving area (A1) in the temporal lobe and then travel to other cortical auditory areas: (1) the **core area**, which includes the primary auditory cortex (A1) and some nearby areas; (2) the **belt area**, which surrounds the core, and (3) the **parabelt area** (Kaas et al., 1999; Rauschecker, 1997, 1998) (**Figure 12.11**). Later in the chapter, we will see that the core and belt areas are important both for auditory localization and for identifying sounds.

The Jeffress Neural Coincidence Model

We begin describing the physiology of localization by describing a neural circuit that was proposed in 1948 by Lloyd Jeffress to show how signals from the left and right ears can be combined to determine the ITD. The **Jeffress model** of auditory localization proposes that neurons are wired so they each receive signals from the two ears, as shown in **Figure 12.12**. Signals from the left ear arrive along the blue axon, and signals from the right ear arrive along the red axon.

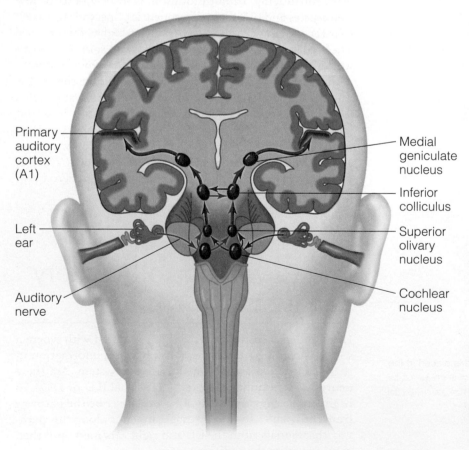

Primary auditory cortex (A1)

Left ear

Auditory nerve

Medial geniculate nucleus

Inferior colliculus

Superior olivary nucleus

Cochlear nucleus

Figure 12.10 Diagram of the auditory pathways. This diagram is greatly simplified, as numerous connections between the structures are not shown. Note that auditory structures are bilateral—they exist on both the left and right sides of the body—and that messages can cross over between the two sides. Adapted from Wever, E. G. (1949). *Theory of hearing.* New York: Wiley.

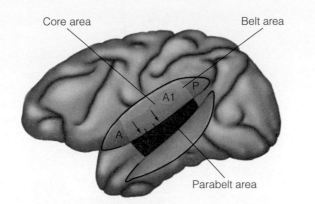

Core area   Belt area

P
A1
A
Parabelt area

Figure 12.11 The three main auditory areas in the monkey cortex: the core area, which contains the primary auditory receiving area (A1); the belt area; and the parabelt area. P indicates the posterior end of the belt area, and A indicates the anterior end of the belt area. Signals, indicated by the arrows, travel from core to belt to parabelt. The dark lines indicate where the temporal lobe was pulled back to show areas that would not be visible from the surface. From Kaas, J. H., Hackett, T. A., & Tramo, M. J. (1999). Auditory processing in primate cerebral cortex. *Current Opinion in Neurobiology, 9*, 164–170.

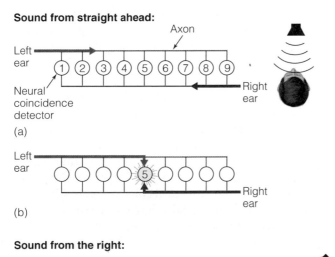

Sound from straight ahead:

Axon

Left ear ① ② ③ ④ ⑤ ⑥ ⑦ ⑧ ⑨

Neural coincidence detector

Right ear

(a)

Left ear

⑤

Right ear

(b)

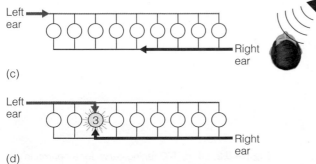

Sound from the right:

Left ear

Right ear

(c)

Left ear

③

Right ear

(d)

Figure 12.12 How the circuit proposed by Jeffress operates. Axons transmit signals from the left ear (blue) and the right ear (red) to neurons, indicated by circles. (a) Sound in front. Signals start in left and right channels simultaneously. (b) Signals meet at neuron 5, causing it to fire. (c) Sound to the right. Signal starts in the right channel first. (d) Signals meet at neuron 3, causing it to fire. Adapted from Plack, C. J. (2005). *The sense of hearing.* New York: Erlbaum.

If the sound source is directly in front of the listener, the sound reaches the left and right ears simultaneously, and signals from the left and right ears start out together, as shown in **Figure 12.12a**. As each signal travels along its axon, it stimulates each neuron along the axon in turn. At the beginning of the journey, neurons receive signals from only the left ear (neurons 1, 2, 3) or the right ear (neurons 9, 8, 7), but not both, and they do not fire. But when the signals both reach neuron 5 together, that neurons fires (**Figure 12.12b**). This neuron and the others in this circuit are called **coincidence detectors**, because they only fire when both signals coincide by arriving at the neuron simultaneously. The firing of neuron 5 indicates that ITD = 0.

If the sound comes from the right, similar events occur, but the signal from the right ear has a head start, as shown in **Figure 12.12c**, and both signals reach neuron 3 simultaneously (**Figure 12.12d**), so this neuron fires. This neuron, therefore, detects ITDs that occur when the sound is coming from a specific location on the right. The other neurons in the circuit fire to locations corresponding to other ITDs.

The Jeffress model therefore proposes a circuit that involves "ITD detectors," and it also proposes that there are a series of these detectors, each tuned to respond best to a specific ITD. According to this idea, the ITD will be indicated by which ITD neuron is firing. This has been called a "place code" because ITD is indicated by the place (which neuron) where the activity occurs.

One way to describe the properties of ITD neurons is to measure **ITD tuning curves**, which plot the neuron's firing rate against the ITD. Recording from neurons in the brainstem of the barn owl, which has excellent auditory localization abilities, has revealed narrow tuning curves that respond best to specific ITDs, like the ones in **Figure 12.13** (Carr & Konishi, 1990; McAlpine, 2005). The neurons associated with the curves on the left (blue) fire when the sound reaches the

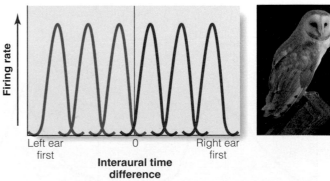

Firing rate

Left ear first   0   Right ear first

Interaural time difference

Niall Benvie/CORBIS

Figure 12.13 ITD tuning curves for six neurons that each respond to a narrow range of ITDs. The neurons on the left respond when sound reaches the left ear first. The ones on the right respond when sound reaches the right ear first. Neurons such as these have been recorded from the barn owl and other animals. However, when we consider mammals, another story emerges. Adapted from McAlpine, D., & Grothe, B. (2003). Sound localization and delay lines: Do mammals fit the model? *Trends in Neurosciences, 26,* 347–350.

left ear first, and the ones on the right (red) fire when sound reaches the right ear first. These are the tuning curves that are predicted by the Jeffress model, because each neuron responds best to a specific ITD and the response drops off rapidly for other ITDs. However, the situation is different for mammals.

Broad ITD Tuning Curves in Mammals

The results of research in which ITD tuning curves are recorded from mammals may appear, at first glance, to support the Jeffress model. For example, **Figure 12.14a** shows an ITD tuning curve of a neuron in the gerbil's superior olivary nucleus (Pecka et al., 2008). This curve has a peak in the middle and drops off on either side. However, when we compare the gerbil curve to the curve for the barn owl in **Figure 12.14b**, we can see from the ITD scales on the horizontal axis that the gerbil curve is much broader than the owl curve. In fact, the gerbil curve is so broad that it extends far outside the range of ITDs that are actually involved in sound localization, indicated by the light bar (also see Siveke et al., 2006).

This broadness of response to different locations also occurs in the auditory cortex of the monkey. **Figure 12.15** shows the responses of a neuron in a monkey's left auditory cortex to sounds located at different positions around the monkey's head. This neuron fires best to sounds on the monkey's right side and is broadly tuned, so even though it responds best when the sound is coming from about 60 degrees (indicated by the star), it also responds strongly to other locations (Recanzone et al., 2011; Woods et al., 2006).

Because of the broadness of the ITD curves in mammals, it has been proposed that coding for localization is based on broadly tuned neurons like the ones shown in **Figure 12.16** (McAlpine, 2005; Grothe, 2010). According to this idea, there are broadly tuned neurons in the right hemisphere that respond when sound is coming from the left and broadly tuned

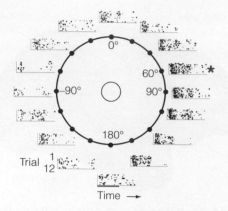

Figure 12.15 Responses recorded from a neuron in the left auditory cortex of the monkey to sounds originating at different places around the head. The monkey's position is indicated by the circle in the middle. The firing of a single cortical neuron to a sound presented at different locations around the monkey's head is shown by the records at each location. Greater firing is indicated by a greater density of dots. This neuron responds to sounds coming from a number of locations on the right. From Recanzone, G. H., Engle, J. R., & Juarez-Salinas, D. L. (2011). Spatial and temporal processing of single auditory cortical neurons and populations of neurons in the macaque monkey. *Hearing Research, 271*, 115–122, Figure 4. With permission from Elsevier. Based on data from Woods et al. (2006).

neurons in the left hemisphere that respond when sound is coming from the right. The location of a sound is indicated by the ratio of responding of these two types of broadly tuned neurons. For example, a sound from the left would cause the pattern of response shown in the left pair of bars in Figure 12.16b; a sound located straight ahead, by the middle pair of bars; and a sound to the right, by the far right bars.

This type of coding resembles the distributed coding we described in Chapter 3, in which information in the nervous system is based on the pattern of neural responding. This is, in fact, how the visual system signals different wavelengths of light, as we saw when we discussed color vision in Chapter 9, in which wavelengths are signaled by the pattern of response of three different cone pigments (Figure 9.11).

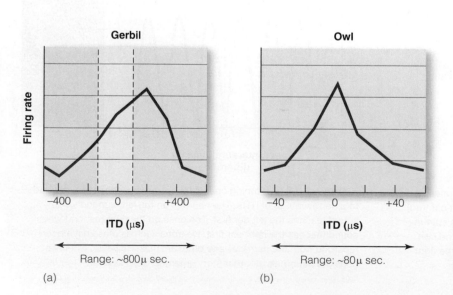

(a) **Gerbil** — Firing rate vs ITD (μs): −400, 0, +400. Range: ~800μ sec.

(b) **Owl** — Firing rate vs ITD (μs): −40, 0, +40. Range: ~80μ sec.

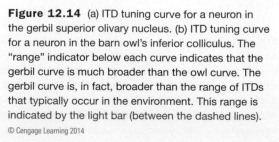

Figure 12.14 (a) ITD tuning curve for a neuron in the gerbil superior olivary nucleus. (b) ITD tuning curve for a neuron in the barn owl's inferior colliculus. The "range" indicator below each curve indicates that the gerbil curve is much broader than the owl curve. The gerbil curve is, in fact, broader than the range of ITDs that typically occur in the environment. This range is indicated by the light bar (between the dashed lines).

© Cengage Learning 2014

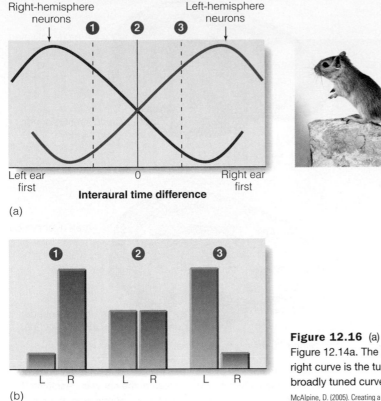

(a)

(b)

Figure 12.16 (a) ITD tuning curves for broadly tuned neurons like the one shown in Figure 12.14a. The left curve represents the tuning of neurons in the right hemisphere; the right curve is the tuning of neurons in the left hemisphere. (b) Patterns of response of the broadly tuned curves for stimuli coming from the left, in front, and from the right. Adapted from McAlpine, D. (2005). Creating a sense of auditory space. *Journal of Physiology, 566,* 21–22.

To summarize research on the neural mechanism of binaural localization, we can conclude that it is based on *sharply tuned* neurons for birds and *broadly tuned* neurons for mammals. The code for birds is a *place code* because the ITD is indicated by firing of neurons at a specific place. The code for mammals is a *distributed code* because the ITD is determined by the firing of many broadly tuned neurons working together. Next, we consider one more piece of the story for mammals, which goes beyond considering how the ITD is coded by neurons to consider how information about localization is organized in the cortex.

Localization in Area A1 and the Auditory Belt Area

We now consider research on where information about localization is processed in the cortex. Researchers have used a number of different techniques to determine whether the primary auditory receiving area, A1, is involved in localization. One technique is to determine how localization is affected by destroying or deactivating A1. Fernando Nodal and coworkers (2010), using the method of brain ablation (or lesioning) in ferrets (see Method: Brain Ablation in Chapter 4, page 83), found that destroying A1 decreased, but did not totally eliminate, the ferrets' ability to localize sounds. The involvement of A1 in localization was also demonstrated by Shveta Malhotra and Stephen Lomber (2007), who showed that deactivating A1 in cats by cooling the cortex

results in poor localization (also see Malhotra et al., 2008). Although both the ferret and cat studies showed that destroying or deactivating A1 affected localization, these studies also showed that destroying or deactivating areas *outside* A1 affected localization.

Research on how higher-order auditory areas, such as the belt or parabelt, affect localization is just beginning. Gregg Recanzone (2000) compared the spatial tuning of neurons in A1 and neurons in the posterior area of the belt (indicated by the "P" in Figure 12.11). He did this by recording from neurons in the monkey and determining how a neuron responded when a sound source was moved to different locations relative to the monkey. He found that neurons in A1 respond when a sound is moved within a specific area of space and don't respond outside that area. When he then recorded from neurons in the posterior belt area, he found that these neurons respond to sound within an even smaller area of space, indicating that spatial tuning is better in the posterior belt area. Thus, neurons in the belt area provide more precise information than A1 neurons about the location of sound sources.

Moving Beyond the Temporal Lobe: Auditory *Where* (and *What*) Pathways

Auditory processing for location extends beyond the auditory areas in the temporal lobe. Two auditory pathways extend from the temporal lobe to the frontal lobe. These pathways, like the *what* and *where* pathways we described

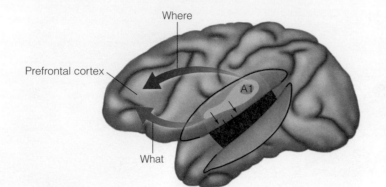

Figure 12.17 Auditory *what* and *where* pathways. The blue arrow from the anterior core and belt is the *what* pathway. The red arrow from the posterior core and belt is the *where* pathway. Adapted from Poremba, A., Saunders, R. C., Crane, A. M., Cook, M., Sokoloff, L., & Mishkin, M. (2003). Functional mapping of the primate auditory system. *Science, 299,* 568–572.

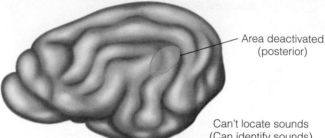

(a) "What" pathway deactivated

(b) "Where" pathway deactivated

Figure 12.18 Results of Lomber and Malhortra's (2008) experiment. (a) When the anterior (*what*) auditory area of the cat was deactivated by presenting a small cooling probe within the purple area, the cat could not identify sounds but could locate sounds. (b) When the posterior (*where*) auditory area was deactivated by presenting a cooling probe within the green area, the cat could not locate sounds but could identify sounds. © Cengage Learning 2014

for vision (see page 84), are called the *what* and *where* pathways for audition (Kaas & Hackett, 1999). The blue arrow in **Figure 12.17** indicates the *what* pathway, which starts in the front (anterior) part of the core and belt (indicated by the "A" in Figure 12.11) and extends to the prefrontal cortex. The *what* pathway is responsible for *identifying* sounds. The red arrow in Figure 12.17 indicates the *where* pathway, which starts in the rear (posterior) part of the core and belt and extends to the prefrontal cortex. This is the pathway associated with *locating* sounds.

The branching of the auditory system into these two pathways or streams is indicated by the difference between how information in the posterior and anterior areas of the belt are processed. We have seen that neurons in the posterior belt have better spatial tuning than neurons in A1. Research has also shown that while monkey A1 neurons are activated by simple sounds such as pure tones, neurons in the anterior area of the belt respond to more complex sounds, such as monkey calls—vocalizations recorded from monkeys in the jungle (Rauschecker & Tian, 2000). Thus, the posterior belt is associated with spatial tuning, and the anterior belt is associated with identifying different types of sounds. This difference between posterior and anterior areas of the belt represents the difference between *where* and *what* auditory pathways.

Additional evidence for *what* and *where* auditory pathways is provided by Stephen Lomber and Shveta Malhortra (2008), who showed that temporarily deactivating a cat's anterior auditory areas by cooling the cortex disrupts the cat's ability to tell the difference between two patterns of sounds, but does not affect the cat's ability to localize sounds (**Figure 12.18a**). Conversely, deactivating the cat's posterior auditory areas disrupts the cat's ability to localize sounds, without affecting the cat's ability to tell the difference between different patterns of sounds (**Figure 12.18b**). If the design of this experiment seems familiar, it is because it is the same as the design of Ungerleider and Mishkin's (1982) experiment that demonstrated *what* and *where* visual pathways in the monkey (compare Figure 12.18 to Figure 4.13). In both experiments, lesioning one area

(for the vision experiment) or deactivating one area (for the hearing experiment) eliminated a *what* function, and lesioning or deactivating another area eliminated a *where* function.

Cases of human brain damage also support the *what/where* idea (Clarke et al., 2002). For example, **Figure 12.19a** shows the areas of the cortex that are damaged in J.G., a 45-year-old man with temporal lobe damage caused by a head injury, and E.S., a 64-year-old woman with parietal and frontal lobe damage caused by a stroke. **Figure 12.19b** shows that J.G. can locate sounds, but his recognition is poor, whereas E.S. can recognize sounds, but her ability to locate them is poor. Thus, J.G.'s *what* stream is damaged, and E.S's *where* stream is damaged. Other researchers have also provided evidence for auditory *what* and *where* pathways by using brain scanning to show that *what* and *where* tasks activate different brain areas in humans (Alain et al., 2001, 2009; De Santis et al., 2007; Wissinger et al., 2001).

We can summarize where information about auditory localization is processed in the cortex as follows: Lesion and cooling studies indicate that A1 is important for localization. However, additional research indicates that processing information about location also occurs in the belt area and then continues farther in the *where* processing stream, which extends from the temporal lobe to the prefrontal area in the frontal lobe.

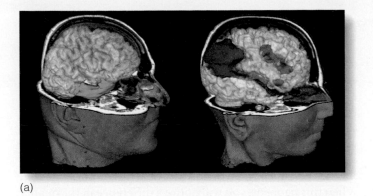

(a)

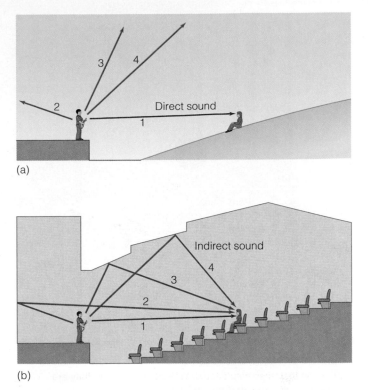

(a)

(b)

Figure 12.19 (a) Colored areas indicate brain damage for J.G. (left) and E.S. (right). (b) Performance on recognition test (green bar) and localization test (red bar). From Clarke, S., Thiran, A. B., Maeder, P., Adriani, M., Vernet, O., Regli, L., Cuisenaire, O., & Thiran, J.-P. (2002). What and where in human auditory systems: Selective deficits following focal hemispheric lesions. *Experimental Brain Research, 147*, 8–15. Reproduced with kind permission of Springer Science and Business Media.

Hearing Inside Rooms

So far in this chapter, and also in Chapter 11, we have seen that our perception of sound depends on various properties of the sound, including its frequency, sound level, location in space, and relation to other sounds. But we have left out the fact that in our normal everyday experience, we hear sounds in a specific setting, such as a small room, a large auditorium, or outdoors. As we consider this aspect of hearing, we will see why we perceive sounds differently when we are outside and inside, and how our perception of sound quality is affected by specific properties of indoor environments.

Figure 12.20 shows how the nature of the sound reaching your ears depends on the environment in which you hear the sound. If you are listening to someone playing a guitar on an outdoor stage, some of the sound you hear reaches your ears after being reflected from the ground or objects like trees, but most of the sound travels directly from the sound source to your ears (**Figure 12.20a**). If, however, you are listening to the same guitar in an auditorium, then a large proportion of the sound bounces off the auditorium's walls, ceiling, and floor

Figure 12.20 (a) When you hear a sound outdoors, you hear mainly direct sound (path 1). (b) When you hear a sound inside a room, you hear both direct sound (1) and indirect sound (2, 3, and 4) that is reflected from the walls, floor, and ceiling of the room. © Cengage Learning

before reaching your ears (**Figure 12.20b**). The sound reaching your ears directly, along path 1, is called **direct sound**; the sound reaching your ears later, along paths like 2, 3, and 4, is called **indirect sound**.

The fact that sound can reach our ears directly from where the sound is originating and indirectly from other locations creates a potential problem because even though the sound *originates* in one place, the sound *reaches the listener* from many directions and at slightly different times. Nonetheless, we generally perceive the sound as coming from only one location. We can understand why this occurs by considering the results of research in which listeners were presented with sounds separated by time delays, as would occur when they originate from two different locations.

Perceiving Two Sounds That Reach the Ears at Different Times

Research on sound reflections and the perception of location has usually simplified the problem by having people listen to sounds coming from two loudspeakers separated in space, as shown in **Figure 12.21**. The speaker on the left is the *lead speaker*, and the one on the right is the *lag speaker*. If a sound is presented in the lead speaker followed by a long delay (tenths of a second), and then a sound is presented in the lag speaker, listeners typically hear two separate sounds—one from the left (lead) followed by one from the right (lag). But when the delay

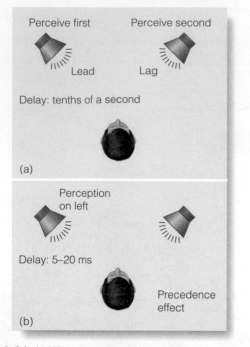

Figure 12.21 (a) When sound is presented first in one speaker and then in the other, with enough time between them, they are heard separately, one after the other. (b) If there is only a short delay between the two sounds, then the sound is perceived to come from the lead speaker only. This is the precedence effect. © Cengage Learning

between the lead and lag sounds is much shorter, something different happens. Even though the sound is coming from both speakers, listeners hear the sound as coming only from the lead speaker. This situation, in which the sound appears to originate from the lead speaker, is called the **precedence effect** because we perceive the sound as coming from the source that reaches our ears first (Litovsky et al., 1997, 1999; Wallach et al., 1949).

The precedence effect governs most of our indoor listening experience. In small rooms, the indirect sounds reflected from the walls have a lower level than the direct sound and reach our ears with delays of about 5 to 10 ms. In larger rooms, like concert halls, the delays are much longer. The precedence effect means that we generally perceive sound as coming from its source, rather than from many different directions at once. You can demonstrate the precedence effect to yourself by doing the following demonstration. **VL**

DEMONSTRATION
The Precedence Effect

To demonstrate the precedence effect, set the controls on your stereo system so that both speakers play the same sounds, and position yourself between the speakers so that you hear the sound coming from a point between both speakers. Then move a small distance to the left or right so that the sound from one of the loudspeakers takes a bit longer to reach your ears. The near and far locations now correspond to the "lead" and "lag" discussed above. When you do this, does the sound appear to be coming from only the nearer speaker?

You perceive the sound as coming from the nearer speaker because the sound from the nearer speaker is reaching your ears first, just as in Figure 12.21b, in which there was a short delay between the sounds presented by the two speakers. But even though you hear the sound as coming from the near speaker, this doesn't mean that you aren't aware of the sound from the far speaker. The sound from the far speaker changes the quality of the sound you hear, giving it a fuller, more expansive quality (Blauert, 1997; Yost & Guzman, 1996). You can demonstrate this by positioning yourself closer to one speaker and having a friend disconnect the other speaker. When this happens, you will notice a difference in the quality of the sound.

Architectural Acoustics

Having solved the location problem for sounds heard in rooms, we now consider how properties of the room can affect the quality of the sound we hear. When we studied vision, we saw that our perception of light depends not only on the nature of the light source but also on what happens to the light between the time it leaves its source and the time it enters our eyes. When light passes through haze on its way from an object to our eyes, the object may seem bluer or fuzzier than it would if the haze were not there. Similarly, our perception of sound depends not only on the sound produced at the source but also on how the sounds are reflected from the walls and other surfaces in a room.

Architectural acoustics, the study of how sounds are reflected in rooms, is largely concerned with how indirect sound changes the quality of the sounds we hear in rooms. The major factors affecting indirect sound are the size of the room and the amount of sound absorbed by the walls, ceiling, and floor. If most of the sound is absorbed, then there are few sound reflections and little indirect sound. If most of the sound is reflected, there are many sound reflections and a large amount of indirect sound. Another factor affecting indirect sound is the shape of the room. This determines how sound hits surfaces and the directions in which it is reflected.

The amount and duration of indirect sound produced by a room is expressed as **reverberation time**—the time it takes for the sound to decrease to 1/1000th of its original pressure (or a decrease in level by 60 dB). If the reverberation time of a room is too long, sounds become muddled because the reflected sounds persist for too long. In extreme cases, such as cathedrals with stone walls, these delays are perceived as echoes, and it may be difficult to accurately localize the sound source. If the reverberation time is too short, music sounds "dead," and it becomes more difficult to produce high-intensity sounds. **VL**

Acoustics in Concert Halls Because of the relationship between reverberation time and perception, acoustical engineers have tried to design concert halls in which the reverberation time matches the reverberation time of halls that are renowned for their good acoustics, such as Symphony Hall in

Boston and the Concertgebouw in Amsterdam, which have reverberation times of about 2.0 seconds. However, an "ideal" reverberation time does not always predict good acoustics. This is illustrated by the problems associated with the design of New York's Philharmonic Hall. When it opened in 1962, Philharmonic Hall had a reverberation time close to the ideal of 2.0 seconds. Even so, the hall was criticized for sounding as though it had a short reverberation time, and musicians in the orchestra complained that they could not hear each other. These criticisms resulted in a series of alterations to the hall, made over many years, until eventually, when none of the alterations proved satisfactory, the entire interior of the hall was destroyed, and the hall was completely rebuilt in 1992. It is now called Avery Fisher Hall.

The experience with Philharmonic Hall, plus new developments in the field of architectural acoustics, has led architectural engineers to consider factors in addition to reverberation time in designing concert halls. Some of these factors have been identified by Leo Beranek (1996), who showed that the following physical measures are associated with how music is perceived in concert halls:

- *Intimacy time:* The time between when sound arrives directly from the stage and when the first reflection arrives. This is related to reverberation but involves just comparing the time between the direct sound and the first reflection, rather than the time it takes for many reflections to die down.

- *Bass ratio:* The ratio of low frequencies to middle frequencies that are reflected from walls and other surfaces.

- *Spaciousness factor:* The fraction of all of the sound received by a listener that is indirect sound.

To determine the optimal values for these physical measures, acoustical engineers measured them in 20 opera houses and 25 symphony halls in 14 countries. By comparing their measurements with ratings of the halls by conductors and music critics, they confirmed that the best concert halls had reverberation times of about 2 seconds, but they found that 1.5 seconds was better for opera houses, with the shorter time being necessary to enable people to hear the singers' voices clearly. They also found that intimacy times of about 20 ms and high bass ratios and spaciousness factors were associated with good acoustics (Glanz, 2000). When these factors have been taken into account in the design of new concert halls, such as the Walt Disney Concert Hall in Los Angeles, the result has been acoustics rivaling the best halls in the world.

In designing Walt Disney Hall, the architects paid attention not only to how the shape, configuration, and materials of the walls and ceiling would affect the acoustics, but also to the absorption properties of the cushions on each of the 2,273 seats. One problem that often occurs in concert halls is that the acoustics depend on the number of people attending a performance, because people's bodies absorb sound. Thus, a hall with good acoustics when full could echo when there are too many empty seats. To deal with this problem, the seat cushions were designed to have the same absorption properties as an "average" person. This means that the hall has the same acoustics when empty or full. This is a great advantage to musicians, who usually rehearse in an empty hall.

Acoustics in Lecture Halls Although the acoustics of glamorous performance spaces such as concert halls receive a great deal of attention, acoustics often receive little attention in the design of lecture halls or classrooms. The ideal reverberation time for a small classroom is about 0.4 to 0.6 seconds, and for an auditorium about 1.0 to 1.5 seconds. These are less than the 2.0-second optimum for concert halls because the goal is not to create a rich musical sound, but to create an environment in which students can hear what the teacher is saying. Even though the ideal reverberation time for classrooms is under 0.6 seconds, many classrooms have reverberation times of 1 second or more (Acoustical Society of America, 2000).

But classrooms face other problems as well. While the main sound present in a concert hall is created by the performers, there are often many sounds in addition to the lecture in a classroom. These sounds, called *background noise*, include noisy ventilation systems, students talking in class (when they aren't supposed to!), and noise from the hall and adjacent classrooms. The presence of background noise has led to the use of **signal-to-noise (S/N) ratio** in designing classrooms. The S/N ratio is the level of the teacher's voice in dB minus the level of the background noise in the room. Ideally, the S/N ratio is +10 to +15 dB or more. At lower S/N ratios, students may have trouble hearing what the teacher is saying.

Having considered how we tell where sounds are coming from, and how we can make sense of sounds even when they are bouncing around in rooms, we are now ready to take the next step in understanding how we make sense of sounds in the environment by considering how we perceptually organize sounds when there are many sound sources.

TEST YOURSELF 12.1

1. How is auditory space described in terms of three coordinates?

2. What is the basic difference between determining the location of a sound source and determining the location of a visual object?

3. Describe the binaural cues for localization. Indicate the frequencies and directions relative to the listener for which the cues are effective.

4. Describe the monaural cue for localization.

5. What happens to auditory localization when a mold is placed in a person's ear? How well can a person localize sound once he or she has adapted to the mold? What happens when the mold is removed after the person has adapted to it?

6. Describe the auditory pathway from cochlea to auditory cortex.

7. Describe the Jeffress model, and how neural coding for localization differs for birds and for mammals.

8. Describe how auditory localization is organized in the cortex. What is the evidence that A1 is important for localization? That areas in addition to A1 are involved in localization? What is the evidence for *what* and *where* pathways in the auditory system?

9. Why does music played outdoors sound different from music played indoors?

10. What is the precedence effect, and what does it do for us perceptually?

11. What are some basic principles of architectural acoustics that have been developed to help design concert halls? What are some special problems in designing classrooms?

Auditory Organization: Scene Analysis

Our discussion so far has focused on localization—where a sound is coming from. We saw that, in contrast to vision, in which objects at different locations in space cast images on different locations on the retina, there is no spatial information on the auditory receptors. Instead, the auditory system uses spectral information and differences in level and timing between the two ears to localize sounds. We now add an important complication that occurs constantly in the environment: multiple sources of sound.

The Problem of Auditory Scene Analysis

At the beginning of the chapter, we described a man talking to a woman, with the sounds of music and other people talking in the background. The array of sound sources at different locations in the environment is called the **auditory scene**, and the process by which the stimuli produced by each of the sources in the scene are separated is called **auditory scene analysis** (Bregman, 1990, 1993; Darwin, 2010; Yost, 2001).

Auditory scene analysis poses a difficult problem because the sounds from different sources are combined into a single acoustic signal, so it is difficult to tell which part of the signal is created by which source just by looking at the waveform of the sound stimulus. We can better understand what we mean when we say that the sounds from different sources are combined into a single acoustic signal by considering the trio in **Figure 12.22**. The guitar, the vocalist, and the keyboard each create their own sound signal, but all of these signals enter the listener's ear together and so are combined into a single complex waveform. Each of the frequencies in this signal causes the basilar membrane to vibrate, but just as in the case of the bird and the cat in Figure 12.2, in which

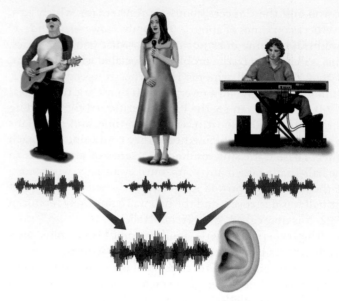

Figure 12.22 Each musician produces a sound stimulus, but these signals are combined into one signal, which enters the ear.
© Cengage Learning

there was no information on the cochlea for the locations of the two sounds, it isn't obvious what information might be contained in the sound signal to indicate which vibration is created by which sound source. **VL**

Separating the Sources

How does the auditory system separate each of the frequencies in the "combined" sound signal into information that enables us to hear the guitar, the vocalist, and the keyboard as separate sound sources? In Chapter 5, we posed an analogous question for vision when we asked how the visual system separates elements of a visual scene into separate objects. For vision, we introduced a number of organizing principles, proposed by the Gestalt psychologists and others, which are based on properties of visual stimuli that usually occur in the environment (see page 100). Now, as we turn to the sense of hearing, we will see that a similar situation occurs for auditory stimuli. There are a number of principles that help us perceptually organize elements of an auditory scene, and these principles are based on how sounds usually organize in the environment. For example, if two sounds start at different times, it is likely that they come from different sources. We will now consider a number of different types of information that are used to analyze auditory scenes.

Location One way to analyze an auditory scene into its separate components would be to use information about where each source is located. According to this idea, you can separate the sound of the vocalist from the sound of the guitar based on localization cues such as the ITD and ILD. Thus, when two sounds are separated in space, the cue of location helps us separate them perceptually. In addition, when a source moves, it typically follows a continuous path rather than jumping erratically from one place to another. For example, this continuous movement of sound helps us perceive the sound from a passing car as originating from a single source.

But the fact that information other than location is also involved becomes obvious when we consider that we can still separate the different sounds when we hear them through a single loudspeaker (or just one earphone of a portable music player), so that all the sounds are coming from the same location (Litovsky, 2012; Yost, 1997).

Onset Time As mentioned above, if two sounds start at slightly different times, it is likely that they came from different sources. This occurs often in the environment, because sounds from different sources rarely start at exactly the same time. When sound components do start together, it is likely that they are being created by the same source (Shamma & Micheyl, 2010; Shamma et al., 2011).

Pitch and Timbre Sounds that have the same timbre or pitch range are often produced by the same source. For example, if we are listening to two instruments with different ranges, such as a flute and a trombone, the timbre of the flute and trombone stay the same no matter what notes they are playing. (The flute continues to sound like a flute, and the trombone sounds like a trombone.) Similarly, the flute tends to play in a high pitch range, and the trombone plays in a low range.

Composers made use of grouping by similarity of pitch long before psychologists began studying it. Composers in the Baroque period (1600–1750) knew that when a single instrument plays notes that alternate rapidly between high and low tones, the listener perceives two separate melodies, with the high notes perceived as being played by one instrument and the low notes as being played by another. An excerpt from a composition by J. S. Bach that uses this device is shown in **Figure 12.23**. When this passage is played rapidly, the low notes sound as though they are a melody played by one instrument, and the high notes sound like a different melody played by another instrument. This separation of different sound sources into perceptually different streams, called *implied polyphony* or *compound melodic line* by musicians, is called **auditory stream segregation** by psychologists (Bregman, 1990; Darwin, 2010; Jones & Yee, 1993; Kondo & Kashino, 2009; Shamma & Micheyl, 2010; Yost & Sheft, 1993).

Albert Bregman and Jeffrey Campbell (1971) demonstrated auditory stream segregation based on pitch by alternating high and low tones, as shown in the sequence in **Figure 12.24**. When the high-pitched tones were slowly alternated with the low-pitched tones, as in **Figure 12.24a**, the tones were heard in one stream, one after another: Hi–Lo–Hi–Lo–Hi–Lo, as indicated by the dashed line. But when the tones were alternated very rapidly, the high and low tones became perceptually grouped into two auditory streams; the listener perceived two separate streams of sound, one high-pitched and one low-pitched, occurring

Figure 12.23 Four measures of a composition by J. S. Bach (Choral Prelude on *Jesus Christus unser Heiland*, 1739). When played rapidly, the upper notes become perceptually grouped and the lower notes become perceptually grouped, a phenomenon called *auditory stream segregation*. © Cengage Learning.

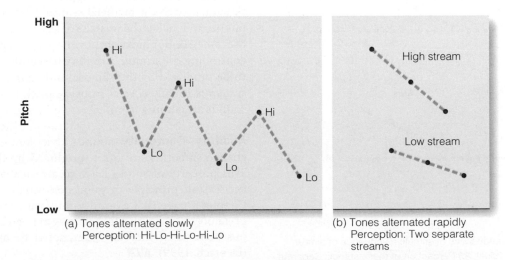

(a) Tones alternated slowly
Perception: Hi-Lo-Hi-Lo-Hi-Lo

(b) Tones alternated rapidly
Perception: Two separate streams

Figure 12.24 (a) When high and low tones are alternated slowly, auditory stream segregation does not occur, so the listener perceives alternating high and low tones. (b) Faster alternation results in segregation into high and low streams. © Cengage Learning

simultaneously (**Figure 12.24b**) (see Heise & Miller, 1951, and Miller & Heise, 1950, for an early demonstration of auditory stream segregation).

This demonstration shows that stream segregation depends not only on pitch but also on the rate at which tones are presented. Thus, returning to the Bach composition, the high and low streams are perceived to be separate if they are played rapidly, but not if they are played slowly.

Figure 12.25 illustrates a demonstration of grouping by similarity of pitch in which two streams of sound are perceived as separated until their pitches become similar. One stream is a series of repeating notes (red), and the other, a scale that goes up (blue) (**Figure 12.25a**). **Figure 12.25b** shows how this stimulus is perceived if the tones are presented fairly rapidly. At first the two streams are separated, so listeners simultaneously perceive the same note repeating and a scale going up. However, when the frequencies of the two stimuli become similar, something interesting happens. Grouping by similarity of pitch occurs, and perception changes to a back-and-forth "galloping" between the tones of the two streams. Then, as the scale continues upward so the frequencies become more separated, the two sequences are again perceived as separated. **VL**

Another example of how similarity of pitch causes grouping is an effect called the **scale illusion**, or **melodic channeling**. Diana Deutsch (1975, 1996) demonstrated this effect by presenting two sequences of notes simultaneously through earphones, one to the right ear and one to the left (**Figure 12.26a**). Notice that the notes presented to each ear jump up and down and do not create a scale. However, Deutsch's listeners perceived smooth sequences of notes in each ear, with the higher notes in the right ear and the lower ones in the left ear (**Figure 12.26b**). Even though each ear received both high and low notes, grouping by similarity of pitch caused listeners to group the higher notes in the right

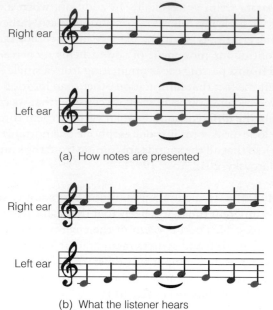

(a) How notes are presented

(b) What the listener hears

Figure 12.26 (a) These stimuli were presented to a listener's left ear (blue) and right ear (red) in Deutsch's (1975) scale illusion experiment. Notice how the notes presented to each ear jump up and down. (b) Although the notes in each ear jump up and down, the listener perceives a smooth sequence of notes. This effect is called the scale illusion, or melodic channeling. From Deutsch, D. (1975). Two-channel listening to musical scales. *Journal of the Acoustical Society of America, 57*, 1156–1160. Copyright © 1975 by the American Institute of Physics. Reproduced by permission.

ear (which started with a high note) and the lower notes in the left ear (which started with a low note).

The scale illusion highlights an important property of perceptual grouping. Most of the time, the principles of auditory grouping help us to accurately interpret what is happening in the environment. It is most effective to perceive similar sounds as coming from the same source because this is what usually happens in the environment. In Deutsch's experiment, the perceptual system applies the principle of grouping by similarity to the artificial stimuli presented through earphones and makes the mistake of assigning similar pitches to the same ear. But most of the time, when psychologists aren't controlling the stimuli, sounds with similar frequencies tend to be produced by the same sound source, so the auditory system is usually correct in using pitch to determine where sounds are coming from.

Auditory Continuity Sounds that stay constant or that change smoothly are often produced by the same source. This property of sound leads to a principle that resembles the Gestalt principle of good continuation for vision (see Chapter 5, page 102). Sound stimuli with the same frequency or smoothly changing frequencies are perceived as continuous even when they are interrupted by another stimulus (Deutsch, 1999). **VL**

Richard Warren and coworkers (1972) demonstrated auditory continuity by presenting bursts of tone interrupted by gaps of silence (**Figure 12.27a**). Listeners perceived these

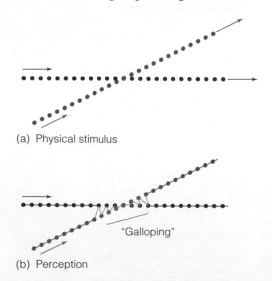

(a) Physical stimulus

"Galloping"

(b) Perception

Figure 12.25 (a) Two sequences of stimuli: a sequence of similar notes (red), and a scale (blue). (b) Perception of these stimuli: Separate streams are perceived when they are far apart in frequency, but the tones appear to jump back and forth between stimuli when the frequencies are in the same range. © Cengage Learning

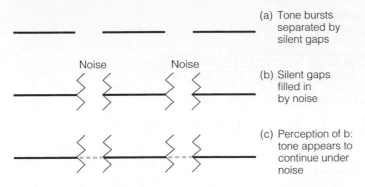

(a) Tone bursts
separated by
silent gaps

(b) Silent gaps
filled in
by noise

(c) Perception of b:
tone appears to
continue under
noise

Figure 12.27 A demonstration of auditory continuity, using tones.

© Cengage Learning

tones as stopping during the silence. But when Warren filled in the gaps with noise (**Figure 12.27b**), listeners perceived the tone as continuing behind the noise (**Figure 12.27c**). This demonstration is analogous to the demonstration of visual good continuation illustrated by coiled rope in Figure 5.17. Just as the rope is perceived as continuous even when it is covered by another coil of the rope, a tone can be perceived as continuous even though it is interrupted by bursts of noise.

Experience The effect of past experience on the perceptual grouping of auditory stimuli can be demonstrated by presenting the melody of a familiar song, as in **Figure 12.28a**. These are the notes for the song "Three Blind Mice," but with the notes jumping from one octave to another. When people first hear these notes, they find it difficult to identify the song. But once they have heard the song as it was meant to be played (**Figure 12.28b**), they can follow the melody in the octave-jumping version shown in Figure 12.28a. **VL**

This is an example of the operation of a **melody schema**— a representation of a familiar melody that is stored in a person's memory. When people don't know that a melody is present, they have no access to the schema and therefore have nothing with which to compare the unknown melody. But when they know which melody is present, they compare what they hear to their stored schema and perceive the melody (Deutsch, 1999; Dowling & Harwood, 1986).

Each of the principles of auditory grouping that we have described provides information about the number and

identity of sources in the auditory environment. But each principle alone is not foolproof, and basing our perceptions on just one principle can lead to error—as in the case of the scale illusion, which is purposely arranged so that similarity of pitch dominates our perception. In most naturalistic situations, we base our perceptions on a number of these cues working together. This is similar to the situation we described for visual perception, in which our perception of objects depends on a number of organizational principles working together, and our perception of depth depends on a number of depth cues working together.

The auditory organization we have been describing involves separation of different sound sources. But sound can also be organized in another way, as a sequence of tones is organized in terms of rhythm and meter.

Auditory Organization: Perceiving Meter

Imagine the first line of *The Star-Spangled Banner*, "Oh say can you see, by the dawn's early light." Putting these words to music in your mind creates a temporal pattern of tones, starting with two short notes (*Oh-oh*), followed by three longer notes (*say, can, you*), then a sustained note (*see*), and so on. The blue lines above the musical notation in **Figure 12.29** indicate this temporal pattern. This series of changes across time is called the **rhythmic pattern**. Different singers might change the rhythmic pattern by holding some notes longer, making others shorter, or adding pauses. Thus, any song or instrumental piece has its own rhythmic pattern, which depends on how the song is written and how it is performed.

There is another, more regular, element of musical time that underlies the rhythmic pattern, called the beat. When you tap your foot to the music, you are tapping the beat. The underlying beat of the music, called the **metrical structure**, is indicated by the red arrows below *The Star-Spangled Banner* in Figure 12.29. Note that the metrical structure is not the same thing as the notes or the rhythmic pattern, because you can feel a beat even if there are pauses in the sound during a song.

Two common meters are duple (represented in musical notation by a 2/4 time signature, which indicates that there

(a)

(b)

Figure 12.28 "Three Blind Mice." (a) Jumping octave version. (b) Normal version. © Cengage Learning

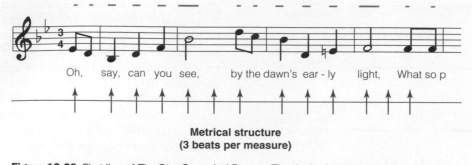

Figure 12.29 First line of *The Star-Spangled Banner*. The rhythmic pattern—the series of changes across time—is indicated by the horizontal blue lines. The metrical structure—the underlying beat of the music, determined by the time signature—is indicated by the red arrows. When the piece is performed, there is an equal amount of time between beats.

© Cengage Learning

are two beats per measure, as in a march) and triple (represented by a 3/4 time signature, which indicates that there are three beats per measure, as occurs in a waltz). Although not a waltz, *The Star-Spangled Banner* is in triple meter, as indicated by the red arrows below the music in Figure 12.29.

We have already seen how different sounds can become organized in auditory scenes, with grouping being based on factors such as similarity of pitch or proximity in time. Now we consider another aspect of auditory organization—how people perceive the metrical structure of sequences of tones. We will see that research using simple strings of tones has added another dimension to our understanding of auditory organization.

Metrical Structure and the Mind

Metrical structure is indicated by the time signature of the composition and, in performance, is typically achieved by accentuating some notes by using a stronger attack or by playing them louder or longer. In doing this, musicians bring an expressiveness to music beyond what is heard by simply playing a string of notes.

But metrical structure can also be achieved by other means, and this is what interests us, because research on how we perceive metrical structure has something to tell us about mechanisms of auditory organization. For example, we often spontaneously form perceptual groups when listening to the beat of a metronome. Thus, even though the metronome creates a series of identical beats with regular spacing, we can perceive the beats in duple meter (TICK-toc) or, with a small amount of effort, in triple meter (TICK-toc-toc) (Nozaradan et al., 2011).

This ability to change metrical structure even when the physical stimulus remains the same is similar to what happens for the visual face–vase display in Figure 5.25. In this case, the display remains the same, but perception can switch back and forth between seeing two faces or a vase. Both the regular auditory beat and the face–vase pattern are examples of *ambiguous stimuli*, because they can be perceived in more than one way.

Just as visual researchers have used ambiguous visual displays to study the mechanisms of visual perception, auditory researchers have used ambiguous repeating beat stimuli to study mechanisms of auditory perception. One of the discoveries that has emerged from this research is that there is a link between the perception of metrical structure and movement.

Metrical Structure and Movement

Music and movement go together. We tap, sway, or dance in time with the beat, and this movement can reflect the metrical structure of the music, as when dancers incorporate the ONE-two-three grouping of a waltz into their footwork. However, the relationship between movement and the beat also occurs in another direction, with movement influencing the perceptual grouping or metrical structure of the beats. Experiments that demonstrate this have been carried out with both adults and infants, so we will describe them together rather than describing the infant research in a separate "Developmental Dimension" section at the end of the chapter.

The idea that how we move may influence how we hear rhythmic patterns was first demonstrated by Jessica Phillips-Silver and Laurel Trainor (2005) in 7-month-old infants. While these infants listened to a regular repeating ambiguous rhythm that had no accents, they were bounced up and down in the arms of the experimenter. These bounces occurred either in a duple pattern (a bounce on every second beat) or in a triple pattern (a bounce on every third beat). After being bounced for 2 minutes, the infants were tested to determine whether this movement caused them to hear the ambiguous pattern in groups of two or in groups of three. To do this, the infants were tested to determine whether they preferred listening to the pattern with accents that corresponded to how they had been bounced. This preference was determined by using a head-turning preference procedure.

Phillips-Silver and Trainor found that infants listened to the pattern they had been bounced to for an average of 8 seconds but only listened to the other pattern for an average of 6 seconds. The infants therefore preferred the pattern they had been bounced to. To determine whether this effect was due to vision, infants were bounced while blindfolded. (Although the infants loved being bounced, they weren't so thrilled about being blindfolded!) The result, when they were tested later using the head-turning procedure, was the same as when they could see, indicating that vision was not a factor. Also, when the infants just watched the experimenter bounce, the effect didn't occur. Apparently *moving* is the key to influencing metrical grouping.

In another experiment, Phillips-Silver and Trainor (2007) tested adults. In this case, the experimenter didn't hold the subject, but the experimenter and subject held hands and bounced together. After bouncing with the experimenter, the adults were tested by listening to duple and triple patterns and indicated which pattern they had heard while bouncing. The adults picked the pattern that matched the way they were bounced on 86 percent of the trials. As with the infants, this result also occurred when the adults were blindfolded, but not when they just watched the experimenter bounce. Remember that during the bouncing experience the adults were *listening to* an ambiguous beat pattern, but when tested, they reported that they had *heard*, or *perceived*, the tones grouped based on how they were bounced.

Based on the results of these and other experiments, Phillips-Silver and Trainor concluded that the crucial factor that causes movement to influence the perception of metrical structure is stimulation of the **vestibular system**—the system that is responsible for balance and sensing the position of the body. To check this idea, Trainor and coworkers (2009) had adults listen to the ambiguous series of beats while electrically stimulating their vestibular system in a duple or triple pattern with electrodes placed behind the ear. This caused the subject to feel as if his or her head were moving back and forth, even though it remained stationary. This experiment duplicated the results of the other experiments, with subjects reporting hearing the pattern that matched the metrical grouping created by stimulating the vestibular system on 78 percent of the trials.

Metrical Structure and Language

Perception of meter occurs not only in response to movement but also under the influence of a longer-term experience—the stress patterns of a person's language. Different languages have different stress patterns, because of the way the languages are constructed. For example, in English, function words like "the," "a," and "to" typically precede content words, as in "the *dog*" or "to *eat*," where *dog* and *eat* are stressed when spoken. In contrast, Japanese speakers place function words after the content words, so "the *book*" in English (with *book* stressed) becomes "*hon* ga" in Japanese (with *hon* stressed). Therefore, the dominant stress pattern in English is *short–long* (*unaccented–accented*), but in Japanese it is *long–short* (*accented–unaccented*).

Comparisons of how native English-speakers and Japanese-speakers perceive metrical grouping supports the idea that the stress patterns in a person's language can influence the person's perception of grouping. John Iversen and Aniruddh Patel (2008) had subjects listen to a sequence of alternating long and short tones (**Figure 12.30a**) and then indicate whether they perceived the tone's grouping as long–short or short–long. The results indicated that English-speakers were more likely to perceive the grouping as short–long (**Figure 12.30b**) and Japanese speakers were more likely to perceive the grouping as long–short (**Figure 12.30c**).

This result also occurs when comparing 7- to 8-month-old English and Japanese infants (see the head-turning procedure described earlier), but it does not occur for 5- to 6-month-old infants (Yoshida et al., 2010). It has been hypothesized that this shift occurs between about 6 and 8 months because that is when infants are beginning to develop the capacity for language.

Returning to the Coffee Shop

The scene in the coffee shop described in Figure 12.1 introduced a number of problems for the auditory system to solve. The first problem was the *problem of auditory localization*: Where is each of the sounds you can hear in the coffee shop coming from? We saw that one solution to this problem involves comparing the sounds that reach the left and right ears, and another solution involves using spectral cues.

The second problem was how to deal with sound reflected from surfaces such as the walls of a room. This is a problem because these reflections create multiple copies of the sound from a single source that reach the listener at different times. This problem is solved by a mechanism that creates the *precedence effect*, which causes the auditory system to give preference to the first sound that arrives.

The third problem, the problem of *auditory scene analysis*, occurs because all of the sounds in the environment are combined, as illustrated for the trio in Figure 12.22. This is

Sound bursts

(a)

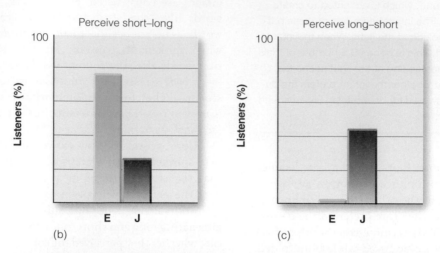

(b)

(c)

Figure 12.30 (a) Subjects listened to sequences of short and long tones. On half the trials, the first tone was short; on the other half, long. The durations of the tones ranged from about 150 ms to 500 ms (durations varied for different experimental conditions), and the entire sequence repeated for 5 seconds. (b) English-speaking subjects (E) were more likely than Japanese-speaking subjects (J) to perceive the stimulus as short–long. (c) Japanese-speaking subjects were more likely than English-speaking subjects to perceive the stimulus as long–short. Based on data from Iversen, J. R., & Patel, A. D. (2008). Perception of rhythmic grouping depends on auditory experience. *Journal of the Acoustic Society of America, 124A,* 2263–2271.

a problem of perceptual organization, because the goal is to separate the sound created by each source from this combined signal. The auditory system solves this problem by using a number of different cues, such as location, timing, pitch, continuity, and experience to separate the individual sources.

Finally, there is the problem of ongoing sequences of sounds in time, which creates a specific beat or "time signature" that organizes the music coming from the coffee shop's speakers. The research we have described on metrical structure shows that people can shift from one meter to another mentally, and also that meter can be influenced by information provided by past experience with a particular language (as demonstrated by comparing English- and Japanese-speakers) or information from another modality, such as movement (as demonstrated by the bouncing experiments).

The link between movement and perceiving meter is significant not only because it demonstrates a mechanism that influences how we perceptually organize sound in time, but also because it provides an example of cross-talk between hearing and the motor system. This cross-talk is related to another problem that the auditory system must solve: how to integrate our perception of sounds with our perception of all the other types of stimuli that exist in the environment in order to create a perception of a coherent world. After all, the coffee shop, or any environment, contains not just "sounds" or "visual stimuli" or "movements" or "smells" or "tastes." All of these things occur together and are often related. In

the next section, we will consider some examples of cross talk between hearing and vision.

SOMETHING TO CONSIDER:
Connections Between Hearing and Vision

The different senses rarely operate in isolation. For hearing, not only is there a connection between perception of musical beat and movement, but there are many examples of connections between hearing and the other senses. We see people's lips move as we listen to them speak; our fingers feel the keys of a piano as we hear the music the fingers are creating; we hear a screeching sound and turn to see a car coming to a sudden stop. All of these combinations of hearing and other senses are examples of **multisensory interactions**. We will focus on interactions between hearing and vision, first perceptually and then physiologically.

Hearing and Vision: Perceptions

One area of multisensory research is concerned with one sense "dominating" the other. If we ask whether vision or hearing is dominant, the answer is "it depends." The

ventriloquism effect, or **visual capture**, is an example of vision dominating audition. It occurs when sounds coming from one place (the ventriloquist's mouth) appear to come from another place (the dummy's mouth). Movement of the dummy's mouth "captures" the sound (Soto-Faraco et al., 2002, 2004).

Another example of visual capture occurs in movie theaters when an actor's dialogue is produced by a speaker located on one side of the screen while the image of the actor who is talking is located in the center of the screen, many feet away. When this happens, we hear the sound coming from its seen location (the image at the center of the screen) rather than from where it is actually produced (the speaker to the side of the screen). In these examples, the sound, even if it actually originates from another location, is captured by vision. Note that because virtually all theaters now have stereophonic sound, binaural cues contribute to the match between sound position and characters on the screen. But before the advent of stereophonic sound, the ventriloquism effect alone caused movie viewers to perceive sound as originating from different places on the screen rather than from off to the side.

But vision doesn't always win out over hearing. Consider, for example, the **two-flash illusion**, which occurs when a single flash is accompanied by two tones and the subject perceives two flashes (**Figure 12.31**) (Shams et al., 2000). In this case, hearing modifies vision.

Another illustration of the auditory–visual connection is shown in **Figure 12.32**. Robert Sekuler and coworkers (1997) presented an animated display that showed two identical objects moving diagonally, one down from the left and the other down from the right, crossing in the middle. Eighty-eight percent of Sekuler's observers perceived these objects as moving past each other and continuing their straight-line motion, as shown in **Figure 12.32a**. The other 12 percent of observers perceived the objects as contacting each

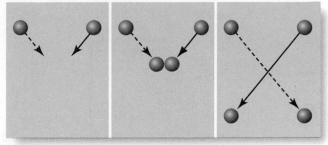

(a) Objects appear to pass by each other

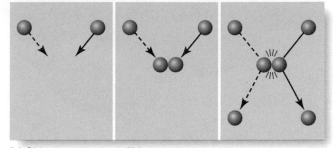

(b) Objects appear to collide

Figure 12.32 Two conditions in the Sekuler et al. (1997) experiment showing successive positions of two balls that were presented so they appeared to be moving. (a) No sound condition: the two balls were perceived to pass each other and continue moving in a straight-line motion. (b) Click-added condition: observers were more likely to see the balls as colliding. © Cengage Learning

other and bouncing off in opposite directions, as shown in **Figure 12.32b**. However, when Sekuler added a brief "click" sound just when the objects appeared adjacent to each other, 63 percent perceived them as colliding and bouncing off in opposite directions. As was the case for visual capture, in which vision influenced hearing, this example, in which hearing influences vision, also reflects the way we normally perceive events in the environment. When a sound occurs just as two moving objects become adjacent to one another, this usually means that a collision has occurred to cause the sound (also see Ecker & Heller, 2005). **VL**

Hearing and Vision: Physiology

The multisensory nature of our experience is reflected in the interconnection of the different sensory areas of the brain, represented in **Figure 12.33** (Murray & Spierer, 2011). These connections between sensory areas contribute to coordinated receptive fields (RFs) like the ones shown in **Figure 12.34** for a neuron in the monkey's parietal lobe that responds to both visual stimuli and sound (Bremmer, 2011; Schlack, 2005). This neuron responds when an auditory stimulus is presented in an area that is below eye level and to the left (**Figure 12.34a**) and when a visual stimulus originates from about the same area (**Figure 12.34b**). **Figure 12.34c** shows that there is a great deal of overlap between these two receptive fields.

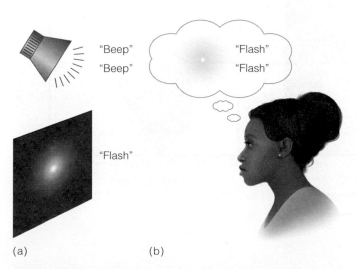

(a)   (b)

Figure 12.31 (a) Stimulus for the two-flash illusion. One flash of light is accompanied by two tones. (b) The illusion occurs when the subject perceives two flashes of light, even though there was just one.
© Cengage Learning 2014

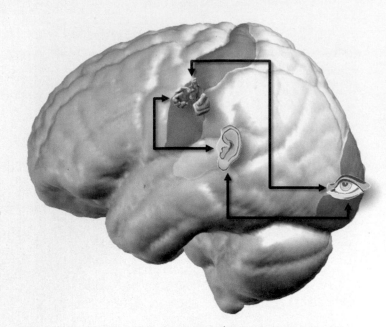

Figure 12.33 There are connections between the primary receiving areas for vision, hearing, and somatosensory sensation (touch, pain). These connections create interactions between the senses. From Murray, M. M., & Spierer, L. (2011). Multisensory integration: What you see is where you hear. *Current Biology, 21,* R229–R231. With permission from Elsevier.

It is easy to see that neurons such as this would be useful in our multisensory environment. When we hear a sound coming from a specific location in space and also see what is producing the sound—a bird singing or a person talking—the multisensory neurons that fire to both sound and vision help us form a single representation of space that involves both auditory and visual stimuli.

Another example of cross talk between the senses occurs when the primary receiving area associated with one sense is activated by stimuli that are usually associated with another sense. For example, some blind people use a technique called *echolocation* to locate objects and perceive shapes in the environment. Their technique is similar to the echolocation used by bats and dolphins, which emit high-frequency sounds and use information from the echoes reflected back from objects to sense the shapes and locations of the objects (see Figure 10.47, page 254).

The blind people make a clicking sound with their tongue and mouth and listen for echoes. Skilled echolocators can detect the positions and shapes of objects as they move through the environment. For example, a person using echolocation can detect a wall as they walk toward it; more impressively, extremely skilled echolocators can identify objects such as cars, large trash cans, and fire hydrants as they are walking along a sidewalk (see www.worldaccess fortheblind.org).

Recently, Lore Thaler and coworkers (2011) had two expert echolocators create their clicking sounds as they stood near objects, and recorded the sounds and resulting echoes with small microphones placed in the ears. The question Thaler and coworkers were interested in is how these sounds would activate the brain. To determine this, they recorded brain activity using fMRI as the expert echolocators and sighted control subjects listened to the recorded sounds that included the echoes. Not surprisingly, they found that the sounds activated the auditory cortex in both the blind and sighted subjects. However, the visual cortex was strongly activated in the echolocators but was silent in the control subjects (**Figure 12.35**).

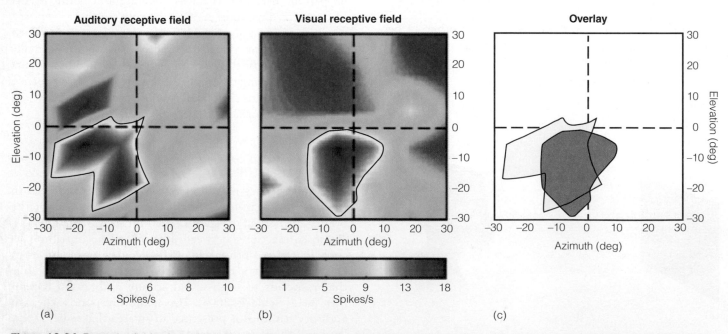

Figure 12.34 Receptive fields of neurons in the monkey's parietal lobe that respond to (a) auditory stimuli that are located in the lower left area of space, and (b) visual stimuli presented in the lower left area of the monkey's visual field. (c) Superimposing the two receptive fields indicates that there is a high level of overlap between the auditory and visual fields. Parts (a) and (b) from Bremmer, F. (2011). Multisensory space: From eye-movements to self-motion. *Journal of Physiology, 589,* 815–823. Reproduced with permission of John Wiley & Sons, Inc. Part (c) © Cengage Learning 2014.

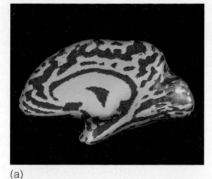

(a)

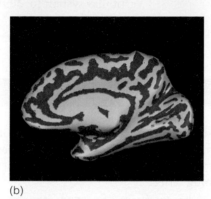

(b)

Figure 12.35 (a) Brain activity for a blind subject listening to sound stimuli. The activity shown here is the activity generated by a stimulus that contained echoes, minus the activity of the same stimulus without the echoes. Because the auditory cortex was activated in both of these conditions, no auditory cortex activation is shown. However, listening to the echo stimulus resulted in activity in the visual cortex shown here. (b) Activity for a sighted subject listening to the same stimuli. Activation with and without echoes was the same, so no activity is shown. From Thaler, L., Arnott, S. R., & Goodale, M. A. (2011). Neural correlates of natural human echolocation in early and late blind echolocation experts. PLoS ONE 6, e20162. doi:10.1371. journal.pone.0020162.

Apparently, the visual area is activated because the echolocators are having what they describe as "spatial" experiences. In fact, some echolocators lose their awareness of the auditory clicks as they focus on the spatial information the echoes are providing (Kish, 2012). This example of multisensory functioning shows that the response of the brain can be based not just on the type of energy entering the eyes or ears but on the perceptual outcome of that energy. Thus, when sound is used to achieve spatial awareness, the visual cortex becomes involved.

TEST YOURSELF 12.2

1. What is auditory scene analysis, and why is it a "problem" for the auditory system?

2. What are the basic principles of auditory grouping that help us achieve auditory scene analysis? Be sure you understand the following experiments: Bregman and Campbell (Figure 12.24); "galloping" crossing streams (Figure 12.25); scale illusion (Figure 12.26); auditory continuity (Figure 12.27); and melody schema (Figure 12.28).

3. What is the difference between the rhythmic pattern and metrical structure?

4. Why can we describe the beating of a metronome as an ambiguous metrical stimulus? Describe the experiments that demonstrate a connection between (a) movement and metrical grouping and (b) a person's language and metrical grouping.

5. Describe the ways that (a) vision "dominates" hearing; (b) hearing dominates vision; (c) sound provides information that influences what we see.

THINK ABOUT IT

1. We can perceive space visually, as we saw in the chapter on depth perception, and through the sense of hearing, as we have described in this chapter. How are these two ways of perceiving space similar and different? (p. 290)

2. How good are the acoustics in your classrooms? Can you hear the professor clearly? Does it matter where you sit? Are you ever distracted by noises from inside or outside the room? (p. 303)

3. How is object recognition in vision like stream segregation in hearing? (p. 304)

4. In the experiments on metrical structure, the stimulus was a steady, accent-free, series of beats, like the sound produced by a metronome. But in most music, specific beats are accented. Determine a number of ways that this accenting is achieved, by listening to a few different kinds of music (p. 305).

5. What are some situations in which (a) you use one sense in isolation, and (b) the combined use of two or more senses is necessary to accomplish a task? (p. 310)

KEY TERMS

Acoustic shadow (p. 292)
Architectural acoustics (p. 302)
Auditory localization (p. 290)
Auditory receiving area (A1) (p. 296)
Auditory scene (p. 304)
Auditory scene analysis (p. 304)
Auditory space (p. 290)
Auditory stream segregation (p. 305)
Azimuth (p. 291)

MEDIA RESOURCES

CourseMate

Go to CengageBrain.com to access Psychology CourseMate, where you will find the Virtual Labs plus an interactive eBook, flashcards, quizzes, videos, and more.

Virtual Labs VL

The Virtual Labs are designed to help you get the most out of this course. The Virtual Lab icons direct you to specific media demonstrations and experiments designed to help you visualize what you are reading about. The numbers below indicate the number of the Virtual Lab you can access through Psychology CourseMate.

12.1 Interaural Level Difference as a Cue for Sound Localization (p. 292)
How the relative loudness of two tones presented by different speakers determines the perceived location of the tone.

12.2 The Precedence Effect (p. 302)
How perception of sound location depends on the lag between sounds presented by two different speakers.

12.3 Reverberation Time (p. 302)
How increasing a tone's reverberation time changes its perceived quality.

12.4 Layering Naturalistic Sounds (p. 304)
How we are able to hear different environmental sounds as being produced by different sound sources, even when they are presented at the same time.

12.5 Grouping by Pitch and Temporal Closeness (p. 306)
How our perception of three tones changes as the tones are presented more rapidly. A demonstration of auditory stream segregation.

12.6 Effect of Repetition on Grouping by Pitch (p. 306)
How the grouping observed in the "Grouping by Pitch and Temporal Closeness" Virtual Lab can be affected by repeating the sequences.

12.7 Grouping by Similarity of Pitch (p. 306)
How the perceptual organization of two sequences of tones changes when their pitches approach each other, illustrating the "galloping" effect.

12.8 Grouping by Similarity of Timbre: The Wessel Demonstration (p. 306)
How similarity of timbre can change the perceived organization of a series of tones if the tones are presented rapidly enough. (The Wessel demonstration is not described in the text.)

12.9 Captor Tone Demonstration (p. 306)
The stimuli used in an experiment by Albert Bregman and Alex Rudnicky, which demonstrated an effect of stream segregation. (This experiment is not described in the text.)

12.10 Auditory Good Continuation (p. 306)
A demonstration of good continuation for auditory stimuli.

12.11 Perceiving Interleaved Melodies (p. 307)
How two familiar melodies are perceived when the notes are interleaved.

12.12 Sound and Vision 1: Crossing or Colliding Balls (p. 311)
Illustrates how sound can influence perception of the paths of two moving balls. (Courtesy of Robert Sekuler)

12.13 Sound and Vision 2: Rolling Ball (p. 311)
Illustrates how sound can affect perception of the path of a rolling ball. (Courtesy of Laurie Heller)

12.14 Sound and Vision 3: Flashing Dot (p. 311)
Illustrates how sound can affect perception of a flashing dot. (Courtesy of Ladan Shams)

12.15 Testing Intermodal Perception in Infants (p. 311)
Stimulus and testing procedure used to test intermodal perception in infants. (Courtesy of George Hollich)

316

Speech Perception

VL The Virtual Lab icons direct you to specific animations and videos designed to help you visualize what you are reading about. Virtual Labs are listed at the end of the chapter, keyed to the page on which they appear, and can be accessed through Psychology CourseMate.

Some Questions We Will Consider:

■ Can computers perceive speech as well as humans? (p. 317)

■ Does each word that we hear have a unique pattern of air pressure changes associated with it? (p. 320)

■ Why does an unfamiliar foreign language often sound like a continuous stream of sound, with no breaks between words? (p. 326)

■ Are there specific areas in the brain that are responsible for perceiving speech? (p. 329)

A lthough we perceive speech easily under most conditions, beneath this ease lurks processes as complex as those involved in perceiving the most complicated visual scenes. One way to appreciate this complexity is to consider attempts to use computers to recognize speech. Many companies now use computer speech recognition systems to provide services such as booking tickets, automated banking, and computer technical support. But if you've ever used one of these systems, it is likely that a friendly computer voice has told you "I can't understand what you said" on more than one occasion.

Computer speech recognition is constantly improving, but it still can't match people's ability to recognize speech. Computers perform well when a person speaks slowly and clearly, and when there is no background noise. However, humans can perceive speech under a wide variety of conditions, including the presence of various background noises, sloppy pronunciation, speakers with different dialects and accents, and the often chaotic give-and-take that routinely

◄ What is going on here? It is safe to assume that the emotions expressed by these people's faces are a response to something someone said. Our ability to perceive sounds created by our speech apparatus as meaningful words is one of our most important means of communication. Just as with other types of perception we have discussed, the ease of speech perception is the end result of complex processes, often involving cognitive mechanisms based on our past experiences.

occurs when people talk with one another (Sinha, 2002; Zue & Glass, 2000). This chapter will help you appreciate the complex perceptual problems posed by speech and will describe research that has helped us begin to understand how the human speech perception system has solved some of these problems.

The Speech Stimulus

We began describing sound in Chapter 11 by introducing pure tones—simple sine-wave patterns with different amplitudes and frequencies. We then introduced complex tones consisting of a number of pure tones, called harmonics, with frequencies that are multiples of the tone's fundamental frequency. The sounds of speech increase the complexity one more level. We can still describe speech in terms of frequencies, but also in terms of the abrupt starts and stops, silences, and noises that occur as speakers form words. It is these words that add an important dimension to speech—the meanings that speakers create by saying words and by stringing them together into sentences. These meanings influence our perception of the incoming stimuli, so that what we perceive depends not only on the physical sound stimulus but also on cognitive processes that help us interpret what we are hearing. We begin by describing the physical sound stimulus, called the *acoustic signal*.

The Acoustic Signal

Speech sounds are produced by the position or the movement of structures within the vocal apparatus, which produce patterns of pressure changes in the air called the **acoustic stimulus**, or the **acoustic signal**. The acoustic signal for most speech sounds is created by air that is pushed up from the lungs past the vocal cords and into the vocal tract. The sound that is produced depends on the shape of the vocal tract as air is pushed through it. The shape of the vocal tract is altered by moving the **articulators**, which include structures such as the tongue, lips, teeth, jaw, and soft palate (**Figure 13.1**).

Let's first consider the production of vowels. Vowels are produced by vibration of the vocal cords, and the specific sounds of each vowel are created by changing the overall shape of the vocal tract. This change in shape changes the resonant frequency of the vocal tract and produces peaks of pressure at a number of different frequencies (**Figure 13.2**). The frequencies at which these peaks occur are called **formants**.

Each vowel sound has a characteristic series of formants. The first formant has the lowest frequency; the second formant is the next highest; and so on. The formants for the vowel /ae/ (the vowel sound in the word *had*) are shown on a **sound spectrogram** in **Figure 13.3** (speech sounds are indicated by setting them off with slashes). The sound

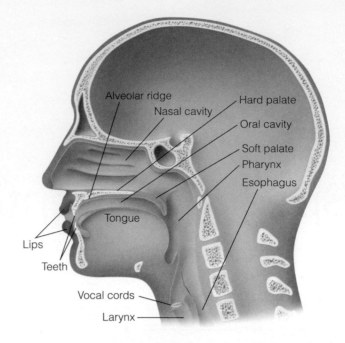

Figure 13.1 The vocal tract includes the nasal and oral cavities and the pharynx, as well as components that move, such as the tongue, lips, and vocal cords. © Cengage Learning

spectrogram indicates the pattern of frequencies and intensities over time that make up the acoustic signal. Frequency is indicated on the vertical axis and time on the horizontal axis; intensity is indicated by darkness, with darker areas indicating greater intensity. From Figure 13.3 we can see that formants are concentrations of energy at specific frequencies, with the sound /ae/ having formants at 500, 1,700, and 2,500 Hz. The vertical lines in the spectrogram are pressure oscillations caused by vibrations of the vocal cord.

Consonants are produced by a constriction, or closing, of the vocal tract. To illustrate how different consonants are produced, let's focus on the sounds /d/ and /f/. Make these sounds, and notice what your tongue, lips, and teeth are doing. As you produce the sound /d/, you place your tongue against the ridge above your upper teeth (the alveolar ridge of Figure 13.1) and then release a slight rush of air as you move your tongue away from the alveolar ridge (try it). As you produce the sound /f/, you place your bottom lip against your upper front teeth and then push air between the lips and the teeth.

These movements of the tongue, lips, and other articulators create patterns of energy in the acoustic signal that we can observe on the sound spectrogram. For example, the spectrogram for the sentence "Roy read the will," shown in **Figure 13.4**, shows aspects of the signal associated with vowels and consonants. The three horizontal bands marked F1, F2, and F3 are the three formants associated with the /e/ sound of *read*. Rapid shifts in frequency preceding or following formants are called **formant transitions** and are associated with consonants. For example, T2 and T3 are formant transitions associated with the /r/ of *read*.

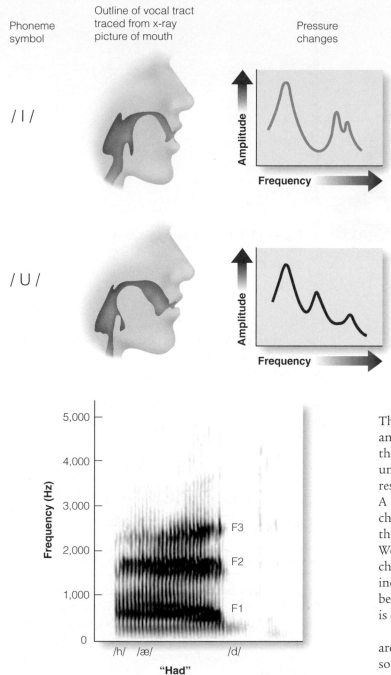

Phoneme symbol

Outline of vocal tract traced from x-ray picture of mouth

Pressure changes

/ I /

Amplitude

Frequency

/ U /

Amplitude

Frequency

Figure 13.2 Left: the shape of the vocal tract for the vowels /I/ (as in *zip*) and /U/ (as in *put*). Right: the amplitude of the pressure changes produced for each vowel. The peaks in the pressure changes are the *formants*. Each vowel sound has a characteristic pattern of formants that is determined by the shape of the vocal tract for that vowel. From Denes, P. B., & Pinson, E. N., *The speech chain*, 2nd ed. Copyright © 1993 by W. H. Freeman and Company. Used with permission of W. H. Freeman and Company.

Figure 13.3 Spectrogram of the word *had*. "Time" is on the horizontal axis. The dark horizontal bands are the first (F1), second (F2), and third (F3) formants associated with the sound of the vowel /ae/. Spectrogram courtesy of Kerry Green.

We have described the physical characteristics of the *acoustic signal*. To understand how this acoustic signal results in *speech perception*, we need to consider the basic units of speech.

Basic Units of Speech

Our first task in studying speech perception is to separate speech sounds into manageable units. What are these units? The flow of a sentence? A particular word? A syllable?

The sound of a letter? A sentence is too large a unit for easy analysis, and some letters have no sounds at all. Although there are arguments for the idea that the syllable is the basic unit of speech (Mehler, 1981; Segui, 1984), most speech research has been based on a unit called the **phoneme**. A phoneme is the shortest segment of speech that, if changed, would change the meaning of a word. Consider the word *bit*, which contains the phonemes /b/, /i/, and /t/. We know that /b/, /i/, and /t/ are phonemes because we can change the meaning of the word by changing each phoneme individually. Thus, *bit* becomes *pit* if /b/ is changed to /p/, *bit* becomes *bat* if /i/ is changed to /a/, and *bit* becomes *bid* if /t/ is changed to /d/.

The phonemes of American English, listed in **Table 13.1**, are represented by phonetic symbols that stand for speech sounds. This table shows phonemes for 13 vowel sounds and 24 consonant sounds. Your first reaction to this table may be that there are more vowels than the standard set you learned in grade school (*a, e, i, o, u,* and sometimes *y*). The reason there are more vowels is that some vowels can have more than one pronunciation, so there are more vowel sounds than vowel letters. For example, the vowel *o* sounds different in *boat* and *hot*, and the vowel *e* sounds different in *head* and *heed*. Phonemes, then, refer not to letters but to speech sounds that determine the meaning of what people say.

Because different languages use different sounds, the number of phonemes varies across languages. There are only 11 phonemes in Hawaiian, but as many as 47 have been identified in American English and up to 60 in some African languages. Thus, phonemes are defined in terms of the sounds that are used to create words in a specific language.

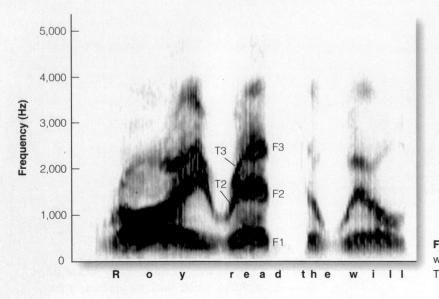

Figure 13.4 Spectrogram of the sentence "Roy read the will," showing formants F1, F2, and F3 and formant transitions T2 and T3. Spectrogram courtesy of Kerry Green.

TABLE 13.1 Major Consonants and Vowels of English and Their Phonetic Symbols

CONSONANTS				VOWELS	
p	pull	s	sip	i	heed
b	bull	z	zip	I	hid
m	man	r	rip	e	bait
w	will	š	should	ε	head
f	fill	ž	pleasure	æ	had
v	vet	č	chop	u	who'd
θ	thigh	ǰ	gyp	U	put
ð	that	y	yip	ʌ	but
t	tie	k	kale	o	boat
d	die	g	gale	O	bought
n	near	h	hail	a	hot
l	lear	ŋ	sing	ə	sofa
				ɨ	many

There are other American English phonemes in addition to those shown here, and specific symbols may vary depending on the source.

© Cengage Learning

It might seem that having identified the phoneme as the basic unit of speech, we could describe speech perception in terms of strings of phonemes. According to this idea, we perceive a series of sounds called phonemes, which create syllables that combine to create words. These syllables and words appear strung together one after another like beads on a string. For example, we perceive the phrase "perception is easy" as the sequence of units "per-sep-shun-iz-ee-zee." But although perceiving speech may seem to be just a matter of processing a series of discrete sounds that are lined up one after another, the actual situation is much more complex.

Rather than following one another, with the signal for one sound ending and then the next beginning, like letters on a page, signals for neighboring sounds overlap one another. In addition, the pattern of air pressure changes for a particular word can vary greatly depending on whether the speaker is male or female, young or old, speaks rapidly or slowly, or has an accent.

The Variable Relationship Between Phonemes and the Acoustic Signal

The main problem facing researchers trying to understand speech perception is that there is a variable relationship between the acoustic signal and the sounds we hear. In other words, a particular sound can be associated with a number of different acoustic signals. Let's consider some of the sources of this variability.

Variability From Context

The acoustic signal associated with a phoneme changes depending on its context. For example, look at **Figure 13.5**, which shows spectrograms for the sounds /di/ and /du/. These are smoothed hand-drawn spectrograms that show the two most important characteristics of the sounds: the formants (shown in red) and the formant transitions (shown in blue). Because formants are associated with vowels, we know that the formants at 200 and 2,600 Hz are the acoustic signal for the vowel /i/ in /di/ and that the formants at 200 and 600 Hz are the acoustic signal for the vowel /u/ in /du/.

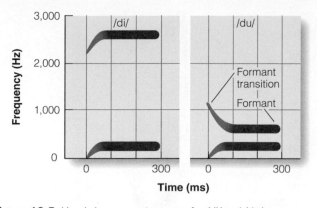

Figure 13.5 Hand-drawn spectrograms for /di/ and /du/. From Liberman, A. M., Cooper, F. S., Shankweiler, D. P., & Studdert-Kennedy, M. (1967). Perception of the speech code. *Psychological Review*, *74*, 431–461. Reproduced by permission of the author.

Because the formants are the acoustic signals for the vowels, the formant transitions that precede the formants must be the signal for the consonant /d/. But notice that the formant transitions for the second (higher-frequency) formants of /di/ and /du/ are different. For /di/, the formant transition starts at about 2,200 Hz and rises to about 2,600 Hz. For /du/, the formant transition starts at about 1,100 Hz and falls to about 600 Hz. Thus, even though we perceive the same /d/ sound in /di/ and /du/, the formant transitions, which are the acoustic signals associated with these sounds, are very different. Thus, the context in which a specific phoneme occurs can influence the acoustic signal that is associated with that phoneme.

This effect of context occurs because of the way speech is produced. Because articulators are constantly moving as we talk, the shape of the vocal tract associated with a particular phoneme is influenced by the sounds that both precede and follow that phoneme. This overlap between the articulation of neighboring phonemes is called **coarticulation**. You can demonstrate coarticulation to yourself by noting how you produce phonemes in different contexts. For example, say *bat* and *boot*. When you say *bat*, your lips are unrounded, but when you say *boot*, your lips are rounded, even during the initial /b/ sound. Thus, even though the /b/ is the same in both words, you articulate each differently. In this example, the articulation of /oo/ in *boot* overlaps the articulation of /b/, causing the lips to be rounded even before the /oo/ sound is actually produced.

The fact that we perceive the sound of a phoneme as the same even though the acoustic signal is changed by coarticulation is an example of *perceptual constancy*. This term may be familiar to you from our observations of constancy phenomena in the sense of vision, such as color constancy (we perceive an object's chromatic color as constant even when the wavelength distribution of the illumination changes) and size constancy (we perceive an object's size as constant even when the size of its image changes on our retina). Perceptual constancy in speech perception is similar. We perceive the sound of a particular phoneme as constant even when the phoneme appears in different contexts that change its acoustic signal.

Variability From Different Speakers

People say the same words in a variety of different ways. Some people's voices are high-pitched and some are low-pitched; people speak with various accents; some talk very rapidly and others speak e-x-t-r-e-m-e-l-y s-l-o-w-l-y. These wide variations in speech mean that for different speakers, a particular phoneme or word can have very different acoustic signals.

Speakers also introduce variability through sloppy pronunciation. For example, say the following sentence at the speed you would use in talking to a friend: "This was a best buy." How did you say "best buy"? Did you pronounce the /t/ of best, or did you say "bes buy"? What about "She is a bad girl"? While saying this rapidly, notice whether your tongue hits the top of your mouth as you say the /d/ in bad. Many people omit the /d/ and say "ba girl." Finally, what about "Did you go to the store?" Did you say "did you" or "dijoo"? You have your own ways of producing various words and phonemes, and other people have theirs. Analysis of how people actually speak has determined that there are 50 different ways to produce the word *the* (Waldrop, 1988).

That people do not usually articulate each word individually in conversational speech is reflected in the spectrograms in **Figure 13.6**. The spectrogram in **Figure 13.6a** is for the question "What are you doing?" spoken slowly and distinctly; the spectrogram in **Figure 13.6b** is for the same question taken from conversational speech, in which "What are you doing?" becomes "Whad'aya doin'?" This difference shows up clearly in the spectrograms. Although the first and last words (*what* and *doing*) create similar patterns in the two spectrograms, the pauses between words are absent or are much less obvious in the spectrogram of Figure 13.6b, and the middle of this spectrogram is completely changed, with a number of speech sounds missing.

The variability in the acoustic signal caused by coarticulation, different speakers, and sloppy pronunciation creates a problem for the listener, who must somehow transform the information contained in this highly variable acoustic signal into familiar words. In the next section, we will consider some of the ways the speech perception system deals with the variability problem.

Perceiving Phonemes

The speech perception system deals with the variability problem in different ways. We first describe a property of the speech system called *categorical perception* and then consider how information provided by the face and by our knowledge of language helps us perceive speech sounds accurately.

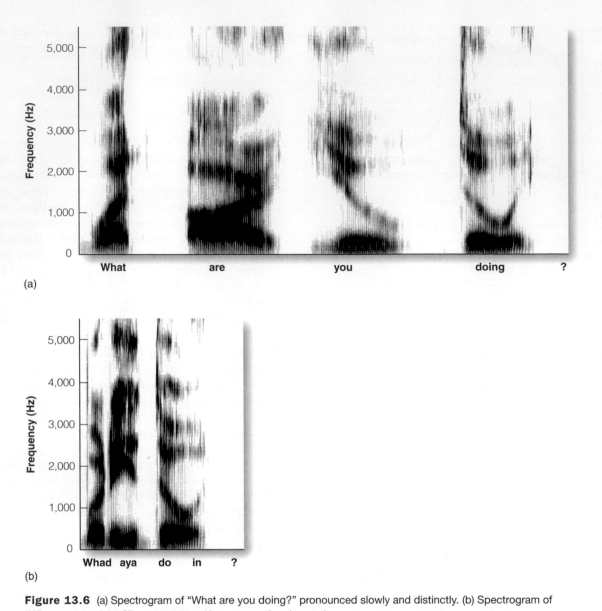

(a)

(b)

Figure 13.6 (a) Spectrogram of "What are you doing?" pronounced slowly and distinctly. (b) Spectrogram of "What are you doing?" as pronounced in conversational speech. Spectrograms courtesy of David Pisoni.

Categorical Perception

Categorical perception occurs when stimuli that exist along a continuum are perceived as divided into discrete categories. For example, consider the visible spectrum in **Figure 13.7**. Starting on the left, at a wavelength of 450 nm, we see blue. As we move toward longer wavelengths, the color remains blue, until suddenly at about 480 nm, we perceive green. Moving along the continuum, we see green all the way to about 570 nm, when the color changes to yellow, then orange, then red. Thus, moving along the entire length of the visible spectrum we encounter just five categories.

Categorical perception in speech occurs in the same way, except the continuum is a property called **voice onset time (VOT)**, the time delay between when a sound begins and when the vocal cords begin vibrating. We can illustrate this delay by comparing the spectrograms for the sounds /da/ and

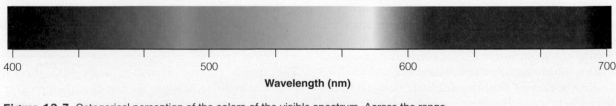

Figure 13.7 Categorical perception of the colors of the visible spectrum. Across the range of wavelengths, five categories of colors are perceived: blue, green, yellow, orange, and red.

© Cengage Learning 2014

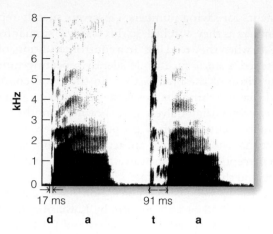

Figure 13.8 Spectrograms for /da/ and /ta/. The voice onset time—the time between the beginning of the sound and the onset of voicing—is indicated at the beginning of the spectrogram for each sound. Spectrogram courtesy of Ron Cole.

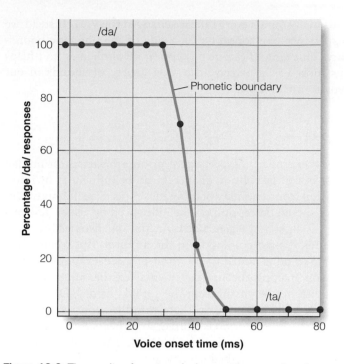

Figure 13.9 The results of a categorical perception experiment indicating a phonetic boundary, with /da/ perceived for VOTs to the left and /ta/ perceived for VOTs to the right. From Eimas, P. D., & Corbit, J. D. (1973). Selective adaptation of linguistic feature detectors. *Cognitive Psychology, 4*, 99–109, Figure 2. Reproduced by permission.

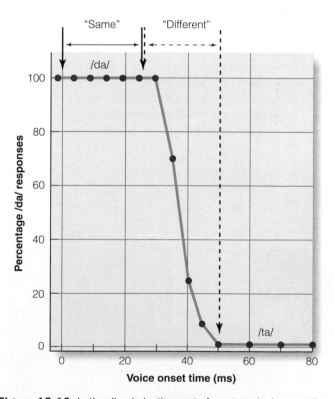

Figure 13.10 In the discrimination part of a categorical perception experiment, two stimuli are presented, and the listener indicates whether they are the same or different. The typical result is that two stimuli with VOTs on the same side of the phonetic boundary (VOT = 0 and 25 ms; solid arrows) are judged to be the same, whereas two stimuli on different sides of the phonetic boundary (VOT = 25 ms and 50 ms; dashed arrows) are judged to be different. © Cengage Learning

/ta/ in **Figure 13.8**. These spectrograms show that the time between the beginning of the sound and the beginning of the vocal cord vibrations (indicated by the presence of vertical stripes in the spectrogram) is 17 ms for /da/ and 91 ms for /ta/. Thus, /da/ has a short VOT, and /ta/ has a long VOT.

By using computers, researchers have created sound stimuli in which the VOT is varied in small steps from short to long. When they vary VOT, using stimuli like the ones shown in Figure 13.8, and ask listeners to indicate what sound they hear, the listeners report hearing only one or the other of the two phonemes, /da/ or /ta/, even though a large number of stimuli with different VOTs are presented.

This result is shown in **Figure 13.9** (Eimas & Corbit, 1973). At short VOTs, listeners report that they hear /da/, and they continue reporting this even when the VOT is increased. But when the VOT reaches about 35 ms, their perception abruptly changes, so at VOTs above 40 ms, they report hearing /ta/. The VOT when the perception changes from /da/ to /ta/ is called the **phonetic boundary**. The key result of the categorical perception experiment is that even though the VOT is changed continuously across a wide range, the listener perceives only two categories: /da/ on one side of the phonetic boundary and /ta/ on the other side.

Once we have demonstrated categorical perception using this procedure, we can run a *discrimination test*, in which we present two stimuli with different VOTs and ask the listener whether they sound the same or different. When we present two stimuli separated by a VOT of 25 ms that are on the same side of the phonetic boundary, such as stimuli with VOTs of 0 and 25 ms, the listener says they sound the same (**Figure 13.10**). However, when we present two stimuli that are separated by the same difference in VOT but are on opposite sides of the phonetic boundary, such as stimuli with VOTs of 25 and 50 ms, the listener says they sound different. The fact that all stimuli on the same side of the phonetic boundary are perceived as the same category is an example of perceptual constancy. If this constancy did not exist, we would perceive different sounds every time we changed the VOT. Instead, we experience one sound on each side of the phonetic boundary. This simplifies our perception of phonemes and helps us more easily perceive the wide variety of sounds in our environment. **VL**

Information Provided by the Face

Another property of speech perception is that it is **multimodal**; that is, our perception of speech can be influenced by information from a number of different senses. One illustration of how speech perception can be influenced by visual information is shown in **Figure 13.11**. At first our listener hears the sounds /ba-ba/ coming from the monitor. But when visual stimulation is added in the form of a videotape showing a person making the lip movements for the sound /ga-ga/, our listener begins hearing the sound /da-da/. Despite the fact that the listener is still receiving the acoustic signal for /ba-ba/, his perception is shifted, so he hears /da-da/.

This effect is called the **McGurk effect**, after the person who first described it (McGurk & MacDonald, 1976). It illustrates that although auditory information is the major source of information for speech perception, visual information can also exert a strong influence on what we hear. This influence of vision on speech perception is called **audiovisual speech perception**. The McGurk effect is one example of audiovisual speech perception. Another example is the way people routinely use information provided by the speaker's lip movements to help understand speech in a noisy environment (also see Sumby & Pollack, 1954). **VL**

The link between vision and speech has been shown to have a physiological basis. Gemma Calvert and coworkers (1997) used fMRI to measure brain activity as observers watched a silent videotape of a person making mouth movements for saying numbers. Observers silently repeated the numbers as they watched, so this task was similar to what people do when they read lips. In a control condition, observers watched a static face while silently repeating numbers. A comparison of the brain activity in these two conditions showed that watching the lips move activated an area in the auditory cortex that Calvert had shown in another experiment to be activated when people are perceiving speech. The fact that the same areas are activated for lipreading and speech perception, suggests Calvert, may be a neural mechanism behind the McGurk effect.

The link between speech perception and face perception was demonstrated in another way by Katharina von Kriegstein and coworkers (2005), who measured fMRI activation as listeners were carrying out a number of tasks involving sentences spoken by familiar speakers (people who also worked in the laboratory) and unfamiliar speakers (people they had never heard before).

Just listening to speech activated the superior temporal sulcus (STS; see Figure 5.52), an area that had been associated in previous studies with speech perception (Belin et al., 2000). But when listeners were asked to carry out a task that involved paying attention to the sounds of familiar voices, the fusiform face area (FFA) was also activated. In contrast, paying attention to the sounds of unfamiliar voices did not activate the FFA. Apparently, when people hear a voice that they associate with a specific person, this activates areas not only for perceiving speech but also for perceiving faces. The link between perceiving speech and perceiving faces, which has been demonstrated in both behavioral and physiological experiments, provides information that helps us deal with the variability of phonemes (also see Hall et al., 2005, and Wassenhove et al., 2005, for more on the link between observing someone speaking and perceiving speech).

Information From Our Knowledge of Language

A large amount of research has shown that it is easier to perceive phonemes that appear in a meaningful context. Philip Rubin, M. T. Turvey, and Peter Van Gelder (1976), for example, presented a series of short words, such as *sin*, *bat*, and *leg*, or nonwords, such as *jum*, *baf*, and *teg*, and asked listeners to respond by pressing a key as rapidly as possible whenever they heard a sound that began with /b/. On average, participants took 631 ms to respond to the nonwords and 580 ms to respond to the real words. Thus, when a phoneme was at the beginning of a real word, it was identified about 8 percent faster than when it was at the beginning of a meaningless syllable.

The effect of meaning on the perception of phonemes was demonstrated in another way by Richard Warren (1970), who had participants listen to a recording of the sentence "The state governors met with their respective legislatures convening in the capital city." Warren replaced the first /s/ in "legislatures" with the sound of a cough and told his subjects

Figure 13.11 The McGurk effect. The woman's lips are moving as if she is saying /ga-ga/, but the actual sound being presented is /ba-ba/. The listener, however, reports hearing the sound /da-da/. If the listener closes his eyes, so that he no longer sees the woman's lips, he hears /ba-ba/. Thus, seeing the lips moving influences what the listener hears.

that they should indicate where in the sentence the cough occurred. None of the participants identified the correct position of the cough, and, even more significantly, none noticed that the /s/ in "legislatures" was missing. This effect, which Warren called the **phonemic restoration effect**, was experienced even by students and staff in the psychology department who knew that the /s/ was missing. **VL**

Warren not only demonstrated the phonemic restoration effect but also showed that it can be influenced by the meaning of words following the missing phoneme. For example, the last word of the phrase "There was time to *ave . . ." (where the * indicates the presence of a cough or some other sound) could be "shave," "save," "wave," or "rave," but participants heard the word "wave" when the remainder of the sentence had to do with saying good-bye to a departing friend.

The phonemic restoration effect was used by Arthur Samuel (1981) to show that speech perception is determined both by the nature of the acoustic signal (bottom-up processing) and by context that produces expectations in the listener (top-down processing). Samuel demonstrated bottom-up processing by showing that restoration is better when a masking sound, such as the hissing sound produced by a TV set tuned to a nonbroadcasting channel, and the masked phoneme sound similar. Thus, phonemic restoration is more likely to occur for a phoneme such as /s/, which is rich in high-frequency acoustic energy, if the mask also contains a large proportion of high-frequency energy. What happens in phonemic restoration, according to Samuel, is that before we actually perceive a "restored" sound, its presence must be confirmed by the presence of a sound that is similar to it. If the white-noise mask contains frequencies that make it sound similar to the phoneme we are expecting, phonemic restoration occurs, and we are likely to hear the phoneme. If the mask does not sound similar, phonemic restoration is less likely to occur (Samuel, 1990).

Samuel demonstrated top-down processing by showing that longer words increase the likelihood of the phonemic restoration effect. Apparently, participants used the additional context provided by the long word to help identify the masked phoneme. Further evidence for the importance of context is Samuel's finding that more restoration occurs for a real word such as *prOgress* (where the capital letter indicates the masked phoneme) than for a similar pseudoword such as *crOgress* (Samuel, 1990; also see Samuel, 1997, 2001, for more evidence that top-down processing is involved in phonemic restoration).

TEST YOURSELF 13.1

1. Describe the speech stimulus. Be sure you understand what phonemes are and how the acoustic signal can be displayed using a sound spectrogram to reveal formants and formant transitions.

2. What are two sources of variability that affect the relationship between the acoustic signals and the sounds we hear? Be sure you understand coarticulation.

3. What is categorical perception? Be sure you understand how it is measured and what it illustrates.

4. What is the McGurk effect, and what does it illustrate about how speech perception can be influenced by visual information? What physiological evidence demonstrates a link between visual processing and speech perception?

5. Describe evidence that shows how perceiving phonemes is influenced by the context in which they appear. Describe the phonemic restoration effect and the evidence for both bottom-up and top-down processing in creating this effect.

Perceiving Words

Just as perceiving phonemes goes beyond simply processing the acoustic signal, perceiving words depends on a number of factors in addition to the acoustic signal. We begin by showing how being in a sentence can influence our perception of words. Then we consider how we are able to distinguish words from one another in a sentence, and how we can perceive words even when they are pronounced differently by different speakers.

Perceiving Words in Sentences

One way to illustrate how being in a sentence can influence our perception of words is to show that words can be read even when they are incomplete, as in the following demonstration.

DEMONSTRATION

Perceiving Degraded Sentences

Read the following sentences:

1. M*R* H*D * L*TTL* L*MB I*S FL**C* W*S WH*T* *S SN*W

2. TH* S*N *S N*T SH*N*NG T*D**

3. S*M* W**DS *R* EA*I*R T* U*D*R*T*N* T*A* *T*E*S

Your ability to read the sentences, even though up to half of the letters have been eliminated, was aided by your knowledge of English words, how words are strung together to form sentences, and perhaps in the first example, your familiarity with the nursery rhyme (Denes & Pinson, 1993).

A similar effect of meaningfulness also occurs for spoken words. An early demonstration of how meaningfulness makes it easier to perceive spoken words was provided by George Miller and Steven Isard (1963), who showed that words are more intelligible when heard in the context of a grammatical sentence than when presented as items in a list of unconnected words. They demonstrated this by creating three kinds of stimuli: (1) normal grammatical sentences, such as *Gadgets simplify work around the house*; (2) anomalous sentences that follow the rules of grammar but make no sense, such as *Gadgets*

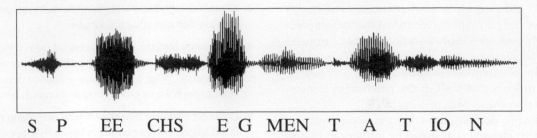

S P EE CHS E G MEN T A TIO N

Figure 13.12 Sound energy for the words "speech segmentation." Notice that it is difficult to tell from this record where one word ends and the other begins. Speech signal courtesy of Lisa Sanders.

kill passengers from the eyes; and (3) ungrammatical strings of words, such as *Between gadgets highways passengers the steal*.

Miller and Isard used a technique called **shadowing**, in which they presented these sentences to subjects through earphones and asked them to repeat aloud what they were hearing. The participants reported normal sentences with an accuracy of 89 percent, but their accuracy fell to 79 percent for the anomalous sentences and 56 percent for the ungrammatical strings. The differences among the three types of stimuli became even greater when the listeners heard the stimuli in the presence of a background noise. For example, at a moderately high level of background noise, accuracy was 63 percent for the normal sentences, 22 percent for the anomalous sentences, and only 3 percent for the ungrammatical strings of words. These results tell us that when words are arranged in a meaningful pattern, we can perceive them more easily. But most people don't realize it is their knowledge of the nature of their language that helps them fill in sounds and words that might be difficult to hear. For example, our knowledge of permissible word structures tells us that ANT, TAN, and NAT are all permissible sequences of letters in English, but that TQN or NQT cannot be English words.

A similar effect of meaning on perception also occurs because our knowledge of the rules of grammar tells us that "There is no time to question" is a permissible English sentence, but "Question, no time there is" is not permissible or, at best, is extremely awkward (unless you are Yoda, who says this in *Star Wars, Episode III: Revenge of the Sith*). Because we mostly encounter meaningful words and grammatically correct sentences, we are continually using our knowledge of what is permissible in our language to help us understand what is being said. This becomes particularly important when listening under less than ideal conditions, such as in noisy environments or when the speaker's voice quality or accent is difficult to understand (see also Salasoo & Pisoni, 1985).

Perceiving Breaks Between a Sequence of Words

Just as we effortlessly see objects when we look at a visual scene, we usually have little trouble perceiving individual words when conversing with another person. But when we look at the speech signal, we see that the acoustic signal is continuous, with either no physical breaks in the signal or

breaks that don't necessarily correspond to the breaks we perceive between words (**Figure 13.12**). The perception of individual words in a conversation is called **speech segmentation**.

The fact that there are usually no spaces between words becomes obvious when you listen to someone speaking a foreign language. To someone who is unfamiliar with that language, the words seem to speed by in an unbroken string. However, to a speaker of that language, the words seem separated, just as the words of your native language seem separated to you. We somehow solve the problem of speech segmentation and divide the continuous stream of the acoustic signal into a series of individual words.

The fact that we can perceive individual words in conversational speech, even though there are no breaks in the speech signal, means that our perception of words is not based only on the energy stimulating the receptors. One thing that helps us tell when one word ends and another begins is knowledge of the meanings of words. The link between speech segmentation and meaning is illustrated in the following demonstration.

DEMONSTRATION
Organizing Strings of Sounds

Read the following words: Anna Mary Candy Lights Since Imp Pulp Lay Things. Now that you've read the words, what do they mean?

If you think this is a list of unconnected words beginning with the names of two women, Anna and Mary, you're right; but read this series of words out loud speaking rapidly and ignoring the spaces between the words on the page. When you do this, can you hear a connected sentence that does *not* begin with the names Anna and Mary? (For the answer, see page 333—but don't peek until you've tried reading the words rapidly.)

If you succeeded in creating a new sentence from the series of words, you did so by changing the perceptual organization of the sounds, and this change was achieved by your knowledge of the meaning of the sounds. Just as the perceptual organization of the forest scene in Figure 5.32 depended on seeing the rocks as meaningful patterns (faces), your perception of the new sentence depended on knowing the meanings of the sounds you created when you said these words rapidly.

Another example of how meaning and prior knowledge or experience are responsible for organizing sounds into words is provided by these two sentences:

Jamie's mother said, "Be a *big girl* and eat your vegetables."

The thing *Big Earl* loved most in the world was his car.

"Big girl" and "Big Earl" are both pronounced the same way, so hearing them differently depends on the overall meaning of the sentence in which these words appear. This example is similar to the familiar "I scream, you scream, we all scream for ice cream" that many people learn as children. The sound stimuli for "I scream" and "ice cream" are identical, so the different organizations must be achieved by the meaning of the sentence in which these words appear.

While segmentation is aided by knowing the meanings of words and making use of the context in which these words occur, listeners use other information as well to achieve segmentation. As we learn a language, we learn that certain sounds are more likely to follow one another within a word, and other sounds are more likely to be separated by the space between two words. For example, consider the words *pretty baby*. In English it is likely that *pre* and *ty* will be in the same word (**pre-tty**) and that *ty* and *ba* will be separated by a space so will be in two different words (pre*ty ba*by). Thus, the space in the phrase *prettybaby* is most likely to be between *pretty* and *baby*.

Psychologists describe the way sounds follow one another in a language in terms of **transitional probabilities**—the chances that one sound will follow another sound. Every language has transitional probabilities for different sounds, and as we learn a language, we not only learn how to say and understand words and sentences, but we also learn about the transitional probabilities in that language. The process of learning about transitional probabilities and about other characteristics of language is called **statistical learning**. Research has shown that infants as young as 8 months of age are capable of statistical learning.

Jennifer Saffran and coworkers (1996) carried out an early experiment that demonstrated statistical learning in young infants. **Figure 13.13a** shows the design of this experiment. During the learning phase of the experiment, the infants heard four nonsense "words" such as *bidaku, padoti, golabu,* and *tupiro,* which were combined in random order to create 2 minutes of continuous sound. An example of part of a string created by combining these words is *bidaku**padoti**go-labu**tupiro**padoti**bidaku.*... In this string, every other word is printed in boldface in order to help you pick out the words. However, when the infants heard these strings, all the words were pronounced with the same intonation, and there were no breaks between the words to indicate where one word ended and the next one began. **VL**

Because the words were presented in random order and with no spaces between them, the 2-minute string of words the infants heard sounds like a jumble of random sounds. However, there was information within the string of words in the form of transitional probabilities, which the infants could potentially use to determine which groups of sounds

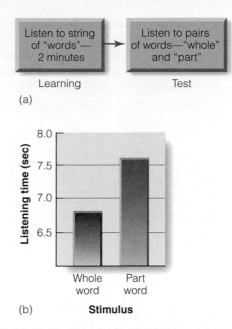

Figure 13.13 (a) Experimental design of the experiment by Saffran and coworkers (1996), in which infants listened to a continuous string of nonsense syllables and were then tested to see which sounds they perceived as belonging together. (b) The results, indicating that infants listened longer to the "part-word" stimuli. © Cengage Learning

were words. The transitional probabilities between two syllables that appeared *within* a word was always 1.0. For example, for the word *bidaku*, when /bi/ was presented, /da/ always followed it. Similarly, when /da/ was presented, /ku/ always followed it. In other words, these three sounds always occurred together and in the same order, to form the word *bidaku*. However, the transitional probabilities between the *end* of one word and the *beginning* of another was only 0.33. For example, there was a 33-percent chance that the last sound, /ku/ from *bidaku*, would be followed by the first sound, /pa/, from *padoti*, a 33-percent chance that it would be followed by /tu/ from *tupiro*, and a 33-percent chance it would be followed by /go/ from *golabu*.

If Saffran's infants were sensitive to transitional probabilities, they would perceive stimuli like *bidaku* or *padoti* as words, because the three syllables in these words are linked by transitional probabilities of 1.0. In contrast, stimuli like *tibida* (the end of *padoti* plus the beginning of *bidaku*) would not be perceived as words, because the components were not linked.

To determine whether the infants did, in fact, perceive stimuli like *bidaku* and *padoti* as words, the infants were tested by being presented with pairs of three-syllable stimuli. One of the stimuli was a "word" that had been presented before, such as *padoti*. This was the "whole-word" test stimulus. The other stimulus was created from the end of one word and the beginning of another, such as *tibida*. This was the "part-word" test stimulus.

The prediction was that the infants would choose to listen to the part-word test stimuli longer than to the whole-word stimuli. This prediction was based on previous research that showed that infants tend to lose interest in stimuli that are repeated, and so become familiar, but pay more attention to novel stimuli that they haven't experienced before. Thus, if the infants perceived the whole-word stimuli as words that had been repeated over and over during the 2-minute learning session, they would pay less attention to these familiar stimuli than to the more novel part-word stimuli that they did not perceive as being words.

Saffran measured how long the infants listened to each sound by presenting a blinking light near the speaker where the sound was coming from. When the light attracted the infant's attention, the sound began, and it continued until the infant looked away. Thus, the infants controlled how long they heard each sound by how long they looked at the light.

Figure 13.13b shows that the infants did, as predicted, listen longer to the part-word stimuli. These results are impressive, especially because the infants had never heard the words before, they heard no pauses between words, and they had only listened to the strings of words for 2 minutes. From results such as these, we can conclude that the ability to use transitional probabilities to segment sounds into words begins at an early age.

Taking Speaker Characteristics Into Account

When you're having a conversation, hearing a lecture, or listening to dialogue in a movie, you usually focus on determining the meaning of what is being said. But as you are taking in these messages, you are also, perhaps without realizing it, taking in characteristics of the speaker's voice. These characteristics, called **indexical characteristics**, carry information about speakers such as their age, gender, place of origin, emotional state, and whether they are being sarcastic or serious. Consider, for example, the following joke:

> A linguistics professor was lecturing to his class one day. "In English," he said, "a double negative forms a positive. In some languages, though, such as Russian, a double negative is still a negative. However, there is no language wherein a double positive can form a negative." A voice from the back of the room piped up, "Yeah, right."

This joke is humorous because "Yeah, right" contains two positive words that, despite the linguistics professor's statement, produce a negative statement that most people who know contemporary English usage would interpret as "I disagree." The point of this example is not just that "Yeah, right" can mean "I disagree," but that the meaning of this phrase is determined by our knowledge of current English usage and also (if we were actually listening to the student's remark) by the speaker's tone of voice, which in this case would be highly sarcastic.

The speaker's tone of voice is one factor that helps listeners determine the meaning of what is being said. But most research on indexical characteristics has focused on how

speech perception is influenced by the speaker's identity. Thomas Palmeri, Stephen Goldinger, and David Pisoni (1993) demonstrated the effect of speaker identity by presenting listeners with a sequence of words. After each word, listeners indicated whether the word was a new word (this was the first time it appeared) or an old word (it had appeared previously in the sequence). They found that listeners reacted more rapidly and were more accurate when the same speaker said all of the words than when different speakers said the words. This means that listeners are taking in two levels of information about the word: (1) its meaning and (2) characteristics of the speaker's voice.

From the results of this experiment and the others we have discussed, we can conclude that speech perception depends both on the bottom-up information provided by the acoustic signal and on the top-down information provided by the meanings of words and sentences, the listener's knowledge of the rules of grammar, and information that the listener has about characteristics of the speaker's voice (**Figure 13.14**).

We can appreciate the interaction between the acoustic signal for speech and the meaning of speech when we realize that although we use the meaning to help us understand the acoustic signal, the acoustic signal is the starting point for determining the meaning. Look at it this way: There may be enough information in my sloppy handwriting so that a person using bottom-up processing can decipher it solely on the basis of the squiggles on the page, but my handwriting is much easier to decipher when, by using top-down processing, the person takes the meanings of the words into account. Just as previous experience in hearing a particular person's voice makes it easier to understand that person later, previous experience in reading my handwriting would make it easier to read the squiggles on the page. Speech perception apparently works in a similar way. Although most of the information is contained in the acoustic signal, taking meaning and indexical properties into account makes understanding speech much easier.

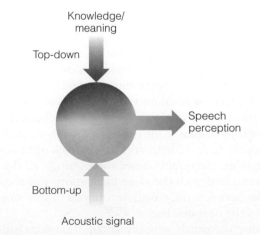

Figure 13.14 Speech perception is the result of top-down processing (based on knowledge and meaning) and bottom-up processing (based on the acoustic signal) working together.
© Cengage Learning

Speech Perception and the Brain

Investigation of the physiological basis for speech perception stretches back to at least the 19th century, but considerable progress has been made only recently in understanding the physiological foundations of speech perception and spoken word recognition.

Cortical Locations of Speech Perception

Based on their studies of brain-damaged patients, 19th-century researchers Paul Broca and Carl Wernicke showed that damage to specific areas of the brain causes language problems, called **aphasias** (**Figure 13.15**). There are numerous forms of aphasia, with the specific symptoms depending on the area damaged and the extent of the damage. Patients with damage to **Broca's area** in the frontal lobe have a condition called **Broca's aphasia**. They have labored and stilted speech and can only speak in short sentences. They are, however, capable of comprehending what others are saying. Patients with damage to **Wernicke's area** in the temporal lobe have **Wernicke's aphasia**. They can speak fluently, but what they say is extremely disorganized and not meaningful. These patients have great difficulty understanding what other people are saying. In the most extreme form of Wernicke's aphasia, the person has a condition called **word deafness**, in which he or she cannot recognize words, even though the ability to hear pure tones remains intact (Kolb & Whishaw, 2003).

Modern research has gone beyond localizing speech production and perception in these two areas through further studies of brain-damaged patients (see Method: Double Dissociations in Neuropsychology, Chapter 4, page 85) and by using brain imaging to locate areas in the brain related to speech. An example of a finding from neuropsychology is that some patients with damage to the parietal lobe have difficulty discriminating between syllables (Blumstein et al., 1977; Damasio & Damasio, 1980). Although we might expect that difficulty in discriminating between syllables would make it difficult to understand words, some patients who have trouble discriminating syllables can still understand words (Micelli et al., 1980). Results such as these illustrate the complex relationship between brain functioning and speech perception.

Measuring brain activity has yielded more straightforward results. For example, Pascal Belin and coworkers (2000) used fMRI to locate a "voice area" in the human superior temporal sulcus (STS) that is activated more by human voices than by other sounds, and Catherine Perrodin and coworkers (2011) recorded from neurons in the monkey's temporal lobe that they called **voice cells** because they responded more strongly to recordings of monkey calls than to calls of other animals or to "non-voice" sounds.

The "voice area" and "voice cells" are located in the temporal lobe, which is part of the *what* processing stream for hearing that we described in Chapter 12 (see page 300). In describing the cortical organization for hearing in Chapter 12, we saw that the *what* pathway is involved in identifying sounds, and the *where* pathway is involved in locating sounds (Figure 12.17). Piggybacking on this dual-stream idea for hearing, a **dual-stream model of speech perception** has proposed a ventral (or *what*) pathway starting in the temporal lobe that is responsible for recognizing speech, and a dorsal (or *where*) pathway starting in the parietal lobe that is responsible for linking the acoustic signal to the movements used to produce speech (**Figure 13.16**; Hickock & Poeppel, 2007).

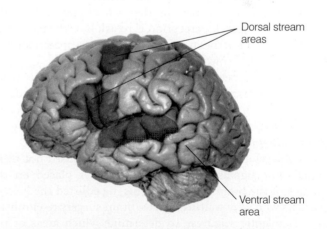

Figure 13.16 The dual-stream model of speech perception proposes a ventral pathway that is responsible for recognizing speech and a dorsal stream that links the acoustic signal and motor movements. The blue areas are associated with the dorsal pathway and the yellow areas with the ventral pathway. The red and green areas are also involved in the analysis of speech stimuli. Adapted from Hickock, G., & Poeppel, D. (2007). The cortical organization of speech processing. *Nature Reviews Neuroscience, 8,* 393–401.

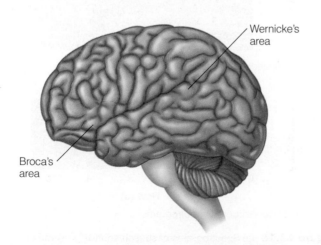

Figure 13.15 Broca's and Wernicke's areas were identified in early research as being specialized for language production and comprehension. © Cengage Learning

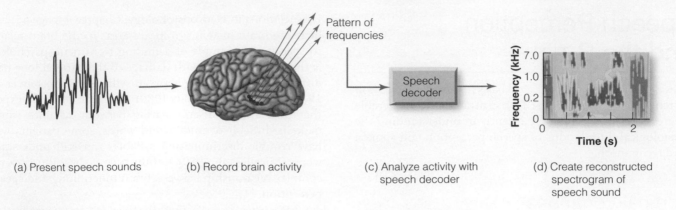

Pattern of frequencies

Speech decoder

(a) Present speech sounds (b) Record brain activity (c) Analyze activity with speech decoder (d) Create reconstructed spectrogram of speech sound

Figure 13.17 Pasley et al. (2012) procedure for creating reconstructed spectrograms from electrical signals recorded from the brain. See text for details. © Cengage Learning 2014

This is similar to the situation we described for perceiving faces in Chapter 5 (page 120). We saw that perceiving faces involves many aspects, including identifying the face, reading expressions, noting where the face is looking, and evaluating the face's attractiveness, and that mechanisms for face perception are therefore distributed across many areas. There are also a number of different aspects to speech perception. It is influenced by cognitive factors such as the meaning of words, the context of sentences, and familiarity with a speaker's voice; it is linked to vision; and it can have a strong emotional component. It is not surprising, therefore, that perceiving speech involves many interconnected areas of the cortex.

Reconstructing Speech From the Cortical Signal

The research described above is concerned with where speech is processed in the cortex. Another way of approaching the physiology of speech perception is to ask how the pattern of electrical signals in the speech areas represents speech sounds. Brian Pasley and coworkers (2012) approached this question by creating a "speech decoder" similar to the visual "scene decoder" we described in Chapter 5, which was able to determine, based on analysis of fMRI signals, the type of scene a person was observing (Naselaris et al., 2009; see "Reading the Brain," Chapter 5, page 116).

To develop a decoder for speech, Pasley used not fMRI signals but signals recorded by electrodes placed on the surface of the brain. To achieve this, he enlisted the help of patients who were waiting to have brain surgery to eliminate severe epileptic seizures. To determine which areas of the brain should be removed to eliminate the seizures, neurosurgeons place electrodes on the surface of the brain and record activity over a period of a week.

As shown in **Figure 13.17**, Pasley presented speech sounds to these patients (**Figure 13.17a**) and recorded the activity picked up by the electrode array (**Figure 13.17b**). Because different frequencies are represented by activity at different locations on the auditory cortex (refer back to Figure 11.31,

page 281), Pasley was able to determine the pattern of frequencies present in the speech stimulus from the activity recorded at the different electrode placements. This pattern of activity was then analyzed by the speech decoder (**Figure 13.17c**), which created a speech spectrogram of the sound that was presented (**Figure 13.17d**). This spectrogram is called a "reconstructed" spectrogram because it is constructed from the electrical signals recorded by the electrode array on the brain. **VL**

The results of this analysis are shown in **Figure 13.18**. Spectrograms of the words being presented are shown in the top row (**Figure 13.18a**), and the corresponding spectrograms created by the speech decoder are shown in the bottom row (**Figure 13.18b**). The correspondence between actual and reconstructed spectrograms is far from perfect, but when a "playback" device is used to convert these frequency patterns into sounds, it is possible to hear speech sounds that, in many cases, can be recognized as the words the patient was hearing.

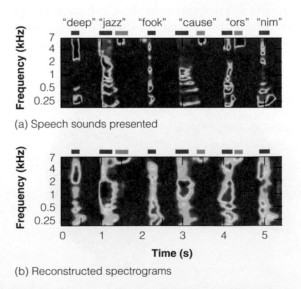

"deep" "jazz" "fook" "cause" "ors" "nim"

(a) Speech sounds presented

(b) Reconstructed spectrograms

Figure 13.18 (a) Spectrograms of speech sounds presented to Pasley's subjects. (b) Speech spectrograms constructed by the speech decoder from electrical signals recorded from auditory cortex.

From Pasley, B. N., David, S. V., Mesgarani, M., Flinker, A., Shamma, S. A., Crone, N. E., et al. (2012). Reconstructing speech from human auditory cortex. *PLoS Biology 10*(1): e1001251.

This result is important because it brings us closer to understanding how speech is represented in the human brain. In addition, being able to determine speech from brain activity could potentially help people who can't talk because of conditions such as ALS (amyotrophic lateral sclerosis; Lou Gehrig's disease), which paralyzes the body while leaving the mind intact. Because thinking about speaking can create brain signals similar to those that occur in actual speech, it is possible that someday it might be possible for people with ALS to communicate by having their thoughts about speaking transformed into sound using a speech decoder similar to the one described here.

SOMETHING TO CONSIDER:
Speech Perception and Action

An important characteristic of speech is that we not only perceive it, we also produce it. This close link between perceiving speech and producing it led Alvin Liberman and coworkers (1963, 1967) to propose a theory called the **motor theory of speech perception**. This theory proposes that (1) hearing a particular speech sound activates motor mechanisms controlling the movement of the articulators, such as the tongue and lips, that are responsible for producing sounds; and (2) activation of these motor mechanisms, in turn, activates additional mechanisms that enable us to *perceive* the sound. Thus, the motor theory proposes that activity of motor mechanisms is the first step toward perceiving speech.

When motor theory was first proposed in the 1960s, it was extremely controversial. In the decades that followed, the theory stimulated a large number of experiments, some obtaining results that supported the theory, but many obtaining results that argued against it. It is difficult for motor theory to explain, for example, how people with brain damage that disables their speech motor system can still perceive speech (Lotto et al., 2009). Evidence such as this has led present-day speech researchers to largely reject the idea that our perception of speech is based on the activation of motor mechanisms.

Although the evidence argues against the idea that activation of motor mechanisms is *necessary* for speech perception, there is evidence for *links* between motor mechanisms and speech perception. One of the results supporting this idea is the discovery of mirror neurons. In Chapter 7, we saw that mirror neurons in monkeys respond both when the monkey carries out an action and when the monkey sees someone else carry out the action. A type of mirror neuron related to hearing is called *audiovisual mirror neurons*. These neurons fire when a monkey *carries out an action that produces a sound* (like breaking a peanut) and when the monkey *hears the sound* (the sound of a breaking peanut) that results from the action (Kohler, 2002; see Chapter 7, page 167). Interestingly, mirror neurons that have been studied in the monkey are found in an area roughly equivalent to Broca's area in humans; for this reason, some researchers have proposed a close link between mirror neurons and language (Arbib, 2001).

But is there any evidence linking *perceiving* speech and *producing* speech in humans? Alessandro D'Ausilio and coworkers (2009) demonstrated a link between production and perception by showing that increasing activation of motor areas associated with making sounds like /b/ and /p/, which involve labial articulation (pursing the lips) aids in the perception of these sounds. Similarly, stimulation of a motor area associated with making sounds like /t/ and /d/, which involve dental articulation (the tongue contacting the back of the teeth) aids in the perception of these sounds.

The subjects' task in D'Ausilio's experiment was to push a button as quickly as possible to indicate which sound they heard on each trial. In the baseline condition, the subjects carried out this task without any stimulation of their brain. In the stimulation condition, brief pulses of *focal transcranial magnetic stimulation*, which can stimulate a small targeted area of the brain, were presented just before the subject heard the sound, either to the area of the motor cortex responsible for creating labial (lip) articulation or the area creating dental (tongue and teeth) articulation. (See Method: Transcranial Magnetic Stimulation (TMS), Chapter 8, page 192.)

Figure 13.19 shows the sites of stimulation on the motor area of the cortex. Stimulation of the lip area resulted in faster responding to labial phonemes (/b/ and /p/) and stimulation of the tongue area resulted in faster responding to the dental phonemes (/t/ and /d/). Based on these results, D'Ausilio suggested that activity in the motor cortex can influence speech perception. Research such as this, along with many other studies, shows that the close link between motor activity and perception holds not only for visual perception (see Chapter 7) but for perceiving speech as well.

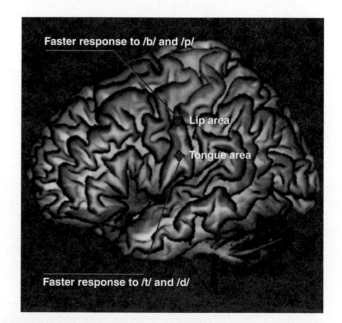

Figure 13.19 Sites of transcranial magnetic stimulation of the motor area for lips and tongue. Stimulation of the lip area increases the speed of responding to /b/ and /p/. Stimulation of the tongue area increases the speed of responding to /t/ and /d/. From D'Ausilio, A., Pulvermuller, F., Salmas, P., Bufalari, I., Begliomini, C., & Fadiga, L. (2009). The motor somatotopy of speech perception. *Current Biology, 19,* 381–385. With permission from Elsevier.

We have seen from Saffran's experiments (Figure 13.13) that infants can use speech statistics to achieve speech segmentation. In addition, research has demonstrated categorical perception in 1-month-old infants.

The Categorical Perception of Phonemes

Categorical perception was first reported for adults in 1967 (Liberman et al., 1967). In 1971, Peter Eimas and coworkers began the modern era of research on infant speech perception by using the habituation procedure to show that infants as young as 1 month old perform similarly to adults in categorical perception experiments. The basis of these experiments was the observation that an infant will suck on a nipple in order to hear a series of brief speech sounds, but as the same speech sounds are repeated, the infant's sucking eventually habituates to a low level. By presenting a new stimulus after the rate of sucking had decreased, Eimas determined whether the infant perceived the new stimulus as sounding the same as or different from the old one.

The results of Eimas and coworkers' experiment are shown in **Figure 13.20**. The number of sucking responses when no sound was presented is indicated by the point at B. When a sound with voice onset time (VOT) of 20 ms (sounds like "ba" to an adult) is presented as the infant sucks, the sucking increases to a high level and then begins to decrease. When the VOT is changed to 40 ms (dashed line; sounds like "pa" to an adult), sucking increases, as indicated by the points to the right of the dashed line. This means that the infant perceives a difference between sounds with VOTs of 20 and 40 ms. The center graph, however, shows that changing the VOT from 60 to 80 ms (both sound like "pa" to an adult) has only a small effect on sucking, indicating that the infants perceive little, if any, difference between the two sounds. Finally, the results for a control group (the right graph) show that when the sound is not changed, the number of sucking responses decreases throughout the experiment.

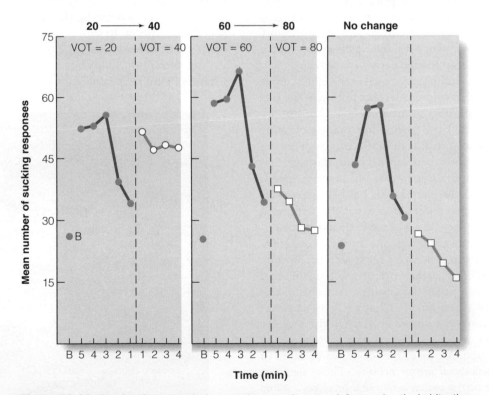

Figure 13.20 Results of a categorical perception experiment on infants using the habituation procedure. In the left panel, VOT is changed from 20 to 40 ms (across the phonetic boundary). In the center panel, VOT is changed from 60 to 80 ms (not across the phonetic boundary). In the right panel, the VOT was not changed. See text for details. From "Speech Perception in Infants," by P. Eimas, E. P. Siqueland, P. Jusczyk, J. Vigorito, 1971, *Science*, 171, 303–306, figure 2. Copyright © 1971 by the American Association for the Advancement of Science. Reproduced by permission.

These results show that when the VOT is shifted across the average adult phonetic boundary (left graph), the infants perceive a change in the sound, and when the VOT is shifted on the same side of the phonetic boundary (center graph), the infants perceive little or no change in the sound. That infants as young as 1 month old are capable of categorical perception is particularly impressive because these infants have had virtually no experience in producing speech sounds and only limited experience in hearing them. But the story regarding phoneme perception extends beyond the discovery that very young infants can perceive phonemes. As we will see in the next section, the ability to perceive phonemes is affected by the language a child hears during its first year.

Learning the Sounds of a Language

If English is your primary language, you may have noticed that many people whose primary language is Japanese say words beginning in "r" with an "l" sound, so they would say "lent" instead of "rent." This difficulty in *producing* some phonemes is related to an inability to *perceive* those phonemes, as indicated by the finding that native Japanese speakers have trouble distinguishing between words like *lent* and *rent*.

What makes this difficulty especially interesting is that young infants in all cultures can tell the difference between sounds that create all of the speech sounds used in the world's languages, but by the age of 1, they have lost the ability to distinguish between some of these sounds (Kuhl, 2000). Thus, 6-month-old Japanese children can tell the difference between the /r/ and /l/ used in American English just as well as American children can. However, by 12 months, Japanese children confuse /r/ and /l/. Over the same period, American children become better at telling the difference between these two sounds (Kuhl et al., 1997; Strange, 1995).

Why does this change occur? The answer involves *experience-dependent plasticity*—a change in the brain's ability to respond to specific stimuli that occurs as a result of experience. We introduced experience-dependent plasticity in Chapter 3 when we described how raising kittens in an environment consisting entirely of vertical lines causes the kitten's brain to contain neurons that respond only to verticals (page 68).

Evidence supporting the idea that the shift in speech perception that occurs sometime after 6 months of age is likely to involve experience-dependent plasticity has been provided by Maritza Rivera-Gaxiola and coworkers (2005), who recorded electrical potentials from the surface of the cortex of 7- and 11-month-old American infants from English-speaking households in response to pairs of sounds that sound the

same to adult English-speakers but are perceived as different by adult Spanish-speakers. At 7 months of age, the electrical response to these two sounds was different in the English-speaking children, but by 11 months of age, the response had become the same.

This result provides a physiological parallel to the experience of young Japanese children described earlier. A pair of sounds can be perceived as different or can cause different physiological responses at an early age, but if the child doesn't have experience discriminating between the two sounds, then the child loses the ability to tell the difference between the two sounds, and physiological responses to the sounds become the same. Apparently, the brain is shaped by experience to respond to sounds that are used in the particular language that the child is learning.

TEST YOURSELF 13.2

1. What is the evidence that meaning can influence word perception?

2. What mechanisms help us perceive breaks between words?

3. How do speaker characteristics influence speech perception?

4. Describe evidence for both bottom-up and top-down processing in speech perception.

5. What did Broca and Wernicke discover about the physiology of speech perception?

6. Describe the following evidence that is relevant to the physiology of speech perception: (1) determining the brain's response to speech stimuli; (2) the dual-stream model of speech perception.

7. Describe Pasley's experiment in which he created a speech "decoder" that made it possible to reconstruct the speech signal. What is a possible practical application of such a speech decoder?

8. What link between perception and motor responding is proposed by the motor theory? Describe what the results of research on mirror neurons and the effect of transcranial magnetic stimulation indicate about the relationship between motor activity and speech perception.

9. Describe the experiment that showed that 1-month-old infants are capable of categorical perception.

10. How does experience-dependent plasticity contribute to a child's development of the ability to perceive phonemes during the first year of life?

Answer to question on page 326:
An American delights in simple playthings.

THINK ABOUT IT

1. How well can computers recognize speech? You can research this question by getting on the telephone with a computer. Dial a service such as the one that books movie tickets. Then, instead of going out of your way to talk slowly and clearly, try talking in a normal conversational voice (but clearly enough that a human would still understand you), and see whether you can determine the limits of the computer's ability to understand speech. (p. 317)

2. How do you think your perception of speech would be affected if the phenomenon of categorical perception did not exist? (p. 322)

KEY TERMS

MEDIA RESOURCES

CourseMate

Go to CengageBrain.com to access Psychology CourseMate, where you will find the Virtual Labs plus an interactive eBook, flashcards, quizzes, videos, and more.

Virtual Labs

The Virtual Labs are designed to help you get the most out of this course. The Virtual Lab icons direct you to specific media demonstrations and experiments designed to help you visualize what you are reading about. The numbers below indicate the number of the Virtual Lab you can access through Psychology CourseMate.

13.1 Categorical Perception (p. 324)
How perception of a tone suddenly changes from one category to another as the characteristics of a tone are slowly changed over a wide range. (Courtesy of Julie Feiz)

13.2 McGurk Effect (p. 324)
How seeing a person's lips move can influence what we hear. (Courtesy of Douglas Whalen, Haskins Laboratory)

13.3 Speechreading (p. 324)
How seeing someone speaking can make it easier to understand what they are saying. (Courtesy of Sensimetrics Corporation)

13.4 Phonemic Restoration (p. 325)
A description of the phonemic restoration effect. (Courtesy of Richard Warren)

13.5 Multiple Phonemic Restoration (p. 325)
A description of phonemic restoration in a natural environment containing many sounds. (Courtesy of Richard Warren)

13.6 Statistical Learning Stimuli (p. 327)
A sample of the string of nonsense words used in Saffran and colleagues' (1996) experiment. (Courtesy of Jennifer Saffran)

13.7 Speech Reconstruction (p. 330)
Video showing spectrograms of original sound stimulus and sound stimulus reconstructed from brain signals. (Courtesy of Brian Pasley)

The Cutaneous Senses

◀ When we touch something or are touched, receptors in the skin provide information about what is happening to the skin and about the object contacting the skin. These fingers are sensing the cell phone's shape and the quality of its surface. As the person enters a number, texts, or searches the Internet, receptors in the skin provide information that helps the person apply the right amount of pressure. In this chapter, we describe perceptions associated with stimulation of the skin, focusing on various qualities of touch, and also consider pain, which involves stimulation of the skin and other processes as well.

VL The Virtual Lab icons direct you to specific animations and videos designed to help you visualize what you are reading about. Virtual Labs are listed at the end of the chapter, keyed to the page on which they appear, and can be accessed through Psychology CourseMate.

Some Questions We Will Consider:

- Are there specialized receptors in the skin for sensing different tactile qualities? (p. 338)
- What is the most sensitive part of the body? (p. 343)
- Is it possible to reduce pain with your thoughts? (p. 355)

When asked which sense they would choose to lose, if they had to lose either vision, hearing, or touch, some people pick touch. This is understandable given the high value we place on seeing and hearing, but making a decision to lose the sense of touch would be a serious mistake. Although people who are blind or deaf can get along quite well, people with a rare condition that results in losing the ability to feel sensations though the skin often suffer constant bruises, burns, and broken bones in the absence of the warnings provided by touch and pain (Melzack & Wall, 1988; Rollman, 1991; Wall & Melzack, 1994).

But losing the sense of touch does more than increase the chance of injury. It also makes it difficult to interact with the environment because of the loss of feedback from the skin that accompanies many actions. As I type this, I hit my computer keys with just the right amount of force, because I can feel pressure when my fingers hit the keys. Without this feedback, typing and other actions that receive feedback from touch would become much more difficult. Experiments in which subjects have had their hands temporarily anesthetized have shown that the resulting loss of feeling causes them to apply much more force than necessary when carrying out tasks with their fingers and hands (Avenanti et al., 2005; Monzée et al., 2003).

A particularly dramatic case that involved losing the ability to sense with the skin, as well as the closely related ability to sense the movement and positions of the limbs, is that of Ian Waterman, a 17-year-old apprentice butcher, who in May 1971 contracted what at first appeared to be a routine case of the flu (Cole, 1995; Robles-De-La-Torre, 2006). He anticipated returning to work after recovering; however, instead of improving, his condition worsened, with an initial tingling sensation in his limbs becoming a total loss of the ability to feel touch below the neck. Ian's doctors, who were initially baffled by his condition, eventually determined that an autoimmune reaction had destroyed most of the neurons that transmitted signals from his skin, joints, tendons, and muscles to his brain. The loss of the ability to feel skin sensations meant that Ian couldn't feel his body when lying in bed, which resulted in a frightening floating sensation, and he often used inappropriate force when grasping objects—sometimes gripping too tightly, and sometimes dropping objects because he hadn't gripped tightly enough.

As difficult as losing sensations from his skin made Ian's life, destruction of the nerves from his muscles, tendons, and joints caused an even more serious problem. The destruction of these nerves eliminated Ian's ability to sense the position of his arms, legs, and body. This is something we take for granted. When you close your eyes, you can tell where your hands and legs are relative to each other and to your body. But Ian had lost this ability, so even though he could move, because the nerves conducting signals from his brain to his muscles were unaffected, he avoided moving, because not knowing where his limbs were made it difficult to control them.

Eventually, after many years of practice, Ian was able to sit, stand, and even carry out movements and tasks such as writing. Ian was able to do these things not because his sensory nerves had recovered (they remained irreversibly damaged), but because he had learned to use his sense of vision to constantly monitor the positions of his limbs and body. Imagine, for a moment, what it would be like to have to constantly look at your hands, arms, legs, and body, so you could tell where they were and make the necessary muscular adjustments to maintain your posture and carry out actions. Ian described the extreme and constant effort needed to do this as making his life like "running a daily marathon" (Cole, 1995).

Ian's problems were caused by a breakdown of his **somatosensory system**, which includes (1) the **cutaneous senses**, which are responsible for perceptions such as touch and pain that are usually caused by stimulation of the skin; (2) **proprioception**, the ability to sense the position of the body and limbs; and (3) **kinesthesis**, the ability to sense the movement of the body and limbs. In this chapter we will focus on the cutaneous senses, which are important not only for activities like grasping objects and protecting against damage to the skin, but also for motivating sexual activity. (Another reason picking touch as the sense to lose would be a mistake.)

When we recognize that the perceptions we experience through our skin are crucial for carrying out everyday activities, protecting ourselves from injury, and motivating sexual activity, we can see that these perceptions are crucial to our survival and to the survival of our species. In fact, we could make a good case for the idea that perceptions felt through the skin and that enable us to sense the positions and movements of our limbs are more important for survival than those provided by vision and hearing. We begin our consideration of the cutaneous senses by focusing on the skin.

Overview of the Cutaneous System

In this section we will describe some basic facts about the anatomy and functioning of the various parts of the cutaneous system.

The Skin

Comel (1953) called the skin the "monumental facade of the human body" for good reason. It is the heaviest organ in the human body, and, if not the largest (the surface areas of the gastrointestinal tract and of the alveoli of the lungs exceed the surface area of the skin), it is certainly the most obvious, especially in humans, whose skin is not obscured by fur or large amounts of hair (Montagna & Parakkal, 1974).

In addition to its warning function, the skin also prevents body fluids from escaping and at the same time protects us by keeping bacteria, chemical agents, and dirt from penetrating our bodies. Skin maintains the integrity of what's inside and protects us from what's outside, but it also provides us with information about the various stimuli that contact it. The sun's rays heat our skin, and we feel warmth; a pinprick is painful; and when someone touches us, we experience pressure or other sensations.

Our main experience with the skin is its visible surface, which is actually a layer of tough dead skin cells. (Try sticking a piece of cellophane tape onto your palm and pulling it off. The material that sticks to the tape is dead skin cells.) This layer of dead cells is part of the outer layer of skin, which is called the **epidermis**. Below the epidermis is another layer, called the **dermis** (**Figure 14.1**). Within the skin are **mechanoreceptors**, receptors that respond to mechanical stimulation such as pressure, stretching, and vibration. **VL**

Mechanoreceptors

Many of the tactile perceptions that we feel from stimulation of the skin can be traced to the four types of mechanoreceptors that are located in the epidermis and the dermis. We can distinguish between these receptors

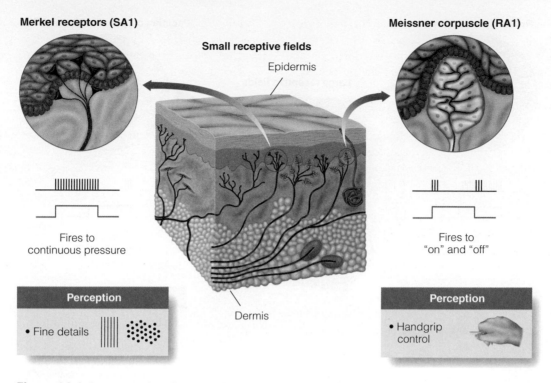

Merkel receptors (SA1)

Meissner corpuscle (RA1)

Small receptive fields

Epidermis

Fires to
continuous pressure

Fires to
"on" and "off"

Perception
• Fine details

Perception
• Handgrip control

Dermis

Figure 14.1 A cross section of glabrous (without hairs or projections) skin, showing the layers of the skin and the structure, firing properties, and perceptions associated with the Merkel receptor (SA1) and Meissner corpuscle (RA1)—two mechanoreceptors near the surface of the skin. © Cengage Learning

by their distinctive structures and by how fibers associated with the receptors respond to stimulation. **Slowly adapting (SA) receptors** respond with prolonged firing to continued pressure. **Rapidly adapting (RA) receptors** respond with bursts of firing just at the onset and offset of a pressure stimulus.

Two mechanoreceptors, the **Merkel receptor (SA1)** and the **Meissner corpuscle (RA1)**, are located close to the surface of the skin, near the epidermis. Because they are located close to the surface, these receptors have small receptive fields; a *cutaneous receptive field* is the area of skin which, when stimulated, influences the firing of the neuron.

Figure 14.1 shows the structure and firing of these receptors in response to a pressure stimulus that is presented and then removed (blue line). The nerve fiber associated with the slowly adapting Merkel receptor fires continuously, as long as the stimulus is on; the nerve fiber associated with the rapidly adapting Meissner corpuscle fires only when the stimulus is first applied and when it is removed. The type of perception associated with the Merkel receptor is sensing fine details, and with the Meissner corpuscle, controlling handgrip.

The other two mechanoreceptors, the **Ruffini cylinder (SA2)** and the **Pacinian corpuscle (RA2 or PC)**, are located deeper in the skin (**Figure 14.2**), so they have larger receptive fields. The Ruffini cylinder responds continuously to stimulation, and the Pacinian corpuscle responds when the stimulus is applied and removed. The Ruffini cylinder is associated with perceiving stretching of the skin, the Pacinian corpuscle with sensing rapid vibrations and fine texture.[1]

Pathways From Skin to Cortex

The receptors for the other senses are localized in one area—the eye (vision), the ear (hearing), the nose (olfaction), and the mouth (taste)—but cutaneous receptors in the skin are distributed over the whole body. This wide distribution, plus the fact that signals must reach the brain before stimulation of the skin can be perceived, creates a travel situation we might call "journey of the long-distance nerve impulses," especially for signals that must travel from the fingertips or toes to the brain.

Signals from all over the body are conducted from the skin to the spinal cord, which consists of 31 segments, each of which receives signals through a bundle called the *dorsal root* (**Figure 14.3**). After the signals enter the spinal cord, nerve fibers transmit them to the brain along two major pathways: the **medial lemniscal pathway** and the **spinothalamic pathway**. The lemniscal pathway has large fibers that carry signals related to sensing the positions of

---

[1]Although Michael Paré and coworkers (2002) have reported that there are no Ruffini receptors in the finger pads of monkeys, Ruffini cylinders are still included in most lists of glabrous (nonhairy) skin receptors, so they are included here.

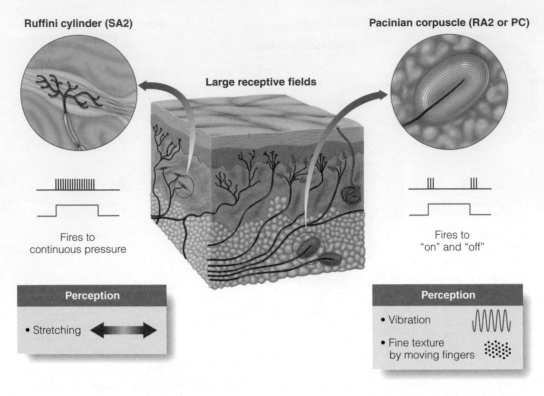

Fires to continuous pressure

Perception
• Stretching ⟷

Fires to "on" and "off"

Perception
• Vibration ∿∿∿∿
• Fine texture by moving fingers

Figure 14.2 A cross section of glabrous skin, showing the structure, firing properties, and perceptions associated with the Ruffini cylinder (SA2) and the Pacinian corpuscle (RA2 or PC)—two mechanoreceptors that are deeper in the skin. © Cengage Learning

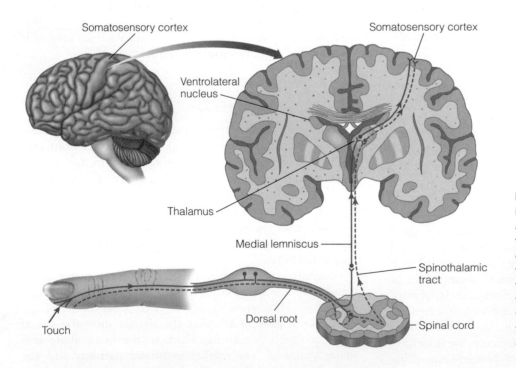

Figure 14.3 The pathway from receptors in the skin to the somatosensory receiving area of the cortex. The fiber carrying signals from a receptor in the finger enters the spinal cord through the dorsal root. The signals then travel up the spinal cord along two pathways: the medial lemniscus and the spinothalamic tract. These pathways synapse in the ventrolateral nucleus of the thalamus and then send signals to the somatosensory cortex in the parietal lobe. © Cengage Learning

the limbs (proprioception) and perceiving touch. These large fibers transmit signals at high speed, which is important for controlling movement and reacting to touch. The spinothalamic pathway consists of smaller fibers that transmit signals related to temperature and pain. The case of Ian Waterman illustrates this separation in function, because although he lost the ability to feel touch and to sense the positions of his limbs (lemniscal pathway), he was still able to sense pain and temperature (spinothalamic pathway).

Fibers from both pathways cross over to the other side of the body during their upward journey to the thalamus. Most of these fibers synapse in the **ventrolateral nucleus** in the thalamus, but some synapse in other thalamic nuclei. (Remember that fibers from the retina and the cochlea also synapse in the thalamus, in the *lateral geniculate nucleus* for vision and the *medial geniculate nucleus* for hearing.) Because the signals in the spinal cord have crossed over to the opposite side of the body, signals originating from the left side of the body reach the thalamus in the right hemisphere of the brain, and signals from the right side of the body reach the left hemisphere.

The Somatosensory Cortex

From the thalamus, signals travel to the **somatosensory receiving area (S1)** in the parietal lobe of the cortex and possibly also to the **secondary somatosensory cortex (S2)** (Rowe et al., 1996; Turman et al., 1998; **Figure 14.4a**). Signals also travel between S1 and S2 and from S1 and S2 to additional somatosensory areas.

An important characteristic of the somatosensory cortex is that it is organized into maps that correspond to locations on the body. The existence of a map of the body on S1 was determined in a classic series of investigations carried out by neurosurgeon Wilder Penfield while operating on awake patients who were having brain surgery to relieve symptoms of epilepsy (Penfield & Rasmussen, 1950). When Penfield stimulated points on S1 and asked patients to report what they perceived, they reported sensations such as tingling

and touch on various parts of their body. Penfield found that stimulating the ventral part of S1 (lower on the parietal lobe) caused sensations on the lips and face, stimulating higher on S1 caused sensations in the hands and fingers, and stimulating the dorsal S1 caused sensations in the legs and feet.

The resulting body map, shown in **Figure 14.4b**, is called the **homunculus**, Latin for "little man." The homunculus shows that adjacent areas of the skin project to adjacent areas in the brain, and that some areas on the skin are represented by a disproportionately large area of the brain. The area devoted to the thumb, for example, is as large as the area devoted to the entire forearm. This result is analogous to the magnification factor in vision (see page 78), in which receptors in the fovea, which are responsible for perceiving visual details, are allotted a disproportionate area on the visual cortex. Similarly, parts of the body such as the fingers, which are used to detect details through the sense of touch, are allotted a disproportionate area on the somatosensory cortex (Duncan & Boynton, 2007). A similar body map also occurs in the secondary somatosensory cortex (S2).

The description above in terms of S1 and S2 and the homunculus is accurate but simplified. Recent research has shown that S1 is divided into four interconnected areas, each with different functions. For example, the area in S1 involved in perceiving touch is connected to another area that is involved in *haptics* (exploring objects with the hand). In addition, there are a number of homunculi both within S1 and S2

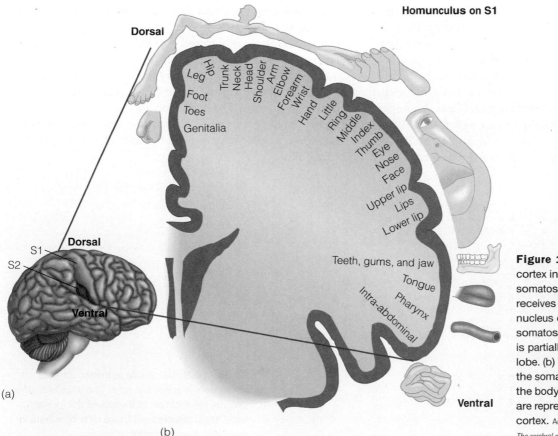

Homunculus on S1

Figure 14.4 (a) The somatosensory cortex in the parietal lobe. The primary somatosensory area, S1 (light purple), receives inputs from the ventrolateral nucleus of the thalamus. The secondary somatosensory area, S2 (dark purple), is partially hidden behind the temporal lobe. (b) The sensory homunculus on the somatosensory cortex. Parts of the body with the highest tactile acuity are represented by larger areas on the cortex. Adapted from Penfield, W., & Rasmussen, T. (1950). *The cerebral cortex of man.* New York: Macmillan.

The Plasticity of Cortical Body Maps

One of the basic principles of cortical organization is that the cortical representation of a particular function can become larger if that function is used often. We introduced this principle, called *experience-dependent plasticity*, when we described how rearing kittens in a vertical environment caused most of the neurons in their visual cortex to respond best to vertical orientations (see page 68) and how training humans to recognize shapes called Greebles caused the fusiform face area of the cortex to respond more strongly to Greeble stimuli (see page 92).

Most of the early experiments that demonstrated experience-dependent plasticity were carried out in the somatosensory system. In one of these early experiments, William Jenkins and Michael Merzenich (1987) measured the cortical areas devoted to each of a monkey's fingers and then trained monkeys to complete a task that involved the extensive use of a particular location on one fingertip. When they compared the cortical maps of the fingertip measured just before the training to the map measured after 3 months of training, they found that the area representing the stimulated fingertip was greatly expanded after the training. Thus, the cortical area representing part of the fingertip, which is large to begin with, became even larger when the area received a large amount of stimulation.

In most animal experiments, like the one we just described, the effect of plasticity is determined by measuring how special training affects the brain. An experiment that measured this effect in humans determined how training affected the brains of musicians. Consider, for example, players of stringed instruments. A right-handed violin player bows with the right hand and uses the fingers of his or her left hand to finger the strings. One result of this tactile experience is that these musicians have a greater than normal cortical representation for the fingers of their left hand (Elbert et al., 1995). Just as in the monkeys, plasticity has created more cortical area for parts of the body that are used more. What this plasticity means is that while we can specify the general area of the cortex that represents a particular part of the body, the exact size of the area representing each part of the body is not totally fixed (Pascual-Leone et al., 2005).

The receptors in the skin make it possible for us to sense different qualities such as small details, vibration, textures of surfaces, the shapes of three-dimensional objects, and potentially damaging stimuli. We will now describe how information for detail, vibration, texture, and object shape are processed by the skin, and then consider pain, which is influenced not only by stimulation of the skin but by other factors as well.

Perceiving Details

One of the most impressive examples of perceiving details with the skin is provided by Braille, the system of raised dots that enables blind people to read with their fingertips. A Braille character consists of a cell made up of from one to six dots. Different arrangements of dots and blank spaces represent letters of the alphabet, as shown in **Figure 14.5**; additional characters represent numbers, punctuation marks, and common speech sounds and words.

Experienced Braille readers can read at a rate of about 100 words per minute, slower than the rate for visual reading, which averages about 250 to 300 words per minute, but impressive nonetheless when we consider that a Braille reader transforms an array of raised dots into information that goes far beyond simply feeling sensations on the skin.

The ability of Braille readers to identify patterns of small raised dots based on the sense of touch depends on tactile detail perception. The first step in describing research on tactile detail perception is to consider how researchers have measured our capacity to detect details of stimuli presented to the skin.

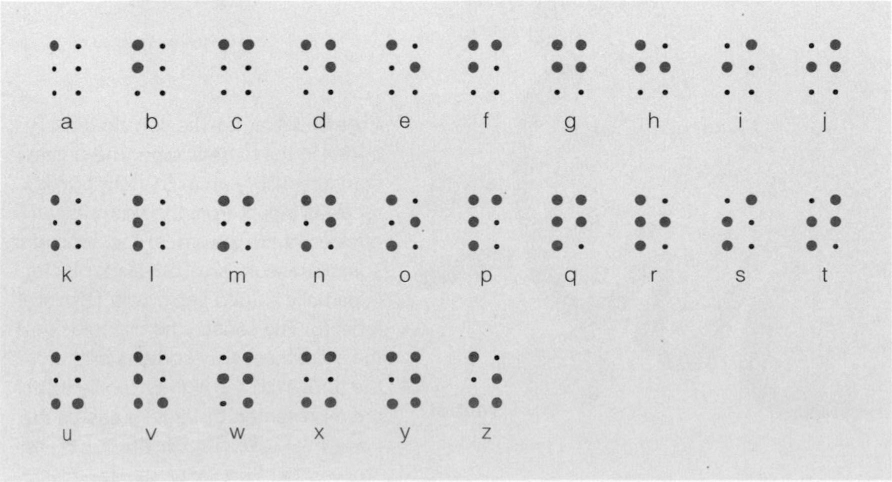

Figure 14.5 The Braille alphabet consists of raised dots in a 2 × 3 matrix. The large blue dots indicate the location of the raised dot for each letter. Blind people read these dots by scanning them with their fingertips. © Cengage Learning

METHOD
Measuring Tactile Acuity

Just as there are a number of different kinds of eye charts for determining a person's visual acuity, there are a number of ways to measure a person's tactile acuity—the ability to detect details on the skin. The classic method of measuring tactile acuity is the **two-point threshold**, the minimum separation between two points on the skin that when stimulated is perceived as two points (**Figure 14.6a**). The two-point threshold is measured by gently touching the skin with two points, such as the points of a drawing compass, and having the person indicate whether he or she feels one point or two.

The two-point threshold was the main measure of acuity in most of the early research on touch. Recently, however, other methods have been introduced. **Grating acuity** is measured by pressing a grooved stimulus like the one in **Figure 14.6b** onto the skin and asking the person to indicate the orientation of the grating. Acuity is measured by determining the narrowest spacing for which orientation can be accurately judged. Finally, acuity can also be measured by pushing raised patterns such as letters onto the skin and determining the smallest sized pattern or letter that can be identified (Cholewaik & Collins, 2003; Craig & Lyle, 2001, 2002).

As we consider the role of both receptor mechanisms and cortical mechanisms in determining tactile acuity, we will see

that there are a number of parallels between the cutaneous system and the visual system.

Receptor Mechanisms for Tactile Acuity

The properties of the receptors are one of the things that determines what we experience when the skin is stimulated. We will illustrate this by first focusing on the connection between the Merkel receptor and associated fibers and tactile acuity. We have indicated that the Merkel receptor is sensitive to details. **Figure 14.7a** shows how the fiber associated with a Merkel receptor fires in response to a grooved stimulus pushed into the skin. Notice that the firing of the fiber reflects the pattern of the grooved stimuli. This indicates that the firing of the Merkel receptor's fiber signals details (Johnson, 2002; Phillips & Johnson, 1981). For comparison, **Figure 14.7b** shows the firing of the fiber associated with the Pacinian corpuscle. The lack of match between the grooved pattern and the firing indicates that this receptor is not sensitive to the details of patterns that are pushed onto the skin.

It is not surprising that there is a high density of Merkel receptors in the fingertips, because the fingertips are the parts of the body that are most sensitive to details (Vallbo & Johansson, 1978). The relationship between locations on the body and sensitivity to detail has been studied psychophysically by measuring the two-point threshold on different parts of the body. Try this yourself by doing the following demonstration.

DEMONSTRATION
Comparing Two-Point Thresholds

To measure two-point thresholds on different parts of the body, hold two pencils side by side (or better yet, use a drawing compass) so that their points are about 12 mm (0.5 in.) apart; then touch both points simultaneously to the tip of your thumb and determine whether you feel two points. If you feel only one, increase the distance between the pencil points until you feel two; then note the distance between the points. Now move the pencil

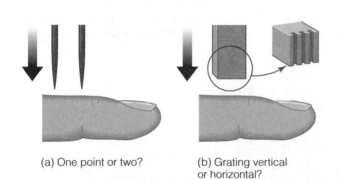

(a) One point or two?   (b) Grating vertical or horizontal?

Figure 14.6 Methods for determining tactile acuity: (a) two-point threshold; (b) grating acuity. © Cengage Learning

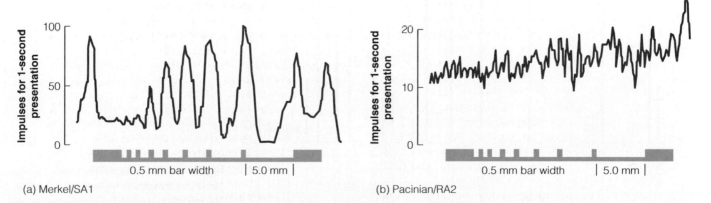

(a) Merkel/SA1   (b) Pacinian/RA2

Figure 14.7 Firing to the grooved stimulus pattern of (a) the fiber associated with a Merkel receptor and (b) the fiber associated with a Pacinian corpuscle receptor. The response to each groove width was recorded during a 1-second indentation for each bar width, so these graphs represent the results for a number of presentations. Adapted from Phillips, J. R., & Johnson, K. O. (1981). Tactile spatial resolution: II. Neural representation of bars, edges, and gratings in monkey primary afferent. *Journal of Neurophysiology, 46,* 1177–1191.

points to the underside of your forearm. With the points about 12 mm apart (or at the smallest separation you felt as two points on your thumb), touch them to your forearm and note whether you feel one point or two. If you feel only one, how much must you increase the separation before you feel two?

A comparison of grating acuity on different parts of the hand shows that better acuity is associated with less spacing between Merkel receptors (**Figure 14.8**). But receptor spacing

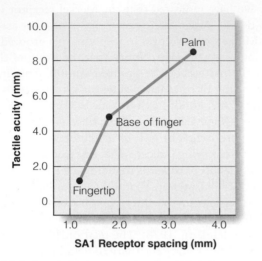

Figure 14.8 Correlation between density of Merkel receptors and tactile acuity. From Craig, J. C., & Lyle, K. B. (2002). A correction and a comment on Craig and Lyle (2001). *Perception & Psychophysics, 64,* 504–506.

can't be the whole story, because although tactile acuity is better on the tip of the index finger than on the tip of the little finger, the spacing between Merkel receptors is the same on all the fingertips. This means that while receptor spacing is part of the answer, the cortex also plays a role in determining tactile acuity (Duncan & Boynton, 2007).

Cortical Mechanisms for Tactile Acuity

Just as there is a parallel between tactile acuity and receptor density, there is also a parallel between tactile acuity and the representation of the body in the brain. **Figure 14.9** indicates the two-point threshold measured on different parts of the male body. By comparing these two-point thresholds to how different parts of the body are represented in the brain (Figure 14.4a), we can see that regions of high acuity, like the fingers and lips, are represented by larger areas on the cortex. As we mentioned earlier, when we described the homunculus, "magnification" of the representation on the brain of parts of the body such as the fingertips parallels the magnification factor in vision (page 78). The map of the body on the brain is enlarged to provide the extra neural processing that enables us to accurately sense fine details with our fingers and other parts of the body.

Another way to demonstrate the connection between cortical mechanisms and acuity is to determine the receptive fields of neurons in different parts of the cortical

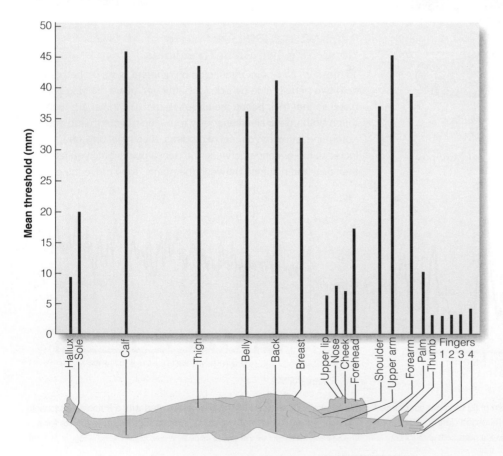

Figure 14.9 Two-point thresholds for males. Two-point thresholds for females follow the same pattern. From Weinstein, S., Intensive and extensive aspects of tactile sensitivity as a function of body part, sex, and laterality. In D. R. Kenshalo (Ed.), *The skin senses,* pp. 206, 207. Copyright © 1968 by Charles C Thomas. Courtesy of Charles C Thomas, Publishers, Springfield, IL.

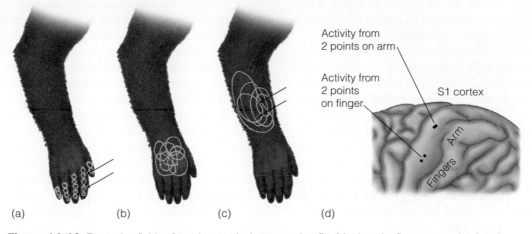

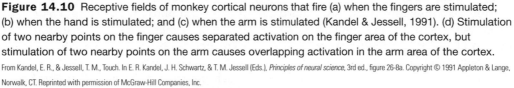

Figure 14.10 Receptive fields of monkey cortical neurons that fire (a) when the fingers are stimulated; (b) when the hand is stimulated; and (c) when the arm is stimulated (Kandel & Jessell, 1991). (d) Stimulation of two nearby points on the finger causes separated activation on the finger area of the cortex, but stimulation of two nearby points on the arm causes overlapping activation in the arm area of the cortex.

From Kandel, E. R., & Jessell, T. M., Touch. In E. R. Kandel, J. H. Schwartz, & T. M. Jessell (Eds.), *Principles of neural science*, 3rd ed., figure 26-8a. Copyright © 1991 Appleton & Lange, Norwalk, CT. Reprinted with permission of McGraw-Hill Companies, Inc.

homunculus. From **Figure 14.10**, which shows the sizes of receptive fields from cortical neurons that receive signals from a monkey's fingers (**Figure 14.10a**), hand (**Figure 14.10b**), and arm (**Figure 14.10c**), we can see that cortical neurons representing parts of the body with better acuity, such as the fingers, have smaller receptive fields. This means that two points that are close together on the fingers might fall on receptive fields that don't overlap (as indicated by the two arrows in Figure 14.10a) and so would cause neurons that are separated in the cortex to fire (**Figure 14.10d**). However, two points with the same separation when applied to the arm are likely to fall on receptive fields that overlap (see arrows in Figure 14.10c) and so could cause neurons that are not separated in the cortex to fire (Figure 14.10d). Thus, the small receptive fields of neurons receiving signals from the fingers translates into more separation on the cortex, which enhances the ability to feel two close-together points on the skin as two separate points.

Perceiving Vibration

The skin is capable of detecting not only spatial details of objects, but other qualities as well. When you place your hands on mechanical devices that produce vibration, such as a car, a lawnmower, or an electric toothbrush, you can sense these vibrations with your fingers and hands. The mechanoreceptor that is primarily responsible for sensing vibration is the Pacinian corpuscle. One piece of evidence linking the Pacinian corpuscle to vibration is that recording from fibers associated with the corpuscle shows that these fibers respond poorly to slow or constant pushing, but respond well to high rates of vibration.

Why do the Pacinian corpuscle fibers respond well to rapid vibration? The answer to this question is that the presence of the corpuscle surrounding the nerve fiber determines which

pressure stimuli actually reach the fiber. The corpuscle, which consists of a series of layers, like an onion, with fluid between each layer, transmits rapidly applied pressure, like vibration, to the nerve fiber, as shown in **Figure 14.11a**, but does not

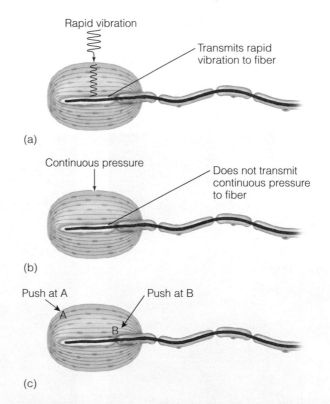

Figure 14.11 (a) When a vibrating pressure stimulus is applied to the Pacinian corpuscle, it transmits these pressure vibrations to the nerve fiber. (b) When a continuous pressure stimulus is applied to the Pacinian corpuscle, it does not transmit the continuous pressure to the fiber. (c) Lowenstein determined how the fiber fired to stimulation of the corpuscle (at A) and to direct stimulation of the fiber (at B). Adapted from Lowenstein, W. R. (1960). Biological transducers. *Scientific American, 203*, p. 103.

transmit continuous pressure, as shown in **Figure 14.11b**. Thus, the corpuscle causes the fiber to receive rapid changes in pressure, but not to receive continuous pressure.

Because the Pacinian corpuscle does not transmit continuous pressure to the fiber, presenting continuous pressure to the corpuscle should cause no response in the fiber. This is exactly what Werner Lowenstein (1960) observed in a classic experiment, in which he showed that when pressure was applied to the corpuscle (at A in **Figure 14.11c**), the fiber responded when the pressure was first applied and when it was removed, but it did not respond to continuous pressure. But when Lowenstein dissected away the corpuscle and applied pressure directly to the fiber (at B in Figure 14.11c), the fiber fired to the continuous pressure. Lowenstein concluded from this result that properties of the corpuscle cause the fiber to respond poorly to continuous stimulation, such as sustained pressure, but to respond well to changes in stimulation that occur at the beginning and end of a pressure stimulus or when stimulation is changing rapidly, as occurs in vibration.

Perceiving Texture

Surface texture is the physical texture of a surface created by peaks and valleys. As can be seen in **Figure 14.12**, visual inspection can be a poor way of determining surface texture because seeing texture depends on the light-dark pattern determined by the angle of illumination. Thus, although the visually perceived texture of the two sides of the post in Figure 14.12 looks very different, moving the fingers across the two surfaces reveals that the texture of the two surfaces is the same.

Touch, which involves direct contact with the surface, therefore provides a more accurate assessment of surface texture than vision. However, this doesn't mean that scanning a surface with the fingers always results in an accurate indication of surface texture. As we will see, our perception of surface texture depends on how the surface is scanned and which mechanoreceptors are activated.

Research on texture perception tells an interesting story, extending from 1925 to the present, that illustrates how psychophysics can be used to understand perceptual mechanisms. In 1925, David Katz proposed that our perception of texture depends on both spatial cues and temporal cues. **Spatial cues** are provided by relatively large surface elements, such as bumps and grooves, that can be felt both when the skin moves across the surface elements and when it is pressed onto the elements. These cues result in feeling different shapes, sizes, and distributions of these surface elements. An example of spatial cues is perceiving a coarse texture such as Braille dots or the texture you feel when you touch the teeth of a comb. **Temporal cues** occur when the skin moves across a textured surface like fine sandpaper. This type of cue provides information in the form of vibrations that occur as a result of the movement over the surface. Temporal cues are responsible for our perception of fine texture that cannot be detected unless the fingers are moving across the surface.

Although Katz proposed that texture perception is determined by both spatial and temporal cues, research on texture perception has, until recently, focused on spatial cues. However, experiments by Mark Hollins and coworkers (2000, 2001, 2002) show that temporal cues are responsible for our perception of fine textures. Hollins called Katz's proposal

(a)   (b)

Figure 14.12 The post in (a) is illuminated from the left. The close-up in (b) shows how the visual perception of texture is influenced by illumination. Although the surface on the right side of the pole appears rougher than on the left, the surface textures of the two sides are identical.

that there are two types of receptors involved in texture perception the **duplex theory of texture perception**.

Hollins and Ryan Risner (2000) presented evidence for the role of temporal cues by showing that when participants touch surfaces without moving their fingers and judge "roughness" using the procedure of magnitude estimation (see Chapter 1, page 15), they sense little difference between two fine textures (particle sizes of 10 μm and 100 μm). However, when participants are allowed to move their fingers across the surface, they are able to detect the difference between the fine textures. Thus, movement, which generates vibration as the skin scans a surface, makes it possible to sense the roughness of fine surfaces.

Additional evidence for the role of vibration in sensing fine textures was provided by using the selective adaptation procedure we introduced in Chapter 3 (see page 66). This procedure involves presenting a stimulus that adapts a particular type of receptor and then testing to see how inactivation of that receptor by adaptation affects perception. Hollins and coworkers (2001) used this procedure by presenting two adaptation conditions. The first condition was 10-Hz (10 vibrations per second) adaptation, in which the skin was vibrated with a 10-Hz stimulus for 6 minutes. This frequency of adaptation was picked to adapt the Meissner corpuscle, which responds to low frequencies. The second condition was 250-Hz adaptation. This frequency was picked to adapt the Pacinian corpuscle, which responds to high frequencies.

Following each type of adaptation, participants ran their fingers over two fine textures—a "standard" texture and a "test" texture. The participant's task was to indicate which texture was finer. Because there were two surfaces, chance performance would be 50 percent, as indicated by the dashed line in **Figure 14.13**. The results indicate that participants could tell the difference between the two textures when they had not been adapted or had received the 10-Hz adaptation. However, after they had been adapted to the 250-Hz vibration, they were unable to tell the difference between two fine textures, as indicated by their chance performance.

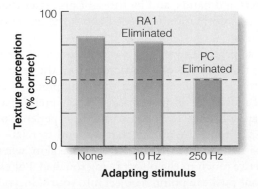

Figure 14.13 Eliminating the action of fibers associated with the Meissner corpuscle by adaptation to a 10-Hz vibration had no effect on perception of a fine texture, but eliminating the action of the Pacinian corpuscle by adapting to a 250-Hz vibration eliminated the ability to sense the fine textures. Data from Hollins, M., Bensmaia, S. J., & Washburn, S. (2001). Vibrotactile adaptation impairs discrimination of fine, but not coarse, textures. *Somatosensory & Motor Research, 18*, 253–262.

Thus, adapting the Pacinian corpuscle receptor, which is responsible for perceiving vibration, eliminates the ability to sense fine textures by moving the fingers over a surface. These results and the results of other experiments (Hollins et al., 2002) support the duplex theory of perception—that the perception of coarse textures is determined by spatial cues and of fine textures by temporal (vibration) cues.

Additional evidence for the role of temporal cues in perceiving texture has been provided by research that shows that vibrations are important for perceiving textures not only when people explore a surface directly with their fingers, but also when they make contact with a surface indirectly, through the use of tools. You can experience this yourself by doing the following demonstration.

DEMONSTRATION
Perceiving Texture With a Pen

Turn your pen over (or cap it) so you can use it as a "probe" (without writing on things). Hold the pen at one end and move the other end over something smooth, such as this page. As you do this, notice that you can sense the smoothness of the page, even though you are not directly touching it. Then, try the same thing on a rougher surface, such as a rug, fabric, or concrete.

Your ability to detect differences in texture by running a pen (or some other "tool," such as a stick) over a surface is determined by vibrations transmitted through the tool to your skin (Klatzky et al., 2003). The most remarkable thing about perceiving texture with a tool is that what you perceive is not the vibrations but the texture of the surface, even though you are feeling the surface remotely, with the tip of the tool (Carello & Turvey, 2004).

TEST YOURSELF 14.1

1. Describe the four types of mechanoreceptors in the skin, indicating (a) their appearance; (b) where they are located; (c) how they respond to pressure; (d) the sizes of their receptive fields; and (e) the type of perception associated with each receptor.

2. Where is the cortical receiving area for touch, and what does the map of the body on the cortical receiving area look like? How can this map be changed by experience?

3. How is tactile acuity measured, and what are the receptor and cortical mechanisms that serve tactile acuity?

4. Which receptor is primarily responsible for the perception of vibration? Describe the experiment that showed that the presence of the receptor structure determines how the fiber fires.

5. What is the duplex theory of texture perception? Describe the series of experiments that led to the conclusion that vibration is responsible for perceiving fine textures and observations that have been made about the experience of exploring an object with a probe.

Perceiving Objects

Imagine that you and a friend are at the seashore. Your friend knows something about shells from the small collection he has accumulated over the years, so as an experiment you decide to determine how well he can identify different types of shells by using his sense of touch alone. When you blindfold your friend and hand him a snail shell and a crab shell, he has no trouble identifying the shells as a snail and a crab. But when you hand him shells of different types of snails that are very similar, he finds that identifying the different types of snails is much more difficult.

Geerat Vermeij, blind at the age of 4 from a childhood eye disease and currently Distinguished Professor of Marine Ecology and Paleoecology at the University of California at Davis, describes his experience when confronted with a similar task. This experience occurred when he was being interviewed by Edgar Boell, who was considering Vermeij's application for graduate study in the biology department at Yale. Boell took Vermeij to the museum, introduced him to the curator, and handed him a shell. Here is what happened next, as told by Vermeij (1997):

> "Here's something. Do you know what it is?" Boell asked as he handed me a specimen.
>
> My fingers and mind raced. Widely separated ribs parallel to outer lip; large aperture; low spire; glossy; ribs reflected backward. "It's a Harpa," I replied tentatively. "It must be Harpa major." Right so far.
>
> "How about this one?" inquired Boell, as another fine shell changed hands. Smooth, sleek, channeled suture, narrow opening; could be any olive. "It's an olive. I'm pretty sure it's Oliva sayana, the common one from Florida, but they all look alike."
>
> Both men were momentarily speechless. They had planned this little exercise all along to call my bluff. Now that I had passed, Boell had undergone an instant metamorphosis. Beaming with enthusiasm and warmth, he promised me his full support. (pp. 79–80)

Vermeij received his PhD from Yale and is now a world-renowned expert on marine mollusks. His ability to identify objects and their features by touch is an example of **active touch**—touch in which a person actively explores an object, usually with fingers and hands. In contrast, **passive touch** occurs when touch stimuli are applied to the skin, as when two points are pushed onto the skin to determine the two-point threshold. The following demonstration compares the ability to identify objects using active touch and passive touch.

DEMONSTRATION
Identifying Objects

Ask another person to select five or six small objects for you to identify. Close your eyes and have the person place an object in your hand. Your job is to identify the object by touch alone, by moving your fingers and hand over the object. As you do this, be aware of what you are experiencing: your finger and hand movements, the sensations you are feeling, and what you are thinking. Do this for three objects. Then hold out your hand, keeping it still, with fingers outstretched, and let the person move each of the remaining objects around on your hand, moving their surfaces and contours across your skin. Your task is the same as before: to identify the object and to pay attention to what you are experiencing as the object is moved across your hand.

You may have noticed that in the active condition, in which you moved your fingers across the object, you were much more involved in the process and had more control over what parts of the objects you were exposed to. In the active part of the demonstration, you were engaging in **haptic perception**—perception in which three-dimensional objects are explored with the fingers and hand.

Identifying Objects by Haptic Exploration

Haptic perception provides a particularly good example of a situation in which a number of different systems are interacting with each other. As you manipulated the objects in the first part of the demonstration above, you were using three distinct systems to arrive at your goal of identifying the objects: (1) the *sensory system*, which was involved in detecting cutaneous sensations such as touch, temperature, and texture and the movements and positions of your fingers and hands; (2) the *motor system*, which was involved in moving your fingers and hands; and (3) the *cognitive system*, which was involved in thinking about the information provided by the sensory and motor systems.

Haptic perception is an extremely complex process because the sensory, motor, and cognitive systems must all work together. For example, the motor system's control of finger and hand movements is guided by cutaneous feelings in the fingers and the hands, by your sense of the positions of the fingers and hands, and by thought processes that determine what information is needed about the object in order to identify it.

These processes working together create an experience of active touch that is quite different from the experience of passive touch. J. J. Gibson (1962), who championed the importance of movement in perception (see Chapter 7, page 154, and Chapter 8, page 182), compared the experience of active and passive touch by noting that we tend to relate passive touch to the sensation experienced in the skin, whereas we relate active touch to the object being touched. For example, if someone pushes a pointed object into your skin, you might say, "I feel a pricking sensation on my skin"; if, however, you push on the tip of the pointed object yourself, you might say, "I feel a pointed object" (Kruger, 1970). Thus, for passive touch you experience stimulation of the skin, and for active touch you experience the objects you are touching.

Psychophysical research has shown that people can accurately identify most common objects within 1 or 2 seconds (Klatzky et al., 1985). When Susan Lederman and Roberta Klatzky (1987, 1990) observed participants' hand movements as they made these identifications, they found that people use a number of distinctive movements, which the researchers called **exploratory procedures (EPs)**, and that the types of EPs used depend on the object qualities the participants are asked to judge.

Figure 14.14 shows four of the EPs observed by Lederman and Klatzky. People tend to use just one or two EPs to determine a particular quality. For example, people use mainly lateral motion and contour following to judge texture, and they use enclosure and contour following to judge exact shape.

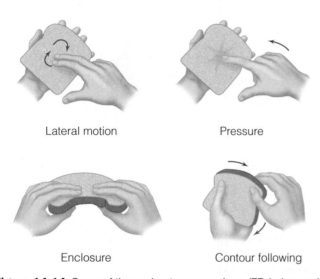

Lateral motion

Pressure

Enclosure

Contour following

Figure 14.14 Some of the exploratory procedures (EPs) observed by Lederman and Klatzky as participants identified objects. From Lederman, S. J., & Klatzky, R. L. (1987). Hand movements: A window into haptic object recognition. *Cognitive Psychology, 19,* 342–368. Reproduced by permission.

The Physiology of Tactile Object Perception

What is happening physiologically as we explore an object with our fingers and hands? Researchers have tried to answer this question by recording from mechanoreceptor fibers in the skin, from neurons in the somatosensory cortex, and from neurons in the parietal and frontal lobes.

In order for the brain to control everyday tasks, such as screwing a lid on a bottle, it needs to have access to information about the size and contour of the lid, and the amount of force needed to grasp the lid. This information is provided by receptors within the body that indicate the position of the joints and by mechanoreceptors in the skin that indicate the textures and contours of the lid.

The information for indicating the contours of the lid is signaled by the pattern of firing of a large number of mechanoreceptors. This is illustrated by the response profiles in **Figure 14.15**, which indicate how fibers in the fingertips respond to contact with two different spheres, one with high curvature relative to the fingertip (**Figure 14.15a**) and one that is more gently curved (**Figure 14.15b**). In both cases, the receptors right at the point where the fingers contact the sphere respond the most, and ones farther away fire less, but the *pattern* of response is different in the two cases. It is this overall pattern that provides information to the brain about the curvature of the sphere (Goodwin, 1998). Returning to the exploratory procedures, we can appreciate that the information on the fingertip corresponds to the EP of pressure. In addition, other EPs, such as enclosing the shape with the hand, contribute to our perception of the shape of three-dimensional objects.

As we move from mechanoreceptor fibers in the fingers toward the brain, we see that neurons become more specialized. This is similar to what occurs in the visual system. Neurons in the ventral posterior nucleus, which is the tactile area of the thalamus, have center-surround receptive

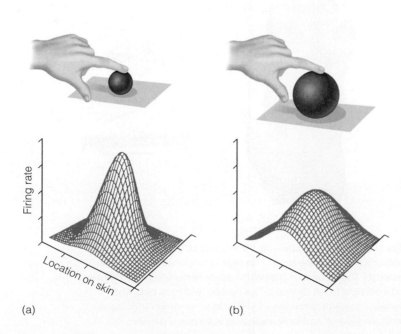

Firing rate

Location on skin

(a)

(b)

Figure 14.15 (a) Response of fibers in the fingertips to touching a high-curvature stimulus. The height of the profile indicates the firing rate at different places across the fingertip. (b) The profile of firing to touching a stimulus with more gentle curvature. From Goodwin, A. W. (1998). Extracting the shape of an object from the responses of peripheral nerve fibers. In J. W. Morley (Ed.), *Neural aspects of tactile sensation* (pp. 55–87). New York: Elsevier Science. By permission of Elsevier.

fields that are similar to the center-surround receptive fields in the lateral geniculate nucleus, which is the visual area of the thalamus (Mountcastle & Powell, 1959; **Figure 14.16**). In the cortex, we find some neurons with center-surround receptive fields and others that respond to more specialized stimulation of the skin. **Figure 14.17** shows stimuli that cause neurons in the monkey's somatosensory cortex to fire. There are neurons that respond to specific orientations (**Figure 14.17a**) and neurons that respond to movement across the skin in a specified direction (**Figure 14.17b**; Hyvärinen & Poranen, 1978; also see Bensmaia et al., 2008; Pei et al., 2011; Yau et al., 2009).

There are also neurons in the monkey's somatosensory cortex that respond when the monkey grasps a specific object (Sakata & Iwamura, 1978). For example, **Figure 14.18** shows the response of one of these neurons. This neuron responds when the monkey grasps the ruler but does not respond when the monkey grasps a cylinder or a sphere (see also Iwamura, 1998).

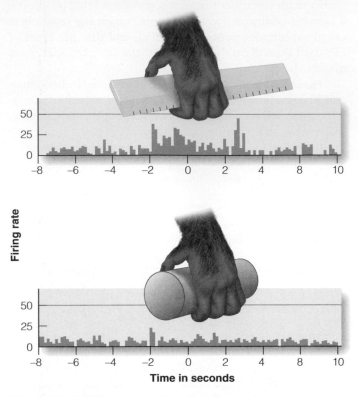

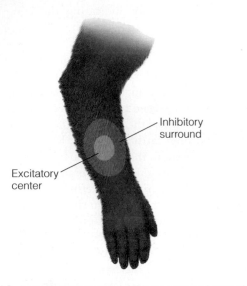

Figure 14.16 An excitatory-center, inhibitory-surround receptive field of a neuron in a monkey's thalamus. © Cengage Learning

Figure 14.18 The response of a neuron in a monkey's parietal cortex that fires when the monkey grasps a ruler but that does not fire when the monkey grasps a cylinder. The monkey grasps the objects at time = 0. From Sakata, H., & Iwamura, Y. (1978). Cortical processing of tactile information in the first somatosensory and parietal association areas in the monkey. In G. Gordon (Ed.), *Active touch* (pp. 55–72). Elmsford, NY: Pergamon Press. Reproduced by permission.

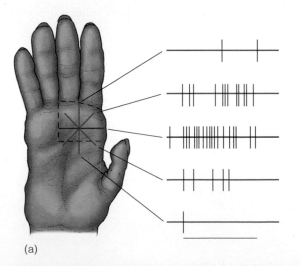

(a)

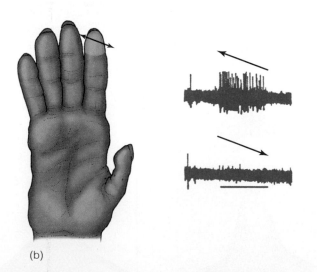

(b)

Figure 14.17 Receptive fields of neurons in the monkey's somatosensory cortex. (a) The records to the right of the hand show nerve firing to stimulation of the hand with the orientations shown on the hand. This neuron responds best when a horizontally oriented edge is presented to the monkey's hand. (b) The records on the right indicate nerve firing for movement of a stimulus across the fingertip from left to right (top) and from right to left (bottom). This neuron responds best when a stimulus moves across the fingertip from right to left. From Hyvärinen, J., & Poranen, A. (1978). Movement-sensitive and direction and orientation-selective cutaneous receptive fields in the hand area of the postcentral gyrus in monkeys. *Journal of Physiology, 283,* 523–537. Copyright © 1978 by The Physiological Society, UK. Reproduced by permission.

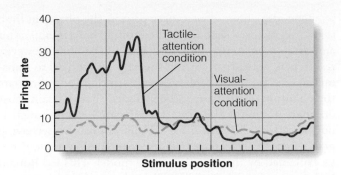

Figure 14.19 Firing rate of a neuron in area S1 of a monkey's cortex to a letter being rolled across the fingertips. The neuron responds only when the monkey is paying attention to the tactile stimulus. From Hsiao, S. S., O'Shaughnessy, D. M., & Johnson, K. O. (1993). Effects of selective attention on spatial form processing in monkey primary and secondary somatosensory cortex. *Journal of Neurophysiology, 70,* 444–447. Copyright © 1993 by The American Physiological Society. Reproduced by permission.

Cortical neurons are affected not only by the properties of the object, but also by whether the perceiver is paying attention. Steven Hsiao and coworkers (1993, 1996) recorded the response of neurons in areas S1 and S2 to raised letters that were scanned across a monkey's finger. In the tactile-attention condition, the monkey had to perform a task that required focusing its attention on the letters being presented to its fingers. In the visual-attention condition, the monkey had to focus its attention on an unrelated visual stimulus. The results, shown in **Figure 14.19**, show that even though the monkey is receiving exactly the same stimulation on its fingertips in both conditions, the response is larger for the tactile-attention condition. Thus, stimulation of the receptors may trigger a response, but the size of the response can be affected by processes such as attention, thinking, and other actions of the perceiver.

If the idea that events other than stimulation of the receptors can affect perception sounds familiar, it is because similar situations occur in vision (see pages 134, 166) and hearing (page 310). A person's active participation makes a difference in perception, not just by influencing what stimuli stimulate the receptors but by influencing the processing that occurs once the receptors are stimulated. This is perhaps most clearly demonstrated for the experience of pain, which is strongly affected by processes in addition to stimulation of the receptors.

Pain

As we mentioned at the beginning of this chapter, pain functions to warn us of potentially damaging situations and therefore helps us avoid or deal with cuts, burns, and broken bones. People born without the ability to feel pain might become aware that they are leaning on a hot stove burner only when they smell burning flesh, or might be unaware of broken bones, infections, or internal injuries—situations that could easily be life-threatening (Watkins & Maier, 2003). The signaling function of pain is reflected in the following definition, from the International Association for the Study of Pain: "Pain is an unpleasant sensory and emotional experience associated with actual or potential tissue damage, or described in terms of such damage" (Merskey, 1991).

Joachim Scholz and Clifford Woolf (2002) distinguish three different types of pain. **Inflammatory pain** is caused by damage to tissue or inflammation of joints or by tumor cells. **Neuropathic pain** is caused by lesions or other damage to the nervous system. Examples of neuropathic pain are carpal tunnel syndrome, which is caused by repetitive tasks such as typing; spinal cord injury; and brain damage due to stroke.

Nociceptive pain is pain caused by activation of receptors in the skin called **nociceptors**, which are specialized to respond to tissue damage or potential damage (Perl, 2007). A number of different kinds of nociceptors respond to different stimuli—heat, chemical, severe pressure, and cold (**Figure 14.20**). We will focus on nociceptive pain. Our discussion will include not only pain that is caused by stimulation of nociceptors in the skin, but also mechanisms that affect the perception of nociceptive pain, and even some examples of pain that can occur when the skin is not stimulated at all.

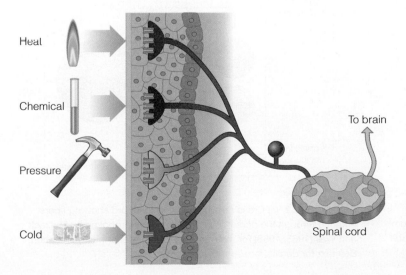

Figure 14.20 Nociceptive pain is created by activation of nociceptors in the skin that respond to different types of stimulation. Signals from the nociceptors are transmitted to the spinal cord and then up the spinal cord in pathways that lead to the brain. © Cengage Learning

Questioning the Direct Pathway Model of Pain

We begin our discussion of pain by considering how early researchers thought about pain, and how these early ideas began changing in the 1960s. In the 1950s and early 1960s, pain was explained by the **direct pathway model of pain**. According to this model, pain occurs when nociceptor receptors in the skin are stimulated and send their signals directly from the skin to the brain (Melzack & Wall, 1965). But in the 1960s, some researchers began noting situations in which pain was affected by factors in addition to stimulation of the skin.

One example was the report by Beecher (1959) that most American soldiers wounded at the Anzio beachhead in World War II "entirely denied pain from their extensive wounds or had so little that they did not want any medication to relieve it" (p. 165). One reason for this was that the soldiers' wounds had a positive aspect: they provided escape from a hazardous battlefield to the safety of a behind-the-lines hospital.

Another example of pain occurring without any transmission from receptor to brain is the phenomena of **phantom limbs**, in which people who have had a limb amputated continue to experience the limb (**Figure 14.21**). This perception is so convincing that amputees have been known to try stepping off a bed onto phantom feet or legs, or to attempt lifting a cup with a phantom hand. For many, the limb moves with the body, swinging while walking. But perhaps most interesting of all, it not uncommon for amputees to experience pain in the phantom limb (Jensen & Nikolajsen, 1999; Katz & Gagliese, 1999; Melzack, 1992; Ramachandran & Hirstein, 1998).

One idea about what causes pain in the phantom limb is that signals are sent from the stump that remains after amputation or from a remaining part of the limb. However, researchers noted that cutting the nerves that used to transmit signals from the limb to the brain does not eliminate the phantom or the pain and concluded that the pain must originate not in the skin, but in the brain. Examples such as not perceiving the pain from serious wounds or perceiving pain when no signals are being sent to the brain could not be explained by the direct pathway model. This led Ronald Melzak and Patrick Wall (1965) to propose the *gate control model* of pain.

The Gate Control Model

The **gate control model** begins with the idea that pain signals enter the spinal cord from the body and are then transmitted from the spinal cord to the brain. In addition, the model proposes that there are additional pathways that influence the signals sent from the spinal cord to the brain. The central idea behind the theory is that the signals from these additional pathways can act to open or close a *gate*, located in the spinal cord, which determines the strength of the signal leaving the spinal cord.

Figure 14.22 shows the circuit that Melzack and Wall (1965) proposed. The gate control system consists of cells in the dorsal horn of the spinal cord (**Figure 14.22a**). These cells in the dorsal horn are represented by the red and green circles in the gate control circuit in **Figure 14.22b**. We can understand

Figure 14.21 The light part of the right arm represents the phantom limb—an extremity that is not physically present, but which the person perceives as existing. © Cengage Learning

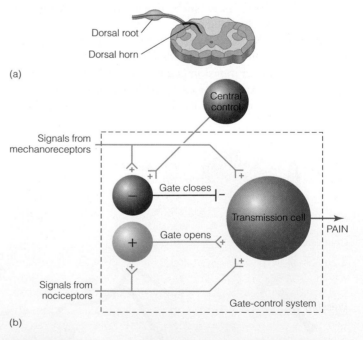

Figure 14.22 (a) Cross section of the spinal cord showing fibers entering through the dorsal root. (b) The circuit proposed by Melzack and Wall (1965, 1988) for their gate control model of pain perception. See text for details. © Cengage Learning

how this circuit functions by considering how input to the gate control system occurs along three pathways:

- *Nociceptors.* Fibers from nociceptors activate a circuit consisting entirely of excitatory synapses, and therefore send excitatory signals to the transmission cells. Excitatory signals from the (+) neurons in the dorsal horn "open the gate" and increase the firing of the transmission cells. Increased activity in the transmission cells results in more pain.

- *Mechanoreceptors.* Fibers from mechanoreceptors carry information about nonpainful tactile stimulation. An example of this type of stimulus would be signals sent from rubbing the skin. When activity in the mechanoreceptors reaches the (−) neurons in the dorsal horn, inhibitory signals sent to the transmission cells "close the gate" and decrease the firing of the transmission cells. This decrease in firing decreases the intensity of pain.

- *Central control.* These fibers, which contain information related to cognitive functions such as expectation, attention, and distraction, carry signals down from the cortex. As with the mechanoreceptors, activity coming down from the brain also closes the gate, decreases transmission cell activity, and decreases pain.

Since the introduction of the gate control model in 1965, researchers have determined that the neural circuits that control pain are much more complex than what was proposed in the original model (Perl & Kruger, 1996; Sufka & Price, 2002). Nonetheless, the idea proposed by the model—that the perception of pain is determined by a balance between input from nociceptors in the skin and nonnociceptive activity from the skin and the brain—stimulated research that provided a great deal of additional evidence for the idea that the perception of pain is influenced by more than just stimulation of the skin (Fields & Basbaum, 1999; Sufka & Price, 2002; Turk & Flor, 1999; Weissberg, 1999). We will now consider some examples of how cognition can influence the perception of pain. **VL**

Cognition and Pain

Modern research has shown that pain can be influenced by what a person expects, how the person directs his or her attention, the type of distracting stimuli that are present, and suggestion made under hypnosis (Rainville et al., 1999; Wiech et al., 2008).

Expectation In a hospital study in which surgical patients were told what to expect and were instructed to relax to alleviate their pain, the patients requested fewer painkillers following surgery and were sent home 2.7 days earlier than patients who were not provided with this information (Egbert et al., 1964). Studies have also shown that a significant proportion of patients with pathological pain get relief from taking a placebo, a pill that they believe contains painkillers but that, in fact, contains no active ingredients (Finniss & Benedetti, 2005;

Weisenberg, 1977). This decrease in pain from a substance that has no pharmacological effect is called the **placebo effect.** The key to the placebo effect is that the patient believes that the substance is an effective therapy. This belief leads the patient to expect a reduction in pain, and this reduction does, in fact, occur. Although many different mechanisms have been proposed to explain the placebo effect, expectation is one of the more powerful determinants (Colloca & Benedetti, 2005).

This effect of expectation in relieving symptoms has been demonstrated in another way by showing that drugs are more effective when the patient knows when they are being administered than if they are unaware of when they are being administered. Martina Amanzio and coworkers (2001) demonstrated this by determining the effectiveness of four widely used painkillers in patients who had just undergone surgery. The "open" group of patients received the drug from a doctor who administered the drug at bedside and told the patient that the drug was a powerful analgesic that should cause the pain to decrease in a few minutes. The "hidden" group of patients received a hidden injection of the same drug through an automatic infusion machine, with no doctor or nurse in the room. Thus, the open group knew when the drug was being given, and the hidden group was unaware of when the drug was being given.

The result of this experiment was that the dose of drug needed to reduce pain by 50 percent was much higher for the hidden presentation. For example, an average of 108 mg of tramadol was necessary in the open condition, but 140 mg was necessary in the hidden condition. The superior effectiveness of the open treatment could be described as a "placebo effect without the placebo," because the effect was caused by expectation, even though no placebo was given. One could say that expectation created by knowledge of the drug's administration functioned as a placebo.

Shifting Attention The perception of pain can increase if perception is focused on the pain or decrease if the pain is ignored or attention is diverted away from it. Examples of the effect of attention on pain were noted in the 1960s (Melzack & Wall, 1965). Here is a recent description of this effect, as reported by a student in my class:

I remember being around five or six years old, and I was playing Nintendo when my dog ran by and pulled the wire out of the game system. When I got up to plug the wire back in I stumbled and banged my forehead on the radiator underneath the living room window. I got back up and staggered over to the Nintendo and plugged the controller back into the port, thinking nothing of my little fall . . . . As I resumed playing the game, all of a sudden I felt liquid rolling down my forehead, and reached my hand up to realize it was blood. I turned and looked into the mirror on the closet door to see a gash running down my forehead with blood pouring from it. All of a sudden I screamed out, and the pain hit me. My mom came running in, and took me to the hospital to get stitches. (Ian Kalinowski)

The important message of this description is that Ian's pain occurred not when he was injured, but when he *realized* he was injured. One conclusion that we might draw from this example is that one way to decrease pain would be to distract a person's attention from the source of the pain. This technique has been used in hospitals using virtual reality techniques as a tool to distract attention from a painful stimulus. Consider, for example, the case of James Pokorny, who received third-degree burns over 42 percent of his body when the fuel tank of the car he was repairing exploded. While having his bandages changed at the University of Washington Burn Center, he wore a black plastic helmet with a computer monitor inside, on which he saw a virtual world of multicolored three-dimensional graphics. This world placed him in a virtual kitchen that contained a virtual spider, and he was able to chase the spider into the sink so he could grind it up with a virtual garbage disposal (Robbins, 2000). **VL**

The point of this "game" was to reduce Pokorny's pain by shifting his attention from the bandages to the virtual reality world. Pokorny reports that "you're concentrating on different things, rather than your pain. The pain level went down significantly." Studies of other patients indicate that burn patients using this virtual reality technique experienced much less pain when their bandages were being changed than patients in a control group who were distracted by playing video games (Hoffman et al., 2000) or who were not distracted at all (Hoffman et al., 2008; also see Buhle et al., 2012).

Content of Emotional Distraction An experiment by Minet deWied and Marinis Verbaten (2001) shows how the content of distracting materials can influence pain perception. The stimuli they used were pictures that had been previously rated as being positive (sports pictures and attractive females), neutral (household objects, nature, and people), or negative (burn victims and accidents). Male subjects looked at the pictures as one of their hands was immersed in cold (2°C) water. They were told to keep the hand immersed for as long as possible but to withdraw the hand when it began to hurt.

The results indicated that subjects who were looking at the positive pictures kept their hands immersed for an average of 120 seconds, but subjects in the other groups removed their hands more quickly (80 seconds for neutral pictures; 70 seconds for negative pictures). Because the subjects' ratings of the intensity of their pain—made immediately after removing their hands from the water—was the same for all three groups, deWied and Verbaten concluded that the content of the pictures influenced the time it took to reach the same pain level in the three groups. In another experiment, Jaimie Rhuddy and coworkers (2005) found that subjects gave lower ratings to pain caused by an electric shock when they were looking at pleasant pictures than when looking at unpleasant pictures. They concluded from this result that positive or negative emotions can affect the experience of pain.

Hypnotic Suggestion Experiences of pain can be induced by hypnotic suggestion (Barber & Hahn, 1964; Dudley et al., 1966; Whalley & Oakley, 2003). Stuart Derbyshire and coworkers (2004) did an experiment in which they attached

a thermal stimulator to the palm of a subject's hand. In the physically induced pain (PI) condition, heat pulses were delivered through the stimulator. In the hypnotically induced pain (HI) condition, subjects received suggestions that painful heat was presented through the stimulator (which was actually inactivated during this condition). In a control group, hypnotized subjects were told that the stimulator was turned off (which was accurate information) and that they should just imagine that heat was increasing at the stimulator. Subjects in all three conditions rated their pain experience on a scale from 0 (no pain) to 10 (extreme pain).

Average pain ratings were 5.7 in the PI condition and 2.8 in the HI condition. A few subjects in the control ("imagine") condition reported feeling some heat, but none reported feeling pain. These results confirm previous research that showed that pain can be induced hypnotically. But Derbyshire went beyond simply asking people to rate physically produced and hypnotically produced pain, by using fMRI to measure his subjects' brain activation as they were making their pain estimates. **Figure 14.23** shows the areas activated in the PI condition (**Figure 14.23a**) and the HI condition (**Figures 14.23b** and **14.23c**). Notice that there is substantial similarity between the PI and HI patterns, with overlap in the thalamus, anterior cingulate cortex, insula, parietal cortex, and prefrontal cortex. Comparing the two HI patterns shows that activation was more widespread for the subject who reported more pain (Figure 14.23b) than for the subject who reported a lower level of pain (Figure 14.23c). (For additional demonstrations of how hypnotic suggestion affects pain perception and brain activity, see also Raij et al., 2005, 2009.)

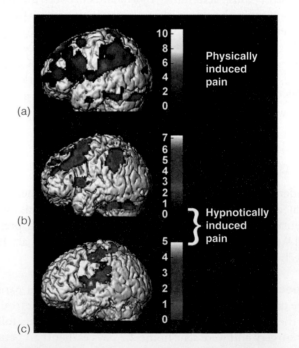

Figure 14.23 Brain activation for individual subjects in Derbyshire et al.'s (2004) experiment. (a) Activation by physically induced pain. (b) Activation for the subject who experienced the highest level of hypnotically induced pain. (c) Activation for the subject who experienced the lowest level of hypnotically induced pain. From Derbyshire, S. W. G., Whalley, M. G., Stenger, V. A. & Oakley, D. A. (2004). Cerebral activation during hypnotically induced and imagined pain. *Neuroimage, 23*, 392–401. Reprinted with permission from Elsevier.

The relation between brain activation and pain experience and the overlap between the physically induced and hypnotically induced pain conditions support the idea that pain can occur without activation of receptors in the skin. This demonstration of a connection between the perception of pain and brain activity leads to our next section, in which we look at more evidence for links between brain activity and perception.

The Brain and Pain

A large number of research studies support the idea that the perception of pain is accompanied by activity that is widely distributed throughout the brain. **Figure 14.24** shows a number of the structures that become activated by pain. They include subcortical structures, such as the hypothalamus, the amygdala, and the thalamus, and areas in the cortex, including the somatosensory cortex (S1), the anterior cingulate cortex (ACC), the prefrontal cortex (PFC), and the insula (an area of the cerebral cortex not visible from the surface that is located in between the temporal and frontal lobes) (Chapman, 1995; Derbyshire et al., 1997; Price, 2000; Rainville, 2002). All of the brain regions that are involved in pain perception, taken together, have been called the **pain matrix** (Melzack, 1999; Tracey, 2005; Wager et al., 2004).

Although pain is associated with the overall pattern of firing in the pain matrix, there is also evidence that certain areas in the matrix are responsible for specific components of the pain experience.

Representation of the Sensory and Affective Components of Pain
The definition of pain on page 351 states that pain is "an unpleasant sensory and emotional experience." This reference to both sensory *and* emotional experience reflects the **multimodal nature of pain**, which is illustrated by how people describe pain. When people describe their pain with words like *throbbing, prickly, hot,* or *dull,* they are referring to the **sensory component of pain**. When they use words like *torturing, annoying, frightful,* or *sickening,* they are referring to the **affective (or emotional) component of pain** (Melzack, 1999).

Evidence that these two components of pain are served by different areas of the brain is provided by an experiment by R. K. Hofbauer and coworkers (2001), in which participants were presented with potentially painful stimuli and were asked to rate (1) subjective pain intensity (the sensory component of pain) and (2) the unpleasantness of the pain (the affective component of pain). Hofbauer and coworkers measured brain activity using PET (see page 79) as participants responded to pain induced by immersing their hands in hot water.

What makes this experiment particularly interesting is that Hofbauer and coworkers not only asked their participants to rate both the sensory and affective components of their pain, but they also used hypnotic suggestion to decrease or increase each of these components. **Figure 14.25a** shows

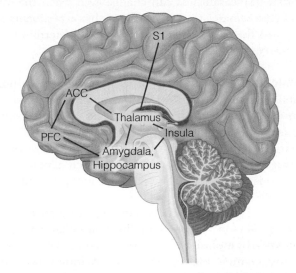

Figure 14.24 The perception of pain is accompanied by activation of a number of different areas of the brain. All of these areas, taken together, are called the pain matrix. Some of the structures in the pain matrix are shown here. ACC is the anterior cingulate cortex; PFC is the prefrontal cortex; S1 is the somatosensory cortex. The positions of the structures are approximate, with some, such as the amygdala, hypothalamus, and insula, located deep within the cortex, and others, such as S1 and PFC, located at the surface. Lines indicate connections between the structures. © Cengage Learning

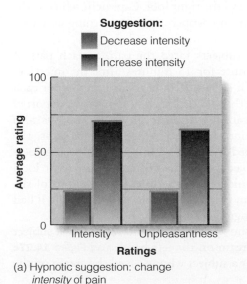

(a) Hypnotic suggestion: change *intensity* of pain

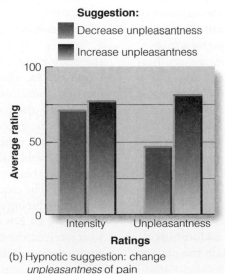

(b) Hypnotic suggestion: change *unpleasantness* of pain

Figure 14.25 Results of Hofbauer et al.'s (2001) experiment. Participants' ratings of the intensity and the unpleasantness of pain were affected by hypnosis. (a) Results of hypnotic suggestion to decrease or increase the pain's *intensity*. (b) Results of suggestion to decrease or increase the pain's *unpleasantness*. © Cengage Learning

that presenting suggestions to decrease or increase *subjective intensity* (sensory component) changed the participants' ratings of both subjective intensity (left pair of bars) and unpleasantness (right pair of bars). These changes were accompanied by changes in activity in S1, the primary somatosensory receiving area.

Figure 14.25b shows that presenting suggestions to decrease or increase the *unpleasantness* (affective component) of the pain did not affect ratings of subjective intensity (left bars) but did affect ratings of unpleasantness (right bars). These changes were accompanied by changes in activity in the anterior cingulate cortex (ACC), but not in S1. From these results, Hofbauer concluded that the ACC is important for determining the affective component of unpleasantness and that unpleasantness can change even when the intensity of pain remains the same. Many other experiments have confirmed the importance of the ACC in determining the affective component of pain (Rainville, 2002).

Chemicals in the Brain Another important development in our understanding of the relationship between brain activity and pain perception is the discovery of a link between chemicals called opioids and pain perception. This can be traced back to research that began in the 1970s on opiate drugs, such as opium and heroin, which have been used since the dawn of recorded history to reduce pain and induce feelings of euphoria.

By the 1970s, researchers had discovered that the opiate drugs act on receptors in the brain that respond to stimulation by molecules with specific structures. The importance of the molecule's structure for exciting these "opiate receptors" explains why injecting a drug called naloxone into a person who has overdosed on heroin can almost immediately revive the victim. Because naloxone's structure is similar to heroin's, it blocks the action of heroin by attaching itself to receptor sites usually occupied by heroin (**Figure 14.26a**).

Why are there opiate receptor sites in the brain? After all, they certainly have been present since long before people started taking heroin. Researchers concluded that there must be naturally occurring substances in the body that act on these sites, and in 1975 neurotransmitters were discovered that act on the same receptors that are activated by opium and heroin. One group of these transmitters is called endorphins, for *endogenous* (naturally occurring) *morphine*.

Since the discovery of endorphins, researchers have accumulated a large amount of evidence linking endorphins to pain reduction. For example, pain can be decreased by stimulating sites in the brain that release endorphins (**Figure 14.26b**), and pain can be increased by injecting naloxone, which blocks endorphins from reaching their receptor sites (**Figure 14.26c**).

In addition to decreasing the analgesic effect of endorphins, naloxone also decreases the analgesic effect of placebos (see page 353). This finding, along with other evidence, led to the conclusion that the pain reduction effect of placebos occurs because placebos cause the release of endorphins. As it turns out, there are some situations in which the placebo

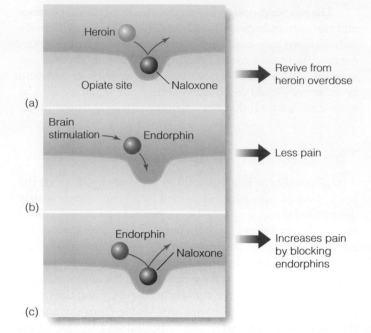

Figure 14.26 (a) Naloxone, which has a structure similar to heroin, reduces the effect of heroin by occupying a receptor site normally stimulated by heroin. (b) Stimulating sites in the brain that cause the release of endorphins can reduce pain by stimulating opiate receptor sites. (c) Naloxone decreases the pain reduction caused by endorphins by keeping the endorphins from reaching the receptor sites. © Cengage Learning

effect can occur without the release of endorphins, but we will focus on the endorphin-based placebo effect by considering the following question, raised by Benedetti and coworkers (1999): Where are placebo-related endorphins released in the nervous system?

Benedetti wondered whether expectation caused by placebos triggered the release of endorphins throughout the brain, therefore creating a placebo effect for the entire body, or whether expectation caused the release of endorphins only at specific places in the body. To answer this question, Benedetti injected subjects with the chemical *capsaicin* just under the skin, at four places on the body: the left hand, the right hand, the left foot, and the right foot. Capsaicin, which is the active component in chili peppers, causes a burning sensation where it is injected.

One group of subjects rated the pain at each part of the body every minute for 15 minutes after the injection. **Figure 14.27a**, which shows the initial pain ratings for each location, indicates that the subjects in this group reported pain at all the locations. Another group of subjects also received the injection, but just before the injections, the experimenter rubbed a cream at one or two of the locations and told subjects that the cream was a potent local anesthetic that would relieve the burning sensation of the capsaicin. The cream was actually a placebo treatment; it had no pain-reducing ingredients.

Figure 14.27b shows the initial pain rating for a subject who received the cream on the left hand, and **Figure 14.27c** shows the result for a subject who received the cream on the

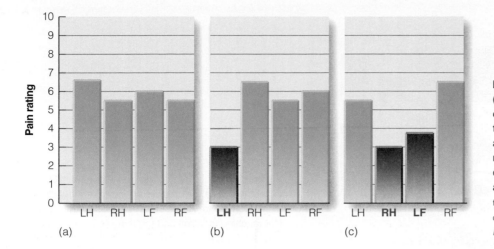

Figure 14.27 The results of Benedetti et al.'s (1999) experiment. (a) Pain ratings, on a scale of 0 (no pain) to 10 (unbearable pain), for pain in the left hand (LH), right hand (RH), left foot (LF), and right foot (RF). These ratings are for when no placebo cream was applied. (b) Placebo cream applied to the left hand. (c) Placebo cream applied to the right hand and left foot. Based on data from Benedetti, F., Arduino, C., & Amanzio, M. (1999). Somatotopic activation of opioid systems by target-directed expectations of analgesia. *Journal of Neuroscience, 19*, 3639–3648.

right hand and left foot. The effect in both of these subjects is striking because the placebo effect occurred only where the cream was applied. To demonstrate that this placebo effect was associated with endorphins, Benedetti showed that injecting naloxone abolished the placebo effect.

What this means, according to Benedetti, is that when subjects direct their attention to specific places where they expect pain will be reduced, pathways are activated that release endorphins at specific locations. The mechanism behind endorphin-related analgesia is therefore much more sophisticated than simply chemicals being released into the overall circulation. The mind, as it turns out, can not only reduce pain by causing the release of chemicals, it can literally direct these chemicals to the locations where the pain would be occurring. Research such as this, which links the placebo effect to endorphins, provides a physiological basis for what had previously been described in strictly psychological terms.

SOMETHING TO CONSIDER:
The Effect of Observing Touch and Pain in Others

How do you feel when you see someone in pain? Do you feel a little pain yourself? Or emotions? A sense of empathy for the person? Or do you turn away because seeing someone in pain can be painful? We can ask a similar question about seeing someone else being touched. Although touch can be pleasant, sometimes it can be threatening. Consider, for example, how you might experience watching the scene from a James Bond movie in which a tarantula crawls on his chest. One reaction might be to shiver, "as if a spider crawled on our own chest" (Keysers et al., 2004, p. 335).

Reacting to observing another person's actions is something we considered in Chapter 7, when we described mirror neurons in the monkey's premotor cortex, which fire both when the monkey sees someone else grasping an object, such as food, *and* when the monkey itself grasps the food.

Research on the somatosensory system has revealed similar phenomena for touch and pain. Watching someone else being touched or experiencing pain activates areas in the somatosensory cortex of the observer that would also be activated in the somatosensory cortex of the person actually being touched or feeling pain. For example, Christian Keysers and coworkers (2004) used fMRI to measure the response of the somatosensory cortex while subjects were being touched on the leg and when the subjects viewed movies of other people or objects being touched.

Not surprisingly, stroking the subject's leg activated the two main somatosensory areas S1 and S2. The interesting result is what happened when the subjects watched films showing touching. **Figure 14.28a** shows the response in area S2 that occurred when the subject viewed the control film when a probe was not touching a person's leg (blue bar on right) and when the subject viewed the experimental film of a probe touching the leg (red bar on right). In this condition, the perception of touching increased the activity of S2.

Figure 14.28b shows that the same result occurred when an object—two white binders—was substituted for the person's leg. Thus, perceiving either another person or an object being touched increased activity in S2. Finally, **Figure 14.28c** shows that this result did not occur when subjects viewed two films of an airplane wing, even though the wing passed over the land in the experimental condition. This shows that it was the touch that was important, not the pattern of visual stimulation. Keysers and coworkers conclude from this result that the brain transforms the visual stimulus of touch into an activation of brain areas involved in our own experience of touch (see also Keysers et al., 2010).

Kaspar Meyer and coworkers (2011) obtained a similar result when subjects watched films of another person's hands haptically exploring common objects like a set of keys, a tennis ball, and the leaves of a plant. **Figure 14.29** shows the increase in brain activation caused by watching the touch films compared to just looking at a fixation cross. The red areas show that activation occurred both in the visual cortex and in somatosensory areas associated with touch.

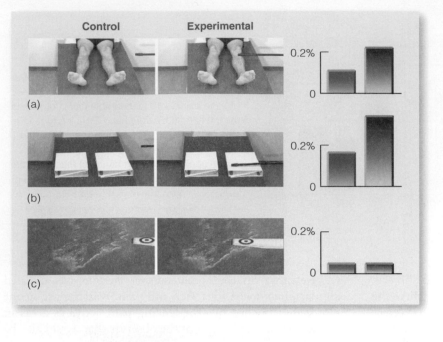

Figure 14.28 Stimuli for the Keysers et al. (2004) experiment. The pictures are stills from control films and experimental films observed by the subjects. (a) Not touching (control) and touching (experimental) legs; (b) not touching and touching object; (c) airplane wing passing over land; no touching. The blue bars are the responses of S2 to the control films. The red bars are the response to the experimental films. Adapted from Keysers, C., Wicker, B., Gazzola, V., Anton, J.-L., Fogassi, L., & Gallese, V. (2004). A touching sight: SII/PV activation during the observation and experience of touch. *Neuron, 42,* 335–346.

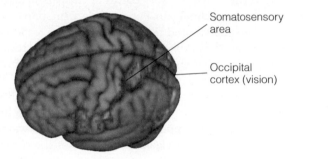

Figure 14.29 Brain activation measured by Meyer et al. (2011) caused by observing films of a person's hands haptically exploring objects. Both visual and somatosensory areas are activated. From Meyer, K., Kaplan, J. T., Essex, R., Damasio, H., & Damasio, A. (2011). Seeing touch is correlated with content-specific activity in primary somatosensory cortex. *Cerebral Cortex, 21,* 2113–2121.

So far we have been describing how somatosensory areas of the brain are activated by observing touch. But what is the observer experiencing? Not all subjects feel touch while watching someone being touched, but some do. Sarah-Jayne Blakemore and coworkers (2005) describe a person with **synesthesia**, a condition in which stimulation of one modality (like vision) results in an experience in another modality (like touch). When this person observes another person being touched, he or she experiences touch on the same part of his or her own body.

But what about people who don't experience synesthesia? When Jody Osborn and Stuart Derbyshire (2010) showed subjects images and films depicting people experiencing pain, such as a person's hand receiving an injection, a diver hitting her head on a diving board, and a soccer player breaking his leg, and asked them to indicate whether they felt any pain sensations, 31 out of 108 subjects reported feeling pain in response to at least one of the images. All subjects reported that the pain occurred in the same part of the body as the pictured injury.

You might wonder how reliable the subjects' pain reports were in this experiment; after all, we have no way of knowing what they were actually experiencing. However, when Osborn and Derbyshire recorded brain activity using fMRI, they observed higher activity in S2 (which is associated with the sensory component of pain) and the insula (which is associated with the affective component of pain) compared to subjects who did not report experiencing any pain from observing the images. Thus, the multimodal nature of pain— both sensory and affective—is reflected in the brain's response to watching another person's pain.

These studies and others have led some researchers to suggest that our response to watching others experience pain reflects our empathy for the other person's negative experience. Tania Singer and coworkers (2004) demonstrated this by bringing romantically involved couples into the laboratory and having the woman, whose brain activity was being measured by an fMRI scanner, either receive shocks herself or watch her male partner receive shocks. The results, shown in **Figure 14.30**, show that a number of brain areas were activated when the woman received the shocks (**Figure 14.30a**), and that some of the same areas were activated when she watched her partner receive shocks (**Figure 14.30b**).

To show that the brain activity caused by watching their partner was related to empathy, Singer had the women fill out "empathy scales" designed to measure their tendency to empathize with others. As predicted, women with higher empathy scores showed higher activation of their ACC. Thus, although the pain associated with watching someone else experience pain may be caused by stimulation that is very different from physical pain, these two types of pain apparently share some physiological mechanisms. (Also see Avenanti et al., 2005; Lamm et al., 2007.)

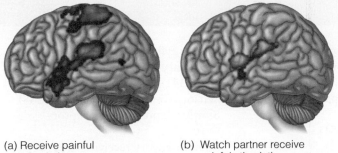

(a) Receive painful stimulation

(b) Watch partner receive painful stimulation

Figure 14.30 Singer and coworkers (2004) used fMRI to determine the areas of the brain activated by (a) receiving painful stimulation and (b) watching another person receive the painful stimulation. Singer proposes that the activation in (b) is related to empathy for the other person. Empathy did not activate the somatosensory cortex but did activate other areas that are activated by pain, such as the insula (tucked between the parietal and temporal lobes) and anterior cingulate cortex (see Figure 14.25). Adapted from Holden, C. (2004). Imaging studies show how brain thinks about pain. *Science, 303,* 1121. Reprinted by permission of Tania Singer.

TEST YOURSELF 14.2

1. What processes are involved in identifying objects by haptic exploration?

2. What are some of the physiological processes involved in recognizing objects by touch?

3. Describe the three types of pain.

4. What is the direct pathway model of pain? What evidence led researchers to question this model of pain perception?

5. What is the gate control model? Be sure you understand the roles of the nociceptors, mechanoreceptors, and central control.

6. Give examples for the following situations, which illustrate how pain is influenced by cognition and experience: expectation, shifting attention, and content of emotional distraction.

7. What is the pain matrix?

8. What does it mean to say that pain is multimodal? Describe the hypnosis experiments that identified areas involved in the sensory component of pain and the emotional component of pain.

9. Describe the role of chemicals in the perception of pain. Be sure you understand how endorphins and naloxone interact at receptor sites, and a possible mechanism that explains why pain is reduced by placebos.

10. Describe the Benedetti et al. (1999) experiment. How did this experiment demonstrate that the placebo's effect can operate on local parts of the body?

11. Describe the following experiments that considered how observers are affected by watching someone being touched or experiencing pain: Keysers et al. (2004); Meyer et al. (2011); Blakemore et al. (2005); Osborn and Derbyshire (2010); Singer et al. (2004).

THINK ABOUT IT

1. One of the themes in this book is that it is possible to use the results of psychophysical experiments to suggest the operation of physiological mechanisms or to link physiological mechanisms to perception. Cite an example of how psychophysics has been used in this way for each of the senses we have considered so far—vision, hearing, and the cutaneous senses.

2. Some people report situations in which they were injured but didn't feel any pain until they became aware of their injury. How would you explain this kind of situation in terms of top-down and bottom-up processing?

How could you relate this situation to the studies we have discussed? (p. 353)

3. Even though the senses of vision and cutaneous perception are different in many ways, there are a number of parallels between them. Cite examples of parallels between vision and cutaneous sensations (touch and pain) for the following: "tuned" receptors, mechanisms of detail perception, receptive fields, plasticity (how changing the environment influences properties of the system), and top-down processing. Also, can you think of situations in which vision and touch interact with one another?

KEY TERMS

Active touch (p. 348)
Affective (or emotional) component of pain (p. 355)
Cutaneous senses (p. 338)
Dermis (p. 338)
Direct pathway model of pain (p. 352)
Duplex theory of texture perception (p. 347)
Endorphin (p. 356)
Epidermis (p. 338)
Exploratory procedures (EPs) (p. 349)
Gate control model (p. 352)
Grating acuity (p. 343)
Haptic perception (p. 348)
Homunculus (p. 341)
Inflammatory pain (p. 351)
Kinesthesis (p. 338)
Mechanoreceptor (p. 338)

Medial lemniscal pathway (p. 339)
Meissner corpuscle (RA1) (p. 339)
Merkel receptor (SA1) (p. 339)
Multimodal nature of pain (p. 355)
Naloxone (p. 356)
Neuropathic pain (p. 351)
Nociceptive pain (p. 351)
Nociceptor (p. 351)
Opioid (p. 356)
Pacinian corpuscle (RA2 or PC) (p. 339)
Pain matrix (p. 355)
Passive touch (p. 348)
Phantom limb (p. 352)
Placebo (p. 353)
Placebo effect (p. 353)
Proprioception (p. 338)
Rapidly adapting (RA) receptor (p. 339)

Ruffini cylinder (SA2) (p. 339)
Secondary somatosensory cortex (S2) (p. 341)
Sensory component of pain (p. 355)
Slowly adapting (SA) receptor (p. 339)
Somatosensory receiving area (S1) (p. 341)
Somatosensory system (p. 338)
Spatial cue (p. 346)
Spinothalamic pathway (p. 339)
Surface texture (p. 346)
Synesthesia (p. 358)
Tactile acuity (p. 343)
Temporal cue (p. 346)
Transmission cell (p. 353)
Two-point threshold (p. 343)
Ventrolateral nucleus (p. 340)

MEDIA RESOURCES

CourseMate 🖥

Go to CengageBrain.com to access Psychology CourseMate, where you will find the Virtual Labs plus an interactive eBook, flashcards, quizzes, videos, and more.

Virtual Labs VL

The Virtual Labs are designed to help you get the most out of this course. The Virtual Lab icons direct you to specific media demonstrations and experiments designed to help you visualize what you are reading about. The numbers below indicate the number of the Virtual Lab you can access through Psychology CourseMate.

14.1 Anatomy of the Skin (p. 338)
Illustrates the skin, with drag-and-drop terms to test your knowledge of the locations of basic skin structures.

14.2 Gate Control System (p. 353)
How different types of stimulation are processed by the gate control system.

14.3 Reducing Pain in the Doctor's Office (p. 354)
Describes research on the effects of distraction and other factors on pain in children visiting the doctor.

The Chemical Senses

DEVELOPMENTAL DIMENSION: **Infant Chemical Sensitivity**

Think About It

VL The Virtual Lab icons direct you to specific animations and videos designed to help you visualize what you are reading about. Virtual Labs are listed at the end of the chapter, keyed to the page on which they appear, and can be accessed through Psychology CourseMate.

Some Questions We Will Consider:

- Are there differences in the way different people experience the taste of food? (p. 369)

- Why is a dog's sense of smell so much better than a human's? (p. 372)

- How do neurons in the cortex combine smell and taste? (p. 381)

We have five senses, but only two that go beyond the boundaries of ourselves. When you look at someone, it's just bouncing light, or when you hear them, it's just sound waves, vibrating air, or touch is just nerve endings tingling. Know what smell is? ... It's made up of the molecules of what you're smelling. (Kushner, 1993, p. 17)

The character speaking these lines in the play *Angels in America* probably did not take a course in sensation and perception and so leaves out the fact that vision and hearing are "just nerve endings tingling" as well. But his point—that smell involves taking molecules into your body—is one of the properties of the chemical senses that distinguishes them from the other senses. Thus, as you drink something, you smell it because molecules in gas form are entering your nose, and you taste it because molecules in liquid form are stimulating your tongue. Smell (which we will

◄ The chemical senses—taste and smell—act both separately and together. Taste creates perceptions by stimulation of receptors in the tongue; smell creates perceptions by stimulation of receptors in the olfactory mucosa within the nose. Taste and smell together collaborate to create flavor, which is the dominant perception we experience when eating or drinking.

refer to as *olfaction*) and taste have been called *molecule detectors* because they endow these gas and liquid molecules with distinctive smells and tastes (Cain, 1988; Kauer, 1987).

Because the stimuli responsible for tasting and smelling are taken into the body, these senses are often seen as "gatekeepers" that (1) identify things that the body needs for survival and that should therefore be consumed and (2) detect things that would be bad for the body and that should therefore be rejected. The gatekeeper function of taste and smell is aided by a large affective, or emotional, component—things that are bad for us often taste or smell unpleasant, and things that are good for us generally taste or smell good. In addition to creating "good" and "bad" affect, smelling an odor associated with a past place or event can trigger memories, which in turn may create emotional reactions.

Because the receptors that serve taste and smell are constantly exposed not only to the chemicals they are designed to sense but also to harmful materials such as bacteria and dirt, they undergo a cycle of birth, development, and death over 5–7 weeks for olfactory receptors and 1–2 weeks for taste receptors. This constant renewal of the receptors, called **neurogenesis**, is unique to these senses. In vision and hearing, the receptors are safely protected inside structures such as the eye and the inner ear, and in the cutaneous senses, under the skin; however, the receptors for taste and smell are relatively unprotected and therefore need to be constantly renewed.

We will consider taste first and then olfaction. We will describe the psychophysics and anatomy of each system and then how different taste and smell qualities are coded in the nervous system. Finally, we will consider flavor, which results from the interaction of taste and smell.

The Taste System

Everyone is familiar with taste. We experience it every time we eat. (Although later in the chapter we will see that what we experience when we eat is actually "flavor," which is a combination of taste and olfaction.) Taste occurs when molecules enter the mouth in solid or liquid form and stimulate taste receptors on the tongue. We will have a lot to say about these receptors, because they are central to our experience of taste. But first we consider some of the functions of taste.

Functions of Taste

We noted that taste and olfaction can be thought of as "gatekeepers" that help us determine which substances we should consume and which we should avoid. This is especially true for taste because we often use taste to choose which foods to eat and which to avoid (Breslin, 2001).

Taste accomplishes its gatekeeper function by the connection between taste quality and a substance's effect. Thus, sweetness is often associated with compounds that have

nutritive or caloric value and that are, therefore, important for sustaining life. Sweet compounds cause an automatic acceptance response and also trigger anticipatory metabolic responses that prepare the gastrointestinal system for processing these substances.

Bitter compounds have the opposite effect—they trigger automatic rejection responses to help the organism avoid harmful substances. Examples of harmful substances that taste bitter are the poisons strychnine, arsenic, and cyanide.

Salty tastes often indicate the presence of sodium. When people are deprived of sodium or lose a great deal of sodium through sweating, they often seek out foods that taste salty in order to replenish the salt their body needs.

Although there are many examples of connections between a substance's taste and its function in the body, this connection is not perfect. People have often made the mistake of eating good-tasting poisonous mushrooms, and there are artificial sweeteners, such as saccharine and sucralose, that have no metabolic value. There are also bitter foods that are not dangerous and do have metabolic value. People can also learn to modify their responses to certain tastes, as when they develop a taste for foods they may have initially found unappealing.

Basic Taste Qualities

Most taste researchers describe taste quality in terms of five basic taste sensations: salty, sour, sweet, bitter, and umami (which has been described as meaty, brothy, or savory, and is often associated with the flavor-enhancing properties of MSG, monosodium glutamate).

Early research that supported the idea of basic tastes showed that people can describe most of their taste experiences in terms of four basic taste qualities (this research was done before umami became the fifth basic taste). In one study, Donald McBurney (1969) presented taste solutions to participants and asked them to make magnitude estimates of the intensity of each of the four taste qualities for each solution (see page 15 to review the magnitude estimation procedure). He found that some substances have a predominant taste and that other substances result in combinations of the four tastes. For example, sodium chloride (salty), hydrochloric acid (sour), sucrose (sweet), and quinine (bitter) are compounds that come the closest to having only one of the four basic tastes, but the compound potassium chloride (KCl) has substantial salty and bitter components (**Figure 15.1**). Similarly, sodium nitrate ($NaNO_3$) results in a taste consisting of a combination of salty, sour, and bitter. **VL**

Results such as these have led most researchers to accept the idea of basic tastes. As you will see in our discussion of the code for taste quality, most of the research on this problem takes the idea of basic tastes as the starting point. (See Erickson, 2000, however, for some arguments against the idea of basic tastes.)

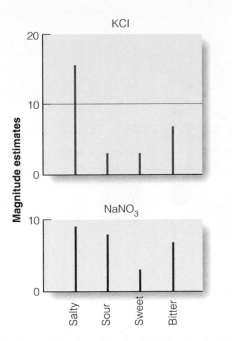

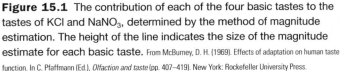

Figure 15.1 The contribution of each of the four basic tastes to the tastes of KCl and NaNO₃, determined by the method of magnitude estimation. The height of the line indicates the size of the magnitude estimate for each basic taste. From McBurney, D. H. (1969). Effects of adaptation on human taste function. In C. Pfaffmann (Ed.), *Olfaction and taste* (pp. 407–419). New York: Rockefeller University Press.

The Neural Code for Taste Quality

One of the central concerns in taste research has been identifying the physiological code for taste quality. We will first describe the structure of the taste system and then describe two proposals regarding how taste quality is coded in this system.

Structure of the Taste System

The process of tasting begins with the tongue (**Figure 15.2a** and **Table 15.1**). The surface of the tongue contains many ridges and valleys caused by the presence of structures called **papillae**, which fall into four categories: (1) filiform papillae, which are shaped like cones and are found over the entire surface of the tongue, giving it its rough appearance; (2) fungiform papillae, which are shaped like mushrooms and are found at the tip and sides of the tongue (see **Figure 15.3**); (3) foliate papillae, which are a series of folds along the back of the tongue on the sides; and (4) circumvilliate papillae, which are shaped like flat mounds surrounded by a trench and are found at the back of the tongue. **VL**

All of the papillae except the filiform papillae contain **taste buds** (**Figures 15.2b** and **15.2c**), and the whole tongue contains about 10,000 taste buds (Bartoshuk, 1971). Because the filiform papillae contain no taste buds, stimulation of the central part of the tongue, which contains only these papillae, causes no taste sensations. However, stimulation of the back or perimeter of the tongue results in a broad range of taste sensations.

Each taste bud contains 50 to 100 **taste cells**, which have tips that protrude into the **taste pore** (Figure 15.2c). Transduction occurs when chemicals contact receptor sites located on the tips of these taste cells (**Figure 15.2d** and **15.2e**). Electrical signals generated in the taste cells are transmitted from the tongue in a number of different nerves: (1) the chorda tympani nerve (from taste cells on the front and sides of the tongue); (2) the glossopharyngeal nerve (from the back of the tongue); (3) the vagus nerve (from the mouth and throat); and (4) the superficial petronasal nerve (from the soft palette—the top of the mouth).

The fibers from the tongue, mouth, and throat make connections in the brain stem in the **nucleus of the solitary tract**. From there, signals travel to the thalamus and then to two areas in the frontal lobe that are considered to be the primary taste cortex—the **insula** and the **frontal operculum cortex**—which are partially hidden behind the temporal lobe (**Figure 15.4**; Finger, 1987; Frank & Rabin, 1989).

Distributed Coding

In Chapter 3 we distinguished between two types of coding: *specificity coding*, the idea that quality is signaled by the activity in individual neurons that are tuned to respond to specific qualities; and *distributed coding*, the idea that quality is signaled by the pattern of activity distributed across many neurons. In that discussion, and in others throughout the book, we have generally favored distributed coding. The situation for taste, however, is not clear-cut, and there are arguments in favor of both types of coding (Frank et al., 2008).

Let's consider some evidence for distributed coding. Robert Erickson (1963) conducted one of the first experiments that demonstrated this type of coding by presenting a number of different taste stimuli to a rat's tongue and recording the response of the chorda tympani nerve. **Figure 15.5** shows how 13 nerve fibers responded to ammonium chloride (NH₄Cl), potassium chloride (KCl), and sodium chloride (NaCl). Erickson called these patterns the **across-fiber patterns**, which is another name for distributed coding. The red and green lines show that the across-fiber patterns for ammonium chloride and potassium chloride are similar to each other but different from the pattern for sodium chloride, indicated by the open circles.

Erickson reasoned that if the rat's perception of taste quality depends on the across-fiber pattern, then two substances with similar patterns should taste similar. Thus, the electrophysiological results would predict that ammonium chloride and potassium chloride should taste similar and that both should taste different from sodium chloride. To test this hypothesis, Erickson shocked rats while they were drinking potassium chloride and then gave them a choice between ammonium chloride and sodium chloride.

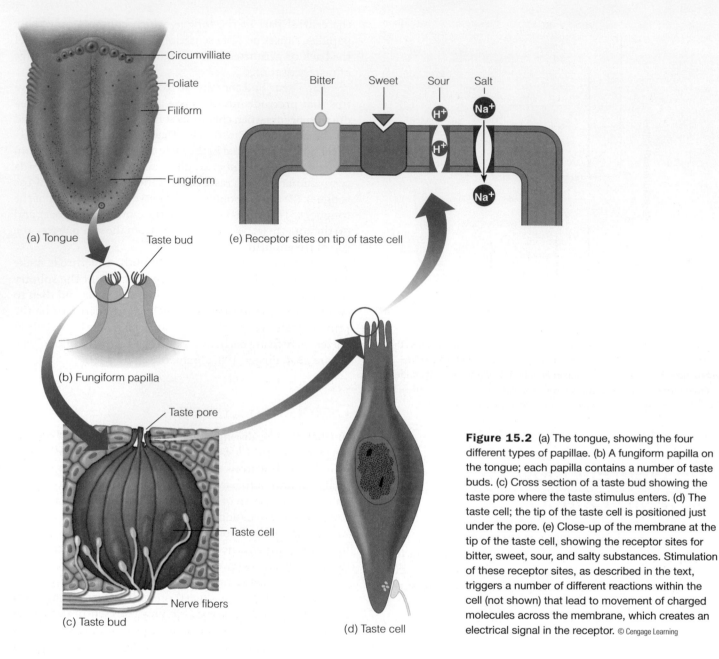

(a) Tongue

Circumvilliate
Foliate
Filiform
Fungiform

(b) Fungiform papilla

Taste bud

(c) Taste bud

Taste pore

Taste cell

Nerve fibers

(e) Receptor sites on tip of taste cell

Bitter   Sweet   Sour   Salt

H⁺   Na⁺

H⁺

Na⁺

(d) Taste cell

Figure 15.2 (a) The tongue, showing the four different types of papillae. (b) A fungiform papilla on the tongue; each papilla contains a number of taste buds. (c) Cross section of a taste bud showing the taste pore where the taste stimulus enters. (d) The taste cell; the tip of the taste cell is positioned just under the pore. (e) Close-up of the membrane at the tip of the taste cell, showing the receptor sites for bitter, sweet, sour, and salty substances. Stimulation of these receptor sites, as described in the text, triggers a number of different reactions within the cell (not shown) that lead to movement of charged molecules across the membrane, which creates an electrical signal in the receptor. © Cengage Learning

TABLE 15.1   Structures in the Taste System

STRUCTURE	DESCRIPTION
Tongue	The receptor sheet for taste. Contains papillae and all of the other structures described below.
Papillae	The structures that give the tongue its rough appearance. There are four kinds, each with a different shape.
Taste buds	Contained on the papillae. There are about 10,000 taste buds.
Taste cells	Cells that make up a taste bud. There are a number of cells for each bud, and the tip of each one sticks out into a taste pore. One or more nerve fibers are associated with each cell.
Receptor sites	Sites located on the tips of the taste cells. There are different types of sites for different chemicals. Chemicals contacting the sites cause transduction by affecting ion flow across the membrane of the taste cell.

© Cengage Learning

If potassium chloride and ammonium chloride taste similar, the rats should avoid the ammonium chloride when given a choice. This is exactly what they did. And when the rats were shocked for drinking ammonium chloride, they subsequently avoided the potassium chloride, as predicted by the electrophysiological results.

But what about the perception of taste in humans? When Susan Schiffman and Robert Erickson (1971) asked

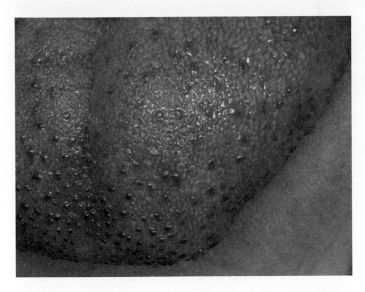

Figure 15.3 The surface of the tongue. The red dots are fungiform papillae. From Shahbake, M. (2008). *Anatomical and psychophysical aspects of the development of the sense of taste in humans*, PhD thesis, University of Western Sydney, pp. 148–153.

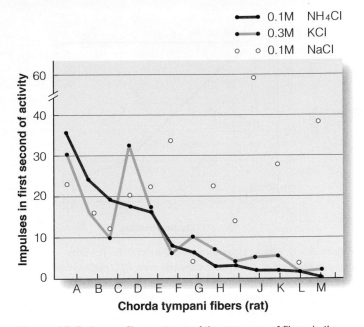

Figure 15.5 Across-fiber patterns of the response of fibers in the rat's chorda tympani nerve to three salts. Each letter on the horizontal axis indicates a different single fiber. Based on "Sensory neural patterns and gustation," by R. P. Erickson, 1963. In Y. Zotterman (Ed.), *Olfaction and taste*, Vol. 1, pp. 205–213, figure 4.

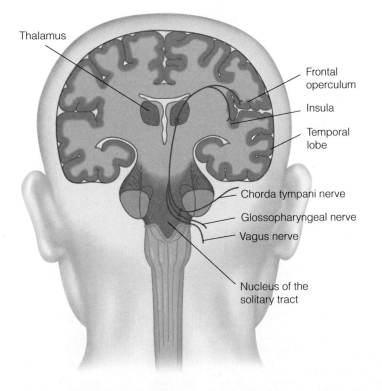

Figure 15.4 The central pathway for taste signals, showing the nucleus of the solitary tract, where nerve fibers from the tongue and the mouth synapse in the medulla at the base of the brain. From the nucleus of the solitary tract, these fibers synapse in the thalamus and then the insula and frontal operculum, which are the cortical areas for taste. From Frank, M. E., & Rabin, M. D. (1989). Chemosensory neuroanatomy and physiology. *Ear, Nose and Throat Journal, 68*, 291–292, 295–296.

humans to make similarity judgments between a number of different solutions, they found that substances that were perceived to be similar were related to patterns of firing for these same substances in the rat. Solutions judged more similar psychophysically had similar patterns of firing, as distributed coding would predict.

Specificity Coding

Most of the evidence for specificity coding comes from research that has recorded neural activity early in the taste system. We begin at the receptors by describing experiments that have revealed receptors for sweet, bitter, and umami.

The evidence supporting the existence of receptors that respond specifically to a particular taste has been obtained by using genetic cloning, which makes it possible to add or eliminate specific receptors in mice. Ken Mueller and coworkers (2005) did a series of experiments using a chemical compound called PTC that tastes bitter to humans but is not bitter to mice. The lack of bitter PTC taste in mice is inferred from the fact that mice do not avoid even high concentrations of PTC in behavioral tests (blue curve in **Figure 15.6**). Because a specific receptor in the family of bitter receptors had been identified as being responsible for the bitter taste of PTC in humans, Mueller decided to see what would happen if he used genetic cloning techniques to create a strain of mice that had this human bitter-PTC receptor. When he did this, the mice with this receptor avoided high concentrations of PTC (red curve in Figure 15.6; see **Table 15.2a**).

In another experiment, Mueller created a strain of mice that *lacked* a bitter receptor that responds to a compound called cyclohexamide (Cyx). Mice normally have this receptor, so they avoid Cyx. But the mice lacking this receptor did not avoid Cyx (**Table 15.2b**). In addition, Cyx no longer caused any

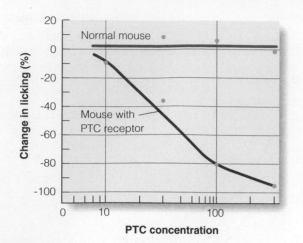

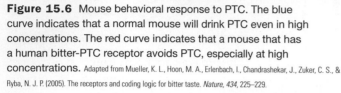

Figure 15.6 Mouse behavioral response to PTC. The blue curve indicates that a normal mouse will drink PTC even in high concentrations. The red curve indicates that a mouse that has a human bitter-PTC receptor avoids PTC, especially at high concentrations. Adapted from Mueller, K. L., Hoon, M. A., Erlenbach, I., Chandrashekar, J., Zuker, C. S., & Ryba, N. J. P. (2005). The receptors and coding logic for bitter taste. *Nature, 434*, 225–229.

TABLE 15.2 Results of Mueller's Experiments

CHEMICAL	NORMAL MOUSE	CLONED MOUSE
(a) PTC	No PTC receptor	Has PTC receptor
	Doesn't avoid PTC	Avoids PTC
(b) Cyx	Has Cyx receptor	No Cyx receptor
	Avoids Cyx	Doesn't avoid Cyx

© Cengage Learning

firing in nerves receiving signals from the tongue. Therefore, when the taste receptor for a substance is eliminated, this is reflected in both nerve firing and the animal's behavior.

It is important to note that in all these experiments, adding or eliminating bitter receptors had no effect on neural firing or behavior to sweet, sour, salty, or umami stimuli. Other research using similar techniques has identified receptors for sugar and umami (Zhao et al., 2003).

The results of these experiments in which adding a receptor makes an animal sensitive to a specific quality and eliminating a receptor makes an animal insensitive to a specific quality have been cited as support for specificity coding—that there are receptors that are specifically tuned to sweet, bitter, and umami tastes. However, not all researchers agree that the picture is so clear-cut. For example, Eugene Delay and coworkers (2006) showed that with different behavioral tests, mice that appeared to have been made insensitive to sugar by eliminating a "sweet" receptor can actually still show a preference for sugar. Based on this result, Delay suggests that perhaps there are a number of different receptors that respond to specific substances like sugar.

Another line of evidence for specificity coding in taste has come from research on how single neurons respond to

taste stimuli. Recordings from neurons at the beginning of the taste systems of animals, ranging from rats to monkeys, have revealed neurons that are specialized to respond to specific stimuli, as well as neurons that respond to a number of different types of stimuli (Lundy & Contreras, 1999; Sato et al., 1994; Spector & Trayors, 2005).

Figure 15.7 shows how three neurons in the rat taste system respond to sucrose (sweet to humans); sodium chloride (NaCl; salty); hydrochloric acid (HCl; sour in low concentrations); and quinine (QHCl; bitter). The neuron in **Figure 15.7a** responds selectively to sucrose, the one in **Figure 15.7b** responds selectively to NaCl, and the neuron in **Figure 15.7c** responds to NaCl, HCl, and quinine. Neurons like the ones

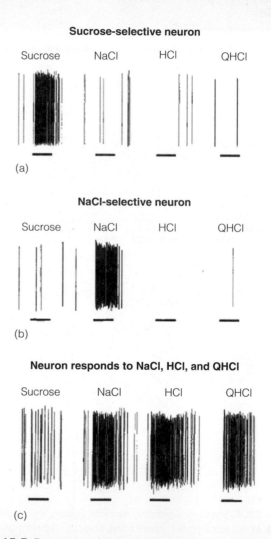

Figure 15.7 Responses of three neurons recorded from the cell bodies of chorda tympani nerve fibers in the rat. Solutions of sucrose, salt (NaCl), hydrochloric acid (HCl), and quinine hydrochloride (QHCl) were flowed over the rat's tongue for 15 seconds, as indicated by the horizontal lines below the firing records. Vertical lines are individual nerve impulses. (a) Neuron responds selectively to sweet stimulus; (b) neuron responds selectively to salt; (c) neuron responds to salty, sour, and bitter stimuli. From Lundy, R. F., & Contreras, R. J. (1999). Gustatory neuron types in rat geniculate ganglion. *Journal of Neurophysiology, 82*, 2970–2988. Reproduced by permission.

in Figure 15.7a and b, which respond selectively to stimuli associated with sweetness (sucrose) and saltiness (NaCl), provide evidence for specificity coding. Neurons have also been found that respond selectively to sour (HCl) and bitter (quinine) (Spector & Trayors, 2005).

Another finding in line with specificity theory is the effect of presenting a substance called **amiloride**, which blocks the flow of sodium into taste receptors. Applying amiloride to the tongue causes a decrease in the responding of neurons in the rat's brainstem (nucleus of the solitary tract) that respond best to salt (**Figure 15.8a**) but has little effect on neurons that respond best to a combination of salty and bitter tastes (**Figure 15.8b**; Scott & Giza, 1990). Thus, eliminating the flow of sodium across the membrane selectively eliminates responding of salt-best neurons but does not affect the response of neurons that respond best to other tastes. As it turns out, the sodium channel that is blocked by amiloride is important for determining saltiness

in rats and other animals, but not in humans. More recent research has identified another channel that serves the salty taste in humans (Lyall et al., 2004, 2005).

What does all of this mean? The results of the experiments involving cloning, recording from single neurons, and the effect of amiloride seem to be shifting the balance in the distributed versus specificity argument toward specificity (Chandrashekar et al., 2006). However, the issue is still not settled. For example, David Smith and Thomas Scott (2003) argue for distributed coding based on the finding that at more central locations in the taste system, neurons are tuned broadly, with many neurons responding to more than one taste quality. Smith and coworkers (2000) point out that just because there are neurons that respond best to one compound like salty or sour, this doesn't mean that these tastes are signaled by just one type of neuron. They illustrate this by drawing an analogy between taste perception and the mechanism for color vision. Even though presenting a long-wavelength light that appears red may cause the highest activation in the long-wavelength cone pigment (Figure 9.11), our perception of red still depends on the combined response of both the long- and medium-wavelength pigments. Similarly, salt stimuli may cause high firing in neurons that respond best to salt, but other neurons are probably also involved in creating saltiness.

Because of arguments such as this, some researchers believe that even though there is good evidence for specific taste receptors, distributed coding is involved in determining taste as well, especially at higher levels of the system. One suggestion is that basic taste qualities might be determined by a specific code, but distributed coding could determine subtle differences between tastes within a category (Pfaffmann, 1974; Scott & Plata-Salaman, 1991). This would help explain why not all substances in a particular category have the same taste. For example, the taste of all sweet substances is not identical (Lawless, 2001).

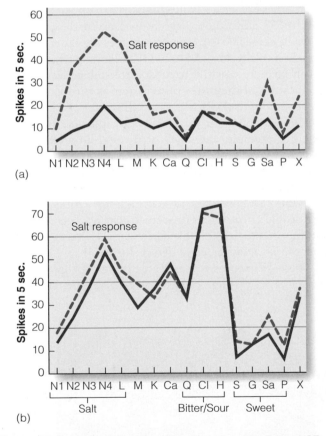

(a)

(b)

Figure 15.8 The blue lines show how two neurons in the rat NST respond to a number of different taste stimuli (along the horizontal axis). The neuron in (a) responds strongly to compounds associated with salty tastes. The neuron in (b) responds to a wide range of compounds. The purple lines show how these two neurons fire after the sodium-blocker amiloride is applied to the tongue. This compound inhibits the responses to salt of neuron (a) but has little effect on neuron (b). Adapted from Scott, T. R., & Giza, B. K., Coding channels in the taste system of the rat, *Science*, 249, 1585–1587, figure 1. Copyright © 1990 by the American Association for the Advancement of Science. Adapted with permission from AAAS.

Individual Differences in Tasting

The "taste worlds" of humans and animals are not necessarily the same. For example, domestic cats, unlike most mammals, don't prefer the sweetness of sugar, even though they display normal taste behavior to other compounds, such as avoiding compounds that taste bitter or very sour to humans. Genetic research has shown that this "sweet blindness" occurs because cats lack a functional gene for formation of a sweet receptor and so, lacking a sweet receptor, have no mechanism for detecting sweetness (Li et al., 2005).

This interesting fact about cats has something to tell us about human taste perception, because it turns out that there are genetic differences that affect people's ability to sense the taste of certain substances. One of the most well-documented effects involves people's ability to taste the bitter substance phenylthiocarbamide (PTC), which we discussed earlier (see page 367). Linda Bartoshuk (1980) describes the discovery of this PTC effect:

> The different reactions to PTC were discovered accidentally in 1932 by Arthur L. Fox, a chemist working at the E. I. DuPont deNemours Company in Wilmington, Delaware. Fox had prepared some PTC, and when he poured the compound into a bottle, some of the dust escaped into the air. One of his colleagues complained about the bitter taste of the dust, but Fox, much closer to the material, noticed nothing. Albert F. Blakeslee, an eminent geneticist of the era, was quick to pursue this observation. At a meeting of the American Association for the Advancement of Science (AAAS) in 1934, Blakeslee prepared an exhibit that dispensed PTC crystals to 2,500 of the conferees. The results: 28 percent of them described it as tasteless, 66 percent as bitter, and 6 percent as having some other taste. (p. 55)

People who can taste PTC are described as **tasters**, and those who cannot are called **nontasters**. More recently, additional experiments have been done with a substance called 6-*n*-propylthiouracil, or PROP, which has properties similar to those of PTC (Lawless, 1980, 2001). Researchers have found that about one-third of Americans report that PROP is tasteless and two-thirds can taste it.

What causes these differences in people's ability to taste PROP? One reason is that people have different numbers of taste buds on the tongue. Linda Bartoshuk used a technique called **video microscopy** to count the taste buds on people's tongues that contain the receptors for tasting (Bartoshuk & Beauchamp, 1994). The key result of this study was that people who could taste PROP had higher densities of taste buds than those who couldn't taste it (**Figure 15.9**).

But the results of an experiment by Jeannine Delwiche and coworkers (2001b) show that the density of taste buds alone cannot explain high sensitivity to PROP. After confirming that PROP tasters do have a higher density of papillae than nontasters, they devised a system for stimulating the same number of papillae in tasters and nontasters. They accomplished this by presenting stimuli to smaller areas of the tongue for the tasters. When participants rated the bitterness of PROP, the tasters' ratings were much higher than nontasters' ratings, even when the same number of papillae were stimulated.

Apparently, another factor in addition to receptor density is involved in determining individual differences in taste. Genetic studies have shown that PROP and PTC tasters have specialized receptors that are absent in nontasters (Bufe et al., 2005; Kim et al., 2003).

What does this mean for everyday taste experience? If PROP tasters also perceived other compounds as being more bitter than nontasters, this would indicate that certain foods might taste more bitter to the tasters. The evidence on this question, however, has been mixed. Some studies have reported differences between how tasters and nontasters rate the bitterness of other compounds (Bartoshuk, 1979; Hall et al., 1975), and others have not observed this difference (Delwiche et al., 2001b). However, it does appear that people who are especially sensitive to PROP, called **supertasters**, may actually be more sensitive to most bitter substances, as if the amplification in the bitter taste system is turned up for all bitter compounds (Delwiche et al., 2001a).

This variability in taste across people also occurs for smell. For example, the smell of the steroid androsterone, which is derived from testosterone, is described negatively ("sweaty," "urinous") by some people, positively by some people ("sweet," "floral"), and as having no odor by others (Keller et al., 2007). Or consider the fact that after eating asparagus some people's urine takes on a smell that has been described as sulfurous, much like cooked cabbage (Pelchat et al., 2011). Some people, however, can't detect this smell.

These differences in smell in different people are, like differences in tasting, caused by genetic differences that

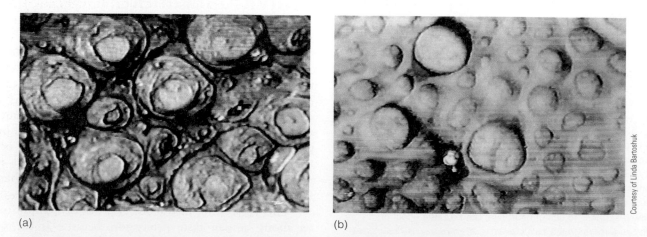

(a)　　　　　　　　　　　　　　　(b)

Courtesy of Linda Bartoshuk

Figure 15.9 (a) Video micrograph of the tongue showing the fungiform papillae of a "supertaster"—a person who is very sensitive to the taste of PROP. (b) Papillae of a "nontaster"—someone who cannot taste PROP. The supertaster has both more papillae and more taste buds than the nontaster.

affect the presence of receptors that respond to different chemicals (Keller et al., 2007; Menashe et al., 2003; Pelchat et al., 2011). Thus, the next time you disagree with someone about the taste of a particular food or smell of a particular odor, don't automatically assume that your disagreement is simply a reflection of your different preferences. It may reflect not a difference in *preference* (you *like* sweet things more than John does) but a difference in *experience* (you *experience* more intense sweet tastes than John does) that could be caused by differences in the types and numbers of taste receptors on the tongue or smell receptors in the nose.

TEST YOURSELF 15.1

1. Describe the anatomy of the taste system, including the receptors and central destinations.

2. What are the five basic taste qualities?

3. What is the evidence for distributed coding and specificity coding in taste? Is it possible to choose between the two?

4. What kinds of evidence support the idea that different people may have different taste and smell experiences? What mechanisms may be responsible for these differences?

5. How can genetics affect taste?

The Olfactory System

Like taste, the sense of smell, or **olfaction**, provides information that can be important for survival. Olfaction provides an alarm system that alerts us to spoiled food, leaking gas, or smoke from a fire. But as important as these signals are to humans, olfaction is even more important in the lives of many other species, because it is often their primary window to the environment (Ache, 1991).

Many animals are **macrosmatic** (having a keen sense of smell that is important to their survival), whereas humans are **microsmatic** (having a less keen sense of smell that is not crucial to their survival). For macrosmatic animals, olfaction provides cues to orient them in space, to mark territory, and to guide them to specific places, other animals, and food sources (Holley, 1991). Olfaction is also extremely important in sexual reproduction because it triggers mating behavior in many species (Doty, 1976; Pfeiffer & Johnston, 1994).

An important aspect of the olfactory world of some animals is the existence of compounds called **pheromones**— molecules that are emitted by members of a species that causes a specific reaction in another individual of the same species (Karlson & Lüscher, 1959; Wyatt, 2010). The term *pheromone*, coined by Peter Karlson and Martin Lüscher, is a combination of two Greek words: *pherein*, to transfer, and *hormon*, to excite. This meaning, "to transfer excitement," is illustrated by many examples of animal behavior—the female silk moth that attracts males from miles away by releasing a chemical *bombykol*; the male mice that release a pheromone that attracts females and causes aggression in other mice (Novotny et al., 1985).

Whether pheromones exist in humans is a matter of debate (Doty, 2010; Schaal & Porter, 1991; Stern & McClintock, 1998; Wysocki & Preti, 2009), but there is evidence that humans can detect odors related to reproduction. Devendra Singh and Matthew Bronstad (2001) demonstrated a connection between men's ratings of women's body odors and the women's menstrual cycle, by showing that men rate the smell of T-shirts that women had worn for three consecutive nights during the ovulatory phase of their menstrual cycle to be more pleasant then the smell of shirts worn during their nonovulatory phase. In another T-shirt experiment, Saul Miller and Jon Maner (2010) showed that when men smelled T-shirts worn by women who were near ovulation, they had higher testosterone levels than when they smelled shirts worn far from ovulation. Olfactory cues can therefore signal a woman's level of reproductive fertility.

Whether these biologically produced olfactory cues actually influence human sexual attraction is unclear. However, from the existence of multibillion-dollar-a-year industries that are devoted to creating pleasing body odors through perfume and deodorants, plus a new billion-dollar-a-year industry called environmental fragrancing, which offers products to add pleasing scents to the air in both homes and businesses, there is no question that the role of smell in our daily lives is not inconsequential (Gilbert & Firestein, 2002; Owens, 1994).

But perhaps the most convincing argument for the importance of smell to humans comes from those who suffer from **anosmia**, the loss of the ability to smell as a result of injury or infection. People suffering from anosmia describe the great void created by their inability to taste many foods because of the close connection between smell and flavor. One woman who suffered from anosmia and then briefly regained her sense of smell stated, "I always thought I would sacrifice smell to taste if I had to choose between the two, but I suddenly realized how much I had missed. We take it for granted and are unaware that everything smells: people, the air, my house, my skin" (Birnberg, 1988; quoted in Ackerman, 1990, p. 42).

Molly Birnbaum (2011), who lost her sense of smell after being hit by a car while crossing the street, also noted the loss of everyday smells she had taken for granted. She described New York City without smell as "a blank slate without the aroma of car exhaust, hot dogs or coffee" and when she gradually began to regain some ability to smell she reveled in every new odor. "Cucumber!" she writes, "their once common negligible scent had returned—intoxicating, almost ambrosial. The scent of melon could bring me to tears" (Birnbaum, 2011, p. 110). These descriptions help us realize that olfaction is more important in our lives than most of us realize. Although it may not be essential to our survival, life is often enhanced by our ability to smell and becomes a little more dangerous if we lose the olfactory warning system that can alert us to danger.

Detecting Odors

Our sense of smell enables us to detect extremely low concentrations of some odorants. The **detection threshold** for odors is the lowest concentration at which an odorant can be detected.

METHOD
Measuring the Detection Threshold

One way to measure the threshold for detecting an odorant is to present different concentrations of an odorant on different trials. The subjects respond either "yes" (I smell something) or "no" (I don't smell anything) on each trial. However, one problem with this procedure is that it is susceptible to bias. Some people will respond "yes" at the merest hint of a smell, whereas others wait until they are sure they smell something before saying "yes" (see Chapter 1, page 16, and Appendix, page 395).

The forced-choice method avoids this problem by presenting subjects with blocks of two trials—one trial contains a weak odorant and the other, no odorant. The subject's task is to indicate which trial has a stronger smell. This eliminates having to decide whether a smell is present, because the subject knows it is present on one of the trials. Threshold can be measured by determining the concentration that results in a correct response on 75 percent of the trials (50 percent would be chance performance). When using this procedure, it is important to wait at least 30 seconds between trials to allow for recovery if an odorant was presented on the first trial. The forced-choice procedure generally indicates greater sensitivity than the yes/no procedure (Dalton, 2002).

Table 15.3 lists thresholds for a number of substances. It is notable that there is a very large range of thresholds. T-butyl mercaptan, the odorant that is added to natural gas, can be detected in very small concentrations of less than 1 part per billion in air. In contrast, to detect the vapors of acetone (the main component of nail polish remover), the concentration must be 15,000 parts per billion, and for the vapor of methanol, the concentration must be 141,000 parts per billion.

Although humans can detect extremely small concentrations of some odorants, they are much less sensitive to odors than many animals. For example, rats are 8 to 50 times more sensitive to odors than humans, and dogs are from 300 to 10,000 times more sensitive, depending on the odorant (Laing et al., 1991). But even though humans are unaware

TABLE 15.3 Human Odor Detection Thresholds

COMPOUND	ODOR THRESHOLD IN AIR (PARTS PER BILLION)
Methanol	141,000
Acetone	15,000
Formaldehyde	870
Menthol	40
T-butyl mercaptan	0.3

Source: Devos et al., 1990.

of odors that other animals can detect, humans' individual olfactory receptors are as sensitive as any animal's. H. deVries and M. Stuiver (1961) demonstrated this by showing that human olfactory receptors can be excited by the action of just 1 molecule of odorant.

Nothing can be more sensitive than 1 molecule per receptor, so how come humans are less sensitive to odors than dogs? The answer is that humans have far fewer receptors than dogs—only about 10 million receptors, compared to about 1 billion for dogs (Dodd & Squirrell, 1980; Moulton, 1977).

Another aspect of odor detection is the *difference threshold*—the smallest *difference* in the concentration of two odors that can be detected. Measurements of the difference threshold highlight one of the most important problems in olfactory research—the control of concentrations in stimulus presentations. For example, when William Cain (1977) carefully measured the difference threshold by placing two odorants of different concentrations on absorbent cotton balls and asked participants to judge which was more intense, he found that the difference threshold averaged 19 percent. However, when Cain analyzed the stimuli he had presented on the cotton balls, he found that stimuli that were supposed to have the same concentration actually varied considerably. This variation was apparently caused by differences in the airflow pattern through the cotton in different samples.

To deal with this problem, Cain remeasured the difference threshold using a device called an **olfactometer**, which presents olfactory stimuli with much greater precision than cotton balls (**Figure 15.10**). Using this more precise method of presenting of stimulus, Cain found that the threshold dropped to 11 percent.

Identifying Odors

When odorant concentrations are near threshold, so a person can just detect the *presence* of an odor, the person

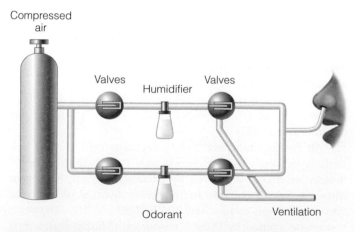

Figure 15.10 This diagram shows the different components of an olfactometer. By adjusting the valves in this system, the experimenter can vary both the humidity and the concentration of olfactory stimuli reaching the subject's nose. © Cengage Learning

usually cannot sense the *quality* of the odor—whether it is "floral" or "pepperminty" or "rancid." The concentration of an odorant has to be increased by as much as a factor of 3 above the threshold concentration before the person can recognize an odor's quality. The concentration at which quality can be recognized is called the **recognition threshold** (Dalton, 2002).

One of the more intriguing facts about odors is that even though humans can discriminate between as many as 100,000 different odors (Firestein, 2001), they often find it difficult to accurately identify specific odors. For example, when people are presented with the odors of familiar substances such as mint, bananas, and motor oil, they can easily tell the difference between them. However, when they are asked to *identify* the substance associated with the odor, they are successful only about half the time (Engen & Pfaffmann, 1960). J. A. Desor and Gary Beauchamp (1974) found, however, that when they presented participants with the names of the substances at the beginning of the experiment and then reminded them of the correct names when they failed to respond correctly on subsequent trials, they could, after some practice, correctly identify 98 percent of the substances.

One of the amazing things about odor identification is that knowing the correct label for the odor actually seems to transform our perception into that odor. Cain (1980) gives the example of an object initially identified as "fishy-goaty-oily." When the experimenter told the person that the fishy-goaty-oily smell actually came from leather, the smell was then transformed into that of leather.

I had a similar experience when sampling the drink aquavit with some friends. Aquavit has a very interesting, but difficult to identify, smell. Odors such as "anise," "orange," and "lemon" were proposed as we tried to identify its smell, but it wasn't until someone turned the bottle around and read the label on the back that the truth became known: "Aquavit (Water of Life) is the Danish national drink—a delicious, crystal-clear spirit distilled from grain, with a slight taste of caraway." When we heard the word *caraway*, the previous hypotheses of anise, orange, and lemon were transformed into caraway. Thus, when we have trouble identifying odors, this trouble results not from a deficiency in our olfactory system, but from an inability to retrieve the odor's name from our memory (Cain, 1979).

DEMONSTRATION
Naming and Odor Identification

To demonstrate the effect of naming substances on odor identification, have a friend collect a number of familiar objects for you and, without looking, try to identify the odors. You will find that you can identify some but not others, but when your friend tells you the correct answer for the ones you identified incorrectly, you will wonder how you could have failed to identify such a familiar smell. Don't blame your mistakes on your nose; blame them on your memory.

Analyzing Odorants: The Mucosa and Olfactory Bulb

How does the olfactory system know what molecules are entering the nose? The first step toward answering this question is to consider some of the difficulties facing researchers who are searching for connections between molecules and perception.

The Puzzle of Olfactory Quality

Although we know that we can discriminate among a huge number of odors, research to determine the neural mechanisms behind this ability is complicated by difficulties in establishing a system to bring some order to our descriptions of odor quality. Such systems exist for other senses. We can describe visual stimuli in terms of their colors and can relate our perception of color to the physical property of wavelength. We can describe sound stimuli as having different pitches and relate these pitches to the physical property of frequency. Creating a way to organize odors and to relate odors to physical properties of molecules, however, has proven extremely difficult.

One reason for the difficulty is that we lack a specific language for odor quality. For example, when people smell the chemical -ionone, they usually say that it smells like violets. This description, it turns out, is fairly accurate, but if you compare -ionone to real violets, they smell different. The perfume industry's solution is to use names such as "woody violet" and "sweet violet" to distinguish between different violet smells, but this hardly solves the problem we face in trying to determine how olfaction works.

Another difficulty in relating odors to molecular properties is that some molecules that have similar structures can smell different (**Figure 15.11a**), and molecules that have very different structures can smell similar (**Figure 15.11b**). But things really become challenging when we consider the kinds of odors we routinely encounter in the environment, which consist of mixtures of many chemicals. Consider, for example, that when you walk into the kitchen and smell freshly brewed coffee, the coffee aroma is created by more than 100 different molecules. Although individual molecules may have their own odors, we don't perceive the odors of individual molecules; we perceive "coffee."

The feat of perceiving "coffee" becomes even more amazing when we consider that odors rarely occur in isolation. Thus, the coffee odor from the kitchen might be accompanied by the smells of bacon and freshly squeezed orange juice. Each of these has its own tens or hundreds of molecules, yet somehow the hundreds of different molecules that are floating around in the kitchen become perceptually organized into smells that refer to three different sources: *coffee*, *bacon*, and *orange juice* (**Figure 15.12**). Sources

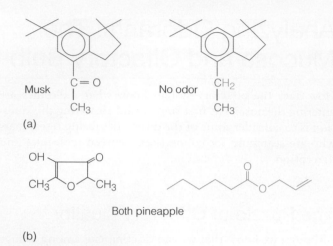

Musk   C=O   No odor   CH₂

CH₃   CH₃

(a)

OH

CH₃   O   CH₃

Both pineapple

(b)

Figure 15.11 (a) Two molecules that have the same structure, but one smells like musk and the other is odorless. (b) Two molecules with different structures but similar odors. © Cengage Learning.

Figure 15.12 Hundreds of molecules from the coffee, orange juice, and bacon are mixed together in the air, but the person just perceives "coffee," "orange juice," and "bacon." This perception of three odor objects from hundreds of intermixed molecules is a feat of perceptual organization.

of odors such as *coffee*, *bacon*, and *orange juice*, as well as non-food sources such as *rose*, *dog*, and *car exhaust*, are called **odor objects**. Our goal, therefore, is to explain not just how we smell different odor qualities, but how we identify different odor objects.

Perceiving odor objects involves olfactory processing that occurs in two stages. The first stage, which takes place at the beginning of the olfactory system in the *olfactory mucosa* and *olfactory bulb*, involves *analyzing*. In this stage, the olfactory system analyzes the different chemical components of odors and transforms these components into neural activity at specific places in the olfactory bulb (**Figure 15.13**). The second stage, which takes place in the olfactory cortex and beyond, involves *synthesizing*. In this stage, the olfactory system synthesizes the information about chemical components received from the olfactory bulb into representations of odor objects. As we will see, it has been proposed that this synthesis stage involves learning and memory. But let's start at the beginning, when odorant molecules enter the nose and stimulate receptors on the olfactory mucosa.

The Olfactory Mucosa

The **olfactory mucosa** is a dime-sized region located on the roof of the nasal cavity just below the **olfactory bulb** (**Figure 15.13a**). Odorant molecules are carried into the nose in an air stream (blue arrows), which brings these molecules into contact with the mucosa. **Figure 15.13b** shows the **olfactory receptor neurons (ORNs)** that are located in the mucosa (colored parts) and the supporting cells (tan area).

Just as the rod and cone receptors in the retina contain visual pigment molecules that are sensitive to light, the olfactory receptor neurons in the mucosa are dotted with molecules called **olfactory receptors** that are sensitive to chemical odorants (**Figure 15.13c**). One parallel between visual pigments and olfactory receptors is that they are both sensitive to a specific range of stimuli. Each type of visual pigment is sensitive to a band of wavelengths in a particular region of the visible spectrum (Figure 2.21, page 34), and each type of olfactory receptor is sensitive to a narrow range of odorants. **VL**

An important difference between the visual system and the olfactory system is that while there are only four different types of visual pigments (one rod pigment and three cone pigments), there are 350 different types of olfactory receptors, each sensitive to a particular group of odorants. The discovery that there are 350 different types of olfactory receptors in the human, and 1,000 different types in the mouse, was made by Linda Buck and Richard Axel (1991), who received the 2004 Nobel Prize in Physiology and Medicine for their research on the olfactory system (also see Buck, 2004).

The large number of olfactory receptors enables us to identify 100,000 or more different odors, but this large number of receptor types increases the challenges in understanding how olfaction works. One thing that makes things slightly simpler is another parallel with vision: Just as a particular rod or cone receptor contains only one type of visual pigment, a particular olfactory receptor neuron (ORN) contains only one type of olfactory receptor.

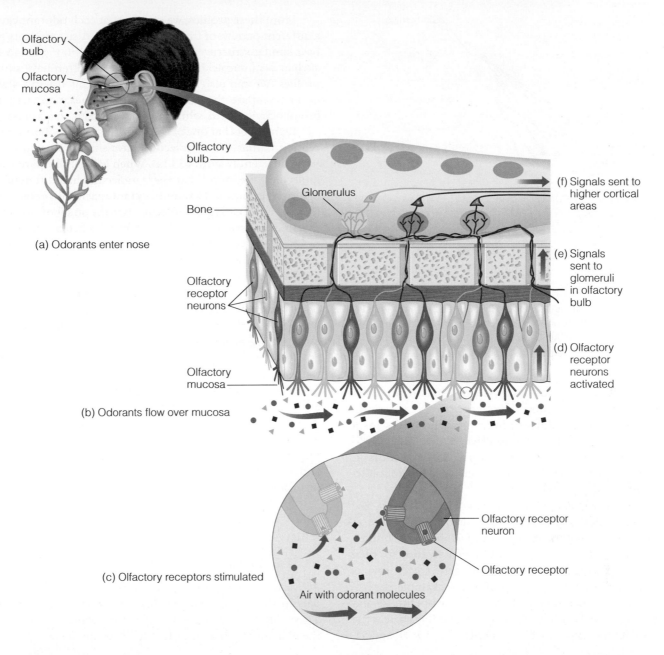

Figure 15.13 The structure of the olfactory system. Odorant molecules flow over the olfactory mucosa, which contains 350 different types of olfactory receptor neurons (ORNs). Three types of neurons are shown here, indicated by different colors. Each type has its own specialized receptors. © Cengage Learning.

Labels in figure:
- Olfactory bulb
- Olfactory mucosa
- (a) Odorants enter nose
- Olfactory bulb
- Glomerulus
- Bone
- (f) Signals sent to higher cortical areas
- Olfactory receptor neurons
- (e) Signals sent to glomeruli in olfactory bulb
- Olfactory mucosa
- (d) Olfactory receptor neurons activated
- (b) Odorants flow over mucosa
- Olfactory receptor neuron
- Olfactory receptor
- (c) Olfactory receptors stimulated
- Air with odorant molecules

How Olfactory Receptor Neurons Respond to Odorants

Figure 15.14a shows the surface of part of the olfactory mucosa. The circles represent ORNs, with two types of ORNs highlighted in red and blue. Remember that there are 350 different types of ORNs in the mucosa in humans. There are about 10,000 of each type of ORN, so the mucosa contains millions of ORNs.

The first step in understanding how we perceive different odorants is to ask how this array of millions of ORNs that blanket the olfactory mucosa respond to different odorants. One way this question has been answered is by using a technique called *calcium imaging*.

METHOD
Calcium Imaging

When an olfactory receptor responds, the concentration of calcium ions (Ca^{++}) increases inside the ORN. One way of measuring this increase in calcium ions is called **calcium imaging**. This involves soaking olfactory neurons in a chemical that causes the ORN to fluoresce with a green glow when exposed to ultraviolet (380 nm) light. This green glow can be used to measure how much Ca^{++} had entered the neuron because *increasing* Ca^{++} inside the neuron *decreases* the glow. Thus, measuring the decrease in fluorescence indicates how strongly the ORN is activated.

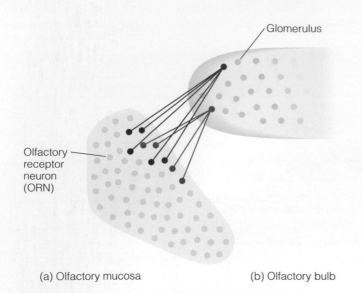

(a) Olfactory mucosa   (b) Olfactory bulb

Figure 15.14 (a) A portion of the olfactory mucosa. The mucosa contains 350 types of ORNs and about 10,000 of each type. The red circles represent 10,000 of one type of ORN, and the blue circles, 10,000 of another type. (b) All ORNs of a particular type send their signals to one or two glomeruli in the olfactory bulb. © Cengage Learning.

Bettina Malnic and coworkers (1999), working in Linda Buck's laboratory, determined the response to a large number of odorants using calcium imaging. The results for a few of her odorants are shown in **Figure 15.15**, which indicates how 10 different ORNs are activated by each odorant. (Remember that each ORN contains only one type of olfactory receptor.)

The response of individual receptors is indicated by the circles in each column. Reading down the columns indicates that each of the receptors, except 19 and 41, respond to some odorants but not to others. The pattern of activation for each odorant, which is indicated by reading across each row, is called the odorant's **recognition profile**. For example, the recognition profile of octanoic acid is weak firing of ORN 79 and strong firing of ORNs 1, 18, 19, 41, 46, 51, and 83, whereas the profile for octanol is strong firing of ORNs 18, 19, 41, and 51.

From these profiles, we can see that each odorant causes a different pattern of firing across ORNs. Also, odorants that have similar structures (shown on the right in Figure 15.15), such as octanoic acid and nonanoic acid, often have similar profiles. We can also see, however, that this doesn't always occur (compare the patterns for bromohexanoic acid and bromooctanoic acid, which also have similar structures).

Remember that one of the puzzling facts about odor perception is that some molecules have similar structures but smell different (Figure 15.11a). When Malnic compared such molecules, she found that these molecules had different recognition profiles. For example, octanoic acid and octanol differ only by one oxygen molecule, but the smell of octanol is described as "sweet," "rose," and "fresh," whereas the smell of octanoic acid is described as "rancid," "sour," and "repulsive." This difference in perception is reflected in their different profiles. Although we still can't predict which smells result from specific patterns of response, we do know that when two odorants smell different, they usually have different profiles.

The idea that an odorant's smell can be related to different response profiles is similar to the trichromatic code for color vision that we described in Chapter 9 (see page 205). Remember that each wavelength of light is coded by a different pattern of firing of the three cone receptors, and that a particular cone receptor responds to many wavelengths. The situation for odors is similar—each odorant is coded by a different pattern of firing of ORNs, and a particular ORN responds to many odorants. What's different about olfaction is that there are 350 different types of ORNs, compared to just three cone receptors for vision.

The Search for Order in the Olfactory Bulb

Activation of receptors in the mucosa causes electrical signals in the ORNs that are distributed across the mucosa. These ORNs send signals to structures called **glomeruli** in the olfactory bulb. Figure 15.14b illustrates a basic principle

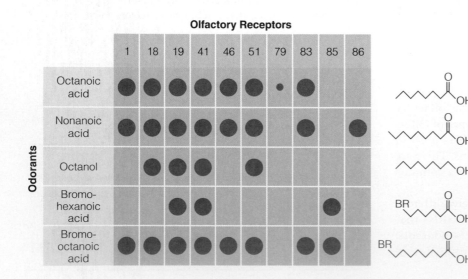

Figure 15.15 Recognition profiles for some odorants. Large dots indicate that the odorant causes a high firing rate for the receptor listed along the top; a small dot indicates a lower firing rate for the receptor. The structures of the compounds are shown on the right. Adapted from Malnic, B., Hirono, J., Sata, T., & Buck, L. B. (1999). Combinatorial receptor codes for odors. Cell, 96, 713–723.

of the relationship between ORNs and glomeruli: All of the 10,000 ORNs of a particular type send their signals to just one or two glomeruli, so each glomerulus collects information about the firing of a particular type of ORN.

We asked how ORNs in the mucosa respond to different odorants, and we now ask the same question for glomeruli in the olfactory bulb. Naoshige Uchida and coworkers (2000) used a technique called *optical imaging* to determine how glomeruli respond to different odorants.

METHOD
Optical Imaging

The technique of **optical imaging** can be used to measure the activity of large areas of the olfactory bulb by measuring how much red light is reflected from the olfactory bulb. The bulb must first be exposed by removing a patch of the skull. Red light is used because when neurons are activated, they consume oxygen from the blood. Blood that contains less oxygen reflects less red light than blood with oxygen, so areas that have been activated reflect less red light and look slightly darker than areas that have not been activated.

The optical imaging procedure involves illuminating the surface of the bulb with red light, measuring how much light is reflected, and then presenting a stimulus and determining which areas of the bulb become slightly darker. These darker areas are the areas that have been activated by the stimulus.

The results of Uchida's optical imaging experiment on the rat are shown in **Figure 15.16**. Each colored area represents the location of clusters of glomeruli in the olfactory bulb that are activated by the chemicals on the right. **Figure 15.16a** shows that each type of carboxylic acid activated a small area, and that there is some overlap between areas. Also notice that as the length of the carbon chain increases, the area of activation moves to the left. **Figure 15.16b** shows that a different group of chemicals—aliphatic alcohols—activates a different location on the olfactory bulb and that the same pattern occurs as before: large chain lengths activate areas farther to the left.

The finding, using optical imaging, that different odorants activate different areas of the olfactory bulb, has also been demonstrated using a procedure called the *2-deoxyglucose technique*.

METHOD
2-Deoxyglucose Technique

The **2-deoxyglucose technique** involves injecting a radioactive 2-deoxyglucose (2DG) molecule into an animal and exposing the animal to different chemicals. The radioactive 2DG contains the sugar glucose, which is taken up by active neurons, so by measuring the amount of radioactivity in the various parts of a structure, we can determine which neurons are most activated by the different chemicals.

Patterns of olfactory bulb activation measured for different chemicals using the 2DG technique are shown in **Figure 15.17**, in which areas of high activation are indicated by yellow and red. These results show that different odorants cause distinctive patterns of activation. Results such as this and the result in Figure 15.16 support the idea that there is a map of odorants in the olfactory bulb. This map has been called a **chemotopic map** to signify that it is based on molecular features of odorants such as carbon chain length or functional groups (Johnson & Leon, 2007; Johnson et al., 2010; Murthy, 2011). Some researchers use the terms **odor map** (Restrepo et al., 2009; Soucy et al., 2009; Uchida et al., 2000) or **odotoptic map** (Nikonov et al., 2005) instead of chemotopic map.

The idea that odorants with different properties create a map on the olfactory bulb is similar to the situation we have described for the other senses. There is a retinotopic map for vision, in which locations on the retina are mapped on the visual cortex (page 78), a tonotopic map for hearing in which frequencies are mapped onto various structures in the auditory system (page 277), and a somatotopic map for the cutaneous senses in which locations on the body are mapped onto the somatosensory cortex (page 341).

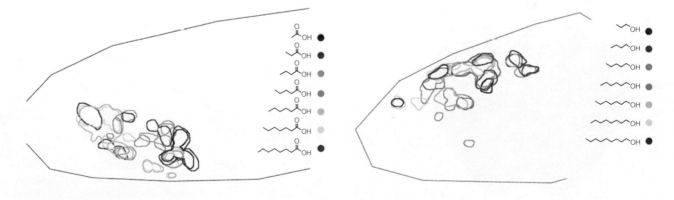

(a) Carboxylic acids

(b) Aliphatic alcohols

Figure 15.16 Areas in the rat olfactory bulb that are activated by various chemicals: (a) a series of carbolic acids; (b) a series of aliphatic alcohols. Reprinted by permission from Macmillan Publishers Ltd.: Uchida, N., Talahashi, Y. K., Tanifuji, M., & Mori, K., Odor maps in the mammalian olfactory bulb: Domain organization and odorant structural features. *Nature Neuroscience, 3,* 1035–1043, Copyright 2000.

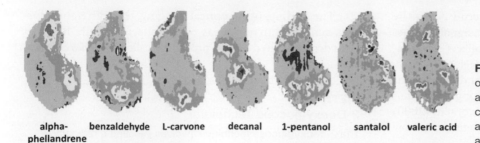

alpha-   benzaldehyde L-carvone   decanal   1-pentanol   santalol   valeric acid
phellandrene

Research on the olfactory map has just begun, however, and much remains to be learned about how odors are represented in the olfactory bulb. Based on what has been discussed so far, it is clear that odorants are at least crudely mapped on the olfactory bulb based on their chemical properties. However, we are far from creating a map based on perception. This map, if it exists, will be a map of different odor experiences arranged on the olfactory bulb (Arzi & Sobel, 2011). But the olfactory bulb represents an early stage of olfactory processing and is not where perception occurs. To understand olfactory perception, we need to follow the output of the olfactory bulb to the olfactory cortex

TEST YOURSELF 15.2

1. What are some of the functions of odor perception?

2. What is the difference between the detection threshold and the recognition threshold?

3. What are some of the factors that need to be taken into account when measuring the detection threshold and the difference threshold?

4. How well can people identify odors? What is the role of memory in odor recognition?

5. Describe the following components of the olfactory system: the olfactory receptors, the olfactory receptor neurons, the olfactory bulb, and the glomeruli. Be sure you understand the relation between olfactory receptors and olfactory receptor neurons, and between olfactory receptor neurons and glomeruli.

6. How do olfactory receptor neurons respond to different odorants, as determined by calcium imaging? What is an odorant's recognition profile?

7. Describe how optical imaging and the 2-deoxyglucose technique have been used to determine a chemotopic map on the olfactory bulb. What is the difference between a chemotopic map and a perceptual map?

Representing Odors in the Cortex

To begin our discussion of how odors are represented in the cortex, let's look at where signals are transmitted when they leave the olfactory bulb. **Figure 15.18a** shows the location of the two main olfactory areas: (1) the **piriform cortex**, which is the **primary olfactory area**, and (2) the **orbitofrontal cortex**, which is the **secondary olfactory area**. **Figure 15.18b** shows the

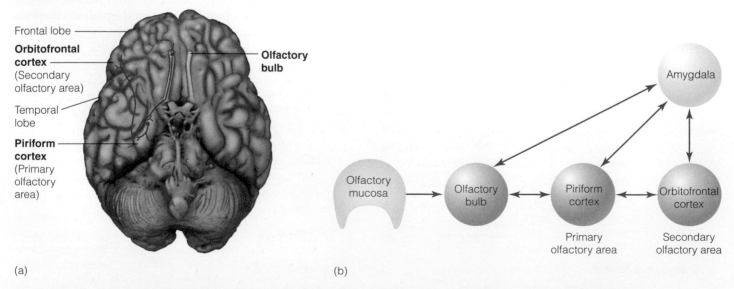

Frontal lobe

Orbitofrontal cortex (Secondary olfactory area)

Temporal lobe

Piriform cortex (Primary olfactory area)

Olfactory bulb

(a)

(b)

Olfactory mucosa → Olfactory bulb ↔ Piriform cortex ↔ Orbitofrontal cortex

Amygdala

Primary olfactory area   Secondary olfactory area

Figure 15.18 (a) The underside of the brain, showing the neural pathways for olfaction. On the left side, the temporal lobe has been deflected to expose the olfactory area. (b) Flow diagram of the pathways for olfaction. (a) Adapted from Frank, M. E., & Rabin, M. D. (1989). Chemosensory neuroanatomy and physiology. *Ear, Nose and Throat Journal, 68,* 291–292, 295–296. (b) Adapted from Wilson, D. A., & Stevenson, R. J. (2006). *Learning to smell.* Baltimore: Johns Hopkins University Press.

olfactory system as a flow diagram and adds the **amygdala**, which is involved in determining emotional reactions not only to smell but also to faces (Chapter 5, page 120) and pain (Chapter 14, page 355). We begin by considering the piriform cortex, where the orderly arrangement of odorants on the olfactory bulb vanishes.

How Odorants Are Represented in the Piriform Cortex

We can appreciate how odorants are represented in the piriform cortex by considering an experiment by Robert Rennaker and coworkers (2007), who used multiple electrodes to measure neural responding in the piriform cortex. **Figure 15.19** shows that isoamyl acetate causes activation across the cortex. Other compounds also cause widespread activity, and there is substantial overlap between the patterns of activity for different compounds.

In another study of how piriform cortex neurons respond to different odorants, Dan Stettler and Richard Axel (2009), using optical imaging, observed the same scattered activation pattern that Rennaker had observed by recording neural responses. **Figure 15.20** shows this scattered activation to hexanol (green) and octanol (red). Each dot is an activated neuron. The yellow dots are neurons activated by both odorants.

What these results mean is that the orderly activation pattern in the olfactory bulb no longer exists in the piriform cortex. The projection from the olfactory bulb is scattered, as indicated by activation patterns like the ones in Figure 15.20 in which activity associated with a single chemical is spread out over a large area, with large spaces between active neurons. Things become even more interesting when we ask what the activation pattern might look like for an odor object such as *coffee*.

How Odor Objects Are Represented

We can appreciate how complicated things become for odor objects by imagining what the pattern of activation would be for *coffee*, which contains a hundred different chemical components. Not only will the pattern be very complicated, but if you are smelling a particular odor for the first time, this raises the question of how the olfactory system is able to determine the identity of this "mystery odor" based on the information in this "first time" response. Some researchers have answered this question by drawing a parallel between recognizing odors and experiencing memories.

(a) Electrode placements (b) Activation by isoamyl acetate

Figure 15.19 (a) Recording sites used by Rennaker and coworkers (2007) to determine activity of neurons in the piriform cortex of the rat. (b) The pattern of activation caused by isoamyl acetate. From Rennaker, R. L., Chen, C.-F. F., Ruyle, A. M., Sloan, A. M., & Wilson, D. A. (2007). Spatial and temporal distribution of odorant-evoked activity in the piriform cortex. *Journal of Neuroscience, 27*, 1534–1542.

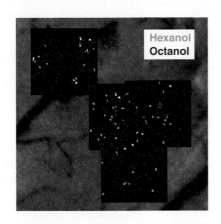

Figure 15.20 Response determined by optical imaging to octanol (red) and hexanol (green) in the rat piriform cortex. In a few instances, both chemicals activate the same neurons (yellow). From Stettler, D. D., & Axel, R. (2009). Representations of odor in the piriform cortex. *Neuron, 63*, 054–064, Figure 4C. With permission from Elsevier.

Figure 15.21 indicates what happens when a memory is formed. When a person witnesses an event, a number of neurons are activated (**Figure 15.21a**). At this point, the memory for the event isn't completely formed in the brain; it is fragile and can be easily forgotten or can be disrupted by trauma, such as a blow to the head. But connections begin forming between the neurons that were activated by the event (**Figure 15.21b**), and after these connections are formed (**Figure 15.21c**), the memory is stronger and more resistant to disruption. Formation of stable memories thus involves a process in which linkages are formed between a number of neurons.

Applying this idea to odor perception, it has been proposed that formation of odor objects involves learning,

Areas in cortex

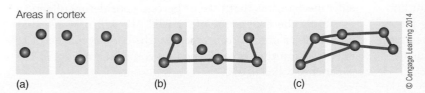

(a)　　　　　(b)　　　　　(c)

Figure 15.21 A model of how memories are formed in the cortex. (a) Initially, incoming information activates a number of areas in the cortex. Tan rectangles are different cortical areas. Red circles are activated areas. (b) As time passes, the neural activity is replayed, which creates connections between activated areas. (c) Eventually, the activated areas for a particular memory are linked, which stabilizes the memory.

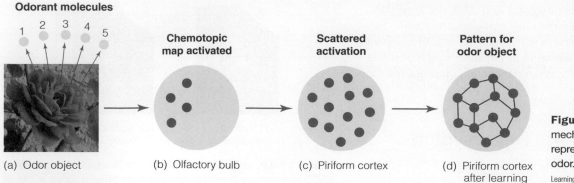

Figure 15.22 Memory mechanism for forming representations of the flower's odor. See text for details. © Cengage Learning 2014. Photo by Barbara Goldstein.

(a) Odor object (b) Olfactory bulb (c) Piriform cortex (d) Piriform cortex after learning

Odorant molecules 1 2 3 4 5

Chemotopic map activated

Scattered activation

Pattern for odor object

which links together the scattered activations that occur for a particular object. We can see how this works by imagining that you are smelling the odor of a flower for the first time. The odor of this flower, just like the odors of coffee and other substances, is created by a large number of chemical compounds (**Figure 15.22a**).

These chemical components first activate the olfactory receptors in the mucosa and then create a pattern of activation on the olfactory bulb that is shaped by the chemotopic map. This pattern occurs any time the flower's odor is presented (**Figure 15.22b**). From the research described above, we know that signals from the olfactory bulb are transformed into a scattered pattern of activation in the piriform cortex (**Figure 15.22c**).

Because this is the first time you have ever experienced the flower's odor, the activated neurons aren't associated with each other. This is like the neurons that represent a new memory, which aren't yet linked (see Figure 15.21a). At this point you are likely to have trouble identifying the odor, and to confuse it with other odors. But after a number of exposures to the flower, which causes the same activation pattern to occur over and over, neural connections form, and the neurons become associated with each other (**Figure 15.22d**). Once this occurs, a pattern of activation has been created that represents the flower's odor. Thus, just as a stable memory becomes established when neurons become linked, odor objects become formed when experience with an odor causes neurons in the piriform cortex to become linked. According to this idea, when the person in Figure 15.12 walks into the kitchen, the activation caused by the hundreds of molecules in the air become three linked networks of activation in the piriform cortex that stand for *coffee*, *orange juice*, and *bacon*.

The idea that learning plays an important role in perceiving odors is supported by research. For example, Donald Wilson (2003) measured the response of neurons in the rat's piriform cortex to two odorants: (1) a *mixture* of isoamyl acetate, which has a banana-like odor, and peppermint and (2) the *component* isoamyl acetate alone. Wilson was interested in how well the rat's neurons could tell the difference between the mixture and the component after the rat had been exposed to the mixture.

Wilson presented the mixture to the rat for either a brief exposure (10 seconds or about 20 sniffs) or a longer exposure (50 seconds or about 100 sniffs) and, after a short pause, measured the response to the *mixture* and to the *component*. Following 10 seconds of sniffing, the piriform neurons responded similarly to the mixture and to the component. However, following 50 seconds of sniffing, the neurons fired more rapidly to the component. Thus, after 100 sniffs of the mixture, the neurons became able to tell the difference between the mixture and the component. Similar experiments measuring responses of neurons in the olfactory bulb did not show this effect.

Wilson concluded from these results that, given enough time, neurons in the piriform cortex can learn to discriminate between different odors, and that this learning may be involved in our ability to tell the difference between different odors in the environment. Numerous other experiments support the idea that a mechanism involving experience and learning is involved in associating patterns of piriform cortex firing with specific odor objects (Choi et al., 2011; Gottfried, 2010; Sosulski et al., 2011; Wilson, 2003; Wilson et al., 2004; Wilson & Sullivan, 2011).

Before leaving our description of how odor objects are represented in the piriform cortex, it is important to note that not all odor objects require learning. Consider, for example, pheromones that trigger stereotyped behaviors that are necessary for survival of a particular species. These pheromone responses may be determined by a second pathway for olfactory perception, which sends signals from the olfactory bulb to the amygdala and which does not depend on experience for identifying odors. According to this "dual pathway" idea, odor objects that depend on experience are served by the piriform cortex, and innate responses to chemicals such as pheromones are served by a separate pathway that creates automatic responses to specific odors (Kobayakawa et al., 2007; Sosulski et al., 2011).

For humans, experience is the most important determinant of the formation of odor objects. But we are now going to take yet another step, beyond the piriform cortex, to consider mechanisms that take us beyond considering olfaction as simply the experience of "smell." We will now see that olfaction is a crucial component of the convergence of taste and olfaction that occurs when we eat, which results in the experience called *flavor*.

The Perception of Flavor

What most people refer to as "taste" when describing their experience of food ("That tastes good, Mom") is usually a combination of taste, from stimulation of the receptors in the tongue, and olfaction, from stimulation of the receptors in the olfactory mucosa. This combination, which is called **flavor**, is defined as the overall impression that we experience from the combination of nasal and oral stimulation (Lawless, 2001; Shepherd, 2012). You can demonstrate how smell affects flavor with the following demonstration.

DEMONSTRATION

"Tasting" With and Without the Nose

While pinching your nostrils shut, drink a beverage with a distinctive taste, such as grape juice, cranberry juice, or coffee. Notice both the quality and the intensity of the taste as you are drinking it. (Take just one or two swallows because swallowing with your nostrils closed can cause a buildup of pressure in your ears.) After one of the swallows, open your nostrils, and notice whether you perceive a flavor. Finally, drink the beverage normally with nostrils open, and notice the flavor. You can also do this demonstration with fruits or cooked foods or try eating a jellybean with your eyes closed (so you can't see its color) while holding your nose.

The reason you may have found it difficult to determine what you were drinking or eating when you were holding your nose is that your experience of flavor depends on a combination of taste and olfaction, and by holding your nose, you eliminated the olfactory component of flavor. This interaction between taste and olfaction occurs at two levels: first in the mouth and nose, and then in the cortex.

Taste and Olfaction Meet in the Mouth and Nose

Chemicals in food or drink cause taste when they activate taste receptors on the tongue. But in addition, food and drink release volatile chemicals that reach the olfactory mucosa by following the **retronasal route**, from the mouth through the **nasal pharynx**, the passage that connects the oral and nasal cavities (**Figure 15.23**). Although pinching the nostrils shut does not close the nasal pharynx, it prevents vapors from reaching the olfactory receptors by eliminating the circulation of air through this channel (Murphy & Cain, 1980).

The fact that olfaction is a crucial component of flavor may be surprising because the flavors of food seem to be centered in the mouth. It is only when we keep molecules from reaching the olfactory mucosa that the importance of olfaction is revealed. One reason this localization of flavor occurs is because food and drink stimulate tactile receptors in the mouth, which creates **oral capture**, in which the sensations we experience from both olfactory and taste receptors are

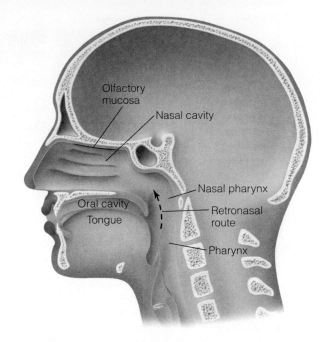

Figure 15.23 Odorant molecules released by food in the oral cavity and pharynx can travel through the nasal pharynx (dashed arrow) to the olfactory mucosa in the nasal cavity. This is the retronasal route to the olfactory receptors. © Cengage Learning.

referred to the mouth (Small, 2008). Thus, when you "taste" food, you are usually experiencing flavor, and the fact that it is all happening in your mouth is an illusion created by oral capture (Todrank & Bartoshuk, 1991).

The importance of olfaction in the sensing of flavor has been demonstrated experimentally by using both chemical solutions and typical foods. In general, solutions are more difficult to identify when the nostrils are pinched shut (Mozell et al., 1969) and are often judged to be tasteless. For example, **Figure 15.24a** shows that the chemical sodium oleate has a strong soapy flavor when the nostrils are open but is judged tasteless when they are closed. Similarly, ferrous sulfate (**Figure 15.24b**) normally has a metallic flavor but is judged predominantly tasteless when the nostrils are closed (Hettinger et al., 1990). However, some compounds are not influenced by olfaction. For example, monosodium glutamate (MSG) has about the same flavor whether or not the nose is clamped (**Figure 15.24c**). In this case, the sense of taste predominates.

Taste and Olfaction Meet in the Nervous System

Although taste and olfactory stimuli occur in close proximity in the mouth and nose, our perceptual experience of their combination is created when they interact in the cortex. **Figure 15.25** is the diagram of the olfactory pathway from Figure 15.18b (in blue) with the taste pathway added (in red), showing connections between olfaction and taste (Rolls et al., 2010; Small, 2012). In addition, vision and touch contribute to flavor

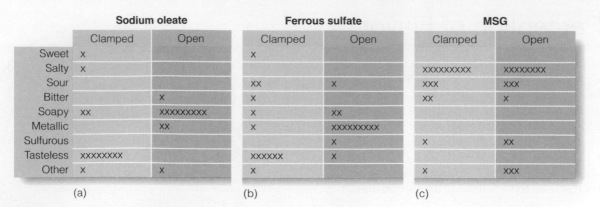

Figure 15.24 How people described the flavors of three different compounds when they tasted them with their nostrils clamped shut and with their nostrils open. Each X represents the judgment of one person. From Hettinger, T. P., Myers, W. E., & Frank, M. E. (1990). Role of olfaction in perception of non-traditional "taste" stimuli. *Chemical Senses, 15,* 755–760, fig. 2, by permission of Oxford University Press.

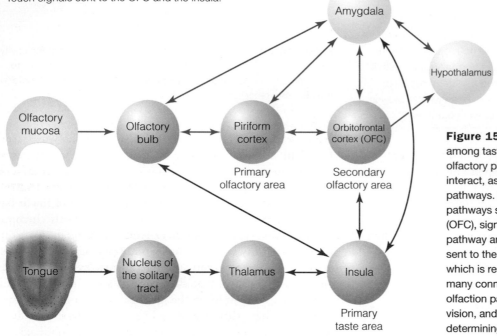

Vision signals sent to the OFC and the amygdala.
Touch signals sent to the OFC and the insula.

Figure 15.25 Flavor is created by interactions among taste, olfaction, vision, and touch. The olfactory pathway (blue) and taste pathway (red) interact, as signals are sent between these two pathways. In addition, both taste and olfactory pathways send signals to the orbitofrontal cortex (OFC), signals from touch are sent to the taste pathway and the OFC, and signals from vision are sent to the OFC. Also shown are the amygdala, which is responsible for emotional responses and has many connections to structures in both the taste and olfaction pathways and also receives signals from vision, and the hypothalamus, which is involved in determining hunger. © Cengage Learning 2014.

by sending signals to the amygdala (vision), structures in the taste pathway (touch), and the orbitofrontal cortex (vision and touch).

All of these interactions among taste, olfaction, vision, and touch underscore the multimodal nature of our experience of flavor. Flavor includes not only what we typically call "taste," but also perceptions such as the texture and temperature of food (Verhagen et al., 2004), the color of food (Spence et al., 2010), and the sounds of "noisy" foods such as potato chips and carrots that crunch when we eat them (Zampini & Spence, 2010).

Because of this convergence of neurons from different senses, the orbitofrontal cortex contains many **bimodal neurons**, neurons that respond to more than one sense. For example, some bimodal neurons respond to both taste and smell, and others respond to taste and vision. An important property of these bimodal neurons is that they often respond to similar qualities. Thus, a neuron that responds to the taste of sweet fruits would also respond to the smell of these fruits. This means that neurons are tuned to respond to qualities that occur together in the environment. Because of these properties, it has been suggested that the orbitofrontal cortex is a cortical center for detecting flavor and for the perceptual representation of foods (Rolls & Baylis, 1994; Rolls et al., 2010). Other research has shown that the insula, the primary taste cortex, is also involved in the perception of flavor (de Araujo et al., 2012; Veldhuizen et al., 2010).

But flavor isn't a fixed response that is automatically determined by the chemical properties of food. Although the chemicals in a particular food may always activate the same pattern of ORNs in the mucosa, by the time the signals reach the cortex they can be affected by many different factors, including a person's expectations and the amount of a particular food the person has consumed.

Flavor Is Influenced by a Person's Expectations

What you expect can influence both what you experience and neural responding. This was demonstrated by Hilke Plassmann and coworkers (2008) by having subjects in a brain scanner judge the "taste pleasantness" of different samples of wine. Subjects were asked to indicate how much they liked five different wines, which were identified by their price. In reality, there were only three wines; two of them were presented twice, with different price labels. The results, for a wine that was labeled either $10 or $90, are shown in **Figure 15.26**. When the wines are presented without labels, the taste pleasantness judgments are the same (**Figure 15.26a**, left bars), but when tasting is preceded by a price label, the "$90 wine" gets a much higher taste rating than the "$10 wine." In addition to influencing the person's judgments, the labels also influence the response of the orbitofrontal cortex, with the $90 wine causing a much large response (**Figure 15.26b**).

What's happening here is that the response of the orbitofrontal cortex is being determined both by signals that begin with stimulation of the taste and olfactory receptors and by signals created by the person's expectations. In another

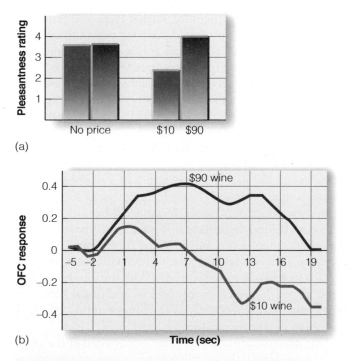

(a)

(b)

Figure 15.26 Effect of expectation on flavor perception, as indicated by the results of Hilke Plassman's (2009) experiment. (a) The red and blue bars indicate ratings given to two presentations of the same wine (although subjects didn't know they were the same). The two bars on the left indicate ratings when there were no price labels on the wines. The two bars on the right indicate that the subject's give higher "taste pleasantness" ratings when the wine is labeled $90, compared to when it is labeled $10. (b) Responses of the OFC when tasting the wines labeled $10 and $90. Part (b) from Plassmann, H., O'Doherty, J., Shiv, B., & Rangel, A. (2008). Marketing actions can modulate neural representations of experienced pleasantness. *Proceedings of the National Academy of Sciences, 105,* 1050–1054, Fig. 2D, p. 1051, with permission. Copyright © 2008 National Academy of Sciences, U.S.A.

experiment, subjects rated the same odor as more pleasant when it was labeled "cheddar cheese" than when it was called "body odor," and the orbitofrontal cortex response was larger for the cheddar cheese label (de Araujo et al., 2005).

Flavor Is Influenced by Food Intake: Sensory-Specific Satiety

Have you ever experienced the first few forkfuls of a particular food as tasting much better than the last? Food consumed to satiety (when you don't want to eat any more) is often considered less pleasurable than food consumed when hungry.

John O'Doherty and coworkers (2000) showed that both the pleasantness of a food-related odor and the brain's response to the odor can be influenced by satiety. Subjects were tested under two conditions: (1) when hungry, and (2) after eating bananas until satiety. Subjects in a brain scanner judged the pleasantness of two food-related odors: banana and vanilla. The pleasantness ratings for both were similar before they had consumed any food. However, after eating bananas until satiety, the pleasantness rating for vanilla decreased slightly (but was still positive), but the rating for banana decreased much more and became negative (**Figure 15.27a**). This larger effect on the odor associated with the food eaten to satiety, called **sensory-specific satiety**, also occurred in the response of the orbitofrontal cortex. The orbitofrontal cortex response decreased for the banana odor but remained the same for the vanilla odor (**Figure 15.27b**). Similar effects also occurred in the amygdala and insula for some (but not all) subjects.

The finding that orbitofrontal cortex activity is related to the pleasantness of an odor or flavor can also be stated in another way: the orbitofrontal cortex is involved in determining the *reward value* of foods. Food is more rewarding when you are hungry and becomes less rewarding as food is consumed, until eventually—at satiety—the reward is gone and eating stops. These changes in the reward value of flavors are important because just as taste and olfaction are important for warning of danger, they are also important for regulating food intake. Also note in Figure 15.25 that the orbitofrontal cortex sends signals to the hypothalamus, where neurons are found that respond to the sight, taste, and smell of food if hunger is present (Rolls et al., 2010).

What we've learned by considering each of the stages of the systems for taste, olfaction, and flavor is that the purpose of the chemical senses extends beyond simply creating experiences of taste, smell, and flavor. Its purpose is to help guide behavior—avoiding potentially harmful substances, seeking out nutrients, and helping control the amount of food consumed.

Does this description of a sense being concerned with behavior sound familiar? You may remember that Chapter 7, Taking Action, presented a similar message for vision: Although early researchers saw the visual system as being concerned primarily with creating visual experiences, later

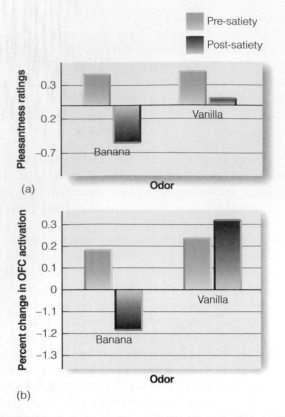

Figure 15.27 Sensory-specific satiety. Results of the O'Doherty et al. (2000) experiment. (a) Pleasantness rating for banana and vanilla odor before eating (left bars) and after eating bananas to satiety (right bars). (b) Response of the orbitofrontal cortex to banana and vanilla odors before and after eating bananas. From O'Doherty, J., Rolls, E. T., Francis, S., Bowtell, R., McGlone, F., Kobal, G., et al. (2000). Sensory-specific satiety-related olfactory activation of the human orbitofrontal cortex. *Neuroreport, 11*, 893–897. Reproduced by permission.

researchers have argued that the ultimate goal of the visual system is to support taking actions that are necessary for survival (see page 169). The chemical senses have a similar ultimate purpose of guiding and motivating actions required for survival. We eat in order to live, and our experience of flavor helps motivate that eating. (Unfortunately, it should be added, the shutoff mechanisms are sometimes overridden by "modern" foods and other factors, with obesity as an outcome—but that's another story.)

SOMETHING TO CONSIDER:
The *Proust* Effect: Memories, Emotions, and Smell

One of the most famous quotes in literature is Marcel Proust's description of an experience after eating a small lemon cookie called a madeleine:

> "The sight of the little madeleine had recalled nothing to my mind before I tasted it … as soon as I had

recognized the taste of the piece of madeleine soaked in her decoction of lime-blossom which my aunt used to give me … immediately the old grey house upon the street, where her room was, rose up like a stage set to attach itself to the little pavilion opening on to the garden which had been built out behind it for my parents … and with the house the … square where I used to be sent before lunch, the streets along which I used to run errands, the country roads we took when it was fine. (Marcel Proust, *Remembrance of Things Past*, 1913)

Proust's description of how taste and olfaction unlocked memories he hadn't thought of for years, now called the **Proust effect**, is not an uncommon experience. I once entered a staircase in an old building. It had wooden walls on either side and dusty old rubber treads on each step, but what hit me was the smell, which was the same smell as the staircase I used to climb as a young boy in my grandfather's house. As soon as I smelled that staircase, I experienced memories of that old house and of my grandfather, who had died years before.

So I have experienced the Proust effect, but is there any scientific evidence for its existence? The answer is that a number of experiments have demonstrated a link between odors and specific aspects of memory. Rachel Herz and Jonathan Schooler (2002) had subjects describe a personal memory associated with items like Crayola crayons, Coppertone suntan lotion, and Johnson's baby powder. After describing their memory associated with the objects, subjects were presented with an object either in visual form (a color photograph) or in odor form (smelling the object's odor) and were asked to think about the event they had described and to rate it on a number of scales. The result was that subjects who smelled the odor rated their memories as more emotional than subjects who saw the picture. They also had a stronger feeling than the visual group of "being brought back" to the time the memory occurred (also see Willander & Larsson, 2007).

What's behind this effect? A physiologically based answer for the high emotionality and feeling of "being brought back" associated with odor-elicited memories is that there are connections from structures involved in both taste and olfaction to the amygdala, which is involved in emotional behavior, and to other structures such as the hippocampus, which is involved in storing memories.

One question raised by this research is whether the emotion associated with the odor-based memories is a perceptual effect that occurs simply because smelling odors activates the amygdala. Or does the effect occur because smelling odors elicits especially emotional memories? There is some evidence that the second explanation is correct (Willander & Larsson, 2007), but more research needs to be done to be sure. Whatever the correct explanation for these effects, it is clear from people's experiences involving odor and memory that there is something special about memories that are associated with odors.

Do newborn infants perceive odors and tastes? Early researchers, noting that a number of olfactory stimuli elicited responses such as body movements and facial expressions from newborns, concluded that newborns can smell (Kroner, 1881, cited in Peterson & Rainey, 1911). However, some of the stimuli used by these early researchers may have irritated the membranes of the infant's nose, so the infants may have been responding to irritation rather than to smell (Beauchamp et al., 1991; Doty, 1991). **VL**

Modern studies using nonirritating stimuli, however, have provided evidence that newborns can smell and can discriminate between different olfactory stimuli. J. E. Steiner (1974, 1979) used nonirritating stimuli to show that infants respond to banana extract or vanilla extract with sucking and facial expressions that are similar to smiles, and they respond to concentrated shrimp odor and an odor resembling rotten eggs with rejection or disgust (**Figure 15.28**). Perhaps the most significant odors for the infant originate from the mother, and infants can recognize their mothers through the sense of smell (Porter et al., 1983; Russell, 1976; Schaal, 1986).

Research investigating infants' reactions to taste has included numerous studies showing that newborns can discriminate sweet, sour, and bitter stimuli (Beauchamp et al., 1991). For example, newborns react with different facial expressions to sweet, sour, and bitter stimuli but show little or no response to salty stimuli (Ganchrow, 1995; Ganchrow et al., 1983; Rosenstein & Oster, 1988; Steiner, 1987).

Research studying how newborns and young infants respond to salt indicates that there is a shift toward greater acceptance of salty solutions between birth and 4 to 8 months of age that continues into childhood (Beauchamp et al., 1994). One explanation for this shift is that it reflects the development of receptors sensitive to salt during infancy. But there is also evidence that infants' preferences are shaped by experience that occurs both before birth and during early infancy. For example, infants born to women who reported suffering from moderate to severe symptoms of morning sickness had significantly higher relative intake of salt solutions at 4 months of age than those whose mothers reported having no more than mild morning sickness (Crystal & Bernstein, 1995, 1998; Lesham, 1998).

Further evidence for the effect of experience before birth is based on the finding that what pregnant women eat can change the smell of the amniotic fluid environment in which the fetus is developing. The amniotic fluid of pregnant women who eat garlic has a stronger or more garlicky smell than the fluid of women who don't eat garlic (Mennella et al., 1995). Evidence that the flavor of the amniotic fluid can influence an infant's preferences is provided by the results of an experiment by Julie Mennella and coworkers (2001).

Mennella's experiment involved three groups of pregnant women, as shown in **Table 15.4**. Group 1 drank carrot juice during their final trimester of pregnancy and water during the first two months of lactation, when they were breastfeeding their infants. Group 2 drank water during pregnancy and carrot juice during the first two months of lactation, and Group 3 drank water during both periods. The infants' preference for carrot-flavored cereal versus plain cereal was tested four weeks after they had begun eating cereal but before they had experienced any food or juice containing a carrot flavor. The results, shown in the right column of Table 15.4, indicate that the infants who had experienced carrot flavor either in utero or in the mother's milk showed a preference for the carrot-flavored cereal (indicated by a score above 0.5), whereas the infants whose mothers had consumed only water showed no preference.

Infant responses to tastes, odors, and flavors are therefore determined both by innate factors and by experience. An important conclusion from the finding that what the mother consumes during pregnancy and lactation influences the odors experienced by the fetus and breastfed infant is that the first step toward ensuring that young children develop good eating habits is for mothers to eat healthy foods both when pregnant and when nursing. Another conclusion is that infants can become familiar with foods common to a particular culture before they are born (Beauchamp & Mennella, 2009).

C. BA/VA FI RE

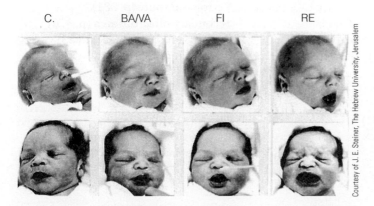

Courtesy of J. E. Steiner, The Hebrew University, Jerusalem

Figure 15.28 The facial expressions of 3- to 8-hour-old infants in response to some food-related odors. Each horizontal row shows the reactions of the same infant to the following stimulation: C = control, odorless cotton swab; BA/VA = artificial solution of banana or vanilla; FI = artificial fish or shrimp odor; RE = Artificial rotten egg odor. The infants were tested prior to the first breast- or bottle-feeding.

TABLE 15.4 **Effect of What the Mother Consumes on Infant Preferences**

GROUP	LAST TRIMESTER	DURING BREAST FEEDING	INTAKE OF CARROT FLAVOR
1	Carrot juice	Water	0.62
2	Water	Carrot juice	0.57
3	Water	Water	0.51

Note: Intake score above 0.50 indicates preference for carrot-flavored cereal.
© Cengage Learning

1. What are the main structures in the olfactory system past the olfactory bulb?

2. How are odors represented in the piriform cortex? How does this representation differ from the representation in the olfactory bulb?

3. How has formation of the representation of odor objects in the cortex been described as being caused by experience? How is this similar to the process of forming memories?

4. What is flavor perception? Describe how taste and olfaction meet in the mouth and nose and then later in the nervous system.

5. Describe the experiment that showed how expectations about a wine's taste can influence taste judgments and brain responding.

6. Describe the experiment that demonstrates sensory-specific satiety.

7. What is the Proust effect? Is there any evidence for it?

8. What is the evidence that newborns can detect different taste and smell qualities? Describe the "carrot juice" experiment and how it demonstrates that what a mother consumes can influence infant taste preferences.

THINK ABOUT IT

1. Consider the kinds of food that you avoid because you don't like the taste. Do these foods have anything in common that might enable you to explain these taste preferences in terms of the activity of specific types of taste receptors? (p. 369)

2. Can you think of situations in which you have encountered a smell that triggered memories about an event or place that you hadn't thought about in years? What do you think might be the mechanism for this type of experience? (p. 384)

KEY TERMS

Across-fiber patterns (p. 365)
Amiloride (p. 369)
Amygdala (p. 379)
Anosmia (p. 371)
Bimodal neuron (p. 382)
Calcium imaging (p. 375)
Chemotopic map (p. 377)
Detection threshold (p. 372)
Flavor (p. 381)
Frontal operculum cortex (p. 365)
Glomeruli (p. 376)
Insula (p. 365)
Macrosmatic (p. 371)
Microsmatic (p. 371)
Nasal pharynx (p. 381)
Neurogenesis (p. 364)

Nontaster (p. 370)
Nucleus of the solitary tract (p. 365)
Odor map (p. 377)
Odor object (p. 374)
Odotoptic map (p. 377)
Olfaction (p. 371)
Olfactometer (p. 372)
Olfactory bulb (p. 374)
Olfactory mucosa (p. 374)
Olfactory receptor neurons (ORNs) (p. 374)
Olfactory receptors (p. 374)
Optical imaging (p. 377)
Oral capture (p. 381)
Orbitofrontal cortex (p. 378)
Papillae (p. 365)

Pheromone (p. 371)
Piriform cortex (p. 378)
Primary olfactory area (p. 378)
Proust effect (p. 384)
Recognition profile (p. 376)
Recognition threshold (p. 373)
Retronasal route (p. 381)
Secondary olfactory area (p. 378)
Sensory-specific satiety (p. 383)
Supertaster (p. 370)
Taste bud (p. 365)
Taste cell (p. 365)
Taste pore (p. 365)
Taster (p. 370)
2-deoxyglucose technique (p. 377)
Video microscopy (p. 370)

MEDIA RESOURCES

CourseMate ⬚

Go to CengageBrain.com to access Psychology CourseMate, where you will find the Virtual Labs plus an interactive eBook, flashcards, quizzes, videos, and more.

Virtual Labs 🔲

The Virtual Labs are designed to help you get the most out of this course. The Virtual Lab icons direct you to specific media demonstrations and experiments designed to help you visualize what you are reading about. The numbers below indicate the number of the Virtual Lab you can access through Psychology CourseMate.

15.1 The Professor Show: How Taste Works (p. 364)
Fast-talking professor describes the basics of taste stimuli in 90 seconds. (Courtesy of Joshua Davis and Tim Harris)

15.2 The Taste System (p. 365)
A drag-and-drop diagram to test your knowledge of structures in the taste system.

15.3 The Olfactory System (p. 374)
A drag-and-drop diagram to test your knowledge of structures in the olfactory system.

15.4 Taste (p. 385)
Research on taste in infants.

15.5 Smell (p. 385)
Research on smell in infants.

The Long and Winding Road

This Epilogue has six sections, each of which focuses on a facet of perception that was discussed in the book. The titles of the sections, which are from Beatles songs, capture the gist of each section.

In our survey of the senses, we have described a number of different senses and how we perceive different qualities within each sense. But you may have noticed that while different chapters may have described different senses or qualities, there were common threads that recurred throughout the book. As different as the structures of the senses are and the experiences that they create, they are all serving the same body and have a similar purpose: to provide information about the environment, to create experiences, and to help the person or animal take actions necessary for survival. The purpose of this epilogue is to recount some of the themes in the book with an emphasis on principles that apply across the senses. It is, therefore, a "survey of the main action" that has occurred in the past 15 chapters. We begin with the perceptual process, which was introduced in Chapter 1 [p. 5] as follows:

> Perception happens at the end of what can be described … as a long and winding road. This road begins outside of you, with stimuli in the environment … and ends with the behavioral responses of perceiving, recognizing, and taking action.

The idea of a long and winding road was introduced to emphasize the complexity of what we were about to describe and also the idea that perception can be conceived of as unfolding in a number of stages. We can also apply the idea of a road in another way, by considering the road of scientific discovery that has stretched from early approaches to perception to what we know today.

Ticket to Ride
Starting Points for the Scientific Study of Perception

The past is prologue to the present.
William Shakespeare, *The Tempest* (adapted)

Every journey has a beginning. The beginning of conjectures about perception can be traced back to Aristotle's and Plato's writings from ancient times. But we will consider some modern precursors to the study of perception by describing trains that took off from different stations in the late 1800s and early 1900s, with ideas about perception that have endured to the present day. One idea was about the connection between neurons and perception; a second was about the nature of perceptual experience; and a third was about ways to measure perception. We call these ideas "tickets to ride" because they provided starting points that were taken up by a series of researchers who eventually created the findings you have read about in this book.

The "neural ticket" was provided by Edgar Adrian, who started his quest to understand the relation between electrical signals in the nervous system and perception in the 1920s in his laboratory at the University of Cambridge. As he states in an early description of his work, *The Basis of Sensation* (1927):

> It turns out that the messages from our sense organs are all made up of a common vocabulary of the simplest kind. They consist of a series of brief impulses in each nerve fibre; all the impulses are very much alike, whether the message is destined to arouse the sensation of light, of touch, or of pain; if they are crowded closely together the sensation is intense, if they are separated by long intervals the sensation is correspondingly feeble. (p. 7)

Adrian was not the first to record electrical signals from the nervous system, but he made use of a new technology—vacuum tube amplifiers—to make visible for the first time nerve impulses in single nerve fibers, and he was awarded the 1932 Nobel Prize in Physiology and Medicine for this achievement.

Notice that Adrian begins with electrical signals but turns to the relationship of these signals to perception when he states, "If electrical signals are crowded together, the sensation is intense, if they are separated by long intervals the sensation is correspondingly feeble." What Adrian is saying is that electrical signals are *representing* the intensity of the stimulus, so light that generates "crowded" electrical signals appears bright, but light that generates signals separated by long intervals appears dim (**Figure 1**). Simple enough. But later researchers tackled more complicated problems. How are colors represented? Complex forms? Musical sounds? The smell of a flower? These are all questions about representation, and we have seen in this book that the answers to these and similar questions are not simple.

Our perception of a tree occurs because the tree is represented by an image on the retina, which is transformed into electrical signals that are transmitted to the brain to form an electrical representation of the tree in the cortex. The simplistic approach to the question of how the tree is represented is that an electrical "picture" of the tree is formed in the brain. But we've seen that the electrical signals that represent the tree may not resemble the tree at all. Instead, they transmit coded electrical information that stands for "tree." This code occurs as signals are transmitted down the road from receptors to the brain and then within the brain [**Ch. 3, p. 70; Ch. 11, p. 280; Ch. 12, p. 300; Ch. 15, p. 378**]. Ideas such as these, which take as their starting point the ability to record from single neurons, are the outcome of a long succession of researchers leading from Adrian to the present day.

The "behavioral (or perceptual experience) ticket" was provided by the Gestalt psychologists when they rejected the structuralists' idea that perceptions are created by adding up tiny sensations. Interestingly, Max Wertheimer, the founder of Gestalt psychology, was actually on a train ride when he bought the toy stroboscope that inspired him to question the struc-

Figure 2 The vase–face display used by the Gestalt psychologists to illustrate figure–ground organization (see Figure 5.25).

© Cengage Learning

turalists' idea of sensations and to propose instead the famous dictum that *the whole is different than the sum of its parts* [**Ch. 5, p. 101**]. The Gestalt psychologists' proposal of principles of organization and their writings on figure–ground segregation emphasized the basic operating principles that determine our perception of what's "out there." Their main interest was not in physiological mechanisms, but in how the elements of the environment become organized into perceptual wholes (**Figure 2**).

Perceptual psychology also had roots in the early ideas of 19th-century physicist Gustav Fechner, who proposed psychophysical methods for measuring thresholds [**Ch. 1, p. 12**]. Many generations after Fechner, researchers still use these methods to make quantitative measurements of thresholds. One reason for measuring thresholds is to determine functions such as dark adaptation and spectral sensitivity curves [**Ch. 2, pp. 29, 33**] and audibility functions [**Ch. 11, p. 267**], and limits such as visual contrast thresholds [**Ch. 3, p. 67**] and tactile and olfactory detection thresholds [**Ch. 14, p. 343; Ch. 15, p. 372**] that define important operating characteristics of sensory systems (**Figure 3**).

But as we have seen throughout this book, measuring thresholds is also crucial for determining the relationship between physiology and perception. Thus, when psychophysical measurements show that we are more sensitive to horizontal lines than to slanted lines, and physiological measurements show that there are more neurons that respond to horizontal lines than to slanted lines, this provides evidence linking physiology and perception [**Ch. 1, p. 11; Ch. 4, p. 91**]. In this example, psychophysical methods devised by Fechner are collaborating with neural recordings descended from Adrian. We now shift our focus from historical precedents that led down a road of discovery, to neurons that create a "roadway" from receptors to the brain.

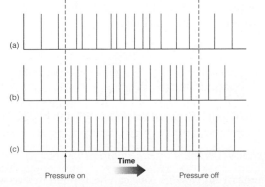

Figure 1 Increases in nerve firing are associated with more intense sensory experiences (see Figure 2.26). © Cengage Learning.

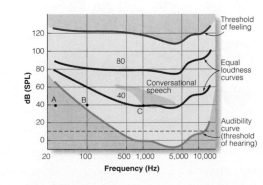

Figure 3 The audibility function (see Figure 11.8). From Fletcher, H., & Munson, W. A. (1933). Loudness: Its definition, measurement, and calculation. *Journal of the Acoustical Society of America,* 5, 82–108. Reproduced by permission.

Here, There, and Everywhere
The Travels and Destinations of Neural Signals

Figure 5 There are neurons in the visual system that respond to faces (see Figure 4.19).

Neural signals reach destinations and create experiences.

One way to describe the neural road would be to say that electrical signals start in the receptors and eventually reach the brain. While this is correct, it is overly simplified because there are many complex routes between receptors and the brain and then within the brain itself **[Ch. 3, p. 63; Ch. 4, p. 83; Ch. 12, p. 396; Ch. 14, p. 340; Ch. 15, p. 382]**. One clue to this complexity appears right at the beginning of the visual system when signals generated in the rod and cone receptors navigate the complex neural pathways of the retina (**Figure 4**) **[Ch. 2, p. 42]**.

Something very important is happening as signals from the receptors are traveling through the retina—the neural representation of the image on the retina is being *processed*. We can't tell this simply by looking at the signals traveling out the back of the eye in the optic nerve, because all nerve impulses look similar. But determining the neuron's receptive field—the area on the retina that causes this neuron to fire—does provide information that indicates the effects of processing **[Ch. 3, p. 60]**. One of the things that measuring receptive fields (and the types of stimuli that cause a neuron to fire) tells us is that the *sequential processing* that occurs as signals move from one nucleus to another toward the brain and within it results in neurons that respond to more and more complex stimuli. Thus, neurons early in the visual system respond best to small spots of light; later neurons respond to faces (**Figure 5**) **[Ch. 2, p. 62; Ch. 4, p. 87]**. Similarly, neurons early in the auditory system respond to pure tones; later neurons respond to complex environmental sounds **[Ch. 12, p. 300; Ch. 13, p. 329]**.

But the neural road doesn't just pass through a linear sequence of structures. There are branches that transmit signals here, there, and everywhere to result in *distributed processing*, so that even a simple object ends up activating many different areas within the brain **[Ch. 3, p. 71; Ch. 4, p. 89; Ch. 5, p. 120; Ch. 7, p. 164; Ch. 8, p. 192; Ch. 9, p. 213; Ch. 12, p. 300; Ch. 14, p. 355; Ch. 15, p. 378]**.

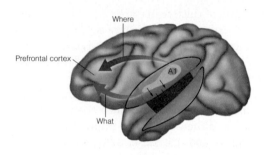

Figure 6 The *what* and *where* streams for the auditory system. Similar streams occur for vision (see Figure 12.17). Adapted from Poremba, A., Saunders, R. C., Crane, A. M., Cook, M., Sokoloff, L., & Mishkin, M. (2003). Functional mapping of the primate auditory system. *Science, 299,* 568–572.

Branching also creates parallel streams, most notably the *what* and *where/how* pathways in vision and hearing (**Figure 6**) **[Ch. 4, p. 83; Ch. 12, p. 299]**. The fact that the same types of pathways occur in both vision and hearing illustrates how the senses can share common mechanisms. In the next section, we consider both commonalities in how the senses operate and how they work together to create the multidimensional quality of everyday perceptions.

All Together Now
The Multidimensional Nature of Perception

A symphony is created by many instruments.

The theme of *All Together Now* can be applied in two ways: (1) the different senses operate according to similar principles; and (2) the different senses interact with each other. The

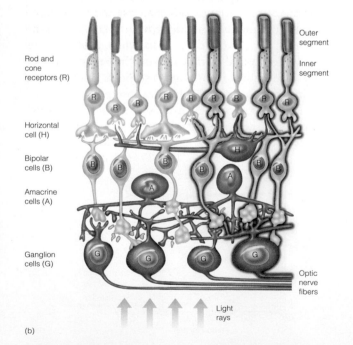

Rod and cone receptors (R)

Outer segment

Inner segment

Horizontal cell (H)

Bipolar cells (B)

Amacrine cells (A)

Ganglion cells (G)

Optic nerve fibers

Light rays

(b)

Figure 4 Cross section of the retina (see Figure 2.32). Based on "Organization of the Primate Retina," by J. E. Dowling and B. B. Boycott, *Proceedings of the Royal Society of London, B,* 1966, 166, p. 80–111, by permission of the Royal Society and John Dowling.

idea that the senses operate according to similar principles isn't surprising given that they all operate within the same nervous system and are often sensing aspects of the same stimuli. One similarity that holds across the senses is the presence of selective receptors. For vision there are separate receptors that respond to different parts of the spectrum [**Ch. 2, p. 34; Ch. 9, p. 208**]; for hearing there are hair cells that, by virtue of their location along the basilar membrane, respond to different frequencies [**Ch. 11, p. 277**]; for touch there are mechanoreceptors specialized for different forms of tactile stimulation (**Figure 7**) [**Ch. 14, p. 338**]; and for taste there are receptors for sweet, salty, sour, bitter, and umami [**Ch. 15, p. 367**].

Another similarity is that there are maps associated with each sense: retinotopic maps of locations in the visual field [**Ch. 4, p. 78**]; tonotopic maps of frequencies [**Ch. 11, p. 277**]; somatotopic maps of locations on the body [**Ch. 14, p. 341**]; and chemotopic maps of chemical properties of odorant molecules [**Ch. 15, p. 377**].

Another example of *All Together Now* is provided by what happens while our observer from Chapter 5 is watching a rolling red ball (**Figure 8**). Because the ball has a number of different qualities—form, color, movement, and depth—the observer is having a multidimensional experience. But even though each of these qualities is processed in different areas

of the brain, the observer experiences them all together, as a coherent whole, because of connections between the areas that process each quality.

Further sensory dimensions occur as the ball creates a sound that follows along with it, and if the person were to catch the ball when it rolls off the end of the table, he would experience cutaneous and haptic perceptions that begin when he sees the ball hit his hand. Going even further and imagining that the ball is an apple, we can bring in the senses of taste and smell as well (but say goodbye to the "ball"). The point of this example is that even though we may have considered different qualities and different senses in separate chapters, our body doesn't work like chapters in a book. All of these qualities and senses work together to create our perception of a coherent world, in which coordination between the senses is the rule [**Ch. 12, p. 310; Ch. 13, p. 324; Ch. 14, p. 357; Ch. 15, p. 381**].

Here Comes the Sun
How Knowledge Illuminates Perception

Neurons receive a little help from what we have learned

Neural signals offer one level of explanation for perception, because without nerve impulses there would be no perception. But because of the complexity of perception and the ambiguous nature of perceptual stimuli (**Figure 9**) [**Ch. 5, p. 97; Ch. 8, p. 189; Ch. 9, p. 220; Ch. 12, p. 304**], achieving accurate perceptions also depends on information from knowledge created by the experiences we bring to a situation. Considered in this way, knowledge is needed to transform the information in coded neural signals into accurate representations of the environment. Perception, according to this idea, is created when bottom-up information created by the receptors is illuminated by top-down information supplied by knowledge [**Ch. 1, p. 9; Ch. 4, p. 84; Ch. 5, p. 111; Ch. 6, p. 131; Ch. 13, p. 324; Ch. 14, p. 353**].

The idea of illuminating perception with knowledge has been approached in a few different ways. We are born into the environment with some built-in capacities. Infants can see rudimentary forms (**Figure 10**) and can distinguish bitter

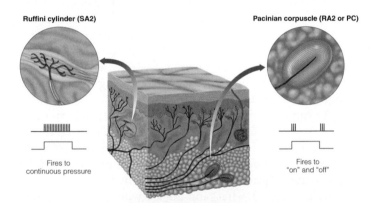

Ruffini cylinder (SA2) Pacinian corpuscle (RA2 or PC)

Fires to continuous pressure   Fires to "on" and "off"

Figure 7 Two types of mechanoreceptors found in the skin that respond to different types of tactile stimulation (see Figure 14.2).
© Cengage Learning.

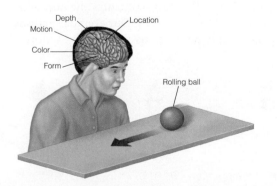

Depth   Location
Motion
Color
Form
Rolling ball

Figure 8 A person observing a rolling red ball. Each quality of the ball is processed in different areas of the brain (see Figure 6.24).
© Cengage Learning.

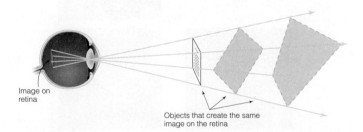

Image on retina

Objects that create the same image on the retina

Figure 9 The image on the retina is ambiguous because the image could potentially be created by many different objects (see Figure 5.6).
© Cengage Learning.

Figure 10 Newborn infants see faces as fuzzy blobs that are created by high-contrast areas of the face (see Figure 5.53).

from sweet [**Ch. 5, p. 120; Ch. 15, p. 385**]. But two things happen as infants grow into children and then into adults: Their perceptual systems mature physically, and they are constantly experiencing their environment, learning about things that occur often, which are called *regularities in the environment* [**Ch. 5, p. 110; Ch. 6, p. 131**].

For example, we learn to expect certain things to occur in certain contexts, so we interpret a blob-like shape differently when it is in different surroundings (**Figure 11**); we learn that when an object is interrupted by an occluding object, the interrupted object continues behind the occluder [**Ch. 5, p. 104**]; and we look longer at objects that violate "everyday rules," such as a printer sitting on a stove [**Ch. 6, p. 131**]. We accomplish these perceptual feats without thinking about "rules" or what we know, just as Hermann von Helmholtz suggested when he proposed his theory of unconscious inference [**Ch. 5, p. 113**].

Not only do experience and knowledge help us "decode" complex stimuli, such as the continuous auditory stimulus created by speech, which we are able to separate into individual words [**Ch. 13, p. 326**], but knowledge also modulates what we experience. Consider, for example the gate control theory of pain, which proposes that pain is determined by stimulation of pain receptors *and* by knowledge and past experience. Thus, even *expecting* that a drug will reduce pain can cause pain reduction, even if the "drug" is a sugar pill placebo [**Ch. 14, p. 353**].

All of the effects we have been describing, both neural and behavioral, are involved in creating our experience of the environment. But what is the purpose of this experience? As we saw in Chapter 7, one important function of perception is to help us survive.

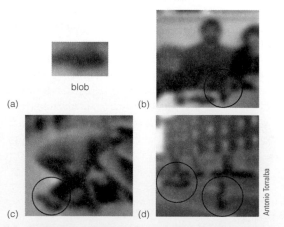

Figure 11 The identity of the blob is determined by the context within which it is seen (see Figure 5.40). Part (d) adapted from Oliva, A., & Torralba, A., The role of context in object recognition, *Trends in Cognitive Sciences*, Vol. 11, 12. Copyright 2007, with permission from Elsevier.

Help!
Why We Need Perception

The point of perception extends beyond having an experience.

One answer to the question "Why do we need perception?" is that perception tells us what is out there in the environment, and this knowledge creates an awareness that helps us survive. Being able to see that the woolly mammoth in the distance is huge—even though it is far away and so creates a small image on the caveman's retina—helps him take appropriate precautions. Hearing the sound of a car bearing down on us alerts us to get out of the way.

What's important about these two examples is that they involve having experiences ("big wooly mammoth out there" and "car coming") and triggering actions ("stay out of sight" and "get out of the way"). The idea that perception is the basis of action has led many researchers to propose that we need perception not only for creating experiences but to help us take action [**Ch. 7, p. 169**].

One starting place for action is attention, which, according to William James, determines a person's experience. "My experience," says James, "is what I agree to attend to" [**Ch. 6, p. 127**]. What are you experiencing right now? A quick guess—the words you are now reading—but what do you experience when you look up? According to James, the answer depends on what you agree to attend to, but we saw in Chapter 6 that our experience is also affected by stimuli such as bright flashes, loud sounds, or moving objects that capture our attention and may help us survive by warning us of possible danger [**Ch. 6, p. 130**].

We can appreciate that action extends beyond attention by remembering the sequence of events that occurred as Serena, sitting in the coffee shop after her bike ride as described in Chapter 7, carries out the simple action of reaching for a cup of coffee (**Figure 12**) [**Ch. 7, p. 164**]. The following actions involve the ventral (what) and dorsal (where/how) pathways that we mentioned earlier: Serena first identifies the cup (ventral), reaches for it (dorsal), perceives the cup's handle (ventral), positions her hand to grip it (dorsal), takes into account how heavy the cup will be based on how much coffee it contains (ventral), and finally, lifts the cup with just the right amount of force (dorsal). Our everyday actions, it turns out, aren't simply perceptions followed by actions. They are

(a) Perceive cup   (b) Reach for cup   (c) Grasp cup

Figure 12 The sequence of recognizing a cup and then reaching out and grasping it involves two separate visual processing streams (see Figure 7.18). From Goldstein, E. B., *Cognitive Psychology*, 3rd ed. © 2011 Wadsworth, a part of Cengage Learning, Inc. Reproduced by permission. www.cengage.com/permissions.

a constant interplay between systems that exist not only in vision but in hearing as well [Ch. 12, p. 299].

As important as perception is for creating action, our ability to get along in the environment depends not only on getting out of the way of dangerous moving objects, and reaching for and grasping stationary objects, but also on interacting with other people. If you have good "social intelligence," you know that people's actions are partially determined by their intentions and that it often helps to be able to appreciate what other people are experiencing in certain situations. It is here that mirror neurons, which fire both when a person carries out an action and when the person observes someone else carrying out the same action, come into play [Ch. 7, p. 166; Ch. 13, p. 331]. Someone who says "I feel your pain" in fact may have a highly developed "mirror" system for experiencing other people's pain [Ch. 14, p. 357]. Perception, it turns out, not only creates representations of the environment, it also helps us take actions within the environment and understand other people's reactions to the environment.

The Fool on the Hill
Things Are Sometimes More Complicated Than They Seem

When we see the sun going down, something else may actually be happening.

Finally, in this last section, we come to the fool on the hill. The fool, the Beatles song informs us, is sitting on a hill watching the sun going down. While this might conjure up an image of someone blankly staring out into the sunset, the fool, as it turns out, is not a fool at all. We know this from the next line of the song, which tells us that while watching the sun go down, he "sees the world spinning 'round." The fool knows that what we see (the sun going down) is not what is actually happening. The earth's rotation is what makes it appear that the sun is going down. Things are not, as the fool realizes, always what they seem.

And so it is with perception. It appears to be one thing—simple because of our effortless perceptual responses to light, sound, pressure, and molecules—but is actually created by processes that are extremely complex and not at all obvious. This idea—that perception appears to be simple but actually isn't—is one of the main messages of this book. So we end this epilogue with two reminders of the difficulty of the problems we face when trying to understand the mechanisms of perception.

The first reminder takes us back to the mind–body problem, described in Chapter 3 [p. 72]: How do physical processes, such as nerve impulses or sodium and potassium molecules flowing across membranes (the body part of the problem), become transformed into the richness of perceptual experience (the mind part of the problem)?

Although researchers have been working to determine the physiological basis of perception for more than a century, the mind–body problem, also called the hard problem of consciousness, is still unsolved. Researchers have had better luck determining the neural correlate of consciousness, which has been called the easy problem of consciousness, through countless experiments linking perception to the firing of single neurons and activation of specific brain areas [Ch. 2, p. 35; Ch. 4, p. 87; Ch. 5, p. 114; Ch. 8, p. 186; Ch. 10, p. 241; Ch. 11, p. 280; Ch. 12, p. 297; Ch. 13, p. 329; Ch. 14, p. 344; Ch. 15, p. 373]. But although great progress has been made toward determining the neural correlate of consciousness, it is important to note that calling this problem "easy" is misleading. It is easy only in relation to a problem that is so difficult that most researchers have abandoned it. At some point the hard problem may be solved, but for now, work continues on the "easy" problem.

The second reminder of the problems we face in trying to understand the mechanisms underlying perception is that most perceptual processes operate "behind the scenes," outside of our awareness. Obviously, we aren't aware of the multitude of nerve impulses and excitatory and inhibitory events at synapses that continually occur in our receptors, neural pathways, and within the brain. But we can also appreciate this behind-the-scenes activity by considering mechanisms such as the what and how pathways for vision that operate as we interact with the environment. When we recognize a coffee cup sitting on a table in front of us and then reach across the table to pick it up, we aren't aware that two separate neural pathways are involved.

V. S. Ramachandran and Sandra Blakeslee (1998), in a book titled *Phantoms in the Brain,* used this example of two pathways to introduce the idea of hidden processes they call *zombies in the brain.* In their explanation of the idea of zombies in the brain, Ramachandran and Blakeslee use the example of D.F., whose what (ventral) pathway was destroyed by carbon monoxide poisoning, so she couldn't recognize objects or determine the orientation of a mail slot. But even though she couldn't determine the orientation of the mail slot, she was able to mail a letter by orienting it so it fit through the slot [Ch. 4, p. 85].

This example and others led Ramachandran and Blakeslee to propose that there are invisible zombies in the brain that control, without our awareness, our ability to carry out actions such as mailing a letter and recognizing objects. "There is," they propose, "another being inside you that goes about his or her business without your knowledge or awareness. And, as it turns out, there is not just one such zombie but a multitude of them inhabiting your brain" (pp. 83–84). While this may seem like a trailer to a Hollywood movie, it is actually one of the challenges to understanding how we perceive. Extremely complex processes, which we are largely unaware of, pose challenges to the ingenuity of perception researchers.

So now we have come to the end of the long and winding road that we have been traveling in our study of perception. As we do this, we return to Adrian, whose accomplishment of recording from single sensory neurons set the stage for the many thousands of experimenters who followed his lead. In a series of 1946 lectures in which Adrian (1947) assessed the state of perception research at the time, he opened by stating that "perhaps the chief impression that will be left by this account is the complete inability of contemporary science to give a satisfactory picture of any kind of mental activity" (p. 1). But within Adrian's lifetime (he died in 1977), he would see advances in our understanding of the physiological basis of perception that might make him reconsider his statement, and if he were alive today he might marvel at how far we have come.

Now, in the second decade of the 21st century, we understand a great deal about how neurons fire to different kinds of stimuli, how parts of the brain are specialized for different functions, how our senses interact, and the way our knowledge of scenes and sounds, smells and textures help us identify what is out there. But just because we know a lot doesn't mean there isn't a great deal more to learn. We have a long way to go before we can say we truly understand how we perceive the enormous complexity of our everyday environment. We are far from understanding everything that's happening both neurally and behaviorally when we take a walk in the woods and perceive trees and leaves blowing in the wind and simultaneously feel the wind on our face, sense a smell in the air, and hear a lone dog barking in the distance. Although we understand aspects of each of these experiences, we understand only a small fraction of what is behind even the simplest of our everyday perceptions.

Picture a student some decades from now, sitting at his or her desk reading a future edition of this book. What new discoveries will he or she be reading about? The answers to this question lie along the road to be paved by the discoveries of future researchers, many of whom, if history is any guide, will have begun their journey of discovery by taking a course in perception much like the one you are taking now.

The songs in the section titles:

"The Long and Winding Road." Paul McCartney (1969). Album: *Let It Be*.

"Ticket to Ride." John Lennon with Paul McCartney (1965). Album: *Help!*

"Here, There, and Everywhere." Paul McCartney (1966). Album: *Revolver*.

"All Together Now." Paul McCartney with John Lennon (1967). Album: *Yellow Submarine*.

"Here Comes the Sun." George Harrison (1969). Album: *Abbey Road*.

"Help!" John Lennon (1965). Album: *Help!*

"The Fool on the Hill." Paul McCartney (1967). Album: *Magical Mystery Tour*.

Signal Detection Theory

At the end of Chapter 1, we described a hypothetical experiment in which two subjects, Regina and Julie, were tested to determine their threshold for detecting a light (Figure 1.17). We saw that the threshold, determined by methods like constant stimuli, can depend on whether the subject is a conservative responder like Regina, who says "yes, I see the light" only if she is very sure she sees the light, or a liberal responder like Julie, who says "yes" any time she thinks the light might possibly have been presented. The difference between these two ways of responding, called a difference in *response criterion*, would cause Julie's threshold to appear to be lower than Regina's, even though the difference could actually be caused by the difference in their response criteria. A technique based on a theory called *signal detection theory* has been used to deal with this problem.

In the next section, we will describe the basic procedure of a signal detection experiment that involves detecting tones and will show how we can tell whether Regina and Julie are, in fact, equally sensitive to the tones even though their response criteria are very different. After describing the signal detection experiment, we will look at the theory on which the experiment is based.

A Signal Detection Experiment

Remember that in a psychophysical procedure such as the method of constant stimuli, at least five different stimulus intensities are presented and a stimulus is presented on every trial. In a signal detection experiment studying the detection of tones, we use only a single low-intensity tone that is difficult to hear, and we present this tone on some of the trials and present no tone at all on the rest of the trials. Thus, a signal detection experiment differs from a classical psychophysical experiment in two ways: in a signal detection experiment, (1) only one stimulus intensity is presented, and (2) on some of the trials, no stimulus is presented. Let's consider the results of such an experiment, using Julie as our participant. We present the tone for 100 trials and no tone for 100 trials, mixing the tone and no-tone trials at random. Julie's results are as follows:

When the tone is presented, Julie

- Says "yes" on 90 trials. This correct response—saying "yes" when a stimulus is present—is called a **hit** in signal detection terminology.
- Says "no" on 10 trials. This incorrect response—saying "no" when a stimulus is present—is called a **miss**.

When no tone is presented, Julie

- Says "yes" on 40 trials. This incorrect response—saying "yes" when there is no stimulus—is called a **false alarm**.
- Says "no" on 60 trials. This correct response—saying "no" when there is no stimulus—is called a **correct rejection**.

These results are not very surprising, given that we know Julie has a low criterion and likes to say "yes" a lot. This gives her a high hit rate of 90 percent but also causes her to say "yes" on many trials when no tone is present at all, so her 90 percent hit rate is accompanied by a 40 percent false-alarm rate. If we do a similar experiment on Regina, who has a higher criterion and therefore says "yes" much less often, we find that she has a lower hit rate (say, 60 percent) but also a lower false-alarm rate (say, 10 percent). Note that although Julie and Regina say "yes" on numerous trials on which no stimulus is presented, that result would not be predicted by classical threshold theory. Classical theory would say "no stimulus, no response," but that is clearly not the case here. By adding a new wrinkle to our signal detection experiment, we can obtain another result that would not be predicted by classical threshold theory.

Without changing the tone's intensity at all, we can cause Julie and Regina to change their percentages of hits and false alarms. We do this by manipulating each person's motivation by means of **payoffs**. Let's look at how payoffs might influence Regina's responding. Remember that Regina is a conservative responder who is hesitant to say "yes." But being clever experimenters, we can make Regina say "yes'" more frequently by adding some financial inducements to the experiment. We tell Regina that we are going to reward her for making correct responses and are going to penalize her for making incorrect responses by using the following payoffs:

Hit:	Win $100
Correct rejection:	Win $10
False alarm:	Lose $10
Miss:	Lose $10

What would you do if you were in Regina's position? Being smart, you analyze the payoffs and realize that the way to make money is to say "yes" more. You can lose $10 if a "yes" response results in a false alarm, but this small loss is more than counterbalanced by the $100 you can win for a hit. Although you decide not to say "yes" on every trial—after all, you want to be honest with the experimenter about whether or not you heard the tone—you do decide to stop being so conservative. You decide to change your criterion for saying "yes." The results of this experiment are interesting. Regina becomes a more liberal responder and says "yes" a lot more, responding with 98 percent hits and 90 percent false alarms.

This result is plotted as data point L (for "liberal" response) in **Figure A.1**, a plot of the percentage of hits versus the percentage of false alarms. The solid curve going through point L is called a **receiver operating characteristic (ROC) curve**. We will see why the ROC curve is important in a moment, but first let's see how we determine the other points on the curve. Doing this is simple: all we have to do is to change the payoffs. We can make Regina raise her criterion and therefore respond more conservatively by means of the following payoffs:

Hit:	Win $10
Correct rejection:	Win $100
False alarm:	Lose $10
Miss:	Lose $10

This schedule of payoffs offers a great inducement to respond conservatively because there is a big reward for saying "no" when no tone is presented. Regina's criterion is therefore shifted to a much higher level, so Regina now returns to her conservative ways and says "yes" only when she is quite certain that a tone is presented; otherwise she says "no." The result of this newfound conservatism is a hit rate of only 10 percent and a minuscule false-alarm rate of 1 percent, indicated by point C (for "conservative" response) on the ROC curve. We should note that although Regina hits on

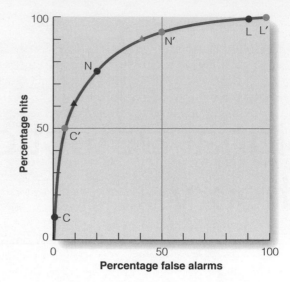

Figure A.1 A receiver operating characteristic (ROC) curve determined by testing Julie (green data points) and Regina (red data points) under three different criteria: Liberal (L and L′), neutral (N and N′) and conservative (C and C′). The fact that Regina's and Julie's data points all fall on this curve means that they have the same sensitivity to the tone. The triangles indicate the results for Julie and Regina for an experiment that did not use payoffs. © Cengage Learning.

only 10 percent of the trials in which a tone is presented, she scores a phenomenal 99 percent correct rejections on trials in which a tone is not presented. (This result follows from the fact that, if there are 100 trials in which no tone is presented, then correct rejections + false alarms = 100. Because there was one false alarm, there must be 99 correct rejections.)

Regina, by this time, is rich and decides to put a down payment on the Miata she's been dreaming about. (So far she's won $8,980 in the first experiment and $9,090 in the second experiment, for a total of $18,070! To be sure you understand how the payoff system works, check this calculation yourself. Remember that the signal was presented on 100 trials and was not presented on 100 trials.) However, we point out that she may need a little extra cash to have a satellite audio system installed in her car, so she agrees to stick around for one more experiment. We now use the following neutral schedule of payoffs:

Hit:	Win $10
Correct rejection:	Win $10
False alarm:	Lose $10
Miss:	Lose $10

With this schedule, we obtain point N (for "neutral") on the ROC curve: 75 percent hits and 20 percent false alarms. Regina wins $1,100 more and becomes the proud owner of a Miata with a satellite radio system, and we are the proud owners of the world's most expensive ROC curve. (Do not, at this point, go to the psychology department in search of the nearest signal detection experiment. In real life, the payoffs are quite a bit less than in our hypothetical example.)

Regina's ROC curve shows that factors other than sensitivity to the stimulus determine a person's response. Remember that in all of our experiments the intensity of the tone has remained constant. Even though we changed only the person's criterion, we succeeded in drastically changing the person's responses.

Other than demonstrating that people will change how they respond to an unchanging stimulus, what does the ROC curve tell us? Remember, at the beginning of this discussion, we said that a signal detection experiment can tell us whether or not Regina and Julie are equally sensitive to the tone. The beauty of signal detection theory is that the person's sensitivity is indicated by the shape of the ROC curve, so if experiments on two people result in identical ROC curves, their sensitivities must be equal. (This conclusion is not obvious from our discussion so far. We will explain below why the shape of the ROC curve is related to the person's sensitivity.) If we repeat the above experiments on Julie, we get the following results (data points L', N', and C' in Figure A.1):

Liberal payoff:
Hits = 99 percent
False alarms = 95 percent

Neutral payoff:
Hits = 92 percent
False alarms = 50 percent

Conservative payoff:
Hits = 50 percent
False alarms = 6 percent

The data points for Julie's results are shown by the green circles in Figure A.1. Note that although these points are different from Regina's, they fall on the same ROC curve as do Regina's. We have also plotted the data points for the first experiments we did on Julie (open triangle) and Regina (filled triangle) before we introduced payoffs. These points also fall on the ROC curve.

That Regina's and Julie's data both fall on the same ROC curve indicates their equal sensitivity to the tones. This confirms our suspicion that the method of constant stimuli misled us into thinking that Julie is more sensitive, when the real reason for her apparently greater sensitivity is her lower criterion for saying "yes."

Before we leave our signal detection experiment, it is important to note that signal detection procedures can be used without the elaborate payoffs that we described for Regina and Julie. Much briefer procedures, which we will describe shortly, can be used to determine whether differences in the responses of different persons are due to differences in threshold or to differences in response criteria.

What does signal detection theory tell us about functions such as the spectral sensitivity curve (Figure 3.21) and the audibility function (Figure 11.9), which are usually determined using one of the classical psychophysical methods? When the classical methods are used to determine these functions, it is usually assumed that the person's criterion remains constant throughout the experiment, so that the function measured is due not to changes in response criterion but to changes in the wavelength or some other physical property of the stimulus. This is a good assumption because changing the wavelength of the stimulus probably has little or no effect on factors such as motivation, which would shift the person's criterion. Furthermore, experiments such as the one for determining the spectral sensitivity curve usually use highly experienced people who are trained to give stable results. Thus, even though the idea of an "absolute threshold" may not be strictly correct, classical psychophysical experiments run under well-controlled conditions have remained an important tool for measuring the relationship between stimuli and perception.

Signal Detection Theory

We will now discuss the theoretical basis for the signal detection experiments we have just described. Our purpose is to explain the theoretical bases underlying two ideas: (1) the percentage of hits and false alarms depends on a person's criterion, and (2) a person's sensitivity to a stimulus is indicated by the shape of the person's ROC curve. We will begin by describing two of the key concepts of signal detection theory (SDT): signal and noise. (See Swets, 1964.)

Signal and Noise

The **signal** is the stimulus presented to the person. Thus, in the signal detection experiment we just described, the signal is the tone. The noise is all the other stimuli in the environment, and because the signal is usually very faint, noise can sometimes be mistaken for the signal. Seeing what appears to be a flicker of light in a completely dark room is an example of visual noise. Seeing light where there is none is what we have been calling a false alarm, according to signal detection theory. False alarms are caused by the noise. In the experiment we just described, hearing a tone on a trial in which no tone was presented is an example of auditory noise.

Let's now consider a typical signal detection experiment, in which a signal is presented on some trials and no signal is presented on the other trials. Signal detection theory describes this procedure not in terms of presenting a signal or no signal, but in terms of presenting signal plus noise (S + N) or noise (N). That is, the noise is always present, and on some trials, we add a signal. Either condition can result in the perceptual effect of hearing a tone. A false alarm occurs when the person says "yes" on a noise trial, and a hit occurs when the person says "yes" on a signal-plus-noise trial. Now that we have defined signal and noise, we introduce the idea of probability distributions for noise and signal plus noise.

Probability Distributions

Figure A.2 shows two probability distributions. The one on the left represents the probability that a given perceptual effect will be caused by noise (N), and the one on the right represents the probability that a given perceptual effect will be caused by signal plus noise (S + N). The key to understanding these distributions is to realize that the value labeled "Perceptual effect (loudness)" on the horizontal axis is what the person experiences on each trial. Thus, in an experiment in which the person is asked to indicate whether or not a tone is present, the perceptual effect is the perceived loudness of the tone. Remember that in an SDT experiment the tone always has the same *intensity*. The *loudness* of the tone, however, can vary from trial to trial. The person perceives different loudnesses on different trials, because of either trial-to-trial changes in attention or changes in the state of the person's auditory system.

The probability distributions tell us what the chances are that a given loudness of tone is due to (N) or to (S + N). For example, let's assume that a person hears a tone with a loudness of 10 on one of the trials of a signal detection experiment. By extending a vertical dashed line up from 10 on the "Perceptual effect" axis in Figure A.2, we see that the probability that a loudness of 10 is due to (S + N) is extremely low, because the distribution for (S + N) is essentially zero at this loudness. There is, however, a fairly high probability that a loudness of 10 is due to (N), because the (N) distribution is fairly high at this point.

Let's now assume that, on another trial, the person perceives a loudness of 20. The probability distributions indicate that when the tone's loudness is 20, it is equally probable that this loudness is due to (N) or to (S + N). We can also see from Figure A.2 that a tone with a perceived loudness of 30 would have a high probability of being caused by (S + N) and only a small probability of being caused by (N).

Now that we understand the curves of Figure A.2, we can appreciate the problem confronting the person. On each trial, she has to decide whether no tone (N) was present or whether a tone (S + N) was present. However, the overlap in the probability distributions for (N) and (S + N) means that for some perceptual effects this judgment will be difficult. As we saw before, it is equally probable that a tone with a loudness of 20 is due to (N) or to (S + N). So, on a trial in which the person hears a tone with a loudness of 20, how does she decide whether or not the signal was presented? According to signal detection theory, the person's decision depends on the location of her criterion.

The Criterion

We can see how the criterion affects the person's response by looking at **Figure A.3**. In this figure, we have labeled three different criteria: liberal (L), neutral (N), and conservative (C). Remember that we can cause people to adopt these different criteria by means of different payoffs. According to signal detection theory, once the person adopts a criterion, he or she uses the following rule to decide how to respond on a given trial: If the perceptual effect is greater than (to the right of) the criterion, say, "Yes, the tone was present"; if the perceptual effect is less than (to the left of) the criterion, say, "No, the tone was not present." Let's consider how different criteria influence the person's hits and false alarms.

To determine how the criterion affects the person's hits and false alarms, we will consider what happens when we present (N) and when we present (S + N) under three different criteria.

Liberal Criterion

1. Present (N): Because most of the probability distribution for (N) falls to the right of the criterion, the chances are good that presenting (N) will result in a loudness to the right of the criterion. This means that the probability of saying "yes" when (N) is presented is high; therefore, the probability of a false alarm is high.

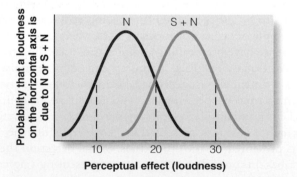

Figure A.2 Probability distributions for noise alone (N, red curve), and for signal plus noise (S + N, green curve). The probability that any given perceptual effect is caused by the noise (no signal is presented) or by the signal plus noise (signal is presented) can be determined by finding the value of the perceptual effect on the horizontal axis and extending a vertical line up from that value. The place where that line intersects the (N) and (S + N) distributions indicates the probability that the perceptual effect was caused by (N) or by (S + N). © Cengage Learning.

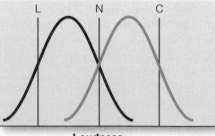

Figure A.3 The same probability distributions from Figure A.2, showing three criteria: liberal (L), neutral (N), and conservative (C). When a person adopts a criterion, he or she uses the following decision rule: Respond "yes" ("I detect the stimulus") when the perceptual effect is greater than the criterion, and respond "no" ("I do not detect the stimulus") when the perceptual effect is less than the criterion. © Cengage Learning.

2. Present (S + N): Because the entire probability distribution for (S + N) falls to the right of the criterion, the chances are excellent that presenting (S + N) will result in a loudness to the right of the criterion. Thus, the probability of saying "yes" when the signal is presented is high; therefore, the probability of a hit is high. Because criterion L results in high false alarms and high hits, adopting that criterion will result in point L on the ROC curve in **Figure A.4**.

Neutral Criterion

1. Present (N): The person will answer "yes" only rarely when (N) is presented because only a small portion of the (N) distribution falls to the right of the criterion. The false-alarm rate, therefore, will be fairly low.

2. Present (S + N): The person will answer "yes" frequently when (S + N) is presented because most of the (S + N) distribution falls to the right of the criterion. The hit rate, therefore, will be fairly high (but not as high as for the L criterion). Criterion N results in point N on the ROC curve in Figure A.4.

Conservative Criterion

1. Present (N): False alarms will be very low because none of the (N) curve falls to the right of the criterion.

2. Present (S + N): Hits will also be low because only a small portion of the (S + N) curve falls to the right of the criterion. Criterion C results in point C on the ROC curve in Figure A.4.

You can see that applying different criteria to the probability distributions generates the solid ROC curve in Figure A.4. But why are these probability distributions necessary? After all, when we described the experiment with Regina and Julie, we determined the ROC curve simply by plotting the results of the experiment. The reason the (N) and (S + N)

distributions are important is that, according to signal detection theory, the person's sensitivity to a stimulus is indicated by the distance (d′) between the peaks of the (N) and (S + N) distributions, and this distance affects the shape of the ROC curve. We will now consider how the person's sensitivity to a stimulus affects the shape of the ROC curve.

The Effect of Sensitivity on the ROC Curve

We can understand how the person's sensitivity to a stimulus affects the shape of the ROC curve by considering what the probability distributions would look like for Jamie Lynn, a person with supersensitive hearing. Jamie Lynn's hearing is so good that a tone barely audible to Regina sounds very loud to Jamie Lynn. If presenting (S + N) causes Jamie Lynn to hear a loud tone, this means that her (S + N) distribution should be far to the right, as shown in **Figure A.5.** In signal detection terms, we would say that Jamie Lynn's high sensitivity is indicated by the large separation (d′) between the (N) and the (S + N) probability distributions. To see how this greater separation between the probability distributions will affect her ROC curve, let's see how she would respond when adopting liberal, neutral, and conservative criteria.

Liberal Criterion

1. Present (N): high false alarms.

2. Present (S + N): high hits.

The liberal criterion, therefore, results in point L′ on the ROC curve of Figure A.4.

Neutral Criterion

1. Present (N): low false alarms. It is important to note that Jamie Lynn's false alarms for the neutral criterion will be lower than Regina's false alarms for the neutral criterion because only a very small portion of

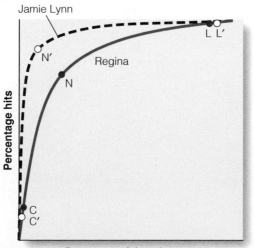

Figure A.4 ROC curves for Regina (solid curve) and Jamie Lynn (dashed curve) determined using liberal (L, L′), neutral (N, N′) and conservative (C, C′) criteria. © Cengage Learning.

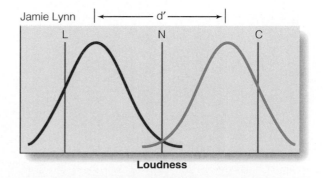

Figure A.5 Probability distributions for Jamie Lynn, a person who is extremely sensitive to the signal. The noise distribution (red) remains the same, but the (S + N) distribution (green) is shifted to the right compared to the curves in Figure A.4. Liberal (L), neutral (N) and conservative (C) criteria are shown. © Cengage Learning.

Jamie Lynn's (N) distribution falls to the right of the criterion, whereas more of Regina's (N) distribution falls to the right of the neutral criterion (Figure A.3).

2. Present (S + N): high hits. In this case, Jamie Lynn's hits will be higher than Regina's because almost all of Jamie Lynn's (S + N) distribution falls to the right of the neutral criterion, whereas less of Regina's does (Figure A.3). The neutral criterion, therefore, results in point N′ on the ROC curve in Figure A.4.

Conservative Criterion

1. Present (N): low false alarms.
2. Present (S + N): low hits. The conservative criterion, therefore, results in point C′ on the ROC curve.

The difference between the two ROC curves in Figure A.4 is obvious because Jamie Lynn's curve is more "bowed." But before you conclude that the difference between these two ROC curves has anything to do with where we positioned Jamie Lynn's L, N, and C criteria, see whether you can get an ROC curve like Jamie Lynn's from the two probability distributions of Figure A.3. You will find that, no matter where you position the criteria, there is no way that you can get a point like point N′ (with very high hits and very low false alarms) from the curves of Figure A.3. In order to achieve very high hits and very low false alarms, the two probability distributions must be spaced far apart, as in Figure A.5.

Thus, increasing the distance (d′) between the (N) and the (S + N) probability distributions changes the shape of the ROC curve. When the person's sensitivity (d′) is high, the ROC curve is more bowed. In practice, d′ can be determined by comparing the experimentally determined ROC curve to standard ROC curves (see Gescheider, 1976), or d′ can be calculated from the proportions of hits and false alarms that occur in an experiment by means of a mathematical procedure we will not discuss here. This mathematical procedure for calculating d′ enables us to determine a person's sensitivity by determining only one data point on an ROC curve, thus using the signal detection procedure without running a large number of trials.

Glossary

The number in parentheses at the end of each entry indicates the chapter in which the term is first used.

Ablation Removal of an area of the brain. This is usually done in experiments on animals, to determine the function of a particular area. Also called lesioning. (4)

Absolute disparity *See* **Angle of disparity**. (10)

Absolute threshold *See* **Threshold, absolute**. (1)

Absorption spectrum A plot of the amount of light absorbed by a visual pigment versus the wavelength of light. (2)

Accommodation (focus) In vision, bringing objects located at different distances into focus by changing the shape of the lens. (2)

Accretion A cue that provides information about the relative depth of two surfaces. Occurs when the farther object is uncovered by the nearer object due to sideways movement of an observer relative to the objects. *See also* **Deletion**. (10)

Achromatic color Color without hue. White, black, and all the grays between these two extremes are achromatic colors. (9)

Acoustic prism The way the cochlea separates frequencies entering the ear to create activity at different places along the basilar membrane. (11)

Acoustic shadow The shadow created by the head that decreases the level of high-frequency sounds on the opposite side of the head. The acoustic shadow is the basis of the localization cue of interaural level difference. (12)

Acoustic signal The pattern of frequencies and intensities of the sound stimulus. (13)

Acoustic stimulus *See* **Acoustic signal**. (13)

Across-fiber patterns The pattern of nerve firing that a stimulus causes across a number of neurons. Also referred to as distributed coding. (15)

Action Motor activities such as moving the head or eyes and locomoting through the environment. Action is one of the major outcomes of the perceptual process. (1)

Action pathway *See* **Dorsal pathway**. (4)

Action potential Rapid increase in positive charge in a nerve fiber that travels down the fiber. Also called the nerve impulse. (2)

Active method (3-D TV) A method used to create 3-D television images. The active method alternates the left-eye and right-eye images on the screen 30 or more times a second. This method is called active because the viewing glasses have a shutter system that is synchronized with the alternating images on the TV screen (10)

Active touch Touch in which the observer plays an active role in touching and exploring an object, usually with his or her hands. (14)

Additive color mixture *See* **Color mixture, additive**. (9)

Adjustment, method of A psychophysical method in which the experimenter or the observer adjusts the stimulus intensity in a continuous manner until the observer detects the stimulus. (1)

Affective (emotional) component of pain The emotional experience associated with pain—for example, pain described as *torturing, annoying, frightful*, or *sickening*. *See also* **Sensory component of pain**. (14)

Affordance The information specified by a stimulus pattern that indicates how the stimulus can be used. An example of an affordance would be seeing a chair as something to sit on or a flight of stairs as something to climb. (7)

Agnosia *See* **Visual form agnosia**. (1)

Akinetopsia A condition in which damage to an area of the cortex involved in motion perception causes blindness to motion. (8)

Amacrine cell A neuron that transmits signals laterally in the retina. Amacrine cells synapse with bipolar cells and ganglion cells. (2)

Ames room A distorted room, first built by Adelbert Ames, that creates an erroneous perception of the sizes of people in the room. The room is constructed so that two people at the far wall of the room appear to stand at the same distance from an observer. In actuality, one of the people is much farther away than the other. (10)

Amiloride A substance that blocks the flow of sodium into taste receptors. (15)

Amplitude In the case of a repeating sound wave, such as the sine wave of a pure tone, amplitude represents the pressure difference between atmospheric pressure and the maximum pressure of the wave. (11)

Amygdala A subcortical structure that is involved in emotional responding and in processing olfactory signals. (15)

Angle of disparity The visual angle between the images of an object on the two retinas. When images of an object fall on corresponding points, the angle of disparity is zero. When images fall on noncorresponding points, the angle of disparity indicates the degree of noncorrespondence. (10)

Angular size contrast theory An explanation of the moon illusion that states that the perceived size of the moon is determined by the sizes of the objects that surround it. According to this idea, the moon appears small when it is surrounded by large objects, such as the expanse of the sky when the moon is overhead. (10)

Anomalous trichromat A person who needs to mix a minimum of three wavelengths to match any other wavelength in the spectrum but mixes these wavelengths in different proportions from a trichromat. (9)

Anosmia Loss of the ability to smell due to injury or infection. (15)

Aperture problem Occurs when only a portion of a moving stimulus can be seen, as when the stimulus is viewed through a narrow aperture. This can result in misleading information about the direction in which the stimulus is moving. (8)

Apex of the cochlea The end of the cochlea farthest from the middle ear. (11)

Aphasia Difficulties in speaking or understanding speech due to brain damage. (13)

Apparent distance theory An explanation of the moon illusion that is based on the idea that the horizon moon, which is viewed across the filled space of the terrain, should appear farther away than the zenith moon, which is viewed through the empty space of the sky. This theory states that because the horizon and zenith moons have the same visual angle but are perceived to be at different distances, the farther appearing horizon moon should appear larger. (10)

Apparent motion See **Apparent movement**. (8)

Apparent movement An illusion of movement that occurs when two objects separated in space are presented rapidly, one after another, separated by a brief time interval. (5, 8)

Architectural acoustics The study of how sounds are reflected in rooms. An important concern of architectural acoustics is how these reflected sounds change the quality of the sounds we hear. (12)

Area V1 The visual receiving area of the brain, called area V1 to indicate that it is the first visual area in the cortex. Also called *striate cortex*. (3)

Articulator Structure involved in speech production, such as the tongue, lips, teeth, jaw, and soft palate. (13)

Atmospheric perspective. A depth cue. Objects that are farther away look more blurred and bluer than objects that are closer because we must look through more air and particles to see them. (10)

Attack The buildup of sound energy that occurs at the beginning of a tone. (11)

Attention The process of focusing on some objects while ignoring others. Attention can enhance the processing of the attended object. (6)

Attentional capture Occurs when stimulus salience causes an involuntary shift of attention. For example, attention can be captured by movement. (6, 8)

Audibility curve A curve that indicates the sound pressure level (SPL) at threshold for frequencies across the audible spectrum. (11)

Audiovisual mirror neuron Neuron that responds to actions that produce sounds. These neurons respond when a monkey performs a hand action *and* when it hears the sound associated with this action. See also **Mirror neuron**. (7)

Audiovisual speech perception A perception of speech that is affected by both auditory and visual stimulation, as when a person sees a tape of someone saying /ga/ with the sound /ba/ substituted and perceives /da/. Also called the McGurk effect. (13)

Auditory canal The canal through which air vibrations travel from the environment to the tympanic membrane. (11)

Auditory localization The perception of the location of a sound source. (12)

Auditory receiving area (A1) The area of the cortex, located in the temporal lobe, that is the primary receiving area for hearing. (12)

Auditory response area The psychophysically measured area that defines the frequencies and sound pressure levels over which hearing functions. This area extends between the audibility curve and the curve for the threshold of feeling. (11)

Auditory scene The sound environment, which includes the locations and qualities of individual sound sources. (12)

Auditory scene analysis The process by which sound stimuli produced by the different sources in an auditory scene become perceptually organized into sounds at different locations and into separated streams of sound. (12)

Auditory space Perception of where sounds are located in space. Auditory space extends around a listener's head in all directions, existing wherever there is a sound. (12)

Auditory stream segregation The effect that occurs when a series of sounds that differ in pitch or timbre are played so that the tones become perceptually separated into simultaneously occurring independent streams of sound. (12)

Autism A serious developmental disorder in which one of the major symptoms is the withdrawal of contact from other people. People with autism typically do not make eye contact with others and have difficulty telling what emotions others are experiencing in social situations. (6)

Axial myopia Myopia (nearsightedness) in which the eyeball is too long. *See also* **Refractive myopia**. (2)

Axon The part of the neuron that conducts nerve impulses over distances. Also called the nerve fiber. (2)

Azimuth In hearing, specifies locations that vary from left to right relative to the listener. (12)

Balint's syndrome A condition resulting from damage to a person's parietal lobe. One characteristic of this syndrome is an inability to focus attention on individual objects. (6)

Base of the cochlea The part of the cochlea nearest the middle ear. (11)

Basilar membrane A membrane that stretches the length of the cochlea and controls the vibration of the cochlear partition. (11)

Bayesian inference A statistical approach to perception in which perception is determined by taking probabilities into account. These probabilities are based on past experiences in perceiving properties of objects and scenes. (5)

Belongingness The hypothesis that an area's appearance is influenced by the part of the surroundings that the area appears to belong to. This principle has been used to explain the perception of lightness in the Benary cross and White's illusion. (3)

Belt area Auditory area in the temporal lobe that receives signals from the core area and sends signals to the parabelt area. (12)

Bimodal neuron A neuron that responds to stimuli associated with more than one sense. (15)

Binaural cue Sound localization cue that involves both ears. Interaural time difference and interaural level difference are the primary binaural cues. (12)

Binding The process by which features such as color, form, motion, and location are combined to create our perception of a coherent object. Binding can also occur across senses, as when sound and vision are associated with the same object. (6)

Binding problem The problem of how neural activity in many separated areas in the brain is combined to create a perception of a coherent object. (6)

Binocular depth cell A neuron in the visual cortex that responds best to stimuli that fall on points separated by a specific degree of disparity on the two retinas. Also called a disparity-selective cell. (10)

Binocular disparity Occurs when the retinal images of an object fall on disparate points on the two retinas. (10)

Binocular rivalry A situation in which one image is presented to the left eye and a different image is presented to the right eye, and perception alternates back and forth between the two images. (5)

Binocularly fixate Directing the two foveas to exactly the same spot. (10)

Biological motion Motion produced by biological organisms. Most of the experiments on biological motion have used walking humans with lights attached to their joints and limbs as stimuli. *See also* **Point-light walker**. (8)

Bipolar cell A retinal neuron that receives inputs from the visual receptors and sends signals to the retinal ganglion cells. (2)

Blind spot The small area where the optic nerve leaves the back of the eye. There are no visual receptors in this area, so small images falling directly on the blind spot cannot be seen. (2)

Border ownership When two areas share a border, as occurs in figure–ground displays, the border is usually perceived as belonging to the figure. (5)

Bottom-up processing Processing that is based on the information on the receptors. Also called data-based processing. (1)

Brain imaging Procedures that make it possible to visualize areas of the human brain that are activated by different types of stimuli, tasks, or behaviors. The two most common techniques used in perception research are positron emission tomography (PET) and functional magnetic resonance imaging (fMRI). (4)

Broca's aphasia Language problems, caused by damage to Broca's area in the frontal lobe, characterized by labored and stilted speech and short sentences. (13)

Broca's area An area in the frontal lobe that is important for language perception and production. One effect of damage is difficulty in speaking. (13)

Calcium imaging A method of measuring receptor activity by using fluorescence to measure the concentration of calcium inside the receptor. This technique has been used to measure the activation of olfactory receptor neurons. (15)

Categorical perception In speech perception, perceiving one sound at short voice onset times and another sound at longer voice onset times. The listener perceives only two categories across the whole range of voice onset times. (13)

Cell body The part of a neuron that contains the neuron's metabolic machinery and that receives stimulation from other neurons. (2)

Center-surround antagonism The competition between the center and surround regions of a center-surround receptive field, caused by the fact that one is excitatory and the other is inhibitory. Stimulating center and surround areas simultaneously decreases responding of the neuron, compared to stimulating the excitatory area alone. (3)

Center-surround organization Arrangement of a neuron's receptive fields in which one area is surrounded by another area, like the hole in a donut (corresponding to the center) and the donut (the surround). Stimulation of the center and surround causes opposite responses. *See also* **Excitatory-center, inhibitory-surround receptive field; Inhibitory-center, excitatory-surround receptive field**. (3)

Center-surround receptive field A receptive field that has a center-surround organization. (3)

Cerebral achromatopsia A loss of color vision caused by damage to the cortex. (9)

Cerebral cortex The 2-mm-thick layer that covers the surface of the brain and contains the machinery for creating perception, as well as for other functions, such as language, memory, and thinking. (3)

Change blindness Difficulty in detecting differences between two visual stimuli that are presented one after another, often with a short blank stimulus interposed between them. Also occurs when part of a stimulus is changed very slowly. (6)

Characteristic frequency The frequency at which a neuron in the auditory system has its lowest threshold. (11)

Chemotopic map The pattern of activation in the olfactory system in which chemicals with different properties create a "map" of activation based on these properties. For example, there is evidence that chemicals are mapped in the olfactory bulb based on carbon-chain length. Also called odor map. (15)

Chromatic adaptation Exposure to light in a specific part of the visible spectrum. This adaptation can cause a decrease in sensitivity to light from the area of the spectrum that was presented during adaptation. (9)

Chromatic color Color with hue, such as blue, yellow, red, or green. (9)

Cilia Fine hairs that protrude from the inner and outer hair cells of the auditory system. Bending the cilia of the inner hair cells leads to transduction. (11)

Classical psychophysical methods The methods of limits, adjustment, and constant stimuli, described by Fechner, that are used for measuring thresholds. (1)

Coarticulation The overlapping articulation that occurs when different phonemes follow one another in speech. Because of these effects, the same phoneme can be articulated differently depending on the context in which it appears. For example, articulation of the /b/ in *boot* is different from articulation of the /b/ in *boat*. (13)

Cochlea The snail-shaped, liquid-filled structure that contains the structures of the inner ear, the most important of which are the basilar membrane, the tectorial membrane, and the hair cells. (11)

Cochlear amplifier Expansion and contraction of the outer hair cells in response to sound sharpens the movement of the basilar membrane to specific frequencies. This amplifying effect plays an important role in determining the frequency selectivity of auditory nerve fibers. (11)

Cochlear implant A device in which electrodes are inserted into the cochlea to create hearing by electrically stimulating the auditory nerve fibers. This device is used to restore hearing in people who have lost their hearing because of damaged hair cells. (11)

Cochlear nucleus The nucleus where nerve fibers from the cochlea first synapse. (12)

Cochlear partition A partition in the cochlea, extending almost its full length, that separates the scala tympani and the scala vestibuli. The organ of Corti, which contains the hair cells, is part of the cochlear partition. (11)

Cognitive influences on perception How the knowledge, memories, and expectations that a person brings to a situation influence his or her perception. (1)

Coherence In research on movement perception in which arrays of moving dots are used as stimuli, the degree of correlation between the direction of the moving dots. Zero percent coherence means all of the dots are moving independently; 100 percent coherence means all of the dots are moving in the same direction. (8)

Coincidence detectors Neurons in the Jeffress neural coincidence model, which was proposed to explain how neural firing can provide information regarding the location of a sound source. A neural coincidence detector fires when signals from the left and right ears reach the neuron simultaneously. Different neural coincidence detectors fire to different values of interaural time difference. *See also* **Jeffress model**. (12)

Color, achromatic *See* **Achromatic color**. (9)

Color, chromatic *See* **Chromatic color**. (9)

Color blindness A condition in which a person perceives no chromatic color. This can be caused by absent or malfunctioning cone receptors or by cortical damage. (9)

Color constancy The effect in which the perception of an object's hue remains constant even when the wavelength distribution of the illumination is changed. *Partial color constancy* occurs when our perception of hue changes a little when the illumination changes, though not as much as we might expect from the change in the wavelengths of light reaching the eye. (9)

Color deficiency People with this condition (sometimes incorrectly called color blindness) see fewer colors than people with normal color vision and need to mix fewer wavelengths to match any other wavelength in the spectrum. (9)

Color mixture, additive The creation of colors that occurs when lights of different colors are superimposed. (9)

Color mixture, subtractive The creation of colors that occurs when paints of different colors are mixed together. (9)

Color-matching experiment A procedure in which observers are asked to match the color in one field by mixing two or more lights in another field. (9)

Common fate, principle of A Gestalt principle of perceptual organization that states that things that are moving in the same direction appear to be grouped together. (5)

Common region, principle of A modern Gestalt principle that states that elements that are within the same region of space appear to be grouped together. (5)

Comparator A structure hypothesized by the corollary discharge theory of movement perception. The corollary discharge signal and the sensory movement signal meet at the comparator to determine whether movement will be perceived. (8)

Complex cell A neuron in the visual cortex that responds best to moving bars with a particular orientation. (3)

Cone of confusion A surface in the shape of a cone that extends out from the ear. Sounds originating from different locations on this surface all have the same interaural level difference and interaural time difference, so location information provided by these cues is ambiguous. (12)

Cone spectral sensitivity curve A plot of visual sensitivity versus wavelength for cone vision. Often measured by presenting a small spot of light to the fovea, which contains only cones. Can also be measured when the eye is light adapted, so cones are the most sensitive receptors. (2)

Cones Cone-shaped receptors in the retina that are primarily responsible for vision in high levels of illumination and for color vision and detail vision. (2)

Conflicting cues theory A theory of visual illusions proposed by R. H. Day, which states that our perception of line length depends on an integration of the actual line length and the overall figure length. (10)

Conjunction search A visual search task in which it is necessary to search for a combination (or conjunction) of two or more features on the same stimulus to find the target. An example of a conjunction search would be looking for a horizontal green line among vertical green lines and horizontal red lines. (6)

Constant stimuli, method of A psychophysical method in which a number of stimuli with different intensities are presented repeatedly in a random order. (1)

Contrast threshold The intensity difference that can just barely be seen between two areas. For vision this is often measured using gratings with alternating light and dark bars. (3)

Convergence (depth cue) *See* **Perspective convergence**. (10)

Convergence (neural) When many neurons synapse onto a single neuron. (2)

Core area The area in the temporal lobe that includes the primary auditory cortex (A1) and some nearby areas. Signals from the core area are transmitted to the belt area of the auditory cortex. (12)

Cornea The transparent focusing element of the eye that is the first structure through which light passes as it enters the eye. The cornea is the eye's major focusing element. (2)

Corollary discharge signal (CDS) A copy of the motor signal that is sent to the eye muscles to cause movement of the eye. The copy is sent to the hypothetical comparator of corollary discharge theory. (8)

Corollary discharge theory The theory that explains motion perception as being determined both by movement of the image on the retina and by signals that indicate movement of the eyes. *See also* **Corollary discharge signal**. (8)

Correct rejection In a signal detection experiment, saying "No, I don't detect a stimulus" on a trial in which the stimulus is not presented (a correct response). (Appendix)

Correspondence problem The problem faced by the visual system, which must determine which parts of the images in the left and right eyes correspond to one another. Another way of stating the problem is: How does the visual system match up the images in the two eyes? This matching of the images is involved in determining depth perception using the cue of binocular disparity. (10)

Corresponding retinal points The points on each retina that would overlap if one retina were slid on top of the other. Receptors at corresponding points send their signals to the same location in the brain. (10)

Cortical magnification Occurs when a disproportionately large area on the cortex is activated by stimulation of a small area on the receptor surface. One example of cortical magnification is the relatively large area of visual cortex that is activated by stimulation of the fovea. An example in the somatosensory system is the large area of somatosensory cortex activated by stimulation of the lips and fingers. (4)

Covert attention Attention without looking. Seeing something "out of the corner of your eye" is an example of covert attention. (6)

Cue approach to depth perception The approach to explaining depth perception that identifies information in the retinal image, and also information provided by aiming and focusing the eyes on an object that is correlated with depth in the scene. Some of the depth cues that have been identified are overlap, relative height, relative size, atmospheric perspective, convergence, and accommodation. (10)

Cutaneous senses The ability to perceive sensations, such as touch and pain, that are based on the stimulation of receptors in the skin. (14)

Dark adaptation Visual adaptation that occurs in the dark, during which the sensitivity to light increases. This increase in sensitivity is associated with regeneration of the rod and cone visual pigments. (2)

Dark adaptation curve The function that traces the time course of the increase in visual sensitivity that occurs during dark adaptation. (2)

Dark-adapted sensitivity The sensitivity of the eye after it has completely adapted to the dark. (2)

Data-based processing Another name for bottom-up processing. Refers to processing that is based on incoming data, as opposed to top-down, or knowledge-based, processing, which is based on prior knowledge. (1)

Decay The decrease in the sound signal that occurs at the end of a tone. (11)

Decibel (dB) A unit that indicates the pressure of a sound stimulus relative to a reference pressure: $dB = 20 \log (p/p_o)$ where p is the pressure of the tone and p_o is the reference pressure. (11)

Deletion A cue that provides information about the relative depth of two surfaces. Deletion occurs when a farther object is covered by a nearer object due to sideways movement of an observer relative to the objects. *See also* **Accretion**. (10)

Dendrites Nerve processes on the cell body that receive stimulation from other neurons. (2)

Depolarization When the inside of a neuron becomes more positive, as occurs during the initial phases of the action potential. Depolarization is often associated with the action of excitatory neurotransmitters. (2)

Dermis The layer of skin below the epidermis. (14)

Desaturated Low saturation in chromatic colors as would occur when white is added to a color. For example, pink is not as saturated as red. (9)

Detached retina A condition in which the retina is detached from the back of the eye. (2)

Detection threshold *See* **Threshold, detection**. (15)

Deuteranopia A form of red–green color dichromatism caused by lack of the middle-wavelength cone pigment. (9)

Dichromat A person who has a form of color deficiency. Dichromats can match any wavelength in the spectrum by mixing two other wavelengths. Deuteranopes, protanopes, and tritanopes are all dichromats. (9)

Difference threshold *See* **Threshold, difference**. (1)

Direct pathway model of pain The idea that pain occurs when nociceptor receptors in the skin are stimulated and send their signals to the brain. This model does not account for the fact that pain can be affected by factors in addition to stimulation of the skin. (14)

Direct sound Sound that is transmitted directly from a sound source to the ears. (12)

Dishabituation An increase in looking time that occurs when a stimulus is changed. This response is used in testing infants to see whether they can differentiate two stimuli. (6)

Disparity-selective cell *See* **Binocular depth cell**. (10)

Disparity tuning curve A plot of a neuron's response versus the degree of disparity of a visual stimulus. The disparity to which a neuron responds best is an important property of disparity-selective cells, which are also called binocular depth cells. (10)

Distance How far a stimulus is from the observer. In hearing, the distance coordinate specifies how far the sound source is from the listener. (12)

Distributed coding Type of neural code in which different perceptual qualities are signaled by the pattern of activity across many neurons. This contrasts with *specificity coding*, in which qualities are signaled by activity in a specific type of neuron. (3)

Dorsal pathway Pathway that conducts signals from the striate cortex to the parietal lobe. The dorsal pathway has also been called the *where*, the *how*, or the *action* pathway by different investigators. (4)

Double dissociation In brain damage, when function A is present and function B is absent in one person, and function A is absent and function B is present in another. Presence of a double dissociation means that the two functions involve different mechanisms and operate independently of one another. (4)

Double-opponent neurons Neurons that have receptive fields in which stimulation of one part of the receptive field causes an excitatory response to wavelengths in one area of the spectrum and an inhibitory response to wavelengths in another area of the spectrum, and stimulation of an adjacent part of the receptive field causes the opposite response. An example of double-opponent responding is when the response of one part of a receptive field is L+M− and the response of an adjacent part is L−M+. (9)

Dual-stream model of speech perception Model that proposes a ventral stream starting in the temporal lobe that is responsible for recognizing speech, and a dorsal stream starting in the parietal lobe that is responsible for linking the acoustic signal to the movements used to produce speech. (13)

Dual-task procedure An experimental procedure in which subjects are required to carry out simultaneously a central task that demands attention and a peripheral task that involves making a decision about the contents of a scene. (6)

Duplex theory of texture perception The idea that texture perception is determined by both spatial and temporal cues that are detected by two types of receptors. Originally proposed by David Katz and named the "duplex theory" by Hollins. (14)

Eardrum Another term for the tympanic membrane, the membrane located at the end of the auditory canal that vibrates in response to pressure changes. This vibration is transmitted to the bones of the middle ear. (11)

Easy problem of consciousness The problem of determining the relationship between physiological processes like nerve firing and perceptual experience. Note that this involves determining a *relationship*, not a *cause*. *See also* **Hard problem of consciousness**. (3)

Echolocation Locating objects by sending out high-frequency pulses and sensing the echo created when these pulses are reflected from objects in the environment. Echolocation is used by bats and dolphins. (10)

Ecological approach to perception This approach focuses on specifying the information in the environment that is used for perception, emphasizing the study of moving observers to determine how their movement results in perceptual information that both creates perception and guides further movement. (7)

Effect of the missing fundamental Removing the fundamental frequency and other lower harmonies from a musical tone does not change the tone's pitch. *See also* **Periodicity pitch**. (11)

Electromagnetic spectrum Continuum of electromagnetic energy that extends from very-short-wavelength gamma rays to long-wavelength radio waves. Visible light is a narrow band within this spectrum. (2)

Elevation In hearing, sound locations that are up and down relative to the listener. (12)

Emmert's law A law stating that the size of an afterimage depends on the distance of the surface against which the afterimage is viewed. The farther away the surface, the larger the afterimage appears. (10)

Endorphin Chemical that is naturally produced in the brain and that causes analgesia. (14)

End-stopped cell A cortical neuron that responds best to lines of a specific length that are moving in a particular direction. (3)

Environmental stimulus The stimulus "out there," in the external environment. (1)

Epidermis The outer layers of the skin, including a layer of dead skin cells. (14)

Equal loudness curve A curve that indicates the sound pressure levels that result in a perception of the same loudness at frequencies across the audible spectrum. (11)

Event A segment of time at a particular location that is perceived by observers to have a beginning and an ending. (8)

Event boundary The point in time when one event ends and another begins. (8)

Excitatory area Area of a receptive field that is associated with excitation. Stimulation of this area causes an increase in the rate of nerve firing. (3)

Excitatory response The response of a nerve fiber in which the firing rate increases. (2)

Excitatory-center, inhibitory-surround receptive field A center-surround receptive field in which stimulation of the center area causes an excitatory response, and stimulation of the surround causes an inhibitory response. (3)

Experience-dependent plasticity A process by which neurons adapt to the specific environment within which a person or animal lives. This is achieved when neurons change their response properties so they become tuned to respond best to stimuli that have been repeatedly experienced in the environment. *See also* **Neural plasticity**; **Selective rearing**. (3)

Expertise hypothesis The idea that human proficiency in perceiving certain things can be explained by changes in the brain caused by long exposure, practice, or training. (4)

Exploratory procedures (EPs) People's movements of their hands and fingers while they are identifying three-dimensional objects by touch. (14)

Extrastriate body area (EBA) An area of the temporal lobe that is activated by pictures of bodies and parts of bodies. (4)

Eye The eyeball and its contents, which include focusing elements, the retina, and supporting structures. (2)

Falling phase of the action potential In the axon, or nerve fiber, the increase in negativity from +40 mV back to –70 mV (the resting potential level) that occurs during the action potential. This increase in negativity is associated with the flow of positively charged potassium ions (K+) out of the axon. (2)

False alarm In a signal detection experiment, saying "Yes, I detect the stimulus" on a trial in which the stimulus is not presented (an incorrect response). (Appendix)

Familiar size A depth cue in which judgment of distance is based on knowledge of the sizes of objects. Epstein's coin experiment illustrated the operation of the cue of familiar size by showing that the relative sizes of the coins influenced perception of the coins' distances. (10)

Far point As a light is moved toward the eye, the distance at which the light becomes focused on the retina. (2)

Farsightedness *See* **Hyperopia**. (2)

Feature detector A neuron that responds selectively to a specific feature of the stimulus such as orientation or direction of motion. (3)

Feature integration theory A theory proposed by Treisman to explain how an object is broken down into features and how these features are recombined to result in a perception of the object. (6)

Feature search A visual search task in which a person can find a target by searching for only one feature. An example would be looking for a horizontal green line among vertical green lines. (6)

Figure When an object is seen as separate from the background (the "ground"), it is called a figure. *See also* **Figure–ground segregation**. (5)

Figure–ground segregation The perceptual separation of an object from its background. (5)

First harmonic *See* **Fundamental frequency**. (11)

Fixation The brief pause of the eye that occurs between eye movements as a person scans a scene. (6)

Flavor The perception that occurs from the combination of taste and olfaction. (15)

Focus of expansion (FOE) The point in the flow pattern caused by observer movement in which there is no expansion. According to J. J. Gibson, the focus of expansion always remains centered on the observer's destination. (7)

Focused attention stage (of perceptual processing) The stage of processing in feature integration theory in which the features are combined. According to Treisman, this stage requires focused attention. (6)

Formant Horizontal band of energy in the speech spectrogram associated with vowels. (13)

Formant transition In the speech stimulus, the rapid shift in frequency that precedes a formant. (13)

Fovea A small area in the human retina that contains only cone receptors. The fovea is located on the line of sight, so that when a person looks at an object, the center of its image falls on the fovea. (2)

Frequency The number of times per second that pressure changes of a sound stimulus repeat. Frequency is measured in Hertz, where 1 Hertz is one cycle per second. (11)

Frequency spectrum A plot that indicates the amplitudes of the various harmonics that make up a complex tone. Each harmonic is indicated by a line that is positioned along the frequency axis, with the height of the line indicating the amplitude of the harmonic. (11)

Frequency tuning curve Curve relating frequency and the threshold intensity for activating an auditory neuron. (11)

Frontal eyes Eyes located in front of the head, so the views of the two eyes overlap. (10)

Frontal lobe Receiving signals from all of the senses, the frontal lobe plays an important role in perceptions that involve the coordination of information received through two or more senses. It also serves functions such as language, thought, memory, and motor functioning. (1, 3)

Frontal operculum cortex An area in the frontal lobe of the cortex that receives signals from the taste system. (15)

Functional magnetic resonance imaging (fMRI) A brain imaging technique that indicates brain activity in awake, behaving organisms. The fMRI response occurs when the response to a magnetic field changes in response to changes in blood flow in the brain. (4)

Fundamental A pure tone with frequency equal to the fundamental frequency of a complex tone. *See also* **Fundamental frequency**. (11)

Fundamental frequency The first harmonic of a complex tone; usually the lowest frequency in the frequency spectrum of a complex tone. The tone's other components, called higher harmonics, have frequencies that are multiples of the fundamental frequency. (11)

Fusiform face area (FFA) An area in the human inferotemporal (IT) cortex that contains neurons that are specialized to respond to faces. (3, 4)

Ganglion cell A neuron in the retina that receives inputs from bipolar and amacrine cells. The axons of the ganglion cells are the nerve fibers that travel out of the eye in the optic nerve. (2)

Gate control model Melzack and Wall's idea that perception of pain is controlled by a neural circuit that takes into account the relative amount of activity in nociceptors, mechanoreceptors, and central signals. This model has been used to explain how pain can be influenced by factors in addition to stimulation of receptors in the skin. (14)

Gestalt psychology An approach to psychology that developed as a reaction to structuralism. The Gestalt approach proposes principles of perceptual organization and figure–ground segregation and states that "the whole is different than the sum of its parts." (5)

Gist of a scene General description of a scene. People can identify most scenes after viewing them for only a fraction of a second, as when they flip rapidly from one TV channel to another. It takes longer to identify the details within the scene. (5)

Global image features Information that may enable observers to rapidly perceive the gist of a scene. Features associated with specific types of scenes include degree of naturalness, degree of openness, degree of roughness, degree of expansion, and color. (5)

Global optic flow Information for movement that occurs when all elements in a scene move. The perception of global optic flow indicates that it is the observer that is moving and not the scene. (8)

Glomeruli Small structures in the olfactory bulb that receive signals from similar olfactory receptor neurons. One function of each glomerulus is to collect information about a small group of odorants. (15)

Good continuation, principle of A Gestalt principle of perceptual organization that states that points that, when connected, result in straight or smoothly curving lines are seen as belonging together, and that lines tend to be seen in such a way as to follow the smoothest path. (5)

Good figure, principle of See **Pragnanz, principle of**. (5)

Gradient of flow In an optic flow pattern, a gradient is created by movement of an observer through the environment. The "gradient" refers to the fact that the optic flow is rapid in the foreground and becomes slower as distance from the observer increases. (7)

Grandmother cell A hypothesized type of neuron that responds only to a very specific stimulus, such as a person's grandmother. See also **Specificity coding**. (3)

Grating acuity In the cutaneous senses, a measure of acuity on the skin that is the narrowest spacing of a grooved surface on the skin for which orientation can be accurately judged. Can also be applied to detecting the orientation of a visual grating stimulus. See also **Two-point threshold**. (14)

Ground In object perception, the background is called the ground. See also **Figure**. (5)

Grouping In perceptual organization, the process by which visual events are "put together" into units or objects. (5)

Habituation Paying less attention to the same stimulus that is presented repeatedly. For example, infants look at a stimulus less and less on each successive trial. See also **Dishabituation**. (6)

Hair cell Neuron in the cochlea that contains small hairs, or cilia, that are displaced by vibration of the basilar membrane and fluids inside the inner ear. There are two kinds of hair cells: inner and outer. (11)

Hair cell, inner Auditory receptor cell in the inner ear that is primarily responsible for auditory transduction and the perception of pitch. (11)

Hair cells, outer Auditory receptor cells in the inner ear that amplify the response of inner hair cells by amplifying the vibration of the basilar membrane. (11)

Haptic perception The perception of three-dimensional objects by touch. (14)

Hard problem of consciousness The problem of determining how physiological processes, such as ion flow across nerve membranes, cause different perceptual experiences. See also **Mind-body problem**. (3)

Harmonics Pure-tone components of a complex tone that have frequencies that are multiples of the fundamental frequency. (11)

Hearing The experience of perceiving sound. (11)

Hermann grid A display that results in the illusion of dark areas at the intersection of two white "corridors." This perception can be explained by lateral inhibition. (3)

Hertz (Hz) The unit for designating the frequency of a tone. One Hertz equals one cycle per second. (11)

Higher harmonics Pure tones with frequencies that are *whole-number* (2, 3, 4, etc.) multiples of the fundamental frequency. See also **Fundamental; Fundamental frequency; Harmonics**. (11)

High-load task Task that involves more processing resources and that therefore uses more of a person's perceptual capacity. (6)

Hit In a signal detection experiment, saying "Yes, I detect a stimulus" on a trial in which the stimulus is present (a correct response). (Appendix)

Homunculus Latin for "little man"; refers to the topographic map of the body in the somatosensory cortex. (14)

Horizontal cell A neuron that transmits signals laterally across the retina. Horizontal cells synapse with receptors and bipolar cells. (2)

Horopter An imaginary surface that passes through the point of fixation. Images caused by a visual stimulus on this surface fall on corresponding points on the two retinas. (10)

How **pathway** See **Dorsal pathway**. (4)

Hue The experience of a chromatic color such as red, green, yellow, or blue or combinations of these colors. (9)

Hypercolumn In the striate cortex, unit proposed by Hubel and Wiesel that combines location, orientation, and ocular dominance columns that serve a specific area on the retina. (4)

Hyperopia A condition causing poor vision in which people can see objects that are far away but do not see near objects clearly. Also called farsightedness. (2)

Hyperpolarization When the inside of a neuron becomes more negative. Hyperpolarization is often associated with the action of inhibitory neurotransmitters. (2)

Illumination edge The border between two areas created by different light intensities in the two areas. (9)

Illusory conjunction Illusory combination of features that are perceived when stimuli containing a number of features are presented briefly and under conditions in which focused attention is difficult. For example, presenting a red square and a blue triangle could potentially create the perception of a red triangle. (6)

Illusory contour Contour that is perceived even though it is not present in the physical stimulus. (5)

Illusory motion Perception of motion when there actually is none. *See also* **Apparent motion**. (8)

Image displacement signal (IDS) In corollary discharge theory, the signal that occurs when an image moves across the visual receptors. (8)

Implied motion When a still picture depicts an action that involves motion, so that an observer could potentially extend the action depicted in the picture in his or her mind based on what will most likely happen next. (8)

Inattentional blindness A situation in which a stimulus that is not attended is not perceived, even though the person is looking directly at it. (6)

Incus The second of the three ossicles of the middle ear. It transmits vibrations from the malleus to the stapes. (11)

Indexical characteristic Characteristic of the speech stimulus that indicates information about a speaker, such as the speaker's age, gender, or emotional state. (13)

Indirect sound Sound that reaches a listener's ears after being reflected from a surface such as a room's walls. (12)

Induced motion The illusory movement of one object that is caused by the movement of another object that is nearby. (8)

Inferior colliculus A nucleus in the hearing system along the pathway from the cochlea to the auditory cortex. The inferior colliculus receives inputs from the superior olivary nucleus. (12)

Inferotemporal (IT) cortex An area of the brain outside Area V1 (the striate cortex), involved in object perception and facial recognition. (3)

Inflammatory pain Pain caused by damage to tissues, inflammation of joints, or tumor cells. This damage releases chemicals that create an "inflammatory soup" that activates nociceptors. (14)

Inhibitory area Area of a receptive field that is associated with inhibition. Stimulation of this area causes a decrease in the rate of nerve firing. (3)

Inhibitory response Occurs when a neuron's firing rate decreases due to inhibition from another neuron. (2)

Inhibitory-center, excitatory-surround receptive field A center-surround receptive field in which stimulation of the center causes an inhibitory response and stimulation of the surround causes an excitatory response. (3)

Inner ear The innermost division of the ear, containing the cochlea and the receptors for hearing. (11)

Inner hair cell *See* **Hair cell, inner**. (11)

Insula An area in the frontal lobe of the cortex that receives signals from the taste system and is also involved in the affective component of the perception of pain. (15)

Interaural level difference (ILD) The difference in the sound pressure (or *level*) between the left and right ears. This difference creates an acoustic shadow for the far ear. The ILD provides a cue for sound localization for high-frequency sounds. (12)

Interaural time difference (ITD) When a sound is positioned closer to one ear than to the other, the sound reaches the close ear slightly before reaching the far ear, so there is a difference in the time of arrival at the two ears. The ITD provides a cue for sound localization. (12)

Invariant information Environmental properties that do not change as the observer moves relative to an object or scene. For example, the spacing, or texture, of the elements in a texture gradient does not change as the observer moves on the gradient. The texture of the gradient therefore supplies invariant information for depth perception. (7)

Inverse projection problem The idea that a particular image on the retina could have been caused by an infinite number of different objects. This means that the retinal image does not unambiguously specify a stimulus. (5)

Ions Charged molecules. Sodium (Na^+), potassium (K^+), and chlorine (Cl^-) are the main ions found within nerve fibers and in the liquid that surrounds nerve fibers. (2)

Ishihara plate A display of colored dots used to test for the presence of color deficiency. The dots are colored so that people with normal (trichromatic) color vision can perceive numbers in the plate, but people with color deficiency cannot perceive these numbers or perceive different numbers than someone with trichromatic vision. (9)

Isomerization Change in shape of the *retinal* part of the visual pigment molecule that occurs when the molecule absorbs a quantum of light. Isomerization triggers the enzyme cascade that results in transduction from light energy to electrical energy in the retinal receptors. (2)

ITD tuning curve A plot of the neuron's firing rate against the ITD (interaural time difference). (12)

Jeffress model The neural mechanism of auditory localization that proposes that neurons are wired to each receive signals from the two ears, so that different neurons fire to different interaural time differences (ITD). (12)

Kinesthesis The sense that enables us to feel the motions and positions of the limbs and body. (14)

Knowledge Any information that the perceiver brings to a situation. *See also* **Top-down processing**. (1)

Landmark discrimination problem The behavioral task used in Ungerleider and Mishkin's experiment in which they provided evidence for the dorsal, or *where*, visual processing stream. Monkeys were required to respond to a previously indicated location. (4)

Landmarks Objects on a route that serve as cues to indicate where to turn; a source of information for wayfinding. (7)

Laser-assisted in situ keratomileuis (LASIK) A process in which the cornea is sculpted with a laser in order to achieve clear vision by adjusting the focusing power of the cornea so it focuses light onto the retina. (2)

Lateral eyes Eyes located on opposite sides of an animal's head, so the views of the two eyes do not overlap or overlap only slightly, as in the pigeon and rabbit. (10)

Lateral geniculate nucleus (LGN) The nucleus in the thalamus that receives inputs from the optic nerve and, in turn, communicates with the cortical receiving area for vision. (3)

Lateral inhibition Inhibition that is transmitted laterally across a nerve circuit. In the retina, lateral inhibition is transmitted by the horizontal and amacrine cells. (3)

Leisure noise Noise associated with leisure activities such as listening to music, hunting, and woodworking. Exposure to high levels of leisure noise for extended periods can cause hearing loss. (11)

Lens The transparent focusing element of the eye through which light passes after passing through the cornea and the aqueous humor. The lens's change in shape to focus at different distances is called accommodation. (2)

Lenticular projection A method used to create 3-D television images. The screen is coated with a film containing two sets of lenses, which results in different images reaching the left and right eyes. (10)

Level Short for sound pressure level or sound level. Indicates the decibels or sound pressure of a sound stimulus. (11)

Light-adapted sensitivity The sensitivity of the eye when in the light-adapted state. Usually taken as the starting point for the dark adaptation curve because it is the sensitivity of the eye just before the lights are turned off. (2)

Light-from-above assumption The assumption that light usually comes from above, which influences our perception of form in some situations. (5)

Lightness The perception of shades ranging from white to grey to black. (3, 9)

Lightness constancy The constancy of our perception of an object's lightness under different intensities of illumination. (9)

Likelihood principle The idea proposed by Helmholtz that we perceive the object that is *most likely* to have caused the pattern of stimuli we have received. (5)

Limits, method of A psychophysical method for measuring threshold in which the experimenter presents sequences of stimuli in ascending and descending order. (1)

Load theory of attention Lavie's proposal that the amount of perceptual capacity that remains as a person is carrying out a task determines how well the person can avoid being distracted by task-irrelevant stimuli. If a person's perceptual load is close to perceptual capacity, the person is less likely to be distracted by task-irrelevant stimuli. *See also* **High-load tasks; Low-load tasks; Perceptual capacity; Perceptual load**. (6)

Local disturbance in the optic array Occurs when one object moves relative to the environment, so that the stationary background is covered and uncovered by the moving object. This local disturbance indicates that the object is moving relative to the environment. (8)

Location column A column in the visual cortex that contains neurons with the same receptive field locations on the retina. (4)

Location cue In hearing, characteristics of the sound reaching the listener that provide information regarding the location of a sound source. (12)

Loudness The quality of sound that ranges from soft to loud. For a tone of a particular frequency, loudness usually increases with increasing decibels. (11)

Low-load task A task that uses only a small amount of the person's perceptual capacity. (6)

Macrosmatic Having a keen sense of smell; usually important to an animal's survival. (15)

Macular degeneration A clinical condition that causes degeneration of the macula, an area of the retina that includes the fovea and a small surrounding area. (2)

Magnitude estimation A psychophysical method in which the subject assigns numbers to a stimulus that are proportional to the subjective magnitude of the stimulus. (1)

Malleus The first of the ossicles of the middle ear. Receives vibrations from the tympanic membrane and transmits these vibrations to the incus. (11)

McGurk effect *See* **Audiovisual speech perception**. (13)

Mechanoreceptor Receptor that responds to mechanical stimulation of the skin, such as pressure, stretching, or vibration. (14)

Medial geniculate nucleus An auditory nucleus in the thalamus that is part of the pathway from the cochlea to the auditory cortex. The medial geniculate nucleus receives inputs from the inferior colliculus and transmits signals to the auditory cortex. (12)

Medial lemniscal pathway A pathway in the spinal cord that transmits signals from the skin toward the thalamus. (14)

Meissner corpuscle (RA1) A receptor in the skin, associated with RA1 mechanoreceptors. It has been proposed that the Meissner corpuscle is important for perceiving tactile slip and for controlling the force needed to grip objects. (14)

Melodic channeling *See* **Scale illusion**. (12)

Melody schema A representation of a familiar melody that is stored in a person's memory. Existence of a melody schema makes it more likely that the tones associated with a melody will be perceptually grouped. (12)

Memory color The idea that an object's characteristic color influences our perception of that object's color. (9)

Merkel receptor (SA1) A disk-shaped receptor in the skin associated with slowly adapting fibers and the perception of fine details. (14)

Metamerism The situation in which two physically different stimuli are perceptually identical. In vision, this refers to two lights with different wavelength distributions that are perceived as having the same color. (9)

Metamers Two lights that have different wavelength distributions but are perceptually identical. (9)

Method of adjustment *See* **Adjustment, method of**. (1)

Method of constant stimuli *See* **Constant stimuli, method of**. (1)

Method of limits *See* **Limits, method of**. (1)

Metrical structure The underlying beat of music. (12)

Microsmatic Having a weak sense of smell. This usually occurs in animals like humans, in which the sense of smell is not crucial for survival. (15)

Microstimulation A procedure in which a small electrode is inserted into the cortex and an electrical current passed through the electrode activates neurons near the tip of the electrode. This procedure has been used to determine how activating specific groups of neurons affects perception. (8)

Middle ear The small air-filled space between the auditory canal and the cochlea that contains the ossicles. (11)

Middle-ear muscles Muscles attached to the ossicles in the middle ear. The smallest skeletal muscles in the body, they contract in response to very intense sounds and dampen the vibration of the ossicles. (11)

Mind–body problem One of the most famous problems in science: How do physical processes such as nerve impulses or sodium and potassium molecules flowing across membranes (the body part of the problem) become transformed into the richness of perceptual experience (the mind part of the problem)? *See also* **Hard problem of consciousness**. (3)

Mirror neuron Neuron in the premotor area of the monkey's cortex that responds when the monkey grasps an object and also when the monkey observes someone else (another monkey or the experimenter) grasping the object. There is also evidence for mirror neuron-like activity in the human brain. *See also* **Audiovisual mirror neuron**. (7)

Misapplied size constancy scaling A principle, proposed by Richard Gregory, that when mechanisms that help maintain size constancy in the three-dimensional world are applied to two-dimensional pictures, an illusion of size sometimes results. (10)

Miss In a signal detection experiment, saying "No, I don't detect a stimulus" on a trial in which the stimulus is present (an incorrect response). (Appendix)

Module A structure that processes information about a specific behavior or perceptual quality. Often identified as a structure that contains a large proportion of neurons that respond selectively to a particular quality, such as the fusiform face area, which contains many neurons that respond selectively to faces. (4)

Monaural cue Sound localization cue that involves one ear. (12)

Monochromat A person who is completely color-blind and therefore sees everything as black, white, or shades of gray. A monochromat can match any wavelength in the spectrum by adjusting the intensity of any other wavelength. Monochromats generally have only one type of functioning receptors, usually rods. (9)

Monochromatic light Light that contains only a single wavelength. (2)

Monocular cue Depth cue—such as overlap, relative size, relative height, familiar size, linear perspective, movement parallax, and accommodation—that can work when we use only one eye. (10)

Moon illusion An illusion in which the moon appears to be larger when it is on or near the horizon than when it is high in the sky. (10)

Motion aftereffect An illusion that occurs after a person views a moving stimulus and then sees movement in the opposite direction when viewing a stationary stimulus immediately afterward. *See also* **Waterfall illusion**. (8)

Motion parallax A depth cue. As an observer moves, nearby objects appear to move rapidly across the visual field, whereas far objects appear to move more slowly. (10)

Motor signal (MS) In corollary discharge theory, the signal that is sent to the eye muscles when the observer moves or tries to move his or her eyes. (8)

Motor theory of speech perception A theory that proposes a close link between how speech is perceived and how it is produced. The idea behind this theory is that when we *hear* a particular speech sound, this activates the motor mechanisms that are responsible for *producing* that sound, and it is the activation of these motor mechanisms that enable us to perceive the sound. (13)

Müller-Lyer illusion An illusion in which two lines of equal length appear to be of different lengths because of the addition of "fins" to the ends of the lines. (10)

Multimodal The involvement of a number of different senses in determining perception. For example, speech perception can be influenced by information from a number of different senses, including audition, vision, and touch. (13)

Multimodal nature of pain The fact that the experience of pain has both sensory and emotional components. (14)

Multisensory interaction Use of a combination of senses. For example, for vision and hearing, seeing a person's lips move while listening to the person speak. (12)

Myopia An inability to see distant objects clearly. Also called nearsightedness. (2)

Naloxone A substance that inhibits the activity of opiates. It is hypothesized that naloxone also inhibits the activity of endorphins and therefore can have an effect on pain perception. (14)

Nasal pharynx A passageway that connects the mouth cavity and the nasal cavity. (15)

Near point The distance at which the lens can no longer accommodate enough to bring close objects into focus. Objects nearer than the near point can be brought into focus only by corrective lenses. (2)

Nearness, principle of *See* **Proximity, principle of**. (5)

Nearsightedness *See* **Myopia**. (2)

Nerve fiber In most sensory neurons, the long part of the neuron that transmits electrical impulses from one point to another. Also called the axon. (2)

Neural circuit A number of neurons that are connected by synapses. (2)

Neural convergence Synapsing of a number of neurons onto one neuron. (2)

Neural correlate of consciousness (NCC) Connections between the firing of neurons and perceptual experience. *See also* **Easy problem of consciousness**. (3)

Neural plasticity The capacity of the nervous system to change in response to experience. Examples are how early visual experience can change the orientation selectivity of neurons in the visual cortex and how tactile experience can change the sizes of areas in the cortex that represent different parts of the body. *See also* **Experience-dependent plasticity**; **Selective rearing**. (3)

Neural processing Operations that transform electrical signals within a network of neurons or that transform the response of individual neurons. (1, 3)

Neurogenesis The cycle of birth, development, and death of a neuron. This process occurs for the receptors for olfaction and taste. (15)

Neuron The structure that transmits electrical signals in the body. Key components of neurons are the cell body, dendrites, and the axon or nerve fiber. (2)

Neuropathic pain Pain caused by lesions or other damage to the nervous system. (14)

Neuropsychology The study of the behavioral effects of brain damage in humans. (4)

Neurotransmitter A chemical stored in synaptic vesicles that is released in response to a nerve impulse and has an excitatory or inhibitory effect on another neuron. (2)

Neutral point The wavelength at which a dichromat perceives gray. (9)

Nociceptive pain This type of pain, which serves as a warning of impending damage to the skin, is caused by activation of receptors in the skin called nociceptors. (14)

Nociceptor A fiber that responds to stimuli that are damaging to the skin. (14)

Noise-induced hearing loss A form of sensorineural hearing loss that occurs when loud noises cause degeneration of the hair cells. (11)

Noncorresponding points Two points, one on each retina, that would not overlap if the retinas were slid onto each other. Also called disparate points. (10)

Nontaster A person who cannot taste the compound phenylthiocarbamide (PTC). (15)

Nucleus of the solitary tract The nucleus in the brain stem that receives signals from the tongue, the mouth, and the larynx transmitted by the chorda tympani, glossopharyngeal, and vagus nerves. (15)

Object discrimination problem The behavioral task used in Ungerleider and Mishkin's experiment in which they provided evidence for the ventral, or *what*, visual processing stream. Monkeys were required to respond to an object with a particular shape. (4)

Oblique effect Enhanced sensitivity to vertically and horizontally oriented visual stimuli compared to obliquely oriented (slanted) stimuli. This effect has been demonstrated by measuring both perception and neural responding. (1)

Occipital lobe A lobe at the back of the cortex that is the site of the cortical receiving area for vision. (1, 3)

Occlusion Depth cue in which one object hides or partially hides another object from view, causing the hidden object to be perceived as being farther away. A monocular depth cue. (10)

Octave Tones that have frequencies that are binary multiples of each other (2, 4, etc.). For example, an 800-Hz tone is one octave above a 400-Hz tone. (11)

Ocular dominance The degree to which a neuron is influenced by stimulation of each eye. A neuron has a large amount of ocular dominance if it responds only to stimulation of one eye. There is no ocular dominance if the neuron responds equally to stimulation of both eyes. (4)

Ocular dominance column A column in the visual cortex that contains neurons that respond best to stimulation of the same eye. (4)

Oculomotor cue Depth cue that depends on our ability to sense the position of our eyes and the tension in our eye muscles. Accommodation and convergence are oculomotor cues. (10)

Odor map. *See* **Chemotopic map**. (15)

Odor object The source of an odor, such as coffee, bacon, a rose, or car exhaust. (15)

Odotoptic map. *See* **Chemotopic map**. (15)

Olfaction The sense of smell. Usually results from stimulation of receptors in the olfactory mucosa. (15)

Olfactometer A device that presents olfactory stimuli with great precision. (15)

Olfactory bulb The structure that receives signals directly from the olfactory receptors. The olfactory bulb contains glomeruli, which receive these signals from the receptors. (15)

Olfactory mucosa The region inside the nose that contains the receptors for the sense of smell. (15)

Olfactory receptor A protein string that responds to odor stimuli. (15)

Olfactory receptor neurons (OR Ns) Sensory neurons located in the olfactory mucosa that contain the olfactory receptors. (15)

Ommatidium A structure in the eye of the *Limulus* that contains a small lens, located directly over a visual receptor. The *Limulus* eye is made up of hundreds of these ommatidia. The *Limulus* eye has been used for research on lateral inhibition because its receptors are large enough so that stimulation can be applied to individual receptors. (3)

Onset time The time at which a specific tone starts. When two tones start at different times, this provides information that they are coming from different sources. (12)

Opioid A chemical such as opium, heroin, and other molecules with related structures that reduce pain and induce feelings of euphoria. (14)

Opponent neuron A neuron that has an excitatory response to wavelengths in one part of the spectrum and an inhibitory response to wavelengths in the other part of the spectrum. (9)

Opponent-process theory of color vision A theory originally proposed by Hering, which claimed that our perception of color is determined by the activity of two opponent mechanisms: a blue–yellow mechanism and a red–green mechanism. The responses to the two colors in each mechanism oppose each other, one being an excitatory response and the other an inhibitory response. In addition, this theory also includes a black–white mechanism, which is concerned with the perception of brightness. *See also* **Opponent neuron**. (9)

Optic array The structured pattern of light created by the presence of objects, surfaces, and textures in the environment. (8)

Optic ataxia A condition in which individuals with parietal lobe damage have trouble pointing to visual stimuli. (7)

Optic flow The flow of stimuli in the environment that occurs when an observer moves relative to the environment. Forward movement causes an expanding optic flow, whereas backward movement causes a contracting optic flow. Some researchers use the term *optic flow field* to refer to this flow. (7)

Optic nerve Bundle of nerve fibers that carry impulses from the retina to the lateral geniculate nucleus and other structures. Each optic nerve contains about 1 million ganglion cell fibers. (2)

Optical imaging A technique that has been used to measure the activity of large areas of the olfactory bulb by measuring the intensity of red light reflected from the bulb. (15)

Oral capture The condition in which sensations from both olfaction and taste are perceived as being located in the mouth. (15)

Orbitofrontal cortex An area in the frontal lobe, near the eyes, that receives signals originating in the olfactory receptors. Also known as the secondary olfactory cortex. (15)

Organ of Corti The major structure of the cochlear partition, containing the basilar membrane, the tectorial membrane, and the receptors for hearing. (11)

Organizing principles In Gestalt psychology, the rules that determine how elements in a scene become grouped together. (5)

Orientation column A column in the visual cortex that contains neurons with the same orientation preference. (4)

Orientation tuning curve A function relating the firing rate of a neuron to the orientation of the stimulus. (3)

Ossicles Three small bones in the middle ear that transmit vibrations from the outer to the inner ear. (11)

Outer ear The pinna and the auditory canal. (11)

Outer hair cells *See* **Hair cells, outer**. (11)

Outer segments Part of the rod and cone visual receptors that contain the light-sensitive visual pigment molecules. (2)

Oval window A small, membrane-covered hole in the cochlea that receives vibrations from the stapes. (11)

Overt attention Attention that involves looking directly at the attended object. (6)

Pacinian corpuscle (RA2 or PC) A receptor with a distinctive elliptical shape associated with RA2 mechanoreceptors. It transmits pressure to the nerve fiber inside it only at the beginning or end of a pressure stimulus, and is responsible for our perception of vibration and fine textures that are perceived when moving the fingers over a surface. (14)

Pain matrix The network of structures in the brain that are responsible for pain perception. (14)

Papillae Ridges and valleys on the tongue, some of which contain taste buds. There are four types of papillae: filiform, fungiform, foliate, and circumvallate. (15)

Parabelt area Auditory area in the temporal lobe that receives signals from the belt area. (12)

Parahippocampal place area (PPA) An area in the temporal lobe that is activated by indoor and outdoor scenes. (4)

Parietal lobe. A lobe at the top of the cortex that is the site of the cortical receiving area for touch and is the termination point of the dorsal (*where* or *how*) stream for visual processing. (1, 3)

Parietal reach region (PRR) A network of areas in the parietal cortex that contains neurons that are involved in reaching behavior. (7)

Partial color constancy A type of color constancy that occurs when changing an object's illumination causes a change in perception of the object's hue, but less change than would be expected based on the change in the wavelengths of light reaching the eye. Note that in complete color constancy, changing an object's illumination causes no change in the object's hue. (9)

Passive method (3-D TV) A method used to create 3-D television images. Polarized light is used to create left and right images—one image is polarized so its vibration is vertical, and the other is polarized so its vibration is horizontal. The TV is viewed through polarizing lenses, which let vertically polarized light into one eye and horizontally polarized light into the other eye, creating the disparity that results in three-dimensional perception. (10)

Passive touch A situation in which a person passively receives tactile stimulation. *See also* **Active touch**. (14)

Payoffs A system of rewards and punishments used to influence a participant's motivation in a signal detection experiment. (Appendix)

Penumbra The fuzzy border at the edge of a shadow. (9)

Perceived magnitude A perceptual measure of stimuli, such as light or sound, that indicates the magnitude of experience. (1)

Perception Conscious sensory experience. (1)

Perceptual capacity The resources a person has for carrying out perceptual tasks. (6)

Perceptual completion The perception of an object as extending behind occluding objects. (6)

Perceptual load The amount of a person's perceptual capacity needed to carry out a particular perceptual task. (6)

Perceptual organization The process by which small elements become perceptually grouped into larger objects. (5)

Perceptual process A sequence of steps leading from the environment to perception of a stimulus, recognition of the stimulus, and action with regard to the stimulus. (1)

Perceptual segregation Perceptual organization in which one object is seen as separate from other objects. (5)

Periodic tone A tone in which the waveform repeats. (11)

Periodicity pitch The constancy of a complex tone's pitch when the fundamental frequency and other lower harmonics are eliminated. *See also* **Effect of the missing fundamental**. (11)

Peripheral retina The area of retina outside the fovea. (2)

Permeability A property of a membrane that refers to the ability of molecules to pass through it. If the permeability to a molecule is high, the molecule can easily pass through the membrane. (2)

Persistence of vision A phenomenon in which perception of any stimulus persists for about 250 ms after the stimulus is physically terminated. (5)

Perspective convergence The perception that parallel lines in the distance converge as distance increases. (10)

PET *See* **Positron emission tomography (PET)**. (4)

Phantom limb A person's continued perception of a limb, such as an arm or a leg, even though that limb has been amputated. (14)

Phase locking Firing of auditory neurons in synchrony with the phase of an auditory stimulus. (11)

Phenomenological method Method of determining the relationship between stimuli and perception in which the observer describes what he or she perceives. (1)

Pheromone Chemical signal released by an individual that affects the physiology and behavior of other individuals. (15)

Phoneme The shortest segment of speech that, if changed, changes the meaning of a word. (13)

Phonemic restoration effect An effect that occurs in speech perception when listeners perceive a phoneme in a word even though the acoustic signal of that phoneme is obscured by another sound, such as white noise or a cough. (13)

Phonetic boundary The voice onset time when perception changes from one speech category to another in a categorical perception experiment. (13)

Physical regularities Regularly occurring physical properties of the environment. For example, there are more vertical and horizontal orientations in the environment than oblique (angled) orientations. (5)

Physiological approach to perception Analyzing perception by determining how a person's perception is related to physiological processes that are occurring within the person. This approach focuses on determining the relationship between stimuli and physiological responding and between physiological responding and perception. (1)

Pictorial cue Monocular depth cue, such as overlap, relative height, and relative size, that can be depicted in pictures. (10)

Pinna The part of the ear that is visible on the outside of the head. (11)

Piriform cortex An area under the temporal lobe that receives signals from glomeruli in the olfactory bulb. Also called the primary olfactory cortex. (15)

Pitch The quality of sound, ranging from low to high, that is most closely associated with the frequency of a tone. (11)

Pitch neurons Neurons that respond to stimuli associated with a specific pitch. These neurons fire to the pitch of a complex tone even if the first harmonic or other harmonics of the tone are not present. (11)

Place theory of hearing The proposal that the frequency of a sound is indicated by the place along the organ of Corti at which nerve firing is highest. Modern place theory is based on Békésy's traveling wave theory of hearing. (11)

Placebo A substance that a person believes will relieve symptoms such as pain but that contains no chemicals that actually act on these symptoms. (14)

Placebo effect A relief from symptoms resulting from a substance that has no pharmacological effect. *See also* **Placebo**. (14)

Point-light walker A biological motion stimulus created by placing lights at a number of places on a person's body and having an observer view the moving-light stimulus that results as the person moves in the dark. (8)

Ponzo illusion An illusion of size in which two objects of equal size that are positioned between two converging lines appear to be different in size. Also called the railroad track illusion. (10)

Positron emission tomography (PET) A brain mapping technique that is used in awake human subjects to determine which brain areas are activated by various tasks. (4)

Power function A mathematical function of the form $P = KS^n$, where P is perceived magnitude, K is a constant, S is the stimulus intensity, and n is an exponent. (1)

Pragnanz, principle of A Gestalt principle of perceptual organization that states that every stimulus pattern is seen in such a way that the resulting structure is as simple as possible. Also called the *principle of good figure* or the *principle of simplicity*. (5)

Preattentive stage (of perceptual processing) An automatic and rapid stage of processing, proposed by Treisman's feature integration theory, during which a stimulus is decomposed into individual features. (6)

Precedence effect The effect that occurs when two identical or very similar sounds reach a listener's ears separated by a time interval of less than about 50 to 100 ms, and the listener hears the first sound that reaches his or her ears. (12)

Precueing A procedure in which a cue stimulus is presented to direct an observer's attention to a specific location where a test stimulus is likely to be presented. This procedure was used by Posner to show that attention enhances the processing of a stimulus presented at the cued location. (6)

Preferential looking technique A technique used to measure perception in infants. Two stimuli are presented, and the infant's looking behavior is monitored for the amount of time the infant spends viewing each stimulus. (2)

Presbycusis A form of sensorineural hearing loss that occurs as a function of age and is usually associated with a decrease in the ability to hear high frequencies. Since this loss also appears to be related to exposure to environmental sounds, it is also called *sociocusis*. (11)

Presbyopia The inability of the eye to accommodate due to a hardening of the lens and a weakening of the ciliary muscles. It occurs as people get older. (2)

Primary auditory cortex (A1) An area of the temporal lobe that receives signals via nerve fibers from the medial geniculate nucleus in the thalamus. (12)

Primary olfactory area A small area under the temporal lobe that receives signals from glomeruli in the olfactory bulb. Also called the piriform cortex. (15)

Primary receiving areas Areas of the cerebral cortex that first receive most of the signals initiated by a sense's receptors. For example, the occipital cortex is the site of the primary receiving area for vision, and the temporal lobe is the site of the primary receiving area for hearing. (1)

Principle of common fate *See* **Common fate, principle of**. (5)

Principle of common region *See* **Common region, principle of**. (5)

Principle of good continuation *See* **Good continuation, principle of**. (5)

Principle of good figure *See* **Pragnanz, principle of**. (5)

Principle of pragnanz *See* **Pragnanz, principle of**. (5)

Principle of proximity (nearness) *See* **Proximity, principle of**. (5)

Principle of representation *See* **Representation, principle of**. (1)

Principle of similarity *See* **Similarity, principle of**. (5)

Principle of simplicity *See* **Pragnanz, principle of**. (5)

Principle of synchrony *See* **Synchrony, principle of**. (5)

Principle of transformation *See* **Transformation, principle of**. (1)

Principle of uniform connectedness *See* **Uniform connectedness, principle of**. (5)

Propagated response A response, such as a nerve impulse, that travels all the way down the nerve fiber without decreasing in amplitude. (2)

Proprioception The sensing of the position of the limbs. (14)

Prosopagnosia A form of visual agnosia in which the person can't recognize faces. (3)

Protanopia A form of red–green dichromatism caused by a lack of the long-wavelength cone pigment. (9)

Proust effect The elicitation of memories through taste and olfaction. Named for Marcel Proust, who described how the taste and smell of a tea-soaked madeleine cake unlocked childhood memories. (15)

Proximity, principle of A Gestalt principle of perceptual organization that states that things that are near to each other appear to be grouped together. Also called the law of nearness. (5)

Psychophysical approach to perception Analyzing perception by determining how a person's perception is related to stimuli in the environment. This approach focuses on determining the relationship between stimuli in the environment and perceptual responding. (1)

Psychophysics Traditionally, the term *psychophysics* refers to quantitative methods for measuring the relationship between properties of the stimulus and the subject's experience. In this book, all methods that are used to determine the relationship between stimuli and perception will be broadly referred to as pychophysical methods. (1)

Pupil The opening through which light reflected from objects in the environment enters the eye. (2)

Pure tone A tone with pressure changes that can be described by a single sine wave. (11)

Purkinje shift The shift from cone spectral sensitivity to rod spectral sensitivity that takes place during dark adaptation. *See also* **Spectral sensitivity**. (2)

Random-dot stereogram A pair of stereoscopic images made up of random dots. When one section of this pattern is shifted slightly in one direction, the resulting disparity causes the shifted section to appear above or below the rest of the pattern when the patterns are viewed in a stereoscope. (10)

Rapidly adapting (RA) receptor Mechanoreceptors that respond with bursts of firing just at the onset and offset of a pressure stimulus. The Meissner corpuscle and the Pacinian corpuscle are rapidly adapting receptors. (14)

Ratio principle A principle stating that two areas that reflect different amounts of light will have the same perceived lightness if the ratios of their intensities to the intensities of their surroundings are the same. (9)

Rat–man demonstration The demonstration in which presentation of a "ratlike" or "manlike" picture influences an observer's perception of a second picture, which can be interpreted either as a rat or as a man. This demonstration illustrates an effect of top-down processing on perception. (1)

Reaction time The time between presentation of a stimulus and an observer's or listener's response to the stimulus. Reaction time is often used in experiments as a measure of speed of processing. (1)

Real motion The physical movement of a stimulus. Contrasts with *apparent motion*. (8)

Real-motion neuron Neuron in the monkey's cortex that responds when movement of an image across the retina is caused by movement of a stimulus, but does not respond when movement across the retina is caused by movement of the eyes. (8)

Receiver operating characteristic (ROC) curve A graph in which the results of a signal detection experiment are plotted as the proportion of hits versus the proportion of false alarms for a number of different response criteria. (Appendix)

Receptive field A neuron's receptive field is the area on the receptor surface (the retina for vision; the skin for touch) that, when stimulated, affects the firing of that neuron. (3)

Receptor A sensory receptor is a neuron sensitive to environmental energy that changes this energy into electrical signals in the nervous system. (1)

Receptor site Small area on the postsynaptic neuron that is sensitive to specific neurotransmitters. (2)

Recognition The ability to place an object in a category that gives it meaning—for example, recognizing a particular red object as a tomato. (1)

Recognition profile The pattern of olfactory activation for an odorant, indicating which ORNs (olfactory receptor neurons) are activated by the odorant. (15)

Recognition threshold *See* **Threshold, recognition**. (15)

Reflectance The percentage of light reflected from a surface. (9)

Reflectance curve A plot showing the percentage of light reflected from an object versus wavelength. (9)

Reflectance edge An edge between two areas where the reflectance of two surfaces changes. (9)

Refractive myopia Myopia (nearsightedness) in which the cornea and/or the lens bends the light too much. *See also* **Axial myopia**. (2)

Refractory period The time period of about 1/1,000th of a second that a nerve fiber needs to recover from conducting a nerve impulse. No new nerve impulses can be generated in the fiber until the refractory period is over. (2)

Regularities in the environment Characteristics of the environment that occur regularly and in many different situations. (5)

Reichardt detector A neural circuit that results in neurons firing to movement in one direction. Excitation and inhibition are arranged so that movement in one direction creates inhibition that reduces or eliminates neural responding, whereas movement in the opposite direction creates excitation that enhances neural responding. (8)

Relative disparity The difference between two objects' absolute disparities. (10)

Relative height A monocular depth cue. Objects that have bases below the horizon appear to be farther away when they are higher in the field of view. Objects that have bases above the horizon appear to be farther away when they are lower in the field of view. (10)

Relative size A cue for depth perception. When two objects are of equal size, the one that is farther away will take up less of the field of view. (10)

Representation, principle of A principle of perception that everything a person perceives is based not on direct contact with stimuli but on representations of stimuli on the receptors and in the person's nervous system. (1)

Representational momentum Occurs when motion depicted in a still picture continues in an observer's mind. (8)

Resonance A mechanism that enhances the intensity of certain frequencies because of the reflection of sound waves in a closed tube. Resonance in the auditory canal enhances frequencies between about 2,000 and 5,000 Hz. (11)

Resonant frequency The frequency that is most strongly enhanced by resonance. The resonance frequency of a closed tube is determined by the length of the tube. (11)

Response compression The result when doubling the physical intensity of a stimulus less than doubles the subjective magnitude of the stimulus. (1)

Response criterion In a signal detection experiment, the subjective magnitude of a stimulus above which the participant will indicate that the stimulus is present. (1)

Response expansion The result when doubling the physical intensity of a stimulus more than doubles the subjective magnitude of the stimulus. (1)

Resting potential The difference in charge between the inside and the outside of the nerve fiber when the fiber is not conducting electrical signals. Most nerve fibers have resting potentials of about −70 mV, which means the inside of the fiber is negative relative to the outside. (2)

Retina A complex network of cells that covers the inside back of the eye. These cells include the receptors, which generate an electrical signal in response to light, as well as the horizontal, bipolar, amacrine, and ganglion cells. (2)

Retinitis pigmentosa A retinal disease that causes a gradual loss of vision, beginning in the peripheral retina. (2)

Retinotopic map A map on a structure in the visual system, such as the lateral geniculate nucleus or the cortex, that indicates locations on the structure that correspond to locations on the retina. In retinotopic maps, locations adjacent to each other on the retina are usually represented by locations that are adjacent to each other on the structure. (4)

Retronasal route The opening from the oral cavity, through the nasal pharnyx, into the nasal cavity. This route is the basis for the way smell combines with taste to create flavor. (15)

Reverberation time The time it takes for a sound produced in an enclosed space to decrease to 1/1,000th of its original pressure. (12)

Reversible figure–ground A figure–ground pattern that perceptually reverses as it is viewed, so that the figure becomes the ground and the ground becomes the figure. The best-known reversible figure–ground pattern is Rubin's vase–face pattern. (5)

Rhythmic pattern In music, the series of changes across time (a mixture of shorter and longer notes) in a temporal pattern. (12)

Rising phase of the action potential In the axon, or nerve fiber, the decrease in negativity from −70 mV to +40 mV (the peak action potential level) that occurs during the action potential. This increase is caused by an inflow of Na^+ ions into the axon. (2)

Rod A cylinder-shaped receptor in the retina that is responsible for vision at low levels of illumination. (2)

Rod–cone break The point on the dark adaptation curve at which vision shifts from cone vision to rod vision. (3)

Rod monochromat A person who has a retina in which the only functioning receptors are rods. (3)

Rod spectral sensitivity curve The curve plotting visual sensitivity versus wavelength, for rod vision. This function is typically measured when the eye is dark adapted by a test light presented to the peripheral retina. (2)

Ruffini cylinder A receptor structure in the skin associated with slowly adapting fibers. It has been proposed that the Ruffini cylinder is involved in perceiving "stretching." (14)

Saccadic eye movement Rapid eye movement between fixations that occurs when scanning a scene. (6)

Saliency map A "map" of a visual display that takes into account characteristics of the display such as color, contrast, and orientation that are associated with capturing attention. (6)

Same-object advantage The faster responding that occurs when enhancement spreads within an object. Faster reaction times occur when a target is located within the object that is receiving the subject's attention, even if the subject is looking at another place within the object. (6)

Saturation (color) The relative amount of whiteness in a chromatic color. The less whiteness a color contains, the more saturated it is. (9)

Scale illusion An illusion that occurs when successive notes of a scale are presented alternately to the left and right ears. Even though each ear receives notes that jump up and down in frequency, smoothly ascending or descending scales are heard in each ear. Also called melodic channeling. (12)

Scene A view of a real-world environment that contains (a) background elements and (b) multiple objects that are organized in a meaningful way relative to each other and the background. (5)

Scene schema An observer's knowledge about what is contained in typical scenes. An observer's attention is affected by knowledge of what is usually found in the scene. (6)

Scene statistics The probability of various things occurring in the environment. (6)

Secondary olfactory area An area in the frontal lobe, near the eyes, that receives signals originating in the olfactory receptors. Also known as the orbitofrontal cortex. (15)

Secondary somatosensory cortex (S2) The area in the parietal lobe next to the primary somatosensory area (S1) that processes neural signals related to touch, temperature, and pain. (14)

Segregation The process of separating one area or object from another. *See also* **Figure–ground segregation**. (5)

Selective adaptation A procedure in which a person or animal is selectively exposed to one stimulus, and then the effect of this exposure is assessed by testing with a wide range of stimuli. Typically, sensitivity to the exposed stimulus is decreased. (3)

Selective rearing A procedure in which animals are reared in special environments. An example of selective rearing is the experiment in which kittens were reared in an environment of vertical stripes to determine the effect on orientation selectivity of cortical neurons. (3)

Selective reflection When an object reflects some wavelengths of the spectrum more than others. (9)

Selective transmission When some wavelengths pass through visually transparent objects or substances and others do not. Selective transmission is associated with the perception of chromatic color. *See also* **Selective reflection**. (9)

Self-produced information Generally, environmental information that is produced by actions of the observer. An example is optic flow, which occurs as a result of a person's movement and which, in turn, provides information that can be used to guide that movement. (7)

Semantic encoding A method for analyzing the patterns of voxel activation recorded from visual areas of an observer's brain, based on the relationship between voxel activation and the meaning or category of a scene. (5)

Semantic regularities Characteristics associated with the functions associated with different types of scenes. These characteristics are learned from experience. For example, most people are aware of the kinds of activities and objects that are usually associated with kitchens. (5)

Sensations Elementary elements that, according to the structuralists, combine to create perceptions. (5)

Sensory component of pain Pain perception described with terms such as *throbbing, prickly, hot,* or *dull*. *See also* **Affective (emotional) component of pain**. (14)

Sensory receptors Cells specialized to respond to environmental energy, with each sensory system's receptors specialized to respond to a specific type of energy. (1, 2)

Sensory-specific satiety The effect on perception of the odor associated with food eaten to satiety (the state of being satiated or "full"). For example, after eating bananas until satiety, the pleasantness rating for vanilla decreased slightly (but was still positive), but the rating for banana odor decreased much more and became negative. (15)

Shadowing Listeners' repetition aloud of what they hear as they are hearing it. (13)

Shortest path constraint In the perception of apparent motion, the principle that apparent movement tends to occur along the shortest path between two stimuli. (8)

Signal The stimulus presented to a participant. A concept in signal detection theory. (Appendix)

Signal detection theory A theory stating that the detection of a stimulus depends both on the participant's sensitivity to the stimulus and on the participant's response criterion. (1)

Signal-to-noise (S/N) ratio The level of a sound signal in decibels minus the level of background noise in decibels. (12)

Similarity, principle of A Gestalt principle stating that similar things appear to be grouped together. (5)

Simple cortical cell A neuron in the visual cortex that responds best to bars of a particular orientation. (3)

Simplicity, principle of *See* **Pragnanz, law of**. (5)

Simultaneous color contrast *See* **Simultaneous contrast**. (9)

Simultaneous contrast The effect that occurs when surrounding one color with another changes the appearance of the surrounded color. Occurs for chromatic and achromatic stimuli. (3, 9)

Single-opponent neuron Neurons that increase firing to long wavelengths presented to the center of the receptive field and decrease firing to short wavelengths presented to the surround (or vice versa). (9)

Size constancy Occurs when the size of an object is perceived to remain the same even when it is viewed from different distances. (10)

Size–distance scaling A hypothesized mechanism that helps maintain size constancy by taking an object's perceived distance into account. According to this mechanism, an object's perceived size, S, is determined by multiplying the size of the retinal image, R, times the object's perceived distance, D. (10)

Slowly adapting (SA) receptor Mechanoreceptors located in the epidermis and the dermis that respond with prolonged firing to continued pressure. The Merkel receptor and the Ruffini cylinder are slowly adapting mechanoreceptors. (14)

Somatosensory receiving area (S1) An area in the parietal lobe that receives inputs from the skin and the viscera associated with somatic senses such as touch, temperature, and pain. *See also* **Secondary somatosensory cortex (S2)**. (14)

Somatosensory system The system that includes the cutaneous senses (senses involving the skin), proprioception (the sense of position of the limbs), and kinesthesis (sense of movement of the limbs). (14)

Sound (perceptual) The perceptual experience of hearing. The statement "I hear a sound" is using *sound* in that sense. (11)

Sound (physical) The physical stimulus for hearing. The statement "The sound's level was 10 dB" is using *sound* in that sense. (11)

Sound level The pressure of a sound stimulus, expressed in decibels. *See also* **Sound pressure level (SPL)**. (11)

Sound pressure level (SPL) A designation used to indicate that the reference pressure used for calculating a tone's decibel rating is set at 20 micropascals, near the threshold in the most sensitive frequency range for hearing. (11)

Sound spectrogram A plot showing the pattern of intensities and frequencies of a speech stimulus. (13)

Sound wave Pattern of pressure changes in a medium. Most of the sounds we hear are due to pressure changes in the air, although sound can be transmitted through water and solids as well. (11)

Sparse coding The idea that a particular object is represented by the firing of a relatively small number of neurons. (3)

Spatial attention Attention to a specific location. (6)

Spatial cue In tactile perception, information about the texture of a surface that is determined by the size, shape, and distribution of surface elements such as bumps and grooves. (14)

Spatial organization How different locations in the environment and on the receptors are represented in the brain. (4)

Specificity coding Type of neural code in which different perceptions are signaled by activity in specific neurons. *See also* **Distributed coding**. (3)

Spectral cue In hearing, the distribution of frequencies reaching the ear that are associated with specific locations of a sound. The differences in frequencies are caused by interaction of sound with the listener's head and pinnae. (12)

Spectral sensitivity The sensitivity of visual receptors to different parts of the visible spectrum. *See also* **Spectral sensitivity curve**. (2)

Spectral sensitivity curve The function relating a subject's sensitivity to light to the wavelength of the light. The spectral sensitivity curves for rod and cone vision indicate that the rods and cones are maximally sensitive at 500 nm and 560 nm, respectively. *See also* **Purkinje shift**. (2)

Speech segmentation The process of perceiving individual words from the continuous flow of the speech signal. (13)

Spinothalamic pathway One of the nerve pathways in the spinal cord that conducts nerve impulses from the skin to the somatosensory area of the thalamus. (14)

Spontaneous activity Nerve firing that occurs in the absence of environmental stimulation. (2)

Stapes The last of the three ossicles in the middle ear. It receives vibrations from the incus and transmits these vibrations to the oval window of the inner ear. (11)

Statistical learning The process of learning about transitional probabilities and other characteristics of the environment. Statistical learning for properties of language has been demonstrated in young infants. (13)

Stereopsis The impression of depth that results from binocular disparity—the difference in the position of images of the same object on the retinas of the two eyes. (10)

Stereoscope A device that presents pictures to the left and the right eyes so that the binocular disparity a person would experience when viewing an actual scene is duplicated. The result is a convincing illusion of depth. (10)

Stereoscopic depth perception The perception of depth that is created by input from both eyes. *See also* **Binocular disparity**. (10)

Stereoscopic vision Two-eyed depth perception involving mechanisms that take into account differences in the images formed on the left and right eyes. (10)

Stevens's power law A law concerning the relationship between the physical intensity of a stimulus and the perception of the subjective magnitude of the stimulus. The law states that $P = KS^n$, where P is perceived magnitude, K is a constant, S is the stimulus intensity, and n is an exponent. (1)

Stimulus salience Characteristics such as bright colors, high contrast, and highly visible orientations that cause stimuli to stand out and therefore attract attention. (6)

Strabismus Misalignment of the eyes, such as crossed-eyes or walleyes (outward looking eyes), in which the visual system suppresses vision in one of the eyes to avoid double vision, so the person sees the world with only one eye at a time. (10)

Striate cortex The visual receiving area of the cortex, located in the occipital lobe. (3)

Structural encoding A method for analyzing the patterns of voxel activation recorded from visual areas of an observer's brain, based on the relationship between voxel activation and structural characteristics of a scene, such as lines, contrasts, shapes, and textures. (5)

Structuralism The approach to psychology, prominent in the late 19th and early 20th centuries, that postulated that perceptions result from the summation of many elementary sensations. The Gestalt approach to perception was, in part, a reaction to structuralism. (5)

Subcortical structure Structure below the cerebral cortex. For example, the superior colliculus is a subcortical structure in the visual system. The cochlear nucleus and superior olivary nucleus are among the subcortical structures in the auditory system. (12)

Subtractive color mixture. *See* **Color mixture, subtractive**. (9)

Superior colliculus An area in the brain that is involved in controlling eye movements and other visual behaviors. This area receives about 10 percent of the ganglion cell fibers that leave the eye in the optic nerve. (3)

Superior olivary nucleus A nucleus along the auditory pathway from the cochlea to the auditory cortex. The superior olivary nucleus receives inputs from the cochlear nucleus. (12)

Supertaster A person who is especially sensitive to 6-*n*-propyl-thiouracil (PROP), a bitter substance. (15)

Surface texture The visual and tactile quality of a physical surface created by peaks and valleys. (14)

Synapse A small space between the end of one neuron (the presynaptic neuron) and the cell body of another neuron (the postsynaptic neuron). (2)

Synchrony, principle of A modern principle of perceptual organization that states that visual events that occur at the same time will be perceived as belonging together. (5)

Synesthesia A condition in which stimulation of one modality (such as vision) results in an experience in another modality (such as touch). For example a person with synesthesia who observes another person being touched may experience touch on the same part of his or her own body. (14)

Tactile acuity The smallest details that can be detected on the skin. (14)

Task-irrelevant stimuli Stimuli that do not provide information relevant to the task at hand. (6)

Taste bud A structure located within papillae on the tongue that contains the taste cells. (15)

Taste cell Cell located in taste buds that causes the transduction of chemical to electrical energy when chemicals contact receptor sites or channels located at the tip of this cell. (15)

Taste pore An opening in the taste bud through which the tips of taste cells protrude. When chemicals enter a taste pore, they stimulate the taste cells and result in transduction. (15)

Taster A person who can taste the compound phenylthiocarbamide (PTC). (15)

Tectorial membrane A membrane that stretches the length of the cochlea and is located directly over the hair cells. Vibrations of the cochlear partition cause the tectorial membrane to bend the hair cells by rubbing against them. (11)

Temporal coding The connection between the frequency of a sound stimulus and the timing of the auditory nerve fiber firing. (11)

Temporal cue In tactile perception, information about the texture of a surface that is determined by the rate of vibrations that occur as we move our fingers across the surface. (14)

Temporal lobe A lobe on the side of the cortex that is the site of the cortical receiving area for hearing and the termination point for the ventral, or *what*, stream for visual processing.

A number of areas in the temporal lobe, such as the fusiform face area and the extrastriate body area, serve functions related to perceiving and recognizing objects. (1, 3)

Texture gradient The visual pattern formed by a regularly textured surface that extends away from the observer. This pattern provides information for distance because the elements in a texture gradient appear smaller as distance from the observer increases. (10)

Theory of unconscious inference The idea proposed by Helmholtz that some of our perceptions are the result of unconscious assumptions that we make about the environment. *See also* **Likelihood principle**. (5)

Threshold, absolute The minimum stimulus energy necessary for an observer to detect a stimulus. (1)

Threshold, detection The minimum amount of energy that can be detected. The detection threshold for smell is the lowest concentration at which an odorant can be detected. This threshold is distinguished from the recognition threshold, which requires a higher concentration of odorant. (15)

Threshold, difference The minimal detectable difference between two stimuli. (1)

Threshold, recognition For smell, the concentration at which the quality of an odor can be recognized. (15)

Tiling The adjacent (and often overlapping) location columns working together to cover the entire visual field (similar to covering a floor with tiles). (4)

Timbre The quality that distinguishes between two tones that sound different even though they have the same loudness, pitch, and duration. Differences in timbre are illustrated by the sounds made by different musical instruments. (11)

Tip links Structures at the tops of the cilia of auditory hair cells, which stretch or slacken as the cilia move, causing ion channels to open or close. (11)

Tone chroma The perceptual similarity of notes separated by one or more octaves. (11)

Tone height The increase in pitch that occurs as frequency is increased. (11)

Tonotopic map An ordered map of frequencies created by the responding of neurons within structures in the auditory system. There is a tonotopic map of neurons along the length of the cochlea, with neurons at the apex responding best to low frequencies and neurons at the base responding best to high frequencies. (11)

Top-down processing Processing that starts with the analysis of high-level information, such as the knowledge a person brings to a situation. Also called knowledge-based processing. Distinguished from bottom-up, or data-based processing, which is based on incoming data. (1)

Transduction In the senses, the transformation of environmental energy into electrical energy. For example, the retinal receptors transduce light energy into electrical energy. (1, 2)

Transformation, principle of A principle of perception that stimuli and responses created by stimuli are transformed, or changed, between the environmental stimulus and perception. (1)

Transitional probabilities In language, the chances that one sound will follow another sound. Every language has transitional probabilities for different sounds. Part of learning a language involves learning about the transitional probabilities in that language. (13)

Transmission cell (T-cell) According to gate control theory, the cell that receives + and – inputs from cells in the dorsal horn. T-cell activity determines the perception of pain. (14)

Traveling wave In the auditory system, vibration of the basilar membrane in which the peak of the vibration travels from the base of the membrane to its apex. (11)

Trichromat A person with normal color vision. Trichromats can match any wavelength in the spectrum by mixing three other wavelengths in various proportions. (9)

Trichromatic theory of color vision A theory proposing that our perception of color is determined by the ratio of activity in three receptor mechanisms with different spectral sensitivities. (9)

Tritanopia A form of dichromatism thought to be caused by a lack of the short-wavelength cone pigment. (9)

Tuning curve, frequency *See* **Frequency tuning curve**. (11)

Tuning curve, orientation *See* **Orientation tuning curve**. (4)

2-deoxyglucose technique A procedure that involves injecting a radioactive 2-deoxyglucose (2DG) molecule into an animal and exposing the animal to oriented stimuli. The 2DG is taken up by neurons that respond to the orientation. This procedure is used to visualize orientation columns in the cortex. (15)

Two-flash illusion An illusion that occurs when one flash of light is presented, accompanied by two rapidly presented tones. Presentation of the two tones causes the observer to perceive two flashes of light. (12)

Two-point threshold The smallest separation between two points on the skin that is perceived as two points; a measure of acuity on the skin. *See also* **Grating acuity**. (14)

Tympanic membrane A membrane at the end of the auditory canal that vibrates in response to vibrations of the air and transmits these vibrations to the ossicles in the middle ear. (11)

Uniform connectedness, principle of A modern Gestalt principle that states that connected regions of a visual stimulus are perceived as a single unit. (5)

Unilateral dichromat A person who has dichromatic vision in one eye and trichromatic vision in the other eye. People with this condition (which is extremely rare) have been tested to determine what colors a dichromats perceive by asking them to compare the perceptions they experience with their dichromatic eye and their trichromatic eye. (9)

Ventral pathway Pathway that conducts signals from the striate cortex to the temporal lobe. Also called the *what* pathway because it is involved in recognizing objects. (4)

Ventriloquism effect *See* **Visual capture**. (12)

Ventrolateral nucleus Nucleus in the thalamus that receives signals from the cutaneous system. (14)

Vestibular system The mechanism in the inner ear that is responsible for balance and sensing the position of the body. (12)

Video microscopy A technique that has been used to take pictures of papillae and taste buds on the tongue. (15)

Viewpoint invariance The condition in which object properties don't change when viewed from different angles. Responsible for our ability to recognize objects when viewed from different angles. (5)

Visible light The band of electromagnetic energy that activates the visual system and that, therefore, can be perceived. For humans, visible light has wavelengths between 400 and 700 nanometers. (2)

Visual acuity The ability to resolve small details. (2)

Visual angle The angle of an object relative to an observer's eyes. This angle can be determined by extending two lines from the eye—one to one end of an object and the other to the other end of the object. Because an object's visual angle is always determined relative to an observer, its visual angle changes as the distance between the object and the observer changes. (10)

Visual capture When sound is heard coming from a seen location, even though it is actually originating somewhere else. Also called the ventriloquism effect. (12)

Visual direction strategy A strategy used by moving observers to reach a destination by keeping their body oriented toward the target. (7)

Visual evoked potential An electrical response to visual stimulation recorded by the placement of disk electrodes on the back of the head. This potential reflects the activity of a large population of neurons in the visual cortex. (2)

Visual form agnosia The inability to recognize objects. (1)

Visual masking stimulus A visual pattern that, when presented immediately after a visual stimulus, decreases a person's ability to perceive the stimulus. This stops the persistence of vision and therefore limits the effective duration of the stimulus. (5)

Visual pigment A light-sensitive molecule contained in the rod and cone outer segments. The reaction of this molecule to light results in the generation of an electrical response in the receptors. (1, 2)

Visual pigment bleaching The change in the color of a visual pigment that occurs when visual pigment molecules are isomerized by exposure to light. (2)

Visual pigment regeneration Occurs after the visual pigment's two components—opsin and retinal—have become separated due to the action of light. Regeneration, which occurs in the dark, involves a rejoining of these two components to reform the visual pigment molecule. This process depends on enzymes located in the pigment epithelium. (2)

Visual receiving area The area of the occipital lobe where signals from the retina and LGN first reach the cortex. (3)

Visual scanning Moving the eyes to focus attention on different locations on objects or in scenes. (6)

Visual search A procedure in which a person's task is to find a particular element in a display that contains a number of elements. (1)

Visuomotor grip cell A neuron that initially responds when a specific object is seen, and then also responds as a hand grasps the same object. (7)

Voice cells Neurons in the temporal lobe that respond more strongly to same-species voices than to calls of other animals or to "non-voice" sounds. (13)

Voice onset time (VOT) In speech production, the time delay between the beginning of a sound and the beginning of the vibration of the vocal chords. (13)

Waterfall illusion An aftereffect of movement that occurs after viewing a stimulus moving in one direction, such as a waterfall. Viewing the waterfall makes other objects appear to move in the opposite direction. *See also* **Movement aftereffect**. (8)

Wavelength For light energy, the distance between one peak of a light wave and the next peak. (2)

Wayfinding The process of navigating through the environment. Wayfinding involves perceiving objects in the environment, remembering objects and their relation to the overall scene, and knowing when to turn and in what direction. (7)

Weber fraction The ratio of the difference threshold to the value of the standard stimulus in Weber's law. (1)

Weber's law A law stating that the ratio of the difference threshold (DL) to the value of the stimulus (S) is constant. According to this relationship, doubling the value of a stimulus will cause a doubling of the difference threshold. The ratio DL/S is called the Weber fraction. (1)

Wernicke's aphasia An inability to comprehend words or arrange sounds into coherent speech, caused by damage to Wernicke's area. (13)

Wernicke's area An area in the temporal lobe involved in speech perception. Damage to this area causes Wernicke's aphasia, which is characterized by difficulty in understanding speech. (13)

What pathway *See* **Ventral pathway**. (4)

Where pathway *See* **Dorsal pathway**. (4)

White's illusion A display in which two rectangles are perceived as differing in lightness even though they both reflect the same amount of light and even though the rectangle that is perceived as lighter receives more lateral inhibition than the one perceived as darker. (3)

Word deafness Occurs in the most extreme form of Wernicke's aphasia, when a person cannot recognize words, even though the ability to hear pure tones remains intact. (13)

Young-Helmholtz theory of color vision *See* **Trichromatic theory of color vision**. (9)

References

Abramov, I., & Gordon, J. (1994). Color appearance: On seeing red, or yellow, or green, or blue. *Annual Review of Psychology, 45,* 451–485.

Abramov, I., Gordon, J., Hendrickson, A., Hainline, L., Dobson, V., & LaBossiere. (1982). The retina of the newborn human infant. *Science, 217,* 265–267.

Ache, B. W. (1991). Phylogeny of smell and taste. In T. V. Getchell, R. L. Doty, L. M. Bartoshuk, & J. B. Snow (Eds.), *Smell and taste in health and disease* (pp. 3–18). New York: Raven Press.

Ackerman, D. (1990). *A natural history of the senses.* New York: Vintage Books.

Acoustical Society of America. (2000). *Classroom acoustics.* Melville, NY: Author.

Addams, R. (1834). An account of a peculiar optical phenomenon seen after having looked at a moving body. *London and Edinburgh Philosophical Magazine and Journal of Science, 5,* 373–374.

Adelson, E. H. (1993). Perceptual organization and the judgment of brightness. *Science, 262,* 2042–2044.

Adelson, E. H. (1999). Light perception and lightness illusions. In M. Gazzaniga (Ed.), *The new cognitive neurosciences* (pp. 339–351). Cambridge, MA: MIT Press.

Aguirre, G. K., Zarahn, E., & D'Esposito, M. (1998). An area within human ventral cortex sensitive to "building" stimuli: Evidence and implications. *Neuron, 21,* 373–383.

Alain, C., Arnott, S. R., Hevenor, S., Graham, S., & Grady, C. L. (2001). "What" and "where" in the human auditory system. *Proceedings of the National Academy of Sciences, 98,* 12301–12306.

Alain, C., McDonald, K. L., Kovacevic, N., & McIntosh, A. R. (2009). Spatiotemporal analysis of auditory "what" and "where" working memory. *Cerebral Cortex, 19,* 305–314.

Alpern, M., Kitahara, K., & Krantz, D. H. (1983). Perception of color in unilateral tritanopia. *Journal of Physiology, 335,* 683–697.

Amanzio, M., Pollo, A., Maggi, G., & Benedetti, F. (2001). Response variability to analgesics: A role for non-specific activation of endogenous opioids. *Pain, 90,* 205–215.

Amso, D. (2010). Perceptual development: Attention. In B. Goldstein (Ed.), *Encyclopedia of perception* (pp. 735–738). Thousand Oaks, CA: Sage.

Anderson, B. A., Laurent, P. A., & Yantis, S. (2011). Value-driven attentional capture. *Proceedings of the National Academy of Sciences, 108,* 10367–10371.

Appelle, S. (1972). Perception and discrimination as a function of stimulus orientation: The "oblique effect" in man and animals. *Psychological Bulletin, 78,* 266–278.

Arbib, M. A. (2001). The mirror system hypothesis for the language-ready brain. In A. Cangelosi & D. Parisi (Eds.), *Computational approaches to the evolution of language and communication.* Berlin: Springer Verlag.

Arzi, A., & Sobel, N. (2011). Olfactory perception as a compass for olfactory and neural maps. *Trends in Cognitive Sciences, 10,* 537–545.

Aslin, R. N. (1977). Development of binocular fixation in human infants. *Journal of Experimental Child Psychology, 23,* 133–150.

Attneave, F., & Olson, R. K. (1971). Pitch as a medium: A new approach to psychophysical scaling. *American Journal of Psychology, 84,* 147–166.

Avenanti, A., Bueti, D., Galati, G., & Aglioti, S. M. (2005). Transcranial magnetic stimulation highlights the sensorimotor side of empathy for pain. *Nature Neuroscience, 8,* 955–960.

Azzopardi, P., & Cowey, A. (1993). Preferential representation of the fovea in the primary visual cortex. *Nature, 361,* 719–721.

Baars, B. J. (2001). The conscious access hypothesis: Origins and recent evidence. *Trends in Cognitive Sciences, 6,* 47–52.

Bach, M., & Poloschek, C. M. (2006). Optical illusions. *Advances in Clinical Neuroscience and Rehabilitation, 6,* 20–21.

Backhaus, W. G. K. (1998). Physiological and psychophysical simulations of color vision in humans and animals. In W. G. K. Backhaus, R. Kliegl, & J. S. Werner (Eds.), *Color vision: Perspectives from different disciplines* (pp. 45–77). New York: Walter de Gruyter.

Backus, B. T., Fleet, D. J., Parker, A. J., & Heeger, D. J. (2001). Human cortical activity correlates with stereoscopic depth perception. *Journal of Neurophysiology, 86,* 2054–2068.

Baird, J. C., Wagner, M., & Fuld, K. (1990). A simple but powerful theory of the moon illusion. *Journal of Experimental Psychology: Human Perception and Performance, 16,* 675–677.

Banks, M. S., & Bennett, P. J. (1988). Optical and photoreceptor immaturities limit the spatial and chromatic vision of human neonates. *Journal of the Optical Society of America, A5,* 2059–2079.

Banks, M. S., & Salapatek, P. (1978). Acuity and contrast sensitivity in 1-, 2-, and 3-month-old human infants. *Investigative Ophthalmology and Visual Science, 17,* 361–365.

Bar, M. (2004). Visual objects in context. *Nature Reviews Neuroscience, 5,* 617–629.

Barber, T. X., & Hahn, K. W. (1964). Experimental studies in "hypnotic" behaviour: Physiologic and subjective effects of imagined pain. *Journal of Nervous and Mental Disorders, 139,* 416–425.

Bardy, B. G., & Laurent, M. (1998). How is body orientation controlled during somersaulting? *Journal of Experimental Psychology: Human Perception and Performance, 24,* 963–977.

Barlow, H. B. (1995). The neuron in perception. In M. S. Gazzaniga (Ed.), *The cognitive neurosciences* (pp. 415–434). Cambridge, MA: MIT Press.

Barlow, H. B., Blakemore, C., & Pettigrew, J. D. (1967). The neural mechanism of binocular depth discrimination. *Journal of Physiology, 193*, 327–342.

Barlow, H. B., Fitzhigh, R., & Kuffler, S. W. (1957). Change of organization in the receptive fields of the cat's retina during dark adaptation. *Journal of Physiology, 137*, 338–354.

Barlow, H. B., & Hill, R. M. (1963). Evidence for a physiological explanation of the waterfall illusion. *Nature, 200*, 1345–1347.

Barlow, H. B., & Mollon, J. D. (Eds.). (1982). *The senses.* Cambridge, UK: Cambridge University Press.

Barry, S. R. (2011). *Fixing my gaze.* New York: Basic Books.

Bartoshuk, L. M. (1971). The chemical senses: I. Taste. In J. W. Kling & L. A. Riggs (Eds.), *Experimental psychology* (3rd ed.). New York: Holt, Rinehart and Winston.

Bartoshuk, L. M. (1979). Bitter taste of saccharin: Related to the genetic ability to taste the bitter substance propylthioural (PROP). *Science, 205*, 934–935.

Bartoshuk, L. M. (1980, September). Separate worlds of taste. *Psychology Today, 243*, 48–56.

Bartoshuk, L. M., & Beauchamp, G. K. (1994). Chemical senses. *Annual Review of Psychology, 45*, 419–449.

Bartrip, J., Morton, J., & deSchonen, S. (2001). Responses to mother's face in 3-week- to 5-month-old infants. *British Journal of Developmental Psychology, 19*, 219–232.

Battaglini, P. P., Galletti, C., & Fattori, P. (1996). Cortical mechanisms for visual perception of object motion and position in space. *Behavioural Brain Research, 76*, 143–154.

Battelli, L., Cavanagh, P., & Thornton, I. M. (2003). Perception of biological motion in parietal patients. *Neuropsychologia, 41*, 1808–1816.

Baylis, G. C., & Driver, J. (1993). Visual attention and objects: Evidence for hierarchical coding of location. *Journal of Experimental Psychology: Human Perception and Performance, 19*, 451–470.

Baylor, D. (1992). Transduction in retinal photoreceptor cells. In P. Corey & S. D. Roper (Eds.), *Sensory transduction* (pp. 151–174). New York: Rockefeller University Press.

Beauchamp, G. K., Cowart, B. J., & Schmidt, H. J. (1991). Development of chemosensory sensitivity and preference. In T. V. Getchell, R. L. Doty, L. M. Bartoshuk, & J. B. Snow (Eds.), *Smell and taste in health and disease* (pp. 405–416). New York: Raven Press.

Beauchamp, G. K., Cowart, B. J., Mennella, J. A., & Marsh, R. R. (1994). *Developmental Psychobiology, 27*, 353–365.

Beauchamp, G. K., & Mennella, J. A. (2009). Early flavor learning and its impact on later feeding behavior. *Journal of Pediatric Gastroenterology and Nutrition, 48*, S25–S30.

Beecher, H. K. (1959) *Measurement of subjective responses.* New York: Oxford University Press.

Behrmann, M., Thomas, C., & Humphreys, K. (2006). Seeing it differently: Visual processing in autism. *Trends in Cognitive Sciences, 10*, 258–264.

Békésy, G. von (1960). *Experiments in hearing.* New York: McGraw-Hill.

Belin, P., Zatorre, R. J., Lafaille, P., Ahad, P., & Pike, B. (2000). Voice-selective areas in human auditory cortex. *Nature, 403*, 309–312.

Benary, W. (1924). Beobachtungen zu einem Experiment uber Helligkeitz-kontrast [Observations concerning an experiment on brightness contrast]. *Psychologische Forschung, 5*, 131–142.

Bendor, D., & Wang, X. (2005). The neuronal representation of pitch in primate auditory cortex. *Nature, 436*, 1161–1165.

Benedetti, F., Arduino, C., & Amanzio, M. (1999). Somatotopic activation of opioid systems by target-directed expectations of analgesia. *Journal of Neuroscience, 19*, 3639–3648.

Bensmaia, S. J., Denchev, P. V., Dammann, J. F., III., Craig, J. C., & Hsiao, S. S. (2008). The representation of stimulus orientation in the early stages of somatosensory processing. *Journal of Neuroscience, 28*, 776–786.

Beranek, L. L. (1996). *Concert and opera halls: How they sound.* Woodbury, NY: Acoustical Society of America.

Berger, K. W. (1964). Some factors in the recognition of timbre. *Journal of the Acoustical Society of America, 36*, 1881–1891.

Berthenthal, B. I., Rose, J. L., & Bai, D. L. (1997). Perception–action coupling in the development of visual control of posture. *Journal of Experimental Psychology: Human Perception and Performance, 23*, 1631–1643.

Bess, F. H., & Humes, L. E. (2008). *Audiology: The fundamentals.* Philadelphia: Lippincott Williams & Wilkins.

Bhalla, M., & Proffitt, D. R. (1999). Visual-motor recalibration in geographical slant perception. *Journal of Experimental Psychology: Human Perception and Performance, 25*, 1076–1096.

Bilalić, M., Langner, R., Ulrich, R., & Grodd, W. (2011). Many faces of expertise: Fusiform face area in chess experts and novices. *Journal of Neuroscience, 31*, 10206–10214.

Birnbaum, M. (2011). *Season to taste.* New York: HarperCollins.

Birnberg, J. R. (1988, March 21). My turn. *Newsweek.*

Blake, R., & Hirsch, H. V. B. (1975). Deficits in binocular depth perception in cats after alternating monocular deprivation. *Science, 190*, 1114–1116.

Blake, R., & Wilson, H. R. (1991). Neural models of stereoscopic vision. *Trends in Neuroscience, 14*, 445–452.

Blakemore, C., & Cooper, G. G. (1970). Development of the brain depends on the visual environment. *Nature, 228*, 477–478.

Blakemore, S.-J., Bristow, D., Bird, G., Frith, C., & Ward, J. (2005). Somatosensory activations during the observation of touch and a case of vision-touch synaesthesia. *Brain, 128*, 1571–1583.

Blaser, E., & Sperling, G. (2008). When is motion "motion"? *Perception, 37*, 624–627.

Blauert, J. (1997). *Spatial hearing: The psychophysics of human sound localization* (Rev. ed.). Cambridge, MA: MIT Press

Block, N. (2009). Comparing the major theories of consciousness. In M. Gazzanaga (Ed.), *The cognitive neurosciences IV.* Cambridge, MA: MIT Press.

Blumstein, S. E., Baker, E., & Goodglass, H. (1977). Phonological factors in auditory comprehension in aphasia. *Neuropsychologia, 15*, 19–30.

Boring, E. G. (1942). *Sensation and perception in the history of experimental psychology.* New York: Appleton-Century-Crofts.

Bornstein, M. H., Kessen, W., & Weiskopf, S. (1976). Color vision and hue categorization in young human infant. *Journal of Experimental Psychology: Human Perception and Performance, 2*, 115–119.

Bouvier, S. E., & Engel, S. A. (2006). Behavioral deficits and cortical damage loci in cerebral achromatopsia. *Cerebral Cortex, 16*, 183–191.

Bowmaker, J. K., & Dartnall, H. J. A. (1980). Visual pigments of rods and cones in a human retina. *Journal of Physiology, 298*, 501–511.

Boynton, R. M. (1979). *Human color vision.* New York: Holt, Rinehart and Winston.

Brainard, D. H., & Wandell, B. A. (1986). Analysis of the retinex theory of color vision. *Journal of the Optical Society of America, A3*, 1651–1661.

Bregman, A. S. (1990). *Auditory scene analysis.* Cambridge, MA: MIT Press.

Bregman, A. S. (1993). Auditory scene analysis: Hearing in complex environments. In S. McAdams & E. Bigand (Eds.), *Thinking in sound: The cognitive psychology of human audition* (pp. 10–36). Oxford, UK: Oxford University Press.

Bregman, A. S., & Campbell, J. (1971). Primary auditory stream segregation and perception of order in rapid sequence of tones. *Journal of Experimental Psychology, 89,* 244–249.

Breslin, P. A. S. (2001). Human gustation and flavour. *Flavour and Fragrance Journal, 16,* 439–456.

Bridgeman, B., & Stark, L. (1991). Ocular proprioception and efference copy in registering visual direction. *Vision Research, 31,* 1903–1913.

Britten, K. H., & van Wezel, R. J. A. (2002). Area MST and heading perception in macaque monkeys. *Cerebral Cortex, 12,* 692–701.

Brown, P. K., & Wald, G. (1964). Visual pigments in single rods and cones of the human retina. *Science, 144,* 45–52.

Buccino, G., Lui, G., Canessa, N., Patteri, I., Lagravinese, G., Benuzzi, F., et al. (2004). Neural circuits involved in the recognition of actions performed by nonconspecifics: An fMRI study. *Journal of Cognitive Neuroscience, 16,* 114–126.

Buck, L. B. (2004). Olfactory receptors and coding in mammals. *Nutrition Reviews, 62,* S184–S188.

Buck, L., & Axel, R. (1991). A novel multigene family may encode odorant receptors: A molecular basis for odor recognition. *Cell, 65,* 175–187.

Bufe, B., Breslin, P. A. S., Kuhn, C., Reed, D. R., Tharp, C. D., Slack, J. P., et al. (2005). The molecular basis of individual differences in phenylthiocarbamide and propylthiouracil bitterness perception. *Current Biology, 15,* 322–327.

Bugelski, B. R., & Alampay, D. A. (1961). The role of frequency in developing perceptual sets. *Canadian Journal of Psychology, 15,* 205–211.

Buhle, J. T., Stevens, B. L., Friedman, J. J., & Wager, T. D. (2012). Distraction and placebo: Two separate routes to pain control. *Psychological Science, 23,* 246–253.

Bukach, C. M., Gauthier, I., & Tarr, M. J. (2006). Beyond faces and modularity: The power of an expertise framework. *Trends Cognitive Science, 10,* 159–166.

Bunch, C. C. (1929). Age variations in auditory acuity. *Archives of Otolaryngology, 9,* 625–636.

Burton, A. M., Young, A. W., Bruce, V., Johnston, R. A., & Ellis, A. W. (1991). Understanding covert recognition. *Cognition, 39,* 129–166.

Bushnell, I. W. R. (2001). Mother's face recognition in newborn infants: Learning and memory. *Infant and Child Development, 10,* 67–74.

Bushnell, I. W. R., Sai, F., & Mullin, J. T. (1989). Neonatal recognition of the mother's face. *British Journal of Developmental Psychology, 7,* 3–15.

Busigny, T., & Rossion, B. (2010). Acquired prosopagnosia abolishes the face inversion effect. *Cortex, 46,* 965–981.

Caggiano, V., Fogassi, L., Rizzolatti, G., Pomper, J. K., Their, P., Giese, M. A., et al. (2011). View-based encoding of actions in mirror neurons of area F5 in Macaque premotor cortex. *Current Biology, 21,* 144–148.

Cain, W. S. (1977). Differential sensitivity for smell: "Noise" at the nose. *Science, 195,* 796–798.

Cain, W. S. (1979). To know with the nose: Keys to odor identification. *Science, 203,* 467–470.

Cain, W. S. (1980). *Sensory attributes of cigarette smoking* (Branbury Report: 3. A safe cigarette?, pp. 239–249). Cold Spring Harbor, NY: Cold Spring Harbor Laboratory.

Cain, W. S. (1988). Olfaction. In R. A. Atkinson, R. J. Herrnstein, G. Lindzey, & R. D. Luce (Eds.), *Stevens' handbook of experimental psychology: Vol. 1. Perception and motivation* (Rev. ed., pp. 409–459). New York: Wiley.

Calder, A. J., Beaver, J. D., Winston, J. S., Dolan, R. J., Jenkins, R., Eger, E., et al. (2007). Separate coding of different gaze directions in the superior temporal sulcus and inferior parietal lobule. *Current Biology, 17,* 20–25.

Calvert, G. A., Bullmore, E. T., Brammer, M. J., Campbell, R., Williams, S. C. R., McGuire, P. K., et al. (1997). Activation of auditory cortex during silent lipreading. *Science, 276,* 593–595.

Campbell, F. W., Kulikowski, J. J., & Levinson, J. (1966). The effect of orientation on the visual resolution of gratings. *Journal of Physiology (London), 187,* 427–436.

Carello, C., & Turvey, M. T. (2004). Physics and psychology of the muscle sense. *Current Directions in Psychological Science, 13,* 25–28.

Carr, C. E., & Konishi, M. (1990). A circuit for detection of interaural time differences in the brain stem of the barn owl. *Journal of Neuroscience, 10,* 3227–3246.

Carrasco, M. (2011). Visual attention: The past 25 years. *Vision Research, 51,* 1484–1525.

Carrasco, M., Ling, S., & Read, S. (2004). Attention alters appearance. *Nature Neuroscience, 7,* 308–313.

Carrasco, M., Loula, F., & Ho, Y.-X. (2006). How attention enhances spatial resolution: Evidence from selective adaptation to spatial frequency. *Perception and Psychophysics, 68,* 1004–1012.

Cartwright-Finch, U., & Lavie, N. (2007). The role of perceptual load in inattentional blindness. *Cognition, 102,* 321–340.

Casagrande, V. A., & Norton, T. T. (1991). Lateral geniculate nucleus: A review of its physiology and function. In J. R. Coonley-Dillon (Vol. Ed.) & A. G. Leventhal (Ed.), *Vision and visual dysfunction: The neural basis of visual function* (Vol. 4, pp. 41–84). London: Macmillan.

Castelhano, M. S., & Henderson, J. M. (2008). Stable individual differences across images in human saccadic eye movements. *Canadian Journal of Psychology, 62,* 1–14.

Cavanagh, P. (2011). Visual cognition. *Vision Research, 51,* 1538–1551.

Cerf, M., Thiruvengadam, N., Mormann, F., Kraskov, A., Quiroga, R. Q., Koch, C., & Fried, I. (2010). On-line voluntary control of human temporal lobe neurons. *Nature, 467,* 1104–1108.

Chandrashekar, J., Hoon, M. A., Ryba, N. J. P., & Zuker, C. S. (2006). The receptors and cells for mammalian taste. *Nature, 444,* 288–294.

Chapman, C. R. (1995). The affective dimension of pain: A model. In B. Bromm & J. Desmedt (Eds.), *Pain and the brain: From nociception to cognition: Advances in pain research and therapy* (Vol. 22, pp. 283–301). New York: Raven.

Chatterjee, S. H., Freyd, J. J., & Shiffrar, M. (1996). Configural processing in the perception of apparent biological motion. *Journal of Experimental Psychology: Human Perception and Performance, 22,* 916–929.

Choi, G. B., Stettler, D. D., Kallman, B. R., Bhaskar, S. T. Fleischmann, A., & Axel, R. (2011). Driving opposing behaviors with ensembles of piriform neurons. *Cell, 146,* 1004–1015.

Cholewiak, R. W., & Collins, A. A. (2003). Vibrotactile localization on the arm: Effects of place, space, and age. *Perception & Psychophysics, 65,* 1058–1077.

Chun, M. M., Golomb, J. D., & Turk-Browne, N. B. (2011). A taxonomy of external and internal attention. *Annual Review of Psychology, 62,* 73–101.

Churchland, P. S., & Ramachandran, V. S. (1996). Filling in: Why Dennett is wrong. In K. Akins (Ed.), *Perception* (pp. 132–157). Oxford, UK: Oxford University Press.

Clarke, S., Thiran, A. B., Maeder, P., Adriani, M., Vernet, O., Regli, L., et al. (2002). What and where in human auditory: Selective deficits following focal hemispheric lesions. *Experimental Brain Research, 147,* 8–15.

Clulow, F. W. (1972). *Color: Its principles and their applications.* New York: Morgan & Morgan.

Cohen, J. D., & Tong, F. (2001). The face of controversy. *Science, 293,* 2405–2407.

Cohen, M. A., Alvarez, G. A., & Nakayama, K. (2011). Natural-scene perception requires attention. *Physiological Science, 22,* 1165–1172.

Cohen, M. R., & Newsome, W. T. (2004). What electrical microstimulation has revealed about the neural basis of cognition. *Current Opinion in Neurobiology, 14,* 169–177.

Cole, J. (1995). *Pride and a daily marathon.* Cambridge, MA: MIT Press.

Collett, T. S. (1978). Peering—a locust behavior pattern for obtaining motion parallax information. *Journal of Experimental Biology, 76,* 237–241.

Colloca, L., & Benedetti, F. (2005). Placebos and painkillers: Is mind as real as matter? *Nature Reviews Neuroscience, 6,* 545–552.

Coltheart, M. (1970). The effect of verbal size information upon visual judgments of absolute distance. *Perception and Psychophysics, 9,* 222–223.

Comel, M. (1953). *Fisiologia normale e patologica della cute umana.* Milan: Fratelli Treves Editori.

Connolly, J. D., Andersen, R. A., & Goodale, M. A. (2003). fMRI evidence for a "parietal reach region" in the human brain. *Experimental Brain Research, 153,* 140–145.

Coppola, D. M., White, L. E., Fitzpatrick, D., & Purves, D. (1998). Unequal distribution of cardinal and oblique contours in ferret visual cortex. *Proceedings of the National Academy of Sciences, 95,* 2621–2623.

Craig, J. C., & Lyle, K. B. (2001). A comparison of tactile spatial sensitivity on the palm and fingerpad. *Perception & Psychophysics, 63,* 337–347.

Craig, J. C., & Lyle, K. B. (2002). A correction and a comment on Craig and Lyle (2001). *Perception & Psychophysics, 64,* 504–506.

Creem-Regehr, S. H., & Kunz, B. R. (2010). Perception and action. *WIRES Cognitive Science, 1,* 800–810.

Crick, F. C., & Koch, C. (2003). A framework for consciousness. *Nature Neuroscience, 6,* 119–127.

Crouzet, S. M., Kirchner, H., & Thorpe, S. J. (2010). Fast saccades toward faces: Face detection in just 100 ms. *Journal of Vision, 10*(4):16, 1–17.

Crystal, S. R., & Bernstein, I. L. (1995). Morning sickness: Impact on offspring salt preference. *Appetite, 25,* 231–240.

Crystal, S. R., & Bernstein, I. L. (1998). Infant salt preference and mother's morning sickness. *Appetite 30*(3), 297–307.

Culler, E. A., Coakley, J. D., Lowy, K., & Gross, N. (1943). A revised frequency-map of the guinea-pig cochlea. *American Journal of Psychology, 56,* 475–500.

Cutting, J. E., & Vishton, P. M. (1995). Perceiving layout and knowing distances: The integration, relative potency, and contextual use of different information about depth. In W. Epstein & S. Rogers (Eds.), *Handbook of perception and cognition: Perception of space and motion* (pp. 69–117). New York: Academic Press.

Dallos, P. (1996). Overview: Cochlear neurobiology. In P. Dallos, A. N. Popper, & R. R. Fay (Eds.), *The cochlea* (pp. 1–43). New York: Springer.

Dalton, D. S., Cruickshanks, K. J., Wiley, T. L., Klein, B. E. K., Klein, R., & Tweed, T. S. (2001). Association of leisure-time noise exposure and hearing loss. *Audiology, 40,* 1–9.

Dalton, P. (2002). Olfaction. In S. Yantis (Ed.), *Stevens' handbook of experimental psychology: Sensation and perception* (3rd ed., pp. 691–756). New York: Wiley.

Damasio, H., & Damasio, A. R. (1980). The anatomical basis of conduction aphasia. *Brain, 103,* 337–350.

Dannemiller, J. L. (2009). Perceptual development: Color and contrast. In E. B. Goldstein (Ed.), *Sage encyclopedia of perception* (pp. 738–742). Thousand Oaks, CA: Sage.

Dartnall, H. J. A., Bowmaker, J. K., & Mollon, J. D. (1983). Human visual pigments: Microspectrophotometric results from the eyes of seven persons. *Proceedings of the Royal Society of London B, 220,* 115–130.

Darwin, C. J. (2010). Auditory scene analysis. In E. B. Goldstein (Ed.), *Sage encyclopedia of perception* (pp. 186–191). Thousand Oaks, CA: Sage.

Datta, R., & DeYoe, E. A. (2009). I know where you are secretly attending! The topography of human visual attention revealed with fMRI. *Vision Research, 49,* 1037–1044.

D'Ausilio, A., Pulvermuller, F., Salmas, P., Bufalari, I., Begliomini, C., & Fadiga, L. (2009). The motor somatotopy of speech perception. *Current Biology, 19,* 381–385.

David, A. S., & Senior, C. (2000). Implicit motion and the brain. *Trends in Cognitive Sciences, 4,* 293–295.

Day, R. H. (1989). Natural and artificial cues, perceptual compromise and the basis of veridical and illusory perception. In D. Vickers & P. L. Smith (Eds.), *Human information processing: Measures and mechanisms* (pp. 107–129). North Holland, The Netherlands: Elsevier Science.

Day, R. H. (1990). The Bourdon illusion in haptic space. *Perception and Psychophysics, 47,* 400–404.

de Araujo, I. E., Geha, P., & Small, D. (2012). Orosensory and homeostatic functions of the insular cortex. *Chemical Perception, 5,* 64–79.

de Araujo, I. E., Rolls, E. T., Velazco, M. I., Margot, C., & Cayeux, I. (2005). Cognitive modulation of olfactory processing. *Neuron, 46,* 671–679.

de Lange, F. P., Spronk, M., Willems, R. M., Toni, I, & Bekkering, H. (2008). Complementary systems for understanding action intentions. *Current Biology, 18,* 454–457.

De Santis, L., Clarke, S., & Murray, M. M. (2007). Automatic and intrinsic auditory "what" and "where" processing in humans revealed by electrical neuroimaging. *Cerebral Cortex, 17,* 9–17.

DeAngelis, G. C., Cumming, B. G., & Newsome, W. T. (1998). Cortical area MT and the perception of stereoscopic depth. *Nature, 394,* 677–680.

DeCasper, A. J., & Fifer, W. P. (1980). Of human bonding: Newborns prefer their mothers' voices. *Science, 208,* 1174–1176.

DeCasper, A. J., & Spence, M. J. (1986). Prenatal maternal speech influences newborns' perception of speech sounds. *Infant Behavior and Development, 9,* 133–150.

DeCasper, A. J., Lecanuet, J.-P., Busnel, M.-C., Deferre-Granier, C., & Maugeais, R. (1994). Fetal reactions to recurrent maternal speech. *Infant Behavior and Development, 17,* 159–164.

Delahunt, P. B., & Brainard, D. H. (2004). Does human color constancy incorporate the statistical regularity of natural daylight? *Journal of Vision, 4,* 57–81.

Delay, E. R., Hernandez, N. P., Bromley, K., & Margolskee, R. F. (2006). Sucrose and monosodium glutamate taste thresholds and discrimination ability of T1R3 knockout mics. *Chemical Senses, 31,* 351–357.

DeLucia, P., & Hochberg, J. (1985). Illusions in the real world and in the mind's eye [Abstract]. *Proceedings of the Eastern Psychological Association, 56,* 38.

DeLucia, P., & Hochberg, J. (1986). Real-world geometrical illusions: Theoretical and practical implications [Abstract]. *Proceedings of the Eastern Psychological Association, 57,* 62.

DeLucia, P., & Hochberg, J. (1991). Geometrical illusions in solid objects under ordinary viewing conditions. *Perception and Psychophysics, 50,* 547–554.

Delwiche, J. F., Buletic, Z., & Breslin, P. A. S. (2001a). Covariation in individuals' sensitivities to bitter compounds: Evidence supporting multiple receptor/transduction mechanisms. *Perception & Psychophysics, 63*, 761–776.

Delwiche, J. F., Buletic, Z., & Breslin, P. A. S. (2001b). Relationship of papillae number to bitter intensity of quinine and PROP within and between individuals. *Physiology and Behavior, 74*, 329–337.

Denes, P. B., & Pinson, E. N. (1993). *The speech chain* (2nd ed.). New York: Freeman.

Derbyshire, S. W. G., Jones, A. K. P., Gyulia, F., Clark, S., Townsend, D., & Firestone, L. L. (1997). Pain processing during three levels of noxious stimulation produces differential patterns of central activity. *Pain, 73*, 431–445.

Derbyshire, S. W. G., Whalley, M. G., Stenger, V. A. & Oakley, D. A. (2004). Cerebral activation during hypnotically induced and imagined pain. *Neuroimage, 23*, 392–401.

Desor, J. A., & Beauchamp, G. K. (1974). The human capacity to transmit olfactory information. *Perception and Psychophysics, 13*, 271–275.

Deutsch, D. (1975). Two-channel listening to musical scales. *Journal of the Acoustical Society of America, 57*, 1156–1160.

Deutsch, D. (1996). The perception of auditory patterns. In W. Prinz & B. Bridgeman (Eds.), *Handbook of perception and action* (Vol. 1, pp. 253–296). San Diego, CA: Academic Press.

Deutsch, D. (1999). *The psychology of music* (2nd ed.). San Diego, CA: Academic Press.

DeValois, R. L. (1960). Color vision mechanisms in monkey. *Journal of General Physiology, 43*, 115–128.

DeValois, R. L., Abramov, I., & Jacobs, G. H. (1966). Analysis of response of LGN cells. *Journal of the Optical Society of America, 56*, 966–977.

DeValois, R. L., & DeValois, K. K. (1993). A multistage color model. *Vision Research, 33*, 1053–1065.

DeValois, R. L., & Jacobs, G. H. (1968). Primate color vision. *Science, 162*, 533–540.

Devos, M., Patte, F., Rouault, J., Laffort, P., & Van Gemert, L. J. (Eds.). (1990). *Standardized human olfactory thresholds*. New York: Oxford University Press.

deVries, H., & Stuiver, M. (1961). The absolute sensitivity of the human sense of smell. In W. A. Rosenblith (Ed.), *Sensory communication*. Cambridge, MA: MIT Press.

deWeid, M., & Verbaten, M. N. (2001). Affective pictures processing, attention, and pain tolerance. *Pain, 90*, 163–172.

Di Pelligrino, G., Fadiga, L., Fogassi, L., Gallese, V., & Rizzolatti, G. (1992). Understanding motor events: A neurophysiological study. *Experimental Brain Research, 91*, 176–180.

Dobson, V., & Teller, D. (1978). Visual acuity in human infants: Review and comparison of behavioral and electrophysiological studies. *Vision Research, 18*, 1469–1483.

Dodd, G. G., & Squirrell, D. J. (1980). Structure and mechanism in the mammalian olfactory system. *Symposium of the Zoology Society of London, 45*, 35–56.

Doty, R. L. (Ed.). (1976). *Mammalian olfaction, reproductive processes and behavior*. New York: Academic Press.

Doty, R. L. (1991). Olfactory system. In T. V. Getchell, R. L. Doty, L. M. Bartoshuk, & J. B. Snow (Eds.), *Smell and taste in health and disease* (pp. 175–203). New York: Raven Press.

Doty, R. L. (2010). *The great pheromone myth*. Baltimore: Johns Hopkins University Press.

Dougherty, R. F., Koch, V. M., Brewer, A. A., Fischer, B., Modersitzki, J., & Wandell, B. A. (2003). Visual field representations and locations of visual areas V1/2/3 in human visual cortex. *Journal of Vision, 3*, 586–598.

Dowling, J. E., & Boycott, B. B. (1966). Organization of the primate retina. *Proceedings of the Royal Society of London, 166B*, 80–111.

Dowling, W. J., & Harwood, D. L. (1986). *Music cognition*. New York: Academic Press.

Downing, P. E., Jiang, Y., Shuman, M., & Kanwisher, N. (2001). Cortical area selective for visual processing of the human body. *Science, 293*, 2470–2473.

Driver, J., & Baylis, G. C. (1989). Movement and visual attention: The spotlight metaphor breaks down. *Journal of Experimental Psychology: Human Perception and Performance, 15*, 448–456.

Driver, J., & Baylis, G. C. (1998). Attention and visual object segmentation. In R. Parasuraman (Ed.), *The attentive brain* (pp. 299–325). Cambridge, MA: MIT Press.

Dudley, D. L., Holmes, T. H., Martin, C. J., & Ripley, H. S. (1966). Hypnotically induced facsimile of pain. *Archives of General Psychiatry, 15*, 258–265.

Duffy, C. J., & Wurtz, R. H. (1991). Sensitivity of MST neurons to optic flow stimuli: 2. Mechanisms of response selectivity revealed by small-field stimuli. *Journal of Neurophysiology, 65*, 1346–1359.

Duncan, R. O., & Boynton, G. M. (2007). Tactile hyperacuity thresholds correlate with finger maps in primary somatosensory cortex (S1). *Cerebral Cortex, 17*, 2878–2891.

Durgin, F. H., Hajnal, A., Li, Z., Tonge, N., & Stigliani, A. (2010). Palm boards are not action measures: An alternative way to the two-systems theory of geographical slant perception. *Acta Psychologica, 134*, 182–197.

Durrant, J., & Lovrinic, J. (1977). *Bases of hearing science*. Baltimore: Williams & Wilkins.

Eames, C. (1977). *Powers of ten*. Pyramid Films.

Ecker, A. J., & Heller, L. M. (2005). Auditory-visual interactions in the perception of a ball's path. *Perception, 34*, 59–75.

Egbert, L. D., Battit, G. E., Welch, C. E., & Bartlett, M. D. (1964). Reduction of postoperative pain by encouragement and instruction of patients. *New England Journal of Medicine, 270*, 825–827.

Egly, R., Driver, J., & Rafal, R. D. (1994). Shifting visual attention between objects and locations: Evidence from normal and parietal lesion subjects. *Journal of Experimental Psychology: General, 123*, 161–177.

Ehrenstein, W. (1930). Untersuchungen über Figur-Grund Fragen [Investigations of figure–ground questions]. *Zeitschrift für Psychologie, 117*, 339–412.

Eimas, P. D., & Corbit, J. D. (1973). Selective adaptation of linguistic feature detectors. *Cognitive Psychology, 4*, 99–109.

Eimas, P. D., & Quinn, P. C. (1994). Studies on the formation of perceptually based basic-level categories in young infants. *Child Development, 65*, 903–917.

Eimas, P. D., Siqueland, E. R., Jusczyk, P., & Vigorito, J. (1971). Speech perception in infants. *Science, 171*, 303–306.

Elbert, T., Pantev, C., Wienbruch, C., Rockstroh, B., & Taub, E. (1995). Increased cortical representation of the fingers of the left hand in string players. *Science, 270*, 305–307.

Emmert, E. (1881). Grossenverhaltnisse der Nachbilder. *Klinische Monatsblätter für Augenheilkunde, 19*, 443–450.

Engel, S. A. (2005). Adaptation of oriented and unoriented color-selective neurons in human visual areas. *Neuron, 45*, 613–623.

Engen, T. (1972). Psychophysics. In J. W. Kling & L. A. Riggs (Eds.), *Experimental psychology* (3rd ed., pp. 1–46). New York: Holt, Rinehart and Winston.

Engen, T., & Pfaffmann, C. (1960). Absolute judgments of odor quality. *Journal of Experimental Psychology, 59*, 214–219.

Epstein, R. A. (2005). The cortical basis of visual scene processing. *Visual Cognition, 12*, 954–978.

Epstein, R., & Kanwisher, N. (1998). A cortical representation of the local visual environment. *Nature, 392*, 598–601.

Epstein, R., Harris, A., Stanley, D., & Kanwisher, N. (1999). The parahippocampal place area: Recognition, navigation, or encoding? *Neuron, 23*, 115–125.

Epstein, W. (1965). Nonrelational judgments of size and distance. *American Journal of Psychology, 78*, 120–123.

Erickson, R. (1975). *Sound structure in music.* Berkeley: University of California Press.

Erickson, R. P. (1963). Sensory neural patterns and gustation. In Y. Zotterman (Ed.), *Olfaction and taste* (Vol. 1, pp. 205–213). Oxford, UK: Pergamon Press.

Erickson, R. P. (2000). The evolution of neural coding ideas in the chemical senses. *Physiology and Behavior, 69*, 3–13.

Fagan, J. F. (1976). Infant's recognition of invariant features of faces. *Child Development, 47*, 627–638.

Fajen, B. R., & Warren, W. H. (2003). Behavioral dynamics of steering, obstacle avoidance and route selection. *Journal of Experimental Psychology: Human Perception and Performance, 29*, 343–362.

Fantz, R. L., Ordy, J. M., & Udelf, M. S. (1962). Maturation of pattern vision in infants during the first six months. *Journal of Comparative and Physiological Psychology, 55*, 907–917.

Farah, M. J., Wilson, K. D., Drain H. M., & Tanaka, J. R. (1998). What is "special" about face perception? *Psychological Review, 105*, 482–498.

Fattori, P., Breveglieri, R., Raos, V., Boco, A., & Galletti, C. (2012). Vision for action in the Macaque medial posterior parietal cortex. *Journal of Neuroscience, 32*, 3221–3234.

Fattori, P., Raos, V., Breveglieri, R, Bosco, A., Marzocchi, N., & Galleti, C. (2010). The dorsomedial pathway is not just for reaching: Grasping neurons in the medial parieto-occipital cortex of the Macaque monkey. *Journal of Neuroscience, 30*, 342–349.

Fechner, G. T. (1966). *Elements of psychophysics.* New York: Holt, Rinehart and Winston. (Original work published 1860)

Fei Fei, L., Iyer, A., Koch, C., & Perona, P. (2007). What do we perceive in a glance of a real-world scene? *Journal of Vision, 7*, 1–29.

Feldman, D. E., & Knudsen, E. I. (1997). An anatomical basis for visual calibration of the auditory space map in the owl's midbrain. *Journal of Neuroscience, 17*, 6820–6837.

Fernald, R. D. (2006) Casting a genetic light on the evolution of eyes. *Science, 313*, 1914–1918.

Ferrari, P. F., Gallese, V., Rizzolatti, G., & Fogassi, L. (2003). Mirror neurons responding to the observation of ingestive and communicative mouth actions in the monkey ventral premotor cortex. *European Journal of Neuroscience, 15*, 399–402.

Fettiplace, R., & Hackney, C. M. (2006). The sensory and motor roles of auditory hair cells. *Nature Reviews Neuroscience, 7*, 19–29.

Fields, H. L., & Basbaum, A. I. (1999). Central nervous system mechanisms of pain modulation. In P. D. Wall & R. Melzak (Eds.), *Textbook of pain* (pp. 309–328). New York: Churchill Livingstone.

Filimon, F., Nelson, J. D., Huang, R.-S., & Sereno, M. I. (2009). Multiple parietal reach regions in humans: Cortical representations for visual and proprioceptive feedback during on-line reaching. *Journal of Neuroscience, 29*, 2961–2971.

Finger, T. E. (1987). Gustatory nuclei and pathways in the central nervous system. In T. E. Finger & W. L. Silver (Eds.), *Neurobiology of taste and smell* (pp. 331–353). New York: Wiley.

Finniss, D. G., & Benedetti, F. (2005). Mechanisms of the placebo response and their impact on clinical trials and clinical practice. *Pain, 114*, 3–6.

Firestein, S. (2001). How the olfactory system makes sense of scents. *Nature, 413*, 211–218.

Fischer, E., Bulthoff, H. H., Logothetis, N. K., & Bartels, A. (2012). Visual motion responses in the posterior cingulated sulcus: A comparison to V5/MT and MST. *Cerebral Cortex, 22*, 865–876.

Fischl, B., & Anders, M. D. (2000). Measuring the thickness of the human cerebral cortex from magnetic resonance images. *Proceedings of the National Academy of Sciences, 97*, 11050–11055.

Fletcher, H., & Munson, W. A. (1933). Loudness: Its definition, measurement, and calculation. *Journal of the Acoustical Society of America, 5*, 82–108.

Fogassi, L., Ferrari, P. F., Gesierich, B., Rozzi, S., Chersi, F., & Rizzolatti, G. (2005). Parietal lobe: From action organization to intention understanding. *Science, 302*, 662–667.

Forster, S., & Lavie, N. (2008). Failures to ignore entirely irrelevant distractors: The role of load. *Journal of Experimental Psychology: Applied, 14*, 73–83.

Fortenbaugh, F. C., Hicks, J. C., Hao, L., & Turano, K. A. (2006). High-speed navigators: Using more than what meets the eye. *Journal of Vision, 6*, 565–579.

Foster, D. H. (2011). Color constancy. *Vision Research, 51*, 674–700.

Fox, C. R. (1990). Some visual influences on human postural equilibrium: Binocular versus monocular fixation. *Perception and Psychophysics, 47*, 409–422.

Fox, R., Aslin, R. N., Shea, S. L., & Dumais, S. T. (1980). Stereopsis in human infants. *Science, 207*, 323–324.

Frank, M. E., Bieber, S. L., & Smith, D. V. (1988). The organization of taste sensibilities in hamster chorda tympani nerve fibers. *Journal of General Physiology, 91*, 861–896.

Frank, M. E., Lundy, R. F., & Contreras, R. J. (2008). Cracking taste codes by tapping into sensory neuron impulse traffic. *Progress in Neurobiology, 86*, 245–263.

Frank, M. E., & Rabin, M. D. (1989). Chemosensory neuroanatomy and physiology. *Ear, Nose and Throat Journal, 68*, 291–292, 295–296.

Franklin, A., & Davies, R. L. (2004). New evidence for infant colour categories. *British Journal of Developmental Psychology, 22*, 349–377.

Freire, A., Lee, K., & Symons, L. A. (2000). The face-inversion effect as a deficit in the encoding of configural information: Direct evidence. *Perception, 29*, 159–170.

Freyd, J. (1983). The mental representation of movement when static stimuli are viewed. *Perception & Psychophysics, 33*, 575–581. (9)

Friedman, H. S., Zhou, H., & von der Heydt, R. (2003). The coding of uniform colour figures in monkey visual cortex. *Journal of Physiology, 548*, 593–613.

Friedman-Hill, S. R., Robertson, L. C., & Treisman, A. (1995). Parietal contributions to visual feature binding: Evidence from a patient with bilateral lesions. *Science, 269*, 853–855.

Fuld, K., Wooten, B. R., & Whalen, J. J. (1981). Elemental hues of short-wave and spectral lights. *Perception and Psychophysics, 29*, 317–322.

Furmananski, C. S., Schluppeck, D., & Engel, S. A. (2004). Learning strengthens the response of primary visual cortex to simple patterns. *Current Biology, 14*, 573–578.

Gallese, V. (2007). Before and below "theory of mind": Embodied simulation and the neural correlates of social cognition. *Philosophical Transactions of the Royal Society B, 362*, 659–669.

Gallese, V., Fadiga, L., Fogassi, L., & Rizzolatti, G. (1996). Action recognition in the premotor cortex. *Brain, 119,* 593–609.

Galletti, C., & Fattori, P. (2003). Neuronal mechanisms for detection of motion in the field of view. *Neuropsychologia, 41,* 1717–1727. (9)

Ganchrow, J. R. (1995). Ontogeny of human taste perception. In R. L. Doty (Ed.), *Handbook of olfaction and gustation* (pp. 715–729). New York: Marcel Dekker.

Ganchrow, J. R., Steiner, J. E., & Daher, M. (1983). Neonatal facial expressions in response to different qualities and intensities of gustatory stimuli. *Infant Behavior and Development, 6,* 473–484.

Ganel, T., Tanzer, M., & Goodale, M. A. (2008). A double dissociation between action and perception in the context of visual illusions. *Psychological Science, 19,* 221–225.

Gardner, M. B., & Gardner, R. S. (1973). Problem of localization in the median plane: Effect of pinnae cavity occlusion. *Journal of the Acoustical Society of America, 53,* 400–408.

Gauthier, I., Skudlarski, P., Gore, J. C., & Anderson, A. W. (2000). Expertise for cars and birds recruits brain areas involved in face recognition. *Nature Neuroscience, 3,* 191–197.

Gauthier, I., Tarr, M. J., Anderson, A. W., Skudlarski, P., & Gore, J. C. (1999). Activation of the middle fusiform face area increases with expertise in recognizing novel objects. *Nature Neuroscience, 2,* 568–573.

Gazzola, V., van der Worp, H., Mulder, T., Wicker, B., Rizzolatti, G., & Keysers, C. (2007). Aplasics born without hands mirror the goal of hand actions with their feet. *Current Biology, 17,* 1235–1240.

Geisler, W. S. (2008). Visual perception and statistical properties of natural scenes. *Annual Review of Psychology, 59,* 167–192.

Geisler, W. S. (2011). Contributions of ideal observer theory to vision research. *Vision Research, 51,* 771–781.

Gelbard-Sagiv, H., Mukamel, R., Harel, M., Malach, R., & Fried, I. (2008). Internally generated reactivation of single neurons in human hippocampus during free recall. *Science, 322,* 96–101.

Gescheider, G. A. (1976). *Psychophysics: Method and theory.* Hillsdale, NJ: Erlbaum.

Gibson, B. S., & Peterson, M. A. (1994). Does orientation-independent object recognition precede orientation-dependent recognition? Evidence from a cueing paradigm. *Journal of Experimental Psychology: Human Perception and Performance, 20,* 299–316.

Gibson, J. J. (1950). *The perception of the visual world.* Boston: Houghton Mifflin.

Gibson, J. J. (1962). Observations on active touch. *Psychological Review, 69,* 477–491.

Gibson, J. J. (1966). *The senses as perceptual systems.* Boston: Houghton Mifflin.

Gibson, J. J. (1979). *The ecological approach to visual perception.* Boston: Houghton Mifflin.

Gilad, S., Meng, M., & Sinha, P. (2009). Role of ordinal contrast relationships in face encoding. *Proceedings of the National Academy of Sciences, 106,* 5353–5358.

Gilbert, A. N., & Firestein, S. (2002). Dollars and scents: Commercial opportunities in olfaction and taste. *Nature Neuroscience, 5,* 1043–1045.

Gilchrist, A. L. (Ed.). (1994). *Lightness, brightness, and transparency.* Hillsdale, NJ: Erlbaum.

Gilchrist, A., Kossyfidis, C., Bonato, F., Agostini, T., Cataliotti, J., Li, X., et al. (1999). An anchoring theory of lightness perception. *Psychological Review, 106,* 795–834.

Glanz, J. (2000, April 18). Art + physics = beautiful music. *New York Times,* pp. D1–D4.

Gobbini, M. I., & Haxby, J. V. (2007). Neural systems for recognition of familiar faces. *Neuropsychologia, 45,* 32–41.

Goffaux, V., Jacques, C., Mauraux, A., Oliva, A., Schynsand, P. G., & Rossion, B. (2005). Diagnostic colours contribute to the early stages of scene categorization: Behavioural and neurophysiological evidence. *Visual Cognition, 12,* 878–892.

Goffaux, V., & Rossion, B. (2006). Faces are "spatial": Holistic face perception is supported by low spatial frequencies. *Journal of Experimental Psychology: Human Perception and Performance, 32,* 1023–1039.

Golarai, G., Ghahremani, G., Whitfield-Gabrieli, S., Reiss, A., Eberhardt, J. L., Gabrieli, J. E. E., et al. (2007). Differential development of high-level cortex correlates with category-specific recognition memory. *Nature Neuroscience, 10,* 512–522.

Goldstein, E. B. (1981). The ecology of J. J. Gibson's perception. *Leonardo, 14,* 191–195.

Goldstein, E. B. (2001a). Cross-talk between psychophysics and physiology in the study of perception. In E. B. Goldstein (Ed.), *Blackwell handbook of perception* (pp. 305–314). Oxford, UK: Blackwell.

Goldstein, E. B. (2001b). Pictorial perception and art. In E. B. Goldstein (Ed.), *Blackwell handbook of perception* (pp. 344–378). Oxford, UK: Blackwell.

Goldstein, E. B., & Fink, S. I. (1981). Selective attention in vision: Recognition memory for superimposed line drawings. *Journal of Experimental Psychology: Human Perception and Performance, 7,* 954–967.

Goodale, M. A. (2011). Transforming vision into action. *Vision Research, 51,* 1567–1587.

Goodale, M. A., & Humphrey, G. K. (1998). The objects of action and perception. *Cognition, 67,* 181–207.

Goodale, M. A., & Humphrey, G. K. (2001). Separate visual systems for action and perception. In E. B. Goldstein (Ed.), *Blackwell handbook of perception* (pp. 311–343). Oxford, UK: Blackwell.

Goodwin, A. W. (1998). Extracting the shape of an object from the responses of peripheral nerve fibers. In J. W. Morley (Ed.), *Neural aspects of tactile sensation* (pp. 55–87). New York: Elsevier Science.

Gottfried, J. A. (2010). Central mechanisms of odour object perception. *Nature Reviews Neuroscience, 11,* 628–641.

Gouras, P. (1991). Color vision. In E. R. Kandel, J. H. Schwartz, & T. M. Jessell (Eds.), *Principles of neural science* (3rd ed., pp. 467–480). New York: Elsevier.

Graham, C. H., Sperling, H. G., Hsia, Y., & Coulson, A. H. (1961). The determination of some visual functions of a unilaterally color-blind subject: Methods and results. *Journal of Psychology, 51,* 3–32.

Granrud, C. E., Haake, R. J., & Yonas, A. (1985). Infants' sensitivity to familiar size: The effect of memory on spatial perception. *Perception and Psychophysics, 37,* 459–466.

Granrud, C. E., & Yonas, A. (1984). Infants' perception of pictorially specified interposition. *Journal of Experimental Child Psychology, 37,* 500–511.

Graziano, M. S. A., Andersen, R. A., & Snowden, R. J. (1994). Tuning of MST neurons to spiral motions. *Journal of Neuroscience, 14,* 54–67.

Gregory, R. L. (1966). *Eye and brain.* New York: McGraw-Hill.

Grelotti, D. J., Gauthier, I., & Schultz, R. T. (2002). Social interest and the development of cortical face specialization: What autism teaches us about face processing. *Developmental Psychobiology, 40,* 213–225.

Grelotti, D. J., Klin, A. J., Gauthier, I., Skudlarski, P., Cohen, D. J., Gore, J. C., et al. (2005). fMRI activation of the fusiform gyrus and amygdala to cartoon characters but not to faces in a boy with autism. *Neuropsychologia, 43*, 373–385.

Griffin, D. R. (1944). Echolocation by blind men and bats. *Science, 100*, 589–590.

Grill-Spector, K., Golarai, G., & Gabrieli, J. (2008). Developmental neuroimaging of the human ventral visual cortex. *Trends in Cognitive Sciences, 12*, 152–162.

Grill-Spector, K., Knouf, N., & Kanwisher, N. (2004). The fusiform face area subserves face perception, not generic within-category identification. *Nature Neuroscience, 7*, 555–562.

Gross, C. G. (2002). The genealogy of the "grandmother cell." *Neuroscientist, 8*, 512–518.

Gross, C. G. (2008). Single neuron studies of inferior temporal cortex. *Neuropsychologia, 46, 841–852.*

Gross, C. G., Bender, D. B., & Roche-Miranda, C. E. (1969). Visual receptive fields of neurons in inferotemporal cortex of the monkey. *Science, 166*, 1303–1306.

Gross, C. G., Rocha-Miranda, C. E., & Bender, D. B. (1972). Visual properties of neurons in inferotemporal cortex of the macaque. *Journal of Neurophysiology, 5*, 96–111.

Grossman, E. D., & Blake, R. (2001). Brain activity evoked by inverted and imagined biological motion. *Vision Research, 41*, 1475–1482.

Grossman, E. D., Batelli, L., & Pascual-Leone, A. (2005). Repetitive TMS over posterior STS disrupts perception of biological motion. *Vision Research, 45*, 2847–2853.

Grossman, E. D., & Blake, R. (2002). Brain areas active during visual perception of biological motion. *Neuron, 56*, 1167–1175.

Grothe, B., Pecka, M., & McAlpine, D. (2010). Mechanisms of sound localization in mammals. *Physiological Review, 90*, 983–1012.

Gulick, W. L., Gescheider, G. A., & Frisina, R. D. (1989). *Hearing.* New York: Oxford University Press.

Gullberg, M., & Holmqvist, K. (2006). What speakers do and what addressees look at. *Pragmatics & Cognition, 14*, 53–82.

Gwiazda, J., Brill, S., Mohindra, I., & Held, R. (1980). Preferential looking acuity in infants from two to fifty-eight weeks of age. *American Journal of Optometry and Physiological Optics, 57*, 428–432.

Haarmeier, T., Their, P., Repnow, M., & Petersen, D. (1997). False perception of motion in a patient who cannot compensate for eye movements. *Nature, 389*, 849–852.

Haber, R. N., & Levin, C. A. (2001). The independence of size perception and distance perception. *Perception & Psychophysics, 63*, 1140–1152.

Hall, D. A., Fussell, C., & Summerfield, A. Q. (2005). Reading fluent speech from talking faces: Typical brain networks and individual differences. *Journal of Cognitive Neuroscience, 17*, 939–953.

Hall, M. J., Bartoshuk, L. M., Cain, W. S., & Stevens, J. C. (1975). PTC taste blindness and the taste of caffeine. *Nature, 253*, 442–443.

Hamer, R. D., Alexander, K. R., & Teller, D. Y. (1982). Rayleigh discriminations in young human infants. *Vision Research, 22*, 575–587.

Hamer, R. D., Nicholas, S. C., Tranchina, D., Lamb, T. D., & Jarvinen, J. L. P. (2005). Toward a unified model of vertebrate rod phototransduction. *Visual Neuroscience, 22*, 417–436.

Hamid, S. N., Stankiewicz, B., & Hayhoe, M. (2010). Gaze patterns in navigation: Encoding information in large-scale environments. *Journal of Vision, 10*(12):18, 1–11.

Handford, M. (1997). *Where's Waldo?* Cambridge, MA: Candlewick Press.

Hansen, T., Olkkonen, M., Walter, S., & Gegenfurtner, K. R. (2006). Memory modulates color appearance. *Nature Neuroscience, 9*, 1367–1368.

Harada, T., Goda, N., Ogawa, T., Ito, M., Toyoda, H., Sadato, N., et al. (2009). Distribution of color-selective activity in the monkey inferior temporal cortex revealed by functional magnetic resonance imaging. *European Journal of Neuroscience, 30*, 1960–1970.

Harris, J. M., & Rogers, B. J. (1999). Going against the flow. *Trends in Cognitive Sciences, 3*, 449–450.

Harris, L., Atkinson, J., & Braddick, O. (1976). Visual contrast sensitivity of a 6-month-old infant measured by the evoked potential. *Nature, 246*, 570–571.

Hartline, H. K. (1938). The response of single optic nerve fibers of the vertebrate eye to illumination of the retina. *American Journal of Physiology, 121*, 400–415

Hartline, H. K. (1940). The receptive fields of optic nerve fibers. *American Journal of Physiology, 130*, 690–699.

Hartline, H. K., Wagner, H. G., & Ratliff, F. (1956). Inhibition in the eye of *Limulus. Journal of General Physiology, 39*, 651–673.

Hartmann, M. (1999). How we localize sound. *Physics Today on the Web.* www.aip.org/pt/nov99/locsound.html

Hayhoe, M., & Ballard, C. (2005). Eye movements in natural behavior. *Trends in Cognitive Sciences, 9*, 188–194.

Hecaen, H., & Angelerques, R. (1962). Agnosia for faces (prosopagnosia). *Archives of Neurology, 7*, 92–100.

Heider, F., & Simmel, M. (1944). An experimental study of apparent behavior. *American Journal of Psychology, 13*, 243–259.

Hubel, D. H., & Wiesel, T. N. (1959). Receptive fields of single neurons in the cat's striate cortex. *Journal of Physiology, 148*, 574–591.

Heise, G. A., & Miller, G. A. (1951). An experimental study of auditory patterns. *American Journal of Psychology, 57*, 243–249.

Held, R., Birch, E. E., & Gwiazda, J. (1980). Stereoacuity of human infants. *Proceedings of the National Academy of Sciences, 77*, 5572–5574.

Helmholtz, H. von (1852). On the theory of compound colors. *Philosophical Magazine, 4*, 519–534.

Helmholtz, H. von. (1911). *Treatise on physiological optics* (J. P. Southall, Ed. & Trans.; 3rd ed., Vols. 2 & 3). Rochester, NY: Optical Society of America. (Original work published 1866)

Henderson, J. M., & Hollingworth, A. (1999). High-level scene perception. *Annual Review of Psychology, 50*, 243–271.

Henderson, J. M., & Hollingworth, A. (2003). Eye movements, visual memory, and scene representation. In M. Peterson & G. Rhodes (Eds.), *Perception of faces, objects, and scenes: Analytic and holistic processes* (pp. 356–383). New York: Oxford University Press.

Hering, E. (1878). *Zur Lehre vom Lichtsinn.* Vienna: Gerold.

Hering, E. (1905). Grundzuge der Lehre vom Lichtsinn. In *Handbuch der gesamter Augenheilkunde* (Vol. 3, Chap. 13). Berlin.

Hering, E. (1964). *Outlines of a theory of the light sense* (L. M. Hurvich & D. Jameson, Trans.). Cambridge, MA: Harvard University Press.

Hershenson, M. (Ed.). (1989). *The moon illusion.* Hillsdale, NJ: Erlbaum.

Herz, R. S., & Schooler, J. W. (2002). A naturalistic study of autobiographical memories evoked by olfactory and visual cues: Testing the Proustian hypothesis. *American Journal of Psychology, 115*, 21–32.

Hettinger, T. P., Myers, W. E., & Frank, M. E. (1990). Role of olfaction in perception of nontraditional "taste" stimuli. *Chemical Senses, 15*, 755–760.

Heywood, C. A., Cowey, A., & Newcombe, F. (1991). Chromatic discrimination in a cortically colour blind observer. *European Journal of Neuroscience, 3*, 802–812.

Hickock, G., & Poeppel, D. (2007). The cortical organization of speech processing. *Nature Reviews Neuroscience, 8,* 393–401.

Hochberg, J. E. (1987). Machines should not see as people do, but must know how people see. *Computer Vision, Graphics and Image Processing, 39,* 221–237.

Hodgetts, W. E., & Liu, R. (2006). Can hockey playoffs harm your hearing? *CMAJ, 175,* 1541–1542.

Hofbauer, R. K., Rainville, P., Duncan, G. H., & Bushnell, M. C. (2001). Cortical representation of the sensory dimension of pain. *Journal of Neurophysiology, 86,* 402–411.

Hoffman, E. J., Phelps, M. E., Mullani, N. A., Higgins, C. S., & Ter-Pogossian, M. M. (1976). Design and performance characteristics of a whole-body positron transaxial tomography. *Journal of Nuclear Medicine, 17,* 493–502.

Hoffman, H. G., Doctor, J. N., Patterson, D. R., Carrougher, G. J., & Furness, T. A., III. (2000). Virtual reality as an adjunctive pain control during burn wound care in adolescent patients. *Pain, 85,* 305–309.

Hoffman, H. G., Patterson, D. R., Seibel, E., Soltani, M., Jewett-Leahy, L., & Sharar, S. R. (2008). Virtual reality pain control during burn wound debridement in the hydrotank. *Clinical Journal of Pain, 24,* 299–304.

Hofman, P. M., Van Riswick, J. G. A., & Van Opstal, A. J. (1998). Relearning sound localization with new ears. *Nature Neuroscience, 1,* 417–421.

Holden, C. (2004). Imaging studies show how brain thinks about pain. *Science, 303,* 1131.

Holley, A. (1991). Neural coding of olfactory information. In T. V. Getchell, R. L. Doty, L. M. Bartoshuk, & J. B. Snow (Eds.), *Smell and taste in health and disease* (pp. 329–343). New York: Raven Press.

Hollins, M., Bensmaia, S. J., & Roy, E. A. (2002). Vibrotaction and texture perception. *Behavioural Brain Research, 135,* 51–56.

Hollins, M., Bensmaia, S. J., & Washburn, S. (2001). Vibrotactile adaptation impairs discrimination of fine, but not coarse, textures. *Somatosensory & Motor Research, 18,* 253–262.

Hollins, M., & Risner, S. R. (2000). Evidence for the duplex theory of texture perception. *Perception & Psychophysics, 62,* 695–705.

Holway, A. H., & Boring, E. G. (1941). Determinants of apparent visual size with distance variant. *American Journal of Psychology, 54,* 21–37.

Hsiao, S. S., Johnson, K. O., Twombly, A., & DiCarlo, J. (1996). Form processing and attention effects in the somatosensory system. In O. Franzen, R. Johannson, & L. Terenius (Eds.), *Somesthesis and the neurobiology of the somatosensory cortex* (pp. 229–247). Basel: Biorkhauser Verlag.

Hsiao, S. S., O'Shaughnessy, D. M., & Johnson, K. O. (1993). Effects of selective attention on spatial form processing in monkey primary and secondary somatosensory cortex. *Journal of Neurophysiology, 70,* 444–447.

Hubel, D. H. (1982). Exploration of the primary visual cortex, 1955–1978. *Nature, 299,* 515–524.

Hubel, D. H., & Wiesel, T. N. (1959). Receptive fields of single neurons in the cat's striate cortex. *Journal of Physiology, 148,* 574–591.

Hubel, D. H., & Wiesel, T. N. (1961). Integrative action in the cat's lateral geniculate body. *Journal of Physiology, 155,* 385–398.

Hubel, D. H., & Wiesel, T. N. (1965). Receptive fields and functional architecture in two non-striate visual areas (18 and 19) of the cat. *Journal of Neurophysiology, 28,* 229–289.

Hubel, D. H., & Wiesel, T. N. (1970). Cells sensitive to binocular depth in area 18 of the macaque monkey cortex. *Nature, 225,* 41–42.

Hudspeth, A. J. (1989). How the ear's works work. *Nature, 341,* 397–404.

Humphrey, A. L., & Saul, A. B. (1994). The temporal transformation of retinal signals in the lateral geniculate nucleus of the cat: Implications for cortical function. In D. Minciacchi, M. Molinari, G. Macchi, & E. G. Jones (Eds.), *Thalamic networks for relay and modulation* (pp. 81–89). New York: Pergamon Press.

Humphreys, G. W., & Riddoch, M. J. (2001). Detection by action: Neuropsychological evidence for action-defined templates in search. *Nature Neuroscience, 4,* 84–88.

Hurvich, L. (1981). *Color vision.* Sunderland, MA: Sinauer Associates.

Hyvärinen, J., & Poranen, A. (1978). Movement-sensitive and direction and orientation-selective cutaneous receptive fields in the hand area of the postcentral gyrus in monkeys. *Journal of Physiology, 283,* 523–537.

Iacoboni, M., Molnar-Szakacs, I., Gallese, V., Buccino, G., Mazziotta, J. C., & Rizzolatti, G. (2005). Grasping the intentions of others with one's own mirror neuron system. *PLoS Biology, 3*(3), e79.

Ilg, U. J., Bridgeman, B., & Hoffmann, K. P. (1989). Influence of mechanical disturbance on oculomotor behavior. *Vision Research, 29,* 545–551.

Ino, T., Doi, T., Hirose, S., Kimura, T., Ito, J., & Fukuyama, H. (2007). Directional disorientation following left retrosplenial hemorrhage: A case report with fMRI studies. *Cortex, 43,* 248–254.

Ishai, A., Pessoa, L., Bikle, P. C., & Ungerleider, L. G. (2004). Repetition suppression of faces is modulated by emotion. *Proceedings of the National Academy of Sciences, U.S.A., 101,* 9827–9832.

Ishai, A., Ungerleider, L. G., Martin, A., & Haxby, J. V. (2000). The representation of objects in the human occipital and temporal cortex. *Journal of Cognitive Neuroscience, 12,* 35–51.

Ishai, A., Ungerleider, L. G., Martin, A., Schouten, J. L., & Haxby, J. V. (1999). Distributed representation of objects in the human ventral visual pathway. *Proceedings of the National Academy of Sciences USA, 96,* 9379–9384.

Ito, M., Tamura, H., Fujita, I., & Tanaka, K. (1995). Size and position invariance of neuronal responses in monkey inferotemporal cortex. *Journal of Neurophysiology, 73,* 218–226.

Ittelson, W. H. (1952). *The Ames demonstrations in perception.* Princeton, NJ: Princeton University Press.

Itti, L., & Koch, C. (2000). A saliency-based search mechanism for overt and covert shifts of visual attention. *Vision Research, 40,* 1489–1506.

Iversen, J. R., & Patel, A. D. (2008). Perception of rhythmic grouping depends on auditory experience. *Journal of the Acoustic Society of America, 124A,* 2263–2271.

Iwamura, Y. (1998). Representation of tactile functions in the somatosensory cortex. In J. W. Morley (Ed.), *Neural aspects of tactile sensation* (pp. 195–238). New York: Elsevier Science.

Jacobson, A., & Gilchrist, A. (1988). The ratio principle holds over a million-to-one range of illumination. *Perception and Psychophysics, 43,* 1–6.

James, W. (1981). *The principles of psychology* (Rev. ed.). Cambridge, MA: Harvard University Press. (Original work published 1890)

Janzen, G., & van Turennout, M. (2004). Selective neural representation of objects relevant for navigation. *Nature Neuroscience, 7,* 673–677.

Jeffress, L. A. (1948). A place theory of sound localization. *Journal of Comparative and Physiological Psychology, 41,* 35–39.

Jenkins, W. M., & Merzenich, M. M. (1987). Reorganization of neocortical representations after brain injury: A neurophysiological model of the bases of recovery from stroke. *Progress in Brain Research, 71*, 249–266.

Jensen, T. S., & Nikolajsen, L. (1999). Phantom pain and other phenomena after amputation. In P. D. Wall & R. Melzak (Eds.), *Textbook of pain* (pp. 799–814). New York: Churchill Livingstone.

Johansson, G. (1973). Visual perception of biological motion and a model for its analysis. *Perception and Psychophysics, 14*, 195–204.

Johansson, G. (1975). Visual motion perception. *Scientific American, 232*, 76–89.

Johnson, B. A., & Leon, M. (2007). Chemotopic odorant coding in a mammalian olfactory system. *Journal of Comparative Neurology, 503*, 1–34.

Johnson, B. A., Ong., J., & Michael, L. (2010). Glomerular activity patterns evoked by natural odor objects in the rat olfactory bulb and related to patterns evoked by major odorant components. *Journal of Comparative Neurology, 518*, 1542–1555.

Johnson, E. N., Hawken, M. J., & Shapley, R. (2008). The orientation selectivity of color-responsive neurons in Macaque V1. *Journal of Neuroscience, 28*, 8096–8106.

Johnson, K. O. (2002). Neural basis of haptic perception. In H. Pashler & S. Yantis (Eds.), *Steven's handbook of experimental psychology* (3rd ed.): *Vol. 1. Sensation and perception* (pp. 537–583). New York: Wiley.

Johnson, S. P., & Aslin, R. N. (1995). Perception of object unity in 2-month-old infants. *Developmental Psychology, 31*, 739–745.

Johnson, S. P., Davidow, J., Hall-Haro, C., & Frank, M. C. (2008). Development of perceptual completion originates in information acquisition. *Developmental Psychology, 44*, 1214–1224.

Johnson, S. P., Slemmer, J. A., & Amso, D. (2004). Where infants look determines how they see: Eye movement and object perception performance in 3-month-olds. *Infancy, 6*, 185–201.

Johnstone, B. M., & Boyle, A. J. F. (1967) Basilar membrane vibrations examined with the Mossbauer technique. *Science, 158*, 390–391.

Jones, M. R., & Yee, W. (1993). Attending to auditory events: The role of temporal organization. In S. McAdams & E. Bigand (Eds.), *Thinking in sound: The cognitive psychology of human audition* (pp. 69–112). Oxford, UK: Oxford University Press.

Jovancevic-Misic, J., & Hayhoe, M. (2009) Adaptive gaze control in natural environments. *Journal of Neuroscience, 29*, 6234–6238.

Judd, D. B., MacAdam, D. L., Wyszecki, G., Budde, H. W., Condit, H. R., Henderson, S. T., et al. (1964). Spectral distribution of typical daylight as a function of correlated color temperature. *Journal of the Optical Society of America, 54*, 1031–1036.

Julesz, B. (1971). *Foundations of cyclopean perception.* Chicago: University of Chicago Press.

Kaas, J. H., & Hackett, T. A. (1999). "What" and "where" processing in auditory cortex. *Nature Neuroscience, 2*, 1045–1047.

Kaas, J. H., Hackett, T. A., & Tramo, M. J. (1999). Auditory processing in primate cerebral cortex. *Current Opinion in Neurobiology, 9*, 164–170.

Kamitani, Y., & Tong, F. (2005). Decoding the visual and subjective contents of the human brain. *Nature Neuroscience, 8*, 679–685.

Kandel, E. R., & Jessell, T. M. (1991). Touch. In E. R. Kandel, J. H. Schwartz, & T. M. Jessell (Eds.), *Principles of neural science* (3rd ed., pp. 367–384). New York: Elsevier.

Kandil, F. I., Rotter, A., & Lappe, M. (2009). Driving is smoother and more stable when using the tangent point. *Journal of Vision, 9*(1):11, 1–11.

Kanisa, G., & Gerbino, W. (1976). Convexity and symmetry in figure-ground organization. In M. Henle (Ed.), *Vision and artifact* (pp. 25–32). New York: Springer.

Kanwisher, N. (2003). The ventral visual object pathway in humans: Evidence from fMRI. In L. M. Chalupa & J. S. Werner (Eds.), *The visual neurosciences* (pp. 1179–1190). Cambridge, MA: MIT Press.

Kanwisher, N. (2010). Functional specificity in the human brain: A window into the functional architecture of the mind. *Proceedings of the National Academy of Sciences, 107*, 11163–11170.

Kanwisher, N., McDermott, J., & Chun, M. M. (1997). The fusiform face area: A module in human extrastriate cortex specialized for face perception. *Journal of Neuroscience, 17*, 4302–4311.

Kaplan, G. (1969). Kinetic disruption of optical texture: The perception of depth at an edge. *Perception and Psychophysics, 6*, 193–198.

Karlson, P., & Lüscher, M. (1959). "Pheromones": A new term for a class of biologically active substances. *Nature, 183*, 55–56.

Katz, D. (1989). *The world of touch* (L. Kruger, Trans.). Hillsdale, NJ: Erlbaum. (Original work published 1925)

Katz, J., & Gagliese, L. (1999). Phantom limb pain: A continuing puzzle. In R. J. Gatchel & D. C. Turk (Eds.), *Psychosocial factors in pain* (pp. 284–300). New York: Guilford Press.

Katzner, S., Busse, L., & Treue, S. (2009). Attention to the color of a moving stimulus modulates motion-signal processing in macaque area MT: Evidence for a unified attentional system. *Frontiers in Systems Neuroscience, 3*, 1–8.

Kauer, J. S. (1987). Coding in the olfactory system. In T. E. Finger & W. C. Silver (Eds.), *Neurobiology of taste and smell* (pp. 205–231). New York: Wiley.

Kaufman, L., & Rock, I. (1962a). The moon illusion. *Science, 136*, 953–961.

Kaufman, L., & Rock, I. (1962b). The moon illusion. *Scientific American, 207*, 120–132.

Kavšek, M., Granrud, C. E., & Yonas. A. (2009). Infants' responsiveness to pictorial depth cues in preferential-reaching studies: A meta-analysis. *Infant Behavior and Development, 32*, 245–253.

Keller, A., Zhuang, H., Chi., Q., Vosshall, L. B., & Matsunami, H. (2007). Genetic variation in a human odorant receptor alters odour perception. *Nature, 449*, 468–472.

Kellman, P., & Spelke, E. (1983). Perception of partly occluded objects in infancy. *Cognitive Psychology, 15*, 483–524.

Kersten, D., Mamassian, P., & Yuille, A. (2004). Object perception as Bayesian inference. *Annual Review of Psychology, 55*, 271–304.

Keysers, C., Kaas, J., & Gazzola, V. (2010). Somatosensation in social perception. *Nature Reviews Neuroscience, 11*, 417–428.

Keysers, C., Wicker, B., Gazzola, V., Anton, J.-L., Fogassi, L., & Gallese, V. (2004). A touching sight: SII/PV activation during the observation and experience of touch. *Neuron, 42*, 335–346.

Khanna, S. M., & Leonard, D. G. B. (1982). Basilar membrane tuning in the cat cochlea. *Science, 215*, 305–306.

Kiefer, J., von Ilberg, C., Reimer, B., Knecht, R., Gall, V., Diller, G., et al. (1996). Results of cochlear implantation in patients with severe to profound hearing loss: Implications for the indications. *Audiology, 37*, 382–395.

Kilner, J. M. (2011). More than one pathway to action understanding. *Trends in Cognitive Sciences, 15*, 352–357.

Kim, U. K., Jorgenson, E., Coon, H., Leppert, M., Risch, N., & Drayna, D. (2003). Positional cloning of the human quantitative trait locus underlying taste sensitivity to phenylthiocarbamide. *Science, 299*, 1221–1225.

King, A. J., Schnupp, J. W. H., & Doubell, T. P. (2001). The shape of ears to come: Dynamic coding of auditory space. *Trends in Cognitive Sciences, 5*, 261–270.

King, W. L., & Gruber, H. E. (1962). Moon illusion and Emmert's law. *Science, 135*, 1125–1126.

Kish, D. (2012, April 13). *Sound vision: The consciousness of seeing with sound.* Presentation at Toward a Science of Consciousness conference, Tucson, AZ.

Kisilevsky, B. S., Hains, S. M., Brown, C. A., Lee, C. T., Cowperthwaite, B., Stutzman, S. S., et al. (2009). Fetal sensitivity to properties of maternal speech and language. *Infant Behavior and Development, 32*, 59–71.

Kisilevsky, B. S., Hains, S. M., Lee, K., Xie, X., Huang, H., Ye, H. H., et al. (2003). Effects of experience on fetal voice recognition. *Psychological Science, 14*, 220–224.

Klatzky, R. L., Lederman, S. J., Hamilton, C., Grindley, M., & Swendsen, R. H. (2003). Feeling textures through a probe: Effects of probe and surface geometry and exploratory factors. *Perception & Psychophysics, 65*, 613–631.

Klatzky, R. L., Lederman, S. J., & Metzger, V. A. (1985). Identifying objects by touch: An "expert system." *Perception and Psychophysics, 37*, 299–302.

Kleffner, D. A., & Ramachandran, V. S. (1992). On the perception of shape from shading. *Perception and Psychophysics, 52*, 18–36.

Klin, A., Jones, W., Schultz, R., & Volkmar, F. (2003). The enactive mind, or from actions to cognition: Lessons from autism. *Philosophical Transactions of the Royal Society of London B, 358*, 345–360.

Knill, D. C., & Kersten, D. (1991). Apparent surface curvature affects lightness perception. *Nature, 351*, 228–230.

Kobatake, E., & Tanaka, K. (1994). Neuronal selectivities to complex object features in the ventral visual pathway of the macaque cerebral cortex. *Journal of Neurophysiology, 71*, 856–867.

Kobayakawa, K., Kobayakawa, R., Matsumoto, H., Oka, Y., Imai, T., Ikawa, M., et al. (2007). Innate versus learned odour processing in the mouse olfactory bulb. *Nature, 450*, 503–510.

Koffka, K. (1935). *Principles of Gestalt psychology.* New York: Harcourt Brace.

Kohler, E., Keysers, C., Umilta, M. A., Fogassi, L., Gallese, V., & Rizzolatti, G. (2002). Hearing sounds, understanding actions: Action representation in mirror neurons. *Science, 297*, 846–848.

Kolb, N., & Whishaw, I. Q. (2003). *Fundamentals of neuropsychology* (5th ed.). New York: Worth.

Kondo, H. M., & Kashino, M. (2009). Involvement of the thalmocortical loop in the spontaneous switching of percepts in auditory streaming. *Journal of Neuroscience, 29*, 12695–12701.

Konorski, J. (1967). *Integrative activity of the brain: An interdisciplinary approach.* Chicago: University of Chicago Press.

Kosaki, H., Hashikawa, T., He, J., & Jones, E. G. (1997). Tonotopic organization of auditory cortical fields delineated by parvalbumin immunoreactivity in Macaque monkeys. *Journal of Comparative Neurology, 386*, 304–316.

Kourtzi, Z., & Kanwisher, N. (2000). Activation of human MT/MST by static images with implied motion. *Journal of Cognitive Neuroscience, 12*, 48–55.

Kroner, T. (1881). Über die Sinnesempfindungen der Neugeborenen. *Breslauer aerzliche Zeitschrift.* (Cited in Peterson & Rainey, 1911)

Kruger, L. E. (1970). David Katz: Der Aufbau der Tastwelt [The world of touch: A synopsis]. *Perception and Psychophysics, 7*, 337–341.

Kuffler, S. W. (1953). Discharge patterns and functional organization of mammalian retina. *Journal of Neurophysiology, 16*, 37–68.

Kuhl, P. K. (2000). Language, mind and brain: Experience alters perception. In M. Gazzaniga (Ed.), *The new cognitive neurosciences* (pp. 99–115). Cambridge, MA: MIT Press.

Kuhl, P. K., Kirtani, S., Deguchi, T., Hayashi, A., Stevens, E. B., Dugger, C. D., et al. (1997). Effects of language experience on speech perception: American and Japanese infants' perception of /ra/ and /la/. *Journal of the Acoustical Society of America, 102*, 3125.

Kuhn, G., & Land, M. F. (2006). There's more to magic than meets the eye. *Current Biology, 16*, R950–R951.

Kujawa, S. G., & Liberman, M. C. (2009). Adding insult to injury: Cochlear nerve degeneration after "temporary" noise-induced hearing loss. *Journal of Neuroscience, 45*, 14077–14085.

Kushner, T. (1993). *Angels in America.* New York: Theatre Communications Group.

Kwee, I., Fujii, Y., Matsuzawa, H., & Nakada, T. (1999). Perceptual processing of stereopsis in humans: GH high-field (3.0 tesla) functional MRI study. *Neurology, 53*, 1599–1601.

LaBarbera, J. D., Izard, C. E., Vietze, P., & Parisi, S. A. (1976). Four- and six-month-old infants' visual responses to joy, anger, and neutral expressions. *Child Development, 47*, 535–538.

Laing, D. D., Doty, R. L., & Breipohl, W. (Eds.). (1991). *The human sense of smell.* New York: Springer.

Lamm, C., Batson, C. D., & Decdety, J. (2007). The neural substrate of human empathy: Effects of perspective-taking and cognitive appraisal. *Journal of Cognitive Neuroscience, 19*, 42–58.

Land, E. H. (1983). Recent advances in retinex theory and some implications for cortical computations: Color vision and the natural image. *Proceedings of the National Academy of Sciences, USA, 80*, 5163–5169.

Land, E. H. (1986). Recent advances in retinex theory. *Vision Research, 26*, 7–21.

Land, E. H., & McCann, J. J. (1971). Lightness and retinex theory. *Journal of the Optical Society of America, 61*, 1–11.

Land, M. F., & Hayhoe, M. (2001). In what ways do eye movements contribute to everyday activities? *Vision Research, 41*, 3559–3565.

Land, M. F., & Horwood, J. (1995). Which parts of the road guide steering? *Nature, 377*, 339–340.

Land, M. F., & Lee, D. N. (1994). Where we look when we steer. *Nature, 369*, 742–744.

Land, M. F., Mennie, N., & Rusted, J. (1999). The roles of vision and eye movements in the control of activities of daily living. *Perception, 28*, 1311–1328.

Larsen, A., Madsen, K. H., Lund, T. E., & Bundesen, C. (2006). Images of illusory motion in primary visual cortex. *Journal of Cognitive Neuroscience, 18*, 1174–1180.

Lavie, N. (1995). Perceptual load as a major determinant of the locus of selection in visual attention. *Perception and Psychophysics, 56*, 183–197.

Lavie, N. (2006). Distracted and confused? Selective attention under load. *Trends in Cognitive Sciences, 9*, 75–82.

Lavie, N. (2010). Attention, distraction, and cognitive control under load. *Current Directions in Psychological Science, 19*, 143–148.

Lavie, N., & Driver, J. (1996). On the spatial extent of attention in object-based visual selection. *Perception and Psychophysics, 58*, 1238–1251.

Lawless, H. (1980). A comparison of different methods for assessing sensitivity to the taste of phenylthiocarbamide PTC. *Chemical Senses, 5*, 247–256.

Lawless, H. (2001). Taste. In E. B. Goldstein (Ed.), *Blackwell handbook of perception* (pp. 601–635). Oxford, UK: Blackwell.

Lederman, S. J., & Klatzky, R. L. (1987). Hand movements: A window into haptic object recognition. *Cognitive Psychology, 19*, 342–368.

Lederman, S. J., & Klatzky, R. L. (1990). Haptic classification of common objects: Knowledge-driven exploration. *Cognitive Psychology, 22,* 421–459.

Lee, D. N., & Aronson, E. (1974). Visual proprioceptive control of standing in human infants. *Perception and Psychophysics, 15,* 529–532.

LeGrand, Y. (1957). *Light, color and vision.* London: Chapman & Hall.

Lesham, M. (1998). Salt preference in adolescence is predicted by common prenatal and infantile mineral fluid loss. *Physiology & Behavior, 63,* 699–704.

Levin, D., & Simons, D. (1997). Failure to detect changes to attended objects in motion pictures. *Psychonomic Bulletin and Review, 4,* 501–506.

Li, F., VanRullen, R., Koch, C., & Perona, P. (2002). Rapid natural scene categorization in the near absence of attention. *Proceedings of the National Academy of Sciences, 99,* 9596–9601.

Li, L., Sweet, B. T., & Stone, L. S. (2006). Humans can perceive heading without visual path information. *Journal of Vision, 6,* 874–881.

Li, X., Li, W., Wang, H., Cao, J., Maehashi, K., Huang, L., et al. (2005). Pseudogenization of a sweet-receptor gene accounts for cats' indifference toward sugar. *PLoS Genetics, 1*(1), e3.

Liberman, A. M., Cooper, F. S., Harris, K. S., & MacNeilage, P. F. (1963). A motor theory of speech perception. *Proceedings of the Symposium on Speech Communication Seminar,* Royal Institute of Technology, Stockholm, Vol. II, Paper D3.

Liberman, A. M., Cooper, F. S., Shankweiler, D. P., & Studdert-Kennedy, M. (1967). Perception of the speech code. *Psychological Review, 74,* 431–461.

Liberman, A. M., & Mattingly, I. G. (1989). A specialization for speech perception. *Science, 243,* 489–494.

Liberman, M. C., & Dodds, L. W. (1984). Single-neuron labeling and chronic cochlear pathology: III. Stereocilia damage and alterations of threshold tuning curves. *Hearing Research, 16,* 55–74.

Lindsay, P. H., & Norman, D. A. (1977). *Human information processing* (2nd ed.). New York: Academic Press.

Litovsky, R. Y. (2012). Spatial release from masking. *Acoustics Today, 8*(2), 18–25.

Litovsky, R. Y., Colburn, H. S., Yost, W. A., & Guzman, S. J. (1999). The precedence effect. *Journal of the Acoustical Society of America, 106,* 1633–1654.

Litovsky, R. Y., Rakerd, B., Yin, T. C. T., & Hartmann, W. M. (1997). Psychophysical and physiological evidence for a precedence effect in the median saggital plane. *Journal of Neurophysiology, 77,* 2223–2226.

Lomber, S. G., & Malhotra S. (2008). Double dissociation of "what" and "where" processing in auditory cortex. *Nature Neuroscience, 11,* 601–616.

Loomis, J. M., DaSilva, J. A., Fujita, N., & Fulusima, S. S. (1992). Visual space perception and visually directed action. *Journal of Experimental Psychology: Human Perception and Performance, 18,* 906–921.

Loomis, J. M., & Philbeck, J. W. (2008). Measuring spatial perception with spatial updating and action. In R. L. Klatzky, B. MacWhinney, & M. Behrmann (Eds.), *Embodiment, ego-space, and action* (pp. 1–43). New York: Taylor and Francis.

Lorteije, J. A. M., Kenemans, J. L., Jellema, T., van der Lubbe, R. H. J., de Heer, F., & van Wezel, R. J. A. (2006). Delayed response to animate implied motion in human motion processing areas. *Journal of Cognitive Neuroscience 18,* 158–168.

Lotto, A. J., Hickok, G. S., & Holt, L. L. (2009). Reflections on mirror neurons and speech perception. *Trends in Cognitive Sciences, 13,* 110–113.

Lowenstein, W. R. (1960). Biological transducers. *Scientific American, 203,* 98–108.

Lundy, R. F., Jr., & Contreras, R. J. (1999). Gustatory neuron types in rat geniculate ganglion. *Journal of Neurophysiology, 82,* 2970–2988.

Lyall, V., Heck, G. L., Phan, T.-H. T., Mummalaneni, S., Malik, S. A., Vinnikova, A. K., et al. (2005). Ethanol modulates the VR-1 variant amiloride-insensitive salt taste receptor: I. Effect on TRC volume and Na+ flux. *Journal of General Physiology, 125,* 569–585.

Lyall, V., Heck, G. L., Vinnikova, A. K., Ghosh, S., Phan, T.-H. T., Alam, R. I., et al. (2004). The mammalian amiloride-insensitive non-specific salt taste receptor is a vanilloid receptor-1 variant. *Journal of Physiology, 558,* 147–159.

Mack, A., & Clarke, J. (2012). Gist perception requires attention. *Visual Cognition, 20,* 300–327.

Mack, A., & Rock, I. (1998). *Inattentional blindness.* Cambridge, MA: MIT Press.

Maguire, E. A., Nannery, R., & Spiers, H. J. (2006). Navigation around London by a taxi driver with bilateral hippocampal lesions. *Brain, 129,* 2894–2907.

Malhotra, S., & Lomber, S. G. (2007). Sound localization during homotopic and heterotopic bilateral cooling deactivation of primary and nonprimary auditory cortical areas in the cat. *Journal of Neurophysiology, 97,* 26–43.

Malhotra, S., Stecker, G. C., Middlebrooks, J. C., & Lomber, S. G. (2008). Sound localization deficits during reversible deactivation of primary auditory cortex and/or the dorsal zone. *Journal of Neurophysiology, 99,* 1628–1642.

Malnic, B., Hirono, J., Sata, T., & Buck, L. B. (1999). Combinatorial receptor codes for odors. *Cell, 96,* 713–723.

Mamassian, P., Knill, D., & Kersten, D. (1998). The perception of cast shadows. *Trends in Cognitive Sciences, 2,* 288–295.

Marino, A. C., & Scholl, B. J. (2005). The role of closure in defining the "objects" of object-based attention. *Perception and Psychophysics, 67,* 1140–1149.

Marois, R., & Ivanoff, J. (2005). Capacity limits of information processing in the brain. *Trends in Cognitive Sciences, 9,* 296–305.

Mather, G., Verstraten, F., & Anstis, S. (1998). *The motion aftereffect: A modern perspective.* Cambridge, MA: MIT Press.

Mayer, D. L., Beiser, A. S., Warner, A. F., Pratt, E. M., Raye, K. N., & Lang, J. M. (1995). Monocular acuity norms for the Teller Acuity Cards between ages one month and four years. *Investigative Ophthalmology and Visual Science, 36,* 671–685.

McAlpine, D. (2005). Creating a sense of auditory space. *Journal of Physiology, 566,* 21–22.

McAlpine, D., & Grothe, B. (2003). Sound localization and delay lines: Do mammals fit the model? *Trends in Neurosciences, 26,* 347–350.

McBurney, D. H. (1969). Effects of adaptation on human taste function. In C. Pfaffmann (Ed.), *Olfaction and taste* (pp. 407–419). New York: Rockefeller University Press.

McCarthy, G., Puce, A., Gore, J. C., & Allison, T. (1997). Face-specific processing in the human fusiform gyrus. *Journal of Cognitive Neuroscience, 9,* 605–610.

McCartney, P. (1970). *The long and winding road* (musical composition). Apple Records.

McFadden, S. A. (1987). The binocular depth stereoacuity of the pigeon and its relation to the anatomical resolving power of the eye. *Vision Research, 27,* 1967–1980.

McFadden, S. A., & Wild, J. M. (1986). Binocular depth perception in the pigeon. *Journal of Experimental Analysis of Behavior, 45,* 149–160.

McGurk, H., & MacDonald, T. (1976). Hearing lips and seeing voices. *Nature, 264,* 746–748.

Mehler, J. (1981). The role of syllables in speech processing: Infant and adult data. *Transactions of the Royal Society of London, B295,* 333–352.

Melzack, R. (1992). Phantom limbs. *Scientific American, 266,* 121–126.

Melzack, R. (1999). From the gate to the neuromatrix. *Pain,* Suppl. 6, S121–S126.

Melzack, R., & Wall, P. D. (1965). Pain mechanisms: A new theory. *Science, 150,* 971–979.

Melzack, R., & Wall, P. D. (1988). *The challenge of pain* (Rev. ed.). New York: Penguin Books.

Menashe, I., Man, O., Lancet, D., & Gilad, Y. (2003). Different noses for different people. *Nature Genetics, 34,* 143–144.

Mennella, J. A., Jagnow, C. P., & Beauchamp, G. K. (2001). Prenatal and postnatal flavor learning by human infants. *Pediatrics, 107*(6), 1–6.

Mennella, J. A., Johnson, A., & Beauchamp, G. K. (1995). Garlic ingestion by pregnant women alters the odor of amniotic fluid. *Chemical Senses, 20,* 207–209.

Menz, M. D., & Freeman, R. D. (2003). Stereoscopic depth processing in the visual cortex: A coarse-to-fine mechanism. *Nature Neuroscience, 6,* 59–65.

Menzel, R., & Backhaus, W. (1989). Color vision in honey bees: Phenomena and physiological mechanisms. In D. G. Stavenga & R. C. Hardie (Eds.), *Facets of vision* (pp. 281–297). Berlin: Springer-Verlag.

Menzel, R., Ventura, D. F., Hertel, H., deSouza, J., & Greggers, U. (1986). Spectral sensitivity of photoreceptors in insect compound eyes: Comparison of species and methods. *Journal of Comparative Physiology, 158A,* 165–177.

Merigan, W. H., & Maunsell, J. H. R. (1993). How parallel are the primate visual pathways? *Annual Review of Neuroscience, 16,* 369–402.

Merskey, H. (1991). The definition of pain. *European Journal of Psychiatry, 6,* 153–159.

Merzenich, M. M., Recanzone, G., Jenkins, W. M., Allard, T. T., & Nudo, R. J. (1988). Cortical representational plasticity. In P. Rakic & W. Singer (Eds.), *Neurobiology of neocortex* (pp. 42 67). New York: Wiley.

Meyer, K., Kaplan, J. T., Essex, R., Damasio, H., & Damasio, A. (2011). Seeing touch is correlated with content-specific activity in primary somatosensory cortex. *Cerebral Cortex, 21,* 2113–2121.

Micelli, G., Gainotti, G., Caltagirone, C., & Masullo, C. (1980). Some aspects of phonological impairment in aphasia. *Brain and Language, 11,* 159–169.

Miller, G. A., & Heise, G. A. (1950). The trill threshold. *Journal of the Acoustical Society of America, 22,* 637–683.

Miller, G. A., & Isard, S. (1963). Some perceptual consequences of linguistic rules. *Journal of Verbal Learning and Verbal Behavior, 2,* 212–228.

Miller, J. D. (1974). Effects of noise on people. *Journal of the Acoustical Society of America, 56,* 729–764.

Miller, S. L., & Maner, J. K. (2010). Scent of a woman: Men's testosterone responses to olfactory ovulation cues. *Psychological Science, 21,* 276–283.

Milner, A. D., & Goodale, M. A. (1995). *The visual brain in action.* New York: Oxford University Press.

Milner, A. D., & Goodale, M. A. (2006). *The visual brain in action* (2nd ed.). New York: Oxford University Press.

Mishkin, M., Ungerleider, L. G., & Macko, K. A. (1983). Object vision and spatial vision: Two central pathways. *Trends in Neuroscience, 6,* 414–417.

Møller, A. R. (2000). *Hearing: Its physiology and pathophysiology.* San Diego: Academic Press.

Mollon, J. D. (1989). "Tho' she kneel'd in that place where they grew . . ." *Journal of Experimental Biology, 146,* 21–38.

Mollon, J. D. (1997). "Tho' she kneel'd in that place where they grew . . .": The uses and origins of primate colour visual information. In A. Byrne & D. R. Hilbert (Eds.), *Readings on color: Vol. 2. The science of color* (pp. 379–396). Cambridge, MA: MIT Press.

Mondloch, C. J., Dobson, K. S., Parsons, J., & Maurer, D. (2004). Why 8-year-olds cannot tell the difference between Steve Martin and Paul Newman: Factors contributing to the slow development of sensitivity to the spacing of facial features. *Journal of Experimental Child Psychology, 89,* 159–181.

Mondloch, C. J., Geldart, S., Maurer, D., & LeGrand, R. (2003). Developmental changes in face processing skills. *Journal of Experimental Child Psychology, 86,* 67–84.

Montagna, W., & Parakkal, P. F. (1974). *The structure and function of skin* (3rd ed.). New York: Academic Press.

Mon-Williams, M., & Tresilian, J. R. (1999). Some recent studies on the extraretinal contribution to distance perception. *Perception, 28,* 167–181.

Monzée, J., Lamarre, Y., & Smith, A. M. (2003). The effects of digital anesthesia on force control using a precision grip. *Journal of Neurophysiology, 89,* 672–683.

Moon, R. J., Cooper, R. P., & Fifer, W. P. (1993). Two-day-olds prefer their native language. *Infant Behavior and Development, 16,* 495–500.

Moore, B. C. J. (1995). *Perceptual consequences of cochlear damage.* Oxford, UK: Oxford University Press.

Moore, C. M., Yantis, S., & Vaughan, B. (1998). Object-based visual selection: Evidence from perceptual completion. *Psychological Science, 9,* 104–110.

More noise than signal [Editorial]. (2007). *Nature Neuroscience, 10,* 799.

Morton, J., & Johnson, M. H. (1991). CONSPEC and CONLEARN: A two-process theory of infant face recognition. *Psychological Review, 98,* 164–181.

Moulton, D. G. (1977). Minimum odorant concentrations detectable by the dog and their implications for olfactory receptor sensitivity. In D. Miller-Schwarze & M. M. Mozell (Eds.), *Chemical signals in vertebrates* (pp. 455–464). New York: Plenum Press.

Mountcastle, V. B., & Powell, T. P. S. (1959). Neural mechanisms subserving cutaneous sensibility, with special reference to the role of afferent inhibition in sensory perception and discrimination. *Bulletin of the Johns Hopkins Hospital, 105,* 201–232.

Movshon, J. A., & Newsome, W. T. (1992). Neural foundations of visual motion perception. *Current Directions in Psychological Science, 1,* 35–39.

Mozell, M. M., Smith, B. P., Smith, P. E., Sullivan, R. L., & Swender, P. (1969). Nasal chemoreception in flavor identification. *Archives of Otolaryngology, 90,* 131–137.

Mueller, K. L., Hoon, M. A., Erlenbach, I., Chandrashekar, J., Zuker, C. S., & Ryba, N. J. P. (2005). The receptors and coding logic for bitter taste. *Nature, 434,* 225–229.

Muir, D., & Field, J. (1979). Newborn infants orient to sounds. *Child Development, 50,* 431–436.

Murphy, C., & Cain, W. S. (1980). Taste and olfaction: Independence vs. interaction. *Physiology and Behavior, 24,* 601–606.

Murphy, K. J., Racicot, C. I., & Goodale, M. A. (1996). The use of visuomotor cues as a strategy for making perceptual judgements in a patient with visual form agnosia. *Neuropsychology, 10,* 396–401.

Murray, M. M., & Spierer, L. (2011). Multisensory integration: What you see is where you hear. *Current Biology, 21,* R229–R231.

Murthy, V. N. (2011). Olfactory maps in the brain. *Annual Review of Neuroscience, 34,* 233–258.

Mythbusters. (2007). Episode 71: Pirate special. Program first aired on the Discovery Channel, January 17, 2007.

Narayan, S. S., Temchin, A. N., Recio, A., & Ruggero, M. A. (1998). Frequency tuning of basilar membrane and auditory nerve fibers in the same cochleae. *Science, 282*, 1882–1884.

Naselaris, T., Prenger, R. J., Kay, K. N., Oliver, M., & Gallant, J. L. (2009). Bayesian reconstruction of natural images from human brain activity. *Neuron, 63*, 902–915.

Nassi, J. J., & Callaway, E. M. (2009). Parallel processing strategies of the primate visual system. *Nature Reviews Neuroscience, 10*, 360–372.

Nathans, J., Thomas, D., & Hogness, D. S. (1986). Molecular genetics of human color vision: The genes encoding blue, green, and red pigments. *Science, 232*, 193–202.

Natu, V., & O'Toole, A. J. (2011). The neural processing of familiar and unfamiliar faces: A review and synopsis. *British Journal of Psychology, 102*, 726–747.

Neisser, U., & Becklen, R. (1975). Selective looking: Attending to visually specified events. *Cognitive Psychology, 7*, 480–494.

Neitz, M., Neitz, J., & Jacobs, G. H. (1991). Spectral tuning of pigments underlying red–green color vision. *Science, 252*, 971–974.

Newsome, W. T., Britten, K. H., & Movshon, J. A. (1989). Neuronal correlates of a perceptual decision. *Nature, 341*, 52–54.

Newsome, W. T., & Paré, E. B. (1988). A selective impairment of motion perception following lesions of the middle temporal visual area (MT). *Journal of Neuroscience, 8*, 2201–2211.

Newsome, W. T., Shadlen, M. N., Zohary, E., Britten, K. H., & Movshon, J. A. (1995). Visual motion: Linking neuronal activity to psychophysical performance. In M. S. Gazzaniga (Ed.), *The cognitive neurosciences* (pp. 401–414). Cambridge, MA: MIT Press.

Newton, I. (1704). *Optiks*. London: Smith and Walford.

Newtson, D., & Engquist, G. (1976). The perceptual organization of ongoing behavior. *Journal of Experimental Psychology: General, 130*, 29–58.

Nikonov, A. A., Finger, T. E. & Caprio, J. (2005). Beyond the olfactory bulb: An odotopic map in the forebrain. *Proceedings of the National Academy of Sciences, 102*, 18688–18693.

Nodal, F. R., Kacelnik, O., Bajo, V. M., Bizley, J. K., Moore, D. R., & King, A. J. (2010). Lesions of the auditory cortex impair azimuthal sound localization and its recalibration in ferrets. *Journal of Neurophysiology, 103*, 1209–1225.

Norcia, A. M., & Tyler, C. W. (1985). Spatial frequency sweep VEP: Visual acuity during the first year of life. *Vision Research, 25*, 1399–1408.

Nordby, K. (1990). Vision in a complete achromat: A personal account. In R. F. Hess, L. T. Sharpe, & K. Nordby (Eds.), *Night vision* (pp. 290–315). Cambridge, UK: Cambridge University Press.

Noton, D., & Stark, L. W. (1971). Scanpaths in eye movements during pattern perception. *Science, 171*, 308–311.

Novotny, M., Harvey, S., Jemiolo, B., & Alberts, J. (1985). Synthetic pheromones that promote inter-male aggression in mice. *Proceedings of the National Academy of Sciences, 82*–2059-2061.

Nozaradan, S., Peretz, I., Missal, M., & Mouraux, A. (2011). Tagging the neuronal entrainment to beat and meter. *Journal of Neuroscience, 31*, 10234–10240.

O'Craven, K. M., Downing, P. E., & Kanwisher, N. (1999). fMRI evidence for objects as the units of attentional selection. *Nature, 401*, 584–587.

O'Doherty, J., Rolls, E. T., Francis, S., Bowtell, R., McGlone, F., Kobal, G., et al. (2000). Sensory-specific satiety-related olfactory activation of the human orbitofrontal cortex. *Neuroreport, 11*, 893–897.

Ohzawa, I. (1998). Mechanisms of stereoscopic vision: The disparity energy model. *Current Opinion in Neurobiology, 8*, 509–515.

Okamoto, H., Teismann, H., Kakigi, R., & Pantev, C. (2011). Broadened population-level frequency tuning in human auditory cortex of portable music player users. *PLoS ONE 6*(3): e17022. Doi:10.1371/journal.pone.0017022.

Oliva, A., & Torralba, A. (2001). Modeling the shape of the scene: A holistic representation of the spatial envelope. *International Journal of Computer Vision, 42*, 145–175.

Oliva, A., & Torralba, A. (2006). Building the gist of a scene: The role of global image features in recognition. *Progress in Brain Research, 155*, 23–36.

Oliva, A., & Torralba, A. (2007). The role of context in object recognition. *Trends in Cognitive Sciences, 11*, 521–527.

Olkkonen, M., Witzel, C., Hansen, T., & Gegenfurtner, K. R. (2010). Categorical color constancy for real surfaces. *Journal of Vision, 10*(9):16, 1–22.

Olshausen, B. A., & Field, D. J. (2004). Sparse coding of sensory inputs. *Current Opinion in Neurobiology, 14*, 481–487.

Olsho, L. W., Koch, E. G., Carter, E. A., Halpin, C. F., & Spetner, N. B. (1988). Pure-tone sensitivity of human infants. *Journal of the Acoustical Society of America, 84*, 1316–1324.

Olsho, L. W., Koch, E. G., Halpin, C. F., & Carter, E. A. (1987). An observer-based psychoacoustic procedure for use with young infants. *Developmental Psychology, 23*, 627–640.

Olson, C. R., & Freeman, R. D. (1980). Profile of the sensitive period for monocular deprivation in kittens. *Experimental Brain Research, 39*, 17–21.

Olson, H. (1967). *Music, physics, and engineering* (2nd ed.). New York: Dover.

Orban, G. A., Lagae, L., Verri, A., Raiguel, S., Xiao, D., Maes, H., et al. (1992). First-order analysis of optical flow in monkey brain. *Proceedings of the National Academy of Sciences, 89*, 2595–2599.

Orban, G. A., Vandenbussche, E., & Vogels, R. (1984). Human orientation discrimination tested with long stimuli. *Vision Research, 24*, 121–128.

Osborn, J., & Derbyshire, W. G. (2010). Pain sensation evoked by observing injury in others. *Pain, 148*, 268–274.

O'Toole, A. J. (2007). Face recognition algorithms surpass humans matching faces over changes in illumination. *IEEE Transactions on Pattern Analysis and Machine Intelligence, 29*, 1642–1646.

O'Toole, A. J., Abdi, H., Jiang, F., & Phillips, P. J. (2007). Fusing face recognition algorithms and humans. *IEEE Transactions on Systems, Man and Cybernetics, 37*, 1149–1155.

O'Toole, A. J., Harms, J., Snow, S. L., Hurst, D. R., Pappas, M. R., & Abdi, H. (2005). A video database of moving faces and people. *IEEE Transactions on Pattern Analysis and Machine Intelligence, 27*(5), 812–816.

Owens, M. (1994, June 6). Designers discover the sweet smell of success. *New York Times*.

Pack, C. C., & Born, R. T. (2001). Temporal dynamics of a neural solution to the aperture problem in visual area MT of macaque brain. *Nature, 409*, 1040–1042.

Pack, C. C., Livingston, M. S., Duffy, K. R., & Born, R. T. (2003). End-stopping and the aperture problem: Two-dimensional motion signals in macaque V1. *Neuron, 59*, 671–680.

Palmer, A. R. (1987). Physiology of the cochlear nerve and cochlear nucleus. In M. P. Haggard & E. F. Evans (Eds.), *Hearing* (pp. 838–855). Edinburgh: Churchill Livingstone.

Palmer, S. E. (1975). The effects of contextual scenes on the identification of objects. *Memory and Cognition, 3*, 519–526.

Palmer, S. E. (1992). Common region: A new principle of perceptual grouping. *Cognitive Psychology, 24*, 436–447.

Palmer, S. E., & Rock, I. (1994). Rethinking perceptual organization: The role of uniform connectedness. *Psychonomic Bulletin and Review, 1*, 29–55.

Palmeri, T. J., Goldinger, S. D., & Pisoni, D. B. (1993). Episodic encoding of voice attributes and recognition memory for spoken words. *Journal of Experimental Psychology: Learning Memory and Cognition, 19*, 309–328.

Paré, M., Smith, A. M., & Rice, F. L. (2002). Distribution and terminal arborizations of cutaneous mechanoreceptors in the glabrous finger pads of the monkey. *Journal of Comparative Neurology, 445*, 347–359.

Parker, A. J. (2007). Binocular depth perception and the cerebral cortex. *Nature Reviews Neuroscience, 8*, 379–391.

Parkhurst, D., Law, K., & Niebur, E. (2002). Modeling the role of salience in the allocation of overt visual attention. *Vision Research, 42*, 107–123.

Parkin, A. J. (1996). *Explorations in cognitive neuropsychology.* Oxford, UK: Blackwell.

Pascalis, O., de Schonen, S., Morton, J., Deruelle, C., & Fabre-Grenet, M. (1995). Mother's face recognition by neonates: A replication and an extension. *Infant Behavior and Development, 18*, 79–85.

Pascual-Leone, A., Amedi, A., Fregni, F., & Merabet, L. B. (2005). The plastic human brain cortex. *Annual Review of Neuroscience, 28*, 377–401.

Pasley, B. N., David, S. V., Mesgarani, M., Flinker, A., Shamma, S. A., Crone, N. E., et al. (2012). Reconstructing speech from human auditory cortex. *PLoS Biology 10*(1): e1001251.

Pasternak, T., & Merigan, E. H. (1994). Motion perception following lesions of the superior temporal sulcus in the monkey. *Cerebral Cortex, 4*, 247–259.

Pecka, M., Bran, A., Behrend, O., & Grothe, B. (2008). Interaural time difference processing in the mammalian medial superior olive: The role of glycinergic inhibition. *Journal of Neuroscience, 28*, 6914–6925.

Pei, Y-C., Hsiao, S. S., Craig, J. C., & Bensmaia, S. J. (2011). Neural mechanisms of tactile motion integration in somatosensory cortex. *Neuron, 69*, 536–547.

Pelchat, M. L., Bykowski, C., Duke, F. F., & Reed, D. R. (2011). Excretion and perception of a characteristic odor in urine after asparagus ingestion: A psychophysical and genetic study. *Chemical Senses, 36*, 9–17.

Pelphrey, K. A., Mitchell, T. V., McKeown, M. J., Goldstein, J., Allison, T., & McCarthy, G. (2003). Brain activity evoked by the perception of human walking: Controlling for meaningful coherent motion. *Journal of Neuroscience, 23*, 6819–6825.

Pelphrey, K. A., Morris, J. P., & McCarthy, G. (2005). Neural basis of eye gaze processing deficits in autism. *Brain, 128*, 1038–1048.

Pelphrey, K. A., Viola, R. J., & McCarthy, G. (2004). When strangers pass. *Psychological Science, 15*, 598–603.

Penfield, W., & Rasmussen, T. (1950). *The cerebral cortex of man.* New York: Macmillan.

Peng, J.-H., Tao, Z.-A., & Huang, Z.-W. (2007). Risk of damage to hearing from personal listening devices in young adults. *Journal of Otolaryngology, 36*(3), 181–185.

Perl, E. R. (2007). Ideas about pain, a historical view. *Nature Reviews Neuroscience, 8*, 71–80.

Perl, E. R., & Kruger, L. (1996). In L. Kruger (Ed.), *Pain and touch* (pp. 179–221). San Diego, CA: Academic Press.

Pero, L. Del, Guan, J., Brau, E., Schlecht, J., & Barnard, K. (2011). Sampling bedrooms. *IEEE Computer Society Conference on Computer Vision and Pattern Recognition (CVPR)*, pp. 2009–2016.

Perrett, D. I., Rolls, E. T., & Caan, W. (1982). Visual neurons responsive to faces in the monkey temporal cortex. *Experimental Brain Research, 7*, 329–342.

Perrodin, C., Kayser, C., Logothetis, N. K., & Petkov, C. I. (2011). Voice cells in the primate temporal lobe. *Current Biology, 21*, 1408–1415.

Peterson, F., & Rainey, L. H. (1911). The beginnings of mind in the newborn. *Bulletin of the Lying-In Hospital, 7*, 99–122.

Peterson, M. A. (1994). Object recognition processes can and do operate before figure-ground organization. *Current Directions in Psychological Science, 3*, 105–111.

Peterson, M. A. (2001). Object perception. In E. B. Goldstein (Ed.), *Blackwell handbook of perception* (Chapter 6, pp. 168–203). Oxford, UK: Blackwell.

Peterson, M. A., & Kimchi, R. (2012). Perceptual organization in vision. In D. Reisberg (Ed.), *Oxford handbook of cognitive psychology.* New York: Oxford University Press.

Peterson, M. A., & Salvagio, E. (2008). Inhibitory competition in figure-ground perception: Context and convexity. *Journal of Vision, 8*(16):4, 1–13.

Pfaffmann, C. (1974). Specificity of the sweet receptors of the squirrel monkey. *Chemical Senses, 1*, 61–67.

Pfeiffer, C. A., & Johnston, R. E. (1994). Hormonal and behavioral responses of male hamsters to females and female odors: Roles of olfaction, the vemeronasal system, and sexual experience. *Physiology and Behavior, 55*, 129–138.

Philbeck, J. W., Loomis, J. M., & Beall, A. C. (1997). Visually perceived location is an invariant in the control of action. *Perception and Psychophysics, 59*, 601–612.

Phillips, J. R., & Johnson, K. O. (1981). Tactile spatial resolution: II. Neural representation of bars, edges, and gratings in monkey primary afferent. *Journal of Neurophysiology, 46*, 1177–1191.

Phillips-Silver, J., & Trainor, L. J. (2005). Feeling the beat: Movement influences infant rhythm perception. *Science, 308*, 1430.

Phillips-Silver, J., & Trainor, L. J. (2007). Hearing what the body feels: Auditory encoding of rhythmic movement. *Cognition, 105*, 533–546.

Pitcher, D., Dilks, D. D., Saxe, R. R., Triantafyllou, C., & Kanwisher, N. (2011). Differential selectivity for dynamic versus static in face-selective cortical regions. *Neuroimage, 11*(11): 654; doi:10.1016/j.neuroimage.2011.03.067.

Plack, C. J. (2005). *The sense of hearing.* New York: Psychology Press.

Plack, C. J., Drga, V., & Lopez-Poveda, E. (2004). Inferred basilar-membrane response functions for listeners with mild to moderate sensorineural hearing loss. *Journal of the Acoustical Society of America, 115*, 1684–1695.

Plassmann, H., O'Doherty, J., Shiv, B., & Rangel, A. (2008). Marketing actions can modulate neural representations of experienced pleasantness. *Proceedings of the National Academy of Sciences, 105*, 1050–1054.

Plug, C., & Ross, H. E. (1994). The natural moon illusion: A multifactor account. *Perception, 23*, 321–333.

Pokorny, J., Shevell, S. K., & Smith, V. C. (1991). Color appearance and color constancy. In P. Gouras (Ed.), *The perception of color: Vol. 6. Vision and visual dysfunction* (pp. 43–61). Boca Raton, FL: CRC Press.

Poremba, A., Saunders, R. C., Crane, A. M., Cook, M., Sokoloff, L., & Mishkin, M. (2003). Functional mapping of the primate auditory system. *Science, 299*, 568–572.

Porter, R. H., Cernoch, J. M., & McLaughlin, F. J. (1983). Maternal recognition of neonates through olfactory cues. *Physiology & Behavior, 30*, 151–154.

Posner, M. I., Nissen, M. J., & Ogden, W. C. (1978). Attended and unattended processing modes: The role of set for spatial location. In H. L. Pick & I. J. Saltzman (Eds.), *Modes of perceiving and processing information*. Hillsdale, NJ: Erlbaum.

Potter, M. C. (1976). Short-term conceptual memory for pictures. *Journal of Experimental Psychology (Human Learning), 2*, 509–522.

Price, D. D. (2000). Psychological and neural mechanisms of the affective dimension of pain. *Science, 288*, 1769–1772.

Prinzmetal, W., Shimamura, A. P., & Mikolinski, M. (2001). The Ponzo illusion and the perception of orientation. *Perception & Psychophysics, 63*, 99–114.

Proffitt, D. R. (2009). Affordances matter in geographical slant perception. *Psychonomic Bulletin & Review, 16*, 970–972.

Puce, A., Allison, T., Bentin, S., Gore, J. C., & McCarthy, G. (1998). Temporal cortex activation in humans viewing eye and mouth movements. *Journal of Neuroscience, 18*, 2188–2199.

Quinn, P. C., Rosano, J. L., & Wooten, B. R. (1988). Evidence that brown is not an elemental color. *Perception and Psychophysics, 43*, 156–164.

Quiroga, R. Q., Reddy, L., Kreiman, G., Koch, C., & Fried, I. (2005). Invariant visual representation by single neurons in the human brain. *Nature, 435*, 1102–1107.

Quiroga, R. Q., Reddy, L., Kreiman, G., Koch, C., & Fried, I. (2008). Sparse but not "grandmother-cell" coding in the medial temporal lobe. *Trends in Cognitive Sciences, 12*, 87–91.

Raffi, M., Squatrito, S., & Maioli, M. G. (2002). Responses to optic flow in the monkey parietal area. *Cerebral Cortex, 12*, 639–646.

Raij, T. T., Numminen, J., Narvarnen, S., Hiltunen, J., & Hari, R. (2005). Brain correlates of subjective reality of physically and psychologically induced pain. *Proceedings of the National Academy of Sciences of the United States of America, 102*, 2147–2151.

Raij, T. T., Numminen, J., Narvarnen, S., Hiltunen, J., & Hari, R. (2009). Strength of prefrontal activation predicts intensity of suggestion-induced pain. *Human Brain Mapping, 30*, 2890–2897.

Rainville, P. (2002). Brain mechanisms of pain affect and pain modulation. *Current Opinion in Neurobiology, 12*, 195–204.

Rainville, P., Hofbauer, R. K., Paus, T., Duncan, G. H., Bushnell, M. C., & Price, D. D. (1999). Cerebral mechanisms of hypnotic induction and suggestion. *Journal of Cognitive Neuroscience, 11*, 110–125.

Ramachandran, V. S. (1992, May). Blind spots. *Scientific American*, 86–91.

Ramachandran, V. S., & Hirstein, W. (1998). The perception of phantom limbs. *Brain, 121*, 1603–1630.

Ratliff, F. (1965). *Mach bands: Quantitative studies on neural networks in the retina*. San Francisco: Holden-Day.

Ratner, C., & McCarthy, J. (1990). Ecologically relevant stimuli and color memory. *Journal of General Psychology, 117*, 369–377.

Rauschecker, J. P. (1997). Processing of complex sounds in the auditory cortex of cat, monkey, and man. *Acta Otolaryngol, 532*(Suppl.), 34–38.

Rauschecker, J. P. (1998). Cortical processing of complex sounds. *Current Opinion in Neurobiology, 8*, 516–521.

Rauschecker, J. P., & Tian, B. (2000). Mechanisms and streams for processing of "what" and "where" in auditory cortex. *Proceedings of the National Academy of Sciences, USA, 97*, 11800–11806.

Reale, R. A., & Imig, T. J. (1980). Tonotopic organization in auditory cortex of the cat. *Journal of Comparative Neurology, 192*, 265–291.

Recanzone, G. H. (2000). Spatial processing in the auditory cortex of the macaque monkey. *Proceedings of the National Academy of Sciences, 97*, 11829–11835.

Recanzone, G. H., Engle, J. R., & Juarez-Salinas, D. L. (2011). Spatial and temporal processing of single auditory cortical neurons and populations of neurons in the macaque monkey. *Hearing Research, 271*, 115–122.

Reddy, L., Moradi, F., & Koch, C. (2007). Top-down biases win against focal attention in the fusiform face area. *Neuroimage, 38*, 730–739.

Regan, D. (1986). Luminance contrast: Vernier discrimination. *Spatial Vision, 1*, 305–318.

Regan, D., & Cynader, M. (1979). Neurons in area 18 of cat visual cortex selectively sensitive to changing size: Nonlinear interactions between responses to two edges. *Vision Research, 19*, 699–711.

Reichardt, W. (1969). Movement perception in insects. In W. Reichardt (Ed.), *Processing of optical data by organisms and by machines*. New York: Academic Press.

Reichl, R. (1994, March 11). Dining in New York. *New York Times*.

Rennaker, R. L., Chen, C.-F. F., Ruyle, A. M., Sloan, A. M., & Wilson, D. A. (2007). Spatial and temporal distribution of odorant-evoked activity in the piriform cortex. *Journal of Neuroscience, 27*, 1534–1542.

Rensink, R. A. (2002). Change detection. *Annual Review of Psychology, 53*, 245–277.

Rensink, R. A., O'Regan, J. K., & Clark, J. J. (1997). To see or not to see: The need for attention to perceive changes in scenes. *Psychological Science, 8*, 368–373.

Restrepo, D., Doucette, W., Whitesell, J. D., McTavish, T. S., & Salcedo, E. (2009). From the top down: Flexible reading of a fragmented odor map. *Trends in Neurosciences, 32*, 525–531.

Rhudy, J. L., Williams, A. E., McCabe, K. M., Thu, M. A. Nguyen, V., & Rambo, P. (2005). Affective modulation of nociception at spinal and supraspinal levels. *Psychophysiology, 42*, 579–587.

Riesenhuber, M., & Poggio, T. (2000). Models of object recognition. *Nature Neuroscience Supplement, 3*, 1199–1204.

Riesenhuber, M., & Poggio, T. (2002). Neural mechanisms of object recognition. *Current Opinion in Neurobiology, 12*, 162–168.

Ringbach, D. L. (2003). Look at the big picture (details will follow). *Nature Neuroscience, 6*, 7–8.

Risset, J. C., & Mathews, M. W. (1969). Analysis of musical instrument tones. *Physics Today, 22*, 23–30.

Rivera-Gaxiola, M., Silva-Pereyra, J., & Kuhl, P. K. (2005). Brain potentials to native and non-native speech contrasts in 7- and 11-month-old American infants. *Developmental Science, 8*, 162–172.

Rizzolatti, G., Forgassi, L., & Gallese, V. (2000). Cortical mechanisms subserving object grasping and action recognition: A new view on the cortical motor functions. In M. Gazzaniga (Ed.), *The new cognitive neurosciences* (pp. 539–552). Cambridge, MA: MIT Press.

Rizzolatti, G., Forgassi, L., & Gallese, V. (2006, November). Mirrors in the mind. *Scientific American*, pp. 54–63.

Rizzolatti, G., & Sinigaglia, C. (2010). The functional role of the parieto-frontal mirror circuit: Interpretations and misinterpretations. *Nature Reviews Neuroscience, 11*, 264–274.

Robbins, J. (2000, July 4). Virtual reality finds a real place. *New York Times*.

Robertson, L., Treisman, A., Friedman-Hill, S., & Grabowecky, M. (1997). The interaction of spatial and object pathways: Evidence from Balint's syndrome. *Journal of Cognitive Neuroscience, 9*, 295–317.

Robinson, D. L., & Wurtz, R. (1976). Use of an extra-retinal signal by monkey superior colliculus neurons to distinguish real from self-induced stimulus movement. *Journal of Neurophysiology, 39,* 852–870.

Robles-De-La-Torre, G. (2006, July–September). The importance of the sense of touch in virtual and real environments. *IEEE Multimedia,* pp. 24–30.

Rocha-Miranda, C. (2011). Personal communication.

Rock, I., & Kaufman, L. (1962). The moon illusion: Part 2. *Science, 136,* 1023–1031.

Rollman, G. B. (1991). Pain responsiveness. In M. A. Heller & W. Schiff (Eds.), *The psychology of touch* (pp. 91–114). Hillsdale, NJ: Erlbaum.

Rolls, E. T. (1981). Responses of amygdaloid neurons in the primate. In Y. Ben-Ari (Ed.), *The amygdaloid complex* (pp. 383–393). Amsterdam: Elsevier.

Rolls, E. T., & Baylis, L. L. (1994). Gustatory, olfactory, and visual convergence within the primate orbitofrontal cortex. *Journal of Neuroscience, 14,* 5437–5452.

Rolls, E. T., Critchley, H. D., Verhagen, J. V., & Kadohisa, M. (2010). The representation of information about taste and odor in the orbitofrontal cortex. *Chemical Perception, 3,* 16–33.

Rolls, E. T., & Tovee, M. J. (1995). Sparseness of the neuronal representation of stimuli in the primate temporal visual cortex. *Journal of Neurophysiology, 73,* 713–726.

Rose, D. (1996). Reflections on (or by?) grandmother cells. *Perception, 25,* 881.

Rosenstein, D., & Oster, H. (1988). Differential facial responses to four basic tastes in newborns. *Child Development, 59,* 1555–1568.

Rossiter, K. J. (1996). Structure-odor relationships. *Chemical Reviews, 96,* 3201–3240.

Rowe, M. J., Turman, A. A., Murray, G. M., & Zhang, H. Q. (1996). Parallel processing in somatosensory areas I and II of the cerebral cortex. In O. Franzen, R. Johansson, & L. Terenius (Eds.), *Somesthesis and the neurobiology of the somatosensory cortex* (pp. 197–212). Basel: Birkhauser Verlag.

Rubin, E. (1958). Figure and ground. In D. C. Beardslee & M. Wertheimer (Eds.), *Readings in perception* (pp. 194–203). Princeton, NJ: Van Nostrand. (Original work published 1915)

Rubin, P., Turvey, M. T., & Van Gelder, P. (1976). Initial phonemes are detected faster in spoken words than in spoken nonwords. *Perception and Psychophysics, 19,* 394–398.

Rushton, S. K., Harris, J. M., Lloyd, M. R., & Wann, J. P. (1998). Guidance of locomotion on foot uses perceived target location rather than optic flow. *Current Biology, 8,* 1191–1194.

Rushton, S. K., & Salvucci, D. D. (2001). An egocentric account of the visual guidance of locomotion. *Trends in Cognitive Sciences, 5,* 6–7.

Rushton, W. A. H. (1961). Rhodopsin measurement and dark adaptation in a subject deficient in cone vision. *Journal of Physiology, 156,* 193–205.

Russell, M. J. (1976). Human olfactory communication. *Nature, 260,* 520–522.

Rust, N. C., Mante, V., Simoncelli, E. P., & Movshon, J. A. (2006). How MT cells analyze the motion of visual patterns. *Nature Neuroscience, 9,* 1421–1431.

Sacks, O. (1985). *The man who mistook his wife for a hat.* London: Duckworth.

Sacks, O. (1995). *An anthropologist on Mars.* New York: Knopf.

Sacks, O. (2006, June 19). Stereo Sue. *The New Yorker,* p. 64.

Sacks, O. (2010). *The mind's eye.* New York: Knopf.

Saffran, J. R., Aslin, R. N., & Newport, E. L. (1996). Statistical learning by 8-month-old infants. *Science, 274,* 1926–1928.

Sakata, H., & Iwamura, Y. (1978). Cortical processing of tactile information in the first somatosensory and parietal association areas in the monkey. In G. Gordon (Ed.), *Active touch* (pp. 55–72). Elmsford, NY: Pergamon Press.

Sakata, H., Taira, M., Mine, S., & Murata, A. (1992). Hand-movement-related neurons of the posterior parietal cortex of the monkey: Their role in visual guidance of hand movements. In R. Caminiti, P. B. Johnson, & Y. Burnod (Eds.), *Control of arm movement in space: Neurophysiological and computational approaches* (pp. 185–198). Berlin: Springer-Verlag.

Salapatek, P., Bechtold, A. G., & Bushnell, E. W. (1976). Infant visual acuity as a function of viewing distance. *Child Development, 47,* 860–863.

Salasoo, A., & Pisoni, D. B. (1985). Interaction of knowledge sources in spoken word identification. *Journal of Memory and Language, 24,* 210–231.

Samuel, A. G. (1981). Phonemic restoration: Insights from a new methodology. *Journal of Experimental Psychology: General, 110,* 474–494.

Samuel, A. G. (1990). Using perceptual-restoration effects to explore the architecture of perception. In G. T. M. Altmann (Ed.), *Cognitive models of speech processing* (pp. 295–314). Cambridge, MA: MIT Press.

Samuel, A. G. (1997). Lexical activation produces potent phonemic percepts. *Cognitive Psychology, 32,* 97–127.

Samuel, A. G. (2001). Knowing a word affects the fundamental perception of the sounds within it. *Psychological Science, 12,* 348–351.

Sato, M., & Ogawa, H. (1993). Neural coding of taste in macaque monkeys. In K. Kurihara, N. Suzuki, & H. Ogawa (Eds.), *Olfaction and taste* (Vol.1, pp. 388–392). Tokyo: Springer-Verlag.

Sato, M., Ogawa, H., & Yamashita, S. (1994). Gustatory responsiveness of chorda tympani fibers in the cynomolgus monkey. *Chemical Senses, 19,* 381–400.

Schaal, B. (1986). Presumed olfactory exchanges between mother and neonate in humans. In J. LeCamus & J. Conier (Eds.), *Ethology and psychology* (pp. 101–110). Toulouse, France: Privat-IEC.

Schaal, B., & Porter, R. H. (1991). "Microsmatic humans" revisited: The generation and perception of chemical signals. In P. J. B. Slater, J. S. Rosenblatt, & Colin Beer (Eds.), *Advances in the study of behavior* (Vol. 20, pp. 135–199). San Diego: Academic Press.

Scherf, K. S., Behrmann, M., Humphreys, K., & Luna, B. (2007). Visual category-selectivity for faces, places and objects emerges along different developmental trajectories. *Developmental Science, 10,* F15–F30.

Schiffman, H. R. (1967). Size-estimation of familiar objects under informative and reduced conditions of viewing. *American Journal of Psychology, 80,* 229–235.

Schiffman, S. S., & Erickson, R. P. (1971). A psychophysical model for gustatory quality. *Physiology and Behavior, 7,* 617–633.

Schinazi, V. R., & Epstein, R. A. (2010). Neural correlates of real-world route learning. *Neuroimage, 53,* 725–735.

Schindler, I., Rice, N. J., McIntosh, R. D., Rossetti, Y., Vighetto, A., & Milner, D.A. (2004). Automatic avoidance of obstacles is a dorsal stream function: Evidence from optic ataxia. *Nature Neuroscience, 7,* 779–784.

Schlack, A., Sterbing-D'Angelo, J., Hartung, K., Hoffmann, K.-P., & Bremmer, F. (2005). Multisensory space representations in the macaque ventral intraparietal area. *Journal of Neuroscience, 25,* 4616–4625.

Schmuziger, N., Patscheke, J., & Probst, R. (2006). Hearing in non-professional pop/rock musicians. *Ear & Hearing, 27*, 321–330.

Schnapf, J. L., Kraft, T. W., & Baylor, D. A. (1987). Spectral sensitivity of human cone photoreceptors. *Nature, 325*, 439–441.

Scholz, J., & Woolf, C. J. (2002). Can we conquer pain? *Nature Neuroscience, 5*, 1062–1067.

Schreiner, C. H., & Mendelson, J. R. (1990). Functional topography of cat primary auditory cortex: Distribution of integrated excitation. *Journal of Neurophysiology, 64*, 1442–1459.

Schubert, E. D. (1980). *Hearing: Its function and dysfunction.* Wien: Springer-Verlag.

Scott, T. R., & Giza, B. K. (1990). Coding channels in the taste system of the rat. *Science, 249*, 1585–1587.

Scott, T. R., & Giza, B. K. (2000). Issues of gustatory neural coding: Where they stand today. *Physiology and Behavior, 69*, 65–76.

Scott, T. R., & Plata-Salaman, C. R. (1991). Coding of taste quality. In T. V. Getchell, R. L. Doty, L. M. Bartoshuk, & J. B. Snow (Eds.), *Smell and taste in health and disease* (pp. 345–368). New York: Raven Press.

Scoville, W. B., & Milner, B. (1957). Loss of recent memory after bilateral hippocampus lesions. *Journal of Neurosurgery and Psychiatry, 20*, 11–21.

Sedgwick, H. (2001). Visual space perception. In E. B. Goldstein (Ed.), *Blackwell handbook of perception* (pp. 128–167). Oxford: Blackwell.

Segui, J. (1984). The syllable: A basic perceptual unit in speech processing? In H. Bouma & D. G. Gouwhuis (Eds.), *Attention and performance X* (pp. 165–181). Hillsdale, NJ: Erlbaum.

Sekuler, R., Sekuler, A. B., & Lau, R. (1997). Sound alters visual motion perception. *Nature, 385*, 308.

Senior, C., Barnes, J., Giampietro, V., Simmons, A., Bullmore, E. T., Brammer, M., et al. (2000). The functional neuoroanatomy of implicit-motion perception or "representational momentum." *Current Biology, 10*, 16–22.

Shahbake, M. (2008). *Anatomical and psychophysical aspects of the development of the sense of taste in humans.* PhD thesis, University of Western Sydney.

Shamma, S. A., Elhilali, M., & Micheyl, C. (2011). Temporal coherence and attention in auditory scene analysis. *Trends in Neurosciences, 34*, 114–123.

Shamma, S. A., & Micheyl, C. (2010). Behind the scenes of auditory perception. *Current Opinion in Neurobiology, 20*, 361–366.

Shams, L., Kamitani, Y., & Shimojo, S. (2000). What you see is what you hear. *Nature, 408*, 788.

Shapley, R., & Hawken, M. J. (2011). Color in the cortex: Single- and double-opponent cells. *Vision Research, 51*, 701–707.

Sheinberg, D. L., & Logothetis, N. K. (1997). The role of temporal cortical areas in perceptual organization. *Proceedings of the National Academy of Sciences, 94*, 3408–3413.

Sheperd, G. M. (2012). *Neurogastronomy.* New York: Columbia University Press.

Sherf, K. S., Behrmann, M., Humphreys, K., & Lina, B. (2007). Visual category-selectivity for faces, places and objects emerges along different developmental trajectories. *Developmental Science, 10*, F15–F30.

Sherman, S. M., & Koch, C. (1986). The control of retinogeniculate transmission in the mammalian lateral geniculate nucleus. *Experimental Brain Research, 63*, 1–20.

Shiffrar, M., & Freyd, J. (1990). Apparent motion of the human body. *Psychological Science, 1*, 257–264.

Shiffrar, M., & Freyd, J. (1993). Timing and apparent motion path choice with human body photographs. *Psychological Science, 4*, 379–384.

Shimamura, A. P., & Prinzmetal, W. (1999). The mystery spot illusion and its relation to other visual illusions. *Psychological Science, 10*, 501–507.

Shimojo, S., Bauer, J., O'Connell, K. M., & Held, R. (1986). Pre-stereoptic binocular vision in infants. *Vision Research, 26*, 501–510.

Shinoda, H., Hayhoe, M. M., & Shrivastava, A. (2001). What controls attention in natural environments? *Vision Research, 41*, 3535–3545.

Silver, M. A., & Kastner, S. (2009). Topographic maps in human frontal and parietal cortex. *Trends in Cognitive Sciences, 13*, 488–495.

Simons, D. J., & Chabris, C. F. (1999). Gorillas in our midst: Sustained inattentional blindness for dynamic events. *Perception, 28*, 1059–1074.

Singer, T., Seymour, B., O'Doherty, J., Kaube, H., Dolan, R. J., & Frith, C. D. (2004). Empathy for pain involves the affective but not sensory components of pain. *Science, 303*, 1157–1162.

Singh, D., & Bronstad, M. P. (2001). Female body odour is a potential cue to ovulation. *Proceedings of the Royal Society of London B, 268*, 797–801.

Sinha, P. (2002). Recognizing complex patterns. *Nature Neuroscience, 5*, 1093–1097.

Siveke, I., Pecka, M., Seidl, A. H., Baudoux, S., & Grothe, B. (2006). Binaural response properties of low-frequency neurons in the gerbil dorsal nucleus of the lateral lemniscus. *Journal of Neurophysiology, 96*, 1425–1440.

Slater, A. M., & Findlay, J. M. (1975). Binocular fixation in the newborn baby. *Journal of Experimental Child Psychology, 20*, 248–273.

Slater, A. M., Morison, V., & Rose, D. (1984). Habituation in the newborn. *Infant Behavior and Development, 7*, 183–200.

Slater, A. M., Morison, V., Somers, M., Mattock, A., Brown, E., & Taylor, D. (1990). Newborn and older infants' perception of partly occluded objects. *Infant Behavior and Development, 13*, 33–49.

Sloan, L. L., & Wollach, L. (1948). A case of unilateral deuteranopia. *Journal of the Optical Society of America, 38*, 502–509.

Small, D. M. (2008). Flavor and the formation of category-specific processing in olfaction. *Chemical Perception, 1*, 136–146.

Small, D. M. (2012). Flavor is in the brain. *Physiology and Behavior.* doi: 10.1016/j.physbeh.2010.04.11

Smith, D. V., & Scott, T. R. (2003). Gustatory neural coding. In R. L. Doty (Ed.), *Handbook of olfaction and gustation* (2nd ed.). New York: Marcel Dekker.

Smith, D. V., St. John, S. J., & Boughter, J. D., Jr. (2000). Neuronal cell types and taste quality coding. *Physiology and Behavior, 69*, 77–85.

Smith, M. A., Majaj, N. J., & Movshon, J. A. (2005). Dynamics of motion signaling by neurons in macaque area MT. *Nature Neuroscience, 8*, 220–228.

Sobel, E. C. (1990). The locust's use of motion parallax to measure distance. *Journal of Comparative Physiology, 167*, 579–588.

Sommer, M. A., & Crapse, T. B. (2010). Corollary discharge. In E. B. Goldstein (Ed.), *Sage encyclopedia of perception* (pp. 325–327). Thousand Oaks, CA: Sage.

Sommer, M. A., & Wurtz, R. H. (2006). Influence of the thalamus on spatial visual processing in frontal cortex. *Nature, 444*, 374–377.

Sommer, M. A., & Wurtz, R. H. (2008). Brain circuits for the internal monitoring of movements. *Annual Review of Neuroscience, 31*, 317–338.

Sosulski, D. L., Bloom, M. L., Cutforth, T., Axel, R., & Sandeep, R. D. (2011). Distinct representations of olfactory information in different cortical centres. *Nature, 472*, 213–219.

Soto-Faraco, S., Lyons, J., Gazzaniga, M., Spence, C., & Kingstone, A. (2002). The ventriloquist in motion: Illusory capture of dynamic information across sensory modalities. *Cognitive Brain Research, 14,* 139–146.

Soto-Faraco, S., Spence, C., Lloyd, D., & Kingstone, A. (2004). Moving multisensory research along: Motion perception across sensory modalities. *Current Directions in Psychological Science, 13,* 29–32.

Soucy, E. R., Albenau, D. F., Fantana, A. L., Murthy, V. N., & Meister, M. (2009). Precision and diversity in an odor map on the olfactory bulb. *Nature Neuroscience, 12,* 210–220.

Spector, A. C., & Travers, S. P. (2005). The representation of taste quality in the mammalian nervous system. *Behavioral and Cognitive Neuroscience Reviews, 4,* 143–191.

Spence, C., Levitan, C. A., Shankar, M. U., & Zampini, M. (2010). Does food color influence taste and flavor perception in humans? *Chemical Perception, 3,* 68–84.

Srinivasan, M. V., & Venkatesh, S. (Eds.). (1997). *From living eyes to seeing machines.* New York: Oxford.

Stark, L., & Bridgeman, B. (1983). Role of corollary discharge in space constancy. *Perception and Psychophysics, 34,* 371–380.

Steiner, J. E. (1974). Innate, discriminative human facial expressions to taste and smell stimulation. *Annals of the New York Academy of Sciences, 237,* 229–233.

Steiner, J. E. (1979). Human facial expressions in response to taste and smell stimulation. *Advances in Child Development and Behavior, 13,* 257–295.

Steiner, J. E. (1987). What the neonate can tell us about umami. In Y. Kawamura & M. R. Kare (Eds.), *Umami: A basic taste* (pp. 97–103). New York: Marcel Dekker.

Stern, K., & McClintock, M. K. (1998). Regulation of ovulation by human pheromones. *Nature, 392,* 177–179.

Stettler, D. D., & Axel, R. (2009). Representations of odor in the piriform cortex. *Neuron, 63,* 854–864.

Stevens, J. A., Fonlupt, P., Shiffrar, M., & Decety, J. (2000). New aspects of motion perception: Selective neural encoding of apparent human movements. *NeuroReport, 111,* 109–115.

Stevens, S. S. (1957). On the psychophysical law. *Psychological Review, 64,* 153–181.

Stevens, S. S. (1961). To honor Fechner and repeal his law. *Science, 133,* 80–86.

Stevens, S. S. (1962). The surprising simplicity of sensory metrics. *American Psychologist, 17,* 29–39.

Stiles, W. S. (1953). Further studies of visual mechanisms by the two-color threshold method. *Coloquio sobre problemas opticos de la vision* (Vol. 1, pp. 65–103). Madrid: Union Internationale de Physique Pure et Appliquée.

Stoffregen, T. A., Smart, J. L., Bardy, B. G., & Pagulayan, R. J. (1999). Postural stabilization of looking. *Journal of Experimental Psychology: Human Perception and Performance, 25,* 1641–1658.

Strange, W. (Ed.). (1995). *Speech perception and linguistic experience: Issues in cross-language research.* Timonium, MD: York.

Sufka, K. J., & Price, D. D. (2002). Gate control theory reconsidered. *Brain and Mind, 3,* 277–290.

Suga, N. (1990, June). Biosonar and neural computation in bats. *Scientific American,* 60–68.

Sumby, W. H., & Pollack, J. (1954). Visual contributions to speech intelligibility in noise. *Journal of the Acoustical Society of America, 26,* 212–215.

Sumner, P., & Mollon, J. D. (2000). Catarrhine photopigments are optimized for detecting targets against a foliage background. *Journal of Experimental Biology, 23,* 1963–1986.

Sun, H.-J., Campos, J., Young, M., Chan, G. S. W., & Ellard, C. G. (2004). The contributions of static visual cues, nonvisual cues, and optic flow in distance estimation. *Perception, 33,* 49–65.

Suzuki, K., Yamadori, A., Hayakawa, Y., & Fujii, T. (1998). Pure topographical disorientation related to dysfunction of the viewpoint dependent visual system. *Cortex, 34,* 589–599.

Svaetichin, G. (1956). Spectral response curves from single cones. *Acta Physiologica Scandinavica Supplementum, 134,* 17–46.

Taira, M., Mine, S., Georgopoulis, A. P., Murata, A., & Sakata, H. (1990). Parietal cortex neurons of the monkey related to the visual guidance of hand movement. *Experimental Brain Research, 83,* 29–36.

Tanaka, J. W., & Presnell, L. M. (1999). Color diagnosticity in object recognition. *Perception & Psychophysics, 61,* 1140–1153.

Tanaka, J. W., Weiskopf, D., & Williams, P. (2001). The role of color in high-level vision. *Trends in Cognitive Sciences, 5,* 211–215.

Tanaka, K. (1993). Neuronal mechanisms of object recognition. *Science, 262,* 684–688.

Tanaka, K., Siato, H.-A., Fukada, Y., & Moriya, M. (1991). Coding visual images of objects in inferotemporal cortex of the Macaque monkey. *Journal of Neurophysiology, 66,* 170–189.

Tanigawa, H., Lu, H. D., & Roe, A. W. (2010). Functional organization for color and orientation in macaque V4. *Nature Neuroscience, 13,* 1542–1548.

Tatler, B. W., Hayhoe, M. M., Land, M. F., & Ballard, D. H. (2011). Eye guidance in natural vision: Reinterpreting salience. *Journal of Vision, 11*(5):5, 1–23.

Tatler, B. W., & Kuhn, G. (2007). Don't look now: The magic of misdirection. In R. P. G. van Gompel, M. H. Fischer, W. S. Murray, & R. L. Hill (Eds.), *Eye movements: A window on mind and brain* (pp. 697–714). Oxford, UK: Elsevier.

Teghtsoonian, R. (1971). On the exponents in Stevens's Law and the constant in Ekman's Law. *Psychological Review, 78,* 78–80.

Teller, D. Y. (1997). First glances: The vision of infants. *Investigative Ophthalmology and Visual Science, 38,* 2183–2199.

Ter-Pogossian, M. M., Phelps, M. E., Hoffman, E. J., & Mullani, N. A. (1975). A positron-emission tomograph for nuclear imaging (PET). *Radiology, 114,* 89–98.

Terwogt, M. M., & Hoeksma, J. B. (1994). Colors and emotions: Preferences and combinations. *Journal of General Psychology, 122,* 5–17.

Thaler, L., Arnott, S. R., & Goodale, M. A. (2011). Neural correlates of natural human echolocation in early and late blind echolocation experts. PLoS ONE 6, e20162. doi:10.1371.journal.pone.0020162.

Todrank, J., & Bartoshuk, L. M. (1991). A taste illusion: Taste sensation localized by touch. *Physiology and Behavior, 50,* 1027–1031.

Tong, F., Nakayama, K., Vaughn, J. T., & Kanwisher, N. (1998). Binocular rivalry and visual awareness in human extrastriate cortex. *Neuron, 21,* 753–759.

Tonndorf, J. (1960). Shearing motion in scalia media of cochlear models. *Journal of the Acoustical Society of America, 32,* 238–244.

Tootell, R. B. H., Nelissen, K., Vanduffel, W., & Orban, G. A. (2004). Search for color "center(s)" in Macaque visual cortex. *Cerebral Cortex, 14,* 353–363.

Torralba, A., Oliva, A. Castelhano, M. S., & Henderson, J. M. (2006). Contextual guidance of eye movements and attention in real-world scenes: The role of global features in object search. *Psychological Review, 113,* 766–786.

Tracey, I. (2005.) Nociceptive processing in the human brain. *Current Opinion in Neurobiology, 15,* 478–487.

Trainor, J. J., Gao, X., Lei, J.-J., Lehtovaara, K., & Harris, L. R. (2009). The primal role of the vestibular system in determining musical rhythm. *Cortex, 45*, 35–43.

Treisman, A. (1986). Features and objects in visual processing. *Scientific American, 255*, 114B–125B.

Treisman, A. (1988). Features and objects: The fourteenth Bartlett memorial lecture. *Quarterly Journal of Experimental Psychology, 40A*, 207–237.

Treisman, A. (1999). Solutions to the binding problem: Progress through controversy and convergence. *Neuron, 24*, 105–110.

Treisman, A. (2005). *Attention and binding.* Presentation to the Cognitive Science Group, University of Arizona, February 4, 2005.

Treisman, A., & Schmidt, H. (1982). Illusory conjunctions in the perception of objects. *Cognitive Psychology, 14*, 107–141.

Tresilian, J., R., Mon-Williams, M., & Kelly, B. (1999). Increasing confidence in vergence as a cue to distance. *Proceedings of the Royal Society of London, 266B*, 39–44.

Truax, B. (1984). *Acoustic communication.* Norwood, NJ: Ablex.

Tsao, D. Y., Freiwald, W. A., Tootell, R. B., & Livingstone, M. S. (2006). A cortical region consisting entirely of face-selective cells. *Science, 311*, 670–674.

Ts'o, D. Y., Roe, A. R., & Gilbert, C. D. (2001). A hierarchy of the functional organization for color, form, and disparity in primate visual area V2. *Vision Research, 41*, 1333–1349.

Tsuchiya, N., & Koch, C. (2009). The relationship between consciousness and attention. In S. Lawreys & G. Tononi (Eds.), *The neurology of consciousness* (pp. 63–79). London: Elsevier.

Turk, D. C., & Flor, H. (1999). Chronic pain: A biobehavioral perspective. In R. J. Gatchel & D. C. Turk (Eds.), *Psychosocial factors in pain* (pp. 18–34). New York: Guilford Press.

Turman, A. B., Morley, J. W., & Rowe, M. J. (1998). Functional organization of the somatosensory cortex in the primate. In J. W. Morley (Ed.), *Neural aspects of tactile sensation* (pp. 167–193). New York: Elsevier Science.

Tye-Murray, N., Spencer, L., & Woodworth, G. G. (1995). Acquisition of speech by children who have prolonged cochlear implant experience. *Journal of Speech and Hearing Research, 38*, 327–337.

Tyler, C. W. (1997a). Analysis of human receptor density. In V. Lakshminarayanan (Ed.), *Basic and clinical applications of vision science* (pp. 63–71). Norwell, MA: Kluwer Academic.

Tyler, C. W. (1997b). *Human cone densities: Do you know where all your cones are?* Unpublished manuscript.

Uchida, N., Takahashi, Y. K., Tanifuji, M., & Mori, K. (2000). Odor maps in the mammalian olfactory bulb: Domain organization and odorant structural features. *Nature Neuroscience, 3*, 1035–1043.

Uchikawa, K., Uchikawa, H., & Boynton, R. M. (1989). Partial color constancy of isolated surface colors examined by a color-naming method. *Perception, 18*, 83–91.

Uddin, L. Q., Iacoboni, M., Lange, C., & Keenan, J. P. (2007). The self and social cognition: The role of cortical midline structures and mirror neurons. *Trends in Cognitive Sciences, 11*, 153–157.

Uka, T., & DeAngelis, G. C. (2003). Contribution of middle temporal area to coarse depth discrimination: Comparison of neuronal and psychophysical sensitivity. *Journal of Neuroscience, 23*, 3515–3530.

Ungerleider, L. G., & Haxby, J. V. (1994). "What" and "where" in the human brain. *Current Opinion in Neurobiology, 4*, 157–165.

Ungerleider, L. G., & Mishkin, M. (1982). Two cortical visual systems. In D. J. Ingle, M. A. Goodale, & R. J. Mansfield (Eds.), *Analysis of visual behavior* (pp. 549–580). Cambridge, MA: MIT Press.

Valdez, P., & Mehribian, A. (1994). Effect of color on emotions. *Journal of Experimental Psychology: General, 123*, 394–409.

Vallbo, A. B., & Johansson, R. S. (1978). The tactile sensory innervation of the glabrous skin of the human hand. In G. Gordon (Ed.), *Active touch* (pp. 29–54). New York: Oxford University Press.

Van Essen, D. C., & Anderson, C. H. (1995). Information processing strategies and pathways in the primate visual system. In S. F. Zornetzer, J. L. Davis, & C. Lau (Eds.), *An introduction to neural and electronic networks* (2nd ed., pp. 45–75). San Diego: Academic Press.

VanRullen, R., & Thorpe, S. J. (2001). The time course of visual processing: From early perception to decision making. *Journal of Cognitive Neuroscience, 13*, 454–461.

Van Wanrooij, M. M., & Van Opstal, A. J. (2005). Relearning sound localization with a new ear. *Journal of Neuroscience, 25*, 5413–5424.

Varner, D., Cook, J. E., Schneck, M. E., McDonald, M., & Teller, D. Y. (1985). Tritan discriminations by 1- and 2-month-old human infants. *Vision Research, 25*, 821–831.

Vecera, S. P., Vogel, E. K., & Woodman, G. F. (2002). Lower region: A new cue for figure–ground assignment. *Journal of Experimental Psychology: General, 131*, 194–205.

Veldhuizen, M. G., Nachtigal, D., Teulings, L., Gitelman, D. R., & Small, D. M. (2010). The insular taste cortex contributes to odor quality coding. *Frontiers in Human Neuroscience, 4*(Article 58), 1–11.

Verhagen, J. V., Kadohisa, M., & Rolls, E. T. (2004). Primate insular/opercular taste cortex: Neuronal representations of viscosity, fat texture, grittiness, temperature, and taste of foods. *Journal of Neurophysiology, 92*, 1685–1699.

Vermeij, G. (1997). *Privileged hands: A scientific life.* New York: Freeman.

Vo, M. L. H., & Henderson, J. M. (2009). Does gravity matter? Effects of semantic and syntactic inconsistencies on the allocation of attention during scene perception. *Journal of Vision, 9*(3), 1–15.

von der Emde, G., Schwarz, S., Gomez, L., Budelli, R., & Grant, K. (1998). Electric fish measure distance in the dark. *Nature, 395*, 890–894.

von Kriegstein, K., Kleinschmidt, A., Sterzer, P., & Giraud, A.-L. (2005). Interaction of face and voice areas in speaker recognition. *Journal of Cognitive Neuroscience, 17*, 367–376.

Wager, T. D., Rilling, J. K., Smith, E. E., Sokolik, A., Casey, K. L., Davidson, R. J., et al. (2004). Placebo-induced changes in fMRI in the anticipation and experience of pain. *Science, 303*, 1162–1167.

Wald, G. (1964). The receptors of human color vision. *Science, 145*, 1007–1017.

Wald, G. (1968). Molecular basis of visual excitation [Nobel lecture]. *Science, 162*, 230–239.

Wald, G., & Brown, P. K. (1958). Human rhodopsin. *Science, 127*, 222–226.

Waldrop, M. M. (1988). A landmark in speech recognition. *Science, 240*, 1615.

Wall, P. D., & Melzack, R. (Eds.). (1994). *Textbook of pain* (3rd ed.). Edinburgh: Churchill Livingstone.

Wallach, H. (1963). The perception of neutral colors. *Scientific American, 208*(1), 107–116.

Wallach, H., Newman, E. B., & Rosenzweig, M. R. (1949). The precedence effect in sound localization. *American Journal of Psychology, 62*, 315–336.

Walls, G. L. (1942). *The vertebrate eye.* New York: Hafner. (Reprinted in 1967)

Wandell, B. A. (2011). Imaging retinotopic maps in the human brain. *Vision Research, 51*, 718–737.

Wandell, B. A., Dumoulin, S. O., & Brewer, A. A. (2009). Visual areas in humans. In L. Squire (Ed.), *Encyclopedia of neuroscience.* New York: Academic Press.

Wandell, B. A., Dumoulin, S. O., & Brewer, A. A. (2007). Visual field maps in human cortex. *Neuron, 56,* 366–383.

Wang, X., Zhang, M., Cohen, I. S., & Goldberg, M. E. (2007). The proprioceptive representation of eye position in monkey primary somatosensory cortex. *Nature Neuroscience, 10,* 640–646.

Wann, J., & Land, M. (2000). Steering with or without the flow: Is the retrieval of heading necessary? *Trends in Cognitive Science, 4,* 319–324.

Warren, R. M. (1970). Perceptual restoration of missing speech sounds. *Science, 167,* 392–393.

Warren, R. M., Obuseck, C. J., & Acroff, J. M. (1972). Auditory induction of absent sounds. *Science, 176,* 1149.

Warren, W. H. (1995). Self-motion: Visual perception and visual control. In W. Epstein & S. Rogers (Eds.), *Handbook of perception and cognition: Perception of space and motion* (pp. 263–323). New York: Academic Press.

Warren, W. H. (2004). Optic flow. In L. M. Chalupa & J. S. Werner (Eds.), *The visual neurosciences* (pp. 1247–1259). Cambridge, MA: MIT Press.

Warren, W. H., Kay, B. A., & Yilmaz, E. H. (1996). Visual control of posture during walking: Functional specificity. *Journal of Experimental Psychology: Human Perception and Performance, 22,* 818–838.

Wassenhove, V. van, Grant, K. W., & Poeppel, D. (2005). Visual speech speeds up the neural processing of auditory speech. *Proceedings of the National Academy of Sciences, 102,* 1181–1186.

Watkins, L. R., & Maier, S. F. (2003). When good pain turns bad. *Current Directions in Psychological Science, 12,* 232–236.

Webster, M. A. (2011). Adaptation and visual coding. *Journal of Vision, 11*(5):3, 1–23.

Weinstein, S. (1968). Intensive and extensive aspects of tactile sensitivity as a function of body part, sex, and laterality. In D. R. Kenshalo (Ed.), *The skin senses* (pp. 195–218). Springfield, IL: Thomas.

Weisenberg, M. (1977). Pain and pain control. *Psychological Bulletin, 84,* 1008–1044.

Weissberg, M. (1999). Cognitive aspects of pain. In P. D. Wall & R. Melzak (Eds.), *Textbook of pain* (4th ed., pp. 345–358). New York: Churchill Livingstone.

Werner, L. A., & Bargones, J. Y. (1992). Psychoacoustic development of human infants. In C. Rovee-Collier & L. Lipsett (Eds.), *Advances in infancy research* (Vol. 7, pp. 103–145). Norwood, NJ: Ablex.

Wertheimer, M. (1912). Experimentelle Studien über das Sehen von Beugung. *Zeitschrift für Psychologie, 61,* 161–265.

Wever, E. G. (1949). *Theory of hearing.* New York: Wiley.

Wexler, M., Panerai, I. L., & Droulez, J. (2001). Self-motion and the perception of stationary objects. *Nature, 409,* 85–88. (9)

Whalley, M. G., & Oakley, D. A. (2003). Psychogenic pain: A study using multidimensional scaling. *Contemporary Hypnosis, 20,* 16–24.

White, M. (1981). The effect of the nature of the surround on the perceived lightness of grey bars within squarewave test gratings. *Perception, 10,* 215–230.

Wiech, K., Ploner, M., & Tracey, I. (2008). Neurocognitive aspects of pain perception. *Trends in Cognitive Sciences, 12,* 306–313.

Wightman, F. L., & Kistler, D. J. (1997). Monaural sound localization revisited. *Journal of the Acoustical Society of America, 101,* 1050–1063.

Wightman, F. L., & Kistler, D. J. (1998). Of Vulcan ears, human ears and "earprints." *Nature Neuroscience, 1,* 337–339.

Wilkie, R. M., & Wann, J. P. (2003). Eye-movements aid the control of locomotion. *Journal of Vision, 3,* 677–684.

Willander, J., & Larsson, M. (2007). Olfaction and emotion: The case of autobiographical memory. *Memory and Cognition, 35,* 1659–1663.

Williams, S. M., McCoy, A. N., & Purves, D. (1998). The influence of depicted illumination on brightness. *Proceedings of the National Academy of Sciences USA, 95,* 13296–13300.

Wilson, D. A. (2003). Rapid, experience-induced enhancement in odorant discrimination by anterior piriform cortex neurons. *Journal of Neurophysiology, 90,* 65–72.

Wilson, D. A., Best, A. R., & Sullivan, R. M. (2004). Plasticity in the olfactory system: Lessons for the neurobiology of memory. *Neuroscientist, 10,* 513–524.

Wilson, D. A., & Stevenson, R. J. (2006). *Learning to smell.* Baltimore: Johns Hopkins University Press.

Wilson, D. A., & Sullivan, R. M. (2011). Cortical processing of odor objects. *Neuron, 72,* 506–519.

Wilson, J. R., Friedlander, M. J., & Sherman, M. S. (1984). Ultrastructural morphology of identified X- and Y-cells in the cat's lateral geniculate nucleus. *Proceedings of the Royal Society, 211B,* 411–436.

Winawer, J., Huk, A. C., & Boroditsky, L. (2008). A motion aftereffect from still photographs depicting motion. *Psychological Science, 19,* 276–283.

Winston, J. S., O'Doherty, J., Kilner, J. M., Perrett, D., I., & Dolan, R. J. (2007). Brain systems for assessing facial attractiveness. *Neuropsychologia, 45,* 195–206.

Wissinger, C. M., VanMeter, J., Tian, B., Van Lare, J., Pekar, J., & Rauschecker, J. P. (2001). Hierarchical organization of the human auditory cortex revealed by functional magnetic resonance imaging. *Journal of Cognitive Neuroscience, 13,* 1–7.

Witt, J. K. (2011). Action's effect on perception. *Current Directions in Psychological Science, 20,* 201–206.

Witt, J. K., & Dorsch, T. E. (2009). Kicking to bigger uprights: Field goal kicking performance influences perceived size. *Perception, 38,* 1328–1340.

Witt, J. K., & Proffitt, D. R. (2005). See the ball, hit the ball: Apparent ball size is correlated with batting average. *Psychological Science, 16,* 937–938.

Witt, J. K., Proffitt, D. R., & Epstein, W. (2010). When and how are spatial perceptions scaled? *Journal of Experimental Psychology: Human Perception and Performance, 36,* 1153–1160.

Witt, J. K., & Sugovic, M. (2010). Performance and ease influence perceived speed. *Perception, 39,* 1341–1353.

Womelsdorf, T., Anton-Erxleben, K., Pieper, F., & Treue, S. (2006). Dynamic shifts of visual receptive fields in cortical area MT by spatial attention. *Nature Neuroscience, 9,* 1156–1160.

Woods, A. J., Philbeck, J. W., & Danoff, J. V. (2009). The various perceptions of distance: An alternative view of how effort affects distance judgments. *Journal of Experimental Psychology: Human Perception and Performance, 35,* 1104–1117.

Woods, T. M., Lopez, S. E., Long, J. H., Rahman, J. E., & Recanzone, G. H. (2006). Effects of stimulus azimuth and intensity on the single-neuron activity in the auditory cortex of the alert macaque monkey. *Journal of Neurophysiology, 96,* 3323–3337.

Wyatt, T. D. (2010). Pheromones and signature mixtures: Defining species-wide signals and variable cues for identity in both invertebrates and vertebrates. *Journal of Comparative Physiology A, 196,* 685–700.

Wysocki, C. J., & Preti, G. (2009). *Human pheromones: What's purported, what's supported* (Sense of Smell Institute white paper). New York: Fragrance Foundation.

Xu, Y. (2005). Revisiting the role of the fusiform face area in visual expertise. *Cerebral Cortex, 15*, 1234–1242.

Yau, J. M., Pesupathy, A., Fitzgerald, P. J., Hsiao, S. S., & Connon, C. E. (2009). Analogous intermediate shape coding in vision and touch. *Proceedings of the National Academy of Sciences, 106*, 16457–16462.

Yonas, A., & Granrud, C. E. (2006). Infants' perception of depth from cast shadows. *Perception and Psychophysics, 68*, 154–160.

Yonas, A., & Hartman, B. (1993). Perceiving the affordance of contact in four- and five-month old infants. *Child Development, 64*, 298–308.

Yonas, A., Pettersen, L., & Granrud, C. E. (1982). Infant's sensitivity to familiar size as information for distance. *Child Development, 53*, 1285–1290.

Yoshida, K. A., Iversen, J. R., Patel, A. D., Mazuka, R., Nito, H., Gerain, J., et al. (2010). The development of perceptual grouping biases in infancy: A Japanese-English cross-linguistic study. *Cognition, 115*, 356–361.

Yoshida, K., Saito, N., Iriki, A., & Isoda, M. (2011). Representation of others' action by neurons in monkey medial frontal cortex. *Current Biology, 21*, 249–253.

Yost, W. A. (1997). The cocktail party problem: Forty years later. In R. H. Kilkey & T. R. Anderson (Eds.), *Binaural and spatial hearing in real and virtual environments* (pp. 329–347). Hillsdale, NJ: Erlbaum.

Yost, W. A. (2001). Auditory localization and scene perception. In E. B. Goldstein (Ed.), *Blackwell handbook of perception* (pp. 437–468). Oxford, UK: Blackwell.

Yost, W. A., & Guzman, S. J. (1996). Auditory processing of sound sources: Is there an echo in here? *Current Directions in Psychological Science, 5*, 125–131.

Yost, W. A., & Sheft, S. (1993). Auditory processing. In W. A. Yost, A. N. Popper, & R. R. Fay (Eds.), *Handbook of auditory research* (Vol. 3). New York: Springer-Verlag.

Young, R. S. L., Fishman, G. A., & Chen, F. (1980). Traumatically acquired color vision defect. *Investigative Ophthalmology and Visual Science, 19*, 545–549.

Young, T. (1802). On the theory of light and colours. *Transactions of the Royal Society of London, 92*, 12–48.

Young-Browne, G., Rosenfield, H. M., & Horowitz, F. D. (1977). Infant discrimination of facial expression. *Child Development, 48*, 555–562.

Yuille, A., & Kersten, D. (2006). Vision as Bayesian inference: Analysis by synthesis? *Trends in Cognitive Sciences, 10*, 301–308.

Yuodelis, C., & Hendrickson, A. (1986). A qualitative and quantitative analysis of the human fovea during development. *Vision Research, 26*, 847–855.

Zacks, J. M. (2004). Using movement and intentions to understand simple events. *Cognitive Science, 28*, 979–1008.

Zacks, J. M., Braver, T. S., Sheridan, M. A., Donaldson, D. I, Snyder, A. Z. Ollinger, J. M., et al. (2001). Human brain activity time-locked to perceptual event boundaries. *Nature Neuroscience, 4*, 651–655.

Zacks, J. M., Kumar, S., Abrams, R. A., & Mehta, R. (2009). Using movement and intentions to understand human activity. *Cognition, 112*, 201–206.

Zacks, J. M., Kurby, C. A., Eisenberg, M. L., & Haroutunian, N. (2011). Prediction error associated with the perceptual segmentation of natural events. *Journal of Cognitive Neuroscience, 23*, 4057–4066.

Zacks, J. M., & Swallow, K. M. (2007). Event segmentation. *Current Directions in Psychological Science, 16*, 80–84.

Zacks, J. M., & Tversky, B. (2001). Event structure in perception and conception. *Psychologial Bulletin, 127*, 3–27.

Zampini, M., & Spence, C. (2010). Assessing the role of sound in the perception of food and drink. *Chemical Perception, 3*, 57–67.

Zeki, S. (1983a). Color coding in the cerebral cortex: The reaction of cells in monkey visual cortex to wavelengths and colours. *Neuroscience, 9*, 741–765.

Zeki, S. (1983b). Color coding in the cerebral cortex: The responses of wavelength-selective and color coded cells in monkey visual cortex to changes in wavelength composition. *Neuroscience, 9*, 767–781.

Zeki, S. (1990). A century of cerebral achromatopsia. *Brain, 113*, 1721–1777.

Zhang, T., & Britten, K. H. (2006). The virtue of simplicity. *Nature Neuroscience, 9*, 1356–1357.

Zhao, G. Q., Zhang, Y., Hoon, M., Chandrashekar, J., Erienbach, I., Ryba, N. J. P., et al. (2003). The receptors for mammalian sweet and umami taste. *Cell, 115*, 255–266.

Zihl, J., von Cramon, D., & Mai, N. (1983). Selective disturbance of movement vision after bilateral brain damage. *Brain, 106*, 313–340.

Zihl, J., von Cramon, D., Mai, N., & Schmid, C. (1991). Disturbance of movement vision after bilateral posterior brain damage. *Brain, 114*, 2235–2252.

Zue, V. W., & Glass, J. R. (2000). Conversational interfaces: Advances and challenges. *Proceedings of the IEEE, 88*, 1166–1180.

Name Index

Subject Index

familiar size depth cue and, 230
haptic perception and, 348–349
pain perception and, 353–355
perception influenced by, 12
speech perception and, 324–325
Coherence, 186
Coincidence detectors, 297
Color
achromatic, 202
chromatic, 202
form related to, 214
mixing, 202–204
reflected, 202
saturation of, 201
transmitted, 202
visualizing, 211
wavelength and, 201–204, 221
Color blindness, 199–200, 209, 213
Color circle, 201
Color constancy, 214–217
chromatic adaptation and, 215–216
demonstrations of, 215, 217
effect of surroundings on, 216–217
illumination and, 215
memory and, 217
partial, 216
Color deficiency, 208–210
anomalous trichromatism, 208
color blindness, 199–200, 209, 213
cortical damage and, 213
dichromatism, 207, 208, 209–210
monochromatism, 208, 209
physiological mechanisms of, 210
receptor-based, 210
tests for, 208
trichromatism, 207, 208
Color-matching experiments, 204
Color perception, 199–225
basic colors in, 201
color constancy and, 214–217
cortex and, 213–214
deficiency of, 199–200, 208–210
demonstrations of, 210, 211, 215, 217, 220
effect of surroundings on, 216–217
functions of, 200–201
infants and, 222–223
lightness constancy and, 217–220
loss or blindness, 199–200
media resources on, 225
memory and, 217
mixed colors and, 202–204
nervous system and, 221–222
opponent-process theory of, 210–213
physiology of, 204–207, 212–213, 221–222
reflectance and, 202, 215
review questions on, 208, 214, 224
taste perception and, 369
thinking about, 224
transmission and, 202
trichromatic theory of, 204–207
wavelengths and, 201–204
Young-Helmholtz theory of, 204

Columnar organization
hypercolumns, 81
location columns, 80, 81
ocular dominance columns, 81n
orientation columns, 80–81
Common fate, principle of, 104
Common region, principle of, 104
Comparator, 183–184
Complex cells, 65, 66
Complex tones, 266–267, 279
Compound melodic line, 305
Computers
face recognition and, 97
object perception and, 97–100
speech recognition and, 317
Concert hall acoustics, 302–303
Condensation, 263
Cone of confusion, 293, 294
Cones, 23, 26
color perception and, 205–206
dark adaptation and, 27, 29–32
distribution of, 28–29
neural convergence and, 41–44
spectral sensitivity and, 33–34
visual acuity and, 43–44, 47
See also Rods
Cone spectral sensitivity curve, 33
Conflicting cues theory, 250
Conjunction search, 144–145
Consciousness, 72–73, 393
Conservative criterion, 399
Consonants, 318, 319, 320
Constancy
color, 214–217
lightness, 217–220
size, 246–247, 248–249
speech perception, 321
Constant stimuli, method of, 14
Context
size perception and, 248
speech perception and, 320–321, 324–325
Continuity errors, 139
Contours, illusory, 101–102
Contrast
perceived, 134–135
simultaneous, 58–59
Contrast threshold, 67
Convergence, 41–44, 228
Convergence angle, 228
Coordinated receptive fields, 311–312
Core area, 296, 297
Cornea, 6, 23
Corollary discharge signal (CDS), 183–184
Corollary discharge theory, 183–186
behavioral demonstrations of, 184–185
physiological evidence for, 185–186
Corrective lenses, 25
Correct rejection, signal detection, 395
Correspondence problem, 241
Corresponding retinal points, 236–237
Cortex
anterior cingulate, 356

auditory areas in, 281–282, 296, 297
color perception and, 213–214
frontal operculum, 365
inferotemporal, 69–70, 87, 142
maps of the body on, 341–342
middle temporal, 186–188, 190, 192
occipital lobe of, 7, 63–64
odor perception and, 378–380
opponent neurons in, 214
orbitofrontal, 378, 382, 383
piriform, 378, 379, 380
primary receiving areas in, 7, 8
retrosplenial, 161, 162
somatosensory, 340, 341–342, 350
speech perception and, 329–330
striate, 64–66, 78, 80–83
tactile acuity and, 344–345
Cortical body maps, 341–342
Cortical magnification factor, 78–80
Cortical organization, 77–93
brain imaging and, 79, 88–89
cortical columns and, 80–81
demonstration of, 80
experience and, 91–92
information streams and, 83–86
magnification factor and, 78–80
media resources on, 93
memory and vision in, 89–91
modularity and, 87–89
retinotopic maps and, 78
review questions on, 83, 91
scene perception and, 81–83
thinking about, 92
Covert attention, 129
Criterion, signal detection, 398–399
Cross-talk, 310
Cue approach to depth perception, 228
binocular cues and, 234–241
monocular cues and, 228–234
oculomotor cues and, 228
Cutaneous senses, 337–360
cortical body maps and, 341–342
demonstrations of, 343–344, 347, 348
detail perception and, 342–345
media resources on, 360
nerve pathways and, 339–341
object perception and, 348–351
pain perception and, 351–357
plasticity of, 342
review questions on, 347, 359
skin receptors and, 338–339
texture perception and, 346–347
thinking about, 359
vibration perception and, 345–346
See also Touch perception

Dark adaptation, 27, 29–32, 48
Dark adaptation curve, 29–31
Dark-adapted sensitivity, 31
Data-based processing, 10
Decay, tone, 270
Decibel (dB), 265, 267

Hearing (*continued*)
range of, 267–268
review questions on, 270, 280, 285–286, 313
scene analysis and, 304–307
sound localization and, 290–301
speech perception and, 309, 310, 317–334
thinking about, 286, 313
timbre and, 269–270
vision related to, 310–313
See also Auditory system; Sound
Hearing impairments, 282–284
age-related, 283
noise-induced, 283–284
Heredity. *See* Genetics
Hermann grid, 55–56
Hertz (Hz), 264
Hidden objects, 99
Higher harmonics, 266
High-load tasks, 142
Hippocampus, 89, 90, 162
Hits, signal detection, 395
Holway and Boring experiment, 243–246
Homunculus, 341
Honeybees, 221, 222
Horizontal cells, 41
Horopter, 237
How pathway, 86, 164
Hubble telescope, 44, 45
Hue, 202
Hypercolumns, 81
Hyperopia, 26
Hyperpolarization, 40
Hypnotic suggestion, 354–355
Hypothalamus, 382, 383

Identifying odors, 372–373
Illumination
color constancy and, 215
lightness constancy and, 218–220
Illumination edge, 219
Illusions
apparent movement, 101
illusory contour, 101–102
Mach bands, 57–58
moon, 252–253
of motion, 101, 178–179
oral capture, 381
scale illusion, 306–307
simultaneous contrast, 58
of size, 248–253
3-D movies and TV, 239–240
two-flash, 311
ventriloquism effect, 311
waterfall, 179
White's illusion, 59
See also Visual illusions
Illusory conjunctions, 143–144
Illusory contours, 101–102
Illusory motion, 178
Image displacement signal (IDS), 183–184
Implied motion, 193, 194–195
Implied polyphony, 305

Inattentional blindness, 138
Incus, 271
Indexical characteristics, 328
Indirect sound, 301
Induced motion, 179
Infants
color vision in, 222–223
depth perception in, 254–256
face perception in, 120–122
habituation in, 147
hearing perception in, 284–285, 308–309
object perception in, 147–149
olfactory perception in, 385
speech perception in, 327–328, 332–333
taste perception in, 385
visual perception in, 45–47
voice recognition in, 284–285
Inference, 112–114
Inferior colliculus, 296
Inferotemporal (IT) cortex, 69–70, 87, 142
Inflammatory pain, 351
Information
disparity, 238–241
environmental, 154–155
invariant, 155
self-produced, 155
Inhibition, 54
Inhibitory area, 61
Inhibitory-center, excitatory-surround receptive fields, 61
Inhibitory response, 40
Inhibitory transmitters, 40, 41
Inner ear, 272–275
Inner hair cells, 273–274
Insects, 254
Insula, 365, 382
Intensity, 16
Intentions, 167–169
Interaural level difference (ILD), 291–293
Interaural time difference (ITD), 291, 292, 293
Intimacy time, 303
Invalid trials, 133
Invariance
viewpoint invariance, 99
invariant information, 155, 157
Inverse projection problem, 98–99
Ions, 38
Ishihara plates, 208
Isomerization, 27, 206
ITD tuning curves, 297–299

Jeffress model, 296–298
Judgmental bias, 170

Kinesthesis, 338
Knowledge
affordances and, 163
attention and, 131
color vision and, 217
epilogue and, 391–393
feature analysis and, 144

feedback and, 84
Gestalt psychology and, 106–107
motion perception and, 175, 194
object perception and, 99, 111, 112, 114
pain and, 353
perceptual process and, 9–11
scene statistics and, 132
size perception and, 229, 255
speech perception and, 321, 324–328
think about it, 122
See also Cognition; Top-down processing
Knowledge-based processing, 10

Landmark discrimination problem, 83, 84
Landmarks, 160–162
Language
learning the sounds of, 333
metrical structure and, 309, 310
mirror neurons and, 331
See also Speech perception
Laser-assisted in situ keratomileusis (LASIK), 26
Lateral eyes, 253–254
Lateral geniculate nucleus (LGN), 35, 63, 64, 66, 341
Lateral inhibition, 54–60
demonstrations of, 56, 58
Hermann grid and, 55–56
Mach bands and, 56–58
simultaneous contrast and, 58–59
White's illusion and, 59–60
Lateral plexus, 54
Lecture hall acoustics, 303
Leisure noise, 283
Length estimation task, 86
Lens, 6, 23
Lenticular projection, 240
Lesioning, 83, 187
Level, sound, 265
Liberal criterion, 398–399
Light
focusing of, 23–24
mixing colored, 202–203
monochromatic, 33
reflected, 5–6
transduction of, 26–27
visible, 22
Light-adapted sensitivity, 30
Light-from-above assumption, 111–112
Lightness, 55, 218
Lightness constancy, 217–220
demonstrations of, 220
illumination and, 218–220
ratio principle and, 218
shadows and, 219–220
surface orientation and, 220
Lightness perception, 54–59
Likelihood principle, 113
Limits, method of, 14
Limulus experiment, 54
Load theory of attention, 141–142
Local disturbance in the optic array, 182